PERSPECTIVES ON CROSS-CULTURAL PSYCHOLOGY

PERSPECTIVES ON CROSS-CULTURAL PSYCHOLOGY

EDITED BY

Anthony J. Marsella

Roland G. Tharp

Thomas J. Ciborowski

Department of Psychology
University of Hawaii
Honolulu, Hawaii

ACADEMIC PRESS   New York San Francisco London 1979

A Subsidiary of Harcourt Brace Jovanovich, Publishers

ACADEMIC PRESS, INC.
111 Fifth Avenue, New York, New York 10003

United Kingdom Edition published by
ACADEMIC PRESS, INC. (LONDON) LTD.
24/28 Oval Road, London NW1 7DX

Library of Congress Cataloging in Publication Data

Main entry under title:

Perspectives on cross—cultural psychology.

    Includes bibliographies and index.
    1. Ethnopsychology. 2. Personality and culture.
I. Marsella, Anthony J. II. Tharp, Roland G. , Date
III. Ciborowski, Thomas P.
GN502.P47   155. 8   79—6950
ISBN 0—12—473550—9

Contents

I
FOUNDATIONS

1
Modes of Thought in Cross-Cultural Psychology:
An Historical Overview   3

Douglass Price-Williams

v

2

Issues in Cross-Cultural Psychology   17

Walter J. Lonner

3

Language and Communication: The Foundations of Culture   47

Jack Bilmes and Stephen T. Boggs

4

Non-Western Psychology: The Search for Alternatives   77

Paul Pedersen

II
COMPLEX HUMAN BEHAVIOR

5

Cross-Cultural Aspects of Cognitive Functioning:
Culture and Knowledge   101

Thomas J. Ciborowski

Contents

10
Culture and Competence   209

Norman Dinges and LorRaine Duffy

11
Cross-Cultural Studies of Mental Disorders   233

Anthony J. Marsella

III
APPLICATIONS

12
Culture and Education   265

Cathie Jordan and Roland G. Tharp

13
Orientation Programs for Cross-Cultural Preparation   287
Richard W. Brislin

14
Culture and Mental Health Services   307
Howard N. Higginbotham

15
Culture and Psychotherapy   333
Wen-Shing Tseng and Jing Hsu

IV
FUTURE

List of Contributors

Numbers in parentheses indicate the pages on which the authors' contributions begin.

J. W. Berry (117), Department of Psychology, Queen's University, Kingston, Ontario, Canada K7L 3N6

Jack Bilmes (47), Department of Anthropology, University of Hawaii, Honolulu, Hawaii 96822

Stephen T. Boggs (47), Department of Anthropology, University of Hawaii, Honolulu, Hawaii 96822

Jerry D. Boucher (159), East-West Center, Culture Learning Institute, University of Hawaii, Honolulu, Hawaii 96848

Richard W. Brislin (287), East-West Center, Culture Learning Institute, University of Hawaii, Honolulu, Hawaii 96848

Thomas J. Ciborowski (101), Department of Psychology, University of Hawaii, Honolulu, Hawaii 96822

James A. Dator (369), Department of Political Science, University of Hawaii, Honolulu, Hawaii 96822

Andrew R. Davidson (137), Department of Psychology, University of Washington, Seattle, Washington 98105

Norman Dinges (209), East-West Center, and Institute of Behavioral Sciences, University of Hawaii, Honolulu, Hawaii 96848

Juris G. Draguns (179), Department of Psychology, Pennsylvania State University, University Park, Pennsylvania 16802

LorRaine Duffy* (209), Department of Psychology, University of Hawaii, Honolulu, Hawaii 96822

George M. Guthrie (349), Department of Psychology, Pennsylvania State University, University Park, Pennsylvania 16802

Howard N. Higginbotham (307), Department of Psychology, University of Hawaii, Honolulu, Hawaii 96822

Jing Hsu (333), St. Francis Hospital, University of Hawaii, Honolulu. Hawaii 96817

Cathie Jordan (265), Kamehameha Early Education Program, Honolulu, Hawaii 96817

Walter J. Lonner (17), Department of Psychology, Western Washington State College, Bellingham, Washington 98225

Anthony J. Marsella (233), Department of Psychology, University of Hawaii, Honolulu, Hawaii 96822

Paul Pedersen (77), Department of Psychology, and East-West Center, Culture Learning Institute, University of Hawaii, Honolulu, Hawaii 96822

Douglass Price-Williams (3), Department of Psychiatry, University of California, Los Angeles, Los Angeles, California 90024

Roland G. Tharp (265), Department of Psychology, University of Hawaii, Honolulu, Hawaii 96822

Harry C. Triandis (389), Department of Psychology, University of Illinois, Champaign-Urbana, Illinois 61820

Wen-Shing Tseng (333), Department of Psychiatry, John A. Burns School of Medicine, University of Hawaii, Honolulu, Hawaii 96822

* PRESENT ADDRESS: Department of Psychology, University of Utah, Salt Lake City, Utah 84112

Preface

Cross-cultural psychology is that area of scientific inquiry concerned with those similarities and differences in human behavior that can be attributed to cultural variables. Although interest in cultural variables can be traced back several centuries, it has only been within the last few decades that systematic efforts have emerged to identify and to document the effects of these variables on human behavior. Today, cross-cultural psychology is a rapidly growing area of specialization with its own research methods, issues, and theories. It is both a distinct discipline and an area of knowledge that transcends all the social sciences.

Although still in its pioneering stages, cross-cultural psychology holds much promise for increasing both our awareness of the ethnocentricity of many of our assumptions about behavior and our sensitivity to the important role of cultural variables in determining the way we think, feel, and act. Much as comparative psychology has added to our knowledge of behavior through comparisons of nervous-system function across species, so can cross-cultural psychology add to our knowledge through comparisons of behavior across different cultures.

The present book provides an overview of cross-cultural psychology: its history, issues, research findings, applications, and future. Each of the chapters represents an original contribution by an acknowledged expert.

Both the topics and the authors were chosen to provide a "perspective" on the field, a viewpoint for grasping both the contributions that have been made and the opportunities for further growth and development. The current book is not a handbook. It does not present an exhaustive review of the literature with regard to all aspects of human behavior. The forthcoming five-volume *Handbook of Cross-Cultural Psychology*,* edited by Harry Triandis, is being produced to serve this function. The present book has as its scope some of the areas in cross-cultural psychology that are being vigorously researched and studied.

All chapters in the present book were first prepared for a conference on cross-cultural psychology held in 1978 at the University of Hawaii, Honolulu, under the auspices of the First Annual Department of Psychology Symposium on "New Directions in Psychology." The authors were invited to present papers on topics that the editors considered important in providing accurate "perspective" on cross-cultural psychology. As the conference symposium progressed, it became clear that the papers were authoritative statements and important resources for students, researchers, teachers, and practitioners interested in cultural similarities and differences in human behavior.

In the present book, those papers are organized into four parts: Foundations, Complex Human Behavior, Applications, and Future. This organization provides a meaningful progression for assimilating the wealth of material included.

Part I, Foundations, contains chapters on historical themes in cross-cultural psychology, major conceptual and methodological issues, role of language and communication, and non-Western psychologies. Even a cursory reading of this section provides a glimpse of the importance of cross-cultural psychology as a distinct field of scientific inquiry with its own unique historical roots, conflicts, and potential.

Part II, Complex Human Behavior, includes chapters on cognition, cognitive style, attitudes, emotions, personality, competence, and psychopathology. The spectrum of topics covered affords rich new insights into the complex role that cultural factors play in human behavior. It is particularly noteworthy that these chapters were written by individuals from diverse disciplinary backgrounds, including developmental, social, and clinical psychology, and anthropology.

Part III, Applications, contains chapters on the applications of cross-cultural psychology to the areas of education, cross-cultural orientation programs, the delivery of mental health services, and psychotherapy. Even in its brief history, cross-cultural psychology has already produced a struc-

---

* These volumes have been cited as 1979 throughout the book. During production of this volume, it was learned that the *Handbook* publication will be delayed until 1980.

ture of knowledge that has practical implications for educating, training, and serving the health needs of the world's people.

The final part, Future, offers some interesting thoughts about the potential of cross-cultural psychology for contributing to the social sciences. The first chapter traces the research "odyssey" of a modern-day pioneer as he pursues such elusive topics as socialization and modernization from the cross-cultural perspective. The second chapter was prepared by a futurist and is concerned with the future of culture and cultures of the future. Futurology, much like cross-cultural psychology, is a new area of study and gives us the chance to test our guesses about what lies ahead. The final chapter deals with the promise of cross-cultural psychology for increasing our knowledge of behavior through new areas of inquiry and application. It was prepared by the president of the International Association of Cross-Cultural Psychology and clearly reflects the author's unique position and long history of contribution.

In brief, the present book should prove valuable in delineating cross-cultural psychology's past, present, and future, and it is from these vantage points that "perspectives" emerge and grow.

The editors wish to thank the Department of Psychology, University of Hawaii, Honolulu, and the University of Hawaii Foundation for financially supporting the preparation of the present book. The authors also wish to thank the editorial staff of Academic Press for their valuable comments and encouragement.

PERSPECTIVES ON
CROSS-CULTURAL
PSYCHOLOGY

I

FOUNDATIONS

1

Modes of Thought in Cross-Cultural Psychology: An Historical Overview[1]

Douglass Price-Williams

Introduction

It is not my intention to provide in this chapter an historical account of cross-cultural psychology. This has been recently and ably done by Klineberg (in press). Rather, my intention is to attempt to discover the recurrent themes and principles that have tended to mold the study of cross-cultural psychology, and see if they can be defined and analyzed. In doing so, connections with the sister disciplines of anthropology and sociology will be mentioned as it is clear that some of the roots of cross-cultural psychology lay in these disciplines.

I suggest that there have been, and still are for that matter, three distinct modes of thought that have influenced the course of the study of cross-cultural psychology. These modes can be represented as a coordinate scheme as shown in Figure 1.1.

The three axes are orthogonal to one another and, although each can be independently analyzed out, they also interact in the real world. The scheme presented is an heuristic device to express guiding principles that are consid-

[1] This chapter was supported in part by the Carnegie Corporation of New York and also by NICHD Mental Retardation Research Grant 04612. Additional assistance was provided by University of California, School of Medicine, and the Socio-behavioral Research Division, Mental Retardation Research Center, University of California, Los Angeles.

3

PERSPECTIVES ON CROSS-CULTURAL PSYCHOLOGY

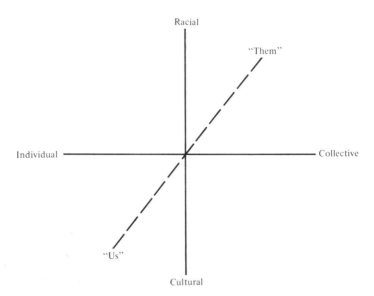

Figure 1.1. A coordinate scheme of three distinct modes of thought that have influenced the course of study of cross-cultural psychology.

ered to be operative in this subject and should not be taken too seriously as a measuring device. It will be noticed that the components of each axis are presented as opposites. Two of them—the racial–cultural and the individual–collective—refer to substantive material. The us–them axis is evaluative.

Racial versus Cultural

Without worrying about very precise definitions (both terms, "racial" and "cultural," have been given all too numerous interpretations in the social science literature), I have simply taken "racial" to pertain to some bodily component—be it genetic or phenotypic—and "cultural" to refer to the manifold of life style. I have chosen the term "racial" for another reason: It is the term adopted by writers in the field that we would now label cross-cultural psychology. However, the difference between racial and cultural is crucial, and the shift in nomenclature occurring in the 1940s and 1950s was an implicit recognition of their lack of equivalence. In this recognition, psychology lagged considerably behind anthropology, as anthropology had focused upon the differences in cultural status and disregarded racial elements, since at least the 1860s (Boas, 1938, pp. 32–33). Of course, it is more natural in the case of psychology, with more of its roots in the biological, that it would concern itself with the racial component. The term "racial" need not be identified with the term "racist," which would constitute the intrusion of our third evaluative axis which will be discussed later. Confusion creeps in when racial and cultural factors are considered synonymous or when cultural factors are disregarded altogether.

The cultural component can be easily traced historically to that field of scholarship that was called folk psychology in the late nineteenth and early twentieth centuries and particularly to one person, Wilhelm Wundt. The importance of folk psychology and Wundt are properly recognized in Klineberg's article, and were given prominence by Gordon Allport in his article on the historical background of modern social psychology (Allport, 1968). Allport pointed out that Wundt bifurcated the field of psychology to the extent that the study of all higher mental processes should be done outside the laboratory, to fall within the province of what he called *Volkerpsychologie*. Wundt had stressed that thinking was heavily conditioned by language, by custom, and by myth, which were the three primary areas of his *Volkerpsychologie*. Allport then summarized Wundt's article as follows:

> When an individual receives sensations from the outer world these commence to combine according to the laws of association, but association depends upon the absorption of an impression into the individual's mass. Impressions enter into a creative relation with memories and contexts stored in this apperceptive mass. But this apperceptive mass is itself a product of culture [Allport, 1968, p. 50].

Although the technical language of associations and apperceptions belongs to the psychological style of the time and no longer has theoretical usage, the actual argument remains relevant. What it says, in effect, is that (at least) our higher psychological processes are saturated through and through with cultural factors to the extent that these processes cannot readily be understood without recourse to cultural factors. It is to be noted that there is no necessary comparative aspect to this thesis, no "cross" prefixed to the psychology, as it were. The problem consists of the relationship of psychology to culture. Of course, this relationship is clarified by comparing cultures so as to identify the nature of the relevant variable. However, the basic question is, namely, how does this or that psychological variable connect with extrapsychological variables.

This question is the basic starting point for a number of varying positions. The recognition that any given psychological process is imbued with cultural factors demands an unraveling of these same factors. Early treatment of this problem led to the taking of causal positions, and an attendance to the relationship between psychology and the social sciences. Rivers (1926), for example, wished to clearly demarcate psychology from sociology, which he did by analogy with the life sciences. He compared the relationship between sociology and psychology with that of geology as compared to physics and chemistry. It was the duty of the geologist to determine the composition of the earth's crust and the history of its constituents in the past. In the same way it was the duty of the sociologist to study the relationships of social phenomena to one another both in the present and in the past. Using the same analogy, Rivers established the basis for the relationship between psychology and sociology. Whereas the geologist has to make assumptions about the physics and chemistry of the situation in order to formulate the mechanism of how the earth's crust came to be as it is, the sociologist has to make assumptions about psychological mechanisms in order to explain why social relations are as they are.

Demarcation, for the sake of analytical analysis, is one thing. Quite how to relate things is another, and it is not always clear exactly how sociology and psychology do relate, despite the analogy of Rivers. Indeed Rivers and Westermarck (see Rivers, 1926, Chap. 1) had a classic argument over the explanatory dominance of the two disciplines. Westermarck wanted to reduce social phenomena to psychological concepts (e.g., the case of the social phenomena of blood feuds—revenge being the reductionist concept). Rivers took issue with this and came out with a statement that indicates the "cultural" component very clearly:

> Just as I believe that it is only through a detailed study of such social processes as the blood-feud that we can expect to understand the real nature of revenge and its place in the mental constitution of different peoples at different levels of development of human society, so do I believe that it is only through the study of social processes in general that we can expect to understand the mental states which underlie these processes. One of the chief interests of sociology is that it affords an avenue by which we may approach and come to understand a most important department of psychology. In place of asking, How can you explain the blood-feud without revenge? I would rather ask, How can you explain the workings of the human mind without a knowledge of the social setting which must have played so great a part in determining the sentiments and opinions of mankind [Rivers, 1926, p. 11]?

This last sentence evokes the same sentiment held by many cross-cultural psychologists today. Indeed, it is a recurrent theme, as Bastian had said much the same thing 40 years before Rivers, indicating that the science of mental life must take cognizance of ethnographic data because "the individual's thinking is made possible only by his functioning in a social group [Lowie, 1937, p. 36]."

Exactly how to take cognizance of ethnographic data is yet a large problem. Like culture, ethnography includes many different kind of factors. What is more, many of these factors are interdependent, a "packaged" variable. For example, in the case of the study of psychological differentiation, it seems that both ecological and socialization factors are involved. Berry deals well with this complexity in his book (1976, Chap. 2) and becomes involved in the kind of argument that was reminiscent of an older environmental determinist school in anthropology and more specifically the cultural ecology viewpoint taken by Julian Steward (1959). The so-called cultural component, then, is complex and, although it can be easily differentiated from the "racial" component, still demands further analysis.

THE RACIAL COMPONENT AND THE US–THEM AXIS

It will be convenient to take the other component of our first axis together with the third evaluative axis, as the history of each has been very much intertwined. As I have mentioned before "racial" can mean "racist" when the evaluative factor intrudes. It is unfortunate that study of the racial component did, in fact, have racist overtones. It provides a legitimacy, if one is needed, for the introduction of the us–them axis in the first place. The us–them distinction is required because there have been, in the history of cultural psychology, evaluative factors that have become entangled with the purely substantive factors. The entanglement is seen when questions of superiority versus inferiority arise—"us" being superior, "them" being inferior; or even when, more subtly, the paradigm of the "us" is taken as a measuring rod against which the "them" is measured. It is noteworthy that Klineberg saw fit to talk about this very thing in his article. He points out that when social scientists took over from pure anecdotal observations and national prejudices, the tendency toward hierarchical conclusions did not go away—the ideas of primitiveness and of genetic lack of endowment helped keep the hierarchical scheme alive. Klineberg goes on to say that this position was maintained by all sorts of beliefs—religious ideas, the natural selection theory, appeals to history—and concludes that:

> Although such a position is still accepted by man, even by some who are identified with the social and biological sciences, the history of cross-cultural research can be characterized in general as a movement away from hierarchy to an appreciation of differences which are considered as variations in life styles rather than as steps on a scale of excellence or progress [Klineberg, in press].

It could not be more clearly expressed. Additionally, whereas Klineberg's point can be addressed to both the cultural and racial components, it is more notable as it applies to racial components. This is probably because cross-cultural psychology primarily focused on similarities and differences in traits, without worrying too much about how these traits were embedded in the cultural medium. Be that as it may, it is clear that some form of a hierarchical notion pervaded the early history of the subject. No doubt prior historical examples could be found, but de Gobineau's (1967) book, *The Inequality of Human Races,* originally published in 1853, set a pattern which has proved to be persistent. In de Gobineau's time the hierarchy was excessively simplistic. For him the mentality of races was a neat scheme with the Negroid races at the bottom, the yellow races in the middle, and the white race at the top.

The author of an early social psychology classic, *The Crowd,* Gustave Le Bon, followed this line of thinking with his book *The Psychology of Peoples,* which was published in English in 1924. There he elaborated on the de Gobineau scheme by postulating that there were primitive, inferior, average, and superior races. Le Bon clearly dips into the cultural side of our axis, as he is concerned with ideas and civilizations, but he is mainly influenced by the notion of racial types. He included in the primitive races the Australian aborigines; Negroes carried the burden of being inferior; Chinese and Japanese were deemed average; and only the Indo-Europeans were classed among the superior races (Le Bon, 1924, p. 27).

It is interesting to note parenthetically that Le Bon was quite specific about those characteristics distinguishing, for him, high and low mentality and levels of social development. Primitive and inferior races were incapable of reasoning, were credulous, and completely lacked the critical spirit. Le Bon considered that the essential point of difference in the social level of peoples was the degree of aptitude for dominating their reflex impulses (1924, pp. 26–27, 30). Unquestionably, Le Bon wove into his intellectual distinctions a characterological component, as is manifest in later chapters of his book.

Although subsequent investigation of different kinds of traits lacked this obvious racist bias, the avalanche of cross-cultural intelligence testing during the first three to four decades of this century did little to offset the pattern set by these early writers. There was heavy emphasis on the racial with little reference to the cultural. The lists are too numerous to cite individually. Garth (1931) published an appendix of experimental and statistical studies on race psychology that indicates the prolific nature of such enterprises up to that time. Additionally, an Office of Education monograph (Cook & Reynolds, 1933) provides a massive collection of studies for the period 1923–1932, broken down into geographical areas.

At the same time it should not be thought that every study of racial differences in mental traits was a mindless effort on the theme of the superiority of the Anglo-Saxon races. Caveats were there from the very beginning. No less a dominant figure in experimental psychology than R. S. Woodworth, in an address to the American Association for the Advancement of Science, cautioned that:

> statements . . . denying to the savage powers of reasoning, or abstraction, or inhibition, or foresight, can be dismissed at once. If the savage differs in these respects from the civilized man, the difference is one of degree, and consistent with considerable overlapping of savage and civilized individuals [Woodworth, 1910, p. 174].

In a later passage he goes on to say:

> Equitable tests of the distinctly intellectual processes are hard to devise, since much depends on the familiarity of the material used. Few tests of this nature have as yet been attempted on different races [Woodworth, 1910, pp. 179–180].

Indeed, even the consideration of this point had to await nearly half a century. Nevertheless there were always reminders. Klineberg himself in his book *Race Differences,* published in 1935, had this important point to make:

> whether our particular criterion of intelligence is applicable to groups with a different background. . . . This relativity in the concept of intelligence has suggested the possibility of devising new tests based upon cultural criteria differing from our own [Klineberg, 1935, pp. 160–161].

Klineberg then goes into the topic of familiarity of tasks. In recent years this has given rise to a whole school of studies on cross-cultural development work, which has been discussed elsewhere (Price-Williams, 1976). There is also a section on the topic of familiarity of tasks in the survey of Piagetian cross-cultural studies (Modgil & Modgil, 1976).

THE CULTURAL COMPONENT AND THE US–THEM AXIS

Although the evaluative factor is more prominent with the racial compo-nent, the cultural side has also been influenced by it. The mere fact that social-sciences terminology has evolved from ''savages'' through ''primi-tives'' through ''underdeveloped'' and presently to ''traditional peoples'' indicates the shifting value distinctions. The evaluative aspect creeps into the cultural component less with the superiority–inferiority complex than with the tacit acceptance that the prevailing standard lies on the ''us'' side. Therefore, when reaction set in against the racial interpretation given to low scores on tests with various ethnic and cultural groups, the scores were seen more as an impairment of environmental, familial, and educational factors. This viewpoint came to be generally known as the ''deficiency'' model.

In a seminal article, Cole and Bruner (1971) articulated the argument by contrasting deficiency with difference. This allowed for a different perspec-tive on other cultures, and subcultures. The value judgment has shrunk to a simple separation: Between ''us'' and ''them'' there are sometimes differ-ences. Such differences do not reflect shortcomings, necessarily, nor do we need to understand them through applying our own standards. This view-point states that other cultures have their own way of making distinctions, forming classifications, perceiving and so on. Therefore, rather than trying to understand these processes by our own standards, we should try to work them out by applying the standards of other people. This is the so-called ''emic'' approach which has been adopted by some scholars (described at length in Chapter 2 by Lonner). However, the us–them distinction continues to hover over scholarship. Francis Hsu particularly has harangued his fellow anthropologists for clinging to distinctions that have no place in the areas that they investigate. One such distinction is the notion that personality is a separate entity, an idea absent in many cultures which identify themselves more with the embedding social structure (Hsu, 1971). In this volume Pedersen has pursued this line of thought with respect to psychology (Chapter 4).

The Collective–Individual Axis

Hsu's point really raises an aspect of the second substantive axis: the collective–individual. At first sight we might say that this reflects only a distinction in disciplines: anthropology and sociology dealing in collectives, psychology focusing on individuals. However, the situation is more complicated than that. First, there is the problem raised in assessing personality cross-culturally. Some investigators have considered it necessary to sample a set number of individuals in order to specify what is meant by a modal personality (e.g., Wallace, 1950). Others, like Benedict (1934), have been content to rely on an impressionistic basis and label entire cultures in terms of personality. Klineberg emphasizes in his chapter (in press) that these two approaches really reflect the differing methodology between psychologists and anthropologists with psychologists evidencing greater interest in individual and subgroup variations within the same cultural or national community than anthropologists. There is also a different kind of question, namely that of the relationship of an individual to society.

As Goldenweiser has indicated, the relationship of an individual to society is a matter of different levels; "the bonds which tie the individual to the group are diverse, some are complex, others simple; some categoric, some loose [1968, p. 64]." What concerns us here is not so much the distinction of a cross-cultural *social* psychology from a cross-cultural *general* psychology (although this can be conceived), but rather a matter of seeing the individual in terms of the collective. If Rivers and others like him are anywhere near correct, it is misleading to focus on the individual apart from those factors that make up his or her milieu. The dilemma of the proper relationship between the individual and the collective confronted Sir Frederic Bartlett who, in his book *Psychology and Primitive Culture* (1923), had this to say on the matter:

> The individual who is considered in psychological theory, in fact, is never an individual pure and simple. The statements about him always have reference to a particular set of conditions. The individual with whom we have to deal may be the individual-in-the-laboratory, or the individual-in-his-everyday-working environment, or—and in social psychology this is always the case—the individual-in-a-given-social-group [Hallowell, 1954, p. 178].

This citation is taken from Hallowell (1954) who, in quoting this from Bartlett, took the opportunity of expatiating on the collective–individual problem as it was reflected in the early pioneers of anthropology and psychology. Hallowell reflected on the Rivers–Westermarck argument already discussed, and made the point that Rivers tended to raise questions without ever settling them one way or the other. This lack of resolution has resulted in various positions being taken that attempt to grapple with the implications of Rivers' arguments. Some, like Leslie White (1949), have reacted by viewing the collective culture as a set of relationships that are quite distinct from the individual and indeed is seen as a phenomenon in its own right, apart from its human carriers. This is the position known as "culturology."

In the realm of psychology this, of course, has not been adopted (there is no room for psychological matters in relation to culture within culturology), but there have been positions taken where culture has been looked upon as an independent unit that may be even inimical to the individuals composing it. Such an interpretation can be given to Freud's (1930) *Civilization and Its Discontents,* wherein the thesis is advanced that the individual is inhibited by the constraints that the culture puts on him or her, and, taken further, that neurosis is the price that mankind pays for the advantages of culture.

An equally deterministic, although nonconflicting, picture is represented by the Russian psychologist, Luria (1976). Luria feels that the mind is shaped by the social forms of human life; that the products of history are social creations in which the child is surrounded; and that human consciousness is thus intimately connected with history. He states, "We began to understand it as the highest form of reflection of reality that sociohistorical development creates: a system of objectively existing agents give birth to it, and causal historical analysis make it accessible to us [Luria, 1976, p. 10]."

Other writers have taken a more individualistic starting point, whereas yet another group again settles for a simple interaction interpretation. Draguns, in the first few pages of Chapter 9, provides examples of the simple interaction interpretation with respect to the relationship between culture and personality. Cross-cultural psychology is in a curious position on the collective–individual issue. On the one hand it has taken the line, as psychology as a whole has always taken, of focusing on individuals as its proper study. Cross-cultural psychology has agreed with the principle that its major function is to formulate laws which would hold for all individuals. Findings on a specified number of individuals thus represent a logical class that would hold for all individuals and thus for human nature. Whereas this agreement is within the mother discipline of psychology, cross-cultural psychology has taken a further step that introduces important modifications about statements said to hold for human nature as a whole.

The search for universals is still there, but now there are qualifications regarding culture. "Culture" therefore becomes a variable to be taken into account, but only to the extent it is needed to throw light on the individual organism. The range of this extent is the crucial question, and although cross-cultural psychology has not yet gone to the limits of conceiving culture in a grander sense, as most anthropologists and some cultural psychologists such as the Soviet School do, there are signs that there are steps in this direction. Cole's (1975) *Ethnographic Psychology of Cognition* indicates the thinking in this direction.

Culture as a Variable

Despite the more radical steps, it is still the position that culture is viewed as a qualifying variable which represents the mainstream of cross-cultural psychology. The thrust of cross-cultural psychology has been to unravel to more definable threads just exactly what is meant by culture. This emphasis was there at the very beginning of systematic experimental researches such as the Cambridge expedition to the Torres Straits and related areas (Haddon, 1901). In that expedition, interest in visual perception and classificatory ability turned to specifications of occupational habits, linguistic structures, and ecological factors. However, the backdrop of the investigations was the state-of-the-art at the time regarding knowledge about visual perception and classificatory ability in general.

In a similar vein, Margaret Mead's (1928) first researches in the South Seas had as a backdrop the existing thought on therapies of adolescence in her home culture. The classic case of Malinowski (1937) finding in the Trobriand Islands a difference in the Oedipal relationship is yet another example. Whiting's (1954) illustration of relating the age of weaning to stress and Albino and Thompson's (1956) study on the effects of sudden weaning with Zulu children show further uses of cross-cultural information in checking findings made from sampling our own culture alone.

In other words, the motive of work done from the 1920s to the 1950s firmly set a pattern which was to be more frequently taken up in the following two decades. This pattern was to extend the range of our psychological knowledge, either through using different types of populations or through using unusual events, in order to broaden and check the domain of psychological knowledge. Although both the disciplines of anthropology and psychology contributed, psychologists put more attention on the process to be tested, while anthropologists used psychological processes to supplement what they knew of the culture.

The Cross-Cultural Method

Whiting (1954) has really covered what needs to be said on the early history of cross-cultural method, but certain aspects of its development need to be highlighted here. As Whiting indicates, the method began with a paper given by Edward Tylor (1889) at the Royal Anthropological Institute of Great Britain called "On a Method of Investigating the Development of Institutions Applied to Laws of Marriage and Descent." This was followed, after a good quarter of a century lag, with Hobhouse, Wheeler, and Ginsberg's (1930) monograph on social institutions. Whereas these early papers were focused on cultural evolution, Whiting accepts the paper by D. C. Horton (1943) as the first application of the cross-cultural method applied to the testing of a hypothesis in behavioral science. The problem examined by Horton was the relationship between the drinking of alcoholic beverages and anxiety. Although Whiting had in mind a more observational type of study than experimental, the logic of the format holds.

The interest for the theme of this chapter is that utilization of the cross-cultural method captures a specific cultural variable, which is then tested for the light it throws on the dependent psychological variable. There is a clear boundary to the cultural variable that avoids becoming entangled in a cultural web, in which cultural factors turn out to be related to one another. This is ideal for an experimental paradigm, so it is easy to see why the pursuit of questions related to this method were undertaken rather than the more complex question of how a psychological process is woven into the culture—a question not so amenable to the comparative method, as it involves the necessity for explicating context.

Cultural Psychology

It is not too much of a digression at this point to make a few comments on the similarities of cross-cultural psychology and comparative psychology. Both of them were influenced by the biological evolutionary theories of Darwin and the social evolutionary ideas espoused by people such as Herbert Spencer. Whereas cross-cultural psychology was, in its early versions, persuaded by the notion of a continuum running from primitive to civilized, comparative psychology had the notion of a continuum from animals to men. Both hold the same principle that one can study the same psychological process in differing organisms (i.e., people of different culture on the one hand, different species on the other hand). Moreover, both had a similar source in the work of Wundt who, as a textbook of comparative psychology (Waters, Rethlingshafer, & Caldwell, 1960) points out, stimulated the use of the comparative method in his *Lectures on Human and Animal Psychology*, published in 1863 in German. Also, in both disciplines, there has been a reaction to the comparative method by stressing the importance of context. In comparative psychology the reaction set in with the advance of ethology. The closeness of the two disciplines can be noted by reference to the name of a chapter in Haddon's (1910) *History of Anthropology*, which is called "Comparative Psychology." This is not just a trick of nominalism; a basic method, the comparative method, was common to the thinking of both disciplines.

The difference between what passes for *cross*-cultural psychology and that branch of inquiry that delves into the contextual background of psychological processes, which one may simply call cultural psychology, deserves further comment. Although cross-cultural psychology may be said to be the logical consequent of cultural psychology, the two can be kept separate as they involve different approaches. It can also be said that cross-cultural psychology, like comparative psychology, has a very clear and distinct methodology.

Cultural psychology, both in terms of concepts and method, is more diffuse. It seems to be anchored in the supposition that "psychology remains incomplete as long as it considers man only as an isolated individual," a remark attributed to the founder of mathematical psychology, Herbart (see Ribot, 1886). It is interesting to note that well-known psychologists who focused on quite other interests—Wundt with physiological psychology, Herbart with mathematical psychology—should have sympathies with cultural psychology, especially as the latter must have seemed less rigorous in both concepts and methods than their main interest. Perhaps this represented a challenge to them. However, although there seemed to be a clear impetus for some kind of psychology, call it cultural or some form of social psychology, it really did not get off the ground.

It is interesting to note that some anthropologists were urging something of the same kind. I do not refer to the obvious psychologically slanted anthropologists whose concern and research were to coalesce in the personality and culture movement, but to anthropologists who were not at all kindly disposed to psychological intrusion into their discipline. I refer to Kroeber (1918) on the one hand, who wrote a plea for a social psychology that I would simply call here cultural psychology, and to Radcliffe-Brown (1957) who looked for an intermediate science that would deal with the relationship of culture to the individual. Cultivators of such an intermediate science for the future would find it rewarding to plough over the old ground first.

References

Albino, R. C., & Thompson, W. J. The effects of sudden weaning on Zulu children. *British Journal of Medical Psychology,* 1956, *29,* 177–210.

Allport, G. W. The historical background of modern social psychology. In G. Lindzey & E. Aronson (Eds.), *The handbook of social psychology* (Vol. 1) (2nd ed.). Reading, Massachusetts: Addison-Wesley, 1968.

Bartlett, F. C. *Psychology and primitive culture.* London: Cambridge Univ. Press, 1923.

Benedict, R. F. Anthropology and the abnormal. *Journal of General Psychology,* 1934, *10* (2), 59–82.

Berry, J. W. *Human ecology and cognitive style.* New York: Wiley, 1976.

Boas, F. *The mind of primitive man.* New York: Macmillan, 1938. (Originally published, 1911.)

Cole, M. An ethnographic psychology of cognition. In R. W. Brislin, S. Bochner, & W. J. Lonner (Eds.), *Cross-cultural perspectives on learning.* New York: Wiley, 1975.

Cole, M., & Bruner, J. S. Cultural differences and inferences about psychological processes. *American Psychologist,* 1971, *26,* 867–876.

Cook, K. M., & Reynolds, F. E. *The education of native and minority groups: A bibliography 1923–1932.* U.S. Office of Education: Bulletin, 1933, No. 12.

de Gobineau, Count A. J. *The inequality of human races.*New York: Howard Fertig, 1967. (Originally published, 1853–1855.)

Freud, S. *Civilization and its discontents.* London: Hogarth Press, 1930.

Garth, T. R. *Race psychology: A study of racial mental differences.* New York: McGraw–Hill, 1931.

Goldenweiser, A. *History, psychology and culture.* Gloucester, Massachusetts: P. Smith, 1968. (Originally published, 1933.)

Haddon, A. C. *Reports of the Cambridge anthropological expedition to Torres Straits* (Vol. 2). Cambridge: Cambridge Univ. Press, 1901.

Haddon, A. C. *History of anthropology.* New York: Putnam, 1910.

Hallowell, A. I. Psychology and anthropology. In J. Gillin (Ed.), *For a science of social man.* New York: Macmillan, 1954.

Hobhouse, L. T., Wheeler, G. C., and Ginsberg, M. *The material culture and social institutions of the simpler peoples.* London: Chapman & Hall, Ltd., 1930.

Horton, D. The functions of alcohol in primitive societies: A cross-cultural study. *Quarterly Journal Studies of Alcohol,* 1943, *4,* 199–320.

Hsu, F. L. K. Psychosocial homeostasis and jen: Conceptual tools for advancing psychological anthropology. *American Anthropologist,* 1971, *73,* 23–43.

Klineberg, O. *Race differences.* New York: Harper, 1935.

Klineberg, O. Historical perspectives: Cross-cultural psychology before 1960. In H. Triandis (Ed.), *Handbook of cross-cultural psychology* (Vol. 1). In press.

Kroeber, A. L. The possibility of a social psychology. *American Journal of Sociology,* 1918, *23,* 633–651.

Le Bon, G. *The psychology of peoples.* New York: G. E. Stechert & Co., reprint 1924.

Lowie, R. H. *The history of ethnological theory.* New York: Holt, 1937.

Luria, A. R. *Cognitive development: Its cultural and social foundations.* Cambridge, Massachusetts: Harvard Univ. Press, 1976.

Malinowski, B. *Sex and repression in savage society.* London: Kegan Paul, Trench, Trubner & Co., Ltd., 1937.

Mcad, M. *Coming of age in Samoa.* New York: Morrow, 1928.

Modgil, S., & Modgil, C. *Piagetian research: Compilation and commentary* (Vol. 8). Rochester, England: Staples Printers, NFER Publishing Co., 1976.

Price-Williams, D. R. Cross-cultural differences in cognitive development. In V. Hamilton & M. D. Vernon, *The development of cognitive processes.* London: Academic Press, 1976.

Radcliffe-Brown, A. R. *A natural science of society.* New York: Free Press, 1957.

Ribot, T. *German psychology to-day.* New York: Scribners, 1886.

Rivers, W. H. R. *Psychology and ethnology.* New York: Harcourt, 1926.

Steward, J. H. The concept and method of cultural ecology. In M. H. Fried (Ed.), *Readings in anthropology* (Vol. 2). New York: Crowell, 1959, 81–93. (Originally published, 1955.)

Tylor, E. B. On a method of investigating the development of institutions: applied to laws of marriage and descent. *Journal of the Anthropological Institute of Great Britain and Ireland,* 1889, *18,* 245–269.

Wallace, A. F. C. The modal personality of the Tuscarora Indians as revealed by the Rorschach test. *Bureau of American Ethnology Bulletin* (150), Washington, D.C., 1950.

Waters, R. H., Rethlingshafer, D. A. & Caldwell, W. E. *Principles of comparative psychology.* New York: McGraw-Hill, 1960.

White, L. A. *The science of culture: A study of man and civilization.* New York: Farrar, Strauss and Giroux, 1949.

Whiting, J. W. M. The cross-cultural method. In G. Lindzey (Ed.), *Handbook of social psychology* (Vol. I). Reading, Massachusetts: Addison-Wesley, 1954.

Woodworth, R. S. Racial differences in mental traits. *Science.* N. S., 1910, *31*, 171–186.

2

Issues in Cross-Cultural Psychology

Walter J. Lonner

Introduction

Cross-cultural psychology has joined anthropology in documenting that interpretations of human behavior are most accurately made in specific sociocultural environments. We know that the behavior evidenced by individuals in one culture is not necessarily "better" or "worse" than behavior found elsewhere, but that it is often manifestly different. We also know (Kuhn, 1970) that the world, as perceived by scientists, is largely determined by what they have been trained to look for, how they go about looking for it, and what they consider to be important topics in contemporary social science. The same situation pertains to any attempt to enumerate "issues" in cross-cultural psychology: perspectives, philosophies, research priorities, and related factors are quite variable, and no single orientation is necessarily "better" than others.

For example, methodological pitfalls to avoid in the conduct of experiments may be of uppermost concern for many scientists. However, concerns of other scientists may have less to do with the complexities of experimental design and analysis and more to do with problems that transcend the narrow boundaries of the field experiment or the theory being tested. Worries about the sociopolitical climate in which research is done as well as cultural sensitivities are prevalent. Additional areas of concern are continuities of

17

PERSPECTIVES ON CROSS-CULTURAL PSYCHOLOGY

research plans, payoffs there may or may not be to the host culture, and the proper placement of cross-cultural psychology within the discipline of psychology. These vexations can be more oppressive than the impersonal domain of the design and analysis of experiments.

Because of such wide variations, as suggested earlier, any attempt to discuss the broad range of issues in cross-cultural psychology is guided by much subjectivity. Using the word "issues" rather than something more tangible like "history of" or "methods in," may be an admission not only that there are many other things requiring attention, but also that we do not yet know where else they may fit. The book, *Issues in Cross-Cultural Research* (Adler, 1977), supports the contention that probably all disciplines, and certainly cross-cultural psychology, need a grab-bag category that can accommodate and examine the leftovers, or the intangibles, until they become clearer and no longer "issues."

Having disclaimed any ownership of the ambiguous title, it can now be said that this chapter will be something of a blend of issues that relate to both methodological concerns and particulars relating to paramethodology. The first part of the chapter is an attempt to summarize a recurrent methodological and epistemological issue permeating all aspects of cross-cultural psychology. The second part is more attuned to problems associated with intercultural sensitivities, cooperation, and options that cross-cultural psychologists may have in the future. The importance of these paramethodological matters cannot be underestimated in such a hybrid orientation as cross-cultural psychology. In the absence of their successful understanding, if not resolution, methodological and epistemological elegance may become mere academic exercises.

Two Methodological Issues Facing
the Comparativist

Two of the most persistent methodological concerns in cross-cultural psychology relate to (*a*) the so-called emic–etic distinction and; (*b*) problems in the establishment of various types of equivalence. They are not totally independent problem areas, but actually are woven together to varying extents in all cross-cultural, psychological research. These two concerns, in fact, are probably what distinguishes psychology from anthropology in culture-comparative strategies more than any other factors.

THE EMIC–ETIC DISTINCTION

This problem has been described and discussed by many authors (e.g., some of the more complete treatments, in chronological order, are Harris, 1964; Berry, 1969; Triandis, Malpass, & Davidson, 1971; Price-Williams,

1974; Jahoda, 1977). The distinction and its implications is such a persistent concern that, in writing about it, one runs the risk of being overly redundant, guilty of plagiarism, or both.

The dilemma has its roots in linguistics, wherein Pike (1966) talked about universal vocal utterances (i.e., phonetics) versus sounds that are culturally unique (i.e., phonemics). Currently, the suffixes have nested themselves securely in the jargon of cross-cultural psychology and so are hardly ever associated with linguistics by members of the cross-cultural guild. In psychological terms, an etic, in its extreme and probably unreachable form, would be some construct, stimulus, or even molar sociological abstraction that is demonstrably and unequivocally recognized everywhere (i.e., no exceptions), and is therefore a universal entity. On the other side of the coin is the emic, or totally unique, construct, stimulus, concept, or abstraction. If the social-scientific world consisted only of etics, comparative research would be no more difficult than standard research done on any college campus or in any research institute or school anywhere in the world. If, on the other hand, we had no universal entities, and instead had only emics, then comparativism would be impossible as no two things (e.g., stimuli, experiments, or cultures) would share anything in common.

If we assume this emic–etic distinction to be a simple bipolar continuum, we can describe certain characteristics at either end, as follows (adapted from Berry & Dasen, 1974);

Perspective Taken by the Researchers

ETIC: The behavior of individuals in one or more cultures is studied from the outside by an outsider or interloper who is not a member of the culture(s) being studied.

EMIC: The behavior of individuals is studied only from within a culture, and then, only by an insider who is intimately familiar with that culture. Published results of such efforts may then be read for this interest value, just as one would read a novel.

Number of Cultures Studied

ETIC: This approach studies as many cultures as possible—the more the merrier—for statistical generalization purposes. (Alternately, it could be argued that to study processes or constructs in one culture is to study processes or constructs in all cultures. A radical behaviorist may argue that to study one organism is to study all organisms.)

EMIC: This approach studies one, and only one, culture at any given time. Generalizations to other cultures are neither contemplated nor desired.

Structure or Constructs Guiding Research

ETIC: These constructs or structures are created by the researcher or the theoretical tradition he follows and are imposed onto the systems being studied.

EMIC: These constructs or structures are discovered by the researcher when and if the structure or constructs manifest themselves as important dimensions in one culture.

Criteria against Which to Compare Behavior in the Culture(s)

ETIC: These criteria are absolute or universal.

EMIC: These criteria are relative to only one culture.

Most of contemporary psychology is an etic enterprise, whereas cultural and social anthropology have traditionally been emic enterprises. However, within each of these disciplines can be found emphases that tend to betray these generalizations. For instance, in psychology certain clinical orientations are more "emic" than other orientations within the discipline (e.g., Rogers' client-centered approach to psychotherapy, and most of the humanistic movement emphasizing and even cherishing individual uniqueness). Likewise, cultural anthropology has research strategies that are highly structured and quantitative, as in the hologeistic, or whole world, method (Naroll, Michik, & Naroll, 1974) or in hypothesis testing through the use of the Human Relations Area Files (Barry, 1979). Both of these methods are unabashedly comparativistic.

Within *cross-cultural* psychology there are even variations of emphases on the opposite poles of this continuum. For example, any psychological approach is at least implicitly "etic" that (*a*) uses tests or standard experiments as if they are universal markers; (*b*) studies more than one culture at a time in the same research program; (*c*) employs a theory or criteria that is not culture-specific; and (*d*) draws generalizations across cultures by using any or all of these factors. An emic psychological approach, of course, would be one that does not rely to any noticeable extent on the above characteristics; to do so would be anathema to the doctrine of cultural relativism.

Exemplars of the Emic–Etic Distinction

Two of the most popular contemporary frameworks within cross-cultural psychology that bring out many of the characteristics of the emic–etic distinction are the research approaches taken by Witkin, Berry, and their colleagues, on the one hand, and by Cole, Scribner, and their colleagues on the other hand. Both frameworks have been energetically and creatively pursued, both make good use of anthropological insight as well as the psychological method, and both have made substantial and convincing contributions. As we shall see, the latter approach tends more toward the "emic" end of our alleged continuum, while the former tends toward the "etic" end. Bear in mind, however, that these researchers are psychologists who over the years have learned a lot of anthropology. One might say that their respective approaches, now to be examined, both reside on the "etic" end, whereas the other "emic" end of the continuum is the province of the classical social or cultural anthropologist.

The Witkin and Berry approach (Witkin & Berry, 1975; Berry, 1976, 1978) is largely guided by Witkin's (Witkin, Dyk, Faterson, Goodenough, & Karp, 1962/1974) theory of psychological differentiation. It is a developmental theory that postulates factors responsible for different "cognitive styles" that range from specific perceptual and cognitive features on the one hand to global personality characteristics on the other. Central concepts in differentiation theory are *field dependence* and *field independence*. People, who through a host of socialization and ecological factors become highly differentiated and are concomitantly guided by internal frames of reference, are characterized as autonomous, self-reliant, and field independent. People who become somewhat less differentiated (but *not* less valuable as persons) being guided more by external situations and generally the social environment are characterized as relatively more socially oriented, sensitive, and field dependent.

The theory is universalistic in its aspirations, and to test its generalizability across the species, it is necessary to attend to at least two important factors. First, dependent variables (measured by tests such as the Embedded Figures Test, and by such tasks as the Asch conformity paradigm) stay relatively constant from study to study, and culture to culture. Second, independent variables (cultural factors that are hypothesized to vary as a function of ecology, acculturation, population density, and other features) are systematically chosen for specific theoretical reasons. In this way the anchoring of dependent variables (behavioral tests and measures) provide for what is hoped to be a relatively common metric with which to assess the effect(s) that the independent variables have on the dependent variables. It has thus been documented that this psychological theory mixes rather well with aspects of anthropological reality in explaining, especially at the group or entire culture level, such phenomena as variations in perception, social conformity, extent of self-disclosure, amount of stress experienced during acculturation, socialization pressures, and so forth.

The strategies employed by Cole, Scribner, and their associates have been radically different from those employed by cognitive style researchers. These workers, who have worked principally in "only" two countries besides the United States—Liberia and Mexico—are, first, not guided by any particular overarching theory that may place constraints on the various paths their research hunches may take them. Moreover, rather than searching for specific factors that may explain the collective and global behavior of an entire culture (as with culture and personality studies), they are interested in more microscopic problems having to do with such basic questions as "what is the role of formal education in development?" "What is cognition?" or "What are the rules that people use when categorizing or naming objects in their environment?" They also want to know exactly how experiments in such research can be situated in the context of the culture of interest.

Second, they accept, as do most cross-cultural psychologists (including Witkin and associates), the assumption taken by anthropologists (e.g., Boas, 1965; Levi-Strauss, 1966) that cognitive *processes* are universal whereas cognitive *content* varies according to cultural values and norms. Because of this assumed common denominator, they see no need to carry their work to as many cultures as possible. In so doing, however, they do not ignore the rather superficial or cosmetic "content" characteristics of the single culture—"superficial" and "cosmetic" not being used pejoratively but as adjectives suggesting that variable cultural uniquenesses barely mask common cognitive processes that are species-wide.

Thus the independent variables (e.g., cultural variations in education or occupational experience) used by experimental anthropologists (as they are sometimes called) are assessed in some detail. Third, their dependent measures (experiments, tests, tasks) are by no means standard or fixed. In fact, it is with respect to the systematic manipulation of the experimental tasks or procedures within the cultural context that tends to emphasize the sharp differences between the two strategies. In short, for cognitive style researchers the context is principally a psychological theory and how it may account for individual and group behavior within or across cultures. The guiding theory can, of course, be modified if new evidence points in that direction. For the experimental anthropologists, in turn, the context is principally a specific culture; attempts are made to situate psychological wisdom (theory) within a unique system.

What does this contrast between research strategies have to do with the etic–emic distinction? As to be explained, I believe that the way in which independent and dependent variables are treated slightly differently in these two traditions is one way to explain a current version of emics and etics, and may prove worthwhile to future researchers in terms of deciding which of these two general strategies—one guided principally by a theoretical context, the other guided principally by a cultural context—they may prefer to take.

In the cognitive style framework, the dependent variables (tests, questions related to socialization practices, etc.) are accorded etic status, whereas the choice of independent variables is more attuned to the adaptive characteristics of the ecosystems of the world, and are therefore more emic. From the viewpoint of experimental anthropology the situation is somewhat reversed.

As psychological processes are assumedly invariant, their independent variables (e.g. characteristic thought patterns of individuals within any culture) are thus more or less fixed, therefore eticlike, whereas the selection of dependent measures is ostensibly more attuned to cultural nuances (e.g., possible communication problems, possible flaws in the experimental design). Dependent measures in experimental anthropology are therefore more emiclike. However, their concern about what the dependent measures "really" mean in a given cultural context leads to a shift in procedures and the nature of what, consequently, becomes the independent variables. Believing that human cognitive skills and processes do not differ qualitatively, Cole, Scribner, and their followers tend to experiment with the dependent variables until populations that once may have *differed* in levels of performance eventually are equal. As Scribner (1976) has said, "This research strategy shifts the principle class of independent variables under investigation from those related to characteristics of populations to those related to characteristics of experiments. Instead of carrying one fixed paradigm to many different cultures, the researcher works with many different variations of a single paradigm within one culture [p. 318]."

The Motorola Quasar as a Cross-Cultural Metaphor

The Motorola Company manufactures a television set that they call the Quasar. A significant portion of the "guts" of the Quasar is in a panel that can easily be removed and immediately replaced with an identical panel in the event of malfunction. Of course, all panels are designed so that they precisely integrate with the rest of the "guts" of the set, including the picture tube, loudspeaker, etc. This is a convenient technical innovation, not unlike a good theory. In the exportation of psychological theories for use in other cultural contexts, the theory is analogous to the removable panel of the Quasar, and the culture is analogous to the chassis with which an integration with theory is being attempted. Now, as any theory in psychology has initially been calibrated on, or integrated primarily within, only one culture, it may be an inestimable error to insert the theory (panel) into another culture (the rest of the chassis) and assume that the same images will appear on the screen and the same sounds will come from the loudspeaker. Any distortions and fuzzy pictures that are seen may be the result of a mismatch of theory and culture (note that it is not culture that is "right" and theory that is "wrong"—only that there may be a mismatch).

It is for reasons similar to this metaphor that Cole and Scribner (1977) have expressed worries about the common practice of the unquestioned exportation of popular psychological theories to other cultures. Skeptical of many of these strategies and the tests they employ, Cole and his associates' contextual experiments deal with a fundamental tenet of classical anthropology: As an item diffuses from one culture to another, its form, function, and meaning may vary independently. In an effort to find the "right" combination of psychological fact and cultural reality, these researchers can become involved in an enormous number of experimental permutations.

Jahoda (1979) criticizes the strategy of Cole and his colleagues on this very point. He notes that Cole has suggested in various writings that a more reasonable way (than using global and sweeping developmental theories such as Piaget's) to study behavior is through the *functional system* approach advanced by Luria (1966). Jahoda seems to think that Luria's system "cannot be regarded as incompatible [with] or even opposed [to]" Piaget's theory. Jahoda (1979) writes:

> If this is correct, it follows that the functional system does not hold out the prospect of a more effective solution of cross-cultural problems. If anything it seems to have some dangers, at least in the way Cole interprets its guidance; for it appears to require extremely exhaustive, and in practice almost endless explorations of quite specific pieces of behavior, with no guarantee of a decisive outcome. This might not be necessary if there were a workable "theory of situations" at our disposal, but as Cole admits there is none. What is lacking in Cole's approach are global theoretical constructs relating to cognitive processes of the kind Piaget provides, and which save the researcher from becoming submerged in a mass of unmanageable materials.

In spite of this critical assessment, Jahoda notes with some enthusiasm the great contribution that Cole, Scribner, and their associates have made, and he is enthusiastic about its inherent value in systems like Piaget's or Witkin's.

Admittedly it may stretch things a trifle to make etics and emics synonymous with dependent and independent variables and to make them analogous to the workings of a television set. The parallel is forced so that a question that prevails in probably all cross-cultural research can be asked: How much confidence, in terms of cultural *comparativism,* can be placed in either of these (or similar) frameworks that tend to treat independent and dependent variables somewhat differently? Since the independent variable in cross-cultural psychology is generally assumed to be in the sphere of macroscopic differences between cultures, it is the emphasis placed on the way in which independent variables are treated that will determine one's principle allegiance to one or the other of these frameworks.

In the cognitive style tradition, comparativism is not only intended and desired (because of standard dependent markers), but it is theoretically postulated in a world that probably has a finite number of ecosystems. Thus, it can lead to a sort of "psychological–ecological" map of the world, where things tend to make best sense against the backdrop of a carefully planned taxonomic system.[1] In the experimental anthropological tradition, com-

---

[1] Berry (personal communication) has said that his research strategy parallels other taxonomic systems. A cross-cultural psychologist may want to collect data in many cultures (e.g., in Berry's case from cultures that are hypothesized to vary with respect to cognitive style). Such

parativism seems, at best, to be either an illusion or incidental to the aims this tradition espouses within the cultural context. Proponents of this viewpoint would first like to know what a test measures in *one* culture before endorsing its use in other cultures.

This brief discussion of two exemplars of the eticlike and emiclike approaches to cross-cultural psychology describe neither the mutual contributions they can make to each other, nor the intermediate positions on the emic–etic continuum occupied by other frameworks. For example, Berry (in press and in Chapter 6 of this volume), has suggested that there are four environmental contexts that produce different organismic effects. The first, and most reductionistic of these, is the *experimental* context, yielding only *scores* (e.g., from tests). The second is the *performance* context, resulting in *responses* to immediate experiences. The third level is the *experiential* context, leading to recurrent *behaviors*. The final context is the *ecological*, accounting for *achievements* or "shared patterns of behavior that can be found in an individual or is distributed in a cultural group", Berry says.

As Berry has pointed out, traditional experimental psychology has the problem of seldom saying anything of value about the performance or experiential contexts while working at the experimental level, let alone saying anything at all about macroscopic behavior in an entire ecological setting. "The problem facing cross-cultural psychology," Berry (in press) says, "tends to be the reverse: rather than failing to ascend the reductionistic–wholistic dimension to achieve ecological validity, cross-cultural psychology has failed to descend the dimension to achieve a specification of experiential and experimental context variables which are responsible for task performance and behavioral variation across natural habitats."

This can be taken to mean that "packaged variables" (Whiting, 1976) of the wholistic variety (where there is power in the cumulative nature of testing large samples within cultures), which Berry, Witkin, and their research associates use as sweeping independent variables, do relatively little to explain variations of scores for *individuals*. On the other hand, the experimental procedures adopted by Cole, Scribner, and their colleagues are refined at the individual level (intentionally using *few* subjects). Therefore, they have not begun the ascension to the ecological level so as to help explain why cultures differ with respect to their institutions, achievements, legacies, and other characteristics that tend to give them a unique identity in the parade of cultures.

It should be mentioned, finally, that these two approaches to the study of cultural factors in basic psychological processes are not in a race so that one will eventually "win." Indeed, there is one reason why they should *not* be

---

strategies may lead to the discovery of how human ecological systems can be explained within a model (taxonomic system) that takes into account all relevant cultural variables affecting individual behavior.

contrasted as *cross*-cultural exemplars. The cognitive style paradigm as outlined by Witkin & Berry (1975) and Berry (1976) is intentionally and enthusiastically cross-cultural, whereas the success of the experimental anthropology framework does not depend upon a sequential and planned investigation of many cultures. The only reason why these two rather different methodological frameworks have been discussed is to shine some light on a major methodological issue. To the extent that they are useful as prototypes of competing strategies that can be generalized to related strategies, this contrast will have served its purpose.

Enough has now been said about these two strategies as they relate to this methodological issue. Those who wish to become more thoroughly acquainted with either or both of them are referred to Witkin and Berry (1975), Berry (1975, 1976, in press) and Witkin (1977, 1978) for outlines of the cognitive style strategy, and to Cole, Gay, Glick, and Sharp (1971), Cole and Bruner (1972), Cole and Scribner (1974, 1977), and Scribner (1976) for the position taken by those who align themselves with the experimental anthropology strategies.

Another, but much briefer, example also highlighting this problem is McClelland's widely used theory of achievement motivation. McClelland (1961) theorized that high (or low) "need achievement" should precede a rise (or decrease) in the rate of national development. He supported his hypothesis by, for example, showing a significant positive correlation between need achievement measured in 1925 and the growth of energy production during the period 1929–1950. However, Finison (1976) failed to replicate this earlier pattern. He found no correlation between need achievement in 1950 and growth in electricity production during 1950–1971 across a sample of 20 countries. Finison also found a *negative* correlation between need achievement in 1950 and national income growth during the same period. As mentioned in his discussion of psychological universals, Lonner (1979) cautioned that such results suggest that the use of generalized models, of which McClelland's is but one of many, may not be appropriate for time periods or societies which do not share the same functional characteristics that existed when the theoretical model was first formulated. So, again we have a possible "assumed etic" that may erode with the passage of time, or with the collection of different samples, or with the use of different strategies. The same *sort* of relationships that McClelland creatively explored may exist everywhere, but perhaps they can be found only through analyses that may be called more emic than etic.

Jahoda (1979) presents an overview of various competing theoretical positions in cross-cultural psychology (including Cole's, Witkin's, and McClelland's) and gives a balanced assessment of the assets and liabilities of these and other theoretical orientations that guide many cross-cultural psychologists. The reader is encouraged to read his excellent review for further guidance on these issues.

The Establishment of Equivalence

If comparisons are to be legitimately made across cultural boundaries, it is first necessary to establish equivalent bases upon which to make such comparisons. Four types of equivalence have received attention from methodologists: functional, conceptual, linguistic (or translation), and metric equivalence. A brief outline of each will be presented.

FUNCTIONAL EQUIVALENCE

The concept of functional equivalence, which is essential for an understanding of the emic–etic distinction as outlined by Berry (1969), is an anthropological concept. It is traceable to Goldschmidt's (1966) "comparative functionalism" approach that seeks to compare the *functions* of institutions at the cultural level rather than the institutions themselves. For example, one institution presumed to be pancultural is some sort of religious ritual (Murdock, 1945; summarized in Lonner, 1979). An uncritical acceptance of religious ritual as a basis for making comparisons of groups as well as individuals may lead to flawed and invalid conclusions. It may be, for instance, that religious ritual in one culture functions as the focal point and highest form of worship of a deity, whereas in another culture a similar ritual may serve as a vehicle to celebrate rites of passage such as marriage or change of status. Conceivably, religious ritual in one culture could be found to have the same function as cosmology or stargazing, not "religion" as literally interpreted by one or two observers, in another culture. As Przeworski and Teune (1970) have so graphically put it, "For specific observation a belch is a belch and nepotism is nepotism. But within an inferential framework a belch is an 'insult' or a 'compliment' and nepotism is 'corruption' or 'responsibility' [cited also in Poortinga, 1975a, p. 23]."

CONCEPTUAL EQUIVALENCE

Functional equivalence is usually viewed from a macroscopic, holocultural level. Conceptual equivalence focuses on the presence (or absence) of meanings that *individuals* attach to specific stimuli such as test items, certain words, the nature of a contrived social psychological experiment, and so forth. It was in the context of this notion of conceptual equivalence that Frijda and Jahoda (1966) questioned the merits of so-called culture-fair testing. Frijda and Jahoda, and others, doubt that anyone will ever develop a truly culture-fair test (which would have to have items either totally familiar or totally unfamiliar to everyone). Perhaps the same specter of pessimism is appropriate when considering any stimuli, tests, experiments, and other dependent variables as well as most of the "manipulated" independent variables for their use in cross-cultural research. In the 1960s and early

1970s, many studies, generally called "comparative social psychological," were undertaken in a wide variety of fairly accessible cultures. These studies were very similar, and usually followed a four-point format:

1. How generalizable is a social psychological concept such as authoritarianism or affiliative need?
2. Test the concept by setting up a contrived laboratory experiment, *patterned after the original Euroamerican laboratory experiments in all important details;*
3. Analyze the results against the backdrop of cultural stereotypes and perhaps anthropological realities (e.g., the "Chinese culture" is authoritarian, or the "Mexican culture" is affiliative); and
4. Conclude, depending upon which direction the results go, that the null hypothesis can be rejected.

In many studies of this type, little attention has been given to the conceptual equivalence of the experiment from the point of view of all cultures that were represented. Sears (1961), who first proposed the notion of conceptual equivalence, contended that it would be difficult to interpret behaviors observed in a given frame without the benefit of additional contextual material.

A simpler example of problems associated with conceptual equivalence can focus on one hypothetical questionnaire item. Suppose we wanted to assess attitudes or aspects of one's personality by asking whether or not one smokes cigarettes. An affirmative answer in the United States could, in the 1970s, characterize one *statistically* as relatively less educated and probably a member of the working class. In many countries (e.g., Mexico) cigarette smoking is not common among the poorer people, perhaps because of the expense. However, it is fairly common among the more affluent and more highly educated people because it may be a symbol that one belongs to the more highly developed and privileged world. Thus the *concept* of cigarette smoking, in this instance, is not equivalent and must be altered somewhat before it can lead to comparable data.

LINGUISTIC (TRANSLATION) EQUIVALENCE

A variant of conceptual equivalence, linguistic equivalence, largely involves both spoken and written language forms for comparative use in questionnaires, interviews, tests, and instructions given during experiments. Of all types of equivalence, the problems associated with linguistic equivalence have received the most consistent attention, with Werner and Campbell (1970); Brislin, Lonner, and Thorndike (1973, Chapter 2); Sechrest, Fay, and Zaidi (1972); and Brislin (1976) providing essential information on the topic. An example will highlight the crux of the problems that must be surmounted if translation equivalence is to be reached.

The statement, "Republican fiscal policies form the backbone of responsible big business," is perfectly understandable as a more or less factual statement in the United States. Literally translated, however, for comparative use elsewhere, it could result in a most nonequivalent statement. First, the concepts of "Republican," "fiscal policies," "backbone," and "big business" are culturally idiographic and culturally isomorphic. Proper translation for more equivalent use elsewhere may result in a statement such as this: "Conservative and thrifty financial policies established by the government are the bases of respected and stable large companies." Linguistically equivalent words, phrases, and sentences should not, however, be translated intuitively and commonsensically with the assumption that one's cultural sensitivities will render the material equivalent. Only through such procedures as back-translation (Brislin, 1976; Sechrest, Fay, & Zaidi, 1972) can one feel reasonably assured that equivalence has been established.

METRIC EQUIVALENCE

A very large percentage of cross-cultural research in psychology is based upon the use of tests and other relatively standardized procedures that yield numerical data. The data are usually scores that place someone on an hypothesized continuous variable (e.g., intelligence) by using an interval scale. Thus children from Culture A may score at Level X on Test Z, whereas children from Culture B may score at Level Y on the same test. In the absence of evidence that the score *levels* are metrically equivalent, any comparisons drawn from the data may be inaccurate, resulting in sets of scores that cannot be compared.

Continuing with this example, as Poortinga (1975a, 1975b) has pointed out, there are three possible interpretations of the score differences between Cultures A and B.

1. The differences are real and absolute, perhaps reflecting genetic differences on the hypothesized attribute (e.g., intelligence).
2. The test *qualitatively* measures different aspects of some hypothesized attribute.
3. The test *quantitatively* measures different aspects of some hypothesized attribute.

Poortinga (1975b, pp. 329–330) has further said that a measure must satisfy three requirements of equivalence if it is to be used for comparisons:

1. It must be *functionally* equivalent, which means that it measures the "same behavioral property in different groups of people." A condition for functional equivalence is that intercorrelation matrices between a set of variables should show equal values for the populations being compared. Poortinga cited a procedure established by Jennrich (1970) as a formal test of this condition.

2. It must be *score equivalent*, meaning that it must measure *quantitatively and qualitatively* the same construct in different populations. In other words, the scores (e.g., on tests) should measure the same things, and at the same level, in other societies.
3. Some tests consist of items that can be used as independent measures. Analysis of the comparability of these items can be done. Item equivalence can be established when each item satisfies the requirements for score equivalence.

Where is Research Done, What Gets Studied, and Who Does It?

WHERE IS RESEARCH DONE?

It is unfair to suggest that cross-cultural psychologists are arbitrary or biased in selecting sites to conduct research. Cross-cultural research is expensive and this reality largely dictates where many people may be able to travel and live for research purposes. Also, cross-cultural psychologists, for all of their independent and pioneering spirit, are nevertheless part of a large professional superstructure that spans the globe. This network of psychological organization ebbs and flows with the *Zeitgeist*[2] and with what holds most currency with funding agencies. Thus cross-cultural psychologists may find themselves doing research that reflects the current trends in mainstream psychology. Both the good and the bad parts of this state of affairs are that cross-cultural psychology extends to other cultures the *Zeitgeist,* and this naturally creates a broader base upon which to develop the science of psychology. The bad part is that cross-cultural psychology is on a tether, so to speak, with relatively limited resources and rare permission to act totally independently.

Nevertheless, the ability to generalize findings in cross-cultural research is limited. The number of distinct and separate world cultures is enormous (Murdock, 1975). However, a large portion of cross-cultural research in psychology is confined to a very small and nonrandom sample of these known cultures. In one small survey (Lonner, 1977) it was shown that the cultures receiving the most attention from cross-cultural psychologists were the United States, India, Israel, Japan, Canada, Australia, and about 10 widely scattered African countries. In the same survey, an even more telling item of information is that the citizenship of authors is generally restricted to these countries plus England, Scotland, Switzerland, and Hong Kong. Although the source of this survey (the *Journal of Cross-Cultural Psychology*'s first 3 years) does not automatically make the picture totally valid, it is fairly evident that data come from a small portion of the world's cultures. The data

---

[2] Spirit of the times.

are dominated by relatively affluent, frequently multilingual, and somewhat adventurous Westerners and their collaborating colleagues who may be native to, but not necessarily representative of, the culture under investigation.

Just as "standard" psychology has been criticized for being largely the psychology of the American college sophomore, cross-cultural psychology runs the risk of being called quasi-cross-cultural, studying human behavior in places that are relatively accessible. Consequently, these studies lean toward the modern, Western lifestyle.

The same criticism about limited generalizability is valid at the *within* culture level. Many samples drawn from within a culture are "samples of convenience" (i.e., in schools, factories, the military, or in railroad stations), and thus are probably not very representative of the entire culture. Yet, in reporting results of research based on such samples of convenience, there is a tendency for researchers to pull the entire culture into the generalization, making sweeping statements about a sort of collectivized individual behavior for that culture. Such statements tend to ignore the tremendous behavioral diversity and variability that each culture is likely to have. Few cross-cultural studies can claim to have used truly representative samples within each of the countries being contrasted—fewer still have gone beyond large initial samples to study within-culture variability.

WHAT TOPICS ARE STUDIED?

A second issue is concerned with the substantive psychological topics that receive attention. The situation here is generally one of feast or near famine. On the one hand, some research strategies have been sustained, integrated, and systematic (e.g., Osgood, May, and Miron's [1975] work with the Semantic Differential Technique, Triandis' [1972] related investigations into subjective culture, Berry's [1976] spreading network of cultures subjected to his ecocultural model, the Six Cultures project [Whiting & Whiting, 1975], and Jahoda's work in Africa, principally Ghana, which has spanned nearly 20 years). These exemplary efforts are heavily offset by the vast number of cross-cultural studies that can be called one-night stands—an affliction that seems to hit just about everyone. There are hundreds of well-conceived and interesting cross-cultural reports in the literature that are not only terminal, but in fact were never planned to extend beyond their limited scope. As a hypothetical example, it would not be very helpful to know how members of a particular caste in India respond to pictorial stimuli without having information about how members from other castes within India respond to the same stimuli. Dozens, if not hundreds, of cross-cultural studies are orphans; no one knows for certain how the results should be interpreted. This situation often leads to very long discussion sections in articles where anthropological musings are indulged. Few researchers seem to have the money, the resources, or the considerable commitment of time to persist in one line of research and to spread the net as far and wide as possible so as to develop an interpretable pattern of results.

In this respect, the last chapter in Cole and Scribner's (1974) book is aptly titled "Trees in Search of a Forest." In that chapter they express concern about how various psychocultural "facts" (their quotes) should be interpreted, when a multitude of possible interpretations are at our disposal. Sechrest (1977) has similarly lamented the lack of theory guiding most cross-cultural research; Malpass (1977) has suggested ways to bridge the gap between theory and cross-cultural research findings.

Until much more triangulation is attempted—using more cultures, different methods, and various research teams replicating the research within the boundaries of a panculturally accepted psychological theory—cross-cultural psychology's interpretations of results will have to be noted with some modesty and caution.

What Is the Purpose of Cross-Cultural Psychology?

A growing number of psychology departments in the United States, Canada, and elsewhere are regularly offering courses that are called "cross-cultural psychology," "sociocultural psychology," "psychology and culture," or something similar. Those who teach such courses typically list the following as objectives:[3]

1. To acquaint the student with the cross-cultural method as used by a growing number of cross-cultural psychologists, and with the potential power of the method. Also, to examine some major differences that exist between cross-cultural psychology, "standard" psychology, and classical cultural anthropology.
2. To give the student a better appreciation for and understanding of human behavior as it occurs in any cultural context.
3. To examine some possible sources of one's ethnocentrism in thought and social interaction.
4. To broaden the base of psychological investigation and inquiry (extending the range of variables and cultural variation).
5. To help prepare students for more advanced courses in psychology and anthropology, or other behavioral sciences, or for work in culturally sensitive areas (e.g., social work, or counseling with minorities). Finally, to make students slightly more aware of cultural sensitivities prior to international travel.

[3] These objectives have been gleaned from my own course syllabi as well as syllabi provided by John Berry and Stephen Bochner.

These objectives cover method and theory, cultural sensitivities, intercultural understanding, and applications. The situation, however, does not seem to be this simple. For what we have here is a distinction between the *teaching* of cross-cultural psychology and the somewhat more problematic situation of conducting research so that there may be something to teach. If cross-cultural research is to continue to thrive and to contribute to objectives such as the ones listed, then the issue of distinguishing basic, theoretical research from application will have to be settled. Let us examine some characteristics of this controversy as it exists in cross-cultural psychology.

In the *Newsletter* of the International Association for Cross-Cultural Psychology there recently appeared a series of editorials that attempted to provide some answers to the question: "What is the purpose of cross-cultural psychology?" The question can be divided into several different parts:

1. Is cross-cultural psychology strictly a methodological frontier which will help psychology develop as a more universally acceptable science by increasing the range of independent variables?
2. Is cross-cultural psychology a methodological frontier plus more: an inherently applied enterprise, that should *always* leave something in its wake that will benefit the cultures in which the research takes place?
3. Is cross-cultural psychology a goldmine for theory testing, or is it a potential contributor to the possible salvation of a troubled, starving, and overpopulated world?
4. Is cross-cultural psychology a combination of the former points or none of them?

Feelings are deep and varied on this issue. They can best be displayed by summarizing some of the main points that were made in several recent editorials published in eight consecutive editions of the IACCP *Newsletter* spanning October, 1976–December, 1977 (Vol. 10, No. 4. through Vol. 11, No. 3). John Berry initiated the series of editorials by suggesting the development of many more "national" psychologies than there presently are, perhaps shelving for the moment any hope of finding international, let alone universal, agreement on the paradigms we use. Berry noted that "most of the world's psychologists, most of the psychological teaching and research, and most of the publishing—in both journals and books—all take place in a single nation state" meaning, of course, the United States.

Harry Triandis's editorial appeared next, and he observed that almost all of cross-cultural psychology (*a*) has to date been concerned with the essential work of testing theories in other cultural contexts; (*b*) has rarely become involved in projects jointly initiated by scientists from several countries; and (*c*) runs the risk of losing credibility and funding if it does not attend to major problems facing nearly all countries instead of appearing as a luxury to many governments. He asks the readers of his editorial: "What can *you* do about that?"

Following Triandis was Mick Bennett, who announced his general disenchantment with cross-cultural psychology, chiding its adherents for still doing too much "airport research" and for perpetuating guildish psychological knowledge that is "either too obstruse [sic], too controversial, or irrelevant." Bennett acknowledged that perhaps cross-cultural psychology should not concern itself with being "problem oriented" or with "in-depth studies of single societies" along the lines established by anthropology and intimated by Berry in his call for nationalistic psychologies. This, Bennett says, would be fine. But, as he fears, such an isolation from reality may "eventually put an end to convenient passive samples from exotic cultures who are prepared to be manipulated to bolster the Western academic reward system." Bennett asks cross-culturalists to ask themselves the question: "Is any person or group I've studied going to benefit anywhere near as much as I?" To Bennett, cross-cultural psychology should be as much an applied enterprise as it is a way to have fun, test favorite theories, and get promoted in the process.

Gustav Jahoda suggested that Triandis's and by implication, Bennett's observations may cause the average cross-cultural psychologist "just to squirm in his chair and resent being made to feel guilty," because there is very little the average cross-cultural psychologist can do of any consequence in a world beset with profound troubles. Jahoda has joined many others in agreeing that psychology needs to make more practical contributions. However, he does not share "the belief that psychology is at present in a position to do a great deal about the long list of major ills which plague the world." Jahoda suggests that we assume a more humble cross-cultural profile and asserts that the ample good will of cross-cultural psychologists should be tapped by psychologists from *within* other cultures, with these psychologists telling us "This is what *you* can do."

In a constructive response to Bennett's tongue-lashing, Roy Malpass suggested that a clearinghouse be developed, where "consultees" (presumably, psychologists or others from developing countries where psychological talent is in short supply) submit descriptions of problem areas, which in turn could be submitted to a number of consultants for reply. Malpass thinks that this process may be workable through an arrangement similar to the sort of consulting board setups that most journals use. He counsels that it would be wise for cross-cultural psychology to take stock of the degree to which it has valuable knowledge to provide, and perhaps to "show a lower profile to the real world until we develop the capacity to actually be of use."

In Diaz-Guerrero's editorial contribution to the possible solutions to this problem, he enumerated six specifications which should guide whether or not papers are allowed to be presented at cross-cultural conferences, or be permitted to grace the pages of journals. These specifications included comments about taking local beliefs into account, shedding light on a local problem, enabling local inhabitants to understand themselves better as a result of research, providing training for local personnel, using at the same time paradigms that have been usefully employed in many cultures, and ensuring that tests and tasks used in the research are adapted for subsequent use by local personnel.

In spite of the idealism and sensitivity contained in these guidelines, my own response to Diaz-Guerrero argued that it would be very difficult to police the conduct of cross-cultural research as well as the processes by which the research is published. The crux of Diaz-Guerrero's thoughtful concerns, however, is embodied in his own quest to develop a "Mexican Psychology" (Diaz-Guerrero, 1977) and a suggestion that others in the Third World follow his suit. A short paragraph in his editorial (IACCP *Newsletter,* Vol. 11, No. 3) speaks for itself:

> To summarize the fundamental theoretical and applied argument, let us say, that cross-cultural psychology up to now has promoted a great deal of application of the instruments developed in the First World. It has done very little to stimulate the development of local instruments that will at least measure socioeconomic characteristics in the Third World, and has been almost completely blind regarding the development of measures sensitive to idiosyncratic cultural and personality dimensions [Diaz-Guerrero, 1977, p. 3].

Ronald Taft, in his editorial (IACCP *Newsletter,* Vol. 11, No. 4) aimed more at the so-called Tapp Report concerning ethical issues in cross-cultural research (Tapp, Kelman, Triandis, Wrightsman, and Coelho, 1974), asked if cross-cultural research is ethically permissible. He implied that cross-cultural psychology, done by both outsiders who "mine" cultures for data and insiders who are usually close colleagues of the latter, is a form of intellectual "colonialism" to the extent that native subjects do not share the same value system of the researchers. Taft claimed that "indigenous scientists have little more right to exploit their people than do outsiders, even though they may make claims based on the common nationality that they share with the subject [p. 5]." The issues Taft raised are, of course, oriented towards the problem of ethics, and it is an ethical problem if, in fact, cross-cultural psychologists who are "only" theory testers or data harvesters are plundering foreign countries for their own gain and leaving nothing of value behind.

It is ironic that the constitution of the International Association for Cross-Cultural Psychology states that the association exists so as to test the range of theories and to develop a more universalistic psychology. Nowhere is it stated that its members must be both theoreticians and society's problem solvers, though perhaps it is implied. It is also ironic—perhaps informative is a better word—that members of the Third World seem not to be unanimously in favor of demanding practical applications of cross-culturalists. Biswanath Roy, of India, asserted in his editorial contribution that cross-cultural psychology is "an applied field." It is his opinion that "No researcher . . . should take up intercultural research just for the sake of doing it." But S. M. Hafeez Zaidi (1978), in a strongly worded opinion about the theory-application–ethics issue, seems not to be concerned about "ethics" or exploiting indigenous people for the sake of collecting data. He asks, "Are subjects in developing countries any better or worse than the children and college sophomores in the United States? Is not the research for the benefit of science and humanity? When students and children are used in a research project, is it not for the benefit of other students and children?"

A problem naturally arises from this complex issue. For example, suppose that some commission of cross-cultural moralists decides that certain research should not be done, simply because an immediate payoff to the culture in terms of bettering life's miserable conditions is not likely. No better example of this dilemma can be used than that of a certain tradition of research in visual perception. A large quantity of very good research has "exploited" ecocultures solely to examine aspects of the nativist–empiricist argument in the perception of visual illusions. For example, Bolton (Bolton, Michelson, Wilde, & Bolton, 1975) and Pollnac (1977) studied aspects of the Müller–Lyer illusion in radically different environments, and Brislin (1974) and Wagner (1977) studied variations in the perception of the Ponzo illusion.

These studies are removed from the kinds of applications that may help Third World countries. One cannot eat visual illusions or use them as diaphragms (although the Müller–Lyer illusion may be an effective I.U.D.). However, it is cross-cultural psychology of a high caliber, at least from the epistemological point of view. That this practice is condoned and even encouraged is attested to by the fact that these purely theoretical articles appeared in the three leading journals oriented more or less exclusively toward cross-cultural psychology.

If, by some ex cathedra pronouncement, cross-cultural psychology were to become strictly an applied enterprise, then, with the door shut on "pure" basic research, we will have lost the first and major characteristic of cross-cultural psychology: extending the range of variables so that psychological theory can be tested in the broadest context possible. There seems to be no good reason why theory and application cannot realize some reciprocal benefits. Applications can suggest problem areas in theory, which can be refined and subsequently applied in another setting. Basic research has been psychology's backbone for over 100 years. To suggest that cross-cultural psychology should now sacrifice theory for application would be to ask that it turn to applications equipped with an incomplete theoretical perspective.

The Issue of the Relative Merits of
Cross- Versus Subcultural Research

Continuing with portions of points raised in the preceding section, a purist may argue that the cross-cultural research method is at its best when theoretical constructs are maximally contrasted, and are relatively free of confounding variables.[4] A characteristic of many of the most influential cross-cultural comparative studies is that they have exploited the widest possible range of "naturally occurring behavior," treating these conditions as manipulations created by nature and not by the laboratory researcher.

For instance, in an effort to create as much behavioral variation as possible, Minturn, Lambert (1964), and their colleagues chose six widely scattered cultures, hoping that this spread would approximate a random, if very small, sample of the world's peoples. Munroe and Munroe (1975) used the same rationale in selecting three cultures, all quite separated by geography and cultural traditions. Segall, Campbell, and Herskovits (1966) studied ecocultural factors in the perception of visual illusions by selecting cultural groups that would maximize the extent to which the independent variable (the carpentered world) would "take" in Segall *et al.*'s attempt to shed some light on the nativist–empiricist argument in perception. Berry (1966) made an extremely wide contrast when he compared the perceptual skills of the Eskimo with those of the Temne tribe in Africa. Price-Williams, Gordon, and Ramirez (1969) contrasted Mexican children with and without experience in pottery making in an effort to study the role of experience in the development of the Piagetian construct of conservation. The entire enterprise of cross-cultural Piagetian research has actually been one of theory testing. The same can be said of Witkin's differentiation hypothesis, the vast majority of the work on culture and perception (Deregowski, 1979), and Osgood's sweeping experimentation with the measurement of metaphorical meaning (Osgood, May, & Miron, 1975).

It is no accident that these well-known research efforts, and others like them, have received high marks by the cross-cultural intelligensia. The results have been rather clear-cut (having been designed that way from the outset). They have been difficult and expensive to implement successfully. The results have cast light on certain theoretical perspectives, and they have been cited with increasing frequency in basic psychological texts.

On the other hand, much research that is termed cross-cultural is in fact better called subcultural or cross-ethnic. Examples of this class of research include contrasts, within one country, of ethnic groups having differential

[4] The problem of confounding in cross-cultural research is the province of the so-called "Galton's Problem," the solutions to which try to untangle "real" (functional) from "diffused" (borrowed or exported) cause–effect relationships. (See Naroll & Cohen, 1970, for an earlier treatment of the problem.)

levels of acculturation, bilingualism, and education. No better example of this is the cross-ethnic research done in the United States, using major subcultural groups such as blacks, Chicanos, and American Indians. In Hawaii this situation has been exploited (e.g., Gallimore, Boggs, & Jordan, 1974) with only a slightly clearer impression that cultural groups there offer more of a contrast. Perhaps subcultural United States research is most energetically pursued among the network of social scientists who live in the southern California basin, within a 75 mile radius of Los Angeles. The number of Spanish-speaking people in Los Angeles makes it one of the largest Spanish-surnamed metropolitan areas in the world. It and its surrounding urban sprawl thus qualify it as a natural laboratory of social scientific research (e.g., to study ethnic identification, self esteem, competitive versus cooperative life styles, active versus passive coping styles). A recent volume by Martinez (1978) demonstrates the wide range of activities pursued by the Chicano research community for the Chicano population; the recent inauguration of the *Hispanic Journal of Behavioral Sciences* is further documentation of this activity. These developments are very wholesome, and certainly have psychological and educational implications for this immediate population. Similar situations exist elsewhere. For example, many Canadians and Israelis are active in cross-ethnic research within their own countries.

Another factor can now be brought to bear on this issue. Although no research is really "easy," it is certainly much more comfortable, usually less expensive, and more immediately productive to do research within ethnically mixed schools and communities that are within easy reach of one's office. Where cross-cultural research has been called "airport research," cross-ethnic or subcultural variations of the same enterprise can be called "subway research," or "mass transit research."

The question can be asked: Should a distinction be made between cross-cultural and subcultural research, or between cross-cultural and cross-national research? Although it may be true that the most clear-cut test of certain theories can be done by using groups that are as widely contrasted and geographically separated as possible, one is also running the risk of simultaneously diminishing the levels of conceptual, functional, and metric equivalence that seem to be requirements for making acceptable comparisons. A serious shortcoming of subcultural, cross-ethnic or cross-national research (to the extent that we are aiming for cross-cultural purity) is that the psychological variables or constructs chosen are for the most part so deeply confounded that any number of alternative hypotheses could account for the result. It is paradoxical that in cross-cultural research of the "pure theoretical" sort the researcher has to weigh any potential gains there may be in using extreme contrasts against what may be lost in attempts to establish equivalence across such a contrast. Conversely, the cross-ethnic or subcultural researcher must be concerned with how much his research may contribute to a more general understanding of a specific theory, weighing this against the inevitability of confounding brought about by studying groups that have much in common.

It certainly cannot be suggested that cross-ethnic or subcultural research be relegated second-class status, or abandoned altogether. It is possible that studies done within one country can be more important or theoretically more defensible than many studies done in more exotic settings. Nevertheless, this issue always returns to the same question: How much of a blend of theory versus application should be demanded of cross-cultural psychology? If cross-cultural psychology is more of a theoretical enterprise, then extending the range of variables by selecting widely contrasting cultural groups is the quickest way to either support or refute a theoretical proposition. In this sort of situation the key variable(s) may be fully exposed. If, however, a measure of application should be demanded of all cross-cultural studies, then the investigation of proximal groups within one country seems most defensible.

The question can be asked in the context of actual practice. Assume that two different studies were competently executed, and that the only substantive difference between the projects was that one study contrasted three widely scattered cultures—Cultures A, M, and Z—and the other focused on three groups—Cultures A, B, and C (with an A–Z contrast representing the most extreme). Which of the two projects should be published first in a periodical or book dealing with cross-cultural psychological research? Assuming that your immediate reaction is to select the "A-M-Z" study over the "A-B-C" study because of the former's assumed "purity," how do you explain this decision to the authors of the latter study?

If subcultural research in pluralistic societies is to be evaluated and accepted on an equal footing—and indeed it should be—with research done across more easily definable and contrasting cultures, then the problem requires some careful attention. Berry (1978) has offered a possible solution.[5] His proposal is essentially a special case of "Galton's Problem" (see footnote 4), the solution to which requires untangling that which is independently *functional* in societies being compared from that which has been borrowed (diffused) from other cultures—including, perhaps, one or more of the cultures being cast in the comparative network.

Diffused cultural artifacts and practices do not meet the test of independence, and therefore violate statistical assumptions. Naroll (Naroll & Cohen, 1970) created the concept of the "cultunit" (culture-bearing unit) in an effort to render comparisons more statistically acceptable. Each of his four cultunits (i.e., the Hopi, the Flathead, the Aztec, and the Aymaran) describe independent and distinct culture types that are based upon mutually exclu-

---

[5] This paper is being modified and is expected to appear in the *Journal of Cross-Cultural Psychology* in late 1979 or early 1980.

sive linguistic and political features. Berry suggests that two of Naroll's cultunits, the Aztec and the Aymaran, and a third, the Ukrainian-Canadian, are descriptive of the cultural and linguistic situations existing in pluralistic societies (e.g., usually a "dominant" culture and various ethnic groups within). In using a new concept, which he has termed the "ethunit," Berry believes that research done with ethnic groups within pluralistic societies can become conceptually more clear. The result of such an advance, the details of which having yet to be settled, would be a significant step in the direction of unconfounding independent variables that may be shared (etic) or idiosyncratic (emic) features of "cultures within cultures."

Keeping Pace with Developments: The Issue of Diffusion and Redefinition

Cross-cultural psychology has been around for only a short time as an active and identifiable entity, with all the accoutrements giving it a measure of professional identity (e.g., its own organization, international meetings, books, journals, and newsletters). Yet cross-culturalists have gained their identity only recently. Prior to about 1965, psychologists who pursued the then rather vague and murky enterprise of cross-cultural comparisons were sometimes spurned by their colleagues and often characterized as rather odd creatures who entertained themselves in the fringes of psychology (Jahoda, 1970; Klineberg, 1979; Price-Williams, Chapter 1 in this volume).

After the well-known Cambridge Expeditions took place (Rivers, 1905), there was a long period of random activity, during which the term "sabbatical opportunism" must have originated. The practice of seeing how well other peoples did on tests, or how well a theory matched an exotic culture, was fairly commonplace, though infrequent enough so that such studies were neither threats to mainstream thinking nor sustained any one substantive area. Then, in 1957, the *Journal of Social Psychology* developed a policy of granting publication priority to such studies under a section titled "Cross-Cultural Notes." Nine years later, in 1966, the *International Journal of Psychology* was inaugurated. With a subvention from UNESCO and sponsorship by the International Union of Psychological Science, part of the policy of the *International Journal of Psychology* has been the publication of cross-cultural research under the scope of its overall policy to "facilitate communication, to develop understanding, and to foster cooperation among psychologists throughout the world." Four years later, in 1970, the *Journal of Cross-Cultural Psychology* was founded.

Exclusively devoted to cross-cultural empirical research, the *Journal of Cross-Cultural Psychology* encouraged manuscripts from neighboring disciplines such as anthropology, linguistics, criminology, and education as long as psychological phenomena, as they naturally occur in other sociocultural contexts, are the targets of the research. Quite a variety of other journals have followed these precedents, and other publications in disciplines congenial to the cross-cultural method very frequently contain articles that are culture-comparative.[6] These additional journals,[7] started during the past few years and the probability of still others to come tend to diffuse published cross-cultural research, making it hard to keep pace with such research. Such a "bandwagon phenomenon" is increasing the difficulty of defining cross-cultural psychology.

There are two other factors contributing to this relative state of confusion. One is that various books, some in series, contain anything *but* a shared definition of cross-cultural psychology. The first of these (Price-Williams, 1969) carried chapters written by researchers representing a wide range of disciplines—from cultural anthropology of the "old school" of Freudian hypothesis testing, to those representing hard-core cognitive psychology. Another (Lambert & Weisbrod, 1971) implied that cross-cultural psychology is largely comparative social psychology, and still another (Cole & Scribner, 1974) serves well as a cross-cultural introduction to cognitive and linguistic material—literally banishing other cross-cultural spheres (notably intelligence testing) to a never-never land of chronic ambiguity. Berry and Dasen's (1974) book probes deeper into cognition.

The other of the two additional factors contributing to some confusion of direction and definition is organizational. At least four associations[8] and, in most instances, their local or regional counterparts express the same goals, share many of the same influential leaders, contribute to the same journals, cite each other sometimes to the point of scandal, and generally run the risk of duplicating efforts to an extent that may not be entirely healthy. This rapid growth of books, journals, and associations will soon have to reach a plateau. Undoubtedly cross-cultural psychology will continue to grow and to reach out in various directions. It will, however, look somewhat different 10 years from now. It will be interesting indeed to monitor developments during the next decade.

Concluding Comments

This chapter began with the disclaimer that the issues to be raised are not necessarily the only ones in cross-cultural research. In the process of dis-

---

[6] *The 1973 Directory of Cross-Cultural Research and Researchers* lists some 30 journals containing cross-cultural research reports.

[7] These are: *Ethos, International Journal of Intercultural Relations, International Journal for the Advancement of Counseling,* and *Culture, Medicine, and Psychiatry.*

[8] The associations are: International Association for Cross-Cultural Psychology, International Council of Psychologists, Society of Cross-Cultural Research, and Society for Intercultural Education Training and Research.

cussing several of them, perhaps other problem areas were overlooked, a situation that can be attributed to my own subjective choices. Others might have chosen differently, had they been invited to discuss their viewpoints.

In any case, the preceding pages may read like a laundry list of formidable obstacles to be overcome, casting some gloom on the cross-cultural enterprise. It may therefore be uplifting to conclude on an upbeat note.

Many cross-cultural psychologists consider psychology an essential and even interesting science, and they respect the cross-cultural approach as a necessary method. Instead of trembling at the altar of a cross-cultural superego and becoming immobilized by the burden of the "issues," they prefer to be ceaselessly curious and empirical—going about their work with an air of detached, scientific pragmatism. To many, there is only one issue: the veridicality of psychological theory. If they happen to encounter problems, in other cultures, in their quest for good and usable data, they will surely be sensitive and wise enough to attempt to solve them. Cross-cultural psychology, as a method, is nearly as interesting as the enormous variations of cultures it attempts to study. One can only hope that an increasing number of psychologists, from all cultures, join in on the fun, misery, and fascination of it all.

References

Adler, L. L. (Ed.) *Issues in cross-cultural research. Annals of the New York Academy of Sciences,* Vol. 285, 1977.

Barry, H. III. Description and uses of the Human Relations Area Files. In H. Triandis & J. Berry (Eds.), *Handbook of cross-cultural psychology,* (Vol. II). Rockleigh, New Jersey: Allyn & Bacon, 1979.

Berry, J. W. Temne and Eskimo perceptual skills. *International Journal of Psychology,* 1966, *1,* 207–229.

Berry, J. W. On cross-cultural comparability. *International Journal of Psychology,* 1969, *4,* 119–128.

Berry, J. W. Ecology, cultural adaptation, and psychological differentiation: traditional patterning and acculturative stress. In R. W. Brislin, S. Bochner, & W. J. Lonner (Eds.), *Cross-cultural perspectives on learning.* Beverly Hills, California: Sage–Halsted, 1975.

Berry, J. W. *Human ecology and cognitive style: Comparative studies in cultural and psychological adaptation.* Beverly Hills, California: Sage–Halsted, 1976.

Berry, J. W. Implications of cross-cultural methods for research in multicultural societies. Paper presented at the symposium, *Theory and practice of cross-cultural research in Canada.* Symposium presented at the meeting of the Canadian Psychological Association, Ottawa, 1978. To appear in the *Journal of Cross-Cultural Psychology* in 1979 or 1980.

Berry, J. W. Ecological analyses for cross-cultural psychology. In N. Warren (Ed.), *Studies in cross-cultural psychology* (Vol. 3). London: Academic Press, in press.

Berry, J. W., & Dasen, P. R. (Eds.). *Culture and cognition: Readings in cross-cultural psychology.* London: Methuen, 1974.

Boas, F. *The mind of primitive man.* New York: Free Press, 1965.

Bolton, R., Michelson, C., Wilde, J., & Bolton, C. The heights of an illusion: On the relationship between altitude and perception. *Ethos,* 1975, *3,* 403–424.

Brislin, R. W., Lonner, W. J., & Thorndike, R. M. *Cross-cultural research methods.* New York: Wiley, 1973.

Brislin, R. W. The Ponzo illusion: Additional cues, age, orientation, and culture. *Journal of Cross-Cultural Psychology,* 1974, *5,* 139–161.

Brislin, R. W. (Ed.). *Translation: Application and research.* New York: Gardner, 1976.

Cole, M., & Bruner, J. Cultural differences and inferences about psychological processes. *American Psychologist,* 1972, *26,* 867–876.

Cole, M., & Scribner, S. *Culture and thought: A psychological introduction.* New York: Wiley, 1974.

Cole, M., & Scribner, S. Developmental theories applied to cross-cultural cognitive research. *Annals of the New York Academy of Sciences,* 1977, *285.*

Cole, M., Gay, J., Glick, J., & Sharp, D. *The cultural context of learning and thinking.* New York: Basic Books, 1971.

Dasen, P. (Ed.). *Piagetian psychology: Cross-cultural contributions.* New York: Gardner, 1977.

Deregowski, J. Perception. In H. Triandis & W. Lonner (Eds.), *Handbook of cross-cultural psychology* (Vol. 3). Rockleigh, New Jersey: Allyn & Bacon, 1979.

Diaz-Guerrero, R. A Mexican psychology. *American Psychologist,* 1977, *32,* 934–944.

Finison, L. J. The application of McClelland's national development model to recent data. *Journal of Social Psychology,* 1976, *98,* 55–59.

Frijda, N., & Jahoda, G. On the scope and methods of cross-cultural research. *International Journal of Psychology,* 1966, *1,* 109–127.

Gallimore, R., Boggs, J., & Jordan, C. *Culture, behavior, and education: A study of Hawaiian-Americans.* Beverly Hills, California: Sage Publications, 1974.

Goldschmidt, W. *Comparative functionalism.* Berkeley: Univ. of California Press, 1966.

Harris, M. *The nature of cultural things.* New York: Random House, 1964.

Jahoda, G. A cross-cultural perspective in psychology. *The Advancement of Science,* 1970, *27,* 1–14.

Jahoda, G. In pursuit of the emic–etic distinction: Can we ever capture it? In Y. H. Poortinga (Ed.), *Basic problems in cross-cultural psychology.* Amsterdam: Swets & Zeitlinger, 1977.

Jahoda, G. Theoretical and systematic approaches in cross-cultural psychology. In H. C. Triandis & W. E. Lambert (Eds.), *Handbook of cross-cultural psychology* (Vol. 1). Rockleigh, New Jersey: Allyn & Bacon, 1979.

Jennrich, R. I. An asymptotic X^2-test for the equality of two correlation matrices. *Journal of American Statistical Association,* 1970, *65,* 904–912.

Klineberg, O. Historical perspectives. In H. Triandis & W. Lambert (Eds.), *Handbook of cross-cultural psychology* (Vol. 1). Rockleigh, New Jersey: Allyn & Bacon, 1979.

Kuhn, T. S. *The structure of scientific revolutions* (2nd ed.) Chicago: Univ. of Chicago Press, 1970.

Lambert, W. E., & Weisbrod, R. *Comparative perspectives on social psychology.* Boston: Little, Brown, 1971.

Levi-Strauss, C. *The savage mind.* Chicago: Univ. of Chicago Press, 1966.

Lonner, W. J. Issues in the publication and dissemination of cross-cultural research data. *Annals of the New York Academy of Sciences,* 1977, *285.*

Lonner, W. J. The search for psychological universals. In H. C. Triandis & W. Lambert (Eds.), *Handbook of cross-cultural psychology* (Vol. 1). Rockleigh, New Jersey: Allyn & Bacon, 1979.

Luria, A. R. *Higher cortical functions in man.* New York: Basic Books, 1966.

Martinez, J. (Ed.). *Chicano psychology.* New York: Academic Press, 1978.

Malpass, R. S. On the theoretical basis of methodology: A return to basics. In Y. H. Poortinga (Ed.), *Basic problems in cross-cultural psychology.* Amsterdam: Swets & Zeitlinger, 1977.

McClelland, D. C. *The achieving society.* Princeton, New Jersey: Van Nostrand, 1961.

Minturn, L., & Lambert, W. *Mothers of six cultures: Antecedents of child rearing.* New York: Wiley, 1964.

Munroe, R. L., & Munroe, R. H. *Cross-cultural human development.* Monterrey, California: Brooks & Cole, 1975.

Murdock, G. P. The common denominator of cultures. In R. Linton (Ed.), *The science of man in the world crisis.* New York: Columbia Univ. Press, 1945.

Murdock, G. P. *Outline of world cultures* (5th ed.). New Haven, Connecticut: Human Relations Area Files, 1975.

Naroll, R., & Cohen, R. (Eds.). *A handbook of method in cultural anthropology.* New York: Doubleday, Natural History Press, 1970.

Naroll, R., Michik, G., & Naroll, F. Hologeistic theory testing. In J. Jorgensen (Ed.), *Harold Driver Festschrift.* New York: HRAF Press; 1974.

Osgood, C. E., May, W., & Miron, M. *Cross-cultural universals of affective meaning.* Champaign, Illinois: Univ. of Illinois Press, 1975.

Pike, K. *Language in relation to a unified theory of the structure of human behavior.* The Hague: Mouton, 1966.

Pollnac, R. Illusion susceptibility and adaptation to the marine environment: Is the carpentered world hypothesis seaworthy? *Journal of Cross-Cultural Psychology,* 1977, *8*, 425–434.

Poortinga, Y. H. Limitations on intercultural comparison of psychological data. *Nederlands Tijdschrift voor de Psychologie,* 1975, *30*, 23–39. (a)

Poortinga, Y. H. Some implications of three different approaches to intercultural comparison. In J. W. Berry and W. J. Lonner (Eds.), *Applied cross-cultural psychology.* Amsterdam: Swets & Zeitlinger, 1975. (b)

Price-Williams, D. (Ed.). *Cross-cultural studies.* Baltimore: Penguin, 1969.

Price-Williams, D. Psychological experiment and anthropology: The problem of categories. *Ethos,* 1974, *2*, 95–114.

Price-Williams, D., Gordon, W., & Ramirez, M. Skill and conservation. *Developmental Psychology,* 1969, *1*, 769.

Przeworski, A., & Teune, H. *The logic of comparative social inquiry.* New York: Wiley, 1970.

Rivers, W. H. R. Observation on the sense of the Todas. *British Journal of Psychology,* 1905, *1*, 321–396.

Scribner, S. Situating the experiment in cross-cultural research. In K. Riegel & J. Meacham (Eds.), *The developing individual in a changing world.* The Hague: Mouton, 1976.

Sears, R. Transcultural variables and conceptual equivalence. In B. Kaplan (Ed.), *Studying personality cross-culturally.* New York: Harper, 1961.

Sechrest, L. On the dearth of theory in cross-cultural psychology: There is madness in our method. In Y. H. Poortinga (Ed.), *Basic problems in cross-cultural psychology.* Amsterdam: Swets & Zeitlinger, 1977.

Sechrest, L., Fay, T., & Zaidi, H. Problems of translation in cross-cultural research. *Journal of Cross-Cultural Psychology,* 1972, *3*, 41–56.

Segall, M., Campbell, D., & Herskovits, M. *The influence of culture on visual perception.* Indianapolis, Indiana: Bobbs-Merrill, 1966.

Tapp, J., Kelman, H. C., Triandis, H. C., Wrightsman, L., & Coelho, G. Continuing concerns in cross-cultural ethics: A report. *International Journal of Psychology,* 1974, *9*, 231–249.

Triandis, H. C., (Ed.). *The analysis of subjective culture.* New York: Wiley, 1972.

Triandis, H., Malpass, R., & Davidson, A. Cross-cultural psychology. In B. Siegel (Ed.), *Biennial Review of Anthropology.* Stanford, California: Stanford Univ. Press, 1971.

Wagner, D. Ontogeny of the Ponzo illusion; Effects of age, schooling and environment. *International Journal of Psychology,* 1977 *12*, 161–176.

Werner, O., & Campbell, D. Translating, working through interpreters, and the problem of decentering. In R. Naroll & R. Cohen (Eds.), *A handbook of method in cultural anthropology.* New York: Doubleday, Natural History Press, 1970.

Whiting, B. The problem of the packaged variable. In K. Riegel & J. Meacham (Eds.), *The developing individual in a changing world* (Vol. 1). The Hague: Mouton, 1976.

Whiting, B., & Whiting, J. *Children of six cultures.* Cambridge, Massachusetts: Harvard Univ. Press, 1975.

Witkin, H. Theory in cross-cultural research: Its uses and risks. In Y. H. Poortinga (Ed.), *Basic problems in cross-cultural psychology.* Amsterdam: Swets & Zeitlinger, 1977.

Witkin, H. *Cognitive styles in personal and cultural adaptation:* Vol. XI of the Heinz Werner Lecture Series. Worcester, Massachusetts: Clark Univ. Press, 1978.

Witkin, H., & Berry, J. Psychological differentiation in cross-cultural perspective. *Journal of Cross-Cultural Psychology,* 1975, *6,* 4–87.

Witkin, H., Dyk, R., Faterson, H., Goodenough, D., & Karp, S. *Psychological differentiation.* Hillsdale, New Jersey: L. Erlbaum, 1974. (Originally published, New York: Wiley, 1962.)

Zaidi, S. *Applied cross-cultural psychology: Submissions of a cross-cultural psychologist from the Third World.* Preliminary draft of a paper presented at the Fourth International Conference of the International Association for Cross-Cultural Psychology, Munich, West Germany, 1978.

3

Language and Communication: The Foundations of Culture

JACK BILMES
STEPHEN T. BOGGS

Introduction

In 1927 Edward Sapir, elaborating on a theme first sounded by Franz Boas, published an article entitled "The Unconscious Patterning of Behavior in Society." This article exhibits, perhaps more clearly than anything preceding it, an awareness of the extent and exquisite detail of social structuring in behavior and of the communicative significance of such structure. For about 30 years following its appearance, progress in uncovering the patterns of communicative behavior was limited largely to the structural study of language. However, even in this area, problems of meaning and of language use were given little attention.

It was not until the 1950's that the ethnographic study of communication (including microsociology) began to reveal its full scope and potential. Social scientists gradually began to appreciate the enormous amount of work that goes into the production and interpretation of communicative behavior as they came to recognize the many ways in which behavior is socially structured. They began, for example, to notice the ways in which people use space (Hall, 1959, 1966), gestures (Birdwhistell, 1952, 1970), and gaze (Kendon, 1967). They noticed the work that is required to synchronize spoken interaction (Chapple, 1970) and coordinate turn taking (Sacks, Schegloff, &

47

PERSPECTIVES ON CROSS-CULTURAL PSYCHOLOGY

Jefferson, 1974), the subtle and mundane cooperation of interactants in mutual face saving (Goffman, 1955), the interpretive artifice which we employ in making sense of what others say to us (Garfinkel, 1967), and the ways in which people unconsciously modify their speech patterns to suit the situation (Labov, 1966). Studies like these are addressed to the "search for the mechanisms which make social facts appear to be what they appear to be [McDermott & Wertz, 1976, p. 166]." As these authors point out, "people are not simply in social structures; they do them [p. 166]." This paper is devoted to describing and discussing some of the issues posed by such studies.

For purposes of this chapter communication must be given a delimitative meaning. It has become something of a truism that all of our behavior is, insofar as it is perceived by someone else, and whether intended or not, communicative. In the words of Watzlawick, Beavin, and Jackson (1967, p. 49), "one cannot *not* communicate." That is, our behavior is (potentially) informative—it carries information about us, the situation we are in, our relationship to others, and so forth. However, as any event whatsoever may "communicate" in this sense (e.g., the falling of a tree may "communicate" something to us about the force of a storm), this conception of communication is too broad for our present purposes.

In this chapter we are concerned with *behavior* that is (intentionally or otherwise) informative. More particularly, we are concerned with studies of the concepts, rules, and procedures used by members of a culture to make and to influence interpretations of one another's behavior—especially those concepts, rules, and procedures shared by group members, and so providing the common ground for agreement on how a piece of behavior is to be interpreted. *Interpretation* is the process by which one recognizes the meaning of an event. It is because events are interpreted that they convey information beyond the bare fact of their own existence. When an event does this we call it a *sign*. A sign is that which is interpreted; if an event is interpreted, then it is a sign.

Recently, increasing attention has been focused upon culture as a system of meanings. The semiotic analysis of culture includes all of those meanings that can be communicated to anyone, and includes the anthropologist's, or other analyst's, interpretations (Umiker-Sebeok, 1977). As implied by the foregoing definitions, such a perspective is too broad, and in one sense too narrow, for our purposes here. Because of space limitations, we have chosen to focus upon the study of everyday native interaction, on the codes and processes which make those interactions intelligible to the native, and on the general mechanisms sustaining the flow of information during interaction. As Birdwhistell has noted, "culture and communication are terms which represent two different viewpoints or methods of representation of patterned and structured human interconnectedness. As 'culture' the focus is upon structure; as 'communication,' it is upon process [1970, p. 318]."

Umiker-Sebeok (1977) has pointed to the lack of articulation in anthropological theory between kinds of symbolic systems and how they are related to social action, adding that students of the one even tend to regard students of the other as opponents. In a parallel way, Evens (1977) has pointed to a "lack of articulation of action and value, process and design" in the analysis of culture. It is exactly this articulation that we seek to develop in this paper. We suggest that the relationship between these features may be found in the emergent properties of culturally structured interaction.[1]

Historical Background

A view of culture as a code for communication is tied to the emergence and development of the concept of culture from the late nineteenth century to the present. Modern awareness of the phenomenon we now call culture grew from circumstances of contact between the expanding Europeans and the various peoples whom they labeled "natives," "primitives," or more perjoratively, "savages." Anthropology very gradually impressed upon European minds (the process is still not complete) the view that the striking differences in action, thought, and feeling, which the European originally perceived in these peoples as due to something intrinsically related to their physical race, were rather something that they had largely acquired as a result of their historic experience in a particular geographic environment. Early in this century this something came under the term "culture" (Stocking, 1968).

Ironically, culture was regarded by Tylor, the first to use the term, as a universal quality, present in the highest degree in European civilization and to a lesser extent in "less advanced" traditions.[2] As Singer (1977; cited in

---

[1] It should be noted that in defining our subject matter we have ruled out of consideration certain areas of anthropological concern that others might have chosen to include under our title. The interpretation of myths as texts, for example, is outside the limits of our concern, in that texts are not behavior. (On the other hand we would be interested in the question of how natives interpret the actual telling of a myth by a specific person on a specific occasion.) Nor are we concerned with ritual, insofar as the ritual is performed on a set schedule and is fixed in regard to participants and content. Although natives can usually offer interpretations of such events, the occurrence of a set ritual is uninformative (to the native)—that is, it is entirely expected and has no element of choice or surprise. If we flip a coin with heads on both sides, we will not be informed when it comes up heads. Also, as we have already implied, we are not concerned with the anthropologist's interpretations as such, but rather with the anthropologist's reconstruction of native methods of interpretation. Nor will we discuss Whorfian and post-Whorfian studies of the relationship between language and cognition, since their central concern is with cognition rather than communication. For practical reasons, we also will not deal with phonology and grammar, even though these are obviously prerequisites for the native's interpretations of verbal communication.

[2] This despite Tylor's famous definition of culture as "that complex whole which includes knowledge, belief, art, law, morals, custom, and any other capabilities and habits acquired by

Umiker-Sebeok 1977) has rightly emphasized, a theory of culture as meaning
(a semiotic theory) could not arise until this ethnocentric, universalist view
gave way to a view of culture as the more or less unique possession of each
society. The scholar most responsible for reaching this alternative view was
Franz Boas. The crucial step was his realization that the universalist view of
culture held by Tylor was unscientific because it was ethnocentric. Boas
reached this conclusion as early as 1888, although his views and their
implications were not fully appreciated for some time. In solving the problem of "alternating sounds," which he and others heard in Indian languages,
Boas came to understand that it was a major error to interpret the sounds of
a language different from one's own as variants of the sounds of one's own
language (Stocking, 1968). As applied eventually to culture by others, this
realization yielded the general proposition that culture constitutes a code for
interpreting the meaning of stimuli of all kinds. This proposition is basic to
the modern study of communicative interaction, although its implications
took a long time to develop, because, for Boas and his students, the important point was that culture governed behavior, not perception. As a consequence, conduct, habit, customs were viewed by many as practically
synonymous with culture for some time. Habitual behavior was regarded as
both unconscious and patterned.

Given this early sensitivity among American anthropologists to the unconscious structure of cultural behavior, it is not surprising that when the study
of nonverbal communication began to emerge as a field, American anthropologists were in the forefront. Gregory Bateson, an English-trained
anthropologist who has worked in the United States and Margaret Mead
(Bateson & Mead, 1942) were pioneers in the analysis of nonverbal behavior
by means of photographic data. Efron (1942) and Birdwhistell (1952, 1970)
initiated the field of kinesics with their microanalyses of body motion. And
Hall's (1959, 1966, 1976) insights into how people from different cultures use
time and space opened new horizons in the study of nonverbal communication.

Another prerequisite for the position developed in the present paper was
provided by the structural–functionalist theory of British social anthropologists stating that entire collective systems of mutually reinforcing
statuses and roles guide the behavior of individuals in each society. Firth
(1951/1965) proposed a modification of this perspective to take account of
individual choice. In this paper we presuppose the reflexive nature of the
social system on the one hand and individual choices on the other. In fact,
the emergent properties of culturally structured interaction depend upon this
reflexive aspect. As for communication, few of the British social an-

man as a member of society." In Tylor's view, knowledge, or morals, constituted culture only
to the extent that they reflected the knowledge and morals of nineteenth-century British
bourgeois society (Stocking, 1968).

thropologists studied it as such, although one, Bronislaw Malinowski, made a signal contribution to this field. His monumental monograph (1935) on the language of gardening in the Trobriand Islands is a landmark in the ethnographic study of language. Even more remarkable, however, is his essay on "The Problem of Meaning in Primitive Languages (1930)," which appeared as a supplement to Ogden and Richards, *The Meaning of Meaning* (1930). In this essay Malinowski advances the principles of contextual interpretation and of meaning as use. To him the meaning of a linguistic expression must be derived from an analysis of its functions in its cultural setting. Language is a "mode of action." Malinowski thus foreshadowed developments in linguistic philosophy (Wittgenstein, 1953; Austin, 1962) and the emergence of sociolinguistics (Hymes, 1962), as well as stimulating the development of British functional linguistics (Firth, 1957).[3]

Another essential ingredient of a communicational view of culture is the concept of symbolic structure—of a code. The idea of culture as a code, not merely a patterned phenomenon, is based largely upon an analogy with language. The analogy leads to a search for rules in other cultural phenomenon, besides language, similar to those constructed for phonology and grammar.[4] Linguistic influence was, in part, responsible for the emergence of ethnosemantics and sociolinguistics within anthropology, both of which are described in a later section of this paper.

Human and Primate Communication

> Lucy is a chimpanzee raised by human foster parents and taught to use American Sign Language in a project directed by Roger Fouts. One day Lucy's human foster mother drove off during a training session. Lucy, who dearly loved car rides, ran to the window to see her foster mother drive off, and as she did so she signed in Ameslan, "cry me, me cry" [Linden, 1974, p. 111].

Recent descriptions of chimpanzee behavior in the laboratory indicate that they have the capacity to use signs systematically as a code to communicate messages that have, like the above, recognizably human social functions. By comparing the ways in which chimpanzees and other nonhuman primates use signs with human sign use, inferences can be drawn as to the universality of certain features of human communication. Such inferences are based on the assumption that similarities represent a minimum inheritance from proto-human ancestors.

It has long been the view that all natural languages share certain common

---

[3] He also anticipated Whorf when he stated (1930) that whereas thought scarcely influences language, thought is greatly influenced by language.

[4] See Burling (1969) for an outstandingly clear statement of how this analogy has been used and Hymes (1970) for a general survey of the influence of linguistics upon anthropology.

features (Greenberg, 1966), but humans have been regarded as the only primate species capable of using language as we know it (Linden, 1974; NOVA, n.d.). The recent experiments conducted by several investigators with chimpanzees indicate that this latter view is no longer tenable. The various systems of signs used by chimps in these experiments possess, to a minimum degree at least, most of the design features which Hockett has proposed as distinguishing characteristics of human languages. Examining the behavior of chimps in the wild, it appears that the social functions of their messages are fully comparable to those of young children using language. It appears likely, therefore, that the basis of human communication is older and broader than had previously been suspected. Pointing to these similarities, on the other hand, throws the unique features of human language into relief. A discussion of these points follows.

The design features of a set of signs in use can be taken as indicators of systematicity (Hockett, 1963; Hockett & Altmann, 1968).[5] Early critics of Washoe, the first chimp taught to use Ameslan, a gestural language widely used by the deaf, argued that she frequently reversed word order, whereas children in the earliest stages of speaking did not, thus proving that her signs lacked systematicity (Linden, 1974, citing Brown, 1970; Bronowski & Bellugi, 1970; Bellugi in Linden, 1974, p. 74). Subsequent experiments by Rumbaugh with Lana, a chimp taught to communicate using a computer programmed to respond only to grammatically correct messages (in "Yerkish," an invented language), have demonstrated this criticism to be without foundation. Lana is competent in using strings which constitute sentences of some complexity, querying, and correcting errors of syntax which are used to test her (NOVA, n.d.).

Although it is beyond the scope of this paper to present the evidence, it appears from the Gardners' (1969, 1971) and Premack's (1970, 1971) results that chimps have the capacity to use a code with at least a minimal degree of arbitrariness, interchangeability, specialization, displacement, cultural transmission, prevarication, and learnability (Hockett & Altmann, 1968). Fouts and his colleagues have provided more evidence to these conclusions from experiments with a number of chimps. They are currently investigating the use of Ameslan by chimps to communicate with one another when not in the presence of humans, and their transmission of these signs to one another (Linden, 1974; Fouts, 1972, 1973; Fouts, Chown, & Goodin, 1976). The design features on which debate is still possible are duality of patterning, reflexiveness, and productivity. Reflexiveness, communicating about communication (Hockett, 1963, p. 13), may be defined narrowly enough to include only human students of language, or broadly to include any use of a

---

[5] It is awkward to refer to all of these features as characteristics of the code, since a number of them depend upon the way the code is used: displacement, for instance. Therefore reference is made here to the code in use.

sign to refer to another sign. Lana uses signs to inquire about the names for objects (Hill, 1978, citing Rumbaugh, 1977). With respect to duality of patterning, it appears that Ameslan combines units at one level, "cheremes," which themselves lack meaning, into signs for words. It is not clear that chimpanzees make use of this feature, however (Hill, 1978, p. 94). On the other hand, it is not clear that a language would need duality in order to function effectively. Finally, debate still rages as to whether the chimps' use of natural and contrived "languages" represent true linguistic productivity, although there is no longer any question about the semantic productivity of their use of signs to create other signs (Hill, 1978).

It can be inferred from the foregoing conclusions that minimal use of most of the design features of human language does not require any neural organization or total brain volume exceeding that of the chimpanzee. The chimpanzee does not speak, however, and attempts to teach him to do so have proven formidably difficult (Hayes, 1951; NOVA, n.d.), thus indicating that the necessary neural basis for articulation is lacking.[6] One would expect to find in humans a neural organization facilitating speech and hearing, while adding to the prelinguistic code capabilities demonstrated by the chimpanzees. Geschwind's description of lateral dominance (the control of speech and language by the left side of the brain) and the localization of specific functions in areas of the left hemisphere, which have distinctive anatomical structures, is consistent with this expectation. Of great significance is his view that language is not a unitary phenomenon behaviorally, but a number of different abilities. This is supported by the fact that specific functions, such as word pronunciation, sentence intonation, mimicry, and the interpretation of words and sentences, appear to be localized in distinct areas. Thus, injury to one of these areas, but not others, results in the loss of one of the abilities whereas the others remain intact (Geschwind, 1970, 1972).

It would appear likely that these neural structures evolved in man along with aural–vocal language. The fact that the associated abilities are distinct, although extensively interrelated as everything in the brain is, might be seen as a result of gradual development from different preexisting capacities. Thus, Hewes (1973) has proposed that gestural language and the use of tools contributed to the evolution of aural–vocal language. The fact that chimpanzees use gestures extensively and are obviously preadapted to the use of gestural language, such as Ameslan, is consistent with part of Hewes' hypothesis. The fact that the right hemisphere in man can, under certain conditions, take over specific langauge functions to a degree (Geschwind, 1970, 1972) is likewise consistent with this hypothesis, as the neural organization normally controlling aural–vocal language in man appears not to be

---

[6] Lieberman (1975) presents a theory that the supralaryngeal anatomy of the nonhuman primates prevented the development of human-like speech. However this may be, areas of neural specialization in the human cortex appear to control articulation, as will be noted.

necessary for some degree of linguistic capacity. Unfortunately, we do not know how the neural organization of the chimpanzee brain relates to their communicative abilities. Presumably it is different, but the correlated behavioral and anatomical research to establish this has not been carried out.

The close relationship between aural–vocal language and gestural communication in primates is indicated by two further observations. One is that gestures, both vocal and nonvocal, continue to provide the most significant framing for human linguistic communication (see the section on nonverbal components of communication following). Another observation is that young children appear to accomplish, by means of aural–vocal language, approximately the same results in their immediate relationships with one another that chimpanzees (and many other mammals) accomplish with gestures. The exchange of threats in disputing is one example.

A threat by a chimp typically takes one or more of the following forms: (*a*) moving confidently up to another animal; (*b*) looking fixedly at the other without blinking or other facial expression ("open-face stare"); (*c*) moving the body in a bobbing motion; and/or (*d*) arm waving. A subordinate animal will typically offer an appeasement gesture in return, such as moving out of the way, grinning without exposing the upper teeth, presenting, or grooming. Occasionally, when rank between the two animals is not established, each will return the threat and the exchange will escalate until one backs down (Sugiyama, 1969; Goodall, 1965; van Lawick-Goodall, 1968, n.d.).

In young children, language functions in a similar way to exchange threats. Consider the following, the climax to an extended verbal dispute between a 4-year-old and her 5-year-old sister:[7]

[1 is the older girl, 2 the younger.]

2: *Five.*	Repeating her claim to be 5 years old.
1: *Her not **five**. Her not in kindəgarten.*	Contradicts 2, offers allegation as argument. 1 is addressing another girl.
2: *Mommy, I to 'schoo'?*	Appeals to mother for evidence.
1: *Da man—Mommy sai'—*	Starts to argue, quoting authority.
2: *No, wha' my mathə say—me an her is* ⌈*fi-ive!*	Argues, quotes authority.
1: ⌊*ae-ae you bu' lia!*	Acting as if contradicted, 1 dismisses, insults 2. (Gloss: 'You are a bull liar!')
2: *You cry I put dis . . . inside you' eye.*	Threatens trial by ordeal. (Gloss: 'You will cry if I put this in your eye.')
1: (pause)	1 does not respond verbally.
2: *Blinked you' eye.*	Claims victory.
1: *You blinked **your** eye.*	Counterclaim.

The referential capabilities of human language obviously go beyond those of nonverbal communication. This in turn has social consequences, among

[7] For complete text see Watson-Gegeo and Boggs, 1977. See also Boggs and Lein, 1978; Boggs, 1978.

others. Thus, children entertain themselves by telling stories about events that they have never witnessed or only imagined (Watson, 1975; Watson-Gegeo & Boggs, 1977). Older children engage in arguments in which they advance propositions to support other statements. These propositions often refer to events far removed in time and space (Brenneis & Lein, 1977; Boggs, 1978). Although chimps trained by humans use signs to refer to events or the outcome of events that are not present when the signs are produced (displacement), there is no evidence that chimps anywhere use signs to tell stories or engage in propositional argument. Additionally, if children differ so much in their referential use of language, it is obvious that adult humans differ to a much greater degree in these forms of discourse, and many others. The difference is great enough to be considered a qualitative difference.

Summarizing, it seems likely, although not yet proven, that a universal human system of communication evolved from an earlier system of nonverbal, vocal, and gestural communication. This nonverbal system is well adapted to the negotiation of social relationships, and human language continues to serve this purpose to a considerable degree. Chimpanzees and some other primates are obviously preadapted to use many of the design features of the human code. Duality of patterning appears to be unique to human languages, at least as we know them, whereas displacement appears to have been developed to a much greater degree among humans and has many social, as well as technological consequences. All of these features, then, are universals in human communication.

The Cultural Code

THE NATURE OF THE CODE

Anthropologists are now widely in agreement that culture is to be conceived as a code. This code is usually thought of as a program or set of rules or body of knowledge whereby culturally appropriate behavior is generated (Geertz, 1965; Goodenough, 1964). Less commonly, culture is viewed primarily as a code which guides *interpretation* of behavior. As Kay (1970) states, "The culture shared by a group of people consists essentially in the cognitive system that makes the actions of one intelligible to another . . . [p. 29]." There is no need, it can be argued, to choose between the two types of definition as there is no essential difference between them. This can be seen through an analogy with Chomsky's concept of grammar as that which links speech sounds to their semantic interpretation. If we take meaning as the starting point, then the grammar is used to generate the appropriate speech behavior. However, if we start with sound, the grammar works in the other direction—it makes the sounds intelligible, it gives them a semantic interpretation. Like grammar, culture links behavior and meaning. Indeed, it has often been said that culture is a kind of grammar. It makes little difference whether we define culture as a code for generating meaningful behavior or as a code for interpreting such behavior, as each definition implies the other.[8]

Having taken a position on this matter, we must immediately qualify it. The analogy between language, as a part of culture, and culture as a whole is not perfect. It is most unlikely that sentences that are not produced in accordance with the rules of English grammar will be interpretable by those rules. When we hear someone speaking Swahili, or Hungarian, or simply making inarticulate noises, we recognize immediately that we cannot provide an interpretation in terms of English grammar. On the other hand, behavior, not generated by reference to the rules of some particular culture, is still open to interpretation by reference to those rules. When this happens between members of different cultures, we speak of *ethnocentrism*. Clearly, cross-cultural misunderstandings of this kind are structured by the cultural code. All behavior generated by cultural code X is also interpreted, at least by the actor himself, in terms of cultural code X. But, not all behavior interpreted in terms of cultural code X is necessarily generated by that code. It follows that a definition of culture as a code for interpretation of behavior is broader (in the sense that it encompasses more phenomena that we would view as culturally structured) than a definition of culture as a code for generating behavior. Accordingly, we favor the former definition.

For Goodenough, the locus of culture is the human mind. This does not mean that any particular mind has complete knowledge of the entire code, but rather that each part of the code exists in the minds of at least some members of the cultural group. Culture is not an entity with its own independent reality—the reality of culture lies in its realization as systems of knowledge in the minds of people. Moreover, the "ultimate locus [of culture] must be in individuals rather than in groups [Goodenough, 1971, p. 20]." Geertz (1973) attacks this view. He uses a Beethoven quartet as an example of an item of culture.

> No one would, I think, identify it with its score, with the skills and knowledge needed to play it, with the understanding of it possessed by its performers or auditors, nor . . . with a particular performance of it or with some mysterious entity transcending material existence. . . . But that a Beethoven quartet is a temporally developed tonal structure, a coherent sequence of modeled sound—in a word, music—and not anybody's knowledge of or belief about anything, including how to play it, is a proposition to which most people are . . . likely to assent [pp. 11–12].[9]

He goes on to say that "Culture is public because meaning is [p. 12]." But when we say that "culture is public" are we not insisting that people

---

[8] Thus, in a single paragraph, Goodenough (1964) can say of culture that it "consists of whatever it is one has to know or believe in order to operate in a manner acceptable to its [i.e., the cultural group's] members" and that "it is the forms of things that people have in mind, their models for perceiving, relating, and otherwise interpreting them [p. 36]."

[9] This and subsequent quotes cited to Geertz (1973) are from *The interpretation of cultures: Selected essays* by Clifford Geertz, © 1973 by Basic Books, Inc., Publishers, New York.

must have knowledge of it? Can it be public and unknown? Suppose that Beethoven had composed a quartet, "a temporally developed tonal structure," decided it was no good, and burned it without showing it to anyone. Is that quartet part of any culture? Any idea of culture as an independent entity of the type proposed by Geertz, it seems, must ultimately be grounded in and derived from an individual-centered concept of culture, such as Goodenough's. However, there is a real sense of which culture is external and prior to any individual. Individuals are the bearers of culture, but the locus of culture is the group. Culture is an intersubjective phenomenon.

In our view, these two conceptions of culture, as put forward by Geertz and Goodenough, are complementary—we do not see any contradiction between them, and we do not feel compelled to choose between them. The relationship between the individual and his culture is what ethnomethodologists would call "reflexive." Culture and the individual are mutually constitutive. The individual perceives, interprets, and acts as he docs (partly) because of his culture, and in perceiving, interpreting, and acting in that way, he (and others) makes his culture what it is. Ultimately, then, our answer to the question, "Where is the cultural code located?" is, "It is located in the individual *and* in the group." Its existence in each is contingent on its existence in the other.

Geertz's view of culture is useful for certain very important purposes. It facilitates insights into structural relationships internal to the code by allowing us to look at the code as a thing-in-itself. Thus, we can tease out relationships among the various parts of the code without reference to variations in the knowledge of its users. (This is the way in which linguists have typically approached language.) When we are seeking to account for culture change, however, an individual-centered concept of culture may be more appropriate. As Wallace (1961) points out, the fact that two individuals may be able to interact with each other in culturally appropriate ways does not necessarily imply that they share the same cognitive maps. This can be a crucial consideration in explaining culture change.

Let us turn now from the question of the locus of the cultural code and consider instead certain features of that code. Geertz asserts that a Beethoven quartet is "music." It seems more accurate to us to say that it is not, strictly speaking, music, except on the occasion of a performance. It is rather a set of rules for making music. Following Searle's (1969) distinction between *constitutive* and *regulative* rules, we may say that a Beethoven quartet is a set of constitutive rules. Constitutive rules "create or define new forms of behavior" whereas regulative rules "regulate antecedently or independently existing forms of behavior [p. 33]." We may think of culture as having both constitutive and regulative aspects. Actually, it may be preferable to think of cultural rules as located on a continuum from purely constitutive to purely regulative.

Constitutive rules are obligatory and rarely broken in the normal course of events. When a constitutive rule is broken—for example, by making one's markings on the lines rather than between them in a game of tic-tac-toe (Garfinkel, 1963)—the result is disorientation and disorganization. In order for it to be noticeable that a constitutive rules is being broken, there must be some sort of frame which establishes the expectation that a certain kind of activity is to take place. The frame may, for example, consist of an announcement naming the activity or it may consist in the performance of part of the activity in accordance with the appropriate constitutive rules. If, with no warning, you approach a piano and begin to hit the keys at random, people may complain, but they are not likely to complain that what you are playing is not "Claire de Lune."

Because of this, one might speculate, the constitutive aspects of culture, at least those governing everyday interaction, are relatively fixed and widely shared within the group to which they apply. Coherent interaction depends on it. There is, however, the possibility of divergent interpretation of "the rule." (Does the knight in chess move one straight and one diagonal, one diagonal and one straight, two straight and one perpendicular, one straight and two perpendicular, or even three straight and one diagonal backward? The possibilities are numerous, but any simple characterization of "the rule" will do, given that all relevant outcomes are equivalent.) Regulative rules (e.g., "Wear whites for tennis") are more likely to be broken. In fact, two persons may successfully carry off an interaction (say, a game of tennis) even though they are using different regulative rules, as long as they do not (relevantly) vary in their interpretation of the constitutive rules.

The relationship between constitutive and regulative rules is a subtle one. In the 1960s, a common way of expressing protest was to take one's clothes off on public occasions, for example, political rallies. This did not change the nature of the occasion, but it did break a regulative rule. However, the breaking of the rule was, in itself, constitutive of the activity of protesting (although it was not the only way of protesting). This brings us to a second kind of distinction that can be made in regard to the cultural code—that between "code rules" and "marking rules [Geoghegan, 1973]." Application of a code rule to a situation yields a "normal," "unmarked," form of behavior. The further application of a marking rule changes this form, and in so doing adds further information. For example, the use of an especially intimate linguistic form may express affection or disrespect. The effective use of marking rules depends on the interactants' shared knowledge of which form is normal and how particular departures from the normal form are to be interpreted. In other words, they must both know the rules. To what degree these rules are constitutive or regulative is a distinct matter and probably varies by situation. Certainly, the rules which distinguish between first and second person pronoun are more constitutive than those which distinguish between different forms of the second person pronoun, insofar as accurate and coherent reference is a condition for, but is not conditional upon, connotations of affection, etc.

However, in the light of our previous discussion, we may say that there is a sense in which any deliberate and visible manipulation of a rule is constitutive. To use an especially intimate form is "to do" affection or disrespect—if one uses a different form, one is doing something else. The important point is that rules are not merely followed or inadvertantly broken. They are *used,* and their use is itself rule-governed, as discussed in the section on communication process. Interpretations of social behavior are possible largely because there are rules for social behavior.

CONTEXT AND COMPETENCE

One of the major trends in recent social science has been the increasing emphasis on the importance of context. In psychology, for example, one finds a new attention to situation as a determinant of individual behavior (Magnusson & Endler, 1977; Endler & Magnusson, 1976). In sociology, the ethnomethodologists stress the indexical (context-bound) nature of meaningful behavior (Garfinkel, 1967). Sociolinguists and other ethnographers of communication have been very much a part of this trend. Indeed, sociolinguistics, by its very nature, must attend to context. As this trend has developed within anthropology and linguistics, two of the major objects of criticism have been Chomskian linguistics and ethnosemantics.

According to Chomsky (1965): "Linguistic theory is concerned primarily with an ideal speaker–listener, in a completely homogeneous speech-community, who knows its language perfectly and is unaffected by such grammatically irrelevant conditions as memory limitations, distraction, shifts of attention and interest, and errors . . . in applying his knowledge of the language in actual performance [p. 3]."[10] (This is more or less in keeping with the "structuralist" approach to the synchronic study of language.) "We thus make a fundamental distinction between *competence* [the speaker–hearer's knowledge of his language] and *performance* [the actual use of language in concrete situations] [p. 4]." Students of language change have attacked this approach on the grounds that speech communities are not homogeneous—ways of speaking vary by age, sex, status, and so forth—and that individual speakers may command several ways of speaking. These facts are crucial and cannot be glossed over if one is to account for language change (Weinreich, Labov, & Herzog, 1968).

More to the point for our present purposes, is Hymes's (1974) critique of Chomsky's concept of competence. It is not the distinction between competence and performance which is in question here, but rather the exact nature of the relationship between them. For Chomsky, a speaker's competence is his knowledge of the grammar (including phonological and semantic, as well as syntactic components) of his language—everything else is performance.

---

[10] This and subsequent quotes cited to Chomsky (1965) are from *Aspects and the theory of syntax* by Noam Chomsky, and are quoted with the permission of the publisher, The MIT Press.

Hymes points out that there are rules of use as well as rules of grammar and that these too must be included as part of a speaker's competence. The speaker who uses grammatical sentences inappropriately, that is, without regard to context, is not a competent speaker as "choice among the alternatives that can be generated from a single base structure depends as much upon a tacit knowledge as does grammar, and can be studied as much in terms of underlying rules as can grammar. . . . linguistic theory must extend the notion of competence to include more than the grammatical [Hymes, 1974, p. 93]."[11]

Hymes (1974, p. 146) distinguishes two kinds of functions served by language, *referential* and *stylistic,* and claims that linguists have typically neglected the latter. It is the aim of sociolinguistics to make up this deficit, to attend to social as well as referential meaning. Hymes (1970) makes three basic points about the sociolinguistic approach.

1. Speech, like language, is structured.
2. The goal of the sociolinguistic approach is to discover underlying knowledge and competence, but the concept of competence is extended to include the knowledge and abilities that underly speaking and, more generally, communicating.
3. "In place of assuming homogeneity of knowledge and use, organized solely around the function of reference, the new approach assumes heterogeneity, and a plurality of functions, including the expressive. It takes as its starting point, not a single language, from which connections to social life may later be sought, but a community's speech economy, of which a particular language is but one component, together with other varieties of language, and modes of communication, within a system of scenes, participants, channels, and acts and genres of speech [Hymes, 1970, p. 308]."

The field of sociolinguistics has flowered since the 1960s, some of the more important collections being Hymes (1964), Fishman (1968, 1971), Gumperz and Hymes (1964, 1972), and Bauman and Sherzer (1974). Sociolinguistics itself (or at least the attempts thus far made in its name) has come under criticism from various quarters within anthropology (e.g., Bloch, 1976; Crick, 1976; Leach, 1976). We do not have the space here to go into the content of these criticisms. Hymes's extended concept of competence is likely to be welcome to most anthropologists both because Hymes is right—speech *is* structured—and because he is asserting the importance of a typically anthropological concern, that is, the effect of social structure on behavior. However, whereas we agree with him on this point, we find his rejection of the more narrowly linguistic viewpoint more problematic.

The linguistic approach, it seems to us, has its uses. "There is a place for

---

[11] Helmer (n.d.) and Basso (1976) make a similar point with reference to Katz and Fodor's (1963) "interpretive semantics."

such functional studies [as advocated by the sociolinguists] certainly, but it should also be recognized that a field growing out of the felt deficiencies of the Chomskian tradition almost deliberately looks away from those paradigmatic structures which, in language as in other systems of human action, are vital to understanding the nature of the phenomena which the recorder of events—in this case speech behavior—registers [Crick, 1976, pp. 64–65]."

The cultural code undoubtedly includes rules of a sociolinguistic as well as a purely linguistic nature. This does not mean, however, that the rules must be treated as somehow separate, equal, and unorganized. The best strategy, we think, is to approach the cultural code as consisting of subsystems of rules, the rules of grammar being one such subsystem. These various subsystems intersect with or frame one another (Bateson, 1955; Goffman, 1974). To give a simple example, it is possible to use words recognized as having antonyms in such a way that the word is understood to convey the conventional meaning of its antonym. However, in our dictionaries, we do not find "bad" listed as one of the meanings of "good," "light" as "heavy," "play" as "work," etc. This would be grossly uneconomical. Instead we recognize a framing operation—sarcasm—that transforms the meaning of a word to its opposite (Bilmes, 1976a). We must conceive the cultural code not simply as a set of rules, but as a set of interrelated subsystems of rules. One of Bateson's major contributions (his concept of metacommunication) follows from his recognition of this property of the code (Bateson, 1951; Bateson, Jackson, Haley, & Weakland, 1972). From this point of view, we can see Chomsky's endeavor as an entirely warranted effort to reveal the properties of a subsystem of the cultural code.

Ethnosemantics has been similarly attacked for its lack of attention to context. The general orientation of the ethnosemantic approach is drawn primarily from Pike (1954) and Goodenough (1951, 1956a, 1964). From these works, ethnosemantics developed the principle of sensitivity to native distinctions and the native point of view, and a concept of culture consistent with this principle (see Footnote 8). The development of a distinctive ethnosemantic methodology began in 1956 with the publication of two articles on componential analysis of kinship terms (Goodenough, 1956b; Lounsbury, 1956).

In a componential analysis, a set of terms belonging to a single domain (e.g., kinship) is analyzed in such a way that each term can be characterized by a unique set of semantic components. These components are values on a relatively small number of dimensions. For certain "well filled-out" sets of terms, we can achieve great economies of description using this technique. For example, consider a set (actually a subset) of terms for "direct" consanguineal relatives (the terminology is that of Romney & D'Andrade, 1964) in English. The set is grandfather, grandmother, father, mother, brother, sister, son, daughter, grandson, granddaughter. The domain of this set can be designated "D"—direct consanguineals. The terms in the set can be differentiated on two dimensions—generation (G) and sex (S). Generation takes five values—G^{+2}, G^{+1}, G^0, G^{-1}, and G^{-2}. Sex takes two values—S_1 (male) and S_2 (female). Using this notation, "grandfather" is uniquely specified as $DG^{+2}S_1$, "sister" is DG^0S_2, "son" is $DG^{-1}S_1$, and so forth. In theory, three bivalued dimensions are capable of differentiating $2^3 = 8$ terms, four bivalued dimensions can differentiate $2^4 = 16$ terms, and so forth. In practice, a componential analysis achieves such descriptive economy only in certain cultural domains, where a large number of terms can be differentiated using a relatively small number of dimensions.

Componential analysis is a technique for relating terms to their referents. If a person is my direct consanguineal relative, male, and in the first ascending generation, I may refer to him as "father." Interesting as this technique is, however, it could not, by itself, generate a movement of such scope as to take on itself the title of "The New Ethnography." Something more was needed. In the late 1950s and early 1960s, Conklin (1957, 1962) and Frake (1961, 1962) began to make known the results of their investigations into the nature of folk taxonomies. Perhaps more than any other single work, Frake's (1961) article on "The Diagnosis of Disease Among the Subanun of Mindanao" was responsible for launching ethnosemantics as a general movement. In this paper, Frake articulated many of the existing elements of the ethnosemantic approach in the context of a taxonomic analysis.

Taxonomic analysis is a technique for relating terms to other terms in the same language. Although there are various kinds of taxonomic relationships, most work has been done on the relationship "inclusion." To say that X includes Y is to say that Y is a kind of X. Figure 3.1 illustrates a taxonomic inclusion structure and shows how it is related to a componential analysis. Notice that terms that are immediately dominated by a single term (as "son" and "daughter" are by "children") contrast with one another (in this case, on the dimension of sex), but are both included in the higher term. At each level of the taxonomy, a new distinction is introduced.

Although ethnosemantics has not had the impact expected by some of its most enthusiastic supporters, its formalist methodology and elicitation techniques have become a standard part of the anthropological tool kit, and its emphasis on native distinctions is still felt. Perhaps because of the inflated claims of some of its supporters, ethnosemantics has been vigorously attacked from many directions. Harris (1968) and Berreman (1966) find it preoccupied with trivialities, Schneider (1965) finds that the cultural domains subjected to analysis tend to be inadequately defined, and Keesing (1972) seems to feel that the approach was obsolete almost from its inception because it was based on an outmoded form of linguistic analysis. Burling (1964) has questioned the psychological validity of componential analyses. (It has generally been taken for granted, on the other hand, that taxonomic analyses directly reflected native cognitive structures.)

Although Hymes has taken a generally favorable view of ethnosemantics, two of his major criticisms of Chomskian linguistics—that it is concerned

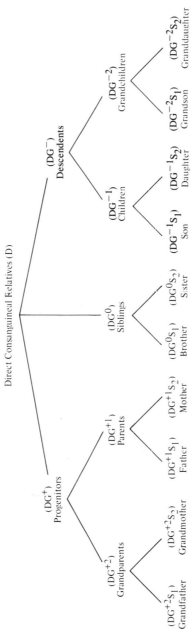

Figure 3.1. The diagram provides an example of a taxonomic inclusion structure: "G" is generation, "S" is sex.

solely with referential meaning and tends to ignore contextual factors—
might be leveled at ethnosemantics as well. As Keesing (1972) writes, "one
deals with only referential usage, not with extended or metaphoric senses,
one sidesteps the slippery problems of polysemy; and one evades the morass
of contextualization [p. 314]."

Wieder (1970) goes so far as to suggest that the critical attributes of a term
vary with the situation, depending on what other objects are present in the
situation from which the object in question must be differentiated. He states
that, "What members might mean when they apply a name would then have
a definite sense for a particular temporally located situation but would have
no necessary stable connection to other situations in which the name was
used [p. 131]." Thus, to adapt an example from Wootton (1976), I may say
"That's not just an assemblage of persons, that's a *mob* [p. 37]." In this
case, I am pointing to some feature that is taken to differentiate a mob from a
mere collection of individuals. In another situation, though, I might refer to a
"mere collection of individuals" as a "mob."

Wieder further points out that, in using a term, we are often intending to
communicate something more than or other than the criterial features of the
term. Thus, when a person says, "I wish I had a rich uncle," the set of
features specifying the reference of "uncle" (e.g., kin, male, first ascending
generation, colineal) are less significant than the notion that an uncle is one
who has certain obligations toward or at least would tend to give aid to, the
speaker. "The sense of the title uncle is thus not restricted by the criteria for
properly using that term but can instead be used as a vehicle for 'recovering'
whatever can be said about uncles by the parties who say and hear the term
[p. 133]." Reconstructing what a person is actually talking about is a
context-dependent activity.

To say that ethnosemanticists have totally ignored the problem of context
would be extreme and incorrect. Frake (1961), for example, gives consideration to the contextual influences on disease term usage, and in 1962 he
writes: "Linguistic forms, whether morphemes or larger constructions, are
not tied to unique chunks of semantic reference like baggage tags; rather it is
the use of speech, the selection of one statement over another in a particular
sociolinguistic context, that points to the category boundaries on a culture's
cognitive map [p. 31]." Additionally, one of the five sections in Tyler's
(1969) edited volume on ethnosemantics is titled "Relevance: Context."
Nor are all ethnosemanticists necessarily advocates of the "white-room,"
"decontextualized" elicitation techniques put forward by Black (1969) and
Black and Metzger (1965).

Frake's studies of Subanun religious behavior (1964), Yakan litigation
(1969), and social usages associated with areas of the Yaken house (1975)
clearly could not have been easily accomplished with "white-room" techniques. Furthermore, in a recent publication (1977), Frake explicitly points
out the weaknesses of such techniques. It might be argued, though, (and
with some justice) that the last four papers mentioned are not typical

ethnosemantic efforts, and that, in general, while the ethnosemanticist may not be ignorant of the effects of contextual variables, neither has he devoted great attention to them.

Hymes (1962, p. 19) formulates the relationship between a linguistic form and its context as follows: "The use of a linguistic form identifies a range of meanings. A context can support a range of meanings. When a form is used in a context, it eliminates the meanings possible to that context other than those that form can signal: the context eliminates from consideration the meanings possible to the form other than those that context can support." Although we have no argument with Hymes on this point, we believe that he has not gone far enough. The relationship between utterance and context is even more intimate than he suggests—it is reflexive. We cannot make a list of possible meanings of the utterance and a list of possible meanings which the context will support, and then match the one with the other. Rather, the meaning emerges in the interaction of utterance and context (Bilmes, 1976a). The possible meaning of the utterance is defined (in part) in context, and the nature of the context is defined (in part) by the utterance. An example from Wieder (1974) illustrates this relationship.

In studying a halfway house, Wieder noted that conversations between inmates and staff were often terminated by the inmate declaring "You know I won't snitch." The remark defines the context—you just asked me to snitch. At the same time, the context—a staff member has asked an inmate to snitch—displays the meaning of the remark. It would have meant something rather different if said in reply to another inmate who had just issued a warning against snitching. In that context, for example, it would not have constituted a refusal to answer.

Sometimes the speaker has available to him a number of referentially identical forms, and his problem is to choose one for use in a particular context. For example, when should one address another with a nickname, a first name, a last name, or with a title plus a last name? Sociolinguists typically approach this problem by searching for a set of contextual criteria which determine "proper" usage (Ervin-Tripp, 1969). However, as Wootton (1976, pp. 46–47) notes, if we know from the context which form will be used, then the use of the form conveys no information. Of course, we do not always know in advance which form will be chosen (we never know to a certainty), and, once again, there is a reflexive relationship between form and context. While context constrains choice of form, it is simultaneously true that "usage itself can crystallize the nature of the context for participants [Wootton, 1976, p. 46]."

A NOTE ON NONVERBAL COMPONENTS OF THE CODE

Most of the preceding discussion in this section applies to nonverbal as well as verbal communication, although the issues have been more clearly articulated with reference to verbal communication. However, certain special issues have arisen in the area of nonverbal studies. Because of space limitations, we can do no more than briefly mention a few of these.

1. Intensive study of nonverbal communication began fairly recently and has tended to concentrate on empirical observation rather than theoretical formulation. Researchers have identified various functions of nonverbal communication, such as supplying redundancy (Cherry, 1957); demarcating, maintaining, and regulating social interaction (Scheflen 1972, 1973a, 1973b); adding new and even contradictory information to that contained in the verbal message (Ekman & Friesen, 1969; Bateson, 1972); and "framing and labeling" verbal messages, and thus determining how they are to be understood (Bateson *et al.*, 1972). However, little has been accomplished in demonstrating how nonverbal phenomena are organized into a system, or a number of systems, or a part of a larger system.

2. It is perhaps indicative of the present state of nonverbal studies that investigators have yet to agree as to whether nonverbal phenomena are digital or analogic in nature. The issue has been most clearly raised in relation to kinesic behavior. Birdwhistell seems to hold that kinesic behavior is digital in nature (1970, pp. 111–113). Watzlawick *et al.* (1967) and Bateson (1972, pp. 411, 423) are among those who find it to be analogic.

3. The study of nonverbal communication raises severe problems of interpretation (different perhaps more in degree than in kind from those raised by the study of verbal performances). Convincing evidence is often lacking for the specific meaning attributed to an event. Moreover, it is not always clear what would constitute adequate evidence. The problem is compounded by the fact that neither the participants nor other native observers can confirm the interpretation. This problem is probably not insoluble, but researchers will have to give more serious attention to this matter of verification eventually.

The Communication Process

> In general, anthropologists have treated realities as if they were the properties of robots. Once people were programmed, they acted out these realities regardless of the contingencies at hand. . . . realities are far more fragile, precarious and subject to the interactional work of their participants; they are constantly in process and under negotiation [McDermott & Wertz, 1976, p. 170].

As noted in the introduction, culture focuses attention upon structure, whereas communication focuses upon process (Birdwhistell, 1970). Within the study of communication, however, there are structural and processual aspects. Harré (1977), for example, writes of templates which are internal structures projected as forms of behavior. A processual approach, on the other hand, emphasizes the negotiated and emergent properties of interaction. Social behavior is something that arises not simply from the participants, but from their interaction with one another.

Perhaps certain members of the symbolic interactionist school of sociology can be credited with the earliest systematic recognition of this property of interaction. Turner's (1962) theoretical discussion of social roles points out that there is a "basic tendency for actors to behave *as if* there were roles [p. 22]."[12] and that "the initial presumption that each actor must be adhering to *some* role created a strong bias in favor of finding a set of interpretations of his behavior which will allow it to be seen as pertaining to a single role [p. 36]." But, on the other hand, "the role becomes the point of reference for placing interpretations on specific actions [p. 24]." In other words, role and setting are reflexive—they emerge together from social interaction. Additionally, because of the flexibility inherent in this process, interactants can negotiate their roles vis-à-vis one another.

Individuals use language in many ways to negotiate their relationships with one another. The dispute quoted in the section on "Human and Primate Communication" is one example. The use of certain forms of speech may signal a status claim among children. Mitchell-Kernan and Kernan (1977), for instance, report that imperatives are much more frequently addressed by older to younger black children, and by adults to children, than vice versa. However, if a younger child addresses an imperative to an older child, it is regarded as an anomalous bid for status. For example a 7-year-old addressed an 11-year-old as follows:

> 7: *Bring you lil' self here.*
> [Laughter from group.]
> 11: *Who do you think you are?*
> 7: *I think I'm somebody big.*

It appears that directness and verbosity characterize the directives of higher to lower status persons, whereas indirectness and nonverbal requests characterize the directives of lower status persons to persons of higher status (Mitchell-Kernan & Kernan, 1977), although there are significant cultural differences in the tendency to use directness (Hollos & Beeman, 1978). Departures from this usual pattern carry a distinct meaning in a given culture. Thus, in American culture an older sister addressing her younger brother with "Would you mind taking your feet off my face?" is understood to be using sarcasm (Mitchell-Kernan & Kernan, 1977).

Not only may speech forms and uses contribute to the establishment of relationships in discourse, they may themselves become metaphors of the relationships they have helped to establish. Iwamura has described the emergent quality of such a development in the dialogue of two girls over a

---

[12] This and subsequent quote cited to Turner (1962) are by Ralph H. Turner, "Role-taking: Process versus conformity" from *Human behavior and social processes,* Arnold Rose, editor. Copyright © 1962 by Houghton Mifflin Company. Used by permission.

10-month period during their third year. As particular verbal routines succeeded during the development of their relationship, they tended to become
ritualized. Their use, thereafter, came to symbolize a reaffirmation of the
relationship in which they were first established. Thus:

> When some routines, such as . . . the You Say routine occurred repeatedly, the
> structure of these routines changed in predictable ways. . . . they seemed to enjoy
> them more. They giggled more and used them as symbols of their friendly (and
> sometimes unfriendly) feelings toward each other. If either girl tried to change such a
> routine, which I call a ritualized routine, the other might become offended by the
> introduction of an unfamiliar element. In this way, familiar parts of a routine could be
> better expressions of friendliness than innovations could be [Iwamura, 1977, p. 311].

Once they have developed as metaphors routines may even be used to
generate interest in situations lacking interest or meaning. This may explain
why boys can spend so much time jockeying for position in line when there is
no practical consequence of the position. Although the status gained is
evanescent and shifting, the game is played with great sophistication and
seriousness. The game itself connotes the struggle for relative status, and
this is a matter of concern to boys.

Just as young children construct a verbal routine to signal and negotiate
their relationships, so have cultures evolved various interaction rituals to the
same ends. In black street culture, the establishment of an individual's
"rep" (status) in each specific gathering by means of highly structured,
variable verbal and nonverbal performances has been noted in all descriptions (Abrahams, 1974, pp. 244–245). The Wolof of Senegal and Maori of
New Zealand have evolved elaborate greeting rituals both to signal and to
negotiate status relations.

Although worlds apart, comparison of the Wolof and Maori reveals certain
underlying similarities. Length of performance is a significant feature of the
encounter in both cultures, although it signals a lowering of status among the
Wolof and superior status among the Maori. Among the Wolof a person of
lower caste, office, age, or other ascribed status, must initiate the greeting
and continue to initiate subsequent, optional, verbal sequences. If he wishes
to emphasize his lower status even further, he can do so by prolonging these
sequences (Irvine, 1974). Among Maori, unlike the Wolof, host group and
visitor(s) vie for status by complicating and extending their respective parts
of each fixed sequence to the point to that the other cannot respond, for
example, by more chants, more fluent oratory, or using more orators than
the other group has (Salmond, 1974), This is, likewise, the way in which
Fijian Indian children when disputing, and blacks when trading ritual in-
sults, win: When the opponent can think of no rejoinder (Lein & Brenneis,
1978; Kochman, 1970). Thus, length of performance is likely to be a culturally significant feature in the negotiation of status in every culture, although
its particular meaning can vary.

There are further resemblances in the means of negotiating status in various cultures. Irvine points out that relative status within an encounter is negotiated among the Wolof by means of paralinguistic features of pitch and stress, rate and verbosity. The reason for this is that these features have become stereotyped, serving as metaphors of the speech of nobles and commoners. These styles can then be used to convey a message within the encounter that is at odds with the role ascribed to the speaker (e.g., that a favor will not be granted if asked, although usually expected). The point of general applicability, here, is that fixed elements ("formula sentences"), by their selection and ordering, signal the ascribed status of the participants, whereas variable elements (paralinguistic phenomena in this case) signal demeanor (i.e., attitude about one's role,Goffman, 1961; Irvine, 1974). Status within an encounter is then negotiated by means of variable elements. A similar statement can be made about Maori rituals of encounter. Although the semantic content of particular sequences is fixed, the form and style of delivery are variable. It is these variable aspects that determine the status judgments made during the encounter (Salmond, 1974).[13]

We see in the use of ritualized routines as metaphors, an analog of the emergent social process wherein values are negotiated. In the cases just discussed the status negotiated in encounters is evanescent. There are times, however, when a single encounter gives rise to a legend that symbolizes an enduring status relationship. Salmond (1974) cites instances in which a visiting official surprised and delighted his Maori hosts by introducing a traditional, but disused, response in the greeting, and was long remembered for it.

The meaning of experience is transformed in the course of social interaction. Becker (1967) has given an example in describing the process by which one became a marihuana user. The study was done in the 1950s when the meaning of this experience was still undefined for most Americans. He points out that in becoming a user one typically goes through a series of stages: "(1) learning to smoke the drug in a way which will produce real effects; (2) learning to recognize the effects and connect them with drug use . . .; and (3) learning to enjoy the sensations he perceives [1967, p. 421]." He demonstrates that this is a process of social learning: The sensation of a marihuana high as pleasurable "occurs, typically, in interaction with more experienced users who . . . teach the novice to find pleasure in this experience . . . [p. 419]." One can surmise that the meaning of this experience has been gradually developing in American culture by just such processes of social interaction.

Meaning is not only defined in social interaction but may be negotiated as well, as the following example indicates. In analyzing a legal discussion, it was found that at a certain point, the conversation turned from a discussion

---

[13] The linguists' preference for studying structure, rather than use, results in a focus upon fixed elements. The social significance of fixed elements, however, does not become clear by focusing upon them alone.

of the legal issues at hand to a discussion in which the topic was the previous conversation itself (i.e., the participants began to negotiate the meanings of what had already been said). The outcome of a discussion of this kind is likely to be profoundly affected by such formulations, which define "what has happened." The person whose formulation prevails has succeeded, to some degree, in controlling the situation. As in Becker's study of marihuana users, the meaning of the experience was defined and transformed within the situation, or, to say it more accurately, the nature of the situation itself was constantly open to reinterpretation by the formulating work of the participants. The participants behaved *as if* what they said had fixed meaning, but in fact their meanings were largely an emergent result of negotiation (Bilmes, in press).

Even such "facts" as norms and motives may not be independent causes or regulators of behavior, firmly fixed in the cultural code. From the perspective of communication as process, they may be seen, instead, as devices for communication and negotiation (Mills, 1940; Wieder, 1974). For example, in a Thai village meeting it was noticed that speakers frequently alluded to certain norms or rules. These were widely accepted as images of desirable forms of behavior or organization. It was further noted, though, that when one speaker invoked a norm, someone else would reply by invoking a different norm having the opposite implications for behavior. It, therefore, became evident that these norms did not govern behavior but rather were rhetorical devices that the villagers used in negotiating behavior. The norms were not so much features of the social structure as of the social *process* (Bilmes, 1976b).

The emergent aspect of interaction is particularly striking in the study of synchronous performance. Such performances belong to no particular participant, but are a property of the interaction in progress. Birdwhistell (1970) has noted that interactants often move in rhythm with one another. Byers (1971), from an examination of onsets and changes in body movement and of voice pulses, shows that there is a rhythmic beat to human behavior, measured in tenths of a second, and that people in interaction synchronize their beats. Even the electroencephalograms of persons in interaction tend to synchronize (Hall, 1976, p. 73). McDermott and Gospodinoff (1976) present a striking example of interactional synchrony in a classroom and the social and educational consequences of the synchrony.

It is shown that children sitting around a table at school arrange themselves, in coordinated ways, into a number of different "positionings." These positionings are a group product, they are done by all at once, and they have significance for how the class functions. They create sanction-defining contexts for children in, and on the periphery of, the group. They limit and indicate what can be accomplished in the group at any given moment (see Bremne & Erickson, 1977 for a similar study). Studies such as these indicate that, to a significant degree, people in interaction cooperate in creating the environment that, in turn, constrains their interaction. Such constraints undoubtedly help to create the cultural code.

Conclusion

In a discussion of cognitive anthropology, Wallace (1968) has noted that anthropologists have been interested primarily in the *what* of cognition, leaving the *how* to psychologists. A parallel observation might be made for the anthropological study of communication. Anthropologists have been interested mainly in the code, the semiotic system, the *what*. They have been interested in the macroprocesses leading to or resulting from culture change, but not in the microinteractional processes through which culture is played out. In the study of communication as an interactive process within which meanings develop over time, the *how* has been left largely to certain schools of sociology (although there is some evidence that this is changing). We can see no advantage and much disadvantage in this arrangement. Interactional sequences are the outcomes of (partly) culturally determined stances and presuppositions of the actors; but they are also the outcomes of the emergent dynamics of interaction itself. The cultural code is a kind of object, but the actual use of a code is work—it involves the continual adjustment and readjustment of the actors to one another and to their setting. It is not enough to ask "What do the actors need to know to do this work?" We must also ask "What kind of work is this? How is this work carried out? Where does it lead?"

References

Abrahams, R. D. Black talking on the streets. In R. Bauman & J. Sherzer (Eds.), *Explorations in the ethnography of speaking*. London: Cambridge Univ. Press, 1974.

Austin, J. L. *How to do things with words*. Cambridge, Massachusetts: Harvard Univ. Press, 1962.

Basso, Keith H. 'Wise words' of the Apache: Metaphor and semantic theory. In K. Basso and H. Selby, Jr. (Eds.), *Meaning in anthropology*. Albuquerque: Univ. of New Mexico Press, 1976.

Bateson, G. Information and codification: A philosophical approach. In J. Ruesch & B. Bateson, *Communication: The social matrix of psychiatry*. New York: Norton, 1951.

Bateson, G. A theory of play and fantasy. *American Psychiatric Association Psychiatric Research Reports II*, 1955.

Bateson, G. Redundancy and coding. In G. Bateson, *Steps to an ecology of mind*. New York: Ballantine, 1972.

Bateson, G., Jackson, D. D., Haley, J., & Weakland, J. H. Toward a theory of schizophrenia. In G. Bateson, *Steps to an ecology of mind*. New York: Ballantine, 1972.

Bateson, G., & Mead, M. Balinese character: A photographic analysis. New York: *Special Publications of the New York Academy of Sciences*, 1942, 2.

Bauman, R., & Sherzer, J. (Eds.). *Explorations in the ethnography of speaking.* New York: Cambridge Univ. Press, 1974.

Becker, H. S. Becoming a marijuana user. In J. G. Manis & B. N. Meltzer (Eds.), *Symbolic interaction: A reader in social psychology.* Rockleigh, New Jersey: Allyn & Bacon, 1967.

Berreman, G. D. Anemic and emetic analyses in social anthropology. *American Anthropologist,* 1966, *68,* 346–354.

Bilmes, J. Meaning and interpretation. *Semiotica,* 1976, *16,* 115–128. (a)

Bilmes, J. Rules and rhetoric: Negotiating the social order in a Thai village. *Journal of Anthropological Research,* 1976, *32,* 44–57. (b)

Bilmes, J. Proposition and codification in a legal discussion. *Semiotica,* in press.

Birdwhistell, R. L. *Introduction to kinesics.* (Photo-offset) Foreign Service Institute. Louisville: Univ. of Louisville Press, 1952.

Birdwhistell, R. L. *Kinesics and context: Essays on body motion communication.* New York: Ballantine, 1970.

Black, M. B. Eliciting folk taxonomies in Ojibwa. In S. A. Tyler, *Cognitive anthropology.* New York: Holt, 1969.

Black, M. B., & Metzger, D. Ethnographic description and the study of law. *American Anthropologist,* 1965, *67*(5, pt. 2), 141–165.

Bloch, M. Review of *Explorations in the ethnography of speaking* by R. Bauman & J. Sherzer (Eds.), *Language in Society,* 1976, *5,* 229.

Boggs, S. T. The development of verbal disputing in part-Hawaiian children. *Language in Society,* 1978, *7,* 325–344.

Boggs, S. T., & Lein, L. Sequencing in children's discourse: Introduction. *Language in Society,* 1978, *7,* 293–297.

Bremne, D. W., & Erickson, F. Behaving and making sense: Some relationships among verbal and nonverbal ways of interacting in a classroom. *Theory into Practice* (Vol. 16). Columbus, Ohio: School of Education, Ohio State Univ., 1977.

Brenneis, D., & Lein, L. 'You fruithead': A sociolinguistic approach to children's dispute settlement. In S. Ervin-Tripp & C. Mitchell-Kernan (Eds.), *Child Discourse.* New York: Academic Press, 1977.

Bronowski, J. S., & Bellugi, U. Language, name, and concept. *Science,* 1970, *168,* 699.

Brown, R. The first sentences of child and chimpanzee. In *Psycholinguistics: Selected papers.* New York: Free Press, 1970.

Burling, R. Cognition and componential analysis: God's truth or hocus-pocus? *American Anthropologist,* 1964, *66,* 20–28.

Burling, R. Linguistics and ethnographic description. *American Anthropologist,* 1969, *71,* 817–827.

Byers, P. *Sentics, rhythms, and a new view of man.* Paper presented at the 138th annual meeting of the American Association for the Advancement of Science, Philadelphia, 1971.

Chapple, E. D. *Culture and biological man: Explorations in behavioral anthropology.* New York: Holt, 1970.

Cherry, C. *On human communication: A review, a survey, and a criticism.* Cambridge, Massachusetts: M.I.T. Press, 1957.

Chomsky, N. *Aspects of the theory of syntax.* Cambridge, Massachusetts: M.I.T. Press, 1965.

Conklin, H. *Ethnobotanical problems in the comparative study of folk taxonomy.* Paper presented at the Ninth Pacific Science Congress, Bangkok, Thailand, 1957.

Conklin, H. Lexicographical treatment of folk taxonomies. In F. W. Householder & S. Saporta (Eds.), *Problems in lexicography.* Supplement to *International Journal of American Linguistics,* 1962, *28* (No. 2), 119–141.

Crick, M. *Explorations in language and meaning: Towards a semantic anthropology.* New York: Wiley, 1976.

Efron, D. *Gesture and environment.* New York: Kings Crown Press, 1942.

Ekman, P., & Friesen, W. V. Non-verbal leakage and clues to deception. *Psychiatry,* 1969, *32,* 88–105.

Endler, N., & Magnusson, D. (Eds.), *Interactional psychology and personality.* Washington, D.C.: Hemisphere, 1976.

Ervin-Tripp, S. M. Sociolinguistics. In L. Berkowitz (Ed.), *Advances in experimental social psychology* (Vol. 4). New York: Academic Press, 1969.

Evens, T. M. S. The predication of the individual in anthropological interactionism. *American Anthropologist,* 1977, *79,* 579–597.

Firth, J. R. *Papers in linguistics, 1934–1951.* London: Oxford Univ. Press, 1957.

Firth, R. *Elements of Social Organization.* Boston: Beacon, 1965. (Originally published, 1951.)

Fishman, J. A. (Ed.). *Readings in sociology of language.* The Hague: Mouton, 1968.

Fishman, J. A. (Ed.). *Advances in the sociology of language* (Vols. 1 & 2). The Hague: Mouton, 1971.

Fouts, R. S. The use of guidance in teaching sign language to a chimpanzee. *Journal of Comparative and Physiological Psychology,* 1972, *80,* 515–522.

Fouts, R. S. Acquisition and testing of gestural signs in four young chimpanzees. *Science,* 1973, *180,* 978–980.

Fouts, R. S., Chown, W., & Goodin, L. Transfer of signed responses in American Sign Language from vocal English stimuli to physical object stimuli by a chimpanzee. *Learning and Motivation,* 1976, *7,* 458–475.

Frake, C. O. The diagnosis of disease among the Subanun of Mindanao. *American Anthropologist,* 1961, *63,* 113–132.

Frake, C. O. The ethnographic study of cognitive systems. In T. Gladwin & W. C. Sturtevant (Eds.), *Anthropology and human behavior.* Washington, D.C.: Anthropological Society of Washington, 1962.

Frake, C. O. A structural description of Subanun "religious behavior." In W. H. Goodenough (Ed.), *Explorations in cultural anthropology.* New York: McGraw-Hill, 1964.

Frake, C. O. Struck by speech: The Yakan concept of litigation. In L. Nader (Ed.), *Law in culture and society.* Chicago: Aldine, 1969.

Frake, C. O. How to enter a Yakan house. In M. Sanches & B. G. Blount (Eds.), *Sociocultural dimensions of language use.* New York: Academic Press, 1975.

Frake, C. O. Plying frames can be dangerous. The Quarterly Newsletter of the Institute for Comparative Human Development, 1977, *1*(3).

Gardner, R. A., & Gardner, B. Teaching sign language to a chimpanzee. *Science,* 1969, *165,* 664–672.

Gardner, R. A., & Gardner, B. Two-way communication with an infant chimpanzee. In A. Schrier & F. Stollnitz (Eds.), *Behavior of non-human primates* (Vol. 4). New York: Academic Press, 1971.

Garfinkel, H. A conception of, and experiments with, "trust" as a condition of stable concerted actions. In O. J. Harvey (Ed.), *Motivation and social interaction.* New York: Ronald Press, 1963.

Garfinkel, H. *Studies in ethnomethodology.* New Jersey: Prentice-Hall, 1967.

Geertz, C. The impact of the concept of culture on the concept of man. In J. R. Platt (Ed.), *New views of man.* Chicago: Univ. of Chicago Press, 1965.

Geertz, C. Thick description: Toward an interpretive theory of culture. In C. Geertz, *The interpretation of cultures: Selected essays by Clifford Geertz.* New York: Basic Books, 1973.

Geoghegan, W. H. Natural information processing rules: Formal theory and applications to ethnography. *Monographs of the Language-Behavior Research Laboratory.* Berkeley, California: Univ. of California Press, 1973.

Geschwind, N. The organization of language and the brain. *Science,* 1970, *170,* 940–944.

Geschwind, N. Language and the brain. *Scientific American,* 1972, *226,* 76–83.

Goffman, E. On face-work: An analysis of ritual elements in social interaction. *Psychiatry: Journal for the study of interpersonal processes,* 1955, *18,* 213–231.

Goffman, E. Role distance. In E. Goffman, *Encounters: Two studies in the sociology of interaction.* Indianapolis, Indiana: Bobbs-Merrill, 1961.

Goffman, E. *Frame analysis: An essay on the organization of experience.* New York: Harper, 1974.

Goodall, J. Chimpanzees of the Gombe Stream Reserve. In I. DeVore (Ed.), *Primate behavior.* New York: Holt, 1965.

Goodenough, W. H. *Property, kin, and community on Truk.* New Haven, Connecticut: Yale Univ. Press, 1951.

Goodenough, W. H. Residence rules. *Southwestern Journal of Anthropology,* 1956, *12,* 22–37. (a)

Goodenough, W. H. Componential analysis and the study of meaning. *Language,* 1956, *32,* 195–216. (b)

Goodenough, W. H. Cultural anthropology and linguistics. In D. Hymes, *Language in culture and society.* New York: Harper, 1964. (Originally published, 1957.)

Goodenough, W. H. Culture, language, and society. Reading, Massachusetts: Addison-Wesley, 1971.

Greenberg, J. H. *Language universals.* The Hague: Mouton, 1966.

Gumperz, J. J., & Hymes, D. (Eds.). The ethnography of communication. *American Anthropologist,* 1964, *66* (6, pt. 2).

Gumperz, J. J., & Hymes, D. (Eds.). *Directions in sociolinguistics: The ethnography of communication.* New York: Holt, 1972.

Hall, E. T. *The silent language.* New York: Doubleday, 1959.

Hall, E. T. *The hidden dimension.* New York: Doubleday, 1966.

Hall, E. T. *Beyond culture.* New York: Doubleday, 1976.

Harré, R. The ethogenic approach: Theory and practice. In L. Berkowitz (Ed.), *Advances in experimental social psychology* (Vol. 12). New York: Academic Press, 1977.

Harris, M. *The rise of anthropological theory.* New York: Crowell-Collier, 1968.

Hayes, C. *The ape in our house.* New York: Harper, 1951.

Helmer, J. *The sociology of language.* n.d.

Hewes, G. W. Primate communication and the gestural origin of language. *Current Anthropology,* 1973, *14,* 5–24.

Hill, Jane H. Apes and language. *Annual Review of Anthropology,* 1978, *7,* 89–112.

Hockett, C. F. The problems of universals in language. In J. Greenberg (Ed.), *Universals of language.* Cambridge, Massachusetts: MIT Press, 1963.

Hockett, C. F., & Altmann, S. A. A note on design features. In T. Sebeok (Ed.), *Animal communication.* Bloomington: Indiana Univ. Press, 1968.

Hollos, M., & Beeman, W. The development of directives among Norwegian and Hungarian children: An example of communicative style in culture. *Language in Society,* 1978, *7,* 345–356.

Hymes, D. The ethnography of speaking. In T. Gladwin & W. Sturtevant (Eds.), *Anthropology and human behavior.* Washington, D. C.: Anthropological Society of Washington, 1962.

Hymes, D. (Ed.). *Language in culture and society.* New York: Harper, 1964.

Hymes, D. Linguistic method in ethnography: Its development in the United States. In P. L. Garvin (Ed.), *Method and theory in linguistics.* The Hague: Mouton, 1970.

Hymes, D. *Foundations in sociolinguistics: An ethnographic approach.* Philadelphia: Univ. of Pennsylvania Press, 1974.

Irvine, J. T. Strategies of status manipulation in the Wolof greeting. In R. Bauman & J. Scherzer (Eds.), *Explorations in the Ethnography of Speaking.* London: Cambridge Univ. Press, 1974.

Iwamura, S. J. *Games and other routines in the conversation of pre-school children: A case study in developmental sociolinguistics.* Unpublished doctoral dissertation, Univ. Hawaii at Manoa, 1977.

Katz, J. J., & Fodor, J. A. The structure of a semantic theory. *Language,* 1963, *39,* 170–210.

Kay, P. Some theoretical implications of ethnographic semantics. In A. Fischer (Ed.), *Current directions in anthropology. Bulletins of the American Anthropological Association,* 1970, *3.* Pp. 19–31.

Keesing, R. M. Paradigms lost: The new ethnography and the new linguistics. *Southwestern Journal of Anthropology,* 1972, *28,* 299–332.

Kendon, A. Some functions of gaze-direction in social interaction. *Acta Psychologica,* 1967, *26,* 22–47.

Kochman, T. Toward an ethnography of Black American speech behavior. In J.Szwed & N. Whitten (Eds.), *Afro-American anthropology: Contemporary Perspectives.* New York: Free Press, 1970.

Labov, W. *The social stratification of English in New York City.* Washington, D.C.: Center for Applied Linguistics, 1966.

Leach, E. Social geography and linguistic performance. *Semiotica,* 1976, *16,* 87–97.

Lein, L., & Brenneis, D. Children's disputes in three speech communities. *Language in Society,* 1978, *7,* 299–324.

Lieberman, P. *On the origins of language: An introduction to the evolution of human speech.* New York: Macmillan, 1975.

Linden, E. *Apes, men, and language.* New York: Penguin, 1974.

Lounsbury, F. G. A semantic analysis of the Pawnee kinship usage. *Language,* 1956, *32,* 158–194.

Magnusson, D., & Endler, N. W. (Eds.). *Personality at the crossroads: Current issues in interactional psychology.* Hillsdale, New Jersey: Lawrence Erlbaum, 1977.

Malinowski, B. The problem of meaning in primitive languages. In C. K. Ogden & I. A. Richards (Eds.), *The meaning of meaning* (3rd ed.). London: Routledge & Kegan Paul, 1930.

Malinowski, B. *Coral gardens and their magic* (Vol. 2). London: Allen & Unwin, 1935.

McDermott, R. P., & Gospodinoff, K. *Social contexts for ethnic borders and school failure: A communicative analysis.* Paper presented to the First International Conference on Non-verbal Behavior, Ontario Institute for Studies in Education, Toronto, 1976.

McDermott, R. P., & Wertz, M. Doing the social order: Some ethnographic advances from communicational analysis and ethnomethodology. *Reviews in Anthropology,* 1976, *3,* 160–174.

Mills, C. W. Situated actions and vocabularies of motive. *American Sociological Review,* 1940, *5,* 904–913.

Mitchell-Kernan, C., & Kernan, K. T. Pragmatics of directive choice among children. In S. Ervin-Tripp & C. Mitchell-Kernan (Eds.), *Child Discourse.* New York: Academic Press, 1977.

NOVA. *The first signs of Washoe.* PBS Network Film, n.d.

Ogden, C. K., & Richards, I. A. *The meaning of meaning* (3rd ed.). London: Routledge & Kegan Paul, 1930.

Pike, K. L. *Language in relation to a unified theory of the structure of human behavior* (Part 1). Glendale, California: Summer Institute of Linguistics, 1954.

Premack, D. The education of Sarah: A chimp learns language. *Psychology Today,* 1970, *4,* 55–58.

Premack, D. Language in the chimpanzee? *Science,* 1971, *172,* 808–822.

Romney, A. K., & D'Andrade, R. G. Cognitive aspects of English kin terms. *American Anthropologist,* 1964, *66* (3, pt. 2), 146–170.

Rumbaugh, D. M. *Language learning by a chimpanzee: The Lana project.* New York: Academic, 1977.

Sacks, H., Schegloff, E. A., & Jefferson, G. A simplest systematics for the organization of turn-taking for conversation. *Language,* 1974, *50,* 696–735.

Salmond, A. Rituals of encounter among the Maori: Sociolinguistic study of a scene. In R. Bauman & J. Sherzer (Eds.), *Explorations in the ethnography of speaking.* London: Cambridge Univ. Press, 1974.

Sapir, E. The unconscious patterning of behavior in society. In E. S. Dummer (Ed.), *The unconscious: A symposium.* New York: Knopf, 1927.

Scheflen, A. E., & Scheflen, A. *Body language and the social order.* Englewood Cliffs, New Jersey: Prentice-Hall, 1972.

Scheflen, A. E. *Communicational structure: Analysis of a psychotherapy transaction.* Bloomington, Indiana: Indiana Univ. Press, 1973. (a)

Scheflen, A. E. *How behavior means.* New York: Anchor, 1973. (b)

Schneider, D. M. American kin terms and terms for kinsmen: A critique of Goodenough's componential analysis of Yankee kinship terminology. *American Anthropologist,* 1965, *67* (5, pt. 2), 288–308.

Searle, J. R. *Speech acts: An essay in the philosophy of language.* London: Cambridge Univ. Press, 1969.

Singer, M. Culture theory's tilt to semiotics. In T. Sebeok (Ed.), *Sight, sound, and sense.* Bloomington, Indiana: Indiana Univ. Press, 1977.

Stocking, G. W., Jr. *Race, culture, and evolution: Essays in the history of anthropology.* New York: Free Press, 1968.

Sugiyama, Y. Social behavior of chimpanzees in the Budongo Forest, Uganda. *Primates,* 1969, *10,* 197–225.

Turner, R. H. Role-taking: Process versus conformity. In A. Rose (Ed.), *Human behavior and social processes.* Boston: Houghton Mifflin, 1962.

Tyler, S. A. (Ed.). *Cognitive anthropology.* New York: Holt, 1969.

Umiker-Sebeok, D. Semiotics of culture: Great Britain and North America. *Annual Review of Anthropology,* 1977, *6,* 121–135.

van Lawick-Goodall, J. A preliminary report on expressive movements and communication in the Gombe Stream chimpanzees. In P. Jay (Ed.), *Primates: Studies in adaptation and variability.* New York: Holt, 1968.

van Lawick-Goodall, J. *Miss Goodall among the wild chimpanzees.* National Geographic Film: Washington, D.C., n.d.

Wallace, A. F. C. *Culture and personality.* New York: Random House, 1961.

Wallace, A. F. C. Cognitive theory. In D. Sills (Ed.), *International encyclopedia of the social sciences* (Vol. 2). New York: Macmillan, 1968.

Watson, K. A. Transferable communicative routines: Strategies and group identity in two speech events. *Language in Society,* 1975, *4,* 53–72.

Watson-Gegeo, K. A., & Boggs, S. From verbal play to talk story: The role of routines in speech events among Hawaiian children. In S. Ervin-Tripp and C. Mitchell-Kernan (Eds.), *Child Discourse.* New York: Academic Press, 1977.

Watzlawick, P., Beavin, J. H., & Jackson, D. *Pragmatics of human communication: A study of interactional patterns, pathologies, and paradoxes.* New York: Norton, 1967.

Weinreich, U., Labov, W., & Herzog, M. I. Empirical foundations for a theory of language change. In W. P. Lehmann & Y. Malkiel (Eds.), *Directions for historical linguistics: A symposium.* Austin, Texas: Univ. of Texas Press, 1968.

Wieder, D. L. On meaning by rule. In J. D. Douglas (Ed.), *Understanding everyday life.* Chicago: Aldine, 1970.

Wieder, D. L. *Language and social reality.* The Hague: Mouton, 1974.

Wittgenstein, L. *Philosophical investigations.* New York: Macmillan, 1953.

Wootton, A. *Dilemmas of discourse: Controversies about the sociological interpretation of language.* New York: Holmes & Meier, 1976.

4

Non-Western Psychology:
The Search for Alternatives

PAUL PEDERSEN

Introduction

Students of psychology often face the dilemma of knowing more about
"non-Western" psychologies than the faculty teaching them. In part, this
relates to the rapidly increasing interest in meditation, Zen, Yoga, and other
non-Western philosophies; in part, it relates to the increased interest in
psychological phenomena by other disciplines studying non-Western cultures; in part, it relates to increased status and power influence of ethnic
minorities whose social traditions often share basic assumptions with non-
Western cultures; and in part, it probably relates to the failure of modern
psychology to escape from a fairly narrow frame of cultural values more
characteristic of white, middle-class males who dominate the field. As a
consequence, some of our best and brightest students of psychology are
searching for alternatives. This movement (Agel, 1971, 1973) is motivated by
a radical rebellion against ''establishment'' psychology on the one hand, and
on the other, a return to the basic questions of consciousness where psychology began (Ornstein, 1972). There are aspects of psychology that have
been developed more extensively in non-Western cultures than in our own
and that provide alternative systems of explaining human behavior.

Much of the writing on the non-Western psychologies has either attempted
to explain non-Western phenomena using Western theoretical constructs or

PERSPECTIVES ON CROSS-CULTURAL PSYCHOLOGY

has described "uniquely" non-Western structures in comparison to Western norms. In either case, we gloss over the reality that most of the world's people do not accept many of the basic assumptions underlying traditional Western psychology. As a consequence, "Western psychology" has become more of a political term reflecting the values of dominant Euro-American society (Surya, 1969). Leading social scientists have articulated non-Western alternatives for some time. Price-Williams (1968) divided all personality theories into two groups: the individualistic, wherein the individual shapes culture; and the culturological, whereby the culture shapes individuals. Singer (1961) identified the three major categories in the relationship of culture to, first, human nature, second, the typical personality, and, third, individual personalities. Nakamura (1964) utilizes a detailed analysis of Asian language to develop a typology of the great variety in the psychological traditions of Asian cultures. The abundance of cross-cultural research indicates that, even in psychobiological processes such as the perception of space and cognition, there are cultural differences (Diaz-Guerrero, 1977).

The consequence of these and other writings to be cited in this chapter is to question the universality of Western psychology as the discipline has been defined. Culture can account for significant variance in the behavioral sciences and there is a basis to speak about "sociocultural psychologies." In developing this theme, Diaz-Guerrero makes it clear that he is "challenging the universality of psychology, not its scientific character [Diaz-Guerrero, 1977, p. 935]," although these two questions have frequently been dealt with as one.

Perhaps the most comprehensive typology of Western and non-Western social systems was developed by Kluckhohn and Strodtbeck (1961) who organized the variety of social systems around five questions:

1. What is the character of innate human nature?
2. What is the relationship of persons to nature (and supernature)?
3. What is the temporal focus of human life?
4. What is the modality of human activity?
5. What is the modality of a person's relationship to other persons?

They approach the typology by getting at the limited number of common human problems for which all peoples at all times must find some solution. Although there are endless solutions available, some are differentially preferred in some societies.

Stewart, Danielian, and Festes (1969) have applied the Kluckhohn and Strodtbeck typology to Western cultures describing it as one where (*a*) self-expression takes place in an activity modality of doing, (*b*) social relationships emphasize equality and informality, (*c*) achievement is a prime motivating force, (*d*) the world is viewed as an object to be exploited or developed for the material benefit of man, and (*e*) the rights, values, and importance of an individual's identity are implicit. Remembering that the prefix "Western" has more of a political than geographical meaning and that many cultures or minorities in Western countries are not characterized by these applications, the typology is nonetheless useful in establishing the assumptions on which Western psychology is founded. Rottenberg (1974) has likewise described the "predestinal dualism" which has dominated "Western psychology" through the Protestant Ethic.

If culture can explain a significant part of the variance in psychological dimensions, the hegemony of Euro-American psychology can reasonably be challenged, especially in perceptual process and coping styles as related to personality and cognitive dimensions. Several psychologists have demonstrated that even those variables that appear to be universal vary from one culture to the next when age, sex, social class, and other specific aspects are taken into account (Diaz-Guerrero, 1977, p. 493).

As a consequence, much of what we consider psychological data is not universally but only relatively true as it applies in the context of those who share the cultural assumptions of the experimenters and writers. Human behavior is incredibly complex, and the validation of conclusions within a prescribed cultural context do not automatically apply universally. Orthodox Western psychology, as it is being taught in the universities, may be guilty of teaching relative facts as universal truth (Tart, 1975, p. 64).

Benaissa (1977) describes how "intrinsic" cultural factors have been influential in cross-cultural studies of child rearing patterns, parent–child interaction, individual–group interactions, dependency, group structure and cohesiveness, conceptual systems, and the sources of gratification or motivation (Barnouw, 1973; Benaissa, 1977; Haring, 1964; Kennedy, 1961; Lambo, 1972; Linton, 1956; Opler, 1959). More recently, the topics of extrinsic social stressors such as biculturalism and acculturation in conflicting value or belief systems as they relate to a revolution of rising expectations far exceeds the possibilities of gratification in non-Western societies (Berry, 1970; Dawson, 1969; Leighton & Murphy, 1965). The need for normative, mental health profiles is apparent from the work of Katz, Sanborn, and Gudeman (1969) and ethnic variations in manifesting depression have been extensively studied by Marsella, Kinzie, and Gordon (1973) and Marsella (1979). Other authors who have written about non-Western psychologies from Asia are cited in Pedersen (1977).

History

Psychological explanations are not Western inventions. Most of the explanations of human behavior developed in non-Western societies have emerged in a political, religious, or philosophical context. At times, the history of such explanations seems so different from what we have come to understand as "psychology" that they are separated from one another, even though the phenomena explained serve the same psychological function in both societies. The non-Western psychological emphasis is on practical or ethical strategies more than on conceptual abstractions.

In India, the first indication we have of psychological explanation is in the religio–philosophical Vedic literature and later Hindu literature of the Rg-Veda, Upanishads, Yoga, and the Bhagavad-Gita. Aryan philosophy contributed a notion of mind, soul, or spirit rooted in the changeless reality of an inner self or *"atman,"* considered to be the core of reality for individuals and as participating in the "Cosmic Unity." Murphy and Murphy (1968, p. 6) describe the *atman* as pure, changeless, honest; dispassionate, and real in all forms of Indian philosophy. The emphasis is not on *atman* as an individual, self-contained unit but part of an absolute core of reality. Through the vehicle of Buddhism, these ideas were to provide a basis for much of Asian psychological thought.

In India, psychological explanations moved from an emphasis on magic and mysticism (the object was to control nature through Hinduism) where they tried to understand nature, into a period of Buddhism, where inner harmony and psychic consciousness became the key to freedom (Pedersen, 1977). Human behavior was explained in terms of *dharma* (codes and rules), *karma* (heritage of previous incarnations and future destiny), *maya* (the illusion of real knowledge), and *atman* (the person as part of the universe). These concepts were illustrated in the Ramayana and Mhabharata legends of religious mythology and the literature of the Upanishads and Bhagavad-Gita, in the struggle between good and evil. The Upanishads ask "Who am I?" in a variety of contexts struggling with the connection between the individual and the universe.

Later, Yoga sought to separate the individual self from the perceiving thought process through self-discipline and training. The Bhagavad-Gita emphasized "self-actualization" beyond the physical or psychological realities of life in a transpersonal psychology of personality. Buddhism emphasized the four noble truths that (a) all life is subject to suffering, (b) desire to live is the cause of repeated existences, (c) only the annihilation of desire gives release from suffering, and (d) the way of escape is through the eightfold path of right belief, right thought, right speech, right action, right livelihood, right effort, right mindfulness, and right concentration to escape from desire.

In China, Buddhism was modified to emphasize social responsibility in Buddha's ethical teachings. The emphasis was on utilitarian reasons for understanding behavior in the everyday context of politics, family life, business, and successful living. Taoism emphasized the "way" to perfection of the personality through mysticism whereas Confucianism emphasized more practical matters, emphasizing the notions of face, filial piety, and proper conduct. Chinese philosophy generally emphasized the social relationships between sovereign–subject, father–son, elder–younger brother, husband–wife, and friend–friend.

The Japanese way of thought was strongly influenced by both India and China from about the sixth century with the emphasis on Confucianism and Buddhism. With the Meiji Restoration in 1868, the Japanese began to emerge with a more distinctive way of thinking that was apparent in the language and philosophies of their literature. Additionally, the Japanese selectively adopted foreign viewpoints to their own unique way of thinking, emphasizing what Nakamura (1964) calls the "limited social nexus" of the Japanese people themselves.

There is a growing interest in the psychological ideas and practices of the non-Western world, particularly of Asia. Popular literature on transcendental meditation has translated psychological insights from Asian religions to American culture. Yoga, likewise, appears to be increasing in popularity in the West as a system of meditation and an exercise discipline. Zen meditative techniques have attempted to emancipate Western culture from the dualistic bondage of subjectivity–objectivity, and mind–body. Biofeedback techniques, in turn, applied sophisticated electronic equipment to the goals of Asian psychology. They have been used to treat muscle-tension problems, to control heart rate and blood pressure, and to solve sexual problems as well as a variety of other difficulties. Biofeedback has been cited as aiding creativity, psychic integration, and improving problem-solving abilities (Brown, 1974).

Each of the non-Western traditions we have discussed has developed its own distinctive psychological point of view that is independent of the religious belief system ordinarily associated with them. In a similar manner, Western psychology can, to some extent, be viewed outside the context of twentieth-century Western culture. By contrast with these non-Western alternatives, Western psychology has dealt very inadequately with the spiritual side of human nature, choosing either to ignore its existence or to label it pathological. Pande (1968) contrasts the two psychological viewpoints citing the Western emphasis on work rather than on relationships and life; self-direction and independence in life, rather than interdependence and acceptance of guidance from others; a directional and linear attitude toward time rather than an ahistorical view of time; encapsulated individual consciousness rather than social if not cosmic consciousness; and a problem-solving cerebral approach to life's conflicts rather than one emphasizing absorption and integration of experience (Pande, 1968, p. 432). Western psychology seeks evidence to verify external experience in objective linear categories and non-Western psychologies suggest that we look inward toward subjective reality in a more philosophical or even religious mode. However, contrasts between Western and non-Western psychologies oversimplify both systems.

The more recent history of non-Western psychologies has expanded to include Third World peoples such as the Asian-Americans, blacks, Chicanos, and native Americans (Sue, Allen, & Conaway, 1978; Sue, McKinney, Allen, & Hall, 1974; Sue & McKinney, 1974) where "social deviance" describes variation across ethnic groups in the way the various communities view and judge emotionally disturbed behavior (Katz & Sanborn, 1976). The psychological perspective of the Chicano or Mexican-American community in contrast to the traditional Western point of view are described by Torrey (1972). He contends that Westernized systems of mental health care services can be described as being largely irrelevant to the needs of the Mexican-American population.

1. Problems of transportation, family responsibilities, and cost factors make such services relatively inaccessible to low-income populations.
2. Mexican-Americans typically were required to use English, which was not their first language.
3. The services were perceived as being class-bound with better services being provided to the more affluent and powerful clients.
4. The services were perceived as being culture-bound, guided by middle-class Anglo-Caucasian values in the defining of problems as well as solutions.
5. The services were perceived as protecting the status-quo point of view.
6. The services were considered to be less effective than those provided by traditional healers such as the curanderos who are readily available to each local population.

Padilla, Ruiz, and Alvarez (1975) discuss these and other factors which are insensitive to Latino culture. Western psychology has been characteristically insensitive to other non-Western or minority cultures as well. Therapists who disregard the discomforting effect of ambiguous and unstructured therapy sessions for Third World clients, or who fail to understand culturally influenced patterns of communication by minority clients, are neglecting their responsibility. Therapists who assume a universally understood and accepted notion of what constitutes mental health, illness, and adjustment are culturally insensitive. Traditional psychology has been encapsulated by criteria of left-brain functioning; emphasizing the distinctly analytical, rational, and verbal aspects of psychology; and searching for cause–effect relationships.

Though Western psychology has been more conservative, individual psychologists have focused on the interplay of sociocultural factors and mental health. Many writers have pointed out the fallacy of universally applying traditional definitions (Pedersen, 1976). The role of social and cultural factors in the occurrence and distribution of mental illness is an issue of some controversy. The social drift or social causation theory has at least three basic assumptions. One is that some cultures may be more immunizing against psychopathology than others; second, that psychiatric disorder will have a different distribution if not a different basis in different cultures; and last, that the stresses and strains of modern industrial society are contributing to an increase in psychological impairment. These attempts to interpret non-Western culture from within a Western framework have been described as oversimplistic in their analysis in a variety of research cited by Benaissa (1977) and Chunnual and Marsella (1975). These authors caution the researcher against ignoring the multidimensional nature of traditionalism—modernism as a personality characteristic.

Critical Issues

Whereas Western psychology seeks the logical integration of personality functions, some non-Western psychologies (e.g., India), seek the dissociation and even detachment from higher and lower functions where the ego is a witness and nonparticipant. The nonrational alternatives rely, instead, on human communication with a higher consciousness that is beyond human control but with a capacity to influence human behavior subjectively. The subjective method emphasizes the importance of "being" more than that of "becoming," experience more than logic. As a result, the criteria of reality in Buddhism, for example, does not always differentiate between actual and ideal or fact and fantasy as clearly as Western explanations.

Existence from this subjective perspective has been compared to a river which has its source in birth and its mouth in death, winding through a continuous process of existence in which consciousness unites all persons with one another and brings together the different moments within our collective and individual lives. All components change in relationship to one another, giving the illusion of constancy, of ego or of an unchanging personality (Pedersen, 1977). The notion of an unchanging personality or identity may itself be an illusion. Subject and object are like two moving systems. When both systems move together, it creates the impression of nonmovement. If they move at different rates or directions, one will appear to move while the other will appear to stand still (Govinda, 1961, p. 130).

Spiritual training leads toward achieving higher levels of consciousness through experience and inner exploration, separating reality from illusion toward the goal of liberation by participating in higher levels of consciousness, as in the achievement of Nirvana in Buddhism. As we examine the critical issues of controversy that separate Western from non-Western psychological alternatives, we might begin by distinguishing the role of rational, intellectual, logical method in Western psychology with the more subjective access to knowledge emphasized in some of the non-Western psychologies.

ACQUISITION OF KNOWLEDGE IS PRIMARILY
AN INTELLECTUAL PROCESS

Knowledge in non-Western societies has many additional forms. There is knowledge by identity through close communion between the knower and the known. Although reasoning is obviously a valuable skill, access to knowledge through intuition is more highly valued in many cultures. At some point, the intellectual process may, in fact, inhibit the quality of life by cutting off sources of information that do not fit comfortably into the logical constructions of a rationally organized and intricately compartmentalized life style (Sandweiss, 1975). Reason is not the "master key" to understanding the relationship between persons and nature.

The presence of logical inconsistency in many non-Western psychologies has discredited that point of view to Western psychologists. Yet, if logic is accepted as only one form of validation, then perhaps logical inconsistency may not be that important. Rottenberg (1974) suggests that the Protestant Ethic has contributed largely to the enhancement of a scientific, rational approach to psychopathology in Western psychology, even though the underlying determinism of the Protestant Ethic is inherently contradictory to the possibility of "people changing systems." It is as though we accept deterministic explanations of human behavior but are so depressed by the possibility of losing our free will that we rationalize and act as if we were free to keep up a positive attitude.

THE NOTION OF PERSONALITY DISTINGUISHES EACH
INDIVIDUAL AS UNIQUE AND SEPARATE FROM
ONE ANOTHER

In many non-Western psychologies, the attachment to individualism can be either a minor consideration or even a direct handicap to attaining spiritual development. The individual development of a person is frequently seen as a lower stage in enlightenment and a diversion from more important spiritual goals. By contrast, Western psychology may describe the individual undifferentiated from peers as lacking in "personality" or distinguishing characteristics. There is a distinction in the meaning of "self" whether as an isolated, individual identity or as participating with other individuals in a corporate reality (e.g., the concept of *atman* in India).

While the ultimate goal may be the recovery or discovery of self in both Western and non-Western psychologies, the spiritual alternative of non-Western psychologies describes the self as participating in a unity with all things and as not limited by the changing manifestations of an illusory and temporary phenomenal world. The emphasis is on the "essence" of the individual, rather than the surface qualities of appearance. In this relational definition of self, the definition of identity is directed toward internalized–

subjective analysis as well as self-affirming extraverted definitions of identity in the context of the external experiences of others. The result is a balance of self and nonself, internal and external experiences, and individual and relational components of identity. How we see ourselves will profoundly affect how we experience life by affecting our cognitive process and perceptions and by systematically distorting the way we see the universe. If I believe that persons are inherently selfish because I am inherently selfish, I will observe selfish behavior in my relationships that will confirm my point of view.

The language used in different cultures provides a valuable cue to the role of the individual. The European languages possess only one pronoun for the first and second person, such as "I," "Thou," "*Ich,*" "*Du.*" By contrast, Kimura (1972) points out that in Japanese there is no single word for translating the pronouns "I" or "Thou," but there are at least two words for "I" and as many for each one of the personal pronouns depending on the situation of the moment. The first person pronoun will be expressed differently depending on whether one is speaking with a man on a higher social level, an equal, or a subordinate; whether one is male or female; whether one is speaking in public or private; and whether one is writing or speaking. Thus, identity is not private property but attached to a web of human relationships. In some cases the personal pronoun is not even expressed and instead of "I see flowers" or "I hear music" you would say in Japanese, "flowers are seen" or "music is heard." The self does not build but rather is built by the situation.

Kimura (1972, p. 107) goes on to quote the Japanese philosopher Dogen, "I do not prove the existence of things, the things come to prove my existence." As another example, Kimura cites the word *ningen,* where *nin* means 'man' and *gen* 'the space between,' emphasizing the space between persons in an encounter. The Western and the Japanese cultures have a different concept of encounter. In the West, it means to step out of one's own self in order to meet the other person who is doing the same. In Japan, the perceiver is already in the "space between." In order to meet the other person, one must first come back to self, while the other person is doing the same (Kimura, 1972, p. 107).

THE CORPORATE IDENTITY OF PERSONS IN RELATIONSHIPS WITH ONE ANOTHER IS THE BASIS OF SELF

While Western psychology has frequently described society as composed of the individuals who have created it, many non-Western cultures concentrate on the relational and cultural differences without specific reference to individuals. There is a humanistic trend in many non-Western psychologies that blurs the distinctions between individuals and human organizations. In Chinese thought, for example, a person was considered a person only through right behavior, excluding birds, animals, barbarians, and extremely immoral individuals from the definition of human (Hsu, 1971). The locus of cultural change or resistance is not the isolated individual but the circle of humanity in interpersonal relationships, and is situation centered by socially controlled criteria. The emphasis is on the space between persons which Hsu (1971) describes as an interpersonal nexus in his theory of psychosocial homeostasis as an alternative to the premises of Western individualism. The emphasis on individual-in-context rather than an individual continuum is more clearly seen in non-Western cultures in the context of developmental emphasis on parent–child interaction or in the configuration of specific social situations where individuals interact with one another. Etymologically, the Chinese word for human, *jen,* is composed of two parts: person and two, meaning goodness in interpersonal relationships (Tseng & Hsu, 1971).

Western and non-Western psychologies take opposite views. The emphasis in Western psychology is on the individual's appropriate role, place, and relationship to other persons, conforming to social reality rather than making reality conform to the individual. The attachment to things that define us as individuals may function to retard human development and keep the individual from going beyond self in an awareness of identity. In contrast with the Western psychological split between ego and environment, Asian cognition provides a relational partnership, fitting into the universe rather than isolating self from it. Psychotherapy in Western cultures attempts to substitute relational understandings of identity in the quest for health and self-understanding, while simultaneously reinforcing an individualistic point of view. Western traditions are based on the self as ego or as the independent observer and potential controller of a world that is experienced as profoundly separate from self (Watts, 1958, p. 760). In contrast, Indian tradition emphasizes self-transcendence rather than self-assertion and the Chinese model their life goals on harmony with nature and integration into a social totality.

MODERNIZED CULTURES TEND TO ADOPT WESTERN PSYCHOLOGICAL VIEWPOINTS AND PATHOLOGY

One of the products of modernization is an increased distance between aspirations and achievements, resulting in dissatisfaction, frustration, low self-esteem, marginality, alienation, and social deviance (Triandis, Malpass, & Davidson, 1972, 1973; Marsella, 1978). In a similar mode, Dohrenwend and Dohrenwend (1967) report consistently higher rates of personality disorder and neurosis in urban areas. In part, this trend is credited to social drift from a "shame" culture, characterized as more typical in less developed societies, toward a "guilt" culture, typically associated with more developed Western societies. While the rigid classifications have not been consistently validated in the research on modernization as polarized on a developmental scale, there is an element of change brought about by modernization that is accompanied by an increase of Western psychological perspectives.

Lebra's (1972) research suggests that guilt arises in the Japanese culture from a breakdown of social reciprocity, whereas shame is likely to result when someone of status finds himself in a situation incongruous with that status. In a monotheistic culture, guilt is a debt owed continuously to one, single, universal creditor. Shame tends to be more specific. In a sociocultic culture, where society itself is deified, shame is generalized and guilt is made specific (Lebra, 1972, p. 21). In traditional Japanese society as a sociocult, shame is generalized in status identification, exposure, and collective sharing of shame. After an exhaustive review of the literature on the psychological impact of modernization, Marsella (1978) points out that while non-Western thought and life styles have had a profound impact on the West in recent years, the non-Western cultures seem more determined than ever to emulate the West as a social model. Some combination of person and situation variables in a multiple determination of behavior to include the physical and psychological context as suggested by Mischel (1977), needs to be worked out in greater detail.

Although we know that culture influences and mediates the symptoms of both health and illness, there is some evidence that the more an afflicted individual is Westernized and urban, the more closely that person's problem parallels those found in Western societies (Benaissa, 1978). This is not to prove, as Dohrenwend and Dohrenwend (1967) point out, that modernization results in an increase of psychopathology as a function of the stresses and strains of modern society, but at least the complexion and symptomatology of the problem is changed. A prominent Nigerian psychologist pointed out that in Western society there is a fear of technological domination that might deteriorate social values and destroy the meaning of traditional culture. Westerners are concerned because of the erosion of spirit that has accompanied the rise of modern technology, while non-Western countries are concerned that the technology will not be available to them. Though technology is important, non-Westerners do not want to lose their souls in the process (Mundy-Castle, 1976, p. 2). Most of us are twentieth-century Westerners, nurtured in the virtues of the scientific method. The task is not to discard what we have learned, but rather to develop alternatives which might integrate or coexist with our own Western cultural heritage.

INTERDEPENDENCE IN PARENT–CHILD RELATIONSHIPS IS A FREQUENT MODEL FOR PERSONALITY DEVELOPMENT

Asian cultures provide models that contrast with the Western family socialization toward independence, speaking out, direct communication, and unrestrained expression of resentment or anger (Tseng & McDermott,

1975). In non-Western families there is a greater acceptance of dependence among interfamily relationships, even as adults, without embarrassment or judgements of immature behavior. The goal of maturity in India may even be described as satisfying and continuous dependency within the family unit (Pedersen, 1977; Carstairs, 1957). At a minimum, the family models a necessary harmony among members, as in the Chinese family, where there is concern about handling hostility between generations or status levels within a generation. In a fight between brothers, both are blamed. The older is blamed for not giving in to the younger, while the younger is scolded for not respecting the older. Both brothers will be punished for their aggressive behavior (Tseng & Hsu, 1971, p. 7).

The term *ho'oponopono*, as practiced by Hawaiians, literally means 'to make things right'. In this tradition, all members of an extended family are assembled by the family head to resolve conflict. After ritual prayers to the gods for help in solving a problem, the different conflicting points of view in a family are expressed directly and openly. In this ritualized context, the family determines guilt, the guilty person apologizes, and the wronged person accepts the apology in a process described by Pukui, Haertig, and Lee (1972).

In Chinese society, the system of filial piety provides the core of society where parents devote themselves to children who, in turn, are expected to support the parents in their old age. Family relationships provide the model for moral virtue in all other aspects of society, with the ideas of family government and harmony being a model for national statesmanship and social harmony.

The Japanese concept of *ie*, or 'family system', implies closely guarded familial relationships as a model of total involvement and absolute loyalty. In Japan, *amae* means 'to expect and to depend upon another's benevolence'. The term originally described a child's relationship with parents, particularly the mother. However, the term can also describe a special relationship between two adults, such as husband and wife or master and subordinate. Again, there is a recognition of mutuality and interdependency.

NON-WESTERN PSYCHOLOGIES DO NOT FIT IN THE DEVELOPMENTAL CATEGORIES DESCRIBING MATURITY IN WESTERN CULTURES

Non-Western psychologies frequently take the view that development is not over upon reaching adulthood, but that the adequately functioning adult member of society has only achieved a preliminary groundwork to begin spiritual development. Western parents are likely to send their maturing children out of the home to gratify hostile or pleasure-seeking impulses outside the family, which would be perceived as "abandonment" in many non-Western cultures. In China, a son's identity is tied to perpetual dependency toward his parents. In Japan, there is a developmental curve which allows the most freedom at infancy and old age, and imposes the most control during the middle range of years. This is nearly the opposite of developmental theory in Western cultures.

Pande (1968) contrasts Western and non-Western notions of development. He states that in the West, a gradual development from infancy to adulthood is anticipated at each stage. Adulthood is the symbolic goal at which point one attains those values overwhelmingly supported by Western culture (e.g., self-reliance, power, achievement, responsibility, work, and sexual fulfillment). Childish behavior in adults (e.g., crying, dependence on others, and excessive emotionality) are considered bad and discouraged (Pande, 1968, p. 429). Again, non-Western cultures may be changing from a postfigurative culture (i.e., children learn primarily from their elders), through a configurative culture (i.e., both children and adults learn from their peers), and ultimately toward a prefigurative culture (i.e., adults learn also from their children).

WESTERN COGNITION IS BASED ON OBJECTS OF CONSCIOUSNESS WHEREAS NON-WESTERN PSYCHOLOGIES EMPHASIZE CONSCIOUSNESS ITSELF

Non-Western psychologies assert that we are more than our physical bodies, including a conception of "soul" or a nonphysical portion, which may be our essence and which may exist independently of our physical selves. This extrasensory self allows learning to occur through uncovering information already existing in the depths of our nature but ordinarily blurred (Tart, 1975, p. 102). Just as there is direct contact between humans, there may also be direct contact between the person and spiritual essence which is not limited by the physical properties of the nervous system. Although our ordinary state of consciousness and perception is "dominated by (the) illusion" of apparent reality surrounding us, non-Western psychologies affirm that it is possible to participate in ultimate or real consciousness. In non-Western psychology, emotion is viewed as a type of consciousness energy or as one aspect in our mind or nervous system more complicated than a mere electrochemical charge, and as a means to attain enlightenment (Tart, 1975, p. 95).

Non-Western psychologies often do not limit reality to physics, but describe a level of reality external to us and perceived through extrasensory perception by the mind which is capable of extending itself outside our bodies. By contrast, Western psychology assumes that we are determined by the physical processes of our nature and surrounding environment, which is a comparatively mechanistic explanation. There is a tendency to discount phenomena that can neither be observed nor measured, even though many of the phenomena we account as important (i.e., love, charity, intelligence, and pleasure) are concepts inferred from behavior and are subjective in their measured impact.

As a consequence of discounting apparent reality, past, present, and future merge, rather than describing discrete stages. In Western thought, time is like water flowing in a stream that flows away once and forever. Western thought moves ahead in one direction and, with a passionate belief in progress, the Western person works in a race against the millennium (Pande, 1968, p. 428). This linear view of time permeates Western psychology where the past is dead and gone, the future does not yet exist, leaving us at an infinitesimally narrow point on the continuum which fades from the future to the past with a more frantic and hectic, if not desperate, urgency.

NON-WESTERN PSYCHOLOGIES AFFIRM PSYCHIC CONNECTION BETWEEN FORMS OF LIFE AND "OBJECTS" IN OUR ENVIRONMENT

The ecology movement has taught us to think of ourselves as part of our own environment, however, many non-Western psychologies go even farther, positing a cosmic participatory unity in a profoundly nonphysical mode. We are not here to control the universe but rather to find our place, through harmony with the universe, beyond the limited view of what might be good for ourselves. The universe is perceived as alive and evolving, with the same properties of life as ourselves, rather than dead, purposeless, and inanimate.

The more typical Western perception of a purposeless universe in which humans are in control, suggests that the only limits on exploiting our environment are economic and ecological—so that we do not disrupt our *own* ecosystem and suffer for it at some later time. With such a perception there is no inherent other reason not to exploit the environment, as long as the exploitation is efficient and "humanitarian." Non-Western psychologies, however, accept that higher nonphysical forces possess consciousness, just as organisms below us on the evolutionary ladder experience consciousness (albeit different from consciousness as we know it). Many non-Western societies acknowledge both positive and hostile forces capable of acting on individuals (Weidman & Sussex, 1971; Yap, 1969), and Wittkower and Weidman (1969) describe the psychologically integrative function of magic in which something that is poorly defined, anxiety arousing, and disruptive is given a name.

HARMONY RATHER THAN INDIVIDUAL ADVANCEMENT CHARACTERIZES HUMAN INTERACTION AS AN IDEAL MODEL

In Chinese philosophy, the interaction between *yin* (female element) and *yang* (male element) provides a model for harmony in nature necessary for individual health and social well-being. Every supernatural belief system depends on a system of laws or rules that defines order in the universe and the route to individual happiness. Westerners are likely to see only part of the African belief system, such as the witch doctor, and wonder how reasonable people can believe in them when Western medicine seems logical by contrast. The African religious–magical system, seen internally, is a great poem. It is allegorical of human experience, and not a literal equation. It is important to include both the poem and the equation in our definition of reality (Lambo, 1978, p. 39).

The supernatural belief systems are harmonious and internally consistent. Reality does not depend on the human ability to master things and advance individually to conquer the world. Reality is rather a soul-based, religious experience of life. Reality is the interaction between one human being and another, and between all people and all spirits (Lambo, 1978, p. 34). There is a unity of life and time which brings apparent opposites into the same harmonious web including the animate and inanimate, natural and supernatural, physical and mental, conscious and unconscious in a dynamic interrelationship that is visible or invisible, past, present, and future so that we experience the same world in our dreams as in daylight. If we were the smartest creatures in the universe, we would have to depend entirely on our own efforts without help rather than acknowledge that help is available to us in a variety of underutilized sources.

PERSONAL HEALTH IS NOT AN INDIVIDUAL BUT A CORPORATE PHENOMENA

Sinclair (1967) described the sequence of indigenous healing rituals in New Guinea where first, at the impact of a crisis, the victim becomes fearful and anxious. Second, a cause of the misfortune is sought through divination in the supernatural. Third, the responsibility for the crisis is transferred to a supernatural agency so that the personal anxiety that threatens the subject's psychological equilibrium becomes identified as the enemy. Likewise, in Africa, the character and effectiveness of medicine depends on the cultural context in which it is practiced. In Africa, health and illness, such as life and death, are intertwined. Health is not separated or isolated but integrated into the community. Health is not the absence of disease but a sign that a person is living in peace and harmony and the healthy person is keeping the laws of the gods and the tribe. Medicine is more than the administration of drugs and potions in promoting a higher quality of life in the community (Lambo, 1978, p. 35). Healing is less often considered a private matter between patient and therapist, but rather an integral part of society and religion involving the whole community. Even death is continuous with this notion of harmony, and some sense of continuous consciousness transcending physical death (either as a personal identity in some systems or as some level of existence that is less personal but more basic) is present (Lambo, 1978; Tart, 1975).

The whole of nature plays a significant role in the emotional and health-related experience of the Japanese (for examples of this relationship see

Tanaka-Matsumi & Marsella, 1976, on clinical depression and other illnesses). The description of health needs to be mediated by the cultural context
in order to be understood. If you were to say that a Chinese woman is
possessed by a male tiger, which has caused her to be aggressive and cruel to
her husband, it will be better understood than identifying her as a phallic
woman who is emotionally castrating her husband. If an American husband,
who has difficulty with his wife, is diagnosed as being born with a fire nature
whereas his wife has a water nature, and therefore, they are poorly matched,
the diagnosis will probably not be very helpful to him (Tseng & McDermott,
1975).

MENTAL HEALTH SERVICES INTENTIONALLY OR
UNINTENTIONALLY IMPOSE, TEACH, AND ENFORCE
CULTURAL VALUES ON THEIR CLIENTS

After cutting through the medical aura and the noninterventional or non-
judgmental orientation of mental health services in Western cultures, we are
still likely to find a hidden agenda of cultural assumptions which are implicit
in the system itself (Pedersen, 1977). The explanation of mental health
problems varies greatly, but the modern tendency has been to shift from
supernatural to natural and from biomedical to sociopsychological in mental
health care (Tseng & McDermott, 1975). Each culture develops its own
cultural interpretation of the problems according to their own characteristics. In agricultural societies dependent on harmony with nature, disharmony with the environment causes psychiatric disturbance whereas in hunting societies, where conquest and competition are valued, conflict and
antagonism are likely to cause problems. Each society defines its own rules
of normality, and the mental health system frequently enforces those rules.
In Chinese society, divination, as a form of therapy, emphasizes conservative and traditional activities. A Chinese client is usually warned in the form
of proverbs or advice not to be too aggressive or too ambitious or to do
things that are inappropriate for his role or status. The client is encouraged
to maintain the existing situation and that it is not good to try to change. The
traditional Chinese way is to remain patient and unaggressive, to accept the
situation rather than to rebel against it (Tseng & McDermott, 1975, p. 383).

In Western cultures, there is a tendency to stigmatize mental illness with
irreversible labels. In East Africa, Edgerton (1969) describes the process and
labels for recognizing mental illness as all negotiable and reversible. Kitano
(1969) likewise describes the social role of the mentally ill in Japan as not
including rejecting attitudes or irreversible labels. Rottenberg (1974)
suggests that the irreversible label may be rooted in the predestinal, dualistic
doctrine of the Protestant Ethic, as the gradual segregation of the insane
seems to be more characteristic of Western societies. By contrast, more
spiritual psychologies take a larger perspective, deemphasizing adjustment

to one's society. If the culture supports behavior judged as delusionary or evil, then spiritual growth would depend on resisting adjustment to that culture—the ultimate conformity not being to the labels of the society but to some external idealistic norm of behavior.

There is an embarrassment evident in Western mental health systems about the degree of direct intervention enforcing social and cultural values through their therapy. We assume that decisions reached in treatment are reached independently and freely by the client. The expertise of the therapist is measured in the ability to evoke right decisions from the patient with a minimum of outside influence (Pande, 1968, p. 427). The therapist seeks to minimize the amount of direct advice, interpretation, and manipulation of the environment through therapy. It is ironic that this process itself enforces the equalitarian cultural values favoring individuality and personal independence. The more reflective and client-centered therapies teach and embody basic values of American culture (e.g., solving your own problems). Berger (1962) has adapted Zen's "no-thought" to counseling through a technique in which the mind can function on its own, free of established forms and practices separating abstractions from case descriptions to perceive the essence unencumbered by details.

Independent of our intentions, mental health professionals perform in similar ways, as pointed out by Torrey (1972). Witch doctors and psychiatrists are both therapists and treat patients using similar techniques with similar results, depending for their validation on the same techniques. The first principle, which Torrey calls the Rumpelstiltskin principle, involves naming the affliction. The second principle relates to the personal qualities of the therapist. The third principle relates to meeting the patient's expectations. The fourth principle relates to establishing credibility through symbols of skill or power and the final principle relates to applying certain techniques to manipulate the affliction and help the patient feel better. There is a degree of basic similarity in approaches to psychological problems independent of the cultural context.

CHANGE AND DEVELOPMENT ARE INHERENTLY GOOD AND DESIRABLE

There is an activist orientation implicit in many Western cultures that change is preferred to no change when given a choice between the two conditions. In Western cultures, if you do not know what to do you are encouraged to "at least do *something*!" By contrast, many non-Western cultures would suggest that "if you don't know what to do, do nothing [Siu, 1957]." There is no single explanation of how this difference evolved, but there is a clear division between Western and non-Western cultures on the issues of change (Capra, 1977).

There is a different perspective on related issues such as cause and effect.

In some non-Western cultures, such as Hinduism, the categories of cause and effect are not separated but are rather part of the same phenomena observed from a different point of view. In contrast, many of the explanations in Western psychology depend profoundly on the separation of cause and effect in relationships. In Western psychology, change is valuable as a cause agent in helping to bring about a desirable rather than an undesirable effect.

THE VALIDITY OF NON-WESTERN PERSPECTIVES ON PSYCHOLOGY CAN BE DEMONSTRATED THROUGH ASSESSMENT TECHNIQUES ACCEPTED BY WESTERN PSYCHOLOGY

There is an extensive literature on the use of personality measurement strategies developed in Western cultures and applied to non-Western cultures (Brislin, Lonner, & Thorndike, 1973; Triandis, 1977). Some of the problems in applying Western measures to non-Western cultures are discussed here, especially in the use of criterion-oriented (empirical) or construct-oriented (theoretical) measures. One problem is that the criteria or theoretical constructs might themselves be culture bound. Osgood, May, and Miron (1975) have developed the semantic differential to measure "affective cross-cultural meaning" so as to identify cultural universals in psychological perspective. Butcher and Pancheri (1976) cite numerous examples of the Minnesota Multiphasic Personality Inventory being used around the world and discovered considerable similarity among normals, although scores were elevated one to two standard deviations above the mean for males in Japan and Pakistan on the scales measuring depression and schizophrenia. There is also clear evidence supporting self-induced, altered states of consciousness as occurs in Zen, Yoga, or Transcendental Meditation, resulting in better mental or physical health and an increased capacity to deal with stress (Benson, Beary, & Carol, 1974).

It is ironic that we apply the measured criteria of achieved effectiveness to validate a psychology that denies and even opposes the values implicit in these assessment techniques. Ultimately, we need to develop new criteria sensitive to the values of the context being examined and, until that happens, we cannot expect an adequate or even accurate assessment of non-Western psychologies.

Conclusion

The objective of this chapter is to briefly discuss some of the value orientations popular in non-Western cultures to explain psychological process, affirming that such alternative explanations do exist, and that those alternatives conflict with assumptions of what is being taught as universal psychological truth in the West. We know that sociocultural factors influence the composition of a psychology through constructs and concepts which are culturally mediated. However, Euro-American cultural values have dominated the field of psychology for so long that these limited value assumptions are being accepted as universal and, consequently, are being imposed on non-Western cultures where alternative assumptions apply. There is a lively interest in Western cultures for examining the non-Western alternatives, particularly among minority groups who do not easily identify with the dominant cultural value systems. As non-Western cultures gain power and prominence, and as increased mobility increases intercultural contact, it will become increasingly important to accomodate non-Western value assumptions into the discipline of psychology. This must occur not just in recognition of their world-wide popularity, but also because, in many cases, their answers fit our questions better than our own.

There are many areas of controversy surrounding the non-Western alternatives. The role of logic and intellectual, rational analysis in psychology is not exclusively or universally accepted as primary. Neither is the role of the individual, which has become the cornerstone of Western perspectives, separated from a cultural context. Clark (1978) coined the concept of "pertext," or person in context, to synthesize the perspectives of Eastern and Western cultures, looking at the corporate context that defines identity in non-Western cultures. As many non-Western cultures modernize, some of their values are replaced or modified to more closely resemble Western values. This trend is causing concern among those wishing to conserve the non-Western alternatives. The erosion of Western values has been particularly threatening in the non-Western family and influences the developmental models for modernizing youth in non-Western cultures.

Some of the Western youth have also adopted elements of non-Western psychology, particularly relating to the more profound and direct experiencing of consciousness. There is an appreciation of the religious and spiritual participation in the universe which comes more naturally and easily through the alternative non-Western assumptions we have discussed. Health and illness are defined in terms of harmony with the universe to help us see ourselves in perspective with the cosmos surrounding us and purposeful for the brief share of time that we are experiencing that cosmos. It is consequently important to be open in our consideration of alternative values rather than closed, accepting of our own incomplete understanding, and sensitive to the implicit cultural bias. If psychology, as it is being taught, can accomodate alternatives to the culturally dominated and politically limited perspective now being taught as universal psychological truth, we are more likely to find psychological enlightenment for ourselves and our students.

References

Agel, J. *The radical therapist*. New York: Ballantine Books, 1971.

Agel, J. *Rough times*. New York: Ballantine Books, 1973.

Barnouw, V. *Culture and personality*. Homewood: Dorsey Press, 1973.

Benaissa, C. *Issues in cross-cultural psychopathology with particular reference to Africa*. Minneapolis: Univ. of Minnesota, 1977.

Benson, H., Beary, J., & Carol, M. The relaxation response. *Psychiatry*, 1974, *37*, 37–46.

Berger, E. M. Zen Buddhism, general psychology, and counseling psychology. *Journal of Counseling Psychology*, 1962, *9*(2), 122–127.

Berry, J. W. Marginality, stress, and ethnic identification in an acculturated aboriginal community. *Journal of Cross-Cultural Psychology*, 1970, *1*, 239–252.

Brislin, R., Lonner, W., & Thorndike, R. *Cross-cultural research methods*. New York: Wiley, 1973.

Brown, B. B. *New mind, new body: Biofeedback: New directions for the mind*. New York: Harper, 1974.

Butcher, J., & Pancheri, P. *A handbook of cross-national MMPI research*. Minneapolis: Univ. of Minnesota Press, 1976.

Capra, F. *The Tao of physics*. New York: Bantam Books, 1977.

Carstairs, M. *The twice born*. London: Hogarth, 1957.

Chunnual, N., & Marsella, A. J. Convergent and discriminant validation of a traditionalism-modernism attitude questionnaire for Thai exchange students. *Journal of Social Psychology*, 1975, *96*, 21–26.

Clark, L. A. Pertextuality, the person in context, theory, and assessment, East and West. Minneapolis: Univ. of Minnesota, 1978.

Dawson, J. L. M. Exchange theory and comparison level changes among Australian aborigines. *British Journal of Social and Clinical Psychology*, 1969, *8*, 133–140.

Diaz-Guerrero, R. A Mexican psychology. *American Psychologist*, 1977, *32*(11), 934–944.

Dohrenwend, B. P., & Dohrenwend, B. S. Field studies of social factors in relation to three types of psychological disorder. *Journal of Abnormal Psychology*, 1967, *72*(4), 369–378.

Edgerton, R. B. On the recognition of mental illness. In S. C. Plog & R. B. Edgerton (Eds.), *Changing perspectives in mental illness*. New York: Holt, 1969.

Govinda, L. A. *The psychological attitude of early Buddhist philosophy*. London: Rider, 1961.

Haring, D. G. *Personal character and cultural milieu*. Syracuse, New York: Syracuse Univ. Press, 1964.

Hsu, F. L. K. Psychosocial homeostasis and Jen: Conceptual tools for advancing psychological anthropology. *American Anthropologist*, 1971, *73*, 23–44.

Katz, M. M., & Sanborn, K. O. Multiethnic studies of psychopathology and normality in Hawaii. In J. Westermeyer (Ed.), *Anthropology and mental health*. The Hague: Mouton, 1976. Pp. 49–57.

Katz, M. M., Sanborn, K. O., & Gudeman, H. Characterizing differences in psychopathology among ethnic groups in Hawaii. In F. Redlich (Ed.), *Social psychiatry*, 1969.

Kennedy, D. Key issues in the cross-cultural study of mental disorders. In B. Kaplan (Ed.), *Studying personality cross-culturally*. New York: Harper, 1961.

Kimura, B. Mitmenschlichkeit in der Psychiatrie: Ein transkultureller Beitrag aus Asiatischer sicht (Interhuman relationships in psychiatry, a transcultural contribution from an Asian perspective). *Zietschrift für Klinische Psychologie und Psychotherapie*, 1971, *19*(1), 3–13. (Abridged by H. Ellenberber in *Transcultural Psychiatric Research Review*, 1972, *9*, 105–108.)

Kitano, H. H. L. Japanese-American mental illness. In S. Plog & R. Edgerton (Eds.), *Changing perspectives in mental illness*. New York: Holt, 1969.

Kluckhohn, F. R., & Strodtbeck, F. L. *Variations in value orientations*. Evanston, Illinois: Harper, 1961.

Lambo, T. A. Psychotherapy in Africa. *Human Nature,* 1978, *1*(3), 32–40.
Lebra, T. S. The social mechanism of guilt and shame: The Japanese case. *Transcultural Psychiatric Research Review,* 1972, *9,* 21–23 (abstract).
Leighton, A., & Murphy, J. Cross-cultural psychiatry. In A. Leighton & J. Murphy (Eds.), *Approaches to cross-cultural psychiatry.* Ithaca, New York: Cornell Univ. Press, 1965.
Linton, R. *Culture and mental disorders.* Springfield, Illinois: Charles Thomas, 1956.
Marsella, A. J. The modernization of traditional cultures: Consequences for the individual. *Overview of Intercultural Education, Training, and Research (Vol. 3).* Washington, District of Columbia: SIETAR, 1978.
Marsella, A. J. Cross-cultural aspects of depressive disorder and affect. In H. Triandis & J. Draguns (Eds.), *Handbook of Cross-cultural psychology: Culture and psychopathology* (Vol. 5). Boston: Allyn & Bacon, 1979.
Marsella, A. J., Kinzie, D., & Gordon, P. Ethnic variations in the expression of dependency. *Journal of Cross-Cultural Psychology,* 1973, *4,* 434–457.
Mischel, W. On the future of personality measurement. *American Psychologist,* 1977, *32,* 246–254.
Mundy-Castle, A. C. Psychology and the search for meaning. Univ. of Lagos, Nigeria, Inaugural lecture, 1976.
Murphy, G., & Murphy, L. *Asian psychology.* New York: Basic Books, 1968.
Nakamura, H. *Ways of thinking of eastern peoples: India, China, Tibet, Japan.* In P. Weiner, (Ed.), Honolulu: Univ. Press of Hawaii, 1964.
Opler, M. K. The cultural backgrounds of mental health. In M. K. Opler (Ed.), *Culture and mental health.* New York: Macmillan, 1959.
Ornstein, R. *The psychology of consciousness.* New York: Viking, 1972.
Osgood, C., May, W. H., & Miron, M. S. *Cross-cultural universals of affective meaning.* Urbana: Univ. of Illinois Press, 1975.
Padilla, S. M., Ruiz, R. A., & Alvarez, R. Community mental health services for the Spanish-speaking/surnamed population. *American Psychologist,* 1975, *30,* 892–905.
Pande, S. The mystique of Western psychotherapy: An Eastern interpretation. *Journal of Nervous and Mental Disorders,* 1968, *46,* 425–432.
Pedersen, P. The field of intercultural counseling. In P. Pedersen, W. Lonner, & J. Draguns (Eds.), *Counseling across cultures.* Honolulu: Univ. Press of Hawaii, 1976.
Pedersen, P. Asian personality theories. In R. Corsini (Ed.), *Current personality theories.* Itaska, New York: Peacock, 1977.
Pedersen, P. The triad model. *The Personnel and Guidance Journal.* October, 1977, *56,* 94–100.
Price-Williams, D. The philosophy of science and the study of personality. In E. Norbeck, D. Price-Williams, & W. McCord (Eds.), *The study of personality: An interdisciplinary appraisal.* New York: Holt, 1968.
Pukui, M. K., Haertig, E. W., & Lee, C. A. *Nana I ke kumu* (Look to the source). Honolulu: Hui Hanai, 1972.
Rottenberg, M. The Protestant Ethic versus Western people-changing sciences. In J. Dawson & W. Lonner (Eds.), *Readings in cross-cultural psychology.* Hong Kong: The International Association for Cross-Cultural Psychology, 1974, 277–294.
Sandweiss, S. H. *Sai Baba: The holy man . . . and the psychiatrist.* San Diego: Birth Day, 1975.
Sinclair, A. *Field and clinical survey report of the mental health of the indigenes of the territory of Papau and New Guinea.* Port Moresby, New Guinea: Government Publishers, 1967.
Singer, M. A. A survey of culture and personality theory and research. In B. Kaplan (Ed.), *Studying personality cross-culturally.* Evanston, Illinois: Row, 1961.
Siu, R. G. H. *The Tao of science: An essay on Western knowledge and Eastern wisdom.* Cambridge, Massachusetts: The MIT Press, 1957.
Stewart, E. C., Danielian, J., & Festes, R. J. *Simulating interultural communication through*

role playing (HumRRO Tech. Rep. 69-16). Alexandria, Virginia: Human Resources Research Organization, 1969.

Sue, S., Allen, D., & Conaway, L. The responsiveness and equality of mental health care to Chicanos and Native Americans. American Journal of Community Psychology, 1978.

Sue, S., & McKinney, H. Asian-Americans in the community mental health care system. American Journal of Orthopsychiatry, 1974, 45, 111–118.

Sue, S., McKinney, H., Allen, D., & Hall, J. Delivery of community mental health services to black and white clients. Journal of Consulting and Clinical Psychology, 1974, 42, 794–801.

Surya, N. C. Ego structure in the Hindu joint family: Some considerations. In W. Caudill & T. Lin (Eds.), Mental health research in Asia and the Pacific. Honolulu: East–West Center Press, 1969.

Tanaka-Matsumi, J., & Marsella, A. J. Cross-cultural variations in the phenomenological experience of depression: I. Word association studies. Journal of Cross-Cultural Psychology, 1976, 1(4), 379–396.

Tart, C. Some assumptions of orthodox Western psychology. In C. Tart (Ed.), Transpersonal psychologies. New York: Harper, 1975, 59–113.

Torrey, E. F. The mind game: Witch doctors and psychiatrists. New York: Emerson Hall, 1972.

Triandis, H. C. Interpersonal behavior. Monterey: Brooks, Cole & Company, 1977.

Triandis, H. C., Malpass, R. S., & Davidson, A. R. Cross-cultural psychology. In B. J. Siegal (Ed.), Biennial review of anthropology. Stanford: Stanford University Press, 1972.

Triandis, H. C., Malpass, R. S., & Davidson, A. R. Psychology and culture. Annual Review of Psychology, 1973, 24, 355–378.

Tseng, W. S., & Hsu, J. Chinese culture, personality formation, and mental illness. International Journal of Social Psychiatry, 1971, 16, 5–14.

Tseng, W. S., & McDermott, J. F. Psychotherapy: Historical roots, universal elements, and cultural variations. American Journal of Psychiatry, 1975, 132(4), 378–384.

Watts, A. W. Asian psychology and modern psychiatry. In C. F. Reed, I. E. Alexander & S. S. Tomkins (Eds.), Psychopathology. New York: Wiley, 1958, 755–762.

Weidman, H. H., & Sussex, J. N. Cultural values and ego functioning in relation to the typical culture bound reactive syndromes. International Journal of Social Psychiatry, 1971, 17(2), 83–100.

Wittkower, E. D., & Weidman, H. Magic, witchcraft, and sorcery in relation to mental health and mental disorder. Social Psychiatry, 1969, 8, 169–184.

Yap, P. M. The culture bound reactive syndromes. In W. Caudill & T. Y. Lin (Eds.), Mental health research in Asia and the Pacific. Honolulu: East–West Center Press, 1969.

II

COMPLEX HUMAN
BEHAVIOR

5

Cross-Cultural Aspects of Cognitive Functioning: Culture and Knowledge

THOMAS J. CIBOROWSKI

Introduction

Granted the usual number of degrees of freedom in producing a paper for any major conference in cross-cultural psychology, it is axiomatic that any of the participants at such a hypothetical conference could serve up an excellent catalogue and synthesis of the major trends and current topical issues bearing on the encompassing relationship between culture and cognitive functioning. To obtain a winning jump on the enterprise one need only consult the work of Berry and Dasen (1974), Cole and Scribner (1974), Wober (1975), Price-Williams (1975), Serpell (1976), Dasen (1977), and Triandis and Berry (1979). This is not said, in any conceivable way, to denigrate the inherent difficulties nor the value and usefulness of the enterprise, but rather to indicate that even a casual glance at the references just mentioned reveals that the available number of degrees of freedom may be quite small in the present case. That is, one wants to produce a new synthesis or possible provocative synoptic view rather than a mere professional recapitulation of the work of one's colleagues in cross-cultural psychology. A rather tall order, indeed!

To compound the situation, a perusal of the references indicates that the established major lines of inquiry within the framework of the relationship between culture and cognitive functioning have been substantially covered

101

PERSPECTIVES ON CROSS-CULTURAL PSYCHOLOGY

by recognized experts. To avoid redundancy, the following substantive areas will, for the most part, be excluded from the present chapter: education, communication, and affect viewed in both its most specific and most general sense. The peripheral issue of the relationship between culture and perception will be briefly discussed later in the chapter

In light of the foregoing, it appears that if I am to say anything on the topic of the relationship between culture and cognitive functioning, I will have to attempt to consider the topic not only in a fundamental sense, but also to resign myself to playing the unfamiliar and uncomfortable role of a provocateur or devil's advocate; this position is hardly by preconceived intent or design, but rather is dictated by the very real constraints discussed previously.

With the previous apologia and/or excuse in mind, I will first attempt to scrutinize the basic relationship between culture and cognitive functioning. Unhappily, we will discover that a number of philosophical skeletons exist in the closet of cross-cultural psychology. These musty skeletons will reek of a definite philosophical odor, but to paraphrase Kessen (1971), the musty odor is not simply the smell of dead issues but rather of issues buried alive. In the wake of this perhaps ideational necrophilia, we will then consider the issue of to what degree the field of cross-cultural psychology has advanced our knowledge of culture and cognitive functioning. Concomitantly, we will consider the important concept of centri-cultural bias, first elucidated by Wober (1969), and examine a number of approaches aimed at diminishing such "bias" in cross-cultural psychology.

In examining these approaches we will briefly consider the work of Lave (1976), Price-Williams, Gordon, and Ramirez (1969), Serpell (1977), and Scribner (1976). Finally, a brief summary will be provided, along with some tentative suggestions for future research. Armed with this sketchy outline, we can now proceed to critically examine the relationship between culture and cognitive functioning.

Culture and Cognitive Functioning Reconsidered

A customary and usually helpful way to begin is to provide some definitions or descriptions so as to map out the general dimensions of the concepts and ideas that will be examined. Although an alarming number of descriptions and definitions of culture abound, and given that this chapter is not the proper forum for sifting through the plethora of offerings, a quite serviceable description was provided by LeVine (1973) who stated that culture can be viewed as an organized collection of rules focusing on the ways in which members of a population should communicate, think, and interact with one another and their environments. This description is not provided in any final or exclusive sense, but rather as a reliable reference point in the present inquiry, and we will return to it after we examine the notion of cognitive functioning.

DEFINING COGNITION

Instead of addressing the outcome or functions of cognitive activity, it seems more appropriate and fitting to address the notion of cognition itself. For those that are unhappy with any definition or description of culture, there is little, if any, solace to be found in an attempt to define cognition. Faced with this unpleasant prospect, and aware of the danger of appearing sophomoric, it seems reasonable to return to basics such as consulting widely respected dictionaries. This seemingly trivial endeavor, however, is itself not without some degree of difficulty. The most current dictionaries, such as the *Webster's Collegiate Dictionary,* start out in the proper direction by equating cognition with the "act or process of knowing" but then cloud the concept by including the notions of "awareness" and "judgment" in the definition. The major shortcoming of such a definition is that it ignores an important philosophical distinction that has long been associated with the concept of cognition. An explicit statement of that distinction can be found in the *Oxford English Dictionary* (1971) which defines cognition as the "action or faculty of knowing, perceiving, conceiving, as opposed to emotion & volition . . . [p. 596]."

As with the definition of culture, the definition of cognition is not provided as *the* definition, but merely as a reliable reference point. I am acutely aware of the dangers involved in committing to paper an explicit definition, no matter how serviceable and reliable it may be. It is of interest to note that in the seminal book *Culture and Thought* by Cole and Scribner (1974), the authors actually frame the questions "What is cognition?" and "What is culture?" even though they never provide an explicit definition of either word.

Unhappily, in other recent impressive scholarly works that actually contain the word "cognition" in the title, one is hard pressed to find an explicit definition (e.g., Weimer & Palermo, 1974; Norman & Rumelhart, 1975). In his recent book, Flavell (1977) tackled the concept of cognition on the very first page, but concluded that is was impossible and undesirable to define it and limit its meaning in any precise or rigid way. Even the most casual observer begins to seriously wonder how the phrases "cognitive activity" or "cognitive functioning" can be so loosely tossed about in the remarkably burgeoning field of cognitive psychology. Obviously, we need to return to fundamentals.

Explicit in the *Oxford English Dictionary* definition of cognition provided is the presence of Cartesian dualism. That is, if we accept the definition, it follows that it is possible to study the processes of acquiring and using knowledge apart from the affective processes. Can what we know be completely separated from what we feel? When I recently (and ingenuously) put this question to a colleague he jokingly replied that of course you could if you happened to be a schizophrenic; the point being that those poor souls who suffer grave problems in living exist as if their intellect is blunted or cut off from their affect. As we are not all schizophrenics, it appears obvious that intellect and affect are inextricably intertwined; and Descartes, even within the tradition of French intellectual thought, has been criticized since the inception of his dualistic position.

More to the point however, is the fact that many researchers within the field of cross-cultural psychology still investigate mental processes as if it were possible to separate, in any clear demonstrable way, knowledge from emotion. This would appear to be especially true of the large body of Piagetian researchers, although I will defer a consideration of Piaget till later in this chapter. To put the equation the other way around, it would appear that the large group of cross-cultural researchers investigating the issues that bear on affect (e.g., personality, attitudes, psychopathology), share equally in the difficulties confronting those that study mental processes. I have raised the specter of Cartesian dualism—not because I am aware of any arcane ritual to exorcise it from our midst, nor do I mean to imply that all of us have not, at some time, speculated on the matter—but rather because I suspect that many of us (including myself) conveniently act as if the matter is inconsequential. I suggest that one need not consider one's self to be a mere crank or moldy closet philosopher to periodically question the very foundations that support our entire enterprise.

Turning to an historical consideration, we are no doubt all aware of the long-standing tradition in cross-cultural psychology that tacitly accepts the premise that mental activity can be dichotomized into thought on the one hand, and affect on the other. The most vigorous proponent of this tradition is, of course, Levy-Bruhl (1910/1977), and he has consistently served as a whipping boy for well over half a century. Levy-Bruhl claimed that the mental activity of a "primitive" (an acceptable term in his day) was not developed enough for him to consider ideas or images of objects separately from the emotions that evoke those ideas or images. According to Levy-Bruhl, the ability to differentiate thought or mental activity from affect was not only reserved for Western man, but that this ability was indeed prima facie evidence for the superiority of Western thinking over the thinking of primitive man. The strong American criticism of Levy-Bruhl was initiated by Boas (1911/1965) who attacked him primarily on methodological grounds by challenging the reliability and authenticity of much of the anecdotal evidence that Levy-Bruhl marshalled. Additionally Boas seriously questioned the notion that one can derive conclusions about thought processes from the traditional beliefs and customs of any cultural group, much less some allegedly primitive group.

It is significant to note that despite the trenchant criticisms of Boas, he did not directly attack the position of the dichotomization of mental processes into the mutually exclusive categories of thought and affect. Though not directly focusing on Cartesian dualism, both Bartlett (1923/1970) and Lévi-Strauss (1966) rejected the notion that the mental processes of primitives differed from those of Western man. Bartlett stated explicitly that primitive man was not only just as capable of learning from experience as any Western man, but that he learned from experience in precisely the same way.

Despite the powerful assaults on the characterization of the thought of traditional peoples as primitive, we find that, by implication, Cartesian dualism apparently applies equally well to all cultural groups. We find Bartlett (1923/1970) stating that "primitives" learn in exactly the same way as "cultivated" people, and we find that Lévi-Strauss (1966) maintains that there are no differences in the basic processes of mental activity from one culture to another. So deeply ingrained is the tacit assumption of dualism in mental activity that it has only been quite recently that we find international figures in the field of cross-cultural psychology suggesting that there may exist modes of thought which do not sharply distinguish intellect and emotion (Price-Williams, 1975). I hazard the suggestion that, as cross-cultural psychologists, we at least admit to the shadowy presence of some form of dualism in our scholarly investigations even though we do not, at the present time, know of methodological techniques to comfortably exorcise the specter.

COGNITION AND KNOWLEDGE

At this point it is appropriate that we focus on another important aspect of cognition and examine the ways it interacts with the notion of culture and the investigations of cross-cultural psychologists. Though cognition may be discussed in a variety of contexts, it is traditional to propose that the central core of whatever we mean by cognition revolves around the issue of knowledge. Running hand-in-hand with this tradition is a chronic philosophical debate on not only what the nature of knowledge is, but also on how the data of experience are transformed into what we call knowledge. As to the question of the nature of knowledge, it is clearly outside the intended scope of the present chapter; those interested in the question should consult Mischel (1971). On the question of how experience enters into the construction of knowledge, I find a Piagetian formulation to be somewhat attractive, although Beilin (1971) and Flavell (1971, 1977) raise a number of well-conceived arguments that tend to diminish that attractiveness.

Nevertheless, if I understand Piaget's formulation correctly, he argues that knowledge is not simply the product of experience, but rather is the outcome of an *interaction* between an active organism and its surrounding environment. As Piaget ascribes this interactive quality of knowledge universally, it follows that members of all cultures (no matter how diverse) go about the business of acquiring knowledge in much the same basic interactive way. However, although we may come to some sort of agreement on the interactive aspect of acquiring knowledge, this does not necessarily mean that there is a consensus between cultures on what is accepted as knowledge. What may be believed to be an irrefutable fact of knowledge in one culture may very well be believed to be a groundless superstition or silly myth by members of another culture who refuse to view particular beliefs and/or cultural traditions as worthy of being called knowledge.

This lack of a consensus has been recognized for quite some time and one outstanding by-product may be labeled as "centri-cultural bias." However, before we turn to a consideration of the well-known centri-cultural bias issue, it is important that I make clear that by the term "knowledge" I do not simply mean an accumulation of beliefs or facts that are held to be true by some cultural group, but I also mean the results of mental activity upon those beliefs or facts. Knowledge is not static, and it may, as in some nonindustrialized cultures, be accepted and respected only if it follows traditional lines. However, this does not necessarily imply that traditional mental activity is either inert or must inevitably lead to the same end point.

If we accept the LeVine (1973) description of culture, and we are willing to grant some degree of credulousness to the proposition that what I am calling knowledge lies at the center of the concept of cognition, then I suspect that, as cross-cultural psychologists, we are faced with another skeleton in our closet. If we view the term cognition in its traditional sense, then it would appear that there is an inseparable link between knowledge and culture.

In LeVine's description of culture we encounter such words as "communication," "thinking," and "behavior;" and these words are used in both an interpersonal and intrapersonal way: They are used not only as a basis of interaction between members of a group, but also between individual members and their own personal views of what each construes their environments to be. If we accept LeVine's description, it follows that it is plausible to assert that one factor (knowledge) cannot be abstracted from nor investigated separately from the other factor (culture) as they are self-mutually interacting factors that defy separation. If this is true, is it not reasonable to suggest that any investigation that attempts to assess the knowledge of some group apart from the culture of that group; and, conversely, any investigation that attempts to assess the culture of some group apart from the knowledge of that group, is inherently confounded? It is immediately obvious that the latter attempt would be rejected by present-day anthropologists, but sadly to say, I suspect that many cross-cultural psychologists have endeavored (and some are still endeavoring) to investigate knowledge apart from the influence of culture. I am hardly the first to call attention to the situation, one need only consider the view of Bruner, Olver, and Greenfield (1966) on the relationship between culture and cognitive growth. Bruner *et al.* (1966) stated that cognitive growth was simply not conceivable without participation in a culture and its linguistic community.

This apparently undeniable confounding brings us sharply back to the familiar and thorny issue of centri-cultural bias, briefly mentioned earlier. Centri-cultural bias is the inherent difficulty encountered by a researcher from one culture who is attempting to explore the mental processes of another culture. Such a researcher is generally lacking a comprehensive understanding of that culture. Cole and Scribner (1974), Berry (1974), and Wober (1969, 1975), to name but a few, have all addressed the problem. Wober (1969) characterized cross-cultural tests and research as essentially centri-cultural (and biased) since they are generated in a technological culture and administered to members of a traditional nontechnological culture with little (or no) modifications. As Wober stated, this is like asking: "How well can they do *our* tricks [p. 52]?" And as Wober quite rightly put it, we should be asking the question: "How well can *they* do *their* tricks [p. 52]?"

Expanding on Wober's theme, many other investigators (e.g., Cole & Scribner, 1974; Dasen, 1977) have called for cross-cultural studies that focus on real-life situations that are culturally relevant to the population being studied. Although coming from a totally different orientation and domain, the same theme is set in a broader context by Estes (1975) when he advocates that the encompassing discipline of cognitive psychology should fundamentally contribute to our understanding of the "acquisition and utilization of the basic intellectual skills of everyday life [p. 12]."

Another characterization of the centri-cultural bias problem is the widely known emic–etic dichotomy (Chapter 2). An emic (derived from phonemics) approach to cross-cultural investigation searches for items, classification schemes, beliefs, events, and phenomena that are meaningful and relevant *within* the culture being studied. An etic (derived from phonetics) approach, on the other hand, stems from a universalist position and *imposes* upon the culture being studied the orientation, training, and beliefs of the investigator's culture, with little (if any) understanding or appreciation of the culture under scrutiny. It is safe to say that but for a few occasional clarion voices in the wilderness (e.g., Price-Williams, 1961, 1962), much of the cross-cultural effort up to the middle 1960s was clearly of an etic nature, and it has only been within the past 10 to 15 years that most cross-cultural psychologists have become increasingly aware of the desperate need for an emic approach. Whether one uses the labels of either a centri-cultural bias or an etic approach however, it is apparent that cross-cultural psychologists should be somewhat uneasy and apprehensive about their entire enterprise. I suggest that there are substantial grounds for this apprehension when we take to heart Wober's (1969) characterization of much of what we label as cross-cultural psychology as essentially centri-cultural psychology.

An objective and dispassionate perusal of the extensive literature within the field of cross-cultural psychology bearing on the relationship between culture and cognition ("knowledge") reveals the disquieting observation that despite much admirable thought, sweat, and labor, our efforts have probably told us precious little about the cultures of the various groups studied. Although some of us might seriously object to, or at least cavil at the above assertion, I suggest that most anthropologists would find it to their liking.

Culture and Cognitive Functioning: Two Major Research Strategies

An illustrative example of the above suggestion is the intensive long term research effort focused on the Kpelle tribe of Liberia by Michael Cole and his colleagues (Cole, Gay, Glick, & Sharp, 1971). To be sure, a considerable body of important psychological problems were investigated in a scholarly and imaginative way, but it seems not entirely unreasonable to say that very little important information about the Kpelle culture itself was unearthed and explicated: I ought to know, after all, I was closely associated with the research group for years and lived amongst the Kpelle on two separate occasions.

Although I have suggested that cross-cultural researchers working within the confines of the relationship between culture and cognition have shed little light on our understanding and appreciation of culture, I do not mean to imply that they are not sensitive to, nor uninterested in, gaining a fuller understanding of traditional cultures: after all, that should be one of the principal concerns of their work. All I am claiming, and it may well be a risky claim to make, is that for all the "cross-cultural-psychological" effort, we have not substantially advanced our understanding of the cultures of traditional peoples.

Considering the other side of the relationship between culture and cognition pertinent to the Cole *et al.* (1971) research effort, an important point needs to be stressed. In using some standard paradigm, such as a free recall task in investigating mnemonic processes, the Cole group was simply not content in obtaining the usual cross-cultural population differences in which the "other" culture performs poorly. Such differences were just the departure point for investigation. Various experimental variables were manipulated until the performance of the "other" cultural group approximated the performance of subjects drawn from the culture that generated the test in the first place. Such a research strategy lends itself to an explication of the presence (or absence) of basic underlying cognitive processes that are manifested in experimental performance.

Despite this laudable approach, however, it is not too harsh an observation to make that comparatively little vital information was unearthed that clearly delineated the basic cognitive processes of the Kpelle tribal people. To be sure, a number of extremely clever, if not ingenious experimental manipulations were performed which led to a marked improvement in test performance by Kpelle tribal people, but many of the performance improvements could be traced to alterations in the general *context* of the experimental setting. In many cases what was essentially unclear was the relationship between the altered experimental context on the one hand, and the basic cognitive processes of the Kpelle on the other hand. In a number of cases, and particularly in investigations of mnemonic processes, it was unclear why some particular experimental manipulations led to increased performance.

Before proceeding any further however, I want to make it clear that, despite the somewhat gloomy picture I seem to have painted of the extensive research effort among the Kpelle as reported in Cole *et al.* (1971), I consider their work to be a seminal contribution to the field of cross-cultural psychology. And since that early work, Cole and his colleagues have pioneered several lines of investigation that should prove invaluable in unraveling the complex relationship between culture and cognition. However, before considering Cole and his colleagues' newer work, it is appropriate that we consider the well-known work of John Berry and his colleagues that bears on the relationship between culture and a hypothetical construct called "perceptual style."

Berry has been working for over 10 years in an effort to explicate the complex relationship between perceptual skills and a very broad conception of culture that includes such encompassing variables as socialization practices and ecological constraints. In the limited space available, it is obvious that a comprehensive treatment of Berry's work is simply out of the question. A full appreciation of Berry's work can be obtained by consulting Berry (1966, 1969, 1971, 1974a, 1974b, Chapter 6 of this volume), Cole and Scribner (1974), Serpell (1976), and Wober (1975).

At the risk of misinterpreting Berry's work however, it would appear that he has hypothesized a crucial link between the ecological demands on a cultural group and the socialization practices of that group. In turn, these demands and practices shape the characteristic manner in which the group perceives and interprets events and phenomena occurring in their daily lives. This characteristic manner has been quantified along a dimension that rates subjects as to the degree of independence or dependence they display upon the elements and components of the "scene" being perceived. A subject who can differentiate among the many elements to produce a variety of holistic perceptual interpretations is labeled as field-independent. A subject who cannot differentiate among the many elements and who cannot mentally rearrange and synthesize them into a variety of perceptual interpretations, is labeled as field-dependent. For Berry, the degree of field-independence or field-dependence is inextricably linked to the complex interaction of ecological and societal factors that determine the cognitive development of a subject within some culture.

Before proceeding, it is important to note that Berry's research enterprise is impressive as it seeks to characterize the influence of such global factors as ecology and socialization upon a major component of cognitive functioning, namely perceptual style. Also, Berry has marshalled a voluminous array of test scores and correlational analyses to support his position. However, despite my admiration for Berry's scholarship and the colossal task that he set for himself, the issues that I raised earlier regarding the relationship between culture and cognition, along with the observations that were made regarding the Cole *et al.* (1971) enterprise among the Kpelle, apply quite forcefully in the present case.

To begin with, the various cultures selected for scrutiny (e.g., the Eskimo and the Temne of West Africa) were essentially chosen from a centri-cultural or etic viewpoint. For example, several Eskimo groups were selected because they supposedly have permissive child-rearing practices and the environment they live in is allegedly a series of barren, featureless plains. According to Berry, this combination of factors promotes independence and necessitates acute perceptual discriminations, leading to high field-independence. However, this characterization is basically etic as what is lacking is a comprehensive understanding of the *knowledge* the Eskimo's possess about their environment and society. What an outsider (like myself) would like to know is the kinds of situations or tasks that the Eskimo themselves believe call for acute perceptual discriminations. Without this kind of culturally biased information or knowledge, any inferences or conclusions about the relative dependence or independence of Eskimo perception, as a fundamental process of cognition, is in fact centri-cultural.

Any inferences or conclusions are also centri-cultural in that the researchers initiated their investigations on the basis of preformed beliefs about the ecological and societal milieu of the cultural groups tested. Without being flippant one might ask whether it is more difficult (and dangerous) to negotiate one's way across a cold barren featureless plain than it is to attempt to cross 45th street and Broadway in New York City at any hour of the day? As with the research effort among the Kpelle, it appears reasonable to suggest that Berry's entire cross-cultural enterprise, classifying people as either field-dependent or field-independent, has shed little light on our understanding of the many cultures that were tested.

Turning to the question of the possible explanation of basic psychological processes as reflected by a score on a hypothetical continuum of field independence–dependence, we encounter a serious methodological difficulty. To a large extent, the entire enterprise of classifying whole cultural groups along such a hypothetical continuum rests almost exclusively upon the use of only two tests, the Embedded Figures Test (EFT) and the Rod and Frame Test (RFT), with the great bulk of the data base stemming from the EFT. What we are faced with is the near classic cross-cultural approach of taking a relatively simple test that was generated in a technological society and administering that test to traditional nontechnological groups for which the test may have but minimal meaning and cultural relevance.

The grave shortcomings of such a basically methodologically etic approach have been echoed by many researchers, particularly Cole and Scribner (1974), Ciborowski (1976), as well as Berry (1974a) himself. To fully appreciate the dangers in such an approach simply recall the Irwin, Schafer, and Freiden (1974) study in which Mano tribal people of Liberia and American undergraduates had to sort material that were familiar to the Mano but not to the Americans. Not surprisingly, the Mano proved significantly "superior" to the American college students. Obviously, when the tables are turned, we are simply not very good at doing "their tricks."

Coming from a different domain, Serpell (1977) has strongly criticized the fundamental conceptualization of field-independence–field-dependence as essentially value laden as the culture which generated the conceptualization in the first place ranks field-independence as quite superior to field-dependence. Serpell states that such a centri-cultural approach "acquires unattractively ethnocentric overtones" and it needs to be "prised free of particular standardized tests [p. 54]."

In light of the preceding discussion it would appear that the notion of field-independence or field-dependence has done very little in advancing our understanding of the basic cognitive processes and knowledge of a wide variety of traditional, nontechnological peoples. An "understanding" has *not emerged* from the research, but rather an "understanding" has been *imposed* upon traditional peoples.

Within the space of a few pages we have briefly examined two distinct research enterprises which I have suggested that, despite their positive aspects, have told us little substantial information about the culture and the basic cognitive activity of the various traditional groups studied. Such an appraisal may seem overly harsh and negative to many, but I suggest that a critical self-examination of their entire enterprise by cross-cultural psychologists is not only warranted but basically healthy and that a number of productive, positive steps are at our disposal.

KNOWLEDGE, COGNITION, AND PERFORMANCE SKILLS

If we understood the relationship between knowledge and performance skills, or at least could specify the ways and contexts in which specific performance skills are manifested as a function of the underlying knowledge of those that we test, then we would be in a much better position to advance assertions about the cognitive activity or cognitive functioning of traditional groups. Fortunately, a number of studies with such an orientation and thrust can be cited. An early (and still ongoing) pioneer in this direction is Price-Williams (1961, 1962) who collected important information about the knowledge and everyday skills of the Tiv people. As if this were not enough, Price-Williams also learned the language of the tribal group before he initiated his investigations, a genuine rarity among cross-cultural psychologists.

Armed with important cultural knowledge as well as Tiv verbal skills, Price-Williams was able to demonstrate that even quite young Tiv children could engage in complex conceptual and classificatory behavioral skills. A few years later, Price-Williams, Gordon, and Ramirez (1969) collected important information concerning the knowledge that sons of potters in Jalisco, Mexico possessed about estimating quantities of clay. This knowledge stemmed from their daily experiences in helping their fathers. The experiential knowledge of these children proved to be very helpful as they were strikingly more competent in a typical Piagetian conservation task of continuous quantity (clay) than the children of nonpotters.

A somewhat ingenuous experiment was conducted by Lave (1976) who first collected extensive information about the everyday working skills (waist and fly measurements, etc.) of tribal tailors in Liberia. Lave constructed a number of arithmetic tests drawn directly from the working activities of the tailors and a comparable arithmetic test from a different domain. In this way, Lave was able to initiate an investigation of the question of the transfer of knowledge gained in daily activities to a different domain. This approach enabled Lave to begin to estimate and quantify the influence of real life knowledge upon performance in tests less germane to the daily activities of the people tested.

In a series of basic studies, Scribner (1975, 1976b) investigated the complex relationship of knowledge and culture of Kpelle and Vai tribal people as seen in their ability to solve logical syllogisms that were culturally relevant. Drawing upon her extensive familiarity with the Kpelle and Vai cultures, Scribner was able to demonstrate clearly that tribal people were quite capable of arriving at a logically airtight conclusion even though, in many cases, one (or even two) of the premises of the syllogism was either outright denied or changed. Without extensive knowledge of the Kpelle and the Vai, Scribner's elegant investigation of tribal modes of thought would have been impossible.

A striking example of the importance of an emic approach can be found in the work of Wober (1974) and Serpell (1972, 1974, 1977) who investigated the concept of intelligence from the point of view of the tribal groups studied. Wober found that Baganda and Batoro villagers in Uganda associated the concept of intelligence with the word "slow" while a group of educated medical students associated the concept with the word "fast." Serpell asked adult Zambian tribal people to rate the intelligence of tribal children and found that the adults cited the qualities of cooperation and obedience in more than half the cases as evidence of "intelligence." Even though coming from the opposite end of Africa, Wober's finding supported that of Serpell when he found that from the point of view of the tribal person, "intelligent behaviour is that which led to respect of and compliance with society's ways [p. 270]." In the face of such evidence the administration of only standardized tests of intelligence (which we now view primarily as tests of acquired knowledge) to tribal people is a pointless enterprise.

We have skimmed rapidly over a number of experimental studies that appear to share in common a deep and vital appreciation of the culture and knowledge of the various groups tested. Concomitantly, the studies show a sensitivity to what is currently called "naturally occurring" situations (i.e., occasions within a culture that occur naturally and frequently, providing clear evidence of culturally relevant cognitive functioning). The trick, of course, is to cleanly (nonetically) identify such "situations" and, without contamination, blend them into an experimental inquiry from which reliable inferences can be drawn. The task is not an easy one even though a number of singular examples have been discussed briefly. Another promising area of "naturally occurring" situations, which Hopkins and Wober (1973) claim has been almost totally ignored, is the area of games and sports.

Although the pressing need for an emic experimental approach focusing on "naturally occurring" situations has been recognized for a number of years, it is unfortunately true that much (if not most) cross-cultural research currently being conducted is essentially of an etic nature. Additionally, even though lines of inquiry that adapt "naturally occurring" situations appear quite promising, there remain a number of important problems still to be considered. For example, we need to know the specific ways in which the knowledge of a tribal group is brought to bear on the day to day problem solving activities of that group. Could the mechanism be the same for all tribal groups? We simply do not know, although it is tempting to believe that some continuity must exist. Furthermore, we need to develop flexible, yet rigorous, methodological techniques for "translating" the "naturally occurring" situations into acceptable experimental paradigms. Such a translation necessitates that the paradigms (yet to be developed) should fit, if not follow from, emerging cognitive theory.

At best, the current bridge between experimental, laboratory-based, cognitive theory and an explication of daily, day-to-day, problem-solving situations is extremely tenuous, if not impossible. However, it would be intellectually myopic to suggest that these problems cannot be solved, or at least reformulated in constructive ways. The body of cross-cultural psychology may indeed be somewhat ill, but it would be too pessimistic to believe that a remedy cannot be found.

Conspicuously absent in the present chapter is a discussion of the voluminous body of Piagetian cross-cultural work. This research was omitted for two reasons. First, to adequately handle the topic would have necessitated a chapter at least four to five times the length of the present one and this was out of the question. Second, Dasen's (1977) book is an excellent review of Piagetian cross-cultural research—particularly Dasen's introduction to the book and the excellent article by Kamara and Easley (1977).

A Brief Summary

I began this chapter by calling attention to the difficult fact that the material which one would most likely expect to find in a chapter focusing on culture and cognitive functioning has already been covered by recognized experts. Therefore I was forced into the position of examining the basic relationship between culture and cognition. An examination of this relationship led us to the suggestion that Cartesian dualism may continue to exist in much of the research dealing with cognition. Following this suggestion, we discovered that any attempt to study the relationship between culture and cognition was probably inherently confounded. I offered no way out of these dilemmas but suggested that it is important for us as cross-cultural psychologists, to periodically recognize their existence: We ignore them at our own peril. A further examination of the relationship between culture and cognition led us into the brier patch of the centri-cultural, (or etic) bias issue; and this led me to tenuously advance the suggestion that, despite all the research on the relationship between culture and cognition, perhaps very little light has been shed on our understanding of culture, and cognition. Finally, I called attention once again to the difficulties facing us if we are to unravel the relationship between culture and cognition.

In so far as offering possible suggestions as to how we can advance the enterprise of explicating the relationship between culture and cognition, I do so with some amount of trepidation. It seems that it is useful when discussing cognition that we deal with the issue of knowledge as I have framed the issue in this chapter. I suspect that instead of trying to devise clever research ideas we can more profitably spend some of our time in an attempt to gain an understanding of the knowledge that traditional peoples possess. Armed with an understanding of this knowledge, I also suspect that experiments will suggest themselves. After all, I take it as a given that we can all think up clever experiments to perform. In our attempt to gain such knowledge I suggest that our anthropological colleagues (or at least those that will talk to us) have much to offer. In our quest to acquire and understand the knowledge that traditional peoples possess, I cautiously suggest that we might profit from examining those aspects of everyday life that face all of us, be we university professors or Kalahari desert bushmen.

References

Bartlett, F. *Psychology and primitive culture*. Cambridge Univ. Press, 1923. Reprint. Westport, Connecticut: Greenwood Press, 1970.
Beilin, H. The development of physical concepts. In T. Mischel (Ed.), *Cognitive development and epistemology*. New York: Academic Press, 1971.
Berry, J. Temne and Eskimo perceptual skills. *International Journal of Psychology*, 1966, *1*, 207–229.

Berry, J. On cross-cultural comparability. *International Journal of Psychology,* 1969, *4*(2), 119–128.

Berry, J. Ecological and cultural factors in spatial perceptual development. *Canadian Journal of Behavioral Science,* 1971, *3,* 324–336.

Berry, J. Radical cultural relativism and the concept of intelligence. In J. Berry & P. Dasen (Eds.), *Culture and cognition.* London: Methuen, 1974.(a)

Berry, J., & Dasen, P. *Culture and cognition.* London: Methuen, 1974.(b)

Boas, F. *The mind of primitive man.* New York: Free Press, 1965. (Originally published, 1911).

Bruner, J., Olver, R., & Greenfield. *Studies in cognitive growth.* New York: Wiley, 1966.

Ciborowski, T. Cultural and cognitive discontinuities of school and home: Remedialism revisited. In D. McElwain & G. Kearney (Eds.), *Aboriginal cognition.* New Jersey: Humanities Press, 1976.

Cole, M., Gay, J., Glick, J., & Sharp, D. *The cultural context of learning and thinking.* New York: Basic Books, 1971.

Cole, M., & Scribner, S. *Culture and thought.* New York: Wiley, 1974.

Dasen, P. *Piagetian psychology: Cross-cultural contributions.* New York: Gardner Press, 1977.

Estes, W. K. The state of the field: General problems and issues of theory and metatheory. In W. K. Estes (Ed.), *Handbook of learning and cognitive processes* (Vol. 1). Hillsdale, New Jersey: Lawrence Erlbaum, 1975.

Flavell, J. Comments on H.Beilin's, The development of physical concepts. In T. Mischel (Ed.), *Cognitive development and epistemology.* New York: Academic Press, 1971.

Flavell, J. *Cognitive development.* Englewood Cliffs, New Jersey: Prentice-Hall, 1977.

Hopkins, B., & Wober, M. Games and sports: Missing items in cross-cultural psychology. *International Journal of Psychology,* 1973, *8,* 5–14.

Irwin, M., Schafer, G., & Freiden, C. Emic and unfamiliar category sorting of Mano farmers and U.S. undergraduates. *Journal of Cross-Cultural Psychology,* 1974, *5,* 407–423.

Kamara, A., & Earley, J. Is the rate of cognitive development uniform across cultures?—A methodological critique with new evidence from Themne children. In P. Dasen (Ed.), *Piagetian Psychology.* New York: Gardner Press, 1977.

Kessen, W. Questions for a theory of cognitive development. In J. Eliot (Ed.), *Human development and cognitive processes.* New York: Holt, 1971.

Lave, J. Cognitive consequences of traditional apprenticeship in West Africa. Unpublished manuscript. Univ. California at Irvine, 1976.

LeVine, R. *Culture, behavior, and personality.* Chicago: Aldine Publishing Company, 1973.

Lévi-Strauss, C. *The savage mind.* Chicago: Univ. of Chicago Press, 1966.

Levy-Bruhl, L. *How natives think* (1910). New York: Washington Square Press, 1977.

Mischel, T. (Ed.). *Cognitive development and epistemology.* New York: Academic Press, 1971.

Norman, D., Rumelhart, D. (Eds.). *Explorations in cognition.* San Francisco, California: Freeman, 1975.

Price-Williams, D. A study concerning concepts of conservation of quantities among primitive children. *Acta Psychologia,* 1961, *18,* 297–305.

Price-Williams, D. Abstract and concrete modes of classification in a primitive society. *British Journal of Educational Psychology,* 1962, *32,* 50–61.

Price-Williams, D. *Explorations in cross-cultural psychology.* San Francisco, California: Chandler & Sharp, 1975.

Price-Williams, D., Gordon, W., & Ramírez, M. Skill and conservation: A study of pottery-making children. *Developmental Psychology,* 1969, *1,* 769.

Scribner, S. Recall of classical syllogisms: A cross-cultural investigation of error on logical problems. In R. J. Falmagne (Ed.), *Reasoning: Representation and process.* Hillsdale, New Jersey: Lawrence Erlbaum, 1975.

Scribner, S. Situating the experiment in cross-cultural research. In K. Riegel & J. Meacham (Eds.), *The developing individual in a changing world (Vol. 1).* Chicago: Aldine, 1976.(a)

Scribner, S. Modes of thinking and ways of speaking: Culture and logic reconsidered. Unpublished manuscript. Rockefeller University, 1976.(b)

Serpell, R. Intelligence tests in the Third World. *Race Today,* 1972, *4,* 46–49.

Serpell, R. Estimates of intelligence in a rural community of Eastern Zambia. *Human Development Research Unit Reports,* 1974, *25.*

Serpell, R. *Culture's influence on behavior.* London: Methuen, 1976.

Serpell, R. Strategies for investigating intelligence in its cultural context. *Quarterly Newsletter of the Institute for Comparative Human Development,* 1977, *1*(3), 2–4.

Triandis, H., & Berry, J. (Eds.). *Handbook of cross-cultural psychology.* Rockleigh, New Jersey: Allyn & Bacon, 1979.

Weiner, W., & Palermo, D. (Eds.). *Cognition and the symbolic processes.* Hillsdale, New Jersey: Lawrence Erlbaum, 1974.

Wober, M. Distinguishing centri-cultural from cross-cultural tests and research. *Perceptual and Motor Skills,* 1969, *28,* 488.

Wober, M. Towards an understanding of the Kiganda concept of intelligence. In J. W. Berry & P. R. Dasen (Eds.), *Culture and cognition: Readings in cross-cultural psychology.* London: Methuen, 1974.

Wober, M. *Psychology in Africa.* Plymouth, Great Britain: Clark, Doble & Brendon, 1975.

6

Culture and Cognitive Style

J. W. Berry

Introduction

This chapter will be concerned with the concept of cognitive style developed by Witkin and his colleagues (Witkin, Dyk, Faterson, Goodenough, & Karp, 1962) known as the *field-dependent–independent* cognitive style. Additionally, the concept of culture will be limited to that derived from the approach known as *cultural ecology*. There are, of course, many other concepts of cognitive style (e.g., the review and work of Kogan, 1976); similarly there are hundreds of approaches to the concept of culture (see' Kroeber & Kluckhohn, 1952), but no comprehensive treatment of them is intended here.

In all of these approaches, however, one feature is held in common: They are all *systematic*. By systematic I mean that both the independent cultural variables and the dependent behavioral variables are thought to consist of clusters of interrelated variables that form complex systems. The basic assumptions of this approach, which can be readily demonstrated, are that many cultural variables cohere in meaningful ways, that many behaviors are also interrelated, and that there are systematic relationships between these cultural and behavioral clusters.

This approach stands in partial contrast to two, well-articulated, contemporary positions in cross-cultural research. One of these (Whiting, 1976)

117

PERSPECTIVES ON CROSS-CULTURAL PSYCHOLOGY

argues that we must try to "unpackage" the complex set of cultural variables with which we work, so that we can specify *which* element of culture is at the root of a behavior. This problem and evidence for the systematic relationships among cultural elements will be taken up on pages 121–125 of this chapter.

The other contrasting position to the systematic one espoused here is that of Cole and Scribner (1974, 1977). In their search for cause and effect relationships between culture and behavior (a goal which all cross-cultural psychologists share) single cultural elements are usually considered in relation to single behavioral elements; little patterning of the cultural context, and no interrelationships among behaviors are examined. In contrast, at the heart of the notion of *cognitive style* is the search for systematic clusters of behaviors that tend to "go together" in fairly consistent ways. The theoretical basis and the empirical evidence for such patterning of behavior, which permit the designation of "styles," is considered on pages 118–121 of this chapter.

Finally, as we have noted, all cross-cultural psychologists are devoted to the search for causal linkages between cultural and behavioral variables. Given the systematic nature of these two sets of variables, in our approach, it should be clear by now that we will also be searching for systematic relationships, using broad comparative sweeps, between these two systems; this we do in pages 125–128 of this chapter.

Thus the term *systematic* has at least three applications in this chapter: Cultural variables are considered to be patterned systematically; behavioral variables are shown to be interrelated systematically yielding a "style"; and the search will be made for systematic relationships between culture and cognitive style. The reader is encouraged to refer to the literature cited earlier before forging ahead with this chapter. Of additional use are the general reviews by Witkin and Berry (1975) and Okonji (1979), a specialized review of sex differences by van Leeuwen (1978), a critical review by Serpell (1976), and a monograph by Berry (1976). The concept of psychological differentiation and the cognitive style of field–dependence–independence has been reviewed by Goodenough and Witkin (1977) and by Witkin and Goodenough (1977a, 1977b, 1977c). Given such a range of sources, this chapter will provide only an outline of some of the broad features of the field.

Differentiation and Cognitive Style

The general concept of differentiation refers to a process of change in a system toward greater specialization. This change occurs over time and constitutes a development in the system. Relatively undifferentiated systems are global, not internally separated in structure or function, whereas relatively differentiated systems have greater structural complexity—they have more parts, and they are more elaborately integrated. Differentiation is a feature of a system as a whole; it refers to the overall structure of, and within, all its component parts.

In psychological systems, the concept of psychological differentiation (Witkin *et al.*, 1962; Witkin & Goodenough, 1977c; Witkin, 1977a) assumes all of these meanings: There is increasing specialization over time (development) and evidence for psychological differentiation is sought in all areas of behavioral functioning—perceptual, cognitive, neurophysiological, social, and affective. One postulate is that this evidence should indicate roughly similar levels of differentiation in each behavioral domain.

The literature reviews referred to earlier generally provide support for all of these basic expectations: Psychological differentiation does increase with chronological age; evidence for individual difference correlations tend to support the organismic interpretation. However as Witkin *et al.* (1962, p. 389) anticipated, continuing research would provide new kinds of evidence that should lead to elaborations and refinements in the development of the theory itself. We now turn to the current conceptualization, and present it schematically in Figure 6.1. The model and its discussion follows closely a tentative proposal taken from Witkin and Goodenough (1977c).

The model is pyramidal in structure, with the highest order construct (psychological differentiation) at the top, and the most specific constructs at the base. It resembles models that are derived from factor analyses, although it is only partly based upon factor analytic evidence. In general, empirical observations are most often concentrated at the base, and inferences are

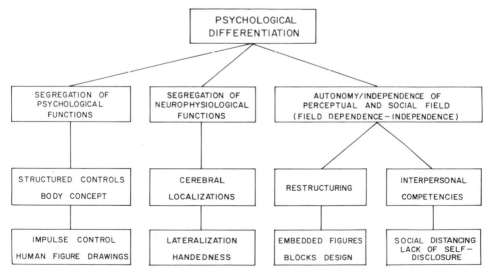

Figure 6.1 The diagram is a schematic representation of a conceptual model of psychological differentiation.

required to ascend the pyramid. In contrast, theoretical interpretations flow from an apex downward.

The most obvious feature of the model is its separation, at one level down from differentiation, into three sectors: segregation of psychological functions, segregation of neurophysiological functions, and autonomy or independence of the perceptual and social fields. The first refers to the specialization of psychological functions—the separation of one behavioral domain from another and the separation of functions within each domain. The second refers to neurophysiological specificity and includes both localization of functions and lateralization. The third refers to the separation of the self from its environment or the field, leading to the use of the terms *field-dependence* and *field-independence*. This category focuses upon two areas of psychological functioning: perceptual–cognitive, and social. The first division is termed "restructuring" and includes such behaviors as disembedding and analysis. The second division, "interpersonal competencies," includes social sensitivity and attention to social cues at one end and social distancing and autonomy at the other.

Taken together, these perceptual–cognitive and social components are designated by Witkin as a field-dependent and field-independent *cognitive style*. Those at the field-dependent end of the dimension tend to rely upon external referents, whereas those at the field-independent end rely upon internal referents. There is now fairly impressive evidence (at least within Western cultural settings) that those who are field-independent on perceptual–cognitive tasks are also socially autonomous and distant in interpersonal relations (Witkin & Goodenough, 1977a).

An important implication of this relationship is that the dimension is bipolar with respect to conventional valuation; there are no clear "high" or "low," "good" or "bad" poles. For example, individuals who are high on restructuring competence tend to be low on interpersonal competencies and vice versa (Witkin & Goodenough, 1977a). The emergence of this relationship has led to a conceptualization of psychological development as proceeding "along different pathways [Witkin, 1977b]." Those who are field-independent employ internal referents in the development of restructuring skills, but do not particularly develop social sensitivity or interpersonal skills. On the other hand, those who are field-dependent employ external referents leading toward the development of interpersonal competencies but not particularly toward cognitive restructuring skills.

Cross-cultural use of the theory has been extensive in recent years. As in the case of much cross-cultural research, there have been three goals to this enterprise. First, there has been an interest in checking the transcultural generality of the theory, both in terms of relationships among behaviors and some of the antecedents (primarily socialization) to the development of differentiation. Second, there has been a search for new examples of differentiated behavior and new antecedents (primarily ecological and sociocultural). Third, there have been some attempts to extend and elaborate the theory to make it more nearly universal in scope (Berry, 1979a). The theoretical formulations we have just examined illustrate this process of theory development.

An Ecocultural Model

A number of models have been developed within which a variety of independent variables have been examined in relation to psychological differentiation. An ecological and cultural model has been developed by Berry (1966, 1971, 1975), and was employed by Witkin and Berry (1975) and by Berry (1976) in their integrative treatments of the topic. A biosocial model has been developed by Dawson (1967, 1969, 1975) which deals more with some biological variables. And van Leeuwen (1978) has incorporated both approaches in her attempt to deal specifically with the origin of sex differences.

The schematic model presented in Figure 6.2 incorporates the main features to be discussed and Tables 6.1 and 6.2 then outline the specific variables thought to be involved. These variables are presented as poles of a dimension; in each case the behavioral expectation is that high psychological differentiation will follow from the variables listed at the left of the dimension whereas lower differentiation will follow from those at the right.

Looking first at the overall structure of Figure 6.2, there are five blocks of variables viewed as a system. Although feedback (bidirectional) relationships are illustrated, the general flow in the system is from Ecology and Acculturation (as exogenous, independent variables) through cultural and biological adaptations, to psychological differentiation (considered as a cluster of dependent variables).

It should be noted that the two input variables of Ecology and Accultura-

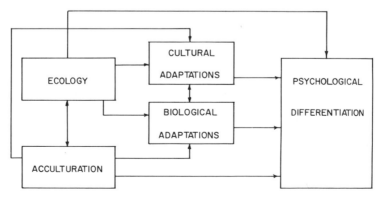

Figure 6.2 The diagram illustrates an ecocultural model of the relationship of independent variables to psychological differentiation.

TABLE 6.1
Antecedent Variables to Psychological Differentiation: Ecological, Cultural, and Biological Adaptation

	Prediction of psychological differentiation	
	High	Low
Ecological adaptations[a]		
Subsistence pattern	Hunting, gathering	Agriculture
Settlement pattern	Nomadic	Sedentary
Population density	Low	High
Cultural adaptations[b]		
Role diversity	Low	High
Stratification	Low	High
Socialization emphases	Assertion	Compliance
Biological adaptations[c]		
Protein intake	High	Low
Hormone balance	Balanced	Imbalanced
Genetic selection	For differentiation	Against differentiation

[a] Interactions among human organisms and groups and their physical environment.
[b] Learned group patterns adaptive to ecological press.
[c] Innate or acquired somatic characteristics adaptive to ecological press.

tion are relatively independent of each other; for that reason, they are separated in Tables 6.1 and 6.2. It should also be noted that within Table 6.1, all variables within a column (left or right) are to be considered to be more or less "packaged" (Whiting, 1976); that is, they represent a cluster of features often found together in the respective subsistence groups. Finally, it is necessary to emphasize that these variables are considered to operate only for societies that are at (or near) subsistence level, where the ecological press is a day-to-day force. Although some of the variables may be important factors in more complex societies, they are sufficiently removed from the ecological press to require their treatment as a separate issue.

Looking at the constituent elements in Tables 6.1 and 6.2, we begin with

TABLE 6.2
Antecedent Variables to Psychological Differentiation: Acculturative Influences

	Prediction of Psychological Differentiation	
Acculturation[a]	High	Low
Education	High	Low
Wage employment	High	Low
Urbanization	High	Low

[a] Cultural and behavioral changes induced by contact.

the ecological variables. An ecological approach asserts that interactions between an organism (in pursuing satisfaction of its primary needs) and its habitat (with a definable set of environmental characteristics) will generate characteristic patterns of economic, demographic, sociocultural, and biological adaptations. The relationships in such a system are probabilistic, rather than deterministic, and the characteristics are to be viewed as likely adaptations, rather than as guaranteed productions. One pervasive set of adaptations has been that of the "nomadic style" (Lee, 1968), and incorporates a nomadic settlement pattern, a low concentration of population, and a hunting and gathering subsistence base. An adaptation in sharp contrast to this may be termed a "sedentary style," and includes a sedentary settlement pattern, a higher population concentration, and an agricultural economic base. Other subsistence activities, such as herding and fishing, have variable relationships to these demographic elements (see Berry, 1976, p. 119). This basic contrast in settlement style is evident in much of the background literature of studies of cultural ecology (e.g., Murdock, 1967, 1969; Murdock & Morrow, 1970).

In adaptation to these contrasting settlement styles are a set of cultural variables. In those societies with a nomadic style, there are likely to be relatively low levels of role diversity and sociocultural stratification; these have been termed "loose" by Pelto (1968). In contrast, those societies with a sedentary style are likely to have higher levels of role diversity and stratification; these have been termed "tight" by Pelto. Essentially, the dimension being outlined is one of "cultural complexity" (Murdock & Provost, 1973). Also lying along the dimension are the characteristic socialization practices examined by Barry, Child, and Bacon (1959). In their classical analysis, they were able to demonstrate that societies with a nomadic style (essentially low in "food accumulation," to use their terms) tended to foster "assertion" during child rearing, whereas those with a sedentary style (higher on food accumulation) tended to foster "compliance."

The importance of these contrasting socialization emphases is that Witkin *et al.* (1962; Dyk & Witkin, 1965; Goodenough & Witkin, 1977) have shown such emphases to be systematically related to the development of psychological differentiation among individuals within Western society. In the Western studies reviewed by Goodenough and Witkin (1977), socialization practices that emphasize strict rules and overprotection tend to foster low levels of psychological differentiation. In contrast, those practices that encourage separation from parental control tend to foster the development of higher levels of psychological differentiation. In the cross-cultural studies reviewed by Witkin and Berry (1975) a similar relationship was evident. But, in addition, there is strong evidence that differences in the broader societal pressures emanating from tight and loose structures may reinforce such specific socialization emphases.

Also, in potential adaptation of the contrasting sets of ecological pressures are some biological variables. Dawson (1969, 1975) has proposed that protein intake levels are likely to vary across the ecological dimension; hunters and gatherers (if successful) maintain high protein-intake levels which have an effect on human development. Dawson (1966) argues that low protein intake may alter the hormonal balance between androgens and estrogens. Inadequate levels (evidenced by the appearance of Kwashiorkor) are associated with androgen imbalance, and such hormonal changes are considered predictive of lower psychological differentiation. More recent studies (Dawson, 1972, 1977) have pursued this relationship between protein intake and hormone balance and spatial skills in laboratory rats. His results tend to confirm the relationship, although generalization from these animal studies is extremely difficult.

Related to this concern for protein intake and hormonal action is the common (but not universal) sex-related difference found in psychological differentiation—females tend to be more field-dependent than males. Waber (1976) has argued that late maturation is associated with both high spatial skills and field-independence. She later (Waber, 1977) added a complex set of genetic, endocrinological, and neurological factors to the model. Essentially, the argument is that the presence of sex-related differences in field-dependence points to the role of those biological factors known to characterize male–female physical differences, and that they should be considered along with the sociocultural emphasis in the Witkin and Berry (1975) review.

Another biological variable is the long-term adaptation to habitat of the gene pool in subsistence-level living. If there is a genetic base for psychological differentiation (as suggested by Goodenough, Gandini, Olkin, Pizzamiglio, Thayer, & Witkin, 1977), then there may be a selective advantage in some habitats. For example, disembedding is clearly demanded of hunters and gatherers in their daily economic activity, although it is less so for farmers. Genetic selection for disembedding, and perhaps other aspects of differentiation, may be ecologically adaptive. Similar arguments are also being made for spatial skills (e.g., Bock & Kolakowski, 1973; Yen, 1975) that may be related to restructuring.

A final set of variables (in Table 6.2) deals with the impact of other cultures on both the traditional culture and individuals in it. These acculturative influences include education (very often of a Western type), a shift from traditional economic activity to wage employment, and an increase in settlement size and population density (urbanization). It is considered that both education and wage employment often encourage the analytic activity included in the field-independent cognitive style. Thus, an increase is likely in field-independence with increasing acculturation.

In summary, we have proposed a model and some constituent elements that are theoretically linked to both individual and group differences in the development of psychological differentiation. This outline has necessarily painted a broad picture, rather than treating any feature in detail; further details are available, however, in the review works cited at the beginning of this and the previous section.

Distribution of Cognitive Style by Ecocultural Setting[1]

In most Western societies, evidence is available to show that there is a developmental change, ontogenetically, in field-dependence–field-independence (FD–FID), with younger children being more field-dependent (FD) (Witkin *et al.*, 1967). There is also evidence for socialization practices contributing to its development: Those individuals raised with an emphasis on autonomy and achievement tend to be more field-independent (FID) whereas those raised in a protective or conforming milieu tend to be more field-dependent (FD) (Goodenough & Witkin, 1977; Witkin, 1969). Thus the dimension is useful in characterizing individual differences based upon at least two background factors.

Moving cross-culturally, it is important both to check the operation of these two factors and to search for other, perhaps novel, features of the cultural ecology for their possible contributions to the patterning of cognitive style. When we consider these latter possibilities, two major classes of variables immediately appear relevant. One is the "ecological engagement" of a group (originally termed "ecological demands," Berry, 1966), and the other is the "cultural supports" available in the group for acquiring a particular cognitive style.

With respect to the ecological factors, it is possible to predict that those peoples who engage the physical environment through hunting and gathering activities will be called upon to develop restructuring skills to a high degree: Tracks, signs, odors, and sounds all need to be isolated from context in order to carry on this subsistence pattern. Furthermore, the nomadic settlement pattern associated with hunting and gathering requires a developed sense of space, complete with an awareness of topographical signs (e.g., streams, mountains, coasts) and angular orientation to other features (such as paths, sun and stars, prevailing winds). It is difficult to conceive of a successful hunter without the skills to find game and to return again to camp. In contrast, these skills are unlikely to be of similar value to agriculturalists.

With respect to cultural factors in a nomadic group, we have already noted that authority pressures generally are weak (social and political stratification is low), and socialization pressures are toward achievement, independence, and self-reliance in hunting and gathering societies. In contrast, social systems tend to be "tight," and socialization practices emphasize compliance in societies engaging in agricultural pursuits in sedentary settlements.

Both the ecological and cultural factors to be found cross-culturally among

---

[1] This section is drawn largely from data contained in the 1976 monograph (Berry, 1976); later sections will be concerned more with the recent analyses and field sites.

subsistence-level peoples are predictive of greater FD among agriculturalists and greater FID among hunters and gatherers. The evidence presented by Berry (1976) for the samples listed in Table 6.3, and the bulk of the evidence reviewed by Witkin and Berry (1975) support this generalization. For example, in the Berry (1976) monograph, cognitive style tasks (such as Kohs Blocks and Embedded Figures Test) correlated with the combined ecocultural index of .73 and .88, respectively, across the 17 samples, and .65 and .84, respectively, across the almost 800 participants in that study. Whether analyzed at the sample or individual level, ecocultural adaptation clearly accounts for a high proportion of group and individual differences in cognitive style development (Berry, 1976). In other words, samples that were nomadic and hunting and gathering in subsistence pattern were relatively FID in contrast to the sedentary agriculturalists.

Influences stemming from acculturation also contribute to the distribution of scores on these tests. The acculturation index correlates at .65 and .38 at the sample level, and .47 and .32 at the individual level. In all cases, though, acculturation (mainly through a form of Westernization in these samples) is less strongly related than is ecocultural adaptation. Given this pattern of both factors contributing, it is worth noting that a combined (ecocultural plus acculturation) analysis pushes the correlations to the .8 range, and a multiple correlation (employing all the variables noted in the outline of the model in a stepwise fashion) pushes the correlation to the .9 range.

Contributing evidence stems from the work of Dawson (1967, 1975); MacArthur (1975), Okonji (1969, 1979) and others. The overall picture supports the generalization made here that individuals develop a cognitive style that is encouraged in their culture, and that is adaptive to their habitat. That this is so may appear to some to be tautological; nevertheless, the analyses of these differences and the demonstration of covariation among behavioral, cultural, and environmental elements within an ecological system seems to be a necessary first step.

A second, but related, set of behaviors has also been explored cross-culturally. In the outline of the concept of cognitive style, mention was made of "social autonomy" being theoretically related to "restructuring" within the FID cognitive style, and of "interpersonal competencies" being related to the FD end of the dimension. Social behaviors may also thus be included within the framework outlined in this chapter.

More specifically, it may be predicted that individuals who grow up in a "tight," stratified, and densely populated society, such as those described in agriculturally based groups, will be more sensitive to group needs and more responsive to group requirements. In contrast, those developing in "loose" social units might be expected to be more independent of authority and less conforming to group pressure. A first approach (Berry, 1967) to this prediction contrasted samples from two cultures (the Temne and the Eskimo, in Table 6.3) on a conformity task. This involved a situation similar to the one

TABLE 6.3
Cultures, Samples and Their Characteristics

Cultural Group	Location	Sample name	N	Ecological index	Cultural index	Ecocultural index	Acculturation index
Temne	West Africa	Mayola	90	-1.98	-1.93	-1.96	-1.68
		Port Loko	32	-1.98	-1.48	-1.66	-.02
Telefol	New Guinea, highlands	Telefomin	40	-1.53	-1.48	-1.51	-1.47
Motu	Coastal New Guinea	Hanuabada	30	-.39	-.53	-.49	+.68
Koonganji	Coastal Australia	Yarrabah	30	-.27	-.53	-.45	-.38
Tsimshian	Coastal British Columbia	Hartley Bay	56	-.27	-.37	-.34	+.74
		Port Simpson	59	-.27	-.37	-.30	+1.42
Carrier	British Columbia mountains	Tachie	60	+.18	-.26	-.11	+.47
		Fort St. James	61	+.18	+.36	+.30	+.95
Ojibway	Northern Ontario	Aroland	39	+.64	+.64	+.64	+.34
		Long Lac	37	+.64	+.25	+.38	+.80
		Sioux Lookout	31	+.64	+.41	+.49	+1.48
Arunta	Central Australia	Santa Teresa	30	+.52	+.80	+.72	-1.26
Cree	Northern Quebec	Wemindji	61	+.86	+.75	+.79	-.69
		Fort George	60	+.86	+.64	+.72	+.26
Eskimo	Baffin Island	Pond Inlet	91	+1.09	+1.58	+1.43	-1.20
		Frobisher Bay	31	+1.09	+1.57	+1.36	-.44

described by Asch (1956) where individuals are requested to judge the length of a line in the face of a false social norm. In field settings, using confederates is impossible for a variety of reasons, and so a group norm was suggested by the researcher as "the one most often chosen by the ____ people." Differences between the two groups were as expected: In the "tight" samples, judgments were significantly closer to the suggested group norm than in the "loose" samples.

At this group level of analysis, there was correspondence between two behavioral domains that are theoretically related in the FD–FID cognitive style. However, at the individual level of analysis (i.e., using individual difference correlations) relationships were not significant. A review by Witkin and Goodenough (1977a) has shown that substantial relationships between restructuring and interpersonal competencies appear only in live or real, rather than simulated, social contexts. Thus the task employed appears, in retrospect, to have been unsuitable for the analysis of individual differences in cognitive style; however, group and individual differences appear to be highly predictable across cultures.

Evidence for this latter generalization has been assembled from the samples listed in Table 6.3, and have been reported in Berry (1979b). Although not as strong as those reported for the restructuring tasks, the correlation with the Ecocultural index across the 17 samples is .70, and across the 800 individuals is .51; and the multiple correlation achieved when all constituent factors are taken into account reaches .75 at the sample level and .43 at the individual level. We are clearly accounting for a substantial amount of the cross-cultural variation in this particular social behavior when we focus on the ecological requirements and sociocultural pressures ("tightness") that characterize these various societies.

Unpackaging Variables

In the past few years there has been an increasing interest in the more detailed specification of the variables, both independent and dependent, that are at work cross-culturally. This effort was termed *unpackaging* by Whiting (1976), who was concerned mainly with independent variables. The term may also be applied to similar efforts directed at dependent variables, although this activity has been more identified with concepts such as *construct validation* (e.g., Irvine, 1979).

Cross-cultural research on cognitive style can obviously benefit from such unpackaging efforts. Berry (in press) has attempted to develop a more refined model focusing specifically on causal relationships between variables in the ecocultural setting and a variety of psychological consequences. This model (see Figure 6.3) represents four arcs or causal linkages between environment and behavior. The structure of the model places the four environmental

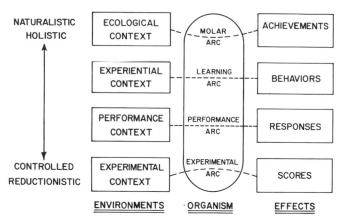

Figure 6.3 The diagram illustrates the causal linkages between environment and behavior.

contexts at the left and the *effects* at the right. Toward the top of the model are natural and holistic contexts and effects, while at the bottom of the model they are more experimental (controlled and reductionistic) contexts.

Looking in detail at the environmental contexts, the first context, the *ecological context*, is the "natural–cultural habitat" of Brunswik (1955), or the "preperceptual world" of Barker (1969). It consists of all the relatively permanent characteristics that provide the context for human action, and includes the "ecological," "traditional culture," and "acculturational influences" aspects of the research model employed earlier (Berry, 1975, 1976).

Nested in this ecological context are two levels of the "life space" or "psychological world" of Lewin (1936). One, the *experiential context*, is that pattern of recurrent experiences that provides a basis for learning. This is, essentially, the set of independent variables which cross-cultural psychology tries to identify as being operative in a particular habitat in the development of behavioral characteristics. The other, the *performance context*, is the limited set of environmental circumstances that may be observed to account for particular behaviors; these are immediate in space and time.

The fourth context, the *experimental context*, represents those environmental characteristics that are designed by the psychologist to elicit a particular response or test score. The experimental context may or may not be nested in the first three contexts. The degree to which it is nested represents the ecological validity of the task.

Paralleling these four contexts are four effects. The first effect, *achievements*, refers to the complex, long-standing, and developed behavior patterns that are in place as an adaptive response to the ecological context. Achievements include established and shared patterns of behavior that can be discovered in an individual or distributed in a cultural group.

The second effect, *behaviors*, are the complex behaviors which have been learned over time in the recurrent experiential context. Included in these are the skills, traits, and attitudes that have been nurtured in particular roles, or acquired by specific training or education (whether formal or informal). A third effect, *responses,* are those performances appearing in response to immediate stimulation or experience. In contrast to behaviors, they are not a function of role experience or long-term training, but appear in reply to immediate experiences.

The fourth effect, *scores,* is composed of those behaviors that are observed, measured, and recorded during psychological experiment or testing. If the experimental context is nested in the other contexts, then the scores may be representative of the responses, behaviors, and achievements of the organism. If the experiment has ecological validity, then the scores will have behavioral validity.

Relationships can be traced between the elements across the model. The *molar arc* operates across the top of the model (see Figure 6.3). It is concerned with the life situation (in physical environmental and cultural terms) of an organism and its accomplishments. At the second level, the *learning arc* is concerned with tying together recurrent independent variables in the experience of an individual with his characteristic behaviors. The third level, the *performance arc*, is interested in more specific acts as a function of immediate and current experience. Finally, at the fourth level, the *experimental arc* is shown and is devoted to the laboratory or other systematic study of relationships between experimental problems and test scores.

A recurrent problem regarding this model for general experimental psychology, is the difficulty in saying anything of value about causal relationships (at the two middle levels) while working almost exclusively with the experimental arc. Brunswik would add to this the further problem of saying anything meaningful, on this basis, about the molar arc as well. The problem facing cross-cultural psychology tends to be the reverse: Rather than failing to ascend the reductionistic–holistic dimension to achieve ecological validity, cross-cultural psychology has failed to descend the dimension to achieve a specification of experiential performance and experimental context variables that are responsible for task performance and behavioral variation across natural habitats. In Campbell's (1957) terms there has been insufficient concern in these two branches of psychology for "external" and "internal" validity, respectively.

The original analyses of Lewin, Brunswik, and Barker, which have stimulated the model presented here, appear to underlie other contemporary analyses. For example, Eckensberger and Kornadt (1977, pp. 222–223) distinguish between group and individual levels of ecological analyses. When groups are the focus, analyses tend to be at the holistic level, with cultural and behavioral achievements being considered as the dependent variables. When individuals are the focus, analyses tend to be at the lower levels, with individual behaviors and performances constituting the dependent variables.

Applying this ecological analysis to the cross-cultural study of cognitive style leads to a number of observations and strategies. It is fair to say that, up till now, the bulk of the cross-cultural study has concentrated upon the molar and experimental arcs. As we have seen, systematic covariation has now been found, across 17 samples, between the ecocultural index and a set of task scores (Berry, 1976). Additionally, this finding is generally supported by the work of others (Witkin & Berry, 1975).

Of course, at the group level, the experiential context has been assessed, but largely because of a lack of individual differences in most of these samples (e.g., in economic roles) individual analyses have been rare. The two analyses which have been attempted (i.e., self-ratings of socialization and experience of Western education) have yielded fairly consistent findings: Socialization for assertion and experience of Western education are both linked with greater FID, with education tending to yield a stronger and more consistent pattern of relationships. Beyond this, only anecdotal evidence has been brought to bear on the issue. Obviously, more work is necessary at the level of the learning arc in order to tie down the specific environmental elements responsible for the development of a particular cognitive style.

At the level of the performance arc as well, work needs to begin in earnest. For example, variations in materials employed to elicit responses need to be developed. These would include emic tasks of such etic[2] dimensions as disembedding, restructuring, and interpersonal distancing.

Finally, across all arc levels, studies need to be conducted that integrate levels within environmental contexts and within behaviors. For the former, experimental materials should be drawn increasingly from the natural, ecological context of the people in a particular study; and for the latter, evidence should be collected to show that responses and behaviors are nested one in the other.

Extensions to Other Ecocultural Settings

Since 1974 a comparative study of Pygmy hunters and gatherers and Bantu farmers has been under way in l'Empire Centrafricain (van de Koppel, 1977). Data analyses are now under way and no results are yet available; but a few comments on *what* data we have will indicate some progress in unpackaging. First, the team includes both an anthropologist and an ecologist whose role is to specify, in great detail, the ecological and cultural features of the two

---

[2] See Berry, 1969, 1979a and Chapter 2 of this volume, for a discussion of the emic and etic approaches to cross-cultural research.

groups. First cuts into these data indicate an extremely rich resource for unpackaging the environmental contexts.

Second, although the four psychologists on the team cover somewhat different areas, their work overlaps on some crucial variables. For example, on the assessment of socialization experience, in addition to the anthropological characterizations of groups and self-ratings by individuals (which were sought in previous work), individual parental interviews were conducted. Furthermore, a standard task was attempted by the child in the presence of parents; this has been filmed and will be analyzed for characteristic interactions.

Third, some of the tests used to assess cognitive style were developed in the second year of the project, based upon pilot data collected and observations made in the field during the first year. These included, for example, an African Embedded Figures Test and an interview assessment of interpersonal distancing.

Finally, work planned for the future includes extensive analyses at the level of the learning arc, employing the concept of role. A comparative study in one agricultural and one hunting culture will try to spot these roles at the individual level and then relate them to the societal context. Each of four features of roles is considered both at the group and at the individual level. Questions to illustrate the approach are indicated in Table 6.4. For example, How many roles are available in a particular society, and how many of these are carried out by a particular individual? are questions that should tell us about role diversity at both levels. By using this strategy of analysis, we hope to be able to specify relationships across the learning arc; that is, to try to link specific, role learning experiences to particular acquired behaviors.

TABLE 6.4
Analysis of Roles at Group and Individual Levels

Role features	Level of analysis	
	Group	Individual
Role diversity	How many roles are identified in the society?	How many roles does an individual carry out?
Role content	What is the function of these roles for society?	What behavior is learned and performed?
Role articulation	How structured are these roles into a system?	How integrated are his roles into the societal system?
Role valuation	How stratified are these roles?	What prestige or reward is attached to each role?

Furthermore, we want to assess, more directly, the question of "value": Is it the case that a FD individual is better adjusted and has higher status in an agricultural society, whereas a FID person holds that position in a hunting and gathering society?

Conclusions

In this chapter an attempt has been made to provide a selective overview of some of the key features of the work relating cognitive style to the cultural context in which it is found. We have argued that (*a*) there are important patterns to be found among elements of culture and among a variety of behaviors; and (*b*) there are systematic relationships between these two clusters of variables. It is the fact of their clustering that permits the use of the terms "culture" and "cognitive style."

Although only one approach to culture (an ecological one) and one approach to cognitive style (that of field-dependence–independence) have been referred to in this chapter, an argument may be made that other conceptions can and should be used. There are other ways of classifying cultures, and other conceptions of cognitive styles, which await innovative research. However, the existence of systematic relationships when the phenomena are "cut" one way, suggests that further systematic relationships will appear when they are "cut" in another. The thrust of this chapter has not been to claim the unique truth arrived at by making one set of "cuts," but to display the value of approaching the cross-cultural study of cognition with the help of systematic models of culture and theories of behavior.

References

Asch, S. E. Studies in independence and conformity 1: A minority of one against a unanimous majority. *Psychological Monographs,* 1956, *70* (416).

Barker, R. G. *Ecological Psychology.* Stanford, California: Stanford Univ. Press, 1969.

Barry, H., Child, I., & Bacon, M. Relation of child training to subsistence economy. *American Anthropologist,* 1959, *61,* 31–63.

Berry, J. W. Temne and Eskimo perceptual skills. *International Journal of Psychology,* 1966, *1,* 207–229.

Berry, J. W. Independence and conformity in subsistence-level societies. *Journal of Personality and Social Psychology,* 1967, *7,* 415–418.

Berry, J. W. On cross-cultural comparability. *International Journal of Psychology,* 1969, *4,* 119–128.

Berry, J. W. Ecological and cultural factors in spatial perceptual development. *Canadian Journal of Behavioural Science,* 1971, *3,* 324–336.

Berry, J. W. An ecological approach to cross-cultural psychology. *Nederlands Tijdschrift voor de Psychologie,* 1975, *30,* 51–84.

Berry, J. W. *Human ecology and cognitive style: Comparative studies in cultural and psychological adaptation.* Beverly Hills, California: Sage–Halsted, 1976.

Berry, J. W. Introduction to methodology. In H. C. Triandis & J. W. Berry (Eds.), *Handbook of cross-cultural psychology* (Vol. 2). Rockleigh, New Jersey: Allyn & Bacon, 1979. (a)

Berry, J. W. A cultural ecology of social behaviour. In L. Berkowitz (Ed.), *Advances in experimental social psychology*. New York: Academic Press, 1979. (b)

Berry, J. W. Ecological analyses for cross-cultural psychology. In N. Warren (Ed.), *Studies in cross-cultural psychology,* London: Academic Press, in press.

Bock, R., & Kolakowski, D. Further evidence of sex-linked major gene influence on human spatial visualizing ability. *American Journal of Human Genetics,* 1973, *25,* 1–14.

Brunswik, E. Representative design and probabilistic theory. *Psychological Bulletin,* 1955, *62,* 193–217.

Campbell, D. T. Factors relevant to the validity of experiments in social settings. *Psychological Bulletin,* 1957, *54,* 297–312.

Cole, M., & Scribner, S. *Culture and thought.* New York: Wiley, 1974.

Cole, M., & Scribner, S. Developmental theories applied to cross-cultural cognitive research. *Annals of the New York Academy of Sciences,* 1977, *285,* 366–373.

Dawson, J. L. M. Kwashiorkor, gynaecomastia and feminization processes. *Journal of Tropical Medicine and Hygiene,* 1966, *69,* 175–179.

Dawson, J. L. M. Cultural and physiological influences upon spatial perceptual processes in West Africa. Parts 1 and 2. *International Journal of Psychology,* 1967, *2* (1 & 2), 115–128; 171–185.

Dawson, J. L. M. Theoretical and research bases of biosocial psychology. *University of Hong Kong Gazette,* 1969, *16,* 1–10.

Dawson, J. L. M. Effects of sex hormones on cognitive style in rats and men. *Behavior Genetics,* 1972, *2,* 21–42.

Dawson, J. L. M. *Psychological effects of bio-social change in West Africa,* New Haven, Connecticut: Hraflex FC1–001, 1975.

Dawson, J. L. M. Theory and method in bio-social psychology. *Annals of New York Academy of Sciences* 1977, *285,* 46–65.

Dyk, R., & Witkin, H. A. Family experiences related to the development of differentiation in children. *Child Development,* 1965, *36,* 21–55.

Eckensberger, L., & Kornadt, H. The mutual relevance of the cross-cultural and the ecological perspective in psychology. In H. McGurk (Ed.), *Ecological factors in human development.* Amsterdam: North Holland, 1977.

Goodenough, D., Gandini, E., Olkin, I., Pizzamiglio,L., Thayer, D., & Witkin, H. A study of X-chromosome linkage with field dependence and spatial-visualization. *Behavior Genetics,* 1977, *7,* 373–387.

Goodenough, D., & Witkin, H. The origins of field-dependent and field-independent cognitive styles. *ETS Research Bulletin,* 1977, RB–77.

Irvine, S. Testing and assessment across cultures: Issues in methodology and theory. In H. C. Triandis & J. W. Berry (Eds.), *Handbook of cross-cultural psychology* (Vol. 2). Rockleigh, New Jersey, Allyn & Bacon, 1979.

Kogan, N. *Cognitive styles in infancy and early childhood.* Hillsdale, New Jersey: Erlbaum, 1976.

Kroeber, A. & Kluckhohn, C. *Culture: A critical review of concepts and definitions.* Cambridge, Massachusetts: Peabody Museum, 1952.

Lee, R. What do hunters do for a living, or how to make out on scarce resources. In R. Lee & I. DeVore (Eds.), *Man the hunter.* Chicago: Aldine, 1968. Pp. 30–48.

Lewin, K. *Principles of topological psychology,* New York: McGraw-Hill, 1936.

MacArthur, R. Differential ability patterns: Inuit, Nsenga and Canadian Whites. In J. W. Berry & W. J. Lonner (Eds.), *Applied cross-cultural psychology.* Amsterdam: Swets & Zeitlinger, 1975.

Murdock, G. P. Ethnographic atlas: A summary. *Ethnology,* 1967, *6,* 109–236.

Murdock, G. P. Correlations of exploitive and settlement patterns. In D. Damas (Ed.), *Ecological essays*, National Museum of Canada Bulletin No. 36, 1969. Pp. 129–146.

Murdock, G. P., & Morrow, D. Subsistence economy and supportive practices: Cross-cultural codes 1. *Ethnology*, 1970, *9*, 302–330.

Murdock, G. P., & Provost, C. Measurement of cultural complexity. *Ethnology*, 1973, *12*, 379; 392.

Okonji, M. O. Differential effects of rural and urban upbringing on the development of cognitive styles. *International Journal of Psychology*, 1969, *4*, 293–305.

Okonji, M. O. *Cognitive styles across cultures*. In N. Warren (Ed.), *Studies in cross-cultural psychology* (Vol. 2). London: Academic Press, 1979.

Pelto, P. The difference between "tight" and "loose" societies. *Transaction*, April 1968, 37–40.

Serpell, R. *Cultures' influence on behaviour*. London: Methuen, 1976.

Van de Koppel, J. M. H. A preliminary report on the Central African Differentiation Project. In Y. Poortinga (Ed.), *Basic problems in cross-cultural psychology*. Amsterdam: Swets & Zeitlinger, 1977.

van Leeuwen, V. M. A cross-cultural examination of psychological differentiation in males and females. *International Journal of Psychology*, 1978, *13*, 87–122.

Waber, D. P. Sex differences in cognition: A function of maturation rate? *Science*, 1976, *192*, 572–574.

Waber, D. P. Biological substrates of field-dependence: Implications of the sex difference. *Psychological Bulletin*, 1977, *84*, 1076–1087.

Whiting, B. The problem of the packaged variable. In K. F. Riegel & J. A. Meacham (Eds.), *The developing individual in a changing world*. The Hague: Mouton, 1976.

Witkin, H. A. Social influences in the development of cognitive style. In D. Goslin (Ed.), *Handbook of socialization theories and research*. Chicago, Illinois: Rand McNally, 1969. Pp. 687–706.

Witkin, H. A. Theory in cross-cultural research: Its uses and risks. In Y. Poortinga (Ed.), *Basic problems in cross-cultural psychology*. Amsterdam: Swets & Zeitlinger, 1977. (a)

Witkin, H. A. *Cognitive styles in personal and cultural adaptation: The 1977 Heinz Werner lectures*. Worcester, Massachusetts: Clark Univ. Press, 1977. (b)

Witkin, H. A. & Berry, J. W. Psychological differentiation in cross-cultural perspective. *Journal of Cross-Cultural Psychology*, 1975, *6*, 4–87.

Witkin, H. A., Dyk, R. B., Faterson, H. F., Goodenough, D. R., & Karp, S. *Psychological differentiation*. New York: Wiley, 1962.

Witkin, H. A., & Goodenough, D. R. Field dependence and interpersonal behaviour. *Psychological Bulletin*, 1977, *84*, 661–689. (a)

Witkin, H., & Goodenough, D. R. Field dependence revisited. *ETS Research Bulletin*, 1977, 77–16. (b)

Witkin, H. A., & Goodenough, D. R. Psychological differentiation: Current status. *ETS Research Bulletin*, 1977, 77–17. (c)

Yen, W. Sex linked major gene influence on selected types of spatial performance. *Behavior Genetics*, 1975, *5*, 281–298.

7

Culture and Attitude Structure and Change

ANDREW R. DAVIDSON

Cultural Differences in Attitude and Belief Content

Major differences in attitudes, beliefs, and values exist among cultures. These dissimilarities, first perceived in terms of such outward characteristics as food preferences, desired clothing styles, and beliefs about physcial attractiveness, extend to practically all aspects of life. Deistic beliefs and religious behavior, long recognized as one of the defining characteristics of culture, obviously vary among groups. Such diversity is made all the more striking by observed religious variations between cultures ostensibly practicing the same religion. At a more mundane level, important differences exist in procreative and family socialization values and behavior; cultural differentials can be observed in desired and actual family size, the appropriate age to wean children, and the preferred mode and level of discipline. In addition, intergroup and internation hostility and alliance patterns continue to remind us that important differences exist between cultures in their beliefs and attitudes about other groups.

Cultural differences in attitudes and beliefs have been the focus of both informal observation and systematic measurement. Although, as we shall see later, many of the instruments developed for systematic observation are extraordinarily complex, the evidence for cultural differences can also be

137

PERSPECTIVES ON CROSS-CULTURAL PSYCHOLOGY

obtained through some rather unencumbered techniques. Perhaps the most direct approach for assessing differences in beliefs among groups is word association. A number of variants of this technique have been used cross-culturally. Rosenzweig (1961), Szalay and Bryson (1973), Szalay and Lysne (1970) and Szalay, Windle, and Lysne (1970) have asked respondents to provide free associations to stimulus words. The perceived antecedents or consequences of an object or behavior (e.g., having a large family) have been obtained (Davidson, Jaccard, Triandis, Morales, & Diaz-Guerrero, 1976; Fawcett, Arnold, Bulatao, Buripakdi, Chung, Iritani, Lee, & Wu, 1974; Triandis, Kilty, Shanmugam, Tanaka, & Vassiliou 1972b). Schaffer, Sundberg, and Tyler (1969) utilized free association (e.g., list ten words that come to mind) and structured associations have been used (e.g., "the _____ butterfly) by Brewer and Campbell (1976), Cole, Gay, Glick, and Sharp (1971), and Jakobovits (1966).

Each of the cited studies have detected significant cultural group differences in the content of beliefs about objects and behavior. For example, in an important comparative study on the value of children, Fawcett *et al.* (1974) asked couples from six countries (i.e., Japan, the Republic of Korea, the Philippines, Taiwan, Thailand, and the United States) open-ended questions about the advantages and disadvantages of having children versus remaining childless. They report that parents in urban middle-class families stressed emotional or psychological benefits as important reasons for having children. These benefits included the happiness and companionship derived from the presence of children as well as the contributions parents felt the children made to their own personal development. For these parents, the potential economic benefits obtainable from children were not an important motivation for having children.

However, as respondents were drawn from successively lower socio-economic groups, the salience of the economic values of children increased. In the rural groups, for example, the help that children were expected to provide around the house, their contribution to family income, and their potential contribution to the old-age security of the parents were all emphasized. A number of intercountry differences in the value of children were also obtained. Parents from the two most economically developed countries of the six surveyed, Japan and the United States, often responded in ways that were quite distinct. As contrasted with parents from other countries, Japanese and American parents tended to agree less often with statements such as "a good reason for having children is that they can help when parents are too old to work" and "a young couple is not fully accepted in the community until they have children."

Davidson *et al.* (1976), studying respondents from Mexico and the United States, also investigated differences in beliefs relevant to family planning behaviors—having a small family and using oral contraceptives. Similar to the results of the Fawcett *et al.* (1974) research, the role of children in ensuring economic security was of greatest importance to respondents of very low socioeconomic status. With regard to oral contraceptive use, the most frequently mentioned disadvantages varied between countries. For example, fear of blood clots was salient only in the United States, whereas nervousness and high blood pressure were salient only in Mexico.

A monograph by Brewer and Campbell (1976) provides examples of cultural differences in attitudes and beliefs from a different content domain. As part of a research project on the intergroup attitudes of 30 East African ethnic tribal groups, respondents were queried about the worst and best traits of the other 29 groups. The findings suggest that belief content varies as a function of the frequency and type of contact between ethnic groups. For example, one group (the Kikuyu) were often mentioned as "sexually loose" by remote outgroups who knew them primarily through contacts in urban centers where displaced Kikuyu women are frequently employed as prostitutes. In contrast, groups familiar with traditional Kikuyu values frequently named them as "most sexually strict." The authors also note that groups that were similar in appearance most frequently named each other as "handsome," reflecting ethnocentric standards of beauty.

A final and interesting example of cultural differences in attitudes and beliefs has resulted from multinational surveys on the quality of life. A number of these investigations have attempted to answer the question, "Does money buy happiness?" The Gallup organization has published preliminary results of a worldwide assessment of satisfaction with the quality of life (Gallup, 1976). The percentage of those interviewed who were highly satisfied was greatest for North America, almost as high for Western Europe, somewhat lower for Latin America, and dramatically lower for Africa and the Far East on almost all of the 10 questions asked. These ratings appear to be roughly correlated with levels of per capita product. Easterlin (1973) also presents multinational data suggesting that feelings of happiness are related to level of income. His findings indicate that the association is even stronger within than among countries.

Methodological Approaches to the Cross-Cultural Study of Attitudes

Cross-cultural differences in belief content have been noted and exemplified because awareness of such differences serves as the starting point for all (i.e., at least all methodologically defensible) cross-cultural studies of beliefs, attitudes, and values. On the basis of this awareness, researchers must make an important decision about the general approach of their research. One can focus on cultural differences in beliefs and attitudes and look for subsets of cultures within which there is maximal similarity in terms of attitudes and beliefs and between which there is maximal heterogeneity.

In other words, one can attempt to develop typologies of cultures—an approach that will be referred to as the *cultural differences approach*. Alternatively, the researcher can look past content differences in beliefs, in an attempt to identify cross-cultural similarities in either belief and attitude structure, or in the processes whereby beliefs combine to form attitudes. This approach will be referred to as the *cultural similarities approach*. It would be inappropriate to assume that only one of these approaches is correct or preferred. Rather, the choice of method and theory should be determined by the objectives of the investigation. We will now turn to a discussion of the research objectives and methodological considerations that would influence the researcher's selection of either the cultural similarities or cultural differences approach. As a detailed presentation of a number of these issues can be found in Davidson and Thomson (1979), they will only be summarized here.

THE CULTURAL DIFFERENCES APPROACH

As Strodtbeck (1964) noted, the most easily conceptualized form of cross-cultural study equates cultural or ecological life experiences with the laboratory treatment administered to an individual subject. If investigators have reason to believe that different types of life experiences lead to the formation of different attitudes and beliefs, and inadequate variance in the life experiences of interest exists within the investigators' own culture, they may then search for other cultures which can serve as a natural experiment to test these ideas. For example, in a classic investigation, Barry, Child, and Bacon (1959) were interested in the effect of the degree of accumulation of food resources on child socialization attitudes and practices. To obtain adequate variation on their independent variable—accumulation of food resources—they were forced to sample a wide range of cultures, including societies in which food accumulation was extremely high (e.g., agricultural and animal husbandry dominant economies) and those in which food accumulation was extremely low (e.g., hunting and fishing dominant economies). They were able to demonstrate that cultures low in food accumulation tended to foster "assertion" during child rearing, while those high in food accumulation fostered "compliance."

In testing their hypothesis, Barry, Child, and Bacon (1959) sampled 104 societies. If they had been forced to dispatch researchers to these societies to collect data, the cost of such a study would have been prohibitive. Fortunately, they were able to use previously collected and compiled anthropological data from each of these societies contained in the Human Relations Area Files (Murdock, 1957). Although gathering data from the accumulated files is easier than conducting surveys in a similar number of cultures, the cultural groups for which data are available are primarily isolated and nonliterate societies—not representative of the cultures in which the vast majority of people live today. In addition, many attitudinal and belief variables of interest are not included in these data. Hence, in many investigations utilizing the cross-cultural differences approach, sampling of cultures is problematic.

One way to make the sampling of cultures more manageable is to examine fewer cultures. Not surprisingly, this is a frequently selected strategy. However, this approach does introduce new difficulties. First, when cultures are the sampling units, the appropriate level of the dependent variable is an aggregated measure of attitude or belief for each culture. Therefore, each culture sampled provides only one observation. As the number of observations decreases, so too does the power of any statistical treatment of the data.

The second sampling problem arises because each culture represents a package of variables (Whiting, 1976). That is, each cultural group can be defined by its position in a hypothetical space in which the dimensions are global variables (e.g., primary economic base, language, climate). In order to separate the effect of one global variable from the effect of other global variables, it is desirable to sample a relatively large number of cultures, in the same manner as individuals are usually sampled. Nuisance variables that are thought to be correlated with the global variable of interest should also be measured so that their effects can be controlled either statistically or by sampling procedures. For example, the societies in the Barry, Bacon, and Child study that were low in food accumulation also tended to have nomadic settlement patterns and low population density, whereas those that were high in food accumulation tended to have sedentary settlements with high population density. To sort out the independent effects of each of these variables on child rearing practices would be extraordinarily difficult, even with their relatively large sample. The situation becomes even more problematic with a greatly decreased sample of societies.

An additional methodological difficulty confronting attitude research utilizing the cultural differences approach concerns the equivalence of measures. Before comparisons can be legitimately made among cultures, it is first necessary to establish equivalent bases on which to make such comparisons. For example, if we accept as valid the previously mentioned finding that Africans are less satisfied with the quality of their lives than are North Americans, it presupposes that we believe that two measurement prerequisites have been met. First, that the translated satisfaction questions are measuring the exact same attribute in different groups of people (functional equivalence). Second, that the response scale is metrically equivalent in each group, that is, if subjects from different national groups obtain an equal satisfaction score they have an equal amount of satisfaction (score equivalence). Poortinga (1975) has demonstrated that a measure must satisfy both the requirements of functional and score equivalence if it is to be used for cross-cultural comparisons.

However, as numerous authors have discussed, when tests are used cross-culturally, score equivalence is rarely achieved (e.g., Cole & Bruner, 1971; Jahoda, 1969; Poortinga, 1975; Triandis, 1977b; Triandis, Malpass, & Davidson, 1973). Consider but a few of the factors that could contribute to the lack of equivalence in our rather simple example concerning life satisfaction: (*a*) differential susceptibility to response sets; (*b*) unequal familiarity with the interview situation or response format; (*c*) differences in the meaning of the interview situation; (*d*) differences in the connotative meaning of items that are correctly translated linguistically; and (*e*) unequal understanding of the test format and directions. The number of variables that might plausibly cause score nonequivalence is so great that it is probably not feasible to measure and control all of them in any one study. Accordingly, in the absence of convincing evidence of score equivalence there are a number of plausible explanations to account for an observed difference in an attitude score between two cultures.

In summary, the researcher adopting the cultural differences approach faces substantial difficulty, both in the sampling of cultures and in demonstrating the equivalence of measures. These difficulties are not always insurmountable however, as is exemplified by the programmatic cross-cultural research on Witkin's differentiation hypothesis (Witkin & Barry, 1975). As is discussed in the following section, the difficulties of both culture sampling and equivalence of measurement are considerably less severe in research which utilizes the cultural similarities approach.

THE CULTURAL SIMILARITIES APPROACH

Triandis, Malpass, and Davidson (1973) argue that concern about the universality of our theories serves as the primary rationale for psychologists venturing to obtain cross-cultural data. To use Willer's (1967) terminology, cross-cultural investigations provide the opportunity to establish the "boundary conditions," for attitudinal models and theories. In the most obvious case, a researcher would test a model or hypothesis that previously has been supported by one cultural group in at least one other culture. Following such a study the researcher could designate, among the cultural groups studied, those for whom the model is valid and those for whom it is not. If appropriate individual level information is obtained in each cultural group, it is frequently possible to do much more.

Depending on the diversity of the group studied and the individual level variables that were measured, the researcher should be able to begin to specify the variables defining the populations for which the model is not valid (e.g., the model is not valid for those with a protein deficiency). With this information it is possible to improve the model by incorporating these boundary conditions in the model. Concern with the universality of theories usually requires that the researcher take the cultural similarities approach and look past superficial differences in cognitive content in an attempt to identify cross-cultural universals in attitude and belief structures and processes.

Testing the universality of psychological models or theories offers two important advantages; both arise from the fact that within each culture the researcher is investigating the relationships among a number of variables. First, only the functional equivalence of measures is required. Second, cultural differences can often be meaningfully interpreted because they tend to appear as a difference in one relationship in the presence of cultural similarities in other relationships.

As Malpass (1977) has outlined, the development of measures that are functionally equivalent is always difficult. However, the difficulty decreases as the strength of the theory or model tested increases. If the terms of the theory are at a high level of abstraction (i.e., not content or method bound) then culturally relevant measures of the theoretical constructs can be constructed (Brislin, 1976; Davidson, 1977; Malpass, 1977; Pike, 1966; Triandis, 1977b). The construct validity of these measures can, in turn, be investigated within each culture to determine, psychometrically, their functional equivalence (Berrien, 1967). Here again, a strong theoretical framework is a help because it indicates how the newly constructed measure should related to other variables in the framework.

On the basis of a general pattern of similarity, one can begin to investigate specific cultural differences in the relationships between variables. For, as Campbell (1964) has observed, differences between cultural groups are only interpretable against a background of considerable similarity. In the absence of demonstrations of similarity, it is impossible to distinguish cultural differences from a large number of alternative explanations that could plausibly account for the difference (e.g., failure to communicate, inadequacy of measures, subject motivation). In the presence of demonstrations of similarity, the plausibility of many of the alternative explanations is decreased.

Problems of culture sampling are also less severe in research that attempts to establish the boundary conditions of psychological models and theories than in research that examines the effects of global-level variables on attitudes. The problems are alleviated, in part, because, in cross-cultural model testing, the attitude and belief measures are appropriately individual level variables and do not have to be aggregated at the cultural level. Hence, the number of cultures studied can be far fewer than in research investigating the effects of cultural and ecological level variables on attitude scores. In addition, the aim in sampling cultures is not to obtain variance on a central variable in the theory being tested, rather it is to select groups that will provide the most stringent test of the generalizability of the theory—cultural groups in which the theory has the greatest a priori probability of not being supported. In attitude research, this approach could, for example, result in studies of groups with very low education and income and groups with maximum linguistic differences.

The following highly selected review of cross-cultural studies of attitude structure and change (chosen from a much broader coverage of the attitude literature by Davidson and Thomson, 1979) is guided by the above methodological discussion. An attempt will be made to focus on studies that have the least severe sampling and equivalence of measurement problems. The majority of the reviewed research utilizes the cultural similarities approach and attempts to investigate the boundary conditions of psychological models and theories.

The Informational Basis of Attitudes

The early attitude theorists, most notably Thurstone (1928) and Doob (1947), recognized that a relationship exists between one's attitude toward an object and one's beliefs about that object. Those familiar with attitude scaling will recognize that belief statements are the items most frequently scaled to obtain a measure of attitude. This procedure is most apparent in Likert and Thurstone scaling. The use of beliefs in this manner implies that an attitude toward an object is some function of the affective value of the attributes associated with that object. If this is the case, a model is needed to specify the exact nature of that relationship. A number of models have been proposed, including the congruity principle (Osgood, Suci, & Tannenbaum, 1957), the summation model (L. Anderson & Fishbein, 1965) and the averaging model (N. Anderson, 1965). According to the congruity principle, a subject weights the evaluation of the attributes that enter into the interaction by their relative polarization. In the summation model the subject is thought to weight the evaluation of each attribute by the probability of its association with the object. The averaging model hypothesizes that an attitude is equal to the sum of the evaluation of each attribute weighted by the importance of the attribute and divided by the sum of the importance weights. Research in the United States has demonstrated the superiority of both the averaging model and the summation model over the congruity principle for predicting attitudes (L. Anderson & Fishbein, 1965; N. Anderson, 1971).

The adequacy of these three models for predicting attitudes has been compared in a number of cross-cultural investigations. Tanaka (1972) obtained evaluative ratings of a nationality component (e.g., America), a noun component (nuclear testing), and then a composite of two components (e.g., American nuclear testing) for Japanese and Finnish college students. Using the congruity model and a variant of the averaging model, predictions concerning the attitude toward the composites were made from the evaluative ratings of the individual components. Both models provided accurate (correlation coefficients ranged from .85 to .93) and similar predictions of composite evaluation. No meaningful differences in the predictive validity of the models could be detected.

Triandis and Fishbein (1963) compared the predictive validity of the congruity and summation models for the evaluation of complex stimulus persons using Greek and Illinois college students as subjects. Evaluative ratings were first obtained separately for each element that would be used in the subsequent construction of stimulus persons. For example, subjects initially rated a variety of races, occupations, religions, and nationalities. Later, they were asked to evaluate a stimulus person constructed from the just mentioned characteristics; for example, a white bank manager who is French and the same religion as you. In Greece and the United States both models provided highly significant correlations with the obtained data. However, in both countries the summation model provided more accurate predictions.

In a similar study, Triandis, Tanaka, and Shanmugam (1966) compared the congruity and summation models using Greek, Japanese, and Indian students as subjects. Complex stimulus persons were constructed from combinations of the characteristics of occupation, sex, age, and religion. Once again, predictions from both models yielded significant correlations with the observed data and the correlations for the summation model were higher than those for the congruity model.

In these tests of the summation model, the subjective probability relating the attitude object and each attribute was assumed to be one. In addition, all subjects were college students. In a later study in Mexico and the United States, which included a sample of women with less than 3 years of education (Jaccard, Davidson, Triandis, Morales, & Diaz-Guerrero, reported in Malpass, 1977), both probability and evaluation were measured for each attribute. Attributes were selected on the basis of their salience for the groups being studied. Results indicated that the summation model accounted for most of the nonerror variance in evaluation of the attitude object. Szalay, Windle, and Lysne (1970) found similar results testing the summation model using indirect methods (frequency of association) for measuring beliefs.

In summary, for the populations and topics reviewed, no culturally determined boundary conditions modifying the models of attitude formation have been detected. However, more studies of noncollege populations are definitely needed. We will now turn our attention to the process of inferential belief formation.

Inferential Belief Formation

The process by which new beliefs are formed is frequently an inferential one. For example, if a subject is informed that a person he does not know is generous, sociable, and popular, and is then asked to state whether he believes the respondent is good-natured or not, he would probably be able to make such a judgment. This type of judgment would be based on inference.

Theorists have suggested that the formation of inferential beliefs may be based either on evaluative consistency (Heider, 1958) or descriptive (probabilistic) consistency (Peabody, 1967). That is, a person known to be friendly might also be judged as sociable, either because the two traits have a common positive evaluation or because of their descriptive similarity with regard to interpersonal pleasantness. In an important study designed to investigate the relative importance of descriptive and evaluative similarity, Peabody (1967) orthogonally manipulated the evaluative and descriptive similarity of adjective pairs. The results of the study clearly indicated that, for American college students, inferences follow lines of descriptive similarity.

A number of cross-cultural studies have also investigated the process underlying inferential belief formation. Initial work in the area of stereotyping (e.g., Buchanan & Cantril, 1953) supported the notion of evaluative consistency. Berrien (1969a) summarized the hypothesizing of many stereotype researchers as follows: "It has generally been held that the characteristics ascribed to persons or groups we dislike are not those of which we approve; and conversely we tend to ascribe favorable characteristics to persons or groups we admire [p. 173]." More recently Peabody (1968), in a cross-cultural extension of his work just cited, once again demonstrated that if descriptive and evaluative similarity are separated, traits assigned to national groups are based to a greater extent on descriptive similarity. In summary, if the effects of evaluative and descriptive consistency are not separated, belief formation may appear to be based on evaluative similarity. However, if the effects are separated, descriptive similarity appears to play the predominant role in inferential belief formation for the cultural groups studied.

THE PROCESS OF INFORMATION UTILIZATION

The process of trait inference was the primary research concern of the reviewed studies of inferential belief formation. In a typical study, a hypothetical stimulus person would be described as possessing trait X, and the subject's task would be to indicate the probability that the stimulus person has trait Y. As Fishbein and Ajzen (1975) have noted, in studies of cue utilization the respondent faces a slightly different task. Both the information provided to the subject and the subject's response represent positions on different content dimensions. For example, a subject might be asked to judge a person's I.Q. from information about his grade point average, aptitude test scores, and number of hours studied per week. When more than one cue is provided, it becomes possible to examine the ways in which different cues are combined to arrive at the criterion judgment and to assess the relative importance of different cues. Studies of cue utilization in the United States (Slovic & Lichtenstein, 1971) have demonstrated that a person's inferences are generally predictable, with considerable accuracy, on the basis of a weighted linear combination of cues.

A good example of a cross-cultural investigation of cue utilization was reported by Cvetkovich and Lonner (1973). College students in West Germany, the Netherlands, India, and the United States made birth-planning decisions for 40 hypothetical family situations. The situations depicted eight familial characteristics (e.g., age of husband and wife, number of children in the family, health of wife, wife's working status) which could be generally descriptive of families in countries where there is monogamous marriage, where it is expected that the husband should be the major provider, and where it is expected that the wife should be primarily responsible for activities involving the home and children.

The respondents' task was to indicate whether they believed each family should have an additional child. The response was regressed against each of the family characteristics depicted. The median regression weights for each characteristic were quite similar across nations, indicating that the samples used similar guidelines in making decisions. In addition, for each national group, a weighted linear combination of the cues yielded a significant prediction of the subject's response.

A large number of cross-cultural studies of cue utilization have been conducted by Triandis and his associates (Triandis, 1963; Triandis, Davis, & Takezawa, 1965; Triandis, Tanaka, & Shanmugam, 1966; Triandis & Triandis, 1960; 1962; Triandis & Vassiliou, 1972). Most of these studies have investigated the effects of such cues as sex, religion, age, race, and occupation on social distance, using a factorial design for the presentation of all possible combinations of cues. For example, Triandis, Davis, and Takezawa (1965) studied the effects of information about race, occupation, religion, and nationality in Germany, the United States, and Japan. Scales of social distance were first independently standardized for each national group. Subjects then gave social distance ratings for hypothetical stimulus persons created from all possible combinations of all levels (two or three) of the above cues. The order of importance of each cue for determining social distance in each culture was as follows:

1. Japan: occupation, race, nationality, and religion
2. Germany: occupation, religion, race, and nationality
3. United States: race, occupation, religion, and nationality

Data from this study and similar studies by Triandis and Triandis (1960, 1962) suggest that the weights given to the four cues are also affected by the demographic characteristics of the subjects (e.g., social class, religion, ethnic background, sex).

It should be noted that this study stands as a good methodological example of many of the issues that we have previously discussed. First, the social distance scale was independently validated in each culture. Second, cultural differences were examined in terms of differences in the relationships among a number of variables. Third, the researchers, in addition to reporting global level (cultural) differences, attempted to determine the boundary conditions of the relationships found using individual level variables (e.g., sex, social class, religion).

The only weakness of the Triandis, Davis, and Takezawa (1965) study is the absence of a theory on which to base predictions of the relative importance of the four cues in each cultural group. However, based on prior subjective culture research Triandis and Vassiliou (1972) were able to make predictions concerning national differences in the relative importance of cues in influencing decisions. American and Greek managers were asked to make employee selection decisions based on information on four characteristics: objective evidence; interview impression; recommended by friend versus unknown person; and recommended by relative versus neighbor. Previous research (Triandis, Vassiliou, & Nassiakou, 1968) had found that Greeks are more sensitive than Americans to whether the person with whom they are interacting is a member of their in-group or not. They also have a narrower definition of the in-group. Hence, Triandis and Vassiliou were able to accurately predict that Greeks would give more weight to the opinions of close friends and relatives than would Americans.

While this programmatic research effort has indicated cultural differences in terms of the importance of different cues in the judgment process, it has also demonstrated many similarities. The most important may be that, although there is clearly some evidence for nonlinear combinations of cues (i.e., interaction effects), most of the variance in judgment can be accounted for by a linear combination (i.e., main effects) rule.

In summary, cross-cultural research on cue utilization suggests that an individuals' inferences are derived in a consistent and predictable manner from the information available to them. Regardless of methodological approach or content area, integration of diverse items of information is found to be well approximated by a weighted linear model. However, all of the studies cited used subjects of relatively high socioeconomic status (e.g., college students, managers). It remains to be demonstrated that these findings hold for groups of lower socioeconomic status.

Determinants of Social Distance and Interpersonal Attraction

Unlike much of the research just reviewed, which suggested that attitudes toward a stimulus are based on information about that stimulus, research on interpersonal attraction has dealt primarily with the noninformational bases of attraction. Of greatest importance is the work which has focused on similarity as a determinant of attraction. Byrne (1971) has developed a model of interpersonal attraction based on the hypothesis that the more similar another person's opinions, interests, or personality characteristics are to those of a perceiver, the more the perceiver will come to like the person. Rokeach (1960) has developed a somewhat similar model based on balance theories of interpersonal attraction (Heider, 1958). He has hypothesized that the primary determinant of social distance is the degree of perceived similarity of belief between the respondent and the stimulus person. The predictions of both Rokeach and Byrne have been supported by data from the United States.

A number of cross-cultural studies have also produced data relevant to these hypotheses. Brislin (1971) investigated friendship choices among members of nine cultural groups attending the University of Guam. Predictions about the amount of interaction were based on objective similarities (language, place of origin, and governmental unit) between specific cultural groups. The amount of interaction was assessed both through sociometric ratings and an unobtrusive measure of seating patterns. Consistent with the hypotheses, interpersonal attraction and the frequency of interaction between groups could be predicted from information on group similarities.

Byrne, Gouaux, Griffitt, Lamberth, Murakawa, Prasad, Prasad, and Ramirez (1971) have conducted laboratory experiments on the relationship between belief similarity and attraction using college students from five countries. In strong support of the model, for each national group, attraction toward a stranger was found to be a linear function of the proportion of similar beliefs expressed by the stranger. Although there was a main effect for culture on the mean level of attraction, culture did not interact with the similarity effect.

Brewer (1968) compared the utility of the predictions from a number of theories—including Rokeach's similarity theory—in accounting for the social distance between 30 East African tribes. In support of Rokeach's theory, perceived similarity accounted for the greatest proportion of nonerror variance in social distance. Further evidence for the similarity–liking relationship can be found in studies by Buchanan and Cantril (1953), Lambert, Anisfeld, and Yeni-Komshian (1965), and Tajfel, Johoda, Nemeth, Campbell, and Johnson (1970).

Ajzen (1974) has presented evidence indicating that attraction is related to similarity because of the empirical association between similarity and evaluation. Ajzen separated the effects of similarity and evaluation in an orthogonal design and reported that, whereas evaluation had a significant effect on attraction, similarity did not. Support for Ajzen's view can also be found in the cross-cultural literature. There is evidence, for example, of the empirical association between similarity ratings of traits and evaluative ratings of traits (Berrien, 1969b; Buchanan & Cantril, 1953; Lambert, Anisfeld, & Yeni-Komshian, 1965). In addition, there is evidence that subjects who negatively evaluate their own traits have a greater degree of liking for dissimilar than similar others. For example, Tajfel, Jahoda, Nemeth, Rim, and Johnson (1972) demonstrated that Israeli children of Oriental origin preferred photos of Israelis of European origin over those of Israelis of Oriental origin. Similarly, Scottish children between the ages of 9 and 11 preferred photos of men they believed to be English over photos of men they believed to be Scottish.

In conclusion, there can be little doubt concerning the empirical association between similarity and attraction or social distance. However, the basis of this relationship is still unclear. From evidence presented in this and the preceding portions of this section, it appears that interpersonal attraction and social distance are a function of the evaluation of the attributes that one associates with the other person or group.

The Structure of Affective Meaning

Osgood and his colleagues (Osgood, 1977; Osgood, May, & Miron, 1975) are currently directing the most extensive cross-culture study of attitudes to date. Their effort has focused on the development of a measurement procedure, the semantic differential. The technique was developed not for the purpose of assessing attitudes, but rather as an instrument for the measurement of meaning. These researchers have theorized that the meaning of an object is its location in a space defined by some number of dimensions, and an attitude toward an object is its projection onto one of these dimensions defined as evaluative. Their initial studies with English-speaking Americans—suggested the existence of three dimensions of connotative meaning—evaluation (E) (good–bad); potency (P) (big–little); and activity (A) (fast–slow). The aims of their cross-cultural project were

1. To test the cross-cultural generality of E, P and A as dimensions of connotative meaning; if such generality can be demonstrated;
2. To construct comparable instruments (semantic differentials) for measuring the dimensions of affective meaning in diverse cultures; and
3. To utilize these instruments in the comparative study of the affective aspects of subjective cultures around the world.

The researchers have made considerable progress in realizing their aims. They have demonstrated the generality of E, P, and A for 21 language or culture communities, constructed comparable semantic differentials for measuring aspects of subjective culture in each community, and utilized these instruments in measuring 620 diverse concepts in the 21 communities. When the final data are completely analyzed they will comprise a world atlas of affective meaning.

As the researchers have carefully developed emic measures for the etic dimensions of *E, P,* and *A,* and since the items comprising the evaluative factor are coming to be the most widely used measure of attitude, their methodology merits special attention. The respondents in each culture were male, monolingual, high school students. They were asked to give the first qualifier (adjective) that occurred to them for each of 100 familiar concepts. The 10,000 responses obtained for each culture were then analyzed in terms of frequency and diversity of usage across the 100 concepts. Those qualifiers which were (*a*) most frequently mentioned, (*b*) highly diverse, and (*c*) relatively independent of each other in their use, were utilized in the construction of semantic differential scales.

A second sample of 200 respondents then rated 100 concepts against 50 such scales; subgroups of 20 respondents each rated a subset of 10 concepts because the task is so time consuming. Within each culture, the mean ratings of the 20 subjects on each scale for each concept were calculated and the scales were then correlated across the 100 concepts. This correlation matrix was submitted to principal components factor analysis, with an orthogonal varimax rotation if the unrotated solution was semantically obscure. Comparisons of the factor structures revealed considerable similarity. In all of the cultures an evaluative factor was present and dominant, and a dynamism factor (i.e., combination of potency and activity) was also observed.

Additional support for the generality of *E, P,* and *A* was obtained from a pancultural factor analysis of the same data set. In this analysis, the mean on each scale, in each culture, and for each concept was computed. The scales were then correlated across the 100 concepts and this matrix was submitted to a principal components factor analysis. The first three factors are clearly recognized as *E, P,* and *A,* and every culture contributed to the definition of these dimensions. The results provide a preview of the overall pattern of findings that can be expected from the world atlas. As the items from all cultures were correlated across concepts, the finding that scales from each culture contributed to *E, P,* and *A* indicates that the concepts mean about the same thing in each culture. That is, the pancultural analysis strongly suggests that a concept that is good, potent, and active in one culture will tend to be good, potent, and active in other cultures. Thus, when the world atlas is completed we can expect to find a general pattern of cross-cultural similarity.

The above studies demonstrate that language, race and nationality do not serve as boundary conditions for the generality of *E, P,* and *A.* Research by Suci (1960) and Schensul (1969) suggest that literacy also is not a boundary condition. Suci studied several Southwest Indian cultures (Hopi, Navajo, Hopi–Tewa) and obtained a pattern of factors quite similar to *E, P,* and *A.* Interviewing rural respondents in Uganda and Northern Minnesota, Schensul also found major similarities between groups in their use of semantic space.

Using a methodological approach similar to that of Osgood, Triandis and his colleagues (Triandis, 1977a) have developed a behavioral differential. Triandis, Vassiliou, and Nassiakou (1968) independently elicited several thousand behaviors in Greece and the United States. Facet analysis was then employed to obtain a small ($N = 60$), maximally heterogeneous sample of behaviors for each group. Factor analyses yielded four etic dimensions (association–dissociation, superordination–subordination, intimacy–formality, and hostility) and a number of emic factors. Osgood (1970) employed a logical analysis of interpersonal intentions and obtained similar etic factors. Additional studies (Triandis *et al.*, 1972a), which obtained data from respondents in five very different cultures, support the existence of these four etic factors.

Attitudes and Behavior

Werner (1977) has recently provided a cogent analysis of much of the cross-cultural work investigating the relationship between attitudes and behavior. His review indicates that most studies do not find a strong correlation between attitudes and behavior. However, this finding is frequently attributable to a discrepancy in the level of specificity between attitude and behavior measures. For example, a researcher might attempt to predict the use or nonuse of a specific contraceptive from more general attitudes toward family planning. Lack of success in such studies is not surprising, for as the degree of specificity between attitudinal and behavioral variables decreases so too does the statistical relationship between the two (Davidson & Jaccard, 1975). When the attitude measure focuses on a specific action predisposition, a reasonable correlation with behavior is generally obtained. In support of this perspective, Freedman, Hermalin, and Chang (1975) found that statements about wanting more children proved to be highly predictive of subsequent fertility for both modern and less advanced segments of the Taiwanese population. Similarly, Kar (1978) found that attitudes toward personal use of available contraceptives were strongly related to the actual use of these contraceptives.

Triandis (1977a) has recently proposed an explicit theoretical model for the prediction of behavior and behavioral intentions from attitudinal and normative beliefs. Davidson *et al.* (1976) have examined the utility of this model for predicting behavioral intentions among samples of both high and low socioeconomic status, from Mexico and the United States. The model states that the intention to perform a behavior is determined by four components: (*a*) affect toward performing the act; (*b*) beliefs about the consequences of performing the behavior and the evaluation of those consequences; (*c*) the perceived appropriateness of the behavior for the subject's reference group (norms) and persons holding similar positions in the social structure (roles); and (*d*) personal normative beliefs with regard to the behavior of interest. The measures for the components were independently constructed within each cultural group (e.g., the salient consequences of performing the behavior were separately elicited for each group).

The model had substantial predictive utility in both countries and at all levels of socioeconomic status. Once this cross-cultural similarity was established it was possible to investigate cultural differences. The relative influence of the components in predicting intentions varied as a function of the cultural group studied. Specifically, in the Mexican and American upper-middle class samples, affect toward the behavior was of greatest importance and in the Mexican lower class sample, personal normative beliefs about the appropriateness of the behavior were most important.

Summary and Conclusions

The analysis of the literature on cross-cultural studies of beliefs and attitudes leads to the following conclusions:

1. Major differences in attitude and belief content exist among cultures.
2. Researchers who are aware of such differences appear to take one of two general approaches to the cross-cultural study of attitudes:
   (*a*) Focus on cultural differences in beliefs and attitudes and look for subsets of cultures within which there is maximal similarity in terms of attitudes and between which there is maximal heterogeneity (the cultural differences approach); or
   (*b*) Look past content differences in beliefs and attitudes and attempt to identify cross-cultural similarities in either belief or attitude *structure* or in the *processes* whereby beliefs combine to form attitudes (the cultural similarities approach).
3. For those taking the cultural differences approach, the primary reason for doing comparative research is to study the effects of global level variables (e.g., climate, sociocultural system) on attitudes and beliefs. For those taking the cultural similarities approach, the primary reason to obtain cross-cultural data is to establish the boundary conditions for attitudinal models and theories.
4. Although the investigation of the effects of global level variables on attitudes is a more easily conceptualized form of cross-cultural study, it introduces sampling (cultures, not individuals, are the sampling units) and equivalence of measurement problems as both functional and score equivalence are required. Such problems are more difficult to solve than are those inherent in the type of research that tests the generality of psychological theories.
5. Three models of attitude formation have been tested cross-culturally—the summation, averaging, and congruity models. Each model has

received considerable support. The data tend to indicate that the predictions from the summation model and the averaging model are more highly correlated with observed attitudes than are the predictions from the congruity model. For the populations and topics reviewed, there appear to be no culturally determined boundary conditions modifying the models of attitude formation.

6. The relative importance of evaluative consistency and descriptive (probabilistic) consistency in determining the formation of inferential beliefs has been investigated in a few cross-cultural studies. The evidence suggests that if the effects of evaluative and descriptive consistency are not separated, belief formation may appear to be based on evaluative similarity. However, if the effects are separated, descriptive similarity appears to play the predominant role in inferential belief formation.

7. Cross-cultural studies on cue utilization suggest that an individual's inferences are derived in a consistent and predictable manner from the available information. Regardless of culture, methodological approach, or content area, integration of diverse items of information is found to be well approximated by a weighted linear nodel. However, all of the studies cited used subjects of relatively high socioeconomic status.

8. Cross-culturally, there is an empirical association between similarity and both attraction and social distance. However, the basis of this relationship is still unclear.

9. There is considerable support for the cross-cultural generality of a basic set of dimensions of attitude and belief structure.

In summary, on the basis of the topics and samples studied to date, nationality, language, and race do not appear to serve as boundary conditions for contemporary theories of attitude formation and attitude structure.

References

Ajzen, I. Effects of information on interpersonal attraction: Similarity versus affective value. *Journal of Personality and Social Psychology,* 1974, *29,* 374–380.

Anderson, L. R., & Fishbein, M. Prediction of attitude from the number, strength, and evaluative aspects of beliefs about the attitude object: A comparison of summation and congruity theories. *Journal of Personality and Social Psychology,* 1965, *2,* 437–443.

Anderson, N. H. Averaging versus adding as a stimulus-combination rule in impression formation. *Journal of Experimental Psychology,* 1965, *70,* 394–400.

Anderson, N. H. Integration theory and attitude change. *Psychological Review,* 1971, *78,* 171–206.

Barry, H. III., Child, I. L., & Bacon, M. Relation of child training to subsistence economy. *American Anthropologist,* 1959, *61,* 51–63.

Berrien, F. K. Methodological and related problems in cross-cultural research. *International Journal of Psychology,* 1967, *2,* 33–43.

Berrien, F. K. Familiarity, mirror imaging and social desirability in stereotypes: Japanese versus American. *International Journal of Psychology,* 1969, *4,* 207–215. (a)

Berrien, F. K. Stereotype similarities and contrasts. *Journal of Social Psychology,* 1969, *78,* 173–183. (b)

Brewer, M. B. Determinants of social distance among East African tribal groups. *Journal of Personality and Social Psychology,* 1968, *10,* 279–289.

Brewer, M. B., & Campbell, D. *Ethnocentrism and inter-group attitudes: East African evidence.* New York: John Wiley–Halstead, 1976.

Brislin, R. W. Interaction among members of nine ethnic groups and belief-similarity hypothesis. *Journal of Social Psychology,* 1971, *85,* 171–179.

Brislin, R. W. Comparative research methodology. *International Journal of Psychology,* 1976, *11,* 215–229.

Buchanan, W., & Cantril, H. *How nations see each other: A study in public opinion.* Urbana, Illinois: Univ. of Illinois Press, 1953.

Byrne, D. *The attraction paradigm.* New York: Academic Press, 1971.

Byrne, D., Gouaux, C., Griffitt, W., Lamberth, J., Murakawa, N., Prasad, M., Prasad, A., & Ramirez, G. III. The ubiquitous relationship: Attitude similarity and attraction. *Human Relations,* 1971, *24,* 201–207.

Campbell, D. T. Distinguishing differences of perception from failure of communication in cross-cultural studies. In *Cross-cultural understandings: Epistemology in anthropology,* F. Northrup & H. Livingston (Eds.), New York: Harper, 1964. Pp. 308–336.

Cole, M., & Bruner, J. S. Cultural differences and inferences about psychological processes. *American Psychologist,* 1971, *26,* 867–876.

Cole, M., Gay, J., Glick, J., & Sharp, D. *The cultural context of learning and thinking: An exploration in experimental anthropology.* New York: Basic Books, 1971.

Cvetkovich, G., & Lonner, W. A transnational comparison of individual birth planning decisions for hypothetical families. *Journal of Cross-Cultural Psychology,* 1973, *4,* 470–480.

Davidson, A. R. The etic–emic dilemma: Can methodology provide a solution in the absence of theory? In Y. H. Poortinga (Ed.), *Basic problems in cross-cultural psychology.* Amsterdam: Swets & Zeitlinger, 1977.

Davidson, A. R., & Jaccard, J. J. Population psychology: A new look at an old problem. *Journal of Personality and Social Psychology,* 1975, *31,* 1073–1082.

Davidson, A. R., & Thomson, E. Cross-cultural studies of attitudes and beliefs. In H. Triandis & R. Brislin (Ed.), *The handbook of cross-cultural psychology* (Volume V). Rockleigh, New Jersey: Allyn & Bacon, 1979.

Davidson, A. R., Jaccard, J. J., Triandis, H., Morales, M., & Diaz-Guerrero, R. Cross-cultural model testing: Toward a solution of the etic–emic dilemma. *International Journal of Psychology,* 1976, *11,* 1–13.

Doob, L. W. The behavior of attitudes. *Psychological Review,* 1947, *54,* 135–156.

Easterlin, R. Does money buy happiness? *The Public Interest,* 1973, *30,* 3–10.

Fawcett, J. T., Arnold, F., Bulatao, R. A., Buripakdi, C., Chung, B. J., Iritani, T., Lee, S. J., & Wu, T. *The value of children in Asia and the United States: Comparative perspectives,* Paper of the East–West Population Institute, Honolulu, Hawaii, No. 32, 1974.

Fishbein, M., & Ajzen, I. *Belief, attitude, intention and behavior.* Reading, Massachusetts: Addison-Wesley, 1975.

Freedman, R., Hermalin, A., & Chang, M. Do statements about desired family size predict fertility? The case of Taiwan, 1967–1970. *Demography,* 1975, *12,* 407–416.

Gallup, G. Americans rate life quality highest. *The Washington Post,* November 7, 1976, p. A–8.

Heider, F. *The psychology of interpersonal relations.* New York: Wiley, 1958.

Jahoda, G. Psychology and social change in developing countries, *Proceedings of the 16th International Congress of Applied Psychology,* Amsterdam: Swets & Zeilinger, 1969.

Jakobovits, L. A. Comparative psycholinguistics in the study of cultures. *International Journal of Psychology*, 1966, *1*, 15–37.

Kar, S. Consistency between fertility attitudes and behavior: A conceptual model. *Population Studies*, 1978, *32*, 173–185.

Lambert, W. E., Anisfeld, M., & Yeni-Komshian, G. Evaluational reactions of Jewish and Arab adolescents to dialect and language variations. *Journal of Personality and Social Psychology*, 1965, *2*, 84–90.

Malpass, R. Theory and method in cross-cultural psychology. *American Psychologist*, 1977, *32*, 1069–1079.

Murdock, G. P. World ethnographic sample. *American Anthropologist*, 1957, *59*, 664–687.

Osgood, C. E. Speculation on the structure of interpersonal intentions. *Behavioral Science*, 1970, *15*, 237–254.

Osgood, C. E. Objective cross-national indicators of subjective culture. In Y. H. Poortinga (Ed.), *Basic problems in cross-cultural psychology*. Amsterdam: Swets & Zeitlinger, 1977.

Osgood, C. E., May, W. H., & Miron, M. S. *Cross-cultural universals of affective meaning.* Urbana, Illinois: Univ. of Illinois Press, 1975.

Osgood, C. E., Suci, G. J., & Tannenbaum, P. *The Measurement of Meaning.* Urbana, Illinois: Univ. of Illinois Press, 1957.

Peabody, D. Trait inferences: Evaluative and descriptive aspects. *Journal of Personality and Social Psychology*, 1967, Monograph 7(Whole No. 644).

Peabody, D. Group judgments in the Philippines: Evaluative and descriptive aspects. *Journal of Personality and Social Psychology*, 1968, *10*, 290–300.

Pike, K. L. *Language in relation to a unified theory of human behavior.* The Hague: Mouton, 1966.

Poortinga, Y. H. Limitations on intercultural comparison of psychological data. *Nederlands Tijdschrift van de Psychologie*, 1975, *30*, 23–39.

Rokeach, M. *The open and closed mind.* New York: Basic Books, 1960.

Rosenzweig, M. R. Comparison among word associations with responses in English, French, German and Italian. *American Journal of Psychology*, 1961, *74*, 347–360.

Schaffer, M., Sundberg, N., & Tyler, L. Content differences on word listing by American, Dutch and Indian adolescents. *Journal of Social Psychology*, 1969, *79*, 139–140.

Schensul, S. *Marginal rural peoples: Behavior and cognitive models among Northern Minnesotans and Western Ugandans.* Unpublished doctoral dissertation, Univ. Minnesota, 1969.

Slovic, P., & Lichtenstein, S. Comparison of Bayesian and regression approaches to the study of information processing in judgment. *Organization Behavior and Human Behavior*, 1971, *6*, 649–744.

Strodtbeck, F. L. Considerations of meta-method in cross-cultural studies. *American Anthropologist*, 1964, *66*, 223–229.

Suci, G. A comparison of semantic structures in American Southwest culture groups. *Journal of Abnormal and Social Psychology*, 1960, *61*, 25–30.

Szalay, L. B., & Bryson, J. A. Measurement of psychocultural distance: A comparison of American Blacks and Whites. *Journal of Personality and Social Psychology*, 1973, *26*, 166–177.

Szalay, L. B., & Lysne, D. A. Attitude research for inter-cultural communication and interaction. *The Journal of Communication*, 1970, *20*, 180–200.

Szalay, L. B., Windle, C., & Lysne, D. A. Attitude measurement by free verbal associations. *The Journal of Social Psychology*, 1970, *82*, 43–55.

Tajfel, H., Jahoda, G., Nemeth, C., Campbell, J. D., & Johnson, N. The development of children's preference for their own country: A cross-national study. *International Journal of Psychology*, 1970, *4*, 245–253.

Tajfel, H., Jahoda, G., Nemeth, C., Rim, Y., & Johnson, N. The devaluation by children of their own national and ethnic group: Two case studies. *Journal of Social and Clinical Psychology*, 1972, *11*, 235–243.

Tanaka, Y. A study of national stereotypes. In H. Triandis (Ed.), *The analysis of subjective culture*. New York: Wiley, 1972. Pp. 117–180.

Thurstone, L. L. Attitudes can be measured. *American Journal of Sociology*, 1928, *33*, 529–554.

Triandis, H. C. Factors affecting employee selection in two cultures. *Journal of Applied Psychology*, 1963, *47*, 89–96.

Triandis, H. C. *Interpersonal behavior*. Monterey, California: Brooks–Cole, 1977. (a)

Triandis, H. C. Some universals of social behavior. *Personality and Social Psychology Bulletin*, 1977, *4*, 1–16. (b)

Triandis, H. C., & Fishbein, M. Cognitive interaction in person perception. *Journal of Abnormal and Social Psychology*, 1963, *67*, 446–453.

Triandis, H. C., & Triandis, L. Race, social class, religion and nationality as determinants of social distance. *Journal of Abnormal and Social Psychology*, 1960, *61*, 110–118.

Triandis, H. C., & Triandis, L. M. A cross-cultural study of social distance. *Psychological Monographs*, 1962, *76*, 1–21.

Triandis, H. C., & Vassiliou, V. Interpersonal influence and employee selection in two cultures. *Journal of Applied Psychology*, 1972, *56*, 140–145.

Triandis, H. C., Davis, E. E., & Takezawa, S. Some determinants of social distance among American, German, and Japanese students. *Journal of Personality and Social Psychology*, 1965, *2*, 540–551.

Triandis, H. C., Kilty, K., Shanmugam, A. V., Tanaka, Y., & Vassiliou, V. A cross-cultural study of role perceptions. In H. Triandis (Ed.), *Analysis of subjective culture*. New York: Wiley, 1972. Pp. 263–298. (a)

Triandis, H. C., Kilty, K., Shanmugam, A. V., Tanaka, Y., & Vassiliou, V. Cognitive structure and the analysis of values. In H. Triandis (Ed.), *Analysis of subjective culture*. New York: Wiley, 1972. Pp. 181–262. (b)

Triandis, H. C. Malpass, R. S., & Davidson, A. R. Psychology and culture. In P. Mussen & M. Rosenzweig (Eds.), *Annual Review of Psychology* (Vol. 24). Palo Alto, California: Annual Reviews, 1973. Pp. 355–378.

Triandis, H. C., Tanaka, Y., & Shanmugam, A. Interpersonal attitudes among American, Indian and Japanese students. *International Journal of Psychology*, 1966, *1*, 177–206.

Triandis, H. C., Vassiliou, V., & Nassiakou, M. Three cross-cultural studies of subjective cultures. *Journal of Personality and Social Psychology*, 1968, Monograph supplement 8, 1–42.

Werner, P. Application of attitude-behavior studies for population research and action. *Studies in Family Planning*, 1977, *11*, 294–299.

Whiting, B. The problem of the packaged variable. In K. Riegel & J. Meacham (Eds.), *The developing individual in a changing world*. The Hague: Mouton, 1976.

Willer, D. *Scientific sociology: Theory and method*. Englewood Cliffs, New Jersey: Prentice-Hall, 1967.

Witkin, H., & Berry, J. Psychological differentiation in cross-cultural perspective. *Journal of Cross-Cultural Psychology*, 1975, *6*, 4–87.

8

Culture and Emotion

JERRY D. BOUCHER

Introduction

Recently I was talking with a friend—a person whose work in emotion I greatly respect. He announced to me that in his most recent manuscript he had offered a definition of emotion. I recall that my reaction was one of surprise, delight, and probably a bit of envy. Surprise, because he would attempt such a formidable task; delight, because at last I could see in print his particular definition; and envy, because I wished I could write my own definition. I am reminded of this incident while preparing the present chapter because I find myself wanting to begin with a definition of the topic, but being in the rather ludicrous position of not being able to do so. How is it that my eminent friend, and myself with pretentions to knowing something about the area, are so challenged by the apparently elementary task of defining the subject matter of our research? The answer to that question is essentially a summation of the state of the art of studies of emotion—we are looking for a definition.

Let us back away from this case of two scientists groping for precision in their studies and look at what the rest of the world thinks. We all know what the experience of emotion is—we have all been happy and sad, we have all felt anger and disgust, and we all know what it means to be surprised and afraid. Furthermore, the Malay knows what it means to feel *marah,* the

159

Spaniard knows *miedo,* the German feels *traurig,* and the second phrase learned by an American in Paris is *"je t'aime"* (the first phrase is *"la plume de ma tante est sur la table de mon oncle"*). Not only do we all know what the experience of emotion is, but, if we stop to think a minute, we will realize that emotion plays an enormously important role in our lives.

Just as emotion is one of the most important aspects of our everyday lives, emotion has been one of the most intriguing topics of research and discussion for social scientists. Long before the attempts to systematically study behavior and thought that led to the inception of psychology as a scientific discipline, philosophers, writers, and physicians were attempting to explain our emotional feelings and behaviors (Boring, 1950). For example, Bell (1847) and Duchenne (1862) performed physiological studies of facial expression that are still being cited, and Darwin (1872) proposed an explanation of the biological basis for the facial expression of emotion that is having a strong effect upon today's thinking about the interplay of culture and biology in affective experience (Ekman, 1973). Although the largest amount of empirical research on emotion is being performed by psychologists, emotion is a primary topic of consideration for philosophers such as Sartre (1948) and Tillman (1967), anthropologists such as LaBarre (1947) and Birdwhistell (1970), and probably every psychiatrist since Freud.

Lest we conclude from the above list of scholars that emotion is a concept growing out of Western philosophical tradition, we should note early in this chapter that one of the earliest (if not *the* earliest) systematic schemes for relating behavior and emotion is *rasa* in the Sanskrit texts of ancient India. DeSilva (1976), a philosopher in Sri Lanka, has written about the role of emotion in Buddhist philosophy in terms that would not be at all unfamiliar to the Western reader. Additionally, the anthropologist David Y. H. Wu has told me (personal communication) of his classical education in China that included learning an elaborate system of relationships between various emotions. He believes that this system is probably derived from the *rasa* system just mentioned.

Beyond the interest shown in human emotional behavior by people in different cultures and scholars in different disciplines, we also find an increasing interest in what appears to be emotional behavior in other animal species. Starting with Darwin's (1872) notion that human emotional behavior is evolved from the "serviceable habits" of lower primates, there is a continuous stream of research in the physiological and ethological disciplines concerned with such topics as the cortical activity of primates showing emotional behavior (e.g., Delgado, 1963), similarities of primate and human facial expression of emotion (e.g., van Hooff, 1972), and the role of emotional behavior in the social organization of primate groups (e.g., van Lawick-Goodall, 1968).

In addition to all of these studies focusing on emotion itself, there is an enormous body of literature on emotion-related studies—studies which focus upon the way in which emotions influence our lives. Within the fields of linguistics and psycholinguistics there is a major emphasis upon affective connotation and the emotional content of language. For example, Osgood and his colleagues (e.g., Osgood, Suci, & Tannenbaum, 1957) have engaged in extensive cross-cultural research on affective meaning, utilizing a semantic differential technique. Numerous books have been written on the place of emotion in music, painting, and literature. And finally, a large proportion of the writing in psychiatry and clinical psychology is concerned with emotional disorder. Although all of these topics are interesting and important, I will limit this chapter to a discussion of those topics that directly address the experience of emotion. That is, we will be looking at the question of what emotion is, rather than what emotion does.

All of this varied interest in the phenomena of emotion is an indication of just how important emotion is in our lives. Unfortunately, and perhaps ironically, it is also an indication of just how much disagreement there is among the many scholars engaged in the study of emotion. One can feel both hope and despair when considering the fact that a hundred years of work by thousands of scholars after Darwin's book have taken many of us back to a reconsideration of his original theory. The source of this disagreement in the field is due, in large part, to the very fact that so many diverse people and disciplines see emotion as a legitimate topic for consideration. Most of the disagreements about the nature of emotion occur along disciplinary lines and are caused by disagreements about what constitutes an adequate method of study, which kinds of data are admissible as evidence, what is the proper unit of analysis, and just plain misunderstanding due to a babel of jargons. For the same reasons, there are disagreements among orthodoxies that cut across disciplines that are even more serious than the interdisciplinary differences.

For example, one of the issues we will be examining is the question of universal versus culture-specific facial expressions—one of the key problems in today's research. This issue is a classic case of where discipline and orthodoxy have intruded to such an extent that two quite distinct camps have formed—apparently because one group refuses to acknowledge the other group's contention that what can be said about gestures and paralinguistic behavior is not necessarily what can be said about facial expression of emotion. Both groups contend that gestures are culturally learned, but by not distinguishing facial expression, the first group precludes any consideration that there may be universal or pancultural commonalities of emotion expression.

THE PLACE OF EMOTION STUDIES IN CROSS-CULTURAL PSYCHOLOGY

The problem that any division such as cross-cultural psychology faces is that it cuts across other divisions, such as personality, social psychology, and subdivisions like emotion studies. In the present case, it is obvious that the study of emotion is not limited to cross-cultural psychologists, and it may be of limited utility to try to separate off those issues of emotion which are of specific interest to the cross-cultural researcher. On the other hand, the cross-cultural issues are of extreme importance to the more general emotion theorists. To ignore the cultural issues would be folly, and indeed, serious consideration of emotion by researchers trained in cross-cultural methodology would be of great benefit in our search for a theory. One goal of the present chapter is to attempt to put the field of emotion study in a perspective that will allow the person whose primary concerns are cross-cultural to make a contribution to the study of emotion.

One of the more important questions to be answered in the study of emotion is the classic "What is learned, what is biological?" Before we go any further, let us reaffirm that we are not playing a zero-sum game. More properly stated, the question should be "What are the relative contributions of learning and biology?", and, in the context of cross-cultural studies, learning implies learning as a function of cultural membership. At this point in the history of emotion studies the evidence is just overwhelming that *something* is going on in the biological domain of the individual experiencing emotion, and thus the most counterproductive course we could take is to continue the "either/or," "nature–nurture" dichotomy.

The difficulty in pursuing this question is, however, the same problem that always seems to plague the social scientist who postulates some biological substrate to behavior: Our knowledge of the biology is not sufficient to give a definitive resolution to the issue, and we often fall back on the exclusionary stance of saying that because we cannot demonstrate learning, we must assume biology. That argument is not sufficient, of course, but may be one we will have to live with for the time being. Furthermore, this argument can be strengthened—here is where the cross-cultural study becomes important—by demonstrating that certain affective phenomena occur in similar ways under dissimilar cultural conditions. If we can go yet a step farther and demonstrate that it is exceedingly unlikely that the phenomena was transmitted across the cultural boundaries, our case is even stronger. By means of careful methodology, we can push this process until it becomes clear that the most parsimonious explanation involves biology. But again, this does not prove the point—only a physiological study can do that.

We need not feel too uncomfortable with this course of action, if we are willing to suspend our commitment to pure orthodoxy. The logic involved is essentially the same as that governing behaviorism—the predominant orthodoxy of twentieth-century psychology—with the variables reversed: Behaviorism in its strict form would have us assume learning until biology is demonstrated. If emotion is a function of both learning and biology, both approaches should bring us to the same end point. However, and I repeat myself because I think it is so important, to the extent that we enter the game with a strong conviction that it is biology *or* learning, our reaching an end point will be delayed.

Although the question of biology and learning may be one of the most important issues in the study of emotion, particularly to the cross-cultural researcher, it is a question of the highest theoretical plane and there is much work to be done that can be pursued without directly addressing this question. Furthermore, one can go a long way in studying the cross-cultural nature of emotion without taking a firm stand on the issue. The decision facing the researcher is to what extent the researcher feels comfortable in studying and reporting observations without using such terms as "cultural learning," "universal," "culture specific." The researcher who works in this mode can then be of best service to the theoreticians by adding "attitude toward learning and biology" to the usual list of biases to be recognized.

The fact that emotion is such an important element of people's lives points to a very rich area of research available on the more applied end of the research continuum. Although I am a firm believer in the Lewinian notion that "nothing is as practical as a good theory," the paucity of available studies of emotion in the cultural domain suggests that a high rate of practical return could be yielded from an investment in studies such as replication of American-based research in other cultures. For example, since a large component of psychiatric practice is based upon affect perception, within-culture studies of affect manifestation could open large areas of proper utilization of existing intervention techniques that cannot be applied at present.

Emotion, Culture, and Nonverbal Behavior

During the last 100 years or so, the vast majority of the studies of emotion have involved study of facial expression and other nonverbal behaviors. This fact will be reflected in the large representation of nonverbal studies in this chapter. There are several reasons for this situation. First, the most reliable indication that a person is experiencing an emotion is the presence of certain facial expressions, even though the validity of this indication has been seriously questioned. Second, the shift away from introspection and toward observation of behavior as the acceptable mode of study for the psychologist, left little more than verbal and nonverbal behavior for the researcher to observe. Third, for a large part of this period the tools necessary for any definitive physiological research were not available. Fourth, some researchers concerned with studies of emotion considered the nonverbal element—primarily facial expression—to be so inextricably linked to the experience of emotion that the study of emotion *meant* the study of nonverbal behavior. And fifth, some studies that focused on nonverbal and verbal behavior, although they were not designed as studies of emotion per se, still became part of that literature.

SOME PROBLEMS OF TERMINOLOGY

The fifth point mentioned earlier (i.e., that many of the studies of emotion behavior were performed as part of more general nonverbal studies) needs a bit of discussion. This situation has been, and continues to be, a source of much of the dissention among the ranks of those concerned with nonverbal behavior and emotion. This is particularly true as it applies to cross-cultural considerations (Ekman, 1977). The very term "nonverbal behavior" is so vague that perhaps we should banish it from our vocabularies: If we wished, all human behavior could be dichotomized into verbal and nonverbal behavior. The concern over this labeling does not appear to be trivial if we consider the many and different kinds of phenomena subsumed under that label. Facial expression of emotion, other facial behavior, hand and body movements, eye contact, interpersonal space, body position and posture, acting and dance movements, and vocal behavior (such as juncture, pause, and intonation) have all been classed as nonverbal behavior at one time or another. There is no denying that indeed these are all nonverbal behaviors, but then so are eating, breathing, and sleeping. There is nothing that holds these behaviors together as a distinct category. But the problem is that there is a strong tendency for people to try to make definitive statements about the class, if for no other reasons than because it *is* a class: It has to be, because it has a label. This goes beyond the case of comparing apples and oranges—it is more like two people defining fruit when one looks only at apples and the other at oranges.

Although there have been some attempts to clarify the issue, the problem is, if anything, getting worse because of the recent explosion of interest in "nonverbal behavior" in the popular press. In particular, the myriad forms of the "personal growth" movement seem to share an almost mystical belief in the power of nonverbal behavior as the key to everyone's problems. To the extent that the term continues to have different meaning to different people, there will continue to be disagreement on the theoretical points as the evidence from these points will come from different domains.

Ekman and Friesen (1967) proposed a system of five categories of nonverbal behavior that, if adopted by researchers in this area, would go a long way toward identifying what is what. Briefly, *emblems* are those body movements (primarily hand movements) that are codified within a culture as having a specific meaning, such as waving "hello," pointing to an object, and beckoning a person to "come here." *Illustrators* are those movements that draw a picture, such as when one attempts to define a spiral. *Regulators* are those behaviors that are used to control the flow of an interaction or pace a verbal exchange, such as a head nod to signal that the listener is listening.

Adaptors are those body movements the individual performs, such as grooming and scratching. Ekman (1977) has since discarded the term adaptors in favor of the more apt *body manipulators*. And *affect displays* or *facial expressions of emotion* refer to those facial behaviors that co-occur with the experience of emotion. Note that the term *gesture* does not occur in this list. All five categories contain behaviors that have been called gestures at different times, and thus the meaning of that term is so loose that it is useless. Most important, this scheme allows a precise separation of facial expression of emotion from all the other types of "nonverbal" behavior, a most advantageous distinction if we are to use evidence from the body behavior domain to further our understanding of emotion.

The situation is a bit more complicated, however. The body, or nonverbal, behavior that occurs during an experience of emotion is not limited to facial expression, and facial behavior may occur that is not linked to the emotion being experienced. For example, body manipulators are more frequent during stress (Ekman & Friesen, 1974), and to the extent that a facial expression is intentionally posed to convey a message, that facial behavior might be more properly labeled an illustrator or emblem. (This latter point will be expanded under the discussion of display rules to follow.) Thus, the researcher who defines the domain of interest as being *nonverbal behavior* will be considering some affective behaviors and a lot of other things. Whereas, the researcher who sees the domain of interest as being *emotion* will be considering some nonverbal behaviors and a lot of other things. Coming back around to where we started this discussion, the confusion in the field has often been because researchers have not taken sufficient notice of this distinction. In this chapter *nonverbal behavior* refers to Ekman's five categories, and *facial expression of emotion* is one of those categories.

CROSS-CULTURAL ISSUES IN THE STUDY OF
FACIAL EXPRESSION

There has recently been an increasing interest in the relationship between culture and the facial expression of emotion (Boucher, 1974a, 1974b; Ekman, 1973; Izard, 1971). The major issue addressed by the cross-cultural studies is the extent to which the facial behavior concomitant with the experience of emotion has cross-cultural generality or is culture specific. In turn, this issue has implications for the larger issue of the relationship of facial expression to the experience of emotion, and ultimately to the issue of whether or not there is a biological basis to emotion that includes facial expression.

The first cross-cultural study of facial expression of emotion was the work of Darwin (1872). Darwin made careful observations of facial affective behavior of people in different cultures, collected accounts of travelers who had observed such behavior in different countries, and also studied the facial behavior of dogs, cats, and other animals. Darwin concluded that there were universal facial expressions among humans, and similarities between human expression and the facial behavior of animals. Based upon his theory of evolution, he proposed that human facial expressions are innate and derived through evolution from the lower animals.

For almost a 100 years, Darwin's work was virtually ignored while the primary concern of the researchers focused upon whether there was even any relationship between the experience of emotion and facial expression. But, bit by bit, a literature on the cultural aspects of emotion began to accumulate and Darwin's work was rediscovered and then celebrated in Ekman's 1973 book.

Although few, if any, of today's researchers would be willing to commit themselves to full support of Darwin's position, a number of us think that the accumulated data do not conflict with Darwin's position, at least with regard to cross-cultural generality, or universality, of facial expression of emotion. There are also a few researchers who continue to argue that there is, in fact, no acceptable evidence for universality, but rather, that the evidence points to facial expression being a culture-specific phenomenon. Let us look at these two positions.

The Culture-Specific Position

The anthropologists LaBarre (1947) and Birdwhistell (1963) have been among the strongest supporters of a culture-specific position. Birdwhistell (1970) has been particularly strong in advocating a culture-specific view of body movement and facial behavior based upon the model and methodology of American structural linguistics (Duncan, 1969). Birdwhistell (1966) argued that both body motion and facial behavior can be studied as a system directly comparable to spoken languages and are therefore specific to a given culture. His system of microkinesic movements, analogous to structural levels of the English language (Birdwhistell, 1966), however, is vague about the basic communication unit in nonverbal behavior. Thus there is a definite breakdown of the analogy between a language structure and microkinesic movements (Weiner, Devoe, Rubinow, & Geller, 1972).

Birdwhistell (1970) argued, for example, that there was little consistency to the phenomenon of smiling, because he saw people smile not only in a pleasant environment but also in an adverse one. Birdwhistell concluded "There are no body motions, facial expressions, or gestures which provoke *identical* responses the world over. . . . A 'smile' in one society portrays friendliness, in another embarassment, and, in still another, may contain a warning that, unless tension is reduced, hostility and attack will follow [1970, p. 34]."

I, too, have seen the smile used to communicate many different messages in many different cultural environments. But as Ekman (1977) points out, the facial behaviors that accompany emotion may be incorporated within a culture's scheme to serve a number of communicative purposes. That does *not* mean that the configuration of facial muscles that constitute a smile is not the same behavior that accompanies the emotion of happiness in many or all cultures. Because we observe that people *dance* differently in different cultures should we therefore argue that *walking* is a culture-specific behavior?

Margaret Mead (1975) came out in favor of the culture-specific position. In her review of Ekman's (1973) research, she concludes that all Ekman has demonstrated is that members of different cultures can be persuaded to produce mutually intelligible simulations. Ekman (1977) replies, however, that Mead ignored one of the most important studies he reported in the same book. Briefly, Japanese subjects produced the same behaviors in the same conditions as American subjects, while both sets of subjects thought they were alone and unobserved.

Although the ethnographic approach provides interesting accounts of facial behavior in different social settings, the investigators utilizing this approach have often failed to distinguish nonverbal behavior of emotion from other forms of nonverbal behavior, such as emblems and illustrators. These other forms, perhaps, are more akin to language, which has socially learned, communicative value (Boucher, 1974b). Furthermore, they often failed to provide information about specific eliciting stimuli for different nonverbal behaviors (Ekman, 1973). If one is to demonstrate specific learning effects of affect displays, one needs to make careful assessment of the social context of the behavior under observation (Mischel, 1968). It is important to recognize that the same social event does not always elicit the same emotion. Thus, identification of the elicitor is not necessarily identification of the emotion.

Given the serious reliability and validity problems of subjective and anecdotal data (Johnson & Balstad, 1973), the confusion of affective behavior with other kinds of nonverbal behaviors, and lack of specificity of context, the proponents of a culture-specific view of emotion have yet to provide any impressive evidence for their position.

The Universalist Position

In contrast to the cultural relativists, most of whom are more comfortable with descriptive ethnographic methods, the universalist position is represented primarily by researchers who are more comfortable with experimental methodologies. Allport (1924), Asch (1952), and Tomkins (1962, 1963) all argued that there are pan-cultural facial expressions of emotion. Ekman (1972) and Izard (1971), both influenced by Tomkin's theory which proposes a neurophysiological basis of emotion that includes the muscles of the face, have performed a number of studies that give strong support to the notion that there are universals of facial expression of emotion.

Ekman and his colleagues (Ekman, Friesen, & Ellsworth, 1972) clarified methodological problems in the study of facial affective behavior, and conducted a series of critical experiments in both laboratory measurement of facial behavior and cross-cultural identification of facial affect. Drawing from the work of Duchenne (1862) and Hjortsjö (1970), who conducted anatomical studies of facial muscles, and examining all of the available stimuli that had been used by other researchers who had studied facial expression, Ekman, Friesen, and Tomkins (1971) constructed the Facial Affect Scoring Technique (FAST). They divided the face into three areas and examined it in terms of wrinkles, tension, and position of features. They then compiled a catalogue of facial components within each of the three facial areas for each of six emotions. The Facial Affect Scoring Technique made it possible to produce experimental stimuli and measure facial behavior objectively (Boucher & Ekman, 1975). A particular benefit of FAST was that the technique now allowed the production of unambiguous, single-affect stimuli—a problem that had plagued virtually every previous study of the communication of affect (Ekman & Friesen, 1969; Tomkins & McCarter, 1964; Nummenmaa, 1964; Plutchik, 1962).

Using photographs of facial expressions that were posed and selected according to FAST criteria, Ekman, Sorenson, and Friesen (1969) found that observers from different cultures—including preliterate cultures with minimal visual contact with Western cultures (Ekman & Friesen, 1971)—were able to identify reliably emotion from these photographs. Boucher (1973) confirmed these findings in Malaysia. Izard (1968, 1971) came to the same conclusion in his cross-cultural studies, although he selected his stimuli independently of Ekman's group and method.

In addition to the five cultures studied by the Ekman group, the nine cultures studied by Izard, and the two cultures studied by Boucher, consistencies between Mexican and American judgments of facial expression were demonstrated by Dickey and Knower (1941). Additionally, Owaki (1971) cites a study by Hariu showing that Japanese accurately identified the Frois-Wittman (1930) photographs of facial expression of emotion. These studies combine to provide strong, data-based support for the existence of universals of facial expression of emotion. In addition Schwartz, Fair, Salt, Mandel, and Klerman (1976) who employed a very different technique—electromyographic measurement of the facial muscles—achieved results quite consistent with the physiological predictions of Tomkins (1962, 1963).

Evidence bearing on the universality of facial expressions also comes from phylogenetic and ontological studies of facial affective behavior. Chevalier-Skolnikoff (1973) reviewed 100 years of literature on facial expressions in nonhuman primates, and concluded that the literature supported Darwin's (1872) hypothesis that the facial expressions of nonhuman primates and humans are remarkably similar and that human facial behavior evolved from the human's primate ancestors.

Similarly, Charlesworth and Kreutzer (1973) reviewed studies relating to the facial expressions of infants and children, and indicated that the three distinct behaviors of crying, smiling, and laughing appear very early in the infant. They also suggested that global expressions, characteristic of adult emotional expressive behavior, also appear in the infant before the end of the second year. Of particular interest is the convergent findings that showed that the laughing, smiling, and crying patterns of congenital blind children have close similarities to those of sighted normal children (Goodenough, 1932; Charlesworth, 1970; Eibl-Eibesfeldt, 1970). The empirical data from cross-cultural, developmental, phylogenetical, and psychophysiological investigations of facial affect strongly suggest that facial expressions of emotion have, not only pan-cultural similarities, but, quite likely, a biological basis as predicted by Darwin in 1872.

The Problem of Cultural Variability

The experimental evidence indicates that there is little doubt that there are commonalities in facial expression of emotion across many cultures, and probably universals across all cultures. This does not mean, however, that there is no variation in affective behavior from culture to culture. Any alert traveler in another culture can attest to problems in the communication of emotion. I have already mentioned the likelihood that affective behavior can be incorporated into the communicative scheme of a culture, as when the smile takes on meaning beyond being the behavior concomitant with happiness. Caudill and Weinstein (1969) and Bond and Shiraishi (1974) suggest that cultures appear to reinforce specific modes of affect display and, therefore, social learning may account for a significant proportion of manifest affect display.

Tomkin's theory (1962, 1963) addresses this issue of cultural variability, as does Ekman and Friesen's neurocultural account of emotion which is based on the work of Tomkins (Ekman, 1972, 1977). This position postulates a facial affect program, located in the nervous system of all human beings, that links particular facial musculature movements with particular emotions. Apparently, cultural differences in the display of emotion are said to be a result of cultural differences in the antecedents to emotional experience and differences in social rules governing the control of affect display—display rules.

Boucher (1974b) elaborated Ekman, Friesen, and Tomkins' concept of display rules. Briefly, this concept proposes that each culture has developed a set of rules that guide a person to display socially acceptable behavior given that a person is experiencing a particular emotion in a particular context. These rules could be studied by (*a*) specifying the emotion that is being experienced; (*b*) specifying the context in which the emotion is being experienced, including such things as the age, sex, and status of the persons involved and the public or private nature of the setting; and (*c*) specifying the proper management technique—intensify, de-intensify, or neutralize the affect display, or mask the emotion that is experienced with the display of another emotion.

Systematic investigation of the potential sources of cultural differences in affective behavior has begun with Friesen's (1972) study of display rules. Subjects from Japanese and American cultures viewed stressful films, both in isolation and with a member of their own culture present. The subjects from both cultures showed very similar facial affect when viewing the films alone. However, when the films were shown with another member of the same culture, differences between the two cultures in affect displays emerged. The Japanese subjects showed less negative affect than their American counterparts. These results demonstrate the influence of interpersonal factors in the displays of emotions (Goffman, 1959) and revealed that display rules in the two cultures are different.

The foregoing review of the literature indicates strong support for commonalities of facial expression of emotion across cultures. Although more data are called for before we can be completely sure of the existence of universals in facial expression, perhaps the ripest area for research is in the area of cultural variability. Friesen's study (1972) is a significant first step toward delineating the social influence of affect displays in different cultures. However, at this writing it is apparently the only published study of display rules that uses a replicable, data-based methodology. The area of social control of affective behavior is also the most likely candidate for research with immediate, applied output. Knowledge of how individuals from different cultures control the expression of emotion and the principles governing the display of emotion across cultures should enhance intercultural communication (Brein & David, 1971).

Identifying the Emotions

So far emotion has been discussed as a single concept, with little being said about the different emotions. One of the major issues for the researcher of emotion—both within and across cultures—is to identify what these emotions are. Are they a set of discrete emotions, such as anger, disgust, and fear? If so, what and how many are there, and what, if any, are the relationships between them? Every researcher concerned with emotion will have to consider that there are many words for emotions in our languages, and any theory of emotion will have to account for these words. For example, we have a study in progress at the East–West Center in which we are working with 230 words that Malays consider to be emotion states, and almost 750 words that Chinese (Taiwanese) consider to be emotion states. Are there, in fact, as many as 750 different emotions, or are there only the 6 or 8 emotions that most investigators study? And if there is only a smaller set, how do we account for the difference between those very different numbers?

Ekman, Friesen, and Ellsworth (1972) report that the emotions of anger, disgust, fear, happiness, sadness, and surprise have been shown to be accurately identified in cross-cultural studies by different investigators. Based on their view, we can proceed with the assumption that these six emotions constitute a set of pan-cultural emotions, at least as far as identification via facial expression is concerned. But what these studies do not tell us—nor did they try to tell us—is what is *the* set of pan-cultural emotions. All of the research that has been considered so far has been performed with an entry point of a predefined set of discrete emotions or emotion dimensions. The majority of these studies were of identification of facial expression, using photographs posed in one culture to represent specific emotions, and observers in another culture who chose their response from a translated list of these same emotions, from stories which represented these emotions, or from an open-ended response which was then referred back to these emotions.

In the case of the two studies by Ekman and Friesen where people in Japan and New Guinea were photographed, the stimuli used to elicit these photographs were chosen according to the investigator's theoretical position. Although these conditions do not detract in the slightest from the stated purposes of these studies, we must be cautious in extrapolating statements from these results about the possible range of emotions. Again, *a* set, not necessarily *the* set, of pan-cultural emotions has been indentified.

A major problem that faces the cross-cultural researcher, and which bears on the issue of identifying the emotions, is that of translation (Brislin, 1976). Not only does the accuracy of the translations affect the comparability of studies across cultures, it also affects the comparability across researchers within the same culture. For example, Ekman, Friesen, and Ellsworth (1972) note that the differences between research they report and Izard (1971) reports may be due to different translations of terms into Japanese. I noticed a particularly insidious problem when I attempted to obtain translation of six emotion categories for a study of facial expression in Malaysia (Boucher, 1973). This problem is that finer shades of meaning may not survive the translation process, even though both languages are capable of the necessary distinctions. For example, anger, rage, and furious were all translated into the single term *marah* by bilingual Malays. These same translators would furnish the single term anger for three distinct but similar anger-type words, such as *marah*, *naik darah*, and *panas hati*. Back-translation would not solve this problem: It takes a knowledge of both languages, knowledge that the problem exists, and the time necessary to tease out what is needed. Whereas this problem is not too acute when a general term is needed, as in the facial expression studies cited above, it does become quite acute when the goal is to explore the range of emotion in different cultures. A rather humorous example of this happened when a collaborator on one of our emotion language studies insisted that Americans were "emotionally constipated" because there were so many more words for emotions in his language than there were in English. Tact made it difficult to convince him that his observation might be because his command of his own language was considerably better than his command of English.

In our study at the East–West Center that was mentioned earlier, we are attacking the problem of the identification of emotion in a very different manner than that used by the investigators of facial expression. Briefly, we are using a variant of the *native taxonomy* approach so common in the anthropological literature. We initially gather a lexicon of emotion terms from one group of members of the culture, attempting to get as complete a list of terms as we can. This lexicon is then given to another group of members of that culture, and each member of that group is instructed to sort the lexicon into any set of categories that he or she derives from the lexicon. Thus, each person is constructing his or her own model of the relationships of the various emotion terms in that language. We then take all of these separate models, combine them and apply a form of cluster analysis. This analysis gives us a model of the relationships of emotion terms for that language. For example, the data might show that Americans think that anger, rage, annoyance, and irritation form one cluster, and sadness, sorrow, despondency, and grief, form another cluster. If these two clusters appear to be independent, we have established both a relationship between similar terms and a nonrelationship between dissimilar terms that would be in accordance with, for example, a Tomkins'-type, discrete-emotion theory.

Note that the basis of this method is the single concept of emotion, whereas the data collection and analysis is carried out within the context of the culture. It is only at the point of attempting cross-cultural comparison that we need to use any language other than the vernacular. Therefore, the descriptive power of this method is limited only by whether or not the concept of emotion has meaning within the context of a particular culture and the extent to which the task itself is appropriate to that culture. Neither of these limitations has yet become apparent in the cultures that have currently been examined.

The intitial development of this method and data collection was carried out by myself in Malaysia in 1972. Since that time, we have expanded the study to include collaborators from ten additional countries. Although we are awaiting completion of all of the analysis before reporting our results, the indication from the Malay data is that the six emotions that Ekman, Friesen, and Ellsworth (1972) reported from studies of facial expression also form the nuclei of clusters in the Malay language data. There is also a strong category for shame and embarassment (which agreed with Tomkins' model) and a small number of other clusters that await interpretation.

One of the practical applications of the emotional language study, in addition to the theoretical issues, is that when completed, we will have a very useful tool for further studies of emotion within the cultures examined. First, the labels of the clusters we obtain could be used as the translations for limited sets of discrete emotions, such as have been used in prior studies of facial expression. Second, open-ended response to stimuli (Izard, 1971) could be used rather than limited responses and the open-ended responses could be verified against the clustering. Boucher and Carlson (in preparation) used this technique in a comparison of Malaysians and Americans on the judgment of facial expression. This might allow for examination of ambiguities in the stimuli that has often been done indirectly by examination of judgment errors. Combining this with the facial coding techniques of the Ekman laboratory could greatly expand our knowledge of the range of possible affective behavior.

Another approach to the problem of identifying the emotions is characterized by attempts to show relationships between the discrete emotions, and if possible, determine the underlying factors that constitute all emotion. This approach stems from at least as far back as Wundt (1896), who proposed that the dimensions of pleasantness–unpleasantness, excitement–quiet, and tension–relaxation were basic to emotional feelings.

The study of Woodworth (1938) and Schlosberg (1941, 1952, 1954) serve as a good example of how the dimensional approach can evolve. (Although these studies are of facial expression, the implication of the studies extends across the larger consideration of emotion.) Woodworth started with six categories of emotion: love–mirth–happiness, surprise, fear–suffering, anger–determination, disgust, and contempt. He then observed that these emotions were related to each other in the order just presented, forming a linear scale. Schlosberg noted that love–mirth–happiness were related to contempt, bending the ends of the linear Woodworth scale around to form a circle. Schlosberg then proposed that if there was such a circular scale there must be a pair of orthogonal dimensions that would adequately describe the circle. He demonstrated that pleasantness–unpleasantness and attention–rejection were two such dimensions. And finally, he suggested that there was a dimension of sleep–tension that was at right angles to the other two dimensions, forming a cone-shaped model. What this model implies is that if one has the scale positions of all three scales for a given facial expression, the discrete-emotion label for that expression can be determined from the cone. For example, and this is how Schlosberg verified his model, a photograph of facial expression that was scored on the unpleasant end of the pleasantness–unpleasantness scale, midway on the attention–rejection scale, and at the tension end of the sleep–tension scale by one group of observers would be seen as anger–determination by another group of observers. Therefore, there is no need to even use such discrete terms as anger—the three dimensions are adequate to describe any emotion, according to this model.

Schlosberg's model has been seriously questioned on a number of grounds (Ekman, Friesen, & Ellsworth, 1972), including the very serious problem that Schlosberg's results did not replicate, even when his own stimuli were retested (Boucher & Ekman, 1965). The more serious question—because it applies to the dimensional approach—is what does it mean to say that there is a relationship between discrete emotions, whether dimensionalized as according to Schlosberg, or scaled as according to Woodworth? Boucher and Ekman (1965) noted three possible meanings to the relationships specified in such a model: (*a*) It might specify the extent to which emotions *feel alike* to the person experiencing them; (*b*) it might specify the probability that emotions could be *experienced simultaneously;* or (*c*) it might specify the extent to which the concomitant facial expressions of emotions *look alike* to the observer. There is a fourth meaning that could be considered: The dimensions may reflect or represent some corresponding physiological process in the individual so that emotion is the interaction of these processes, rather than physiological processes being more specific to the discrete emotions. With this interpretation the experience of anger, for example, would be due to the relative action of the three physiological components (e.g., pleasantness, attention, and tension, using Schlosberg's dimensions) rather than a specific process for anger. This interpretation is quite similar to Tomkins' notion that the "gradient of neurological firing" is a component that distinguishes the discrete emotions in his theory.

Perhaps the most crucial question to be asked of the dimensional approach is whether the approach is being used because of theoretical reasons or because of methodological reasons. It is one thing to say that a method such as factor analysis accounts for a certain proportion of the experimental variance. It is quite another thing to say that the derived factors are, in fact, measures of some real-world phenomena. Although we may gain statistical power by using a scaler mode of measurement such as occurs in factor analysis, and that power is very attractive when the alternative is nominal measurement, that power may be illusory if the phenomena being measured is in fact nominal. Thus, to discover that anger differs from happiness on a pleasantness scale becomes informative only when pleasantness is defined as something other than one end of the experimenter's bipolar scale.

Triandis and Lambert (1958) report the only cross-cultural study of actual facial expression utilizing the dimensional approach, although there are many single-culture dimensional studies. They compared Greeks and Americans on the Schlosberg model, obtaining both similarities and differences between the two cultures. Cuceloglu (1970) used Osgood's (1966) semantic differential methodology to measure Japanese, American, and Turkish interpretations of abstract line drawings of faces. Marsella, Murray, and Golden (1974) report a semantic differential study of shame among Caucasian-Americans, Chinese-Americans, and Japanese-Americans. Although it is not a dimensional approach in the context of this discussion, the latter study utilizes a method that would bear upon the issue of dimensionality if they had reported the results they obtained for the emotions other than shame. And finally, Osgood's monumental cross-cultural study of affective meaning (Osgood, May, & Miron, 1975) with it's demonstration of universals in the semantic space, has implications for a dimensional approach to emotions.

Conclusion

The most important concern for the researcher of emotion is to gain a better understanding of emotion itself; a tightening-up of our definitions and substantiation of our theories. A critical element in this process is the need to know more about the interaction of biology and social learning in regard to the phenomena of emotion. This, in turn, suggests cross-cultural research on both universal and culture-specific aspects of emotion.

UNIVERSAL ASPECTS

The preponderence of the research to date strongly supports the notion that there are consistencies of emotion across many—perhaps all—cultures. The most frequently studied component of affective experience—facial expression—has commonalities in every culture studied. Furthermore, six emotions (anger, disgust, fear, happiness, sadness, and surprise) have been consistently identified via both studies of facial expression and language in many different cultures, giving credence to the notion that these discrete emotions have meaning beyond a simple linguistic convention of any particular language. The question of whether there are more than these six, and if so what they are, remains to be answered. Likewise, the extent to which there are relationships between these discrete emotions has not been sufficiently specified. Both the small number of cross-cultural studies, and the conflict between theory and methodology of the within-culture studies that utilize a dimensional approach, leave this as an area for further research.

CULTURE-SPECIFIC ASPECTS

What we know about the social learning side of emotion involves a curious paradox. On the one hand, some scholars challenge the conclusions of the previous paragraph. I have concurred with other reviewers that this reasoning stems from confusion of affective and nonaffective behavior and from observations that do not get beyond the socially learned aspects of emotion. On the other hand, systematic studies of the socially learned aspects of emotion in the cross-cultural context are extremely small in number. Except for a few studies of the antecedents to emotional experience (which are beyond the scope of this chapter) and a single study of display rules, the existing literature primarily consists of anecdotal observations. Even with these sketchy data, it seems quite evident that people can control, to a

certain extent, their manifest affective behavior, and it is quite likely that
this control is subject to social conventions and culture-based "display
rules." A further expansion of our knowledge is called for, and there is much
work to be done in this area.

  Combining these two main propositions—that the affective episode consists of some socially learned behaviors overlaying a universally human
substrate—suggests many research topics that could have virtually immediate applications, in addition to contributing to our theories. The most
apparent of these studies would occur in the realms of trans-cultural
psychiatry and intercultural communication.

References

Allport, F. H. *Social psychology*. Cambridge, Massachusetts: Houghton, 1924.

Asch, S. E. *Social psychology*. Englewood Cliffs, New Jersey: Prentice-Hall, 1952.

Bell, C. *The anatomy and philosophy of expression as connected with the fine arts* (4th ed.), London: John Murray, 1847.

Birdwhistell, R. L. The kinesic level in the investigation of the emotions. In P. H. Knapp (Ed.), *Expression of the emotions in man*. New York: International Univ. Press, 1963.

Birdwhistell, R. L. Some relationships between American kinesics and spoken American English. In A. G. Smith (Ed.), *Communication and culture*. New York: Holt, 1966.

Birdwhistell, R. L. *Kinesics and context: Essays in body motion communication*. Philadelphia: Univ. of Pennsylvania Press, 1970.

Bond, M. H., & Shiraishi, D. The effects of body lean and status of an interviewer on the non-verbal behavior of Japanese interviewees. *International Journal of Psychology*, 1974, *9*, 117–128.

Boring, E. G. *A history of experimental psychology*. New York: Appleton, 1950.

Boucher, J. D. *Facial behavior and the perception of emotion: Studies of Malays and Temuan Orag Asli*. Paper presented to the Conference on Psychology and Related Disciplines in Malaysia, Univ. of Kebangasaan Malaysia, Kuala Lumpur, 1973.

Boucher, J. D. Culture and the expression of emotion. *International and Intercultural Communication Annal*, 1974, *1*, 82–86. (a)

Boucher, J. D. Display rules and facial affective behavior: A theoretical discussion and sugges-tions for research. *Topics in Culture Learning*, Honolulu, East–West Culture Learning Institute, 1974, *2*, 87–101. (b)

Boucher, J. D., & Carlson, G. A three-culture study of facial expression of emotion. (Manu-script in preparation)

Boucher, J. D., & Ekman, P. *A replication of Schlosberg's evaluation of Woodworth's scale of emotion*. Paper presented to the Western Psychological Association, Honolulu, Hawaii, 1965.

Boucher, J. D., & Ekman, P. Facial areas and emotional information. *Journal of Communica-tion*, 1975, *25*, 21–29.

Brein, M., & David, K. H. Intercultural communication and the adjustment of the sojourner. *Psychological Bulletin*, 1971, *76*, 215–250.

Brislin, R. W. (Ed.). *Translation: Applications and research*. New York: Gardner, 1976.

Caudill, W., & Weinstein, H. Maternal care and infant behavior in Japan. *Psychiatry*, 1969, *32*, 12–43.

Charlesworth, W. R. Surprise reactions in congenitally blind and sighted children. National Institute of Mental Health Progress Report, 1970.

Charlesworth, W. R., & Kreutzer, M. A. Facial expressions of infants and children. In P. Ekman (Ed.), *Darwin and facial expression*. New York: Academic Press, 1973.

Chevalier-Skolnikoff, S. Facial expressison of emotion in non-human primates. In P. Ekman (Ed.), *Darwin and facial expression*. New York: Academic Press, 1973.

Cuceloglu, D. Perception of facial expressions in three different cultures. *Ergonomics,* 1970, *13,* 93–100.

Darwin, C. *The expression of the emotions in man and animals.* London: Murray, 1872.

Delgado, J. M. R. Effect of brain stimulation on task-free situations. In R. N. Peon (Ed.), *The physiological basis of mental activity,* 1963.

deSilva, P. *The psychology of emotions in buddhist perspective.* Kandy, Sri Lanka: Buddhist Publication Society, 1976.

Dickey, E. C., & Knower, F. H. A note on some ethnological differences in recognition of simulated expressions of the emotions. *American Journal of Sociology,* 1941, *47,* 190–193.

Duchenne, G. B. *Méchanisme de la physionomie humaine.* Paris: Bailliere, 1862.

Duncan, S. Nonverbal communication. *Psychological Bulletin,* 1969, *72,* 118–137.

Eibl-Eibesfeldt, I. *Ethology: The biology of behavior.* New York: Holt, 1970.

Ekman, P. Universality and cultural differences in facial expressions of emotion. In J. K. Cole (Ed.), *Nebraska Symposium on motivation, 1971.* Lincoln, Nebraska: Univ. of Nebraska Press, 1972.

Ekman, P. (Ed.). *Darwin and facial expression: A century of research in review.* New York: Academic Press, 1973.

Ekman, P. Biological and cultural contributions to body and facial movement. In J. Blacking (Ed.), *The anthropology of the body,* A. S. A. Monograph 15. London: Academic Press, 1977.

Ekman, P., & Friesen, W. V. *Origin, usage and coding: The basis for five categories of nonverbal behavior.* Paper presented at the Symposium on Communication Theory and Linguistic Models, Buenos Aires, 1967.

Ekman, P., & Friesen, W. V. The repertoire of nonverbal behavior: Categories, origin, usage, and coding. *Semiotica,* 1969, *1,* 49–97.

Ekman, P., & Friesen, W. V. Constants across cultures in the face and emotion. *Journal of Personality and Social Psychology,* 1971, *17,* 124–129.

Ekman, P., & Friesen, W. V. Detecting deception from the body or face. *Journal of Personality and Social Psychology,* 1974, *29,* 288–298.

Ekman, P., Friesen, W. V., & Ellsworth, P. *Emotion in the human face: Guidelines for research and an integration of findings.* New York: Pergamon Press, 1972.

Ekman, P., Friesen, W. V., & Tomkins, S. S. Facial Affect Scoring Technique: A first validity study. *Semiotica,* 1971, *3,* 37–38.

Ekman, P., Sorenson, E. R., & Friesen, W. V. Pan-cultural elements in facial displays of emotion. *Science,* 1969, *164,* 86–88.

Friesen, W. V. Cultural differences in facial expressions in a social situation: An experimental test of the concept of display rules. Unpublished doctoral dissertation, Univ. of California, 1972.

Frois-Wittman, J. The judgment of facial expression. *Journal of Experimental Psychology,* 1930, *13,* 113–151.

Goffman, E. *The presentation of self in everyday life.* Garden City, New York: Doubleday, 1959.

Goodenough, F. L. Expression of the emotions in a blind–deaf child. *Journal of Abnormal and Social Psychology,* 1932, *27,* 328–333.

Hjortsjö, C. H. *Man's face and mimic language.* Lund, Sweden: Studentlitteratur, 1970.

Izard, C. E. *The emotions and emotion constructs in personality and culture research.* In R. B. Cattell (Ed.), *Handbook of modern personality theory.* Chicago: Aldine, 1968.

Izard, C. E. *The face of emotion.* New York: Appleton, 1971.

Johnson, S. M., & Balstad, D. D. Methodological issues in naturalistic observation: Some problems and solutions for field research. In L. A. Hamerlynck, L. K. Handy, & E. J. Mash (Eds.), *Behavior change methodology, and practice.* Champaign, Illinois: Research Press, 1973.

LaBarre, W. The cultural basis of emotions and gestures. *Journal of Personality,* 1947, *16,* 49–68.

Marsella, A. J., Murray, M. D., & Golden, C. Ethnic variations in the phenomenology of emotions: I. Shame. *Journal of Cross-Cultural Psychology,* 1974, *5,* 312–328.

Mead, M. Review of Darwin and Facial Expression, P. Ekman (Ed.). *Journal of Communication,* 1975, *25,* 209–213.

Mischel, W. *Personality and assessment.* New York: Wiley, 1968.

Nummenmaa, T. *The language of the face. Jyvaskyla studies in education, psychology, and social research.* Jyvaskyla, Finland: Jyvaskylan Yllopiostoyhdistys, 1964.

Osgood, C. E. Dimensionality of the semantic space for communication via facial expression. *Scandinavian Journal of Psychology,* 1966, *7,* 1–30.

Osgood, C. E., May, W. H., & Miron, M. S. *Cross-cultural universals of affective meaning.* Urbana, Illinois: Univ. of Illinois Press, 1975.

Osgood, C. E., Suci, G. J., & Tannenbaum, P. H. *The measurement of meaning.* Urbana, Illinois: Univ. of Illinois Press, 1957.

Owaki, Y. *Psychology of emotion* (in Japanese) Tokyo: Baifukan, 1971.

Plutchik, P. *The emotions: Facts, theories, and a new model.* New York: Springer, 1962.

Sartre, J. P. *The emotions: Outline of a theory.* (B. Frechtman, trans.) New York: Philosophical Library, 1948.

Schlosberg, H. A scale for the judgment of facial expression, *Journal of Experimental Psychology,* 1941, *29,* 497–510.

Schlosberg, H. The description of facial expression in terms of two dimensions. *Journal of Experimental Psychology,* 1952, *44,* 229–237.

Schlosberg, H. Three dimensions of emotion. *Psychological Review,* 1954, *61,* 81–88.

Schwartz, G. E., Fair, P. L., Salt, P., Mandel, M. R., & Klerman, G. L. Facial muscle patterning to affective imagery in depressed and nondepressed samples. *Science,* 1976, *192,* 489–492.

Tillman, F. On perceiving persons. In J. Edie (Ed.), *Phenomonology in America.* Chicago: Quadrangle, 1967.

Tomkins, S. S. *Affect, imagery, consciousness. Volume I: The positive affects.* New York: Springer, 1962.

Tomkins, S. S. *Affect, imagery, consciousness. Volume II: The negative affects.* New York: Springer, 1963.

Tomkins, S. S., & McCarter, R. What and where are the primary affects? Some evidence for a theory. *Perceptual and Motor Skills,* 1964, *18,* 119–158.

Triandis, H. C., & Lambert, W. W. A restatement and text of Schlosberg's theory of emotion with two kinds of subjects from Greece. *Journal of Abnormal and Social Psychology,* 1958, *56*(3), 321–328.

van Hooff, J. A. R. A. M. A comparative approach to the phylogeny of laughter and smiling. In R. A. Hinde (Ed.), *Nonverbal communication.* Cambridge: Cambridge Univ. Press, 1972.

van Lawick-Goodall, J. The behavior of free-living chimpanzees in the Gombe Stream Reserve. *Animal Behaviour Monographs,* 1968, *1*(3), 161–311.

Weiner, M., Devoe, S., Rubinow, S., & Geller, J. Nonverbal behavior and nonverbal communication. *Psychological Review,* 1972, *79,* 185–214.

Woodworth, R. S. *Experimental psychology.* New York: Holt, 1938.

Wundt, W. *Grundriss der Psychologie.* Leipzig: Englemann, 1896.

9

Culture and Personality

JURIS G. DRAGUNS

Introduction

The theme of this chapter is the triangular relationship between culture, behavior, and personality. Do different cultures produce individuals who differ (*a*) in the internal organization of their behavior (personal organization); (*b*) in the distribution of various personal dispositions, dimensions, and traits (interindividual differences); and (*c*) in the range of equivalence of various stimuli and situations (intraindividual consistency)? These topics constitute the three abiding concerns of personality research (see Draguns, 1975, 1979).

The question then, whether cultures differ in personality, is not easily nor lightly answered. On the one hand, it is intuitively plausible that culture, which shapes all of our experience and behavior, would leave an imprint on the "internal" organization of behavior and would produce different "types of people" or, at least, different distributions of such types in various cultures.

Equally as plausible, however, is the notion of a "psychic unity of mankind [Tylor, 1873/1958]" in which cultures produce divergent external trappings of custom and behavior while leaving the inner core of human experience untouched. According to this view, all of us are brothers or sisters

PERSPECTIVES ON CROSS-CULTURAL PSYCHOLOGY

under the skin, our individuality resulting from the idiosyncrasies of our personal, but not cultural, shaping.

The question just posed, but not answered, can be introduced in another way. The rapidly increasing cross-cultural literature richly documents dif- ferences across cultures in various domains of behavior such as perception, cognition, learning, motivation, and social interaction (Malpass, 1977; Ser- pell, 1976; Triandis, 1977). Do these documented differences in behavior "add up to" or, at some point, become transformed into differences in personality? To answer this question, we must have criteria for differentiat- ing personality differences from mere differences in behavior. LeVine (1973) cautioned against inferring personality characteristics from normative be- havior evidenced where there are sanctions against its violation; personality-related behavior, according to LeVine, is more likely to be distributed in the form of overlapping curves. LeVine also suggested, how- ever, that the study of behavioral norms and of categorical differences was a useful adjunct to the study of overlapping curves of distribution in two or more cultures. Presumably, it would provide the background for those behaviors in which personality would have a wider scope to operate and a greater role to play.

Elsewhere (Draguns, 1979) the tripartite division of social influence, formulated by Kelman (1958), has been proposed as a point of departure for specifying behavioral differences germane to the investigation of per- sonality. Behavior, under conditions of compliance or brought about by external constraint, is of peripheral interest to the student of personality. A personality investigator is concerned with actions that result from identifica- tion, imitation, or internalization (i.e., the act of becoming "absorbed" into the individual's self—his or her own pattern of behavior). The lines between any two of these three avenues of influence, originally introduced in the more specific context of opinion change, are not hard and fast, nor can I defend the proposition that compliance, under all circumstances, is irrele- vant to personality. People can, and have been demonstrated to differ in conformity behavior, both within (e.g., Crutchfield, 1955; Marsella & Mur- ray, 1974) and across (e.g., Huang & Harris, 1973) cultures. Typically, however, research and conceptualization on personality are focused upon behavior that is enduring, characteristic, and not limited to a narrow range of situations.

Another aspect of the relationship of culture to personality concerns behavior and culture. Culture produces, changes, and shapes behavior. Behavior, in turn, alters and patterns cultures. Cross-cultural psychologists traditionally investigated culture as an independent variable. Concretely, two or more cultures were compared and the main effects of this variable upon behavior and/or personality were noted. This tradition was shared by the anthropologists and psychoanalysts who created and developed culture and personality as a coherent subject of study. In both cases, the individual was construed as a product, not a creator of culture. By the time a social scientist got into the field, the culture was already there. It is, in fact, a lot easier and more practical to study individuals as a function of culture, rather than to investigate a culture as a function of individuals. Steward (1958) went further when he said: "Personality is shaped by culture, but it has never been shown that culture is affected by personality [p. 7]."

Few contemporary readers, I believe, would be inclined to agree completely with the above statement. Historical evidence is abundant in documenting the impact of at least individual personalities, or groups of such personalities, upon customs and institutions. Less dramatically, changes in personality have been shown to precede spurts of economic achievement (McClelland, 1961) of "overall modernity" or other aspects of modernization (Guthrie, Azores, Juanico, Luna, & Ty, 1970; Inkeles, 1966, 1977). Nonetheless, the professional bias of cross-cultural psychologists, and of their colleagues in anthropology and other social disciplines, is slanted toward assuming culture to be immutable—at least for the duration of a given research project. Cross-cultural investigation of personality has, as yet, not fully responded to the fact that this relationship is not only triangular, but bilateral and reciprocal. To elaborate, behavior influences personality and is in turn determined by it. Culture shapes behavior and personality and behavior rooted in individual personalities produces cultural change—from infinitesimal to major and from imperceptibly gradual to dramatically sudden. Of course, not all individuals are equal in their impact as agents of cultural change, but none are excluded from participation in this process.

The issue just raised has its origins in a broader domain of psychological concern. Its source can be traced to Kurt Lewin's (1935) famous formula: B = f (P,E), where B refers to behavior, P to the person and E to the environment. The renewal of interest in this relationship has been sparked by the social learning movement (e.g., Bandura, 1978) which is no longer content to consider behavior as the sole function of environment as it was construed by the radical behaviorists (Skinner, 1953). Rather, Bandura (1978) emphasizes the active role of the person in influencing both behavior and environment and acknowledges the reciprocal nature of interchanges among these three variables. Similar issues have been sporadically raised in other quarters, for example, among psychoanalysts (Brisset, 1963) critical of the one-sided culturalism of Neo-Freudians who tend to view culture as a cause rather than as effect of behavior.

Culture–personality research, then, has yet to overcome the unwitting and unintentional simplification of the implicit concept of culture. Culture is not simply "something that makes things happen," a deus ex machina. Rather, there is a subtle and dynamic equilibrium among behavior, culture, and personality, each of the three components to this transaction being capable of influencing and being influenced by either of the others.

Historical Considerations

According to Bruner (1974, pp. 395–396), "[T]here has been one magnificent failure in cross-cultural studies and that is the area of personality and culture. This is a splendid failure and men good and true have tried it." Siegel (1970) has voiced similar sentiments. The renaming of what used to be known as "culture and personality studies" to that of "psychological anthropology," a development in which Hsu (1971a, 1971b) has played a central role, is symptomatic of this disenchantment. Reviews of cross-cultural psychological research (Pelto, 1968; Triandis, Malpass, & Davidson, 1971, 1973), and of the interface between psychology and anthropology, document the relative decline of personality as a bridge between the two disciplines.

These developments have come about for a variety of methodological, substantive, and conceptual reasons. Hsu (1971b), for example, has expressed doubts concerning whether personality, itself a historically traceable, Western, culture-bound concept (see Herrmann, 1971; Wikse, 1978, for detailed consideration of its historical, ideological, and philosophical roots) is a useful and adequate vehicle of cross-cultural integration and comparison. No doubt the decline of the psychodynamic theory as a unifying framework of culture and personality studies has accelerated this development. The clear-cut division of labor that characterized such historically influential collaborations as those of Linton (1945) and Kardiner (1945) has, perhaps, not completely broken down, but rather, been greatly strained. There was a time when anthropologists went into the field and collected data that were then interpreted by psychoanalysts. By contrast, even modern psychoanalytically inspired investigations (e.g., Parin, Morgenthaler, & Parin-Matthey, 1963, 1971) rely upon the team approach. More generally, the question as to the status of the concept of personality and its usefulness within anthropology has been vigorously debated (see Williams, 1975). Such debate centers around two questions: To what extent does the science of culture need to describe or understand the personalities of the groups it investigates and, to what extent, if any, can this be realistically and fruitfully done?

Methodological disenchantment has set in with the realization that the relationship between culturally mediated socialization experience and the resulting personality is neither as powerful, nor as simple, as the enthusiasts of the culture and personality approach had supposed. Although this is an oversimplification, unfair no doubt to a great many sensitive pioneers of the culture and personality movement, the optimal outcome of culture and personality studies was widely envisaged as a single personality type characteristic of a single culture. This notion, questionable even in its application to small-scale, nontechnological tribe and band cultures (see Wallace, 1970), is easily reduced to absurdity when extended to the cultures of the large-scale, modern, nation state (e.g., Italy, Argentina, Finland, France, China, Japan).

Yet, the field is scattered with attempts—too numerous to list and too embarrassing to mention—of doing just that. The conceptual umbrella for these efforts was the concept of national character (see reviews, critiques, and discussions by Bell, 1968; Duijker & Frijda, 1960; Inkeles & Levinson, 1968; Vexliard, 1970) predicated, in its simplest form, upon the expectation of a single personality type within a large cultural–political unit. In fairness to the proponents of the concept of national character, this is not the only meaning that can be attributed to the notion. Nonetheless, the obtrusive reality of intragroup variabilities within all large-scale national cultures, including our own, did much to dampen the enthusiasm for and to usher in disenchantment with not only research on national character, but also with the promise of finding worthwhile and solid links between cultural characteristics and behavioral parameters.

In addition to overestimating uniformity in their dependent variables, personality dimensions, and patterns, the early proponents of the culture–personality approach probably erred in their estimates of the uniformity of the effects of socialization. The traditional view proceeded from the assumption of one set of culturally prescribed socialization practices, tenable in the case of the Alorese (DuBois, 1944), but questionable in its application to Great Russians (Gorer & Rickman, 1949) or Japanese (LaBarre, 1945).

More subtly, the exponents of the culture–personality approach, and some of the more recent investigators as well, fell prey to what Wrong (1961) called the "oversocialized conception of mankind." The distinction was lost between what the culture set out to accomplish, and the manner in which this design was realized in practice. Particularly, in the case of modern, ideologically governed societies, a great deal of "slippage" may exist between the cultural blueprint of creating (e.g., the "new Soviet man" discussed in Bauer, 1952) and the means of bringing about this goal. Bronfenbrenner's (1970) book on childhood in the U.S.A. and in the U.S.S.R. is, for the most part, about the explicit cultural design; the question is open as to how close this design is to cultural practice. The discrepancy between design and practice, however, is not unique to ideologically impregnated cultures. Its effects may be seen in the interindividual and intraindividual variability in socialization practices and in the gap between the learning of culture through socialization and the results of that learning. The relationship between culture and personality then can only be approximate, probabilistic, and complex; yet it was expected to result in definite, simple, and qualitative links.

Another source of methodological scepticism has its roots in research on personality. Over the last decade, the concept of personality has been called into question on its home grounds. Mischel (1968, 1973, 1977) is centrally associated with this development. Although his position has undergone a number of changes in substance and emphasis over the years, its gist continues to be twofold: (*a*) the role of personality in determining behavior has been historically overestimated on a number of illusory grounds, and (*b*) such personality variables as exist are more narrow in scope and more variable across persons than has been commonly supposed. The objective is to study a person in the complexity of his or her multifaceted interactions with environments (Mischel, 1977), rather than compare uniform variables across a great many people. Obviously then—although Mischel does not speak to this issue—there is little point to comparing people across culture lines in dimensions or variables that are questionable in their generality even in the milieus of their origin.

These contentions have kicked up a lot of dust and have stimulated a great deal of thinking. The emerging consensus is an interactionist position (Magnusson & Endler, 1977) which allows room for both situational and dispositional determinants of behavior in a variety of complex and individual combinations. Nonetheless, this position, which does not deny the usefulness and reality of the concept of personality, but limits its scope, calls into question many of the traditional tools of investigating personality and culture (e.g., projective tests, inventories, accounts of dreams, and interpretations of artistic productions). All of these instruments of appraisal share the feature of providing a narrow base for far-reaching and wide-ranging personal inferences. It is the scope of how much information can be extracted from these measures that the situationalists and interactionists have called into question. One of the few authors who addressed himself to this issue in the culture–personality literature is LeVine (1973) who advocated the reliance on specific, observational, naturalistic measures as the basic source of information about personality in various cultural milieus. Escovar (1974) and Guthrie (1975) provided programmatic statements on cross-cultural research from the social-learning point of view. The research by Gallimore, Boggs, and Jordan (1974) proceeded from the social-learning position in analyzing the contingencies of aggressive, achievement-related, and affiliative acts among Hawaiian children in the school setting. Guthrie *et al.* (1970) relied upon the principles of operant conditioning both to explain traditional behavior in the rural Philippines, and to induce change in it toward modernization. These several contributions share a concern with a personally characteristic behavior in the context of its occurrence. People in situations are being characterized, rather than being imbued with general and abiding characteristics. These studies deal with the traditional phenomena of personality, but with minimal assumptions about their scope, consistency, and stability.

The final reason for the ebbing of enthusiasm regarding cross-cultural personality comparisons, is the gloomy evaluation of the quality and quantity of evidence produced during several decades of culture and personality study. Barnouw (1973) and LeVine (1973) do not go as far as Bruner in their general appraisal of the field, but they, too, feel that the area of personality and culture is ripe for reassessment and for a new start. Distinctive of

LeVine's (1973) approach is the search for both new methods and new theoretical frameworks—the methods should be less interpretive and inferential, the theoretical frameworks more inclusive, and encompassing, yet transcending the traditional Western-based notions of personality. Barnouw's (1973) suggestions converge, in some respects, with LeVine's, particularly in emphasizing the potential of unobtrusive methods (Webb *et al.*, 1966) as an avenue of data gathering on personality in culture. Williams' (1975) conclusions are cautious and tentative: "[T]he substantive questions . . . must be answered if psychological anthropology is to move on to the production of generalizations of a high level of validity, authority, and scope [Williams, 1975, p. 23]."

There is then an aura of self-scrutiny and reflectiveness over the traditional research enterprise of culture and personality. But while the evaluators of this field have been giving vent to their scepticism and disenchantment, another body of researchers, oblivious of these doubts, has been accumulating information about culture and personality interrelationships, with little reference to the accumulation of the traditional culture–personality literature. A perusal of such publications as the *Journal of Cross-Cultural Psychology*, *International Journal of Psychology*, *Journal of Social Psychology*, *Psychologia*, and *Interamerican Journal of Psychology* reveals a substantial, if variable, proportion of articles directly or indirectly concerned with personality concepts, variables, and measures. This work has, as yet, been nowhere integratively and exhaustively reviewed, although coverage of personality material has been included in a number of more comprehensive and general reviews (Triandis, Malpass, & Davidson, 1971, 1973; Malpass, 1977; Serpell, 1976; Triandis, 1977, see also Draguns, 1979).

The distinguishing features of this accumulation of findings are that it is concerned with components, rather than with the global organization of personality, that it is based on quantitative comparisons across two or more cultures rather than on the qualitative capture of coherence within one unique cultural pattern, and that, for the most part, this work is undertaken by psychologists, "cross-cultural" and other, rather than by cultural anthropologists. A subsidiary and perhaps less characteristic feature is that the focus has shifted from the small-scale, traditional "archaic" or "primitive" cultures in which, historically, the bulk of anthropological field work has been done, to modern nation states, or their ethnically distinct components, as units of observation and comparison.

Another line of research, less prominent in quantity, but gradually rising, involves multicultural or even hologeistic comparison on the basis of archival data. Human Research Area Files have been intensively utilized by social scientists in their search for worldwide, empirically based findings (Barry, Bacon, & Child, 1957; Murdock, 1957), especially on the effects of various socialization practices.

Critical Issues

How deeply does the culture cut into the individual's dreams, thoughts, wishes, and fears—the stuff of which personality, or at least its internal subjective side, is made? The issue is germane to the question raised, outside of the cross-cultural context, by Monte (1977): Is personality, as the etymological origin of the term implies, a mask, or is it the core, or at least the knot by which our behavior is tied? Similarly, do outward differences in behavior, for example, in relation to aggression, imply differences in personality, or are they role-determined and situation-bound? Conversely, is personality concerned with the "public presentation of self in everyday life [Goffman, 1959]." What kinds of criteria would satisfy contemporary experts or personality as being indicative of personality differences across cultures? The question is complicated by the fact that measures, situations, and methods change meaning as they are transposed across cultural lines.

Serpell's (1976) suggestion that the widely used indicators of field-dependence measure cognitive style in modern, organized populations and perceptual skill in traditional, rural settings comes to mind in this connection. It is particularly salient because it pertains to an object- and content-free measure that, on the face of it, would appear to be particularly immune to cultural shaping or taint. The cross-cultural variation in the stimulus-value of projective stimuli, even such relatively acultural ones as inkblots, has by this time been the subject of such extensive critical literature and commentary (Abel, 1973; Delpech, 1971; Kaplan, 1961; Lindzey, 1961; Spain, 1972) as to make elaborations and restatements superfluous. Suffice it to say that, with few dissenting voices (e.g., DeVos, 1965), it is recognized that the signs derived from these tests differ in their meaning across cultures, mediated as they are by cultural variations in the meaning attached to the situation, communication, and stimuli. It is a rare contemporary user of projective measures who will readily and hastily impose the same interpretations on results obtained in several cultural settings.

The readiness and ease of responding to paper-and-pencil personality measures (Brislin, Lonner, & Thorndike, 1973; Sharma, 1977), are matters of cultural variation. Apart from the more specific issues of appropriateness and equivalence of content across linguistic and cultural boundaries, the readiness to engage in structured, impersonal, and standardized self-revelation is an activity in which members of some cultures are socialized and those of others are not. The United States and Canada are probably the most test-oriented cultures in the world, and the typical form that this testing takes is that of the limited-option, paper-and-pencil, self-descriptive variety. These considerations should give those investigators pause who, all too readily, pack their favorite questionnaires and scales as they travel around the world. The psychological equivalence of taking such a personality measure has rarely been demonstrated across cultural settings, although by this time self-report personality measures have literally been used in scores of languages.

Added to this are the more restricted problems of assuring linguistic equivalence. We know more than we did only a decade ago about the safeguards to employ in translating personality inventories and avoiding the pitfalls of misleading, inexact, or erroneous translation (Brislin, 1970; Sechrest, Fay & Zaidi, 1972; Wagatsuma, 1977). Major projects of translating, adapting, and revalidating a number of prominent personality scales have been completed in the case of such instruments as the Minnesota Multiphasic Personality Inventory (M.M.P.I.) (Butcher & Pancheri, 1976; Glatt, 1969; Spreen, 1961), Spielberger's State–Trait Anxiety Inventory (Spielberger & Diaz-Guerrero, 1976; Sharma, 1977), Zung Self-Rating Depression Scale (Conde Lopez & Chamorro, 1974; Zung, 1972) and many other tools. The common feature of these efforts is what has been called "decentering" (Brislin *et al.*, 1973).

Through decentering, content equivalence is sacrificed to, or at least given lower priority than, cultural appropriateness. The result, then, is a tool adapted to a specific culture for use for research and clinical purposes, but no longer automatically or easily comparable to the original from which it has been derived. Thus, comparative studies across two or more cultures occupy a minor place in the recent reports on the cross-cultural readaptation of these instruments (e.g., Butcher & Pancheri, 1976; Spielberger & Diaz-Guerrero, 1976); in the case of the few cross-cultural comparisons, their preliminary and tentative nature is stressed (e.g., Sharma, 1977). The objective of constructing a comparable version of a psychological instrument is more easily attained in the case of a short, concretely descriptive, unidimensional, and transparent instrument, such as the Zung Self-Rating Depression Scale (e.g., Zung, 1972) than in the case of "broad-band," omnibus inventories with a wide range of content and style of items, such as the M.M.P.I. In either case, the task of the translator and revalidator is often complicated by the subtlety of emotional meanings and their difference in connotation, intensity, and frequency of usage (Draguns, 1977; Wagatsuma, 1977).

If both projective techniques and questionnaires pose problems in crosscultural research that are not easily removed once and for all, what is left? Cross-cultural experiments in personality, specifically involving manipulation of independent variables and measurement of dependent variables, have been few in number (Sechrest, 1977). When experiments have been simultaneously conducted across culture lines, or replicated in two or more cultures, the question as to the culturally mediated meaning of the experimental conditions, instructions, and settings becomes a problem. Lazarus *et al.* (1966) demonstrated that the experience of being examined overrode the specific-threat value of highly arousing stimuli with Japanese subjects. A psychological experiment, with its paraphernalia of automatic recording and measurement, may be a strange cultural import in many countries; the connotations of being examined, observed, and tested may be both less specific and more intense at many sites of cross-cultural investigation.

LeVine's (1973) recommendation of naturalistic, observational techniques, resting minimally on interpretive operations and inferential meaning, has limited applicability as their relevance to personality is not clear. The observational findings by Caudill and Weinstein (1969) and Caudill and Plath (1966) are the exceptions that prove the rule. On the basis of time samples of mother–infant interaction in Japan and the United States, these investigators discovered important, culturally characteristic features of early socialization experience which have plausibly been related to a variety of patterns of behavior of normal Americans and Japanese. Gallimore *et al.* (1974) contributed similarly valuable information on the culture-specific Hawaiian nexus of affiliation, aggression, and achievement with a minimum of special tools and inference. Instances of such research are, as yet, uncharacteristic and rare, and I, for one, harbor some doubts as to the potential scope of such efforts. What it comes down to is a question of how easily and readily personality is inferred from behavior. On this score, I admit to a rather pessimistic and sceptical position. Like Mischel (1977), but for different reasons, I am impressed with the complexity of behavior–personality relationships. It is fortuitous when such relationships clearly and directly emerge, but I see no grounds for expecting many instances of such emergence.

If behavioral observation is limited in its applicability and promise, one can try out for size what, for lack of a better term, might be called personality research without personality measures. What is substituted for them are the plausible effects of personality characteristics. Measurement of aggression in several cultures may be a thorny problem, but the comparison of homicide rates, and those of violent assault, may be possible by comparing already available police statistics—on the assumption that these statistics are uniformly and constantly kept, an assumption that, in many instances, is subject to question. Lynn (1971) has probably gone furthest in practicing this approach in his comparison of anxiety and hostility levels in 16 developed industrialized countries. His attempt has received a great deal of criticism, in part because of his unconventional reliance on genetic and even "racial" factors for explanation of cross-cultural differences and in part because of the questionable comparability of national data on such subjects as alcohol and tobacco consumption, caloric intake, and automobile accident rates. On the other side of the ledger, some of the results of Lynn's statistical bird's-eye view of the countries of Western Europe, North America, Australia, New Zealand, and Japan has sparked more direct research comparisons (Lynn & Hampson, 1975) and is consonant with independently collected evidence (Cattell, 1957; Cattell & Scheier, 1961).

Lynn's (1971) undertaking was not all that different from the use of the Human Research Area Files for personality purposes. Although a rigorous and elaborate coding system is imposed on raw ethnographic data, and a set of complex precautions is applied, the limitations of original sources of information can be minimized, but not overcome. That is why Rohner (1975, 1976) advocates a "triangular" research attack composed of hologeistic studies of socialization antecedents and behavioral consequences, intensive investigation of these variables in one or more culture, and laboratory studies, involving analogue situations and/or animal populations. It is this approach that he applied to the study of the effects of acceptance and rejection in a worldwide perspective.

The options open to the cross-cultural investigator of personality are numerous, yet imperfect. None of the methods enumerated is useless; each is limited in its inference value and applicability. Use of imperfect tools with the realization of their limitations is an indispensable expedient, not only in cross-cultural psychology. Combining several imperfect instruments is another useful corrective; all too many cross-cultural investigations are based on the investigator's sole favorite measure. Overshadowing all of these precautions is, however, the willingness to observe and learn the culture before plunging into research. The writings of the last decade have been replete with admonitions of bilaterality in the conduct and execution of cross-cultural studies (e.g., Berrien, 1970; Brislin *et al.*, 1973); these admonitions are widely agreed to, and equally widely disregarded.

The flow of concepts, tools, and measures still proceeds, for the most part, unilaterally from the countries of the West (especially the United States, Canada, and Great Britain) to the Orient and to the developing countries of the Third World. Increasingly, calls are being heard for the reorientation of cross-cultural psychology from an etic assumption of the universality of Western concepts and measures, to an emic emphasis upon the implicit, indigenous taxonomy, nomenclature, and conceptualization of behavior (Berry, 1969; Price-Williams, 1974). These proposals on the international scale are paralleled, in the pluralistic microcosm of the United States by proposals for a black (Jones, 1972), Chicano (Martinez, 1977), and Indian (Trimble, 1975) psychology. All of these kinds of programs are a lot easier to propose than to implement.

For better or worse, psychology as a scientific discipline in the late 1970s remains a Western cultural product, rooted in the formal philosophical systems and the informal patterns of thought ("common sense") of Western Europe and North America of the late-nineteenth century. Psychology's spread around the globe, a movement which is gathering momentum and increasing in speed, has involved the spread of problems, methods, and instruments which variously originated in Leipzig, Paris, Chicago, or London. Rather than scrapping this accumulation of method, evidence, and instrumentation, the question is one of producing a creative blend of cultural reality and psychological conceptualization. The ideal solution is starting at both, or several, sites of cultural comparison and converging toward mutually acceptable and equally fitting measures and methods. Yet, this is rarely done; the less developed the country, the fewer the local psychologists and the more likely they are to be in the imitative and adaptational stage in respect to Western psychology. Thus, emic constructs, with their strange and exotic names, are invoked post hoc in explanation of findings obtained by means of "imported" measures.

Yet, there are exceptions, studies where blending has occurred. For example, the Japanese concept of *amae* (akin to, but not synonymous with, passive dependence) has not only been extensively described and analyzed, mainly on the basis of clinical material by Doi (1973), but operationalized by means of a preliminary paper-and-pencil measure, applied in both Japanese and English (Yamada, 1970). In addition, the Greek folk-notion of *philotimo*, referring to culturally valued role-appropriate behavior, has been systematically investigated in relation to its implicative meaning (Vassiliou & Vassiliou, 1973). These are but bare beginnings, yet they suggest that a combination of concepts drawn from folk psychology and scientific methods of investigation is feasible. Moreover, the concepts embedded in the informal psychological systems of a specific space and time may not be unique to its specific site or period. Rather, they may be "in focus" in the consciousness of members of a particular group. Doi (1973) in his more recent writings articulates this possibility; *amae* is something the Japanese have a word for, but that many non-Japanese may be capable of experiencing.

The other side of the coin is that an unknown proportion of supposedly universal etic concepts that originated in Europe or America are actually emic notions of their respective cultural sources, questionable in their application on a worldwide basis. Alas, there is no sure way to tell which of our cherished concepts are culture-specific and which are general. "Adjustment" is cumbersome to translate into German, French, Spanish, or Russian; the dictionary equivalents of this term are in less frequent use in any of these languages than "adjustment" is in English; courses in the "psychology of adjustment" are unthinkable at European universities. What about achievement motivation, locus of control, and field independence, to mention only few of the recent or current topics of active and productive cross-cultural investigation?

Several safeguards come to mind—to be applied before, during, and after the research project. The first of these is the use of local informants, not necessarily limited to social psychologists, as to the fit of the concept, content, and format of the variable being investigated. How meaningful is it to translate the F-Scale (Adorno *et al.*, 1950) in a culture where the authority of the chief or of the elite is unquestioned and absolute? How useful is the investigation of the need for achievement (McClelland, 1961) in a subsistance economy in which opportunities for entrepreneurial behavior and social mobility are nil? These are extreme examples, but subtler instances of the lack of fit of a concept to a culture can be discovered upon this kind of inquiry. The factorial composition of the measure in question may then be ascertained empirically in its new milieu. Kuo and Marsella (1977) found that Christie's (Christie & Geis, 1970) Macchiavellianism scale, which in the United States measures successful social manipulativeness, is greatly contaminated in Taiwan by the admixture of individual differences in social reserve.

The factorial approach can be extended to several measures; Guthrie and Bennett (1971) used multivariate techniques as an empirical avenue for ascertaining a particular culture's "implicit personality theory," its unverbalized formulation of what traits "go together." At the postinvestigation stage, a further check can be performed on the coherence of the findings obtained with other available sources of information on the culture. The studies by Carment (1974) and Carment and Hodgkin (1973) are notable for integrating differences in locus of control between Indian and Canadian subjects with other psychological findings on the two cultures and with a broader understanding of human functioning in the two cultures. What, at first glance, might have appeared an isolated, even trivial, finding is effectively blended with the understanding of the opportunities and limitations in the Indian and the Canadian cultures.

A recent approach developed by Brislin and Holwill (1977) is worth recommending in this connection. Subjects of cross-cultural investigations can be used as informants and critics of findings pertaining to their own culture. This approach has not yet been applied to the results of personality research, but would appear to be applicable here also. In some, although not all, cross-cultural personality studies, participants in the research could shed valuable light on the meaning of the results obtained. Finally, the pattern of findings, from a variety of perspectives and by means of a variety of measures, is almost always superior to a single finding, no matter how significant. It is in this connection that the several approaches to cross-cultural investigation, from the much disdained projective measures, through the easily applied questionnaires to the time samples of behavior, all acquire their partial and complementary significance.

Once the problem of choosing measures is settled, the cross-cultural student of personality must tackle the problem of intragroup variability. The rejection of national character as a unimodal construct has already been discussed. The investigator must come to grips with the notion that probably all cultures allow for more than one formula of adaptation among their members and that this applies even more so to the large-scale modern national cultures. The "typical" American, Korean, or German is a stereotype which, as Bruner and Perlmutter (1957) demonstrated, thrives on scarcity of contact. But does this mean that personality differences among *groups* of individuals from several cultures are illusory and stereotypical?

And, moreover, is there nothing, in the words of Dufrenne (1953) that "makes a Comanche a Comanche and a Frenchman a Frenchman" other than political allegiance and language?

In response to the first question, differences in a variety of personality parameters have been demonstrated, but they, as a rule, assume the form of overlapping curves with significant differences in central tendency and, sometimes, in dispersion. Moreover, cultural groups are likely to vary on several dimensions and to form several factors, similar or different across culture lines. It may be helpful to conceive of these differences as paths differing in ease or resistance. Thus, it is easier for a Mexican than for a North American to learn to respond to challenging and stressful situations stoically and passively (Diaz-Guerrero, 1967, 1970; Holtzman, Diaz-Guerrero, & Swartz, 1975); both personal experience of socialization and the historically transmitted "wisdom" of the Mexican culture makes such a response appear sensible and graceful. Yet, there are a great many North Americans who are more passive than most Mexicans; nor is there perfect consistency across the situations of both of these groups (although this aspect of the problem is, to the extent of my knowledge, as yet not systematically investigated).

An adequate cultural psychology of personality must also account for meaningful variation of personality characteristics among its members. Aronoff (1967) sharply contrasted the needs and personality constellations of the fishermen and cane-cutters on St. Kitts of the West Indies. Edgerton (1971), in a comparative study of four East African cultures, identified the overriding dichotomy of agriculturalists and pastoralists as the determinant of a variety of differences in behaviors, values, and attitudes—especially in relation to conformity. In Japan, a contrast exists in the socialization of the offspring of businessmen and salaried employees, clearly prepared for different slots in life, with different values (Vogel, 1963). The authors of these reports restricted themselves to the descriptions of subgroups in their particular milieus, without speculating on the commonalities of fisherman, businessmen, or agriculturalists across a variety of settings. The possibility is not precluded of investigating the interaction between cultures and various subcultural roles within them. Is there a pancultural peasant personality, as Redfield (1953) proposed? The answer to this question must await the implementation of such studies.

Not only is there intragroup variability that complicates cross-cultural comparison of personality; intraindividual variability—across situations, from the social-learning point of view, and across levels of consciousness, from the psychodynamic perspective—must be integrated into culture–personality study. The prototypical approach has been to assume the unity of personality within culture. Casual observation, clinical study, and systematic research converge in suggesting that such a monolithic state is an exception rather than a rule. This is especially evident in countries undergoing rapid economic, social, and political transformation, and among the strata of the population centrally involved in these processes.

Benoit (1969), described his clientele in Martinique as French on the surface and Antillean inside. In the process of psychotherapy, the metropolitan veneer was shed and the local beliefs, attitudes, values, and fears came to the fore. Bulatao (1969) coined the term ''split-level personality'' to describe the skillful shuttling of many educated Filipinos between the modern and traditional world. An analogous phenomenon was investigated by Boesch (1970) in Thailand. Here the ambivalent and seemingly inconsistent behavior of the elites may spring from conflict between traditional static values, and modern demands for performance and achievement. Intraindividually and interindividually, the complexities of the relationship between personality and culture intrude upon and obstruct the establishment of clear-cut links between cultural characteristics and personality variables.

To turn to the second issue, a number of proposals have been formulated that allow for a possibility of a common cultural heritage within the individual's subjective, culturally shared world. Vexliard (1970), on the basis of a historical review of the older works on national character, suggested reformulating the concept as a ''structure in depth'' composed of a ''central nucleus of meaning.'' Without proposing specific alternatives, Vexliard inveighed against fragmented cross-cultural studies, exemplified by the comparison of the number of Rorschach white-space responses in the United States and Samoa. The bibliography of Duijker and Frijda (1960), according to Vexliard, is replete with molecular, isolated studies of this type which, neither cumulatively nor discretely, bring us any closer to the central, nationally shared nucleus of meanings that may be harbored by individuals of shared culture, but differing personalities.

Independently of this proposal, the concept of ''subjective culture'' and the methods for assessing it have been developed. Triandis *et al.* (1972, p. 4) consider subjective culture to be ''a cultural group's characteristic ways of perceiving the man-made part of its environment.'' Systematic techniques for capturing a group's subjective culture have been devised. These revolve around the tasks of categorizing and relating a wide variety of concepts, activities, and role titles. A complex network of relationships is thus obtained which yields both emic and etic data. Emically, information is provided on the culture-specific meaning of particular roles, abstractions, and relationships. What is expected of a ''boss'' in India and of a ''scholar'' in Japan is ascertained in this manner. Etically, factor analyses of subjective culture data have yielded four dimensions which remain unchanged across cultures: association–dissociation, superordination–subordination, intimacy, and hostility (Triandis *et al.*, 1972). It is these four modes of social interaction to which a multitude of roles and relationships are panculturally reduced. Subjective culture appears to underlie, yet is not synonymous with, cultural personality or national character. All people partaking of a specific subjective culture must not necessarily share personality characteristics.

According to Triandis (1977), subjective culture predicts a little more than half of the social behavior. At this point it is unknown what share of the remaining variance is captured by personality and how it relates to subjective culture. Yet, blending of investigations of personality characteristics with subjective culture would appear to be a meaningful way for rescuing the realistic aspects of national character from oblivion and for closing the gap between social determinants of behavior and their individually patterned expressions.

Theories and Findings

CULTURAL VARIABLES

What are the antecedents of personality differences on the plane of culture? Few such characteristics have been identified, let alone conclusively studied. At this point, one of the most promising leads is the parallel between cultural and personal (usually called, cognitive) complexity, stressed by Triandis (1977). In the simplest case, socially, politically, and economically, simple societies produce individuals low in cognitive complexity. Triandis feels cognitive complexity thrives in social settings characterized by specialized economic activities, elaborate systems of governance, and an intricate system of social graduation and differentiation. Factor analyses of data from the Human Relations Area Files (Carneiro, 1970; Lomax & Berkowitz, 1972; Murdock & Provost, 1973) do indeed demonstrate that a factor of cultural complexity emerges from these analyses. Several lines of psychological investigation, reviewed by Triandis (1975, 1977), point to cognitive complexity as an organizing principle of individual behavior, even though there is no merger of the several independently developed traditions of measuring cognitive complexity as yet. Triandis *et al.* (1965) have produced evidence that these several measures merge into a single factor. What remains to be done is to relate, systematically, the indicators of individual and cognitive complexity and to establish, empirically, the degree of this correspondence.

The likelihood of such overlap appears to be plausible, even though a number of conflicting bits of evidence have to be considered. Anticipating the consideration of Witkin and Berry's (1975) formulation on the relationship of types of subsistence economy and cognitive style, it is the hunters and gatherers who have been found to exceed in field-independence; the sedentary agriculturalists, even though soil-tilling activities usually are associated with higher socioeconomic complexity. Moreover, intracultural work in field-dependence (see Musahl, 1976; Schulte, 1974; Fröhlich, 1972;

Huteau, 1975) has, on occasion, brought to the fore the high specificity of field-independence measures. There is no doubt that interrelationships are complex within the domain of social and individual complexity. The expectation of a one-to-one relationship between these two variables is probably illusory, rather an imperfect link (subject to a variety of currently unidentified mediating variables) is a more realistic possibility.

The other cultural variable discussed in Triandis' (1977) review is that of tight and loose cultures introduced by Pelto (1968). At the one end of the continuum, societies are characterized by a great deal of ambiguity and even anomie concerning division of labor, status, and norms of behavior. At the opposite extreme, a system of tight prescriptions regulates, but also restricts, the individual and social behavior. Triandis hypothetically links this dimension of social organization to the variable or overtness–vicariousness in individual behavior. Loose societies would foster overt behavior, including outbursts of impulses. Tight societies would predispose their members toward "projective," vicarious, fantasy expression. This proposal remains a hypothesis to be tested biculturally, multiculturally, and hologeistically.

Pelto's division overlaps with the much earlier proposal by Arsenian and Arsenian (1948) of tough and easy cultures, differing in the severity and pervasiveness of sanctions over social rule breaking. The Arsenians' concern, in an article which, as far as I know, was never followed up, was with the psychopathological consequences of these two social regimens: differences in suicide rates, stress-related illnesses, and other related social indicators. It is possible to broaden their concern and to ask the question of what personality constellations would be produced in "tough" and "easy" societies.

SOCIALIZATION TECHNIQUES AND EXPERIENCES

Cross-cultural investigators have identified several parameters of socialization experience that noticeably vary across cultures, but might easily be overlooked in studies limited to one culture. Socialization research was the central concern of the culture–personality movement in the narrow sense of the word from the 1930s through the 1950s. The objective of the investigators operating within this tradition was to establish the variations in the interrelationship of psychoanalytically postulated variables within a universal framework and universally applicable. Anthropologists and their psychoanalytic collaborators looked at various cultures as "laboratories of nature" for testing tenets of psychoanalytic theory. In modern terminology, they felt that they were in possession of an etic framework which allowed for emic variations in the structuring of such experiences as weaning, toilet training, or Oedipal conflict. LeVine (1973), Barnouw (1973), Honigmann (1967), Wallace (1970), and Williams (1975) have reviewed the yield of these studies.

Perhaps one of the reasons for the relative decline of this approach was the gradual realization by cross-cultural students of personality that the formative experiences postulated by psychoanalysis capture but a share of the total variance of cross-culturally active, and influential, socialization variables (e.g., Guthrie & Jacobs, 1966). Cultures, to be sure, differ in weaning, cleanliness training, and handling of childhood sexuality, but they differ in many variables besides. Balanced reviews of cross-cultural socialization and development (e.g., LeVine, 1973; Munroe & Munroe, 1975) document and discuss this realization, in addition to the mixed picture of partial corroboration and partial refutation of psychoanalytically inspired hypotheses.

One of the cross-culturally relevant socialization variables is the nature of child–mother contact, even in the earliest periods of infancy. Caudill and Weinstein (1969) discovered that the behavior of Japanese and American infants differed in the earliest weeks of their lives and that these differences were traceable to the cultural modes of interaction between baby and mother. To simplify, American mothers talked and vocalized more whereas their Japanese counterparts relied upon direct bodily and tactile contact. A lot of personality contrasts, between Japan, the United States, and other Western countries can be at least speculatively related to this early childhood experience (see Kimura, 1971; Morsbach, 1973; Norbeck & DeVos, 1972; Tanaka-Matsumi & Marsella, 1976). Further substantiation of this link awaits the implementation of cross-cultural longitudinal studies.

Another variable that the cross-cultural observation of socialization experiences has brought to light is the respective role of peers and parents in the process of socialization. Bronfenbrenner (1967) deserves credit for identifying this cross-cultural variable which, according to him, operates differently in a variety of countries. Peers have more influence as agents of socialization in the United States than in countries of Western Europe such as Great Britain, West Germany, and Switzerland (Devereux, Bronfenbrenner, and Suci, 1962; Rodgers, Bronfenbrenner, and Devereux, 1968). The Soviet Union and the United States are roughly similar in using peers as socializers, but in the Soviet Union, the roles of peers and adults are complementary, whereas in the United States these roles are antagonistic (Bronfenbrenner, 1967). For the moment, let us gloss over the fact already mentioned that not all aspects of this formulation have been confirmed; the important thing is the identification of an important antecedent which could be meaningfully investigated in relation to personality characteristics in children, adolescent, and adults. Guthrie and Jacobs (1966) make the point that the child-care tasks in the rural Philippines are largely entrusted to the siblings; this situation no doubt obtains in a lot of other non-Western settings as well (see Ainsworth, 1967, on the Baganda).

Related to this, one could posit a continuum from the nuclear family socialization, such as we know it in the United States, through the extended family of a great many Oceanic and African settings (see Munroe & Munroe, 1975) to the predominance of extrafamilial influences in the socialization experience, perhaps best exemplified in the Israeli kibbutzim.[1] The role of extrafamilial and nonparental socializers has been grossly neglected in Western-based theories of socialization. Cross-cultural research can make a contribution here that would benefit all of psychology.

To elaborate, all of the variables enumerated operate not only across, but within cultures. Because of their relatively limited range of variation, they, however, are not readily visible and are easily overlooked in a culturally unitary milieu. In this manner then cross-cultural psychology can fulfill one of its primary objectives, that is, expand the range of observations so as to identify new and active variables.

However, this contribution does not exhaust the potential of cross-cultural socialization research. Two recently reported projects (Rohner, 1975; Whiting & Whiting, 1975) illustrate another potential of this kind of investigation. Rohner's project is a hologeistic analysis of the factors surrounding parental rejection and acceptance, a pair of intuitively understandable "folk variables," which have a central role to play in a number of formulations of child development. Whiting and Whiting conducted an intensive analysis of the day-to-day interactions between parents and children in six widely different cultures, with particular emphasis on the children's social behavior in a variety of categories. The common features of these two projects is that they tap universal characteristics, variable both within and across cultures, and readily inferable from observable and coded behavior.

The impact of later social influences upon personality has been neglected in the cross-cultural research extant. This relationship could be investigated by tracing the effect of values and implicit personality theories upon members of different cultures. Personality can be influenced not only "from below," that is, through child rearing practices and parental attitudes, but also "from above," through that which the culture considers right and valuable. Instruments have been devised to this end (e.g., Morris, 1955) and cross-culturally tested (e.g., Kilby, 1971), but not, as yet, related to personality. However, Green's (1964) research, among others, demonstrates that values of parents shape the goals of socialization of their children. Presumably, they exercise an influence on actual socialization practices as well.

SOME CROSS-CULTURALLY RELEVANT PERSONALITY CHARACTERISTICS: THE RESULTS OF DIFFERENT SOCIAL ENVIRONMENTS

The range of personality characteristics investigated cross-culturally at one time or another is extremely wide. An exhaustive bibliography of this

---

[1] Even the kibbutzim are experiencing considerable strain as a result of competition between the community and the family for the child's attention, affection, and time (see Beit-Hallahmi & Rabin, 1977; Endleman, 1977).

work is nowhere compiled, nor is an integration of this work available, in article, monograph, or book form. Nonetheless, it is possible to construct a tentative and preliminary hierarchy of various types of personality-related cross-cultural investigations.

Lowest on the list are episodic, instrument-centered studies bereft of hypotheses or theory. The investigators pack their favorite scales as they prepare for a sabbatical abroad and come back with a comparative study of their instruments. Next are the instrument-centered studies, undertaken with a view to their revalidation in another cultures. There is no pejorative intent in listing these kinds of study so low on the scale, as some of them are methodologically sophisticated and practically useful. The point is that this research rarely yields cross-cultural information of substance. Its primary purpose is to adapt an instrument for use in another culture. Only after this is done, is it worthwhile and practical to turn to cross-cultural comparisons. On the third rung of the ladder are the systematic and sequential investigations of phenomena in which meaningful cross-cultural variation may, on a theoretical or common sense basis, be plausibly expected. The remainder of this subsection will be devoted to a rather arbitrary selection of topics which share the feature of sparking a lot of recent effort and attention.

At this time, field dependence is the subject of probably the most coherent cross-cultural personality research program extant. The availability of recent reviews (Witkin & Berry, 1975; Witkin & Goodenough, 1977) and of Berry's chapter (Chapter 6) in this volume make it superfluous to consider the details of this work. A chain of links has been forged between the nature of subsistence economy, mode of socialization, and cognitive style. In the application of this theoretical scheme to more complex and differentiated societies, problems arise; In the figurative sense, there are "hunters" as well as "peasants" in each one of the modern nation–state societies; their comparison requires additional sources of hypotheses and principles of explanation.

By contrast, the newer cross-cultural topic of "locus of control" has neither been comprehensively reviewed nor has it currently yielded a coherent body of data. The notions that oriental, welfare-oriented, and traditional–magical cultures are characterized by greater externality has received some support, as well as refutation (Carment, 1974; Hsieh, Shybut, & Lotsof, 1969; Jahoda, 1970; Lao, 1978; Mahler, 1974; Parsons, Schneider, & Hanson, 1970; Schneider & Parsons, 1970; Yamada, 1970). Moreover, subscales within the paper-and-pencil locus-of-control measures and the items within them are more useful for cross-cultural differentiation than global scores. All of this tentatively suggests that the construct of locus of control is more cross-culturally useful than its current American-based measures. Redesigning these scales at the several sites of cross-cultural comparison might be a useful remedy to this situation. Next, cultural characteristics and social antecedents for the transmission of an external versus an internal locus of control would need to be specified.

Another major body of personality-related work is focused on need for achievement, but remarkably, not to the same extent upon the other two parallel motivational variables, need for power and need for affiliation (McClelland, 1961; Serpell, 1976; Veroff & Veroff, 1972). Again, as in the case of field independence, there are plausible cross-culturally varied socialization antecedents and there are differences across cultures in the need for achievement. Moreover, the social and economic consequences of these differences are of great importance. As DeVos (1960) demonstrated in Japan, achievement in real life is not inextricably linked to need for achievement; ambitious striving may have a lot of other antecedents. Gallimore *et al.* (1974) showed that, among Hawaiian Americans, affiliation fosters and stimulates, rather than impedes, achievement in the school setting. McClelland's (1965) own demonstration that achievement in behavior can be effectively fostered on a short-range, situational basis, casts doubts on the extent to which achievement striving is a personality characteristic rather than a reflection of what Veroff, Atkinson, Feld, and Gurin (1960) called "the individual's situation in life."

That cultural groups differ in self-rating depression scales has been demonstrated in the worldwide macrocosm of cross-national comparison (Zung, 1972) and in the multicultural microcosm of Hawaii (e.g., Marsella, Walker, & Johnson, 1973). Currently lacking is a comprehensive statement of cultural and social antecedents that predispose normal individuals to, or protect them from, the expression of melancholy affect. A complex pattern of expectations, opportunities for their fulfillment, self-sufficiency, dependence, and internalization of one's own standards combines to determine how "high" or "low" a person feels in a given cultural setting and how willing and able he or she is to report this state verbally (see Marsella, in press, for a review of depression across cultures).

By contrast, research on active–passive coping, which is centered upon a series of comparisons between Mexico and the United States (Diaz-Guerrero, 1967, 1970; Holtzman *et al.*, 1975), but is potentially relevant to the contrast between Latin America and North America and is perhaps applicable on a worldwide basis, is grounded in the theory of "sociocultural premises" which are reflected in socialization, response to stress, and everyday coping. The interrelated set of findings of differences between Mexicans and Americans on this dimension, in its various manifestations, makes it another promising concept to explore and to pursue.

No appraisal of cross-cultural personality research is complete without reference to psychoanalytically inspired studies, at one time the dominant current of thought in culture and personality, now only a trend among others. The appraisal by Kline (1977) absolves me of the necessity of sharing the details of the status of this research area; in a balanced review, he registers several failures and notes some successes. Thus, Stephens' (1962) hologeistic study of the Oedipal complex hypothesis produced evidence that a variety of socialization antecedents that could realistically be assumed to intensify the Oedipal experience, led to the theoretically expected results. Similarly, Lee's (1958) studies among the Zulus corroborated a number of Freudian hypotheses in a culture where the knowledge of Freudian symbolism could not yet have spread. Work by Parin and Parin-Matthey (1976), which is comparative in research design, but qualitative in data analysis, brought to the fore differences in superego and ego functioning between two groups of analysands who were close in language and culture, but divergent in recent historical and political experience (i.e., Germans and Swiss). But these results are, of necessity, more suggestive than conclusive sources of hypotheses to be followed up by psychoanalytic and nonpsychoanalytic means. Kline (1977) concluded that conclusive tests of Freudian hypotheses demand both theoretical knowledge and methodological skill, a combination which has not been abundant among the cross-cultural investigators of psychoanalytic propositions.

To switch the evaluation from personality variables to cultures, what have we learned about the personality functioning in specific cultural milieus? Information would appear to be substantial in the case of Japan (see Caudill, 1973; Norbeck & DeVos, 1972), suggestive in the case of Mexico (Diaz-Guerrero, 1970) and the Philippines (Guthrie, 1968), and scattered and fragmentary in the case of most other cultures around the world. In particular, little substantive and integrated knowledge has emerged from the manifold speculation on our culturally closest neighbors—the various countries of Western Europe. Culture and personality studies started with the archaic, proceeded to the exotic—from the Western point of view—and have yet to immerse themselves in the cultural variation closest to their origin. Americans, who are more frequently used as "control groups" in bicultural and multicultural investigations than citizens of any other nation, have rarely been the focus of cross-cultural study. It is an interesting and open question as to what information all these unreviewed and unintegrated data may yield about personality functioning in interplay with the American historical experience and contemporary milieu. Perhaps it is a task worth tackling.

Conclusions

On the basis of the material reviewed, culture–personality research appears to be neither "magnificent" nor a "failure," to echo the words of Bruner's (1974) appraisal. The burden seems to have shifted from illustrative monocultural, qualitative studies to bilateral, multilateral, and hologeistic comparisons. While the unity of the movement for culture–personality studies has disappeared, the relationship of these topics has remained an active and productive area of investigation. The focus is no longer upon the pattern of personality characteristics in a culture; it is upon dimensions of personality across cultures. Yet, what these dimensions are, and what their scope is, continue to be matters of debate. Hence, the impression of confusion and uncertainty that the current state of culture and personality research conveys. Beyond this impression, there is the prospect of integration of strands and fragments of information already gathered, and the promise of their contributing to the sum of knowledge of general psychology. Our perspectives on socialization have already been broadened through cross-cultural research; other contributions are not sure, but likely to come.

References

Abel, T. M. *Psychological testing in cultural contexts.* New Haven, Connecticut: College & University Press, 1973.

Adorno, T. W., Frenkel-Brunswik, E., Levinson, D. J., & Sanford, R. N. *The authoritarian personality.* New York: Harper, 1950.

Ainsworth, M. D. S. *Infancy in Uganda.* Baltimore, Maryland: Johns Hopkins Press, 1967.

Aronoff, J. *Psychological needs and cultural systems: A case study.* Princeton, New Jersey: Van Nostrand-Reinhold, 1967.

Arsenian, J., & Arsenian, J. Tough and easy cultures: A conceptual analysis. *Psychiatry,* 1948, *11,* 377–385.

Bandura, A. The self-system in reciprocal determinism. *American Psychologist,* 1978, *33,* 344–358.

Barry, H. III, Bacon, M. K., & Child, I. L. A cross-cultural survey of some sex differences in socialization. *Journal of Abnormal and Social Psychology,* 1957, *55,* 327–332.

Barnouw, V. *Culture and personality* (Rev. ed.). Homewood, Illinois: Dorsey, 1973.

Bauer, R. *The new man in Soviet psychology.* Cambridge, Massachusetts: Harvard Univ. Press, 1952.

Beit-Hallahmi, B., & Rabin, A. I. The Kibbutz as a social experiment and as a child-rearing laboratory. *American Psychologist,* 1977, *32,* 532–541.

Benoit, G. *A propos d'une recherche en matière de psychiatrie transculturelle.* Paper presented at the Second International Congress of Social Psychiatry, London, 1969.

Bell, D. National character revisited: A proposal for renegotiating the concept. In: E. Norbeck, D. Price-Williams, & W. M. McCord (Eds.), *The study of personality: An interdisciplinary appraisal.* New York: Holt, 1968.

Berrien, F. K. A super-ego for cross-cultural research. *International Journal of Psychology,* 1970, *5,* 1–9.

Berry, J. W. On cross-cultural comparability. *International Journal of Psychology,* 1969, *4,* 119–128.

Boesch, E. E. *Zwiespältige Eliten: Eine sozialpsychologische Untersuchung über administrative Eliten in Thailand.* Berne: Huber, 1970.

Brislin, R. W. Back-translation for cross-cultural research. *Journal of Cross-Cultural Psychology,* 1970, *1,* 185–216.

Brislin, R. W., & Holwill, F. Reaction of indigenous people to writings of behavioral and social scientists. *International Journal of Intercultural Relations,* 1977, *1,* 15–34.

Brislin, R. W., Lonner, W. J., & Thorndike, R. M. *Cross-cultural research methods.* New York: Wiley, 1973.

Brisset, C. Le culturalisme en psychiatrie. *Evolution psychiatrique,* 1963, *28,* 369–402.

Bronfenbrenner, U. Responses to pressure from peers vs. adults among Soviet and American school children. *International Journal of Psychology,* 1967, *2,* 199–208.

Bronfenbrenner, U. *Two worlds of childhood: U.S. and U.S.S.R.* New York: Russell Sage Foundation, 1970.

Bruner, J. S. Concluding comments and summary of conference. In J. L. M. Dawson & W. J. Lonner (Eds.), *Readings in cross-cultural psychology.* Hong Kong: Univ. of Hong Kong Press, 1974.

Bruner, J. S., & Perlmutter, H. V. Compatriot and foreigner: A study of impression formation in three countries. *Journal of Abnormal and Social Psychology,* 1957, *55,* 253–261.

Bulatao, J. Westernization and the split-level personality in the Philippines. In W. Caudill & T. Lin (Eds.), *Mental health research in Asia and the Pacific.* Honolulu: East–West Center Press, 1969.

Butcher, J. N., & Pancheri, P. *A handbook of cross-cultural MMPI research.* Minneapolis: Univ. of Minnesota Press, 1976.

Carment, D. W. Internal versus external locus of control in India and Canada. *International Journal of Psychology,* 1974, *9,* 45–50.

Carment, D. W., & Hodgkin, B. Coaction and competition in India and Greece. *Journal of Cross-Cultural Psychology,* 1973, *4,* 459–469.

Carneiro, R. L. Scale analysis, revolutionary sequence and the rating of cultures. In R. Naroll & R. Cohen (Eds.), *A handbook of method in cultural anthropology.* New York: Columbia Univ. Press, 1970.

Cattell, R. B. *Personality and motivation: Structure and measurement.* New York: World Book Company, 1957.

Cattell, R. B., & Scheier, I. H. *Measurement of neuroticism and anxiety.* New York: Ronald Press, 1961.

Caudill, W. The influence of social structure and culture on human behavior in Japan. *Journal of Nervous and Social Disease,* 1973, *157,* 249–258.

Caudill, W., & Plath, D. Who sleeps by whom? Parent–child involvement in urban Japanese families. *Psychiatry,* 1966, *29,* 344–366.

Caudill, W., & Weinstein, H. Maternal care and infant behavior in Japan and America. *Psychiatry,* 1969, *32,* 12–43.

Christie, R., & Geis, F. L. *Studies in Machiavellianism.* New York: Academic Press, 1970.

Conde Lopez, V., & Chamorro, T. deE. Contribución al estudio de la S.D.I. de Zung in una muestra estratificada de población normal. *Revista de psicología general y aplicada,* 1974, *29,* 515–553.

Crutchfield, R. S. Conformity and character. *American Psychologist,* 1955, *10,* 191–198.

Delpech, B. Les techniques projectives dans l'exploration de la personnalité socioculturelle. *Psychopathologie Africaine,* 1971, *7,* 239–284.

Devereux, E. C., Bronfenbrenner, U., & Suci, G. J. Patterns of parent behavior in the United States of America and the Federal Republic of Germany: A cross-cultural comparison. *International Social Sciences Journal,* 1962, *14,* 488–506.

DeVos, G. The relation of guilt toward parents to achievement and arranged marriage among the Japanese. *Psychiatry,* 1960, *23,* 287–301.

DeVos, G. Transcultural diagnosis of mental health by means of psychological tests. In A. V. S. DeReuck & E. Porter (Eds.), *Transcultural psychiatry.* Boston: Little Brown, 1965.

Diaz-Guerrero, R. The active and the passive syndromes. *Revista interamericana de psicologia,* 1967, *1,* 263–272.

Diaz-Guerrero, R. *Estudios de psicología del mexicano* (Tercera edición). Mexico City: Trillas, 1970.

Doi, L. T. *The anatomy of dependence* (J. Bester, trans.). Tokyo: Kodansha, 1973.

Draguns, J. G. Assessment of personality. In C. N. Cofer & H. E. Fitzgerald (Eds.), *Psychology: A programmed modular approach.* Homewood, Illinois: Learning Systems Company, 1975.

Draguns, J. G. Advances in the methodology of cross-cultural psychiatric assessment. *Transcultural Psychiatric Research Review,* 1977, *14,* 125–143.

Draguns, J. G. Cultura y personalidad. In J. O. Whittaker (Ed.), *La psicología social en el mundo de hoy.* Mexico City: Trillas, 1979, 287–322.

DuBois, C. *The people of Alor*. Minneapolis: Univ. of Minnesota Press, 1944.

Dufrenne, M. *La personnalité de base*. Paris: Presses universitaires de France, 1953.

Duijker, H. C. J., & Frijda, N. H. *National character and national stereotypes*. Amsterdam: North Holland Publishing Company, 1960.

Edgerton, R. B. *The individual in cultural adaptation*. Berkeley: Univ. of California Press, 1971.

Endleman, R. Familistic social change in the Israeli Kibbutz. In L. L. Adler (Ed.), *Annals of the New York Academy of Sciences*, 1977, *285*, 605–611.

Escovar, L. A. Consideraciones teóricas necessarias en la aplicación de los principios de conductismo al cambio social. *Revista interamericana de psicología*, 1974, 8, 309–324.

Fröhlich, W. D. Sozialisation und kognitive Stile. In C. F. Graumann (Ed.), *Handbuch für Psychologie. Band VIII: Sozialpsychologie*. Göttingen, West Germany: Verlag für Psychologie, 1972.

Gallimore, R., Boggs, J. W., & Jordan, C. *Culture, behavior and education*. Beverly Hills, California: Sage–Halsted, 1974.

Glatt, K. M. An evaluation of the French, Spanish, and German translation of the MMPI. *Acta psychologica*, 1969, *29*, 65–84.

Goffman, E. *The presentation of self in everyday life*. New York: Doubleday, 1959.

Gorer, G., & Rickman, J. *The people of Great Russia*. London: Grosset, 1949.

Green, H. B. Socialization values in Negro and East-Indian subcultures of Trinidad. *Journal of Social Psychology*, 1964, *64*, 1–20.

Guthrie, G. M. The Philippine temperament. In G. M. Guthrie, *Six perspectives on the Philippines*. Manila: Bookmark, 1968.

Guthrie, G. M., Azores, F. M., Juanico, M. B., Luna, M. P. A., & Ty, T. P. *The psychology of modernization in the rural Philippines*. Manila: Institute of Philippine Culture, 1970.

Guthrie, G. M. A behavioral analysis of culture learning. In. R. W. Brislin, S. Bochner & W. Lonner (Eds.), *Cross-cultural perspectives on learning*. New York: Wiley, 1975.

Guthrie, G. M., & Bennett, A. B., Jr. Cultural differences in implicit personality theory. *International Journal of Psychology*, 1971, *6*, 305–312.

Guthrie, G. M., & Jacobs, P. J. *Child rearing and personality development in the Philippines*. University Park, Pennsylvania: Pennsylvania State Univ. Press, 1966.

Herrmann, T. *Lehrbuch der empirischen Persönlichkeitsforschung*. Göttingen, West Germany: Verlag für Psychologie, 1971.

Holtzman, W., Diaz-Guerrero, R., & Swartz, J. D. *Personality development in two cultures*. Austin: Univ. of Texas Press, 1975.

Honigmann, J. J. *Personality in culture*. New York: Harper, 1967.

Hsieh, T. Y., Shybut, J., & Lotsof, E. J. Internal versus external control and ethnic group membership: A cross-cultural comparison. *Journal of Consulting and Clinical Psychology*, 1969, *33*, 122–124.

Hsu, F. L. K. (Ed.) *Psychological anthropology*. (Rev. ed.). Cambridge, Massachusetts: Schenkman, 1971. (a)

Hsu, F. L. K. Psychological homeostasis and jen: Conceptual tools for advancing psychological anthropology. *American Anthropologist*, 1971, *73*, 23–33. (b)

Huang, L. C., & Harris, M. B. Conformity in Chinese and Americans: A field experiment. *Journal of Cross-Cultural Psychology*, 1973, *4*, 427–434.

Huteau, M. Un style cognitif: La dépendence–indépendence a l'égard du champ. *L'année psychologique*, 1975, *75*, 198–262.

Inkeles, A. The modernization of man. In M. Weiner (Ed.), *Modernization: The dynamics of growth*. New York: Basic Books, 1966.

Inkeles, A. Individual modernity in different ethnic and religious groups. Data from the six-nation study. In L. L. Adler (Ed.), Issues in cross-cultural research. *Annals of the New York Academy of Sciences*, 1977, *285*, 539–564.

Inkeles, A., & Levinson, D. J. National character: The study of modal personality and sociocultural systems. In G. Lindzey & E. Aronson (Eds.), *Handbook of social psychology* (Vol. 4, 2nd ed.). Reading, Massachusetts: Addison-Wesley, 1968.

Jahoda, G. Supernatural beliefs and changing cognitive structures among Ghanaian university students. *Journal of Cross-Cultural Psychology,* 1970, *1,* 115–130.

Jones, R. L. (Ed.). *Black psychology.* New York: Harper, 1972.

Kaplan, B. Cross-cultural use of projective techniques. In F. L. K. Hsu (Ed.), *Psychological anthropology.* Homewood, Illinois: Dorsey, 1961.

Kardiner, A. *Psychological frontiers of society.* New York: Columbia Univ. Press, 1945.

Kelman, H. C. Compliance, identification, and internalization: Three processes of attitude change. *Journal of Conflict Resolution,* 1958, *2,* 51–60.

Kilby, R. W. Values of Indian, American, and Japanese university students. *Psychologia,* 1971, *14,* 53–66.

Kimura, B. Mitmenschlichkeit in der Psychiatrie: Ein transkultureller Beitrag aus asiatischer Sicht, *Zeitschrift für klinische Psychologie,* 1971, *19,* 3–15.

Kline, P. Cross-cultural studies and Freudian theory. In: N. Warren (Ed.), *Studies in cross-cultural psychology* (Vol. 1). London: Academic Press, 1977.

Kuo, H. K., & Marsella, A. J. The meaning and measurement of Macchiavellianism in Chinese and American college students. *Journal of Social Psychology,* 1977, *101,* 165–173.

La Barre, W. Some observations on character structure in the Orient: The Japanese. *Psychiatry,* 1945, *8,* 319–342.

Lao, R. C. Levenson's IEC (Internal–External Control) scale: A comparison of Chinese and American students. *Journal of Cross-Cultural Psychology,* 1978, *9,* 113–124.

Lazarus, R. S., Opton, E., Tomita, M., & Kodama, M. A cross-cultural study of stress reaction patterning in Japan. *Journal of Personality and Social Psychology,* 1966, *4,* 622–633.

Lee, S. G. Social influences in Zulu dreaming. *Journal of Social Psychology,* 1958, *47,* 265–283.

LeVine, R. A. *Culture, behavior, and personality.* Chicago: Aldine, 1973.

Lewin, K. *A dynamic theory of personality.* New York: McGraw-Hill, 1935.

Lindzey, G. *Projective techniques and cross-cultural research.* New York: Appleton, 1961.

Linton, R. *The cultural background of personality.* New York: Appleton, 1945.

Lomax, A., & Berkowitz, N. The evolutionary taxonomy of culture. *Science,* 1972, *177,* 228–239.

Lynn, R. *Personality and national character.* Oxford: Pergamon Press, 1971.

Lynn, R., & Hampson, S. I. National differences in extroversion and neuroticism. *British Journal of Social and Clinical Psychology,* 1975, *14,* 223–240.

Magnusson, D., & Endler, N. S. (Eds.). *Personality at the crossroads: Current issues in interactional psychology.* Hillsdale, New Jersey: Lawrence Erlbaum, 1977.

Mahler, I. A comparative study of locus of control. *Psychologia,* 1974, *11,* 135–139.

Malpass, R. S. Theory and method in cross-cultural psychology. *American Psychologist,* 1977, *32,* 1069–1079.

Marsella, A. Depressive affect and disorder across cultures. In H. Triandis & J. Draguns (Eds.), *Handbook of cross-cultural psychology* (Vol. 5). Rockleigh, New Jersey: Allyn & Bacon, in press.

Marsella, A. J., & Murray, M. D. Diagnostic type, gender, and consistency vs. specificity in behavior. *Journal of Clinical Psychology,* 1974, *30,* 484–488.

Marsella, A. J., Walker, E., & Johnson, F. Personality correlates of depressive disorders in female college students of different ethnic groups. *International Journal of Social Psychiatry,* 1973, *19,* 77–82.

Martinez, J. (Ed.). *Chicano psychology.* New York: Academic Press, 1977.

McClelland, D. *The achieving society.* Princeton, New Jersey: Van Nostrand, 1961.

McClelland, D. Toward a theory of motive acquisition. *American Psychologist,* 1965, *20,* 321–333.

Mischel, W. *Personality and assessment.* New York: Wiley, 1968.

Mischel, W. Toward a cognitive social learning reconceptualization of personality. *Psychological Review*, 1973, *80*, 252–283.

Mischel, W. On the future of personality measurement. *American Psychologist*, 1977, *32*, 246–254.

Monte, C. F. *Beneath the mask: An introduction to theories of personality*. New York: Holt, 1977.

Morris, C. *Varieties of human value*. Chicago: Univ. of Chicago Press, 1955.

Morsbach, H. Aspects of non-verbal communication in Japan. *Journal of Nervous and Mental Disease*, 1973, *157*, 262–278.

Munroe, R. L., & Munroe, R. H. *Cross-cultural human development*. Monterey, California: Brooks–Cole, 1975.

Murdock, G. P. World ethnographic sample. *American Anthropologist*, 1957, *59*, 664–687.

Murdock, G. P., & Provost, C. Measurement of cultural complexity. *Ethnology*, 1973, *12*, 379–392.

Musahl, H. P. *Untersuchungen zum Konzept der sogenannten Feldabhängigkeit (Witkin): Eine experimentelle Grundlagenstudie*. Opladen: Westdeutscher Verlag, 1976.

Norbeck, E., & DeVos, G. Culture and personality: The Japanese. In F. L. K. Hsu (Ed.), *Psychological anthropology* (New ed.). Cambridge, Massachusetts: Schenkman, 1972.

Parin, P., & Parin-Matthey, G. Typische Unterschiede zwischen Schweizern und Süddeutschen aus dem gebildeten Kleinbürgertum. *Psyche*, 1976, *30*, 1028–1048.

Parin, P., Morgenthaler, F., & Parin-Matthey, G. *Die Weissen denken zuviel*. Zurich, Switzerland: Atlantis, 1963.

Parin, P., Morgenthaler, F., & Parin-Matthey, G. *Fürchte deinen Nächsten wie dich selbst*. Frankfurt: Suhrkamp, 1971.

Parsons, O. A., Schneider, J. M., & Hansen, A. S. Internal-external locus of control and national stereotypes in Denmark and the United States. *Journal of Consulting and Clinical Psychology*, 1970, *35*, 30–37.

Pelto, P. J. The difference between "tight" and "loose" societies. *Transaction*, 1968 (April), 37–40.

Price-Williams, D. Psychological experiment and anthropology: The problem of categories. *Ethos*, 1974, *2*, 95–114.

Redfield, R. *The primitive world and its transformations*. Ithaca, New York: Cornell Univ. Press, 1953.

Rodgers, R. R., Bronfenbrenner, U., & Devereux, E. C. Standards of social behavior among school children in four cultures. *International Journal of Psychology*, 1968, *3*, 31–42.

Rohner, R. P. Parental acceptance–rejection and personality development: A universalistic approach to behavioral science. In R. W. Brislin, S. Bochner, & W. J. Lonner (Eds.), *Cross-cultural perspectives of learning*. New York: Wiley, 1975.

Rohner, R. P. *They love me, they love me not*. New Haven, Connecticut: Human Research Area Files Press, 1976.

Schneider, J. M., & Parsons, O. A. Categories on the locus of control scale and cross-cultural comparison in Denmark and the United States. *Journal of Cross-Cultural Psychology*, 1970, *1*, 131–138.

Schulte, D. *Feldabhängigkeit in der Wahrnehmung*. Meisenheim, West Germany: Hain, 1974.

Sechrest, L. On the need for experimentation in cross-cultural research. In L. L. Adler (Ed.), Issues in cross-cultural research. *Annals of the New York Academy of Sciences*, 1977, *285*, 104–118.

Sechrest, L., Fay, T. L., & Zaidi, S. M. H. Problems of translation in cross-cultural research. *Journal of Cross-Cultural Psychology*, 1972, *3*, 41–57.

Serpell, R. *Culture's influence on behaviour*. London: Methuen, 1976.

Sharma, S. Cross-cultural comparisons of anxiety: Methodological problems. *Topics in Culture Learning*, 1977, *5*, 166–173.

Siegel, B. J. Foreword. In *Biennial review of anthropology*. Palo Alto, California: Annual Reviews, Inc. 1971.

Skinner, B. F. *Science and human behavior*. New York: Macmillan, 1953.

Spain, D. H. On the use of projective techniques for psychological anthropology. In F. L. K. Hsu (Ed.), *Psychological anthropology* (New ed.). Cambridge, Massachusetts: Schenkman, 1972.

Spielberger, C. D., & Diaz-Guerrero, R. *Cross-cultural anxiety*. Washington: Hemisphere Press, 1976.

Spreen, O. Problems of translation and revalidation of questionnaires for clinical and cross-cultural purposes. *Acta Psychologica*, 1961, *19*, 1–12.

Stephens, W. N. *The Oedipus-complex: Cross-cultural evidence*. New York: Free Press of Glencoe, 1962.

Steward, J. H. *Theory of culture change*. Urbana, Illinois: Univ. of Illinois Press, 1958.

Tanaka-Matsumi, J., & Marsella, A. J. Cross-cultural variation in the phenomenological experience of depression. *Journal of Cross-Cultural Psychology*, 1976, *7*, 379–396.

Triandis, H. Culture training, cognitive complexity, and interpersonal attitudes. In R. Brislin, S. Bochner, & W. Lonner (Eds.), *Cross-cultural perspectives on learning*. New York: Wiley, 1975.

Triandis, H. C. Cross-cultural social and personality psychology. *Personality and Social Psychology Bulletin*, 1977, *3*, 143–158.

Triandis, H., Hall, E., & Ewen, R. B. Member heterogeneity and dyadic creativity, *Human Relations*, 1965, *18*, 33–55.

Triandis, H. C., Malpass, R. S., & Davidson, A. H. *Cross-cultural psychology*. *Biennial Review of Anthropology*, 1971, 1–84.

Triandis, H. C., Malpass, R. S., & Davidson, A. H. Psychology and culture. *Annual Review of Psychology*, 1973, *24*, 355–378.

Triandis, H. C., Vassiliou, V., Vassiliou, G., Tanaka, Y., & Shanmugam, A. V. *The analysis of subjective culture*. New York: Wiley, 1972.

Trimble, J. E. The intrusion of Western psychological thought on Native American ethos. In J. W. Berry & W. J. Lonner (Eds.), *Applied Cross-cultural psychology: Selected papers from the Second International Conference of I.A.C.C.P.* Amsterdam: Swets & Zeitlinger, 1975.

Tylor, Sir E. B. *Primitive culture*. New York: Harper, 1958. (Originally published in 1873.)

Vassiliou, V. G., & Vassiliou, G. The implicative meaning of the Greek concept of *philotimo*. *Journal of Cross-Cultural Psychology*, 1973, *4*, 326–341.

Veroff, J., Atkinson, J. W., Feld, S., & Gurin, G. The use of thematic apperception to assess motivation in a nationwide interview study. *Psychological Monographs*, 1960, *74* (Whole No. 499).

Veroff, J., & Veroff, J. B. Reconsiderations of a measure of power motivation. *Psychological Bulletin*, 1972, *78*, 279–291.

Vexliard, A. *Le caractère national: Une structure en profondeur*. Istanbul: Istanbul Universitesi Edebiyat Fakultesi, 1970.

Vogel, E. *Japan's middle class*. Berkeley: Univ. of California Press, 1963.

Wagatsuma, H. Problems of language in cross-cultural research. In L. L. Adler (Ed.), Issues in cross-cultural research. *Annals of the New York Academy of Sciences*, 1977, *285*, 141–150.

Wallace, A. F. C. *Culture and personality* (2nd ed.). New York: Random House, 1970.

Webb, E., Campbell, D. T., Schwartz, R. D., & Sechrest, L. *Unobtrusive measures: Nonreactive research in the social sciences*. Chicago, Illinois: Rand McNally, 1966.

Whiting, B. B., & Whiting, J. W. M. *Children of six cultures: A psychocultural analysis*. Cambridge, Massachusetts: Harvard Univ. Press, 1975.

Wikse, J. R. *About possession: The self as private property*. University Park, Pennsylvania: Pennsylvania State Univ. Press, 1978.

Williams, T. R. Introduction. In T. R. Williams (Ed.), *Psychological anthropology*. The Hague: Mouton, 1975.

Witkin, H. A., & Berry, J. W. Psychological differentiation in cross-cultural perspective. *Journal of Cross-Cultural Psychology*, 1975, *6*, 4–87.

Witkin, H. A., & Goodenough, D. R. Field dependence and interpersonal behavior. *Psychological Bulletin*, 1977, *84*, 661–689.

Wrong, D. H. The oversocialized conception of man in modern sociology. *American Sociological Review*, 1961, *26*, 183–193.

Yamada, E. M. *The personality variables of "Amaeru" and locus of control as functions of culture: A cross-cultural study of Japan and the United States*. Unpublished master's thesis, Pennsylvania State University, 1970.

Zung, W. W. K. A cross-cultural survey of depressive symptomatology in normal adults. *Journal of Cross-Cultural Psychology*, 1972, *3*, 177–184.

10

Culture and Competence[1]

NORMAN DINGES
LORRAINE DUFFY

Introduction

It is the sad fate of anyone who attempts to examine the relationship of culture and competence that he or she must deal simultaneously with disparate theoretical and empirical literatures that show little awareness or concern with one another's existence. It is probably only in the subdiscipline of personality and culture research that the notion of competence implicitly enters the areas of the overlapping concerns of the major disciplines of anthropology and psychology. As culture and personality research has not enjoyed a prominent position or engaged a large share of the research energies of either psychology or anthropology, it is also not surprising that research linking competence and culture has drawn relatively little attention. The psychological research tradition has emphasized research on the incompetent or maladjusted person and the anthropological research tradition has focused more on the ideal person who embodies the cultural norm.

Although simple neglect due to more pressing disciplinary concerns may account for the paucity of research on culture and competence, there may be other, more serious, scientifically based reasons for the apparent neglect.

[1] Preparation of this chapter was supported in part by the Office of Naval Research, Organizational Effectiveness Research Program, contract No. N00014–77–C–0345.

209

For example, one must ask if the concept of competence contributes anything new conceptually, or merely serves as a synonymous term for other
more easily operationalized, and more frequently used, concepts that are
already well established in the literature. Heath (1977), for example,
suggests that the terms, such as self-actualization, mental health, and competence, all of which connote effectiveness of functioning, may be subsumed
under the concept of maturity. He also asserts that there is considerable
agreement in the literature about the dimensions that define a maturing
person.

Perhaps more serious than the terminological issues are the problems of
metapsychology implied by the concept of competence when viewed from
different cultural standpoints. Examining the relationship of culture and
competence may require dealing with ultimate questions about what people
are to be in their cultures, and may involve inevitable value assumptions that
neither anthropology nor psychology wish to make. Considered from the
cultural ecology standpoint, there are those who would assert the relativist
position in which no general criteria of cultural or behavioral excellence are
possible (e.g., Berry, 1975). It may also be that the predominantly
nonspiritual stance of Western psychology, by contrast with the pervasive
spiritual orientation toward life in general of many non-Western psychologies, produces a clash of paradigms which is currently insurmountable.

Despite these drawbacks, there are compelling reasons to refocus research
attention on the positive end of the spectrum of human adaptation with
which culture and competence would be concerned. We have applied the
term competence to that complex array of internal and external human
activities that constitute a core of culturally valued behaviors denoting
effective adaptation by a given culture's terms. In this chapter we have had
the relatively modest goal of providing a sample of psychological models of
competence that seem relevant to culture factors. We have also attempted to
consider some of the variables that may provide for a meaningful integration
of both psychological and anthropological concepts bearing on the relationship of culture to competence. This is a murky area indeed, and one in which
theoretical pitfalls are encountered at every turn.

Historical Background

Considered from a Western perspective, the notion of competence has a
relatively long history. For example, Goldfried and D'Zurilla (1969) quote
the ultimate source, Socrates, who defined competence as follows:

> Those who manage well the circumstances which they encounter daily, and who
> possess judgment which is accurate in meeting occasions as they arise and rarely miss
> the expedient course of action [p. 155].

This definition contains most of the important elements of contemporary Western views of competence, even though operational terminology may make them appear much more scientific, and greater specificity of its components has indeed improved upon it. Although there were undoubtedly many other theorists of competence both before and after Socrates, it appears to have been given its greatest scientific recognition in the twentieth century.

Three contemporary Western orientations are discernible in the research which bears on competence and competent behavior: (*a*) the drive–instinct–motive orientation; (*b*) the self-concept–autonomy orientation, (*c*) the personality trait orientation.

White (1959) has probably been the foremost proponent of the drive–instinct–motive orientation to competence, although Groos (1901) was one of the first to postulate a need that humans have for producing effects (e.g., the child's "joy in being a cause"). Hendrick (1942) subsequently proposed an instinct to mastery, based upon an inborn drive to do and to learn how to do. By contrast, Fenichel (1945) presented the psychoanalytic view by attributing mastery of the environment as an aim to reduce anxiety, rather than an instinctually based component, and Mowrer (1950) reinforced the view that anxiety reduction was the motivating factor in ego development. Mittleman (1954) proposed a "motility" concept as a basic urge, along with Freudian oral, excretory, and genital urges. Dollard and Miller (1950) followed with their concept of drive and attendant reinforcement theory. Obviously, all of these theorists were heavily influenced by Freudian drive theory and based their thinking on physiological views of human behavior.

The self-concept–autonomy orientation closely paralleled the instinct–drive–motive theory. Angyal (1941), perhaps the most renowned proponent of the organism's active striving for mastery over the environment, proposed a "general dynamic trend" toward an increase in autonomy. He was also one of the first contemporary theorists to view humans as internally determining dominators of the environment, as opposed to purely reactive organisms.

From a Freudian perspective, Kardiner (1947) proposed an effective ego (i.e., an autonomous energy source) built along the same lines as the psychoanalytic model of ego development, but more positively oriented to the successful rather than the conflictual experiences in life. Hartmann (1950) developed the psychoanalytic trend with his conception of the autonomous factor in the developed ego, which in turn mediated instinctual drives and environmental demands. Erikson (1952) originated the concept of ego identity and "a sense of industry" while developing his thoughts on libido theory and the sequential development of the ego. Erikson's views, perhaps more than any other, epitomized the growing discontentment with the instinct–drive–motive theories. With the parallel growth of Murray's (1938) need–press theory and Allport's (1937) insistence on the functional autonomy of motives, it was only a matter of time before the original assumption of Goldstein's (1940) master tendency toward self-actualization was developed and consolidated by Maslow (1954) and Rogers (1961).

With the influence of the major theorists of the trait orientation (e.g., Cattell, 1965; Eysenck & Eysenck, 1969; Guilford, 1959) the 1950s and 1960s saw a dramatic increase in research along these lines and there remains a lively debate in the literature regarding the proper role of traits in explaining human behavior (e.g., Argyle & Little, 1972; Epstein, 1977). Parallel with these developments was the emergence of environmental theorists dating back to Lewin (1939) who stressed the importance of situation variables in the determination of human behavior. The combination of the trait and the environmentalist views of human behavior, and their relevance to issues of competence, is probably best expressed in the current trends of interactional psychology, which appear to foreshadow important changes in the direction of future research (e.g., Endler & Magnusson, 1976; Magnusson & Endler, 1977).

Considered from the standpoint of competence, these lines of development in Western psychology have perhaps been best summarized by Goldfried and D'Zurilla (1969) who identify three major definitions:

1. The achievement approach emphasizes the social attainments of the individual in the various major areas of living within a particular society (e.g., Phillips & Cowitz, 1953; Lanyon, 1967).
2. The internal antecedents approach identifies the attitudes, motives, personality dynamics, and traits which are presumed to bear some relationship to effective behavior (e.g., Doll, 1953a; Foote & Cottrell, 1955; Brewster-Smith, 1966).
3. The behavior–environment interactionism approach operationally translates into an analysis of effective responses to specific problematic life situations (e.g., Hamburg & Adams, 1967; Goldfried & D'Zurilla, 1969).

All of the approaches described above constitute a personality theory, whether implicit or explicit, in which the locus of competence is firmly rooted in the individual. These approaches are also based on a relatively short tradition of scientific personality research in Western psychology which contrasts with the considerably longer tradition of personality theory in many non-Western psychologies. It is therefore instructive to contrast Western views with non-Western views of personality for the light they may shed on the relationship of culture and competence.

Tart (1975) is probably the foremost proponent of the contribution that the non-Western "spiritual psychologies," many of which are based on centuries old traditions, can make to an understanding of human personality. He has extensively examined the assumptions underlying Western scientific psychology in an attempt to bridge the existing gaps between it and spiritual psychologies, such as Zen Buddhism, Indian yoga, and Sufism. It is his analysis of Western assumptions about personality that are most pertinent to the examination of the relationship of culture and competence. The following example of an assumption of Western psychology, followed by the non-Western view of a similar human experience illustrates the contrasting approaches that may be taken (Tart, 1975, p. 86).

> *Western assumption:* A healthy personality is one that allows the individual to be well adjusted in terms of his culture.
> *Non-Western view:* The spiritual psychologies, taking a longer and wider perspective, would see adjustment to one's society as a relatively minor achievement, and, if the culture perpetuates patterns judged as delusory or evil, then someone who actually wishes to grow spiritually should definitely *not* be well adjusted to his or her culture, although he or she may have to dissimulate adjustment in order to avoid friction and harassment that would divert energies from his or her spiritual goals.

In what is the only currently available summary of Asian personality theory, Pedersen (1977) reiterates many of Tart's points, but takes a slightly different focus on certain personality variables that are more directly related to Western theories. He presents Western psychologies as stressing the individual, achievement motivation, rationally defined evidence, the scientific method, and direct self-disclosure. By contrast, Asian theories are characterized as emphasizing corporate welfare, experiential evidence, intuitive logic, religiophilosophical methods, and subtle indirection in personal relationships. Of greatest pertinence for the relationship of competence to culture is the assertion that the Asian view of basic personality structure is relational and focused on the space between individuals, rather than individualistic as in Western personality theories. Pedersen also makes a number of other assertions, all of which are in need of empirical verification, that stand in bold contrast to Western views of competence. For example, the notion that the "Hindu ideal of maturity emphasizes continuous dependency relations" or "interdependence in parent–child relationships is the Chinese ideal for personality development [p. 375]" will be seen to contradict Heath's Western-based model of maturity and competence (Heath, 1977).

Whereas Tart and Pedersen present an apparently stark contrast between Western and non-Western views of personality and the definitions of competence that may be derived from them, it is apparently possible to reach different conclusions for the same non-Western sources of information about personality. Heath (1977) concludes from the psychological analysis of mental health principles and views of healthy adult development represented in a number of summaries of non-Western sources on the subject (e.g., Bellah, 1976; Bouwsma, 1976; Goleman, 1976; Lapidus, 1976; Neki, 1975; Rohlen, 1976; Wei-Ming, 1976) that religious traditions agree in most of their basic assumptions about healthy adult growth, but disagree in their emphasis on others. Heath's goal in his analysis was to find evidence for his model of maturing, which is rooted in Western empirical research on a number of personality dimensions. Coding of the desirable human traits hypothesized by traditional religions which could be included in his model of maturing, produced suggestive but very unreliable results. Heath allows that more thorough and objective analyses are needed, but also concludes that his cursory survey suggests that a transculturally universal model of maturing remains a reasonable possibility.

It has been the primary goal of this all too brief contrast of Western and non-Western views of competence to show the widely divergent views that can be taken of culturally desirable, human behavior. As there has been so little scientific–scholarly exchange on the metapsychologies that inform the Western and non-Western traditions relating to the relationship of culture to competence, it is hoped that the foregoing material will provide the minimal theoretical background with which to proceed to an analysis of available models of human competence. This will not be an exhaustive analysis. Models of competence have been selected which have either attempted to include cultural variables in their conceptual framework, or hold substantial promise of including such variables in future research. With the exception of Arasteh (1975), they are Western in origin.

Selected Theories of Competence

EDGAR DOLL: THE VINELAND LABORATORY

In *The Measurement of Social Competence: A Manual for the Vineland Social Maturity Scale* (1953a), Doll describes the work which took place in the 1930s and 1940s at the Vineland Laboratory. The essential goal was the assessment of social competence, defined as "the synthesized expression of the progressive independence and responsibility which signify social maturation [p. 17]." The explicit assumptions were that (*a*) social competence is defined as a functional ability; (*b*) competence could be measured in terms of maturation; and (*c*) social competence may be seen as a dynamic and functional composite of human traits. Possibly anticipating future trends, Doll defined social competence as the "social adequacy of the individual as a whole (with due regard for age and culture) conceived as a social end result of the physical, physiological, intellectual, habitual, emotional, volitional, educational, occupational aspects of personal growth, adjustment, and attainment which ensue from his constitutional predispositions and environmental impacts [p. 2]." Obviously, Doll was a trait theorist, but he still managed to encompass all three of the approaches identified by Goldfried and D'Zurilla (1969).

Doll also integrated cross-cultural research undertaken with American minorities, such as Longwell's (1935) study of preadolescent Pueblo Indians, Sill's (1936) study of Jewish and Italian subnormal girls, and Eugene Doll's (1937/1953b) research on blacks (which interestingly found that blacks are constantly retarded in development, but mature relatively early when compared to Caucasians).

His measurement scale was blatantly middle-class and severely limited by its emphasis on verbal output and inherent assumptions of individual independence, responsibility, and competence—which all lack cross-cultural validity.

FOOTE AND COTTRELL: INTERPERSONAL COMPETENCE

Foote and Cottrell (1955) were among the first to use a process definition of competence. They defined competence as synonymous with ability and credited Sullivan (1950) as the originator of the use of the word "competence" to denote such an ability. According to Foote and Cottrell, competence was "a satisfactory degree of ability for performing certain implied kinds of tasks [p. 36]." Their's was an essentially behavior-bound definition, incorporating "health, intelligence, empathy, autonomy, judgement, and creativity [p. 41]." They defined behavior as dynamic, episodic, and situationally specific and expanded the temporal dimension to refer to the utilization of past experiences and future aspirations in an effective organization of present effort. They also expanded the social basis of their definition of competence by asserting that competence is "not dependent upon direction from without but capable of integrating goals with those of others and collaborating in their realization [p. 50]."

Foote and Cottrell elaborated Doll's definition, but were culture-bound by a trait orientation and an ethnocentric emphasis on the value of autonomy and independence for the individual. Their emphasis on the interpersonal aspect of competence, although immature in development, was an innovation and an indication of the future trend of interactional psychology. They shared an awareness of the cultural issues by recognizing the cultural and subcultural influences on the achievement of interpersonal competence. Unfortunately, they never elaborated on nor accounted for this influence in their approach.

ROBERT WHITE: MOTIVATION FOR COMPETENCE (EFFECTANCE)

Robert White (1959), in an article which marked the turning point in the social trend of competence theory, postulated not only the achieved capacity of competence but also found it necessary to make competence a motivational concept "because it satisfies an intrinsic need to deal with the environment [p. 318]." White proposed the term "effectance" for the motivational aspect of competence, used to refer to "an organism's capacity to interact effectively with its environment [p. 297]." Effectance referred to neurogenic "energy" derived from the living cells making up the nervous system.

The importance of the learning process in developing competence was also emphasized by White, particularly relationships between the stimulus fields and the effects that can be produced by the individual. White also pointed out the importance of play and investigatory behavior of children, noting the adaptive value of a motivation independent of primary drives in learning about one's environment.

White literally ignored all cross-cultural reference probably because of the assumed universality of his effectance motive. His contribution lies in the area of crossing the boundary into a comparative-physiological psychology. On a physiological level, White's theory may prove cross-culturally applicable (assuming all human physiology is the same), but it may not prove comprehensive enough to cover the territory designated by the term competence.

WALLACE: AN ABILITIES CONCEPTION OF PERSONALITY

Wallace (1966) proposes an entirely different view of competent behavior with considerable potential for cross-cultural use. He makes a discrimination between "response predisposition and response capability" and argues that when theorists assume the existence of a need (Murray, 1938) or trait, what they are in fact referring to is a response capability. Wallace (1966) actually questions the necessity of referring to motivational inferences, if we have an accurate knowledge of the "breadth and diversity of extant behavioral repertoires in conjunction with detailed knowledge of specific stimulus situations [p. 133]."

An important contribution to the competence research made by Wallace is the focus on the conditions under which behavior occurs. His reference to Szasz's (1961) plea for greater situational analysis of psychiatric operations is well directed. It is one of the first attempts to criticize the stronghold of trait theorists in the area of personality and personality assessment.

Wallace, like White, provides an innovative scheme without considering the implications for cross-cultural research. Although this seriously affects the generality of his model, the application of such an approach would be an asset in cross-cultural competence research. However, the implications of such an approach (assuming a learning deficit) could lead to subtle forms of ethnocentrism.

GOLDFRIED AND D'ZURILLA: A BEHAVIORAL–ANALYTIC MODEL FOR ASSESSING COMPETENCE

This model focuses primarily on the assessment of competence and takes, as its unit of analysis, the effective response of the individual (influenced by past social learning) to the specific life situations being examined (Goldfried & D'Zurilla, 1969). Following the lead first developed by Argyris (1965a,1965b), Goldfried and D'Zurilla define an effective response as a response "to a problematic situation which alters the situation so that it is no longer problematical, and at the same time produces a maximum of other positive consequences and a minimum of negative ones [p. 158]." An individual's total reaction constitutes an effective response, and the evaluation of the response is dependent upon the consequences generated by that response. Competence is defined operationally as the "effectiveness or adequacy with which an individual is capable of responding to the various problematic situations which confront him [p. 161]."

The behavioral–analytic technique developed by Goldfried and D'Zurilla involves (*a*) situational analysis; (*b*) response enumeration; (*c*) response evaluation; (*d*) development of a measuring instrument format; and (*e*) an evaluation of that measure. Situational analysis involves generating specific, but meaningful situations which the individual will encounter and must attempt to deal effectively with. Situations eliciting automatic effective responses are not included in this analysis. Response enumeration entails a tally of possible responses and is also used to further define the situation. Response evaluation requires significant others in a person's environment in order to judge the effectiveness of those responses enumerated. This is done to improve reliability and validity. Development of a measurement format is a direct extension of the first three steps: Content of the items to be used in the measurement instrument and the criteria for scoring are simply derived from the first three steps. The final step, evaluation of the measure, follows the usual criteria for evaluation used in psychological research.

A basic assumption of Goldfried and D'Zurilla is that overall competence is increased when an individual learns to cope independently with problematic situations. In other words, a learning-how-to-learn (deutero-learning) approach is the best approach, according to the authors, and this would appear to have considerable significance for the learning of cultural behaviors.

With its value-based emphasis on individuality and independence as the most effective problem-solving strategy, this model may have limited cross-cultural applicability, but it appears eminently adaptable as a research strategy if the criteria of effectiveness can be made more culturally appropriate.

FRENCH, RODGERS, AND COBB: ADJUSTMENT AS PERSON–ENVIRONMENT FIT

Another Western model that would appear to have potential for cross-cultural use is that of French, Rodgers, and Cobb (1974) who define adjustment as the goodness of fit between the characteristics of the person and the properties of his environment. This entails an objective and subjective dimension to self-concept and environment. There are two demands made of the individual, the motive of the person and the demands located in the environment (e.g., role requirements). The supplies needed to meet these demands are simply a person's abilities or the environment's abilities to meet demands with which a person is faced.

Four criteria of mental health are proposed: (a) objective person–environment fit; (b) subjective person–environment fit; (c) contact with reality; and (d) accuracy of self-assessment.

This model provides for eight adjustive behaviors depending upon the conditions of person and environment. It is a mathematically oriented outgrowth of Lazarus, Averill, and Opton's (1974) original psychodynamic model and may be adaptable to cross-cultural situations, although problems may arise in applying the concepts of needs and demands as were originally proposed by Murray's (1938) need–press theory. It is also unclear whether this model could be adapted to the variety of interpersonal tasks found in different sociocultural environments. Another essential lack for cross-cultural research purposes is an affective variable beyond simple, subjective, person–environment fit.

M. BREWSTER-SMITH: SOCIALIZATION FOR COMPETENCE

One of the first to link competence with a cross-cultural perspective is M. Brewster-Smith (1968). Brewster-Smith defines competence as involving effective, role performance for self and society and posits a core of interrelated personal attributes that play a crucial role in the effectiveness of the person's interaction with the environment. A circular developmental path of causation is suggested that underlies a cluster of traitlike characteristics of effectiveness. These traitlike characteristics are to be found in the "attitudes and the motives related to the self, as the entity around which a person's enduring orientations to the world are organized [p. 278]." Thus, early effective interaction with the environment leads the individual to accrue an effective orientation to the world that is continually strengthened by current and former successes. Changing an individual's effective orientation involves breaking into these well-entrenched circles of social causation and turning vicious into benign circles.

In Brewster-Smith's model the competent self incorporates an inner sense of efficacy or potency (a positive attitude toward the self), an attitude of hope (a positive attitude toward the world), and a concomitant behavioral orientation that places the person into the kinds of interactions that bring closure to the benign circle. The generalized core of attitudes and behavioral orientations, which constitute the core of the competent self, are suggested as panculturally relevant in principle, even though different cultures would value the competence syndrome differently in terms of specific goals and the knowledge and skill required to achieve them. Cross-cultural, empirical verification of the hypothesis has yet to be demonstrated.

An important aspect of the "competent self" in this model lies in the socialization of the child. Brewster-Smith asserts that there are two major constructive (or destructive, as the case may be) forces influencing the development of the sense of self: (*a*) The feedback the child gets about his–her effect on the physical environment; and (*b*) perhaps more importantly, the feedback from the individual's social environment through the mirror of social response and appraisal. These two forces intertwine to influence the individual's perception of self.

Brewster-Smith is one of the first theorists to deal with the relationship of social structure to competence. There are three strategic aspects of social structure that directly influence the competent self: opportunity, respect, and power. Power is considered crucial because it leads to respect and opportunity. However, it is at this point that Brewster-Smith's model begins to break down when considered cross-culturally, as he suggests that opportunity offered without the sharing of power breeds paternalism, accentuates dependence, and leads to a resentment that can be viewed as ingratitude. Although these arguments are fortified with examples of the inadequacy of "paternalism," Brewster-Smith neglects at least one very important exception—the Japanese, and probably other Asian cultures as well. According to theorists of these cultures, there is no sharing of social power between the horizontal levels of hierarchical structures, and no resentment ensues (Nakane, 1972). Despite these limitations, Brewster-Smith's framework is heuristic in suggesting the existence of a limited dynamic core of characteristics of the competent individual which may be operationalized for a given culture and tested empirically.

Brewster-Smith is also one of the few theorists to deal with "deviant" forms of competence. He notes, for example, that many slum youth in American culture channel all their competence into socially unrewarded directions. Although he focuses on juvenile delinquents, these concepts can be expanded to include other "marginal" persons, such as the mentally ill (e.g., Dabrowski, 1964). There are many other examples of nominal incompetence, that may, in fact, be highly competent when situation and culture variables are considered.

ARASTEH: FINAL PERSONALITY INTEGRATION

Arasteh (1975) is a non-Western psychologist, with a background in Sufi mysticism, who has contributed to the theoretical research on personality integration. Arasteh relies heavily on Erikson's (1959) theory of identity development in children, but goes beyond both Erikson and Sullivan (1953) by emphasizing the continuous nature of identity acquisition beyond adolescence. According to Arasteh (1975), there are multiple identities, hierarchies of identities, and a succession of identities that culminate in an "autonomous person who has mastered the last and most critical crisis of existential identity formation [p. 24]."

Arasteh notes that, in Western terms, ultimate maturity is the objectification of the ego and the social institution. Eastern rationalism at one time held a similar view. His concept of final personality integration, "does not concern itself with the objectification of the ego, but with the liberation from the ego. The fact that man can liberate himself from social drives, devaluate systems, and reintegrate himself, demonstrates that he is an autonomous being. This autonomy reveals man's independence from cultural drives in the transcultural state (the view of rational Eastern thinkers—the point past objectification of the ego) [p. 55]." Final integration is a universal state transcending time, place, and degree of culture. It is a universal in every sense of the word, including applicability to all other cultures.

Arasteh provides a brief description of what final integration entails in several diverse cultures. In Zen Buddhist cultures, final integration is the state of deciphering *koan* (the state of enlightenment). *Koan* is "what everyone brings into this world at his birth and tries to decipher before he dies," whereas enlightenment is the situation in which a person is completely oriented to reality outside and within himself; he is fully aware of his state (Fromm, Suzuki, & Martino, 1965, p. 115). "In Sufism, it is an individuality in nonindividuality; becoming creative truth; passing from I-ness to he-ness to one-ness. . . . The Chinese express it as *Tao*, a fulfillment, a beginning, and end, and complete realization of the meaning of existence in innate things. . . . Comparatively, in Western thought, it is expressed as insight in the dynamic sense [Arasteh, 1975, p. 56]."

The concept of reality proposed by Arasteh is related to maturity through the awareness of various realities and the appreciation of multiple realities. It is significant that all Western and Eastern ways of attaining maturity in the adult personality have recognized, as an essential quality, the ability to become aware of multiple realities (Stein & Vidich, 1960). "Final integration is marked by an 'intense awareness of various spheres of reality' [Arasteh,

1975, p. 81]." The developmental stages of this awareness (going from a closed system to an open system of rationalism and transculturalism) are viewed by Arasteh as similar for both Far Eastern and Western cultures.

Arasteh's model reads, at times, like a Far Eastern paradox making moot the relationship of culture to competence by positing a final stage of independence from cultural drives to the transcultural state. It is invaluable in its insight into what other cultures designate as final integration. Unfortunately, even Arasteh is caught up in Western logic in his writing. His use of autonomy and identity are relatively different from the Western connotation, yet he continues to use these terms without emphasizing this difference. This provides a confusing orientation to his concept of reality and the "attainment" of successive identities and multiple realities. Nonetheless, this is one of the few introductions to non-Western structures of maturity. In this analysis, one could substitute the concept of competence for maturity (following Heath's example, 1977), and produce a non-Western view of ultimate competence.

WILLIAM BOWERMAN: SUBJECTIVE COMPETENCE

One of the most comprehensive recent theoretical approaches to competence has been proposed by Bowerman (1978). Based on two motivational assumptions, (*a*) that people want to act effectively, and (*b*) that people try to maximize their self-esteem, this theory takes Heider (1944) a step further in delineating an attributional process that determines subjective competence. Self-referent, causal attributions and their relationship to behavior and the effects of behavior form the core of the theory. The components of self-referent, causal attributions include actor, action, effect, and affect. Subjective competence is an interaction (or multiple function) of these attribution components. Bowerman, like Lazarus, *et al.* (1974), is one of the first theorists to include an affective component, and expands the definition of competence beyond simple effectiveness to one involving interaction with the physical and social environment.

Of major importance in this theory is the manner in which the individual posits causal elements in an action–effect–affect sequence. Positive and negative subjective competence are derived from differing combinations of these components, and by varying the positive or negative loading of the attributional links between them, different subjective competence structures are formed. For example, positive subjective competence is described by the following behavior sequence: The actor approaches (+) the prevention (−) of a negative affect (−). Thus, the actor actively prevents an action that would have caused the occurrence of a negatively loaded affect. An example of negative, subjective competence is described in the following sequence: An actor approaches (+) an action that causes (+) a negative affect (−).

Three attributional components vary in these sequences: (*a*) an actor either approaches (+) or avoids (−); (*b*) causes (+) or does not cause (−) an action; and (*c*) which leads to positive (+) or negative (−) affect.

These attributional sequences form "paths" to positive or negative subjective competence with several factors influencing these paths. Included among influencing factors are content, perceived affective consequences of action, the locus of attribution, temporal perspective, evaluative criteria, generality of the sequence, certainty of belief about the sequence, awareness of one's position as actor in a behavioral sequence, flexibility of the values in the attribution sequence, accuracy of fit with reality, and contact with the environment. This is obviously a very complicated multidimensional theory that is not easily presented in summary form.

The motivational hypothesis underlying the theory is that the individual will attempt to maximize subjective competence. An important aspect involves predicting the particular sequence of action the individual will choose. Bowerman makes an innovative contribution by asserting that the individual will opt for a sequence of less subjective utility (contrary to the achievement motivation hypothesis, or cost–benefits theory), if the action is associated with much higher personal responsibility. He fortifies his arguments with White's (1959) notions of effectance motivation and deCharm's (1968) origin–pawn concept, both of which emphasize the individual's perception of him–herself as the source of effects on their environment. Of potentially critical importance for understanding culturally different attributional processes, is Bowerman's notion of higher-order competence, which involves one's view of one's own subjective competence. Space does not permit an examination of the complex attributional linkages between overt behaviors and covert behaviors, but the implications for understanding culturally "inscrutable" behaviors should be apparent.

Bowerman has melded four theoretical approaches (effectance motivation, origin–pawn concept, dissonance theory, and attribution theory) into the framework of subjective competence. Although its eventual value is to be determined, even the cursory discussion of it here is some indication of its breadth. By integrating a number of former, less adequate theories into a new framework which better explains a particular phenomena, it fulfills one of the major requirements of a "new" theory. Its application to cross-cultural research on competence has not been developed. Hopefully, Bowerman will include the cultural dimension in a future presentation of the theory, thereby increasing the validity of generalizations derived from it.

DOUGLAS HEATH: MATURITY AND COMPETENCE

Heath (1977) provides the first comprehensive and rigorous model of maturity directed at cross-cultural issues. "Maturity refers to universal genotypic developmental dimensions . . . and is inferred from the type and

range of tasks, roles, and situations in which a person functions effectively. . . . . Competence refers to effectiveness in relating to some specific
environmental expectation or task . . . to identify competence requires that
we evaluate a person's level of skill in relation to what is required by the task
[p. 35]." Maturity can be viewed as a determinant of generalized competence.

The model, which was induced from previous research, theories about
healthy persons, and longitudinal studies of student development in college,
postulates a number of hypotheses concerning how the mature person differs
from the immature person. More mature persons are viewed as more aware
of their (a) cognitive process, (b) self-concept, (c) values, and (d) their
relationships to others. These four personality dimensions are systematically
related to dimensions of maturity and include (a) symbolization (language,
the ability to represent reality through image production), (b) allocentrism
(the ability to take a multiplicity of perspectives), (c) integration (a growing
coherence, an increased synthesis), (d) stability, and (e) autonomy (stable
structure which provides the basis for autonomous self-regulation). Thus,
the hypothesis for any combination of personality and maturity variables is
linear positive (i.e., the mature person is better able to use symbolization
processes to enhance the self-concept; the mature person is more allocentric
in personal relations).

Maturity is a systemic property of the model. A major assumption of the
model is that "a person is a constantly changing, open, organized system
dependent both on his means of adaptation to others and on the environment
for his fulfillment and survival [p. 22]." A second assumption is that all the
dimensions of the model are interdependent. Heath also assumes that every
viable living system "has an intrinsic equilibrating or self-regulating principle that preserves its structural integrity [p. 24]."

It is important to note that Heath's model is primarily trait based (although
he does make passing reference to situational variables) in that he believes
that the study of effectively functioning or competent persons in diverse
cultures will lead to the identification of a universal or recurring set of
common, core traits. He also contends that the identification of such a
recurring set of core traits that are descriptive of competent persons and
selected by numerous and diverse judges from diverse cultural areas, will
free the concepts of maturity and competence from idiosyncratic personal
and cultural values.

To test his model, Heath used a multifaceted and multilevel assessment
methodology to compare mature and immature college men with five cultural
groups: Mid-Atlantic United States, Sicily, Northern Italy, Eastern and
Western Turkey. According to the results, a common core set of traits were
found to define maturity in the groups studied. As Heath (1977) states, these
were the "ability to anticipate consequences; calm, clear thinking; fulfilling
potential; ordered; predictable; purposeful; realistic; reflective; strong con-

victions; and unshakable [p. 204]." The model's predictions about differences between *psychologically test-defined* mature and immature men of the
three cultures were generally supported. The social judgements and the
psychological test indices of maturity when combined confirmed 40%,
weakly confirmed 50%, and neither confirmed nor disconfirmed 10% of the
model's hypotheses.

Although based on a small and relatively restricted cultural sample,
Heath's study is a landmark in culture and competence research. It is
innovative in many regards and one would hope that subsequent research
would be equally innovative in finding measures and methodologies that are
not predetermined by trait orientations, which minimize the contribution of
situational variance to judged effective functioning in different cultural
milieus. A variety of measures were used, from the Rorschach, to independent judge ratings, to objective tests. The combination of these measures
greatly enhanced the validity of the results (Hersen & Bellack, 1977). The
author's recognition of the limitations of the project insofar as it did not
include an Asian sample is reassuring. However, the model has not yet been
widely disseminated, nor has there been sufficient time to fully digest the
many findings and refine the interpretations in light of speculations that
might derive from a greatly expanded sample. The Western flavor of the
model and the criteria of competence that were provided to judges for
making their selections of subjects was defended as not "imperious" as none
of the indigenous study collaborators complained about it. One is reminded
of Barnlund's dictum to the effect that when cross-cultural, research collaborators reach easy agreement on the definition of the variables of interest,
the study should be suspect as not truly cross-cultural (Barnlund, 1978).

The major conceptual problem with Heath's model is the Western orientation seen most vividly in the definition of the dimensions and variables he
used. For example, as one moves across cultures, the concept of individual
autonomy may be defined differently, or may not even exist in some Far
Eastern cultures. While one may agree quite easily with Heath about the
possibility of a pancultural, universal model of competence and maturity, a
major doubt remains about its validity until data from a sample of Far
Eastern cultures can be collected.

EUGENE WEINSTEIN: INTERPERSONAL COMPETENCE

In this model, interpersonal competence is defined as the ability to accomplish interpersonal tasks involving the elicitation of the desired response or
set of responses from others. It is similar to the goal-orientation aspects of
Doll (1953a) and the process-orientation of Foote and Cottrell (1955).

Weinstein's model is developed through successive definitions of the three
major elements entailed in the process of establishing and maintaining desired personal identities, both for one's self and for others. This process is

founded on the capacity for empathy, which requires the "actor to correctly predict the impact that various lines of action will have on alter's definition of the situation [Weinstein, 1969, p. 757]." Capacities underlying empathy include intelligence and cue sensitivity through selective focusing. A second critical element of interpersonal competence is the possession of a large and varied repertoire of lines of action. The third critical element is the intrapersonal resources for employing effective tactics in appropriate situations.

In developmental terms, empathy evolves from the capacity to distinguish self from nonself; to projective role taking involving perception of the situation as it impinges on the other; to positional role taking involving reciprocal role enactment (e.g., learning to be a patient to a doctor); and then to personality stereotyping which requires placing the other in a category based on central features of the person. The final stage of individuation involves the willingness to abandon stereotypes and base role taking on direct experience with a specific other.

Weinstein's model is explicitly nonpurposive in that he asserts that people are socialized primarily for the skills of role acquisition, acquisition of norms, and learning to take the role of others, all of which involve learning to behave appropriately, and not necessarily effectively. Social learning theory is called on to explain the acquisition of the basic elements of interpersonal competence through incidental learning.

Although clearly relevant to the relationship of culture to competence, cross-cultural generality remains to be demonstrated with this model. It is not backed by a strong base of empirical research, even though its explicit assumptions are apparent in implicit form in many of the other competence models in this review. If Weinstein's elements of interpersonal competence are cross-culturally applicable, it should be possible to demonstrate it empirically by systematically varying the cultures of actor and alter and examining empathic accuracy in different life situations. Doing so would also contribute to an understanding of intercultural competence in terms of the dissimilarity–similarity of actor and alter.

A Dimensional Analysis of Selected
Theories of Competence

A schematic summary of the theories of competence is provided in Figure 10.1. An attempt has been made to show the relative degree of emphasis (high or low) that each theorist places on the dimensions selected for comparison. Although this simplifies the task of comparison and contrast between the different theories, there are some difficulties in interpreting the varying approaches to competence. For example, Arasteh's (1975) treatment of autonomy as a form of transcendence does not follow the use of the same concept by Western theorists (e.g., Foote & Cottrell, 1955). A more careful

Figure 10.1. A dimensional analysis of selected theories of competence. H = high emphasis; L = low or negligible emphasis.

Dimension	Doll (1953a)	Foote and Cottrell (1955)	White (1959)	Wallace (1966)	Goldfried and D'Zurilla (1969)	French, Rogers, and Cobb (1974)	Weinstein (1969)	Bowerman (1978)	Arasteh (1975)	M. Brewster-Smith (1968)	Heath (1977)
Subjective: deals with the effectiveness of internal (covert) behaviors	L	L	H	L	L	H	H	H	H	H	H
Stability: competence defined as formation of integrative capacities	H	H	L	L	L	H	L	H	H	H	H
Socialization: defines adequacy of socialization as basis of competence	L	H	H	L	L	L	H	L	H	H	H
Self-symbol formation: focuses on personal identity formation as primary goal of competence	L	H	L	L	L	L	H	L	H	H	H
Process: competence defined as a developmental sequential phenomena	L	H	H	L	H	H	H	H	H	H	H
Objective: deals with effectiveness of external (overt) behaviors	H	H	H	H	H	H	H	L	H	H	H
Motivation: defines competence primarily as a drive, motive, or instinct	L	L	H	L	L	L	L	H	H	H	H
Microlevel: identifies individual behaviors as unit of analysis for competence	H	H	H	H	H	H	H	H	H	H	H
Macrolevel: identifies social system level as unit of analysis for competence	L	L	L	L	L	L	L	L	H	H	L
Interpersonal: deals with the capability/skill for human relationships	L	H	L	H	L	H	L	H	H	H	H
Interactional: deals with situation-response as unit of analysis for competent behavior	L	L	H	H	H	H	H	L	H	L	H
Ethnocultural: deals with ethnic and cultural aspects of competence	L	L	L	L	L	L	L	L	H	H	H
Cognition: deals with cognitive differentiation as essential component of competence	H	H	H	H	H	H	H	H	H	H	H
Autonomy: competence defined primarily in terms of striving for increased self-direction	H	H	H	H	H	L	H	H	H	H	H
Affect: deals with emotional attributional processes as essential component of competence	L	L	L	L	L	L	H	H	L	L	L

226

reading of each theorist's concept of competence is recommended for deeper analysis of the differences in emphasis and content.

Although caution is required in interpreting the various theories, certain trends are easily discernible. For example, five major dimensions are strongly emphasized in nearly all the models: (*a*) autonomy; (*b*) cognition; (*c*) microlevel analysis; (*d*) objective view; and (*e*) process. One exception occurs to the relatively strong emphasis on the autonomy dimension: Rather than *emphasizing* it, French, Rogers, and Cobb's (1974) "subjective demands" concept *implies* the autonomous dimension. There is uniformly strong emphasis on both the cognitive and microlevel dimensions, which is an indication of their importance in the predominantly behavioristic–Western orientation of the theories.

An objective view of competence is taken by all the theorists with the exception of Arasteh (1975) and Bowerman (1978). Arasteh works primarily from a "subjective experience" level and does not deal with the objective aspects of competence, even though he does not negate their existence or importance. Bowerman's (1978) emphasis is on what he considers the neglected dimension of "subjective competence" and he does not pursue the objective dimension with the same intensity as other theorists.

The process approach, which is common to most of the theories, may be an artifact of the trend in psychological literature that is based on social learning and developmental theories. Doll (1953a) implies a process emphasis in his theory, but does not develop it in detail. Wallace (1966) views competence from the "here-and-now" perspective, without discussing what precedes competent behaviors, or what may determine future competent behaviors.

Those dimensions which are characterized by a mixed emphasis include (*a*) self-symbol formation; (*b*) interactional approach; (*c*) interpersonal approach; (*d*) stability; and (*e*) subjective view. Possibly because content and structure are difficult to define for purposes of comparison, the self-symbol formation dimension is treated very unevenly, and is lacking more often than not. If used, in the conventional sense, as a personal self-symbol (i.e., self-image), it could be very important for comparative analysis. It is a concept implied by almost all the theories, but the level of conceptual development varies considerably. Doll (1953a), White (1959), Wallace (1966), and Goldfried and D'Zurilla (1969) really never define how the self-image effects competent behavior, nor the reciprocal effects of competent behavior on the self-image.

The interactional dimension, which is at the center of one of the major current controversies in personality theory (e.g., Magnusson & Endler, 1977), is dealt with in a majority of the theories. Doll (1953a) and Foote and Cottrell (1955) predate the more explicit theorists (e.g., Endler & Magnusson, 1976) in this area, whereas Arasteh (1975) and Heath (1977) are more concerned with personality factors, rather than the interaction between the person and the environment or situation–response units of analysis.

The interpersonal dimension is about evenly divided in emphasis among the theories and reflects the social level of analysis that is characteristic of the theory being considered. The dimension of stability is also present as an aspect of most theories; however, several of the more fully developed theories (e.g., White, 1959; Wallace, 1966; Goldfried & D'Zurilla, 1969; Weinstein, 1969) deal with the integrative capacities involved in competence in an indirect way or suggest its importance without developing it.

The subjective dimension, which places emphasis on the efficacy of internal behaviors, is present in the majority of the theories but varies in the explicitness with which it is treated. It is closely related to the cognitive dimension which is an element of all the theories but relates more to the effectiveness of the cognitions involved in competence. Bowerman (1978) is easily the most explicit theorist in this regard, even though French, Rogers & Cobb (1974) acknowledge the subjective dimension in their theoretical equations. Arasteh (1975) develops subjective competence as successive "integrations" on a strictly private level, and Brewster-Smith (1968) points to the primacy of one's feelings of efficacy. Heath (1977) also emphasizes this in his theory. White (1959), Brewster-Smith (1968) and Heath (1977) all contend that feedback about the effects of one's behavior on the environment are required for effective functioning, but how this process works is left to Bowerman (1978) to delineate in detail.

Socialization is a relatively neglected dimension in all the theories. How competence develops is, of course, an important question and one not easily answered with available theories. Those theorists who were characterized as giving socialization low emphasis were primarily concerned with current competent behaviors and not with the precursors of these behaviors. Weinstein (1969) is perhaps the most explicit source on the socialization of individuals, but is concerned almost exclusively with the socialization of interpersonal competence. Brewster-Smith (1968) discusses the relationship of social structure to competence and the effects on the socialization of the self-symbol, but does not develop the point extensively. The role of socialization processes on competent behaviors is also present in Foote and Cottrell (1955), White (1959), and Heath (1977) but at a more superficial level than either Weinstein or Brewster-Smith.

There are several seriously neglected dimensions that will be important to consider in future research on competence. These include: (*a*) affect, (*b*) cultural influences, (*c*) macrolevel analysis, and (*d*) motivation. Affect is not present as a dimension of competence until Weinstein (1969) and Bowerman (1978) discuss it, which may reflect the tendency to ignore affect in much of the behaviorally-oriented literature of the 1950s and 1960s. The neglect of the cultural dimension also appears to reflect the relative recency of cross-cultural research on competence. Arasteh (1975) is the only non-Western theorist in the group and is valuable alone for the contrasts he presents. Brewster-Smith (1968) is very general in his approach to the cultural factors involved in competence, whereas Heath (1977) provides the first and apparently only empirical cross-cultural study of competence. Such work is extremely useful in gaining an understanding of the many variables involved in an empirical analysis of the cultural factors related to competent behavior.

The motivational factors involved in competent behavior are a major neglected dimension. White (1959) was the first to tie it to the physiological realm and is the single source on this topic. Bowerman (1978) and Brewster-Smith (1968) develop the Heiderian notion of the primacy of the self-symbol as a motivational concept, although Bowerman pursues it in the sense of self-esteem maintenance, rather than a broader notion of self-symbol formation. Additionally, macrolevel analysis is both a poorly defined and undeveloped dimension. Brewster-Smith (1968) is the only theorist to deal with the social-systems aspects of competence with his notions of circles of social causation and the position effects of social structure on self-efficacy.

Conclusions and Recommendations for Future Research

It should be clear by this point that the available conceptual frameworks for studying the relationship of culture and competence are primarily Western in origin, and limited by the cultural assumptions which underlie the disciplines of psychology and anthropology. Moreover, and more telling for future research in this area, they almost all posit the locus of competence within the individual. Having been derived primarily from Western traditions, there is very little emphasis on social system variables and the superorganismic aspects of culture which might provide a more cross-culturally useful framework for examining the relationship of culture and competence.

It should be equally obvious that the empirical basis of culture and competence research is extremely weak and based almost entirely on male samples from a restricted culture range. With these faults of the existing literature in mind, the following questions seem salient for future research:

1. Is an empirically verifiable, transcultural, sex-independent model of competence possible?
2. Is there an invariant sequence, pattern, process, and structure of competence attainment for all cultures?
3. What are the characteristics of a model of competence that can deal with the variety of cultural differences in the social environments to which human beings must adapt?
4. Is it possible to link the immediately effective coping strategies used in meeting the day-to-day situational demands of a culture, to the enabling conditions that cultures may provide for achieving competence?

5. Would situational taxonomies, derived from varying cultures, aid in the assessment of competence within cultures?
6. Is it possible to establish a nonindividual locus of competence at the group, subculture, or the social-system level of a culture, and to assess adaptive effectiveness on those levels?
7. What are the most effective means of transmitting competence within a culture, and what level of cultural organization is most effective for transmitting what competencies?
8. What criteria shall be used to assess competence, and can these be applied cross-culturally?

References

Allport, G. *Personality: A psychological interpretation.* New York: Holt, 1937.
Angyal, A. *Foundation for a science of personality.* New York Commonwealth Fund, 1941.
Arasteh, A. R. *Toward final personality integration.* New York: Schenkman Publishing Co., 1975.
Argyle, M., & Little, B. R. Do personality traits apply to social behavior? *Journal of Social Behavior,* 1972, *2,* 1–35.
Argyris, C. Explorations in interpersonal competence I and II. *Journal of Applied Behavioral Science,* 1965, *1,* 58–83. (a)
Argyris, C. Explorations in interpersonal competence I and II. *Journal of Applied Behavioral Science,* 1965, *1,* 255–269. (b)
Arsenian, J., & Arsenian, J. M. Tough and easy cultures: A conceptual analysis. *Psychiatry,* 1948, *11,* 377–385.
Barnlund, D. Personal communication, 1978.
Bellah, R. To kill and survive or to die and become: The active life and the contemplative life as ways of being adult. *Daedalus,* 1976, *105,* 57–76.
Berry, J. W. An ecological approach to cross-cultural psychology. *Nederlands Tijdschrift Voor De Psychologie,* 1975, *30,* 51–84.
Bouwsma, W. J. Christian adulthood. *Daedalus,* 1976, *105,* 77–92.
Bowerman, W. Subjective competence: The structure, process, and function of self-referent causal attributions. *Journal for the Theory of Social Behavior,* 1978.
Brewster-Smith, M. Explorations in competence: A study of Peace Corps teachers in Ghana. *American Psychologist,* 1966, *21,* 555–566.
Brewster-Smith, M. Socialization for competence. In J. Clausen (Ed.), *Socialization and society.* Boston: Little, Brown, 1968.
Cattell, R. B. *The scientific analysis of personality.* Chicago: Aldine, 1965.
Dabrowski, K. *Positive disintegration.* Boston: Little, Brown, 1964.
deCharms, R. *Personal causation: The internal affective determinants of behavior.* New York: Academic Press, 1968.
Doll, E. *The measurement of social competence: A manual for the Vineland Social Maturity Scale.* New York: Educational Publishing, 1953. (a)
Doll, E. A pilot study of the Vineland Social Maturity Scale with Negro subjects. (Originally published in 1937.) In E. Doll, *The measurement of social competence.* New York: Educational Publishing, 1953. (b)
Dollard, J., & Miller, N. *Personality and psychotherapy.* New York: McGraw-Hill, 1950.
Endler, N., & Magnusson, D. (Eds.), *Interactional psychology and personality.* New York: Wiley, 1976.

Epstein, S. Traits are alive and well. In D. Magnusson & N. Endler (Eds.), *Personality at the crossroads.* Hillsdale, New Jersey: Erlbaum, 1977, 83–89.

Erikson, E. *Childhood and society.* New York: Norton, 1952.

Erikson, E. Identity and the life cycle. *Psychological Issue,* 1959 (Whole No. 1).

Eysenck, H. I., & Eysenck, S. B. G. *Personality structure and measurement.* San Diego, California: Knapp, 1969.

Fenichel, O. *The psychoanalytic theory of neurosis.* New York: Norton, 1945.

Foote, N., & Cottrell, L., Jr. *Identity and interpersonal competence: A new direction in family research.* Chicago: Univ. of Chicago Press, 1955.

French, J., Jr., Rodgers, W., & Cobb, S. Adjustment as person-environment fit. In G. Coehlo, D. Hamburg, & J. Adams (Eds.), *Coping and adaptation.* New York: Basic Books, 1974, 316–333.

Fromm, E., Suzuki, D. T., & Martino, R. *Psychoanalysis and Zen Buddhism.* New York: Harper, 1950.

Goldfried, M. R., & D'Zurilla, T. A behavioral-analytic model for assessing competence. In C. D. Spielberger (Ed.), *Current topics in clinical and community psychology.* New York: Academic Press, 1969, 151–196.

Goldstein, K. *Human nature in the light of psychopathology,* Cambridge, Massachusetts: Harvard Univ. Press, 1940.

Goleman, D. Meditation and consciousness: An Asian approach to mental health. *American Journal of Psychotherapy,* 1976, *30,* 41–54.

Groos, K. *The play of man* (E. L. Baldwin, trans.). New York: D. Appleton, 1901.

Guilford, J. P. *Personality.* New York: McGraw-Hill, 1959.

Hamburg, D., & Adams, J. A perspective on coping behavior: Seeking and utilizing information in major transitions. *Archives of General Psychiatry,* 1967, *17,* 277–284.

Hartman, H. Comments on the psychoanalytic theory of the ego. *Psychoanalytic Study of the Child,* 1950, *5,* 74–95.

Heath, D. *Maturity and competence: A transcultural view.* New York: Gardner, 1977.

Hendrick, I. Instinct and the ego during infancy. *Psychoanalytic Quarterly,* 1942, *11,* 33–58.

Hersen, M., & Bellack, A. Assessment of social skills. In A. Chiminero, K. Calhoun, & H. Adams (Eds.), *Handbook of behavioral assessment.* New York: Wiley, 1977.

Kardiner, A. In H. Spiegel (Ed.), *War stress and neurotic illness.* New York: Hoeber, 1947.

Lanyon, R. I. Measurement of social competence in college males. *Journal of Consulting Psychology,* 1967, *31,* 495–498.

Lapidus, I. M. Adulthood in Islam: Religious maturity in the Islamic tradition. *Daedalus,* 1976, *105*(2), 93–108.

Lazarus, R. S., Averill, J. & Opton, E., Jr. The psychology of coping: Issues of research assessment. In G. Coehlo, D. Hamburg, & J. Adams (Eds.), *Coping and adaptation.* New York: Basic Books, 1974.

Lewin, K. Field theory and experiment in social psychology concepts and methods. *American Journal of Sociology,* 1939, *44,* 868–896.

Longwell, S. G. Exploratory use of the Vineland and Social Maturity Scale with 10 preadolescent Pueblo Indians in a bicultural environment. 1935. In E. Doll (Ed.), *The measurement of social competence.* New York: Educational Publishing, 1953.

Magnusson, D., & Endler, N. S. *Personality at the crossroads: Current issues in interactional psychology.* Hillsdale, New Jersey: Lawrence Erlbaum, 1977.

Maslow, A. *Motivation and personality.* New York: Harper, 1954.

Mittleman. Motility in infants, children, and adults. *Psychoanalytic Study of the Child,* 1954, *9,* 142–177.

Mowrer, O. *Learning theory and personality dynamics.* New York: Ronald Press, 1950.

Murray, H. A. *Explorations in personality.* New York: Oxford Press, 1938.

Nakane, C. *Japanese society.* Berkeley: Univ. of California Press, 1972.

Neki, J. S. Jaha Ja: An Indian ideal of mental health. *Psychiatry*, 1975, *38*, 1–10.

Pedersen, P. Asian personality theory. In R. Corsini (Ed.), *Current personality theories*. Itasca, Illinois: F. E. Peacock Publishers, 1977, 367–398.

Phillips, L., & Cowitz, B. Social attainment and reactions to stress. *Journal of Personality*, 1953, *22*, 270–283.

Rogers, C. *On becoming a person*. Boston: Houghton, 1961.

Rohlen, T. P. The promise of adulthood in Japanese spiritualism. *Daedalus*, 1976, *105*, 125–143.

Sill, J. B. A comparative study of non-institutionalized Jewish and Italian subnormal girls by the use of the Vineland Social Maturity Scale. 1936. In E. Doll, *The measurement of social competence*. New York: Educational Publishers, 1953.

Stein, M., & Vidich, A. J. (Eds.), Identity and history: An overview. In *Identity and anxiety*. New York: The Free Press of Glencoe, 1960.

Sullivan, H. S. Tensions, interpersonal and international: A psychiatrist's view. In H. Cantril (Ed.), *Tensions that cause wars*. Urbana: Univ. of Illinois Press, 1950.

Sullivan, H. S. *Conceptions of modern psychiatry*. New York: Norton, 1953.

Szasz, T. *The myth of mental illness: Foundations of a theory of personal conduct*. New York: Hoeber-Harper, 1961.

Tart, C. T. (Ed.), Transpersonal psychologies. New York: Harper, 1975.

Wallace, J. An abilities conception of personality: Some implications for personality measurement. *American Psychologist*, 1966, *21*, 132–138.

Wei-Ming, T. The Confucian perception of adulthood. *Daedalus*, 1976, *105*, 109–123.

Weinstein, E. The development of interpersonal competence. In D. A. Goslin (Ed.), *Handbook of socialization theory and research*. Chicago: Rand McNally, 1969.

White, R. Motivation reconsidered: A concept of competence. *Psychological Review*, 1959, *66*, 297–333.

11

Cross-Cultural Studies of Mental Disorders[1]

ANTHONY J. MARSELLA

Introduction

The last two decades have witnessed an increased interest in the cross-cultural study of mental disorders. This interest has manifested itself across a variety of disciplines and has served as an impetus for the development of a number of subdisciplinary specialties, which have been variously termed *vergleichende psychiatrie* or comparative psychiatry (Kraepelin, 1904), primitive psychiatry (Devereux, 1940), culture and psychopathology (Slotkin, 1955), ethnopsychiatry (Devereux, 1961), comparative psychopathology (Kaelbling, 1961), transcultural psychiatry (Wittkower & Rin, 1965), cross-cultural psychiatry (Murphy & Leighton, 1965), psychiatric sociology (Weinberg, 1967), cultural psychiatry (Kennedy, 1973), and the "new" transcultural psychiatry (Kleinman, 1977). Regardless of the different names that have been applied to the area, the major concerns have been the same. Essentially, these concerns can be divided into four basic questions:

1. Is there a universal concept of "normal" and "abnormal" behavior?
2. Are there differences in the rates of mental disorders across cultures?

[1] Preparation of this chapter was partially supported by NIMH Research Grant 5R-12-MH-31016-01 awarded to the author for participation in the WHO International Collaborative Study of Schizophrenia.

233

PERSPECTIVES ON CROSS-CULTURAL PSYCHOLOGY

3. Are there differences in the manifestations or patterns of mental disorders across cultures?
4. Are there relationships between the sociocultural milieu and various aspects of mental disorders?

A number of previous publications have attempted to review the relevant research literature that has been concerned with these questions. The first of these reviews was published by Benedict and Jacks (1954). Since that time, many others have appeared. Among the most recent reviews, some have focused on the spectrum of mental disorders (e.g., Draguns & Phillips, 1971; Guthrie, 1972; Kiev, 1972; Pfeiffer, 1970; Draguns, 1979) whereas others have addressed themselves to more specific forms of mental disorders, such as schizophrenia (e.g., Sanua, 1969) and depression (e.g., Marsella, 1979).

The purpose of the present chapter is to continue the efforts toward synthesizing and integrating the data on cross-cultural studies of mental disorders, with the hope that these efforts can lead to a better understanding of the role of cultural factors in the etiology, expression, and experience of mental disorders. Other chapters in the current volume will address themselves to the implications that the research literature has for the design and delivery of culturally relevant mental health services and therapies. Before examining the questions raised earlier, let us first take a look at the history of the topic and the influence that culture may have on mental disorders.

Historical Perspectives

In my opinion, the history of the cross-cultural study of mental disorders can be divided into four basic periods: (a) Pre–1900, (b) 1900–1950, (c) 1950–1970, (d) 1970 and beyond. The basis of these time period distinctions are the shifts in the conceptual and research foci among investigators. The periods will be discussed in order.

PRE–1900

The first systematic concern for the role of cultural factors in the etiology of mental disorders can be traced, in my opinion, to the words of the famous Swiss philosopher, Jean Jacques Rousseau. In 1749, Rousseau claimed that "Man is by nature good, and only our institutions have made him bad [Durant & Durant, 1967, p. 19]." These words, historians such as Durant and Durant have argued, served as the basis for the entire romanticist movement and became a rallying cry for social reformers throughout the world. For example, the "vices of civilization" soon became a target for the reform efforts of several physicians such as George Burrows, who in 1828 wrote:

> Many of the causes inducing intellectual derangement and which are called moral, have their origin not in individual passions or feelings, but in the state of society at large and the more artificial, i.e., civilized, society is, the more do these causes multiply and extensively operate [Burrows, 1828, in Rosen, 1959, p. 17].

In 1851, Jarvis, a psychiatrist in New England voiced similar thoughts. He stated,

> Insanity is then a part of the price we pay for civilization. The causes of the one increase with the developments and results of the other. . . . The increase of knowledge, the improvement in the arts, the multiplication of comforts, the amelioration of manners, the growth of refinement, and the elevation of morals, do not of themselves disturb men's cerebral organs and create mental disorder. But with them come more opportunities and rewards for great and excessive mental action, more uncertain and hazardous employments, and consequently more disappointments, more means and provocations for sensual indulgences, more dangers of accidents and injuries, more groundless hopes, and more painful struggle to obtain that which is beyond reach or to effect that which is impossible [Jarvis, 1851, in Rosen, 1959, p. 21].

Amidst the extensive discontent with "civilization", it was natural for many individuals to point out the virtues of life in the primitive societies of the "noble savage." For example, Andrews, in 1887, stated,

> The small percentage of insane among the aborigines and Chinese is fully in accord with the observations of writers upon the causes productive of mental disease. There is much less refinement of civilization; less competition and struggle for place, power, wealth, and as a consequence, less mental deterioration [Andrews, 1887, quoted in Rosen, 1959, p. 25].

These early observations were soon to yield to more systematic efforts to examine the role of the cultural milieu in mental disorders.

1900–1950

In 1904, Kraepelin, the acknowledged father of modern psychiatric thought, reported cultural differences in the expression and frequency of mental disorders among various populations in Indonesia, albeit that he chose to attribute the differences to diet and climate. Within a few years, a growing number of reports emerged on the so called "culture-specific disorders" like arctic hysteria (Brill, 1913), *latah* (Van Brero, 1895), *myriachit* (Czapligka, 1914), hysterical neuroses (Coriat, 1915), *amok* and *latah* (Van Loon, 1927), and *mali-mali* (Musgrave & Sison, 1910). In addition, a number of investigators began to comment on "Western" disorders in non-Western cultural groups in Africa (e.g., Gordon, 1934), Australia (Cleland, 1928), Canada (e.g., Saindon, 1933), India (e.g., Dhunjiboy, 1930), Indonesia (e.g., Van Wulfften-Palthe, 1936), Japan (e.g., Uchimura, 1938), and New Guinea (e.g., Seligman, 1929). Additionally, of course, how can we forget the publication in 1922 of Sigmund Freud's famous work, *Civilization and Its Discontents,* which once again targeted "society" as the root of mankind's problems.

The 1930s witnessed the emergence of yet another important research direction, for it was during this time period that the first psychiatric epidemiology studies were initiated to identify the rates of mental disorders in such countries as Germany (Brugger, 1931, 1933, 1937), Japan (Akimoto, Sunazaki, Okada, & Hanashiro, 1942; Tsugawa, Okada, Hanashiro, Asai, Takuma, & Morimura, 1942; Uchimura, Akimoto, Kan, Abe, Takahashi, Inose, Shimazaki, & Ogawa, 1940), and the United States (Faris & Dunham, 1939; Lemkau, Tietze, & Cooper, 1942; Roth & Luton, 1943).

1950–1970

The next two decades saw a proliferation of publications directed toward four topical areas including (*a*) the epidemiology of mental disorders (e.g., Eaton & Weil, 1955; Lin, 1953); (*b*) the role of cultural factors in mental disorders (e.g., A. Leighton, Lambo, Hughes, Leighton, Murphy, & Macklin, 1963; D. Leighton, Harding, Macklin, Macmillan, & Leighton, 1963; Srole, Langner, Michael, Opler, & Rennie, 1962); (*c*) the role of cultural factors in the expression of both "Western" disorders (e.g., Carothers, 1948; Dai, 1959; Enright & Jaeckle, 1963; Gaitonde, 1959; Murphy, Wittkower, & Chance, 1964) and "culture-specific" disorders (e.g., Rin, 1965; Rubel, 1964; Yap, 1951); and (*d*) the role of cultural factors in the conceptualization and treatment of mental disorders (e.g., Kiev, 1964).

Within this same time period, several new journals and newsletters were published with specific interests in the cross-cultural study of mental disorders including *Transcultural Psychiatric Research Review and Newsletter,* the *International Journal of Social Psychiatry,* and the *International Mental Health Research Newsletter.* McGill University in Canada emerged as special training center for cross-cultural psychiatry under the leadership of Eric Wittkower and H. B. M. Murphy. In addition, the National Institute of Mental Health funded a Culture and Mental Health Training Program at the University of Hawaii for the period 1966–1972 under the directorship of William Lebra to provide interdisciplinary training for both behavioral scientists and psychiatrists. Many research studies conducted by the participants in this program were published in Caudill and Lin (1969) and Lebra (1972, 1974, 1976).

1970 AND BEYOND

Our proximity to the present limits our ability to develop an accurate perspective on where we currently are, and where we are going with regard to the cross-cultural study of mental disorders. However, in my opinion two trends are emerging. First, a number of signs are visible which suggest greater sensitivity to the ethnocentricity of many Western concepts about the expression and treatment of mental disorder (e.g., Kleinman, 1977; Marsella, Kinzie, & Gordon, 1973; Tanaka-Matsumi & Marsella, 1976; Torrey, 1972). Now more than ever before, there appears to be a recognition of the cultural variations in the expression and the experience of mental disorders and also a recognition of the need for culturally relevant interventions (e.g., Higginbotham, 1976, and chapter 14 of this volume; Kleinman, 1978; Sue, 1977).

Second, there is reason to believe that research efforts will be directed toward a pursuit of cultural variations across many aspects of given mental disorder. For example, the new WHO–NIMH study on the sociocultural determinants of the course and outcome of schizophrenic disorders represents an effort to refine our knowledge on why schizophrenia seems to have a different time course and prognostic outcome among non-Western people (Sartorius, Jablensky, & Shapiro, 1978). It will involve simultaneous studies of nine countries on case identification criteria, family dynamics, life stress, and impairment profiles.

Another example is my own research program on cultural differences in depressive affect and disorders. My program involves comparisons of the epidemiology, expression, experience, measurement, personality correlates, antecedent–consequences, and psychophysiological correlates of depression among ethnocultural groups in Hawaii. These approaches offer us a greater opportunity to more fully understand the influence of culture on mental disorders and to develop theoretical frameworks for linking culture and mental disorders.

The Multiple Influences of Culture on Mental Disorders

Is it reasonable to expect cross-cultural differences in mental disorders? The answer to this question is, of course, yes! As all behavior is inextricably linked to culture and as cultures vary, it is logical to expect cross-cultural differences in mental disorders. But, what aspects of a culture are important for mental disorders? Several researchers have attempted to delineate the important sources of cultural influence (e.g., Leighton & Hughes, 1961; Marsella, Kinzie, & Gordon, 1973; Wittkower & Dubreil, 1973). In general, these sources can be divided into three categories: (*a*) cultural variations in stress inducers; (*b*) cultural variations in defining abnormality; and (*c*) cultural variations in personality. These will be discussed in order.

CULTURAL VARIATIONS IN STRESS INDUCERS

Cultures vary with regard to both the amount and the type of stress they induce in their members. In certain instances, the stresses may be so numerous and so severe that cultural disintegration may occur (see Leighton, 1959). Some of the culturally related stresses which have been investigated include the following:

1. *Value Conflict Stress*: This type of stress occurs when there are many conflicting values in a given society. These conflicts serve to elicit psychological uncertainty and confusion because a stable frame of reference is absent.

2. *Social Change Stress*: When a culture is forced to change under such pressures as urbanization or modernization, stress develops because of the many challenges to the previous habitual forms of adaptation. However, as Fried (1964) has pointed out, the effects of social change on mental health are a function of the meaning and functional significance of the changes, and these factors depend on the social situations, group characteristics, and so forth. Reviews of the literature on the effects of social change have been published by Murphy (1961), Inkeles and Smith (1970), and Marsella (1978a).

3. *Acculturation Stress*: Unlike social change stress, acculturation stress typically involves the changes set in motion when different cultures come into contact with one another. Several authors have written about the different types of acculturation that can occur (e.g., Baldauf, 1975; Teske & Nelson, 1974). In some instances, acculturation pressures have been considered to have very pernicious effects on mental health (e.g., Hallowell, 1950; Sampath, 1974; Spindler, 1955).

4. *Life Events Stress*: Many life events are capable of evoking stress within the organism because they elicit new adaptive responses which require change in ongoing patterns of adjustment. Some life event changes obviously require greater life readjustment than others, and cultures vary with regard to the number of life event changes to which their members are exposed and the particular ordering of their implications (e.g., Woon, Masuda, Wagner, & Holmes, 1971; Masuda & Holmes, 1967). Coverage of the literature on this topic is available in Dohrenwend and Dohrenwend (1974) and Rabkin and Struening (1976).

5. *Goal-Striving Discrepancy Stress*: This type of stress is present in cultures in which there are large discrepancies between aspirations and achievements. For example, in many developing countries, a revolution of rising expectations is occurring as a result of the increased awareness fostered by the communication media. When the goal-striving discrepancies are high, there is greater risk of mental disorder

present (e.g., Marsella, Escudero, & Brennan, 1975; Marsella, Escudero, & Gordon, 1972; Parker & Kleiner, 1966).

6. *Role Discrimination Stress*:   Many cultures have a great deal of stress associated with certain social strata (e.g., age groups, gender, or race). This type of status discrimination places pressure on individuals by fostering feelings of inadequacy and self-worth (e.g., Dohrenwend & Dohrenwend, 1969; Weissman & Klerman, 1977).

7. *Role Conflict*:   In many cultures, the roles which people play are in conflict with one another. The disparities can elicit stress because of the continual switching in role requirements and demands. A good example of this type of stress is the role requirements in dual-career families or the gaps that exist when women may be the major money earner, but then have to defer to males within the home.

CULTURAL VARIATIONS IN THE DEFINITION OF "ABNORMALITY"

Since "normality" and "abnormality" are relative to particular cultural milieus, it stands to reason that particular definitions of "abnormality" may tolerate greater or lesser degrees of deviancy. By defining "normality" and "abnormality" each culture conditions certain patterns of acceptable behavior. For example, withdrawal may not be considered pathogenic in one culture while in another it may be a stimulus for hospitalization. The question of "normality" will be discussed in a later section of this chapter.

CULTURAL VARIATIONS IN PERSONALITY

Abnormal behavior is continuous with normal behavior. The former reflects the stylistic features and orientations of the latter. Within this context, personality is the basis of both normal and abnormal behavior. And, as personality structure and dynamics vary across cultures, it is logical to expect cross-cultural differences in mental disorders.

In my opinion, it would appear that personality variations across cultures are related to the etiology, experience, and expression of mental disorders. From the point of view of etiology, certain personality patterns may be more or less resistant to stress by virtue of either temperament styles, cognitive and physiological coping patterns, and general personality orientations. Similarly, personality is also related to the actual experiences associated with mental disorders, as well as the particular forms they assume.

For example, I reported that there were numerous differences in the expression of depression across cultures (Marsella, 1979). In Western cultures, depression appears to be characterized by disturbances in somatic, affective, and cognitive–existential aspects of functioning, whereas in non-Western cultures, somatic features tend to dominate the symp-tomatological presentation. I speculated (see Marsella, 1978b) that the ex-perience and expression of depression is related to several important vari-ables. These are language, self-structure, and experiential mode of reality. Some cultures tend to have objective epistemological orientations. Such an orientation is related to the use of abstract languages, individuated self-structures, and lexical mediation of reality. In contrast, other cultures tend to have subjective epistemological orientations. This orientation is related to metaphorical languages, unindividuated self-structures, and imagistic media-tion of reality. These relationships and their association with the experience and expression of depression are depicted in Figure 11.1. Although this approach is admittedly speculative, it does provide an example of the possi-ble linkages between personality factors and mental disorders across cul-tures. Now, let me address the four major questions raised in the introduc-tion.

Are the Concepts of "Normal" and "Abnormal" Behavior Universal?

The first challenges to the assumption about the universality of "normal" and "abnormal" behavior emerged in the early 1930s with the writings of such famous cultural anthropologists as Sapir, Hallowell, and Benedict. Sapir (1932) wrote:

> Cultural anthropology has the healthiest of scepticisms about the validity of the concept of "normal behavior" . . . . It [cultural anthropology] is valuable because it is constantly rediscovering the normal. For the psychiatrist and the student of per-sonality in general, this is of the greatest importance, for personalities are not con-ditioned by a generalized process of adjustment to the "normal" but by the necessity of adjustment to the greatest possible variety of idea and action patterns according to the accidents of birth and biography [p. 230].

A few years later, Benedict (1934) and Hallowell (1934) published strong statements on the relativity of normal behavior based on the growing number of culture and personality studies. Hallowell's words are as meaningful today as when he wrote them. He stated (Hallowell, 1934) that the cross-cultural investigator must:

> have an intimate knowledge of the culture as a whole, he must also be aware of the normal range of individual behavior within the cultural pattern and likewise understand what the people themselves consider to be extreme deviations from this norm. In short, he must develop a standard of normality with reference to the culture itself, as a means of controlling an uncritical application of the criteria that he brings with him from our civilization [p. 2].

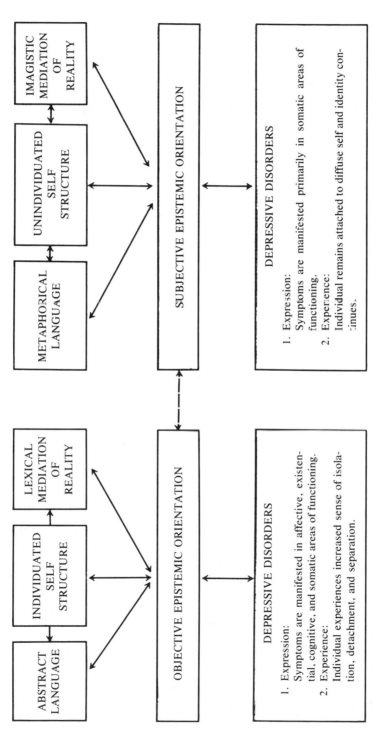

Figure 11.1. Continuum of objective versus subjective epistemological relationships (from Marsella, 1978b).

One of the first medical people to respond to the growing ideas about the relativity of normality was Ackerknecht (1942). He suggested that behavior could be divided into four categories: (a) *autopathological* (behavior abnormal in the culture in which it is found, but normal in other cultures); (b) *autonormal* (behavior normal in the culture in which it is found, but abnormal in other cultures); (c) *heteropathological* (behavior which is abnormal in all cultures); and (d) *heteronormal* (behavior which is normal in all cultures). Obviously Ackerknecht's system represents an oversimplification of a complex problem as it is doubtful that behaviors could be so easily classified. But, it served to sensitize researchers to cultural differences.

Honigmann (1953), another cultural anthropologist, approached the problem by defining ''abnormality'' as a behavior which was characterized by one or more of eight signs including anxiety, sensorimotor dysfunction, reality distortion, derangement of intellectual capacities, and so forth. However, this approach did not resolve the problem as many of these criteria were not relevant to non-Western cultures.

A different approach was taken by Katz, Gudeman, and Sanborn (1969). They attempted to rate behavior of normal and abnormal individuals from different ethnocultural groups in Hawaii on a standardized adjustment scale measuring ten behavior categories (e.g., negativism, belligerence, confusion, withdrawal). They were then able to develop a profile of normal and abnormal Japanese, Chinese, Filipinos, Caucasians, Hawaiians, and Samoans on these behavior categories. The profiles obtained could then be compared within and across ethnocultural groups. The basic shortcoming of this approach is that the items composing the various categories were derived from factor analysis of Caucasians, and thus do not reflect the possible variations which may exist for the other groups. Nevertheless, this approach represents one of the most systematic efforts to date to cross-culturally study ''normal'' and ''abnormal'' behavior in an empirical manner.

Draguns (1977) concluded that what is needed at this point are the following: (a) a clear, unambiguous standard of disturbance, cross-culturally acceptable, at least for purposes of comparative research; (b) operational measures that embody this concept in a manner applicable across cultures; and (c) demonstrations of equivalence of these measures in different cultural locales. The state of affairs would be less disturbing if researchers were more willing to acknowledge, and be responsive to, cultural differences in defining normality and abnormality. However, with few exceptions, most research is characterized by an imposition of Western standards.

It would be refreshing to find a study that first, made an effort to understand indigenous concepts of health and disorder, and then proceeded to examine the people from both Western and non-Western standards looking for contrasts and similarities. This approach would require researchers to know both the indigenous categories of disorders and the indigenous conceptions of cause. It would also be important to know the signs for including individuals within the various categories of disorder. Figure 11.2 displays the type of matrix suggested. These matrices could be developed for different cultural groups and then compared. This would enable us to meet both etic and emic standards, and could provide a rich source of data for understanding mental disorders.

A universal standard of normality and abnormality has been the goal of many researchers. A possible approach within this context is the "efficiency" concept developed by Wishner (1955). Briefly, *efficiency* is the ratio of focused to diffuse energy expended by an individual in meeting a task demand. Wishner's research indicated that more inefficiency is associated with psychopathology. Unfortunately, Wishner's concept has never been tested cross-culturally.

In brief, what I am suggesting is that we must be sensitive to the relativity of normality and abnormality if we are to avoid psychiatric "imperialism." It is my impression that steps toward resolving the question can be taken by conducting empirical studies of the conceptualizations of health and disorder

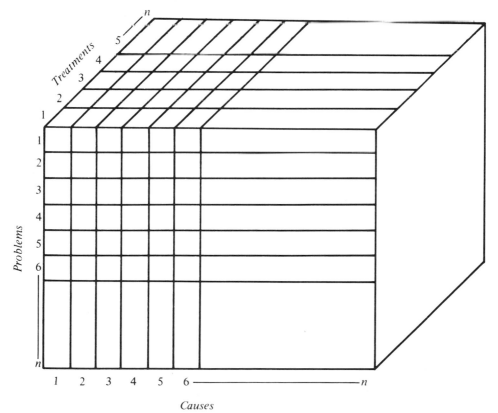

Causes

Figure 11.2. Research matrix for investigating problem, cause, and treatment interactions.

held by different cultures. Then, we could proceed to examine individuals in a given culture from both the emic and the etic perspectives for purposes of comparison. At the present time, there is a growing knowledge regarding cultural variations in conceptions of health and disorder. The fact that these conceptions are available, but not used as legitimate categories for comparative research is an unfortunate commentary on the ethnocentricity of our researchers.

Do Rates of Mental Disorders Differ Across Cultures?

The second major question which has characterized the study of culture and mental disorders is whether rates of mental disorder vary across cultures. Research on cultural variations in the frequency of mental disorders is essentially the province of psychiatric epidemiology, that branch of public health concerned with the distribution of mental disorders. According to Opler (1965), the first impetus for psychiatric epidemiology studies was provided by Emerson in 1930 at the First International Congress on Mental Hygiene when he identified mental disorders as a major public health problem and called for extensive research. Within a brief period of time, a number of studies were initiated in Germany, Japan, and the United States.

Since that time, numerous psychiatric epidemiology studies have been conducted in dozens of countries. The results of these studies can be divided into two different groups: (*a*) studies concerned with rates of mental disorders in general; and (*b*) studies concerned with rates of specific mental disorders such as depression. Let us examine the findings in that order.

MENTAL DISORDERS IN GENERAL

The most exhaustive review of general, psychiatric epidemiology studies have been published by Dohrenwend and Dohrenwend (1965, 1969). Table 11.1 displays an overview of the studies examined by Dohrenwend and Dohrenwend. As Table 11.1 indicates, there are substantial differences in the rates of mental disorder for the different countries. However, the essential question is whether the rates are an accurate portrayal of reality, or a function of differences in the definitions of disorder used, the criteria for case inclusion, and the extent of case contact. Clearly, differences in these areas could yield profound differences in rates of mental disorder. As research methods were not standardized across the studies, it is extremely difficult to reach any substantive conclusions about cultural variations in mental disorders. Therefore the existing figures can only serve as tantalizing prods for future research efforts.

TABLE 11.1
Percentage of Psychological Disorder Reported according to Geopolitical Area[a]

Site	North America	Northern Europe	Asia	Africa
Rural	1.7 (Eaton & Weil, 1955)	1.1 (Kaila, Study 2)	.8 (Uchimura et al., 1940)	40.0 (A. Leighton et al., 1963)
	1.9 (Rosanoff, 1917)	1.3 (Brugger, 1931)	1.0 (Lin, small town, 1953)	
	6.9 (Roth & Luton, 1943)	1.3 (Kaila, Study 1)	1.1 (Lin, village, 1953)	
	18.0 (Trussel et al., 1956)	3.5 (Brugger, 1937)	2.7 (Akimoto et al., 1942)	
	50.0+ (D. Leighton et al., 1963)	4.2 (Strömgren, 1950)		
	64.0 (Llewellyn-Thomas, 1960)	7.5 (Brugger, 1933)		
		9.0 (Mayer-Gross, 1948)		
		11.9 (Fremming, 1951)		
		13.2 (Primrose, 1962)		
		13.6 (Essen-Möller, 1956)		
		23.2 (Bremer, 1951)		
Urban	1.8 (Lemkau et al., 1942)	1.0 (Kaila, Study 1)	1.1 (Lin, city, 1953)	45.0 (A. Leighton et al., 1963)
	2.3 (Cohen et al., 1939)	1.1 (Kaila, Study 2)	3.0 (Tsuwaga et al., 1942)	
	3.4 (Manis et al., 1964)	15.6 (Gnat et al., 1964)		
	10.9 (Pasamanick et al., 1959)	33.0 (Taylor & Chave, 1964)		
	23.4 (Srole et al., 1962)			
	32.0 (Cole et al., 1957)			

[a] From Dohrenwend and Dohrenwend, 1965.

SPECIFIC MENTAL DISORDERS

Several researchers have reviewed the epidemiological studies of depression across cultures (e.g., Marsella, 1978c; Sartorius, 1973; Silverman, 1968). In general, these reviews indicate that the rates of depression appear to be smaller for non-Western cultures whether we are using treated or untreated prevalences. For the few exceptions where depression rates were high in non-Western cultures, the studies were based on highly urbanized populations. Recent reviews of other disorders such as schizophrenia, psychosomatic illnesses, etc., have not, to my knowledge, been published. However, there have been many epidemiological studies of these disorders—especially schizophrenia (e.g., Hollingshead & Redlich, 1958; Mishler & Scotch, 1963). An overview suggests that schizophrenia rates vary considerably across cultures (Dunham, 1965). However, this too may be due to measurement artifacts.

Methodological differences among the epidemiological studies conducted of mental disorders make it difficult to reach any conclusions about the frequency of mental disorders in different cultural milieus. In those epidemiological studies that examined the treated prevalence rates for specific disorders such as depression, there is a greater homogeneity in the research methods: However, the treated prevalence rates may be biased because of differences in the accessibility of clinical services, and the fact that the expression of depression varies so much across cultures (see Marsella, 1978c).

Marsella (1978c) has suggested that cross-cultural epidemiological studies can be improved by implementing new procedures including

1. An emic determination of mental disorder categories for different cultures.
2. The establishment of symptom frequency, and duration baselines for both normal and abnormal populations.
3. The objective generation of symptom patterns through the use of factor analysis.
4. The use of similar research methods (i.e., house to house survey with actual case contact) in different cultures, but with culturally relevant definitions of mental disorder.

Does the Expression of Mental Disorder Differ Across Cultures?

The third question which has dominated the thinking of researchers in the area of culture and mental health is whether the expression of mental disorder differs across cultures. As was the case for the other two questions, the answer to this question is quite complicated. Essentially, many of the same behaviors that are labeled as being disordered in the Western world, are also considered to be disordered in non-Western cultures (e.g., extreme sadness, agitation, hostility, motor retardation). However, it is the patterning of the disordered behaviors which varies considerably across cultures.

The research is clear in pointing out extensive cultural variability in the manifestation of mental disorders. The grouping of symptoms according to the patterns that Western psychiatrists have traditionally used (i.e., neurotic depression, sociopathic personality, paranoid schizophrenia) are not universally found. Indeed, there is even a growing discontent among Western mental health professionals regarding the existence of the Western "textbook" patterns of mental disorders. Many professionals feel that mental disorders are quite unique for individuals and cultures and do not fit the neat "textbook" descriptions that they are taught in training.

The study of cultural variations in the manifestation of mental disorders has been characterized by five major research strategies: (*a*) culture-specific disorders, (*b*) matched diagnosis, (*c*) matched sample, (*d*) international survey, and (*e*) factor analysis. Findings from these strategies will be discussed in that order.

CULTURE-SPECIFIC DISORDERS

As was pointed out in the history section of this chapter, researchers long ago identified mental disorders which are unique to certain cultural settings. Some of the more popularly researched disorders falling into this category are *Latah, Koro,* and *Pibloktoq. Latah* is found in many parts of the Orient and Southeast Asia. It is characterized by hysteria, echolalia, echopraxia, hypersuggestibility, and anxiety. *Koro* is found among Chinese males and is characterized by a fear that one's penis is shrinking into the body. *Pibloktoq,* or Arctic hysteria, is found among certain Eskimo populations and is characterized by anxiety, amnesia, agitation, and fear. Oftentimes the victims will take off all their clothes and run naked in the snow. Yap (1951) has written an excellent review of the clinical signs of these and other culture-specific disorders.

Although it has been assumed that many of the culture-specific disorders are unique to a given culture, some researchers have argued that variants of them can be found around the world (Kiev, 1972). Yet, it is clear that these dysfunctions seem to show great cultural coloring in their manifestation, and most explanations of their etiology and form emphasize factors unique to given cultures.

The culture-specific disorder, research strategy supports the conclusion that cultural variations in the manifestation of mental disorders do exist. Indeed, I have even taken the radical position that culture-specific disorders are not exotic syndromes; instead, all disorders are culture-specific disorders, regardless of the cultural milieu in which they are found, as all mental disorders must ultimately be expressed through the filter of cultural experience.

MATCHED DIAGNOSIS

A second strategy used to study cultural variations in the manifestation of mental disorders is the matched diagnosis. In this approach individuals who are from different cultural groups and who share a common diagnosis are compared for symptom variations.

For example, Opler and Singer (1959) compared Italian and Irish schizophrenic patients and found that the Irish tended to have more guilt and sin preoccupations, more systematic delusions, more drinking problems, and less affective troubles than the Italians. Enright and Jaeckle (1963) compared Japanese and Filipino paranoid schizophrenics in Hawaii and found that the Filipinos were more active, belligerent, hostile, and agitated whereas the Japanese were more withdrawn, passive, and cooperative. Sunshine (1971) compared black and Puerto Rican schizophrenics in New York and found that the latter group were more active, possessed more florid symptomatology, and tended to somatize more often than the former group. A study by DeHoyos and DeHoyos (1965) also found symptom differences between black and white schizophrenic patients.

Cultural variations in depression have also been reported using the matched diagnosis strategy. For example, Simon, Fliess, Gurland, Stiller, and Sharpe (1973) compared black and white depressive patients and found numerous differences in symptoms leading them to conclude that blacks "have a quality of their depression different from whites [p. 509]." Similarly, Kimura (1965) reported variations in the expression of depression between German and Japanese depressives, especially with regard to guilt, suicide, and the quality of depression.

MATCHED SAMPLES

A third strategy used to study cultural variations in the manifestation of mental disorders is the matched diagnosis approach. This approach matches individuals from different cultural groups according to such variables as age, education, gender, social class, and rural–urban residence. The different cultural groups are then compared with regard to variations in the frequency or severity of different symptoms. The basic idea is that, with these variables held constant, it is possible to attribute any differences in the symptom pictures to cultural factors.

A series of studies comparing matched samples in Argentina and the United States (Fundia, Draguns, & Phillips, 1971) and Japan and the United States (Draguns, Phillips, Broverman, Caudill, & Nishimae, 1971) found profound differences in the symptom pictures of the contrasting cultures. In general, the differences were in the direction of exaggerations of the normal, behavior patterns of the various cultural groups. Stoker, Zurcher, and Fox (1968) compared symptom profiles of Mexican-American and Anglo-American females and found the Mexican pattern was characterized by greater hostility, hyperactivity, crying, sleeplessness, somatic complaints, and withdrawal. The Anglo pattern was characterized by greater guilt feelings and psychomotor retardation.

Sechrest (1969) compared patients from Chicago and the National Mental Hospital of the Philippines. A dramatic finding was that only 3% of the Filipino cases were described as depressed. Guilt feelings and suicidal threats and attempts were also quite low in the Philippines. There were also differences in the frequency and content of the hallucinations reported.

INTERNATIONAL SURVEY

The international survey approach to studying cultural variations in the manifestation of mental disorders is one of the oldest methods used. In the early 1960s, H. B. M. Murphy and Eric Wittkower initiated a series of international surveys to compare the symptom pictures associated with schizophrenia and depression in numerous countries around the world. In both instances, cultural differences were found in the expression of the different disorders.

For example, a survey of depression in 30 countries revealed (Murphy, Wittkower, & Chance, 1964), that in 9 countries (mainly non-Western) there was a rarity in depressed mood, insomnia, mood variation, and loss of interest in the environment. Yet, these symptoms are considered part of the classic picture of depression in the Western world. A similar survey comparing symptom profiles of schizophrenic patients in different countries also revealed numerous differences in the symptom patterns (Murphy, Wittkower, Fried, & Ellenberger, 1963).

A more recent effort by the Division of Mental Health of the World Health Organization examined schizophrenia in nine countries around the world using highly standardized interview forms (World Health Organization, 1973). Although many similarities were found in the symptom profiles of patients from the nine centers, there were also a number of variations. One of the most interesting findings to emerge was that the prognosis, or outcome, for schizophrenia varied considerably across cultures (Sartorius, Jablensky, & Shapiro, 1978).

FACTOR ANALYSIS

The most recent research strategy used to study cultural variations in the manifestation of mental disorders is factor analysis. Throughout psychiatry's history, patterns of disorder have usually been identified through clinical observation. Based on these observations, clinicians suggest clusters of symptoms which appear to fall together. If there is agreement across clinicians, then a syndrome is usually posited. In the case of factor analysis, the clustering of the symptoms is done objectively, through a set of mathematical operations, rather than subjectively by a clinician. This objective approach often yields different patterns of symptoms from those reported by clinical observation. As a result, factor analysis lends itself to efforts to understand symptom patterns in different cultures as it reduces the risks of automatically adopting Western notions about the existence of certain patterns of psychiatric disturbance.

For example, using factor analysis, Caudill and Schooler (1969) found certain patterns of disorders among Japanese psychiatric patients that were not found among other ethnocultural groups (e.g., *shinkeishitzu*). Similarly, Marsella, Kinzie, and Gordon (1973) found depressive disorders among Chinese-Americans, Japanese-Americans, and Caucasian-American differed in terms of symptom profiles. The Chinese-Americans emphasized somatic complaints whereas the Japanese-Americans evidenced more interpersonal dysfunctions (e.g., not wanting to talk to people, not caring for appearance, wanting to have privacy). In contrast, Caucasian-Americans presented more existential complaints (e.g., life has no meaning, depressive affect, feelings of worthlessness).

SOME CONCLUDING COMMENTS

Regardless of the research strategy used, the results demonstrate that cultures differ in the manifestation of mental disorders. That this is the case should not be surprising! Clearly, there is no reason to believe that cultural variables should have any less influence on deviant behavior patterns than they do on "normal" behavior patterns. Even if certain biochemical processes may be universally operative in the etiology of mental disorders, it is obvious that the appraisal and behavioral responses to these processes must be filtered through culturally conditioned experience. Furthermore, the social response to the behavior pattern must also reflect cultural influences. Certain cultural traditions may (by the response they condition to various behavior patterns) maintain, enhance, and encourage their development.

Yet another important point regarding cultural variations in the manifestation of mental disorders, is the fact that many cultural groups do not have similar words or concepts to describe the mental disorders "reported" in the Western world. This also should not be surprising as the diagnostic and classification systems used in the Western world grew largely from the work of Emil Kraepelin in nineteenth-century Germany. Today, even in the Western world, there is a growing discontent with the "acknowledged" patterns of mental disorder.

Over the course of the past two decades numerous changes have been made in the *Diagnostic and Statistical Manual* (DSM) of the American Psychiatric Association. In addition to the changes in the DSM, many clinicians and researchers have advanced alternative classification systems that bear little resemblance to the traditional patterns of mental disorder (e.g., Karl Menninger, Hans Eysenck, Maurice Lorr).

The fact that many cultural groups do not have terms approximating the patterns of mental disorder accepted in other cultures, is important because it supports the empirical findings. For example, a number of researchers have pointed out that there are no equivalent terms for depression among Nigerians (Leighton *et al.*, 1963), Chinese (Tseng & Hsu, 1969), Japanese (Tanaka-Matsumi & Marsella, 1976), Malaysians (Resner & Hartog, 1972), and various Canadian-Indian groups (Terminsen & Ryan, 1970). This finding is a function of the fact that depression, as we know it in the West, does not have a similar pattern nor meaning in many non-Western cultures. However, even within Western cultural groups, there are important language differences which limit equivalency. For example, Stengel (1961) reported that German psychiatrists look for a symptom of *Gedankenentzug* in diagnosing schizophrenics, whereas there is no use of the symptom among American or British psychiatrists. Stengel (1961) wrote:

> symptoms which to psychiatrists using one language appear very important do not exist for psychiatrists and patients using another language, because there are no words for them. Take the example of the symptom of Gedankenentzug, which many German psychiatrists regard as a basic schizophrenic symptom. You find no reference to it in British or American textbooks, and patients using the English language do not complain about this experience [p. 59].

In brief, cultures do vary in the manifestation of mental disorders and this finding should not surprise even the most ardent supporters of the universalist position. To deny such a finding would not only be tantamount to rejecting the research which has been conducted, but also to denying that cultural differences exist in behavior.

What Are the Relationships Between Culture and Mental Disorder?

This is the fourth and final question discussed and, in many respects, it is perhaps the most important one, for this question involves the issue of theoretical frameworks for understanding the relationships between culture and mental disorders. There are very few theories or models which have been advanced to explain culture and mental disorder relationships. Of the few which have been posited, two basic types emerge.

One type has attempted to explain differences in the frequency and/or expression of mental disorders in particular cultural milieus by reference to a major theoretical construct such as "cultural disintegration" or "social change." The other type has attempted to explain the frequency and/or expression of particular categories of disorder like depression or schizophrenia. Thus, Type 1 theories and models are invoked to explain cross-cultural variations in the rate and/or expression of mental disorder in general, whereas Type 2 theories and models are used to explain cross-cultural variations in the rate and/or expression of specific disorder.

TYPE 1: WHY CULTURES DIFFER IN THE RATE AND/OR EXPRESSION OF MENTAL DISORDERS IN GENERAL

As was noted in the history section of the present chapter, one of the earliest explanations of cultural differences in mental disorders was based on the perceived role of "civilization." The more civilized a society, the more mental disorders! Civilization was associated with excitement of the passions, competition, struggle for place, and so forth. Primitive society, in contrast, was considered to be much more congruent with man's basic nature. Years later, of course, Freud was to pick up on this idea in his book *Civilization and Its Discontents,* albeit that he believed any societal imposition on man's essential biological nature was destined to produce neurosis. This point of view, needless to say, is much too simplistic and, as research by Cawte (1975) has indicated, simply untrue. High rates of mental disorder do exist in some primitive societies!

A model advanced by Arsenian and Arsenian (1948) suggested that differences in the rates of mental disorder across cultures might be due to the "toughness" or "easiness" of a culture. "Tough" cultures foster psychopathology by producing psychological tension both through the goals fostered, and the pathways to these goals. The following characteristics or properties of the goals and paths were considered important by Arsenian and Arsenian.

1. Properties of paths
   A. Effectiveness—Do paths lead one to the goal?
   B. Efficiency—How much time and/or energy are necessary to get to the goal?
   C. Number—Are the paths few or numerous?
   D. Accessibility—How many people have access to the path?
   E. Clarity—Are certain paths more clearly discernible than others?
   F. Approval—Are certain paths more honorific than others?
   G. Substitutivity—What paths are mutually exclusive though having some direction?
   H. Congruence—To what extent are there oppositions among paths?
   I. Cognizance—To what extent is the population explicitly or inexplicitly acquainted with the properties of the paths?

2. Properties of goals
   A. Number—Are there a number of things which are valuable?
   B. Approval—Are some goals more valuable as tension terminates?
   C. Distribution—What proportion of the population has access to tension terminals?
   D. Clarity—Are the goals well defined?
   E. Substitutivity—Are there alternative goals?
   F. Congruence—How aware is the population of the properties of the goals?

Although this framework is filled with a number of enticing hypotheses, it has, unfortunately, never been examined. There is face validity to the approach. However, what is needed is an actual study in which different cultures arc typed on the basis of the path–goal properties, and then the rates of mental disorder determined. It would also be interesting to test the dynamics that might emerge between specific goal–path relationships, such as the presence of few goals and the lack of acquaintance with their properties.

Perhaps the most detailed theory proposed is Alexander Leighton's notions regarding "integrated" versus "disintegrated" cultures. In his excellent book, *My Name Is Legion* (Leighton, 1959), Leighton set forth a series of postulates about the relationships between cultural disintegration and mental disorder. He followed this book with two others which offered empirical tests of his theory (A. Leighton, *et al.*, 1963; D. Leighton, *et al.*, 1963).

Briefly, Leighton speculated that all individuals exist in the act of striving toward a universal end, which is the maintenance and achievement of the "essential psychical condition" (*EPC*). The *EPC* is a state of optimum tension and certain cultural milieus may interfere with reaching the *EPC* whereas others may facilitate reaching it. Interference is especially high among "disintegrated" cultures.

According to Leighton, there are ten patterns of strivings which are necessary to attain the *EPC*. These strivings include: physical security, sexual satisfaction, expression of love, expression of hostility, and so forth. When certain cultural characteristics are present, cultures become disintegrated and this disintegration interferes with the essential strivings and, ultimately, the attainment of the *EPC*. Some of the cultural characteristics associated with "cultural disintegration" include many broken homes, few leaders, high crime, secularization, migration, poverty, and so forth.

Leighton tested his theory in several small communities in Nova Scotia, Canada. He found higher rates of mental disorder in the culturally disintegrated communities, thus supporting his theory. He subsequently carried out further research in Nigeria (A. Leighton, *et al.*, 1963). Leighton's results have been subjected to careful scrutiny by a number of researchers. One of the most careful evaluations of his thinking was published by Kunitz (1970). Kunitz, though respectful of Leighton's efforts, is quite critical of the logic of the theory which he claims is a "series of hidden tautologies." However, criticism aside, Leighton's work stands as the most thorough effort to date to uncover cultural relationships to mental disorders.

Yet another example of this type of theory was advanced by Marsella and Escudero in their work in the Philippines (e.g., Marsella, Escudero, & Gordon, 1972; Marsella, Escudero, & Santiago, 1969). This model was subsequently explored in Taiwan (Kuo, 1976) and Korea (e.g., Lee, 1977; Marsella & Kim, 1973). Essentially, the Marsella and Escudero model proposes that symptom patterns will differ across cultures because of cultural variations in the patterns of stresses and coping resources. Marsella and his coworkers examined stress levels in a number of different areas of life functioning (e.g., housing, marriage, child rearing, employment, interpersonal relations, health). Stress was assessed by either frequency measures, goal-striving discrepancies, or psychological conflict models. Coping was examined in terms of philosophies-of-life and crisis behaviors. Finally, more than 50 symptoms regarding cognitive, affective, interpersonal, and somatic functioning were examined. The scores for the stresses, coping resources, and symptoms were then factor analyzed to determine the unique interrelationships among these variables for distinct cultural groups.

The results of the Marsella studies suggested that stresses, resources, and symptom patterns are related, and that the relationships vary across cultures. However, it is still too early to determine the utility of this approach because the research did not sample a large enough spectrum of stresses or coping resources. Furthermore, the studies were community based and did not focus on mentally-disordered populations. Even so, the "ecological" orientation of the research does have interesting implications for cross-cultural research.

TYPE 2: WHY CULTURES DIFFER IN THE AMOUNT OR EXPRESSION OF SPECIFIC MENTAL DISORDERS

A number of investigators have advanced theories, models, and hypotheses to explain cultural differences in the amount and/or expression of specific forms of mental disorder. Perhaps the best example of this type of explanatory system is related to the topic of depressive disorders. A previous publication (i.e., Marsella, 1979) reviewed these cultural explanations for depression so the present chapter will simply summarize them.

Depression

A number of investigators have suggested that depression is rare in many non-Western societies because of the family structure and relationship patterns. For example, Stainbrook (1954) speculated that frustrations are minimized in some cultures because of "multiple mothering" and the "generalization of object interest to several family members." Both Collomb (1967), and Tseng and Hsu (1969) also commented on the important role of the extended family in minimizing the risk of early loss of a parent which is associated with a predisposition to depression. Vitols (1967) observed that the extended family of the American black helps share the burdens of life and death.

Other investigators have hypothesized that depression is related to the social cohesion of a society (e.g., Chance, 1964). A test of this hypothesis was conducted by Murphy, Wittkower, and Chance (1964) through the use of an international survey. The results indicated support for this viewpoint. However, the investigation may have been limited by the definitions of depression used in the survey since depression appears to express itself differently across cultures.

Another hypothesis about the differences in the rates and/or expression of depression across cultures emphasizes the role of psychological defense. For example, both Stainbrook (1954), and Savage and Prince (1967) contended that the use of projection as a defense mechanism by certain cultural groups reduces the risk of self-blame associated with depression, and thus limits its chance of occurring.

Mourning rituals have also been invoked by several investigators to explain cultural differences in depression. For example, both Tseng and Hsu (1969), and Vitols (1967) pointed out the value of overt grieving in Chinese and American black cultural groups, respectively. Furthermore, Yamamoto, Okonogi, Iwasaki, and Yoshimura (1969) observed that in Japan, the practice of ancestor worship reduces grief because the love objects are not thought to end through death.

Some investigators have suggested that depression rates will drop in a culture which provides outlets for the externalizing of aggression (e.g., Kendall, 1970). A test of this hypothesis in Northern Ireland by Lyons (1972) supported this view. This approach is closely linked to psychoanalytic thinking which conceived of depression as hostility which is inwardly directed. Thus, if an opportunity is present to externalize the hostility, the depression should be reduced.

Marsella, Kinzie, and Gordon (1973) hypothesized that the expression of depression was related to a culture's conditioning of the self-structure. They claimed that cultures which condition a sense of self in terms of somatic functioning will have somatic complaints dominating the portrayal of depression, whereas a culture which conditions a sense of self in terms of existential functioning will have existential complaints dominating the depressive picture.

More recently, I (e.g., Marsella, 1978b; Tanaka-Matsumi & Marsella,

1976) speculated that the actual experience of depression will vary across cultures because of differences in basic epistemological orientations. Essentially, I argued that cultural groups which have subjective, as opposed to objective, epistemological orientations toward life will tend to depsychologize experience, and thus not experience the sense of loneliness, isolation, guilt, and detachment associated with depression. I noted that the language, self-structure, and mode of experiencing reality are the dominant influences in the development of an epistemological orientation. Figure 11.1, which was discussed earlier in the chapter, summarizes this viewpoint.

Schizophrenia

Although there have been many cross-cultural studies of schizophrenia (see Chase, 1978; Jablensky & Sartorius, 1975; Sanua, 1979), few sociocultural explanations derived from cross-cultural research have been advanced. Furthermore, among the explanations which have been posited, few have gained much support, including "downward drift" (e.g., Faris & Dunham, 1939; Cooper, 1961), "poverty (e.g., Hollingshead & Redlich, 1958; Clausen & Kohn, 1959), "religion" (e.g., Malzberg, 1962; Kleiner & Lavell, 1962) and "modernization" (e.g., Torrey, Torrey, & Burton-Bradley, 1974). Indeed, even the many "family" hypotheses based on everything from family communication to family structure have failed to influence current notions. One reason for this may be the lingering belief that schizophrenia will ultimately prove to be a genetic and/or biochemical problem.

Yet, if one considers the tremendous number of studies which have revealed ethnocultural variations in the epidemiology, expression, and prognosis of schizophrenia, our failure to advance more elaborate sociocultural explanations of schizophrenia is quite puzzling. The World Health Organization's new multinational study may ultimately illuminate the role of sociocultural factors in schizophrenia—especially with regard to family communication patterns, life stress, and early experience.

One of the things which is quite clear from even a cursory review of the literature on the cross-cultural study of mental disorders, is that there are few theories available for understanding cultural differences in mental disorders. In certain respects, this is probably due to the relative youth of the field. It has only been within the last two decades that the sociocultural approach to mental disorders has even gained a modicum of support against the more firmly entrenched genetic, biochemical, and psychodynamic positions. As a result, there are still few accepted theories about the role of the sociocultural milieu in the etiology and expression of mental disorders, and the differences appearing across cultures are left unexplained. Nevertheless, there is every reason to believe that the critical mass of evidence which has now emerged will serve as an impetus to the growth of more and better theoretical explanations within the next decade.

References

Ackerknecht, E. Psychopathology, primitive medicine, and primitive culture. *Bulletin of the History of Medicine*, 1942, *14*, 30–67.

Akimoto, H., Sunazaki, T., Okada, K., & Hanashiro, S. Demographic und psychiatrische Untersuchung über abgegrenzte Kleinstadtgevolkerung. *Psychiatria et Neurologia Japonica*, 1942, *47*, 351–374.

Arsenian, J., & Arsenian, J. Tough and easy cultures. *Psychiatry*, 1948, *11*, 377–385.

Baldauf, R. *Acculturation and value change as predictors of academic achievement in Samoan students*. Unpublished doctoral dissertation, Univ. of Hawaii, 1975.

Benedict, R. Anthropology and the abnormal. *Journal of General Psychology*, 1934, *10*, 59–80.

Benedict, P., & Jacks, I. Mental illness in primitive societies. *Psychiatry*, 1954, *17*, 377–389.

Brill, A. Pibloktoq or hysteria among Perry's Eskimos. *Journal of Nervous and Mental Diseases*, 1913, *40*, 514–520.

Brugger, C. Versuch einer Geisteskrankenzahlung in Thuringe. *Zeitschrift für die Gesamte Neurologie Psychiatrie*, 1931, *133*, 352–390.

Brugger, C. Psychiatrische ergebrisse einer medizenischen, anthropologischen, und soziologischen Bevolkerunguntersuchung. *Zeitschrift für die Gesamte Neurologie Psychiatrie*, 1933, *146*, 489–524.

Brugger, C. Psychiatrische Bestandaufnahme im gebiet eines medizinisch anthropologischen Zenzus in der Nahe von Rosenheim. *Zeitschrift für die Gesamte Neurologie Psychiatrie*, 1937, *160*, 189–207.

Carothers, J. A study of mental derangement in Africans and an attempt to explain its peculiarities more especially in relation to the African attitude to life. *Psychiatry*, 1948, *11*, 47–86.

Caudill, W., & Lin, T. J. (Eds.). *Mental health research in Asia and the Pacific*. Honolulu, Hawaii: East–West Center Press, 1969.

Caudill, W., & Schooler, C. Symptom patterns and background characteristics of Japanese psychiatric patients. In W. Caudill & T. Y. Lin (Eds.), *Mental health research in Asia and the Pacific*. Honolulu, Hawaii: East–West Center Press, 1969.

Cawte, J. *Cruel, poor, and brutal nations*. Honolulu, Hawaii: Univ. Press of Hawaii, 1975.

Chance, N. A cross-cultural study of social cohesion and depression. *Transcultural Psychiatric Research Review*, 1964, *1*, 19–24.

Chase, L. Culture and schizophrenia. In A. Marsella (Ed.), *Culture and psychopathology annotated bibliography series* (Vol. 4). The Queen's Medical Center, Honolulu, Hawaii, 1978.

Clausen, J., & Kohn, M. Relations of schizophrenia to the social structure of a small city. In B. Pasamanick (Ed.), *Epidemiology of mental disorders*. Washington, D.C.: American Association for the Advancement of Science, 1959.

Cleland, J. Mental diseases amongst Australian aborigines. *Journal of Tropical Medicine*, 1928, *31*, 326–330.

Collomb, H. Methodological problems in cross-cultural research. *International Journal of Psychiatry*, 1967, *3*, 1–9.

Cooper, B. Social class and prognosis in schizophrenia. *British Journal of Preventive and Social Medicine*, 1961, *15*, 17–41.

Coriat, I. Psychoneuroses among primitive tribes. *Journal of Abnormal and Social Psychology*, 1915, *10*, 201–208.

Czaplicka, M. *Aboriginal Siberia*. Oxford, England: Clarendon Press, 1914.

Dai, B. Obsessive-compulsive disorders in Chinese culture. In M. Opler (Ed.), *Culture and mental health*. New York: Macmillan, 1959.

DeHoyos, A., & DeHoyos, G. Symptomatology differentials between Negro and white schizophrenics. *International Journal of Social Psychiatry*, 1965, *11*, 245–255.

Devereaux, G. Primitive psychiatry. *Bulletin of the History of Medicine*, 1940, *8*, 1194–1213.
Devereaux, G. *Mohave ethnopsychiatry and suicide: The psychiatric knowledge and disturbances of an Indian tribe*. Washington, D.C.: Smithsonian Institution, 1961.
Dhunjiboy, J. A brief resume of the types of insanity commonly met with in India. *Journal of Mental Science*, 1930, *16*, 254–264.
Dohrenwend, B., & Dohrenwend, B. The problem of validity in field studies of psychological disorder. *Journal of Abnormal Psychology*, 1965, *70*, 52–66.
Dohrenwend, B., & Dohrenwend, B. *Social status and psychological disorder: A causal inquiry*. New York: Wiley, 1969.
Dohrenwend, B., & Dohrenwend, B. *Stressful life events*. New York: Wiley, 1974.
Draguns, J. Problems of defining and comparing abnormal behavior across cultures. *Annals of the New York Academy of Sciences*, 1977, *285*, 664–679.
Draguns, J. Psychological disorders of clinical severity. In H. Triandis & J. Draguns (Eds.), *Handbook of cross-cultural psychology* (Vol. 5). Rockleigh, New Jersey: Allyn & Bacon, 1979.
Draguns, J., & Phillips, L. *Culture and psychopathology: The quest for a relationship*. Morristown, New Jersey: General Learning Press, 1971.
Draguns, J., Phillips, L., Broverman, I., Caudill, W., & Nishimae, S. Symptomatology of hospitalized psychiatric patients in Japan and in the United States: A study of cultural differences. *The Journal of Nervous and Mental Diseases*, 1971, *152*, 3–16.
Dunham, W. Community and schizophrenia: An epidemiological analysis. Detroit, Michigan: Wayne State Univ. Press, 1965.
Durant, W., & Durant, A. *The story of civilization* (Vol. 10). New York: Simon & Schuster, 1967.
Eaton, J., & Weil, R. *Culture and mental disorders*. Glencoe, Illinois: Free Press, 1955.
Enright, J., & Jaeckle, W. Psychiatric symptoms and diagnosis in two subcultures. *International Journal of Social Psychiatry*, 1963, *9*, 12–17.
Faris, R., & Dunham, H. *Mental disease in urban areas*. Chicago: Univ. of Chicago Press, 1939.
Fried, M. Effects of social change on mental health. *American Journal of Orthopsychiatry*, 1964, *34*, 3–247.
Fundia, T., Draguns, J., & Phillips, L. Culture and psychiatric symptomatology: A comparison of Argentine and United States patients. *Social Psychiatry*, 1971, *6*, 11–20.
Gaitonde, M. Cross-cultural study in outpatient clinics in Bombay, India and Topeka, Kansas. *International Journal of Social Psychiatry*, 1959, *4*, 98–108.
Gordon, H. Psychiatry in Kenya Colony. *Journal of Mental Science*, 1934, *80*, 167.
Guthrie, G. *Culture and mental disorder*. Reading, Massachusetts: Addison-Wesley, 1972.
Hallowell, A. Culture and mental disease. *Journal of Abnormal and Social Psychology*, 1934, *29*, 1–9.
Hallowell, A. Values, acculturation, and mental health. *American Journal of Orthopsychiatry*, 1950, *20*, 732–743.
Higginbotham, H. Culture and the delivery of mental health services. In A. Marsella (Ed.), *Culture and psychopathology annotated bibliography series* (Vol. 1). The Queen's Medical Center, Honolulu, Hawaii, 1976.
Hollingshead, A., & Redlich, F. *Social class and mental illness*. New York: Wiley, 1958.
Honigman, J. Toward a distinction between social and psychiatric abnormality. *Social Forces*, 1953, *31*, 274–277.
Inkeles, A., & Smith, D. The fate of personal adjustment in the process of modernization. *International Journal of Comparative Sociology*, 1970, *11*, 81–114.
Jablensky, A., & Sartorius, N. Culture and schizophrenia. *Psychological Medicine*, 1975, *5*, 113–124.
Kaelbling, R. Comparative psychopathology and psychotherapy. *Acta Psychotherapeutica*, 1961, *9*, 10–28.

Katz, M., Gudeman, H., & Sanborn, K. Characterizing differences in psychopathology among ethnic groups in Hawaii. In F. Redlich (Ed.), *Social psychiatry*. Baltimore, Maryland: Williams & Wilkins, 1969.

Kendall, R. Relationships between aggression and depression: Epidemiological implications of a hypothesis. *Archives of General Psychiatry, 1970, 22,* 308–318.

Kennedy, J. Cultural psychiatry. In J. Honigmann (Ed.), *Handbook of social and cultural anthropology*. Chicago: Rand McNally, 1973.

Kiev, A. *Magic, faith, and healing*. New York: Free Press, 1964.

Kiev, A. *Transcultural psychiatry*. New York: Free Press, 1972.

Kimura, B. Vergleichende Untersuchungen über depressive Erkrankungen in Japan und in Deutschland. *Fortschritte der Neurologie und Psychiatrie, 1965, 33,* 202–215.

Kleiner, R., & Lavell, M. Mental disorder and status based on protestant subgroup membership. *Journal of Social Psychology, 1962, 58,* 345–348.

Kleinman, A. Depression, somatization, and the "new transcultural psychiatry." *Social Science and Medicine, 1977, 11,* 3–9.

Kleinman, A. Rethinking the social and cultural context of psychopathology and psychiatric care. In T. Manschreck & A. Kleinman (Eds.), *Renewal in psychiatry*. New York: Halstead Press, 1978.

Kunitz, S. Equilibrium theory in social psychiatry: The work of the Leightons. *Psychiatry, 1970, 33,* 312–328.

Kuo, H. K. *Social stress and psychological adjustment in urban Taiwan*. Unpublished doctoral dissertation, Univ. of Hawaii, 1976.

Kraepelin, E. Vergleichende psychiatrie. *Zentralblatt für Nervenherlkande und Psychiatrie, 1904, 15,* 433–437.

Lebra, W. (Ed.). *Transcultural research in mental health*. Honolulu, Hawaii: Univ. Press of Hawaii, 1972.

Lebra, W. (Ed.). *Youth, socialization, and mental health*. Honolulu, Hawaii: Univ. Press of Hawaii, 1974.

Lebra, W. (Ed.). *Culture-bound syndromes, ethnopsychiatry, and alternate therapies*. Honolulu, Hawaii: Univ. Press of Hawaii, 1976.

Lee, H. K. Social stress and psychological adjustment in urban Korea. Unpublished doctoral dissertation, Univ. of Hawaii, 1977.

Leighton, A. *My name is legion*. New York: Basic Books, 1959.

Leighton, A., & Hughes, J. Cultures as causative of mental disorder. In *Causes of mental disorders: A review of epidemiological knowledge*. New York: Milbank Memorial Fund, 1961.

Leighton, A., Lambo, T., Hughes, C., Leighton, D., Murphy, J., & Macklin, D. *Psychiatric disorder among the Yoruba*. Ithaca, New York: Cornell Univ. Press, 1963.

Leighton, D., Harding, J., Macklin, D., Macmillan, A., & Leighton, A. *The character of danger*. New York: Basic Books, 1963.

Lemkau, P., Tietze, C., & Cooper, M. Mental hygiene problems in an urban district. *Mental Hygiene, 1942, 26,* 100–118.

Lyons, H. Depressive illness and aggression in Belfast. *British Medical Journal, 1972, 1,* 342–344.

Malzberg, B. The distribution of mental disease according to religious affiliation in New York State, 1941–1951. *Mental Hygiene, 1962, 46,* 510–522.

Marsella, A. J. Modernization: Consequences for the individual. In D. Hoopes, P. Pedersen, & G. Renwick (Eds.), *Overview of intercultural education, training, and research* (Vol. 3). La Grange, Illinois: Intercultural Network, Inc., 1978. (a)

Marsella, A. J. *Toward a conceptual framework for understanding cross-cultural variations in depressive affect and disorder*. Invited address to School of International Studies, Univ. of Washington, Seattle, Washington, April 18, 1978. (b)

Marsella, A. J. Thoughts on cross-cultural studies on the epidemiology of depression. *Culture, Medicine, and Psychiatry,* 1978c, *2,* 343–357.

Marsella, A. J. Depressive affect and disorder across cultures. In H. Triandis & J. Draguns (Eds.), *Handbook of cross-cultural psychology* (Vol. 5). Rockleigh, New Jersey: Allyn & Bacon, 1979.

Marsella, A. J., Escudero, M., & Brennan, J. Goal-striving discrepancy stress in urban Filipino men: I: Housing. *International Journal of Social Psychiatry,* 1975, *21,* 282–291.

Marsella, A. J., Escudero, M., & Gordon, P. Stresses, resources, and symptom patterns in urban Filipino men. In W. Lebra (Ed.), *Transcultural research in mental health.* Honolulu, Hawaii: Univ. Press of Hawaii, 1972.

Marsella, A. J., Escudero, M., & Santiago, C. *Stresses, resources, and symptom patterns in the Philippines.* Paper presented at the Second Conference on Culture and Mental Health in Asia and the Pacific, East–West Center, Honolulu, Hawaii, 1969.

Marsella, A. J., & Kim, K. S. Social change and psychiatric adjustment in Korea. Unpublished data. Univ. of Hawaii, 1973.

Marsella, A. J., Kinzie, D., & Gordon, P. Ethnocultural variations in the expression of depression. *Journal of Cross-Cultural Psychology,* 1973, *4,* 435–458.

Masuda, M., & Holmes, T. The social readjustment rating scale: A cross-cultural study of Japanese and Americans. *Journal of Psychosomatic Research,* 1967, *11,* 227–237.

Mishler, E., & Scotch, N. Sociocultural factors in the epidemiology of schizophrenia. *Psychiatry,* 1963, *26,* 315–351.

Murphy, H. B. M. Social change and mental health. In *Causes of mental disorders: A review of epidemiological knowledge.* New York: Milbank Memorial Fund, 1961.

Murphy, H. B. M., Wittkower, E., & Chance, N. Cross-cultural inquiry into the symptomatology of depression. *Transcultural Psychiatric Research Review,* 1964, *1,* 5–21.

Murphy, H. B. M., Wittkower, E., Fried, J., & Ellenberger, H. A cross-cultural survey of schizophrenic symptomatology. *International Journal of Social Psychiatry,* 1963, *9,* 237–249.

Murphy, J., & Leighton, A. (Eds.). *Approaches to cross-cultural psychiatry.* Ithaca, New York: Cornell Univ. Press, 1965.

Musgrave, W., & Sison, A. Mali-mali: A mimic psychosis in the Philippine Islands. *Philippine Journal of Sciences,* 1910, *5,* 335.

Opler, M. *Culture, psychiatry, and human values.* Springfield, Illinois: Thomas, 1965.

Opler, M., & Singer, J. Ethnic differences in behavior and psychopathology: Italian and Irish. *International Journal of Social Psychiatry,* 1959, *2,* 11–23.

Parker, S., & Kleiner, R. *Mental illness in the urban Negro community.* New York: Free Press, 1966.

Pfeiffer, W. *Transkulturelle Psychiatrie: Ergebnisse und Probleme.* Stuttgart: Thieme, 1970.

Rabkin, J., & Struening, E. Life events, stress, and illness. *Science,* 1976, *194,* 1013–1020.

Resner, J., & Hartog, J. Concepts and terminology of mental disorder among Malays. *Journal of Cross-Cultural Psychology,* 1972, *1,* 369–381.

Rin, H. A study of the etiology of Koro in respect to the Chinese concept of illness. *International Journal of Social Psychiatry,* 1965, *11,* 7–13.

Rosen, G. Social stress and mental disease from the 18th century to the present. *The Milbank Memorial Fund Quarterly,* 1959, *11,* 1–31.

Roth, W., & Luton, F. The mental hygiene program in Tennessee. *American Journal of Psychiatry,* 1943, *99,* 662–675.

Rubel, A. The epidemiology of a folk illness: Susto in Hispanic America. *Ethnology,* 1964, *3,* 268–283.

Saindon, J. E. Mental disorders among the James Bay Cree. *Primitive Man,* 1933, *6,* 1–12.

Sampath, H. Prevalence of psychiatric disorders in a southern Baffin Island Eskimo community. *Canadian Psychiatric Association Journal,* 1974, *19,* 363–367.

Sanua, V. Sociocultural aspects of schizophrenia. In L. Bellak & L. Loeb (Eds.), *The schizophrenic syndrome*. New York: Grune & Stratton, 1969.

Sanua, V. Schizophrenia across cultures. In H. Triandis & J. Draguns (Eds.), *Handbook of cross-cultural psychology* (Vol. 5). Rockleigh, New Jersey: Allyn & Bacon, 1979.

Sapir, E. Cultural anthropology and psychiatry. *Journal of Abnormal and Social Psychiatry*, 1932, *27*, 229–242.

Sartorius, N. Culture and the epidemiology of depression. *Psychiatria, Neurologia, et Neurochirugia*, 1973, *76*, 479–487.

Sartorius, N., Jablensky, A., & Shapiro, R. Cross-cultural differences in the short-term prognosis of schizophrenic psychoses. *Schizophrenia Bulletin*, 1978, *4*, 102–113.

Savage, C., & Prince, R. Depression among the Yoruba. In W. Muensterberger (Ed.), *The psychoanalytic study of society*. New York: International Universities Press, 1967.

Sechrest, L. Philippine culture, stress, and psychopathology. In W. Caudill & T. Y. Lin (Eds.), *Mental health research in Asia and the Pacific*. Honolulu, Hawaii: Univ. Press of Hawaii, 1969.

Seligman, G. Temperament, conflict, and psychosis in a stone age population. *British Journal of Medical Psychology*, 1929, *9*, 187–202.

Silverman, C. *The epidemiology of depression*. Baltimore, Maryland: Johns Hopkins Press, 1968.

Simon, R., Fliess, J., Gurland, B., Stiller, P., & Sharpe, L. Depression and schizophrenia in hospitalized Black and White mental patients. *Archives of General Psychiatry*, 1973, *28*, 509–512.

Slotkin, J. Culture and psychopathology. *Journal of Abnormal and Social Psychiatry*, 1955, *51*, 269–275.

Spindler, G. Socio-cultural and psychological processes in Menominic acculturation. Berkeley: Univ. of California Press, 1955.

Srole, L., Langner, T., Michael, S., Opler, M., & Rennie, T. *Mental health in the metropolis: The midtown Manhattan study*. New York: McGraw-Hill, 1962.

Stainbrook, E. A cross-cultural evaluation of depressive reactions. In P. Hoch & J. Zubin (Eds.), *Depression*. New York: Grune & Stratton, 1954.

Stengel, E. Problems of nosology and nomenclatuure in the mental disorders. In J. Zubin (Ed.), *Field studies in the mental disorders*. New York: Grune & Stratton, 1961.

Stoker, D., Zurcher, L., & Fox, W. Women in psychotherapy: A cross-cultural comparison. *International Journal of Social Psychiatry*, 1968, *14*, 5–22.

Sue, S. Community mental health services to minority groups. *American Psychologist*, 1977, *32*, 616–624.

Sunshine, N. *Cultural differences in schizophrenia*. Unpublished doctoral dissertation, City Univ. New York, 1971.

Tanaka-Matsumi, J., & Marsella, A. J. Cross-cultural variations in the phenomenological experience of depression: Word associations. *Journal of Cross-Cultural Psychology*, 1976, *7*, 379–396.

Terminsen, J., & Ryan, J. Health and disease in a British Columbian community. *Canadian Psychiatric Association Journal*, 1970, *15*, 121–127.

Teske, R., & Nelson, B. Acculturation and assimilation: A clarification. *American Ethnologist*, 1974, *1*, 351–367.

Torrey, E. F. *The mind game: Witch doctors and psychiatrists*. New York: Emerson Hall, 1972.

Torrey, E. F., Torrey, B., & Burton-Bradley, B. The epidemiology of schizophrenia in Papua-New Guinea. *American Journal of Psychiatry*, 1974, *131*, 567–573.

Tseng, W., & Hsu, J. Chinese culture, personality formation, and mental illness. *International Journal of Social Psychiatry*, 1969, *16*, 5–14.

Tsugawa, T., Okada, K., Hanashiro, S., Asai, T., Takuma, T., Morimura, S., & Tsuboi, F.

Uber die psychiatrische Zenzusuntersuchung in einem Stadtbezirk von Tokyo. *Psychiatria et Neurologia Japonica,* 1942, *46,* 204–208.

Uchimura, Y. The syndrome of Imu in the Ainu race. *American Journal of Psychiatry,* 1938, *94,* 1467–1469.

Uchimura, Y., Akimoto, H., Kan, O., Abe, Y., Takahashi, K., Inose, Y., Shimazaki, T., & Ogawa, N. Uber die vergleichende psychiatrische und erbpathologische Untersuchung auf einer Japanischen Isel. *Psychiatria et Neurologia Japonica,* 1940, *44,* 745–782.

Van Brero, P. Latah. *Journal of Mental Sciences,* 1895, *41,* 537–538.

Van Loon, F. Amok and latah. *Journal of Abnormal and Social Psychology,* 1927, *21,* 434–444.

Van Wulfften-Palthe, P. Psychiatry and neurology in the tropics. In A. Lichtenstein (Ed.), *A clinical textbook of tropical medicine.* Batavia, Indonesia: de Langen, 1936.

Vitols, M. *Patterns of mental disturbance in the Negro.* Unpublished paper. Cherry Hospital, Goldsboro, North Carolina, 1967.

Weinberg, K. (Ed.). *The sociology of mental disorders.* Chicago: Aldine Press, 1967.

Weissman, M., & Klerman, G. Sex roles and the epidemiology of depression. *Archives of General Psychiatry,* 1977, *34,* 98–111.

Wishner, J. The concept of efficiency in psychological health and psychopathology. *Psychological Review,* 1955, *62,* 62–80.

Wittkower, E., & Dubreil, G. Psychocultural stress in relation to mental illness. *Social Science and Medicine,* 1973, *7,* 691–704.

Wittkower, E., & Rin, H. Transcultural psychiatry. *Archives of General Psychiatry,* 1965, *13,* 387–394.

Woon, T., Masuda, M., Wagner, N., & Holmes, T. The social readjustment rating scale: A cross-cultural study of Malaysians and Americans. *Journal of Cross-Cultural Psychology,* 1971, *2,* 373–386.

World Health Organization. *International Pilot Project on Schizophrenia.* Geneva, Switzerland: World Health Organization, 1973.

Yamamoto, J., Okonogi, K., Iwasaki, T., & Yoshimura, S. Mourning in Japan. *American Journal of Psychiatry,* 1969, *125,* 1660–1665.

Yap, P. M. Mental disease peculiar to certain cultures: A survey of comparative psychiatry. *Journal of Mental Science,* 1951, *97,* 313–327.

III

APPLICATIONS

12

Culture and Education

CATHIE JORDAN
ROLAND G. THARP

Introduction

From the perspective of cross-cultural psychology, "education" is a vast domain. The term can refer to early infant socialization, to belly-dancing classes, and to the modern university. It occurs at the mother's breast, in fishing boats, at the cobbler's last, in eighth-grade discussion groups, and graduate seminars. Beginning with birth and ending with breath, education— in some form—seems always with us.

In this chapter, we will first survey this broad domain. Then, narrowing our focus, we will discuss the concept of a transnational culture of schooling and the kinds of problems that can arise when the schools' culture conflicts with that of the population they purport to serve. We will examine the different kinds of explanations which have been proposed for one such problem, that of minority academic underachievement. Finally, we will present a case study of one effort to confront and deal with minority underachievement—the Kamehameha Early Education Program (KEEP).

The Varieties of Education

Although we will eventually focus our discussion in this chapter on that narrow band of education known as "schools," it is necessary to consider

PERSPECTIVES ON CROSS-CULTURAL PSYCHOLOGY

the full range of educational activities, however briefly, to provide a framework within which to define that segment of education to be discussed in this chapter. This framework will also demonstrate that, even in the context of the most formal "school," other aspects of education are always present and interacting. Indeed, these little-noticed aspects are often the small stones which send the great wheel of formal education lurching from the road.

A commonly used system of classification distinguishes among types of education according to their social organization (e.g., Scribner & Cole, 1973). The types so distinguished are (*a*) informal education; (*b*) noninstitutional formal education; and (*c*) institutional formal education. *Informal education* designates the everyday process by which children (and to a lesser extent, adults) learn to participate increasingly in their culture, without, however, any particular place, time, personnel, or activity being set aside expressly for the purpose of teaching. A child imitating with a small broom an adult who is sweeping the floor, or one person watching another repair a car, thus storing up information about cars and their workings, would be examples. *Noninstitutional formal education* is a process of cultural transmission in which there are particular activities, with specified personnel in designated circumstances, which are expressly designed to transmit a particular body of cultural information. However, this last is usually fairly limited in scope and the occasions of transmission occupy limited time periods. Examples would be the instruction of adolescents that precedes initiation rituals in many traditional societies, or the pre-Confirmation classes run by some churches in our own. *Institutional formal education* shows the characteristics mentioned above, but has the added attributes of being carried out by professional teachers operating in a graded, hierarchical system which exists continually over a long period of time. It takes place in relatively permanent sites and is responsible for the transmission of a broad spectrum of information. It is this last type of education that we will now consider.

INSTITUTIONAL FORMAL EDUCATION

Although concentrating on institutional formal education, we cannot, even in that context, afford to completely ignore the other types. Thomas La Belle (1975), in proposing a model for considering rural education, asserts that different types of education are perhaps best seen as "modes of emphasis or predominance" rather than separate entities, and that a particular mode can have "secondary characteristics" of other modes. His point is well taken. Within the context of formal institutional education, noninstitutional and informal education can also take place. An example of the former situation would be the training of a choir group or a football squad; of the latter, the information transmission that takes place among peers when they are brought together in a formal educational setting. If we take these secondary characteristics of formal educational institutions into account and also keep in mind that participants in institutional formal education are, at other times, being educated in noninstitutional and informal "modes," it becomes evident that institutional formal education does not exist in a vacuum. When there are important differences between the content or processes of one mode or another, or between different aspects of the same mode, there is potential conflict.

Most issues currently of interest in the cross-cultural study of education occur at the interface of institutional formal education and other educational modes or characteristics. For example, the minority child in a multicultural society often finds different goals emphasized in the formal institutional school than in his informal home education. Indeed, such conflicts may be found between different aspects of the school: The goals and methods of arithmetic class are not the same as the education of the playground. We will devote a major portion of this chapter to examining such areas of conflict, and the last section of this chapter will illustrate methods of resolving these conflicts in a multicultural society. But before undertaking that task, it is necessary to clarify the nature of the school itself.

The Transnational Culture of the School and the Effects of Education

This chapter concentrates on formal institutional education as it has developed in technological, literate societies. Formal institutional education can be distinguished from other kinds of education in several ways, some of which have already been mentioned. To these can be added that formal educational institutions of literate, technological societies—or "schools" as we will refer to them from this point on—tend to undertake the following functions:

1. They attempt to teach broad-based, *generalizable skills,* such as reading, writing, and ciphering.
2. They bear explicit responsibility for the transmission of some *cultural information,* such as the history of the society, scientific knowledge, community standards, and the nature of civic responsibilities. In a multicultural society, such cultural information usually pertains to the majority or dominant culture which operates the school.
3. Schools also bear, in a less explicit way, the burden of transmitting a large freight of *cultural norms* which, again, in a multicultural society, usually represent those of the public or dominant culture. This latter transmission is not often a formally imposed obligation, but it is felt as an implicit responsibility by teachers.

In our opinion, schooling is so similar from country to country that it is best seen as a culture unto itself, a transnational culture, the culture of the school. These similarities are present in schools' architecture, their social organization, their goals, their responsibilities, and, most especially, their personnel's adaptation to the institution. It is when the transnational culture of the school conflicts with the recipient culture that we see the crucial current issues in culture and education.

The concept of a transnational culture of the school has not yet been clearly enough formulated to allow detailed study—it is currently no more than an hypothesis. However, it is often taken as an assumption. The general inquiry into the effects of education, internationally, seems to presuppose that education in Ghana is like education in Mexico, and also like that in London. The logic of this assumption would be strengthened if it were found that education everywhere has the same effects on the child. That inquiry is unfortunately beset with methodological and conceptual problems.

The study of the cross-cultural effects of education has an odd history. Because in Western countries, age and amount of education are so highly correlated, developing intellectual capacities cannot be clearly attributed to environmental effects (education) or to maturation. (See Chapter 5 in this volume for a discussion of this issue.) To disentangle these effects, developmental and cognitive psychologists have compared the schooled versus unschooled members of many exotic cultures, in an effort to see whether the typical course of cognitive development of Western children is in fact maturational and universal, or whether it is a result of Western education, formal and informal.

As a result of this enterprise, the cross-cultural educational psychologist finds a detritus of data in which schooled versus unschooled children of many cultures are compared—Liberians, Guatemalans, Soviets, Native Americans and so forth—and in order to make general statements, must assume that "school" in the African bush is in some important way equivalent to the "school" of the Yucatecan Mayan. Even in those exceptional studies whose purpose is to determine school effects in a particular population (e.g., Cole, Sharp, & Lave, 1976), ethnographic descriptions of the schools are rarely included. In our own view, however, there is a modal tendency of schools transnationally, and the concept should guide research toward its clarification.

For example, many researchers have emphasized that learning in the school is characteristically "decontextualized"; that is, compared to traditional societies' teaching, school removes skill learning from those situations to which the skill is to be applied. Thus, one does not learn to count beads or bags, one learns to count; rather than memorizing a list of trail markers, one learns to memorize lists. The assumption of psychologists and educators has been that this "context-free" learning produces generally applicable skills, ones which can then transfer to many contexts. Cole and Scribner and their associates have been the group most vigorously pursuing these issues, and while once sanguine for the identification of these transferable operations (Scribner & Cole, 1973), they lucidly presented the measurement pitfalls in cross-cultural comparison (Cole & Scribner, 1974); and then somewhat gloomily speculated that perhaps schooled-skills were applicable after all only to school situations (Cole, Sharp, & Lave, 1976). In the recent works of Lave (1977a, 1977b), there may be data encouraging to a more intermediate position; that is, learned skills, wherever learned, will transfer to situations which are similar enough to the context of original learning.

This position accords well with logic, and with the known laws of stimulus generalization. It also forces us to a somewhat more sophisticated view of schools; they are not to be seen as "decontextualized," but rather as being a *specific context*. If transfer is to be predicted, we must have a precise description of schools, and a precise description of to-be-transferred-to situations—in short, a taxonomy of situations, which will allow predictions of transfer according to principles of generalization.

In the meantime, useful and stimulating suggestions as to where to look for school similarities continue to be made. Olson (1977), in a brilliant though unpersuasive essay, suggests that the features that are characteristic of the culture of the school flow from the characteristics of written prose, upon which school learning ultimately rests. However, Scribner's recent North African data (1977) indicate that it is the way that written prose is *taught* which predicts general cognitive strategies, such as short-term mnemonic techniques. "School-ness" is apparently more than written prose itself.

Can general, transferable skills be identified at all? It is at this question that current knowledge pauses for breath. Several paths of inquiry are now open. As a single example, Ciborowski's (1977) recent Liberian data suggest that schooled and unschooled children can learn a new rule equally well, through induction from repeated instances. This is reasonable, since the discernment of regularities in experience is surely a primary survival competence. However, once the rule is acquired (either through induction or by direct instruction), schooled children apply it more frequently to subsequent, similar cases.

Do schools in fact ask for the re-application of rules to new instances? Ethnography is needed to answer that question. Whether or not the rule-application skill will survive into the eventual catalog of schooled strategies, such matchings of performance with the specifics of the school context will be required for the field to advance.

In spite of the difficulties just discussed, we will proceed on the tentative assumption that, whatever may prove to be the details of the school context, the general outlines are similar enough from country to country that a transnational culture of the school is a useful working concept. We will now examine problems which arise when the school is so different from the culture of some of its children, that the two conflict significantly.

Problems in Cross-Cultural Education

Cross-cultural issues in education are of more than theoretical interest; passions of citizens and vexations of educators are present whenever the schools of a dominant culture undertake the education of the children of a minority, whether in the United States, Nigeria, Australia, Mexico, or Guatemala. The Kamehameha Early Education Program (KEEP) is a Hawaiian educational research and development program where we and our colleagues have, for a number of years, addressed these issues. It will be used as a "case study" to illustrate many of these problems and some attempts at their solution. First, however, we will examine issues, explanations, and potential solutions in a broader perspective.

Conflicts at the interface between schools and the populations that they serve may arise over what is to be transmitted (content), the efficacy of transmission, or both. "What is to be transmitted" can be characterized as general skills (e.g., reading and writing), cultural information (e.g., geography or history), or cultural norms (e.g., "working hard" or "honesty"). The kinds of problems that arise tend to differ according to the goal of transmission.

Goals in the areas of *general skills,* more often than goals in the other areas, tend to be explicit and to be shared by dispensing and client populations. That is to say, even minority group parents frequently favor these goals. They want their children to learn reading, arithmetic, and, often, mastery of the dominant language or dialect. Conflicts and problems in this area tend to be, not over the nature of the goals, but over their implementation. Difficulties arise when schools fail to effectively transmit the general skills that they claim to teach. (A good deal of the failure to transmit general skills can result from cultural norm disparities, as we will see.)

The second area, that of *cultural information,* is one in which the goals are usually explicit, but may well *not* be shared by client and dispensing populations. Problems may arise, either because of failure to transmit such information effectively, or from disagreements about the appropriate cultural information to transmit. Examples of the latter would be the current conflicts in some areas of the United States between black community members and schools over the variety of history to be taught, or the resistence of Old Order Amish parents to their children learning conventional geography, due to the supposed ill effects of such learning on important cultural norms (Hostetler & Huntington, 1971).

The third area, that of *cultural norms,* involves goals which are often neither explicit nor shared, such as competition versus cooperation, group versus individual achievement, expressiveness verses reticence, etc. Difficulties arising in this area tend to be rather subtle ones, because, due to the implicit nature of the goals involved, client and dispensing populations may not clearly understand what is at issue. Again, however, the kinds of conflicts that arise can be seen as two-fold: difficulties arising over the failure to transmit cultural norms effectively, and/or disparities in the cultural norms which are held by the client and dispensing populations.

Minority Academic Underachievement

Whereas issues in all three of these areas can overlap, and difficulties in one area can contribute to problems in the others, we will limit our focus here to problems arising from the failure to transmit general skills valued by both recipient and dispensing populations. In other words, we will examine the problem of minority academic underachievement.

There are two basic models that have been used in considering minority underachievement. One is the *deficiency* model, which can take many forms, from hypotheses that certain ethnic or social groups are genetically inferior (e.g., Jensen, 1969) to cultural deprivation models. The latter assume capacities that are equal, but posit that some cultural or social groups do not provide their children with certain essential socialization experiences. Deficiency models have been called into serious question (e.g., Keddie, 1973), and are not much in favor in the social science community today. However, they are still very much alive in the classroom, and their assumptions are often taken for granted by members of the education community and its controlling bureaucracy. They are also held by some minority group people, both parents and children. In addition, their more benevolent forms still appear not infrequently in literature on minority underachievement.

The second model, and the one we will use, is that of *cultural difference*. It takes the general position that minority underachievement results from some lack of congruence between the assumptions, norms, values, and behaviors of school personnel, and the assumptions, norms, values, and behaviors of minority student populations.

Different varieties of the cultural-difference model can be distinguished by the specific lack of congruence posited as the cause of the problems between school and child. On this basis, most of the major hypotheses can be viewed as falling into one of six categories; these are (*a*) cultural understandings and misunderstandings; (*b*) motivation; (*c*) cognition; (*d*) language; (*e*) social organization; and (*f*) political issues.

CULTURAL UNDERSTANDINGS AND MISUNDERSTANDINGS

Explanations for minority school failure falling under this heading, attribute the problem to misunderstandings between pupils and teachers arising from different culturally-based assumptions, or to misunderstandings on the part of educators about the nature of culture and cultural differences (e.g., the use of deficiency models as the bases for designing school programs). For example, Valentine (1971) suggests that schools cause minority group failure because they assume that cultural differences interfere with education and, therefore, attempt to wipe out such differences. Rosenfeld (1971) places part of the responsibility for slum school failure on teachers who "give up" on their pupils as unteachable, partly because they do not understand their students' culturally different social organization and motivation. Wax and Wax (1971) attribute the inappropriacy of many educational programs designed for minority children to the use of a "vacuum" or cultural deficiency model for minority cultures. In the Hawaiian case, previous research has demonstrated that simply educating educators about cultural differences, in the hope of alleviating such misunderstandings, is not by itself effective in remedying underachievement (MacDonald & Gallimore, 1971). An alternative approach will be discussed in the case study in this chapter.

MOTIVATION

Motivational explanations are those which attribute academic underachievement on the part of minority children to their failure to perform the necessary learning activities in school. Although a deficiency model may attribute such nonperformance to individual or cultural weaknesses, in the cultural difference framework it is postulated to occur because the conventional school environment does not contain the proper cues to effectively elicit learning behaviors from minority children (e.g., McDermott, 1974). Some workers suggest that the school environment is so inimical to minority children that they may actively rebel and refuse to do what is asked of them by the school, in a show of hostility toward teachers or the system (e.g., Rosenfeld, 1971), or in a perhaps not-altogether-unconscious attempt to preserve their own cultural identity and dignity (e.g., Howard, 1973). KEEP, in one of its major lines of research (Tharp & Gallimore, 1976), has trained teachers to shape the classroom environment in ways that are conducive to a willing engagement in school tasks on the part of Hawaiian children. However, the resulting industriousness proved to be a necessary but not sufficient condition for effective learning.

COGNITION

Explanations having to do with culturally derived differences in cognition are increasingly popular among psychologists. Unfortunately they encounter problems because of the difficulty of measuring cognition across cultures, or even across situations. As a further complexity, one can view the problems of minority students as due to differences in the *organization* of cognitive operations (e.g., Cole & Scribner, 1974); that is, pupils may fail to learn because their cognitive operations, though adequate, are organized in systems which do not mesh well with the way the school presents information.

Further controversy exists around issues of "cognitive training." Will the performance of the pupil be improved by formal cognitive training as Ann Brown (in press) and others have suggested? Or, is it necessary instead, to only engage or elicit the appropriate cognitive processes, which are assumed to already be present and well-developed, by changes of context? Furthermore, would the teaching behaviors generated by those two hypotheses be, in fact, any different? In our opinion, effective innovations in the cognitive area are difficult to separate conceptually from innovations generated by sociolinguistic hypotheses, to which we now turn.

LANGUAGE ISSUES

Two kinds of explanations can be included in this category. One is that of actual code interference. According to this explanation, failure to learn may occur because material is presented in a school, or "standard" code (i.e., language or dialect), which is unfamiliar to the student. For example, the student may not understand the code well enough to absorb the content, whereas his teacher may not understand the student's first language or dialect well enough to recognize and be able to mobilize his real academic potential; or there may be interference between specific features of the two codes which produce learning difficulties, especially in reading. The recent bicultural, bilingual impetus in education (e.g., Torres-Trueba, 1976) has grown partially out of these concerns.

The other variety of explanation involving language is sociolinguistic. Even if teacher and pupil share the same language code, it may well be that the ways in which they use that code (i.e., the particular social circumstances of speech and the paralinguistic acts surrounding it) are sufficiently different that they effectively hamper communication. Sociolinguistic explanations emphasize social circumstances of speech acts and the ways that language is used in interaction. These vary widely from one cultural group to another. Laura Lein (1975), for example, points out how differences in sociolinguistic rules result in mutual misinterpretations by teachers and black American migrant children; and Boggs (1972) has reported similar phenomena for Hawaiian children and their teachers. Cazden, Bond, Epstein, Matz, and Savignon (1977), among others, have emphasized the great difficulty of even evaluating the linguistic repertoire of minority children, because of misfits between the sociolinguistic parameters of school and conventional testing situations, on the one hand, and those of the settings in which such children will produce the full range of language performance, on the other. The failure of schools to fully engage the cognitive and linguistic capacities of minority children is a source of consternation to educators, as well as social scientists; and sociolinguistic analyses are more and more looked to for solutions. An example of one solution will be discussed in some detail further on.

SOCIAL ORGANIZATION OF THE CLASSROOM AND OF
THE TEACHING PROCESS

Even within the transnational school culture, there are a variety of classroom social organizations possible, ranging from that symbolized by the traditional self-contained ranks and files of desks, through small-group formats, to individual tutorial systems, and to the radical, "free-school", minimum-organization style. Social organizations willy-nilly emphasize different interaction styles (e.g., competition or cooperation, individualization or group-linking, personal or impersonal teacher relationships, formality or informality of teaching style, peer–peer or student–teacher relationships) which, in turn, implicate cultural norms. Discongruities between preferred types of social interactions, and even social norm conflicts, can result from a classroom social organization which is alien to the child's culture.

Although this kind of hypothesis is not common among educators, or even recipient-culture parents, it is of interest and concern to the cross-cultural social scientist, and a number of workers have placed major responsibility for cross-cultural educational problems on misfits in this area. Frederick Erikson (1977), for instance, has argued that social interactional "styles" of being a student and being a teacher need to be matched with each other in order for satisfactory educational achievement to occur. Rosen (1977), although he sees social interaction issues in the classroom as ultimately stemming from the social class divisions of society as a whole (a "political" explanation), advocates change of the social organization *within* classroom and school as at least a partial solution. Cazden and John (1971), among others, cite "discontinuities" between instructional methods and the customary learning interaction styles of American Indian children and suggest that instructional processes could be better adapted to that style. Hypotheses concerning the social organization of the classroom and of teaching–learning interactions seem potentially fruitful for educational innovations. An example of one such innovation will be discussed later.

SOCIOPOLITICAL ISSUES

This last category of explanation attributes educational problems in cross-cultural circumstances to the structure of the larger society and the relationship of minority or subordinate groups to the dominant group which controls the educational institutions. Eleanor Leacock (1971), for example, has given some support to this position as a result of a comparative study of black and white low- and middle-income schools. In the same volume, Thomas and Wahrhaftig (1971) come to a similar conclusion from work with Cherokee Indian and folk, Anglo-Saxon populations.

Proponents of political explanations often see solutions to cross-cultural educational problems as resulting only from changes in the larger society, or at least from a drastic reorganization of the total school system. Although they may concede that the immediate problems experienced by minority and subordinate-group children in school can be due to factors included in any of the other five categories, solutions to these problems cannot be reached, these theorists feel, by changes which are confined to the classroom alone. Only by alterations in the larger sociopolitical frame, can effective and lasting educational change be produced.

Researchers in cross-cultural education must recognize the reality of sociopolitical issues. However, educational research and political action are separate spheres of activity with different ways of proceeding. The researcher, in so far as he remains a researcher, must most often attack classroom issues directly, in the hope that making the transnational culture of the school operate more effectively for minority students will help to alleviate one root issue—political discontent.

The above categories, we believe, subsume most of the cultural difference explanations for difficulties in minority group encounters with the culture of the school. We would now like to present our case study of mutual accommodation and adaptation between children of a minority culture and the transnational school, the Kamehameha Early Education Program (KEEP). We see this case study as presenting, not the ideal pattern for a solution of all such issues, but a model of a process for proceeding toward solutions, and an illustration of the use of hypotheses falling in several of the aforementioned areas. The outcome of KEEP's work, at this time, is a school situation which seems comfortable for both students and teachers, and which also results in greatly increased academic achievement on the part of the children. The school has been changed in what may seem minor ways, but ones which take into account several possible sources of conflict at the cultural interface.

A Case Study: The Kamehameha
Early Education Program

Like other American minority children, those of Polynesian-Hawaiian ancestry do not ordinarily prosper in the public schools of their state. A case can be made that Hawaiian children experience the lowest level of academic achievement among the United States' ethnic minorities. In the Hawaiian instance, it is particularly clear that such educational frustration does flow from a failure of fit between the two cultures of school and child, because intellectual equipage for school work, even by conventional measures, is demonstrably present in Hawaiian children. In our own laboratory school, for example, the measured mean Wechsler Preschool and Primary Scale of Intelligence IQs of post-kindergarten, pre-first-grade pupils has repeatedly been 100, in classes drawn randomly from a sample stratified for socioeconomic proportions. Yet, by the fourth grade, state-wide testing on Stanford Achievement Tests in reading has placed the means of schools with predominantly Hawaiian populations in the first and lowest stanine of national norms.

Upwards of 35,000 Hawaiian and part-Hawaiian children attend the public schools of Hawaii. However, Hawaiian adults are sharply underrepresented in the teaching and administrative personnel of the state; the State Department of Education is predominantly Japanese-American, and is characteristically successful in educating Japanese, Caucasian, and Chinese children. Curricula, procedures, and school organization are largely indistinguishable from those of the mainstream U. S. and may be seen as an example of the efficient operation of the transnational culture of the school.

This is a situation, then, particularly well suited for cross-cultural inquiry: Hawaiian children who require only a year of kindergarten preparation to bring their school-success prediction scores to parity with the general population; an efficient transnational school system; and a disastrous educational result. Neither the children, nor the schools are incompetent for the tasks of learning and teaching, yet in the outcome, little evidence of teaching or learning can be found.

The Kamehameha Early Education Program operates a laboratory and demonstration school in Honolulu, enrolling primarily Hawaiian and part-Hawaiian, urban, poor children in kindergarten through the third grade. KEEP is a multidisciplinary research and development program, involving psychologists, anthropologists, linguists, and educators. The school is under the immediate control of researchers, and its purpose is to design and demonstrate an effective school program for Hawaiian children.

The basic assumption of KEEP operations has been a two-culture model: There is a culture of the school and teachers, and a culture of the child. In the Hawaiian instance, they do not interact to the advantage of either. In order to design accommodations between the two, a careful knowledge of both is required.

Knowledge of modern Hawaiian culture was gained through 3 years of ethnographic, and experimental, psychological research on Hawaiian communities (Gallimore, Boggs, & Jordan, 1974; Howard, 1974), and through extensive sociolinguistic research with Hawaiian children (Day, 1975a, 1975b; Gallimore, 1978; Watson-Gegeo & Boggs, 1977). Knowledge of the school culture was obtained by creating a school and observing it intensively. That is, we hired a staff of teachers, with conventional training and experience (except that they were sympathetic to our ultimate revisionist goals), built a conventional school building (except that it was equipped with extensive observational facilities), and let a typical school emerge.

We populated the school with educationally at-risk Hawaiian children, and were able to observe, at firsthand, the dramatic two-culture conflict played out below our observation deck. As long as the traditional school culture remained intact, the KEEP children did no better on standardized test results than did control children in public schools. A typical result was a mean 27th percentile on the Gates-MacGinitie Tests of reading achievement.

Such results continued for some 4 years, despite a vigorous multidisciplinary research program, a dedicated and generous teaching staff, and effort after effort at educational innovation. Only after that time were we able to create an effective mix of cultural accommodations. At this writing, KEEP children are achieving at levels considerably above national norms. Class means above the 50th percentile on the Gates-MacGinitie Reading Tests are typical.

Before turning to an examination of the detailed cultural–psychological issues, an operational principle of KEEP work should be specified—that which we call the principle of *least change*. In creating the accommodated educational culture for which KEEP aimed, we wished to effect only those changes in either school or child culture which would be necessary to produce the good learning desired by both the schools and Hawaiian parents. Neither the researchers, nor the parents, wanted the children culturally changed in values, attitudes, social relationships, and the like; and certainly a least-changed school model would be the most acceptable to the public schools which KEEP hoped to influence. As a result of these least-changes, casual visitors to the KEEP school see Hawaiian children acting very much like Hawaiian children; they see a school which looks very much like the transnational school. Only close scrutiny will reveal anything very different. The sophisticated educator will often comment that KEEP school success is due entirely to sound educational practice carefully executed, and that cultural considerations are probably minimal in effect. Culturally sophisticated observers emphasize the Hawaiian elements in the program, and attribute success to those features. In the opinion of the writers, both attributions are correct in part. We have attempted to employ many elements which are features of, and grow solely from, educational science. We have attempted also to retain and emphasize in the classroom those characteristics of the children's culture which facilitate their learning and personal growth in the school environment (Au & Jordan, 1978a, 1978b). The accommodated school culture looks like both of the two cultures, but *is* neither.

Descriptions of the educational-science portions of the KEEP program (data-based, minimum objective system; comprehension-based reading instruction; quality control system) have been described elsewhere (Crowell, 1976, 1977; O'Neal & Bogert, 1977) and are not the proper focus for this chapter. This does not imply a denigration of the transnational elements; the accommodated culture requires the strengths of both school and child. However, we will discuss here those elements of the culture of the child which have been retained, emphasized, or compensated for in the accommodated culture.

Ethnographic research has revealed features of the culture of the

Hawaiian child which are distinctive and of profound importance educationally. Those features are the system of *sibling caretaking; affiliation motivation;* and *peer orientation* (Gallimore, Boggs, & Jordan, 1974). It is possible
to see sibling caretaking as the foundational system for affiliation motives
and peer orientation; and KEEP children are heavily involved in sibling
caretaking. Twenty-seven percent of KEEP mothers report that their 5- to
8-year-old children "seldom" or "never" perform caretaking for their
younger siblings, but 73% said "sometimes," "often," or "always"
(Weisner, 1978). Gallimore, Boggs and Jordan (1974) suggest that siblings
are often best seen as primary socialization agents.

     As a group, Hawaiian children are vigorous, mutually helpful, socially
skilled, talkative, affectionate, and aggressive. These are traits which would
arise naturally from the peer- and sibling-oriented culture. However, these
traits in an ordinary classroom can produce chaos, and teachers are more
likely to describe Hawaiian children as "rowdy, restless, inattentive, lazy,
uninvolved, and provocative." Hawaiian children in the school continue to
be, as they are at home, highly peer oriented; the schools are designed for
adult orientation. Hawaiian children typically *avoid* adults; the school adult
is inescapable. The school adult is designed to *teach;* the child's expectation
of her is to be an "auntie." In short, the school's expectation of close
attention, approach, and clear orientation to the teacher produces an immediate failure of fit between the two cultures of school and Hawaiian child.

     In our effort to adapt the school and the child into an harmonious and
productive unit, we have adopted several strategies. Some require changes
in the teachers' behaviors; some produce changes in the behavior of the
children. The main cultural accommodations that have resulted can be seen
as falling into three different areas according to the framework discussed
earlier: motivation–industriousness; classroom social organization; and
sociolinguistic–cognitive facilitation.

MOTIVATION–INDUSTRIOUSNESS

     Public school teachers typically view the Hawaiian child as lazy, unin-
volved, and unconcerned with learning. These traits are blamed on "the
home," and the teacher often views the school as powerless to overcome a
massive cultural lethargy. KEEP children, in the accommodated school
culture, are industrious, involved, and enthusiastic. The changes in teacher
behavior by which these differences are effected can be clearly specified and
have been developed into reliable training programs for interested teachers
(Sloat, Tharp, & Gallimore, 1977; Speidel & Tharp, 1978; Tanaka-Matsumi
& Tharp, 1977).

     First, during the early days of kindergarten, the teacher creates a new role
identity for herself and for the children. They are taught that she is a warm,
loving, and approachable person whose role is to teach them many things,

and her plentiful praises, hugs, and smiles melt the hearts of even the wariest child. We conceptualize this early, high diet of affection and physical warmth as reminiscent of the "baby" role characteristic of the Hawaiian family, in which much expressive closeness between adult and child is present. In the Hawaiian family, the baby role terminates as the "baby" is promoted to "child" and moves into the sibling culture. We think that this brief return serves to initiate important interpersonal ties between the children and their teacher and helps to establish the teacher as an adult who has high social relevance for the children—a status which is not automatically accorded to all adults by Hawaiian children, but must be earned.

At the same time, the children are taught to address the teacher as "Mrs. Lee," not as "auntie." They learn that Mrs. Lee has definite expectations of them and that the role of student has rules. The teacher makes all this known by clear and consistent statements and modelings of correct behaviors, by clear praises, and by clear desists.

After perhaps 6–8 weeks of kindergarten, the rich broth of praise and warmth is continued, but along a pattern of contingency, especially in the academic domain. The children need success experiences in school, along with a view of the teacher as one who controls important interpersonal resources. Therefore, our teachers constantly look for opportunities to "catch the children being good," and so to recognize good work or helpful deportment. The idea is (*a*) to provide success experiences and encourage self-regard in the school context; and (*b*) to alter the children's habits toward orientation to and engagement with teacher-organized educational activities.

In summary, KEEP teachers use praise much more, and punishment much less, than any comprison group of teachers that we have found. The KEEP observation deck and videotape equipment allow for close observation of the classroom, and we have records of the rates of praise and punishment that each teacher uses. We have also observed in comparison classrooms in the public schools. Several years of these data have been assembled and reported in Tharp and Gallimore (1976). The summary statement would be this: KEEP teachers use up to five times more praise than comparison schools and employ so little punishment that it cannot be reliably counted. Rates of praise are highest in kindergarten and gradually become lowest in third grade.

It should be noted that the pattern of high praise–low scold is *not* characteristic of Hawaiian family life, nor is it characteristic of the culture of public education. It is an adaptation of both, designed to meet their mutual goals.

Now let us examine the results for the children. The change in teacher behavior produces *industrious* children. We index industriousness by what we call *on-task rate;* that is, the percentage of time in which a child is engaged in the learning task being asked of him at the moment. We have also made comparison observations in public schools, in classes of children similar to our own. By these measures, our children are on-task about 90%

of the time. These rates are, on the average, some 20% higher than comparison schools. We attribute this industriousness to our strategy of high rates of praise and encouragement, both verbal and nonverbal.

Again, it should be emphasized that this explicitly encouraging, richly reinforcing culture is not typical of either the home culture or the school culture. It is an example of an element of the accommodated culture which derives from neither; but in the warm and affectionate climate it creates for both teacher and child, it is felicitous for their engagements in their mutual tasks.

CLASSROOM SOCIAL ORGANIZATION

Following also from the peer- and sibling-oriented culture are considerations of social organization in the classroom. The strong affiliation tendencies in Hawaiian culture, creating patterns of cooperation and mutuality in task accomplishment, have been documented by ethnographic and experimental analysis of children (Gallimore, Boggs, & Jordan, 1974) and adults (Howard, 1974). Ethnographic observation of KEEP classrooms has revealed large amounts of peer interaction, whenever teachers allow children access to one another. Included in these interactions are many teaching–learning sequences between children (Jordan, 1978).

Group incentives and rewards have been found more effective than individual ones for older Hawaiian students (Sloggett, 1969), as well as for KEEP children. In several formats (Speidel, 1976; Tharp, Au, & O'Neal, n.d.), group instruction has been found more effective than individual instruction, even though the response opportunities for children are reduced in the group format.

Given these considerations, it would appear that the most effective social organization of the classroom would not be individual tutorials, even should such massive resources be available. Neither should it be large group, teacher-dominated, whole-class formats, which reduce the opportunities for the child–child interactions and fellow-feeling, characteristic of the small groups into which the children tend to spontaneously organize themselves.

Rather, the appropriate format would appear to be small-group, and this is the characteristic KEEP system. Children are organized into continuing groups, whose membership is semifluid, based on current objectives. These groups have identities, self-chosen names, etc., and during reading instruction meet with a teacher daily for face-to-face lessons. Supportive, teacher-independent desk work is also performed in small groups, meeting at one of several "centers," each identified by its characteristic activity ("library center," "listening center," etc.). This system has been described in detail by O'Neil and Bogert (1977). During one day's language arts instruction period of 2 hours, each child may work at up to six centers, at each of which he or she will be in the company of a somewhat different group of from one to six other children.

The reader familiar with the literature of education can see immediately that such a format is often advocated by the transnational school, and educators on the KEEP staff have developed these recommendations without regard to Hawaiian cultural issues, on the basis of sound school-culture practice. KEEP culturalists have recommended, concurred in, and elaborated these formats, solely on the basis of child-culture considerations.

In the earlier section on motivation–industriousness, we observed that the element was a new, accommodated one, neither "Hawaiian" nor "school." The social organization format represents another type of accommodated element, one which is *both* "Hawaiian" and "school," simultaneously.

SOCIOLINGUISTIC FACILITATION

In formal education, it is necessary to fully engage the linguistic and cognitive capacities of children. It is reasonable to assume that when Hawaiian children perform poorly in conventional education, their linguistic and cognitive capabilities have not been engaged.

Stephen Boggs, Richard Day, and Karen Watson-Gegeo have conducted extensive sociolinguistic explorations with Hawaiian children in order to discover those social settings in which children display maximal, linguistic and cognitive complexity. Perhaps the richest of these settings is that called "talk-story" or a subtype of "talk-story," called "storytelling" (Watson-Gegeo & Boggs, 1977). Among the features present in such settings are: a small group of children, a sympathetic and receptive adult, informality, turn taking, overlapping speech, and co-narration. The image is of a group of children under a tree with a friendly adult, all enthusiastically creating or recalling a story together. Under such circumstances, verbal sequences of great richness and complexity are produced by quite young Hawaiian children. This is an image quite different from the listless, disinterested, or resistant Hawaiian child often seen in the the school setting. The KEEP program evolved an element which duplicates many features of the "talk-story–storytelling" format.

During the daily small-group, direct-instruction reading lessons, about five children are seated in a semicircle before the teacher. Typically, there is a text present for each person, and often a brief period of silent reading occurs. Then the teacher begins to ask questions about the story at hand. Details, main ideas, alternate outcomes, speculations about the characters' motives or feelings, and related personal experiences of the children—all are interwoven into a group discussion which is experienced by the teacher as planned instruction, *but is experienced by the child as "storytelling"* (Au & Jordan, 1978a). Many of the features described by Watson-Gegeo and Boggs are present: co-narration, overlapping speech, and enthusiastic engagement. However, there are differences: The teacher does enforce roughly equal opportunities for each child to speak, over a period of days—apparently the self-regulating, equal-time principle, characteristic of the fully developed adult form of Hawaiian "talk-story" activity, does not develop until about age 12 (Boggs, 1977). The teachers do not, however, enforce a rigid turn-taking system, nor do they demand responses from a child who is not ready to participate, thus preserving the child-experienced informality of the enterprise, which is vital to the child's continued engagement.

In this sociolinguistic element, we see a third type of accommodated-culture feature—one which has clear progenitors in the school and in the child culture, but which, itself, is a hybrid, a compromise. For example, the system of "comprehension" instruction in reading is advocated by many transnational educators, and when this meaning-emphasis approach to a text is employed in small groups, it looks much like the KEEP system. But in "pure" form, the group lesson might be more orderly, more Socratic, more teacher controlled than is the case at KEEP. On the other hand, the element is by no means "pure" talk-story or storytelling. The teacher does have an agenda (though its artful embedding in informality is characteristic) and the teacher does select and order the stories. Whether this offspring element resembles more the mother-culture or the father-culture depends, in the opinion of the writers, on the slant of the light.

Conclusions

It is in minority-group formal education that cultures can be seen to clearly cross. In this applied case-study discussion, we have attempted to demonstrate that cross-cultural psychology, in cooperation with its sister disciplines of anthropology, linguistics, and education, can contribute to an analysis of cultural conflicts in the school, and also work toward a reversal of educational failures. Such work is in its infancy, and we will risk only one general conclusion. The successful accommodated-school is not likely to bear a simple isomorphic relationship to the culture of the child, however appealing such a vision might be. Neither will the pure-form transnational school, however perfected, be uniformly successful with minority-culture children. However, we cannot disregard either culture. The successful accommodated-school will take from both the strengths appropriate to their common goals, creating a system in which teachers and children can work harmoniously and with self-respect. But the accommodated-school will be neither the culture of the child, nor the standard culture of the school. It will be something new, a third culture.

References

Au, K. H., & Jordan, C. Teaching reading to Hawaiian children: Finding a culturally appropriate solution. In C. Jordan, T. Weisner, R. G. Tharp, R. Gallimore, & K. H. Au. *A multidisciplinary approach to research in education: The Kamehameha Early Education Program.* (Tech. Rep. No. 81). Honolulu, Hawaii: The Kamehameha Schools, The Kamehameha Early Education Program, 1978. (a)

Au, K. H., & Jordan, C. *Creating the cross-cultural classroom: A case study.* Paper presented at the meeting of the American Anthropological Association, Los Angeles, 1978. (b)

Boggs, S. T. The meaning of questions and narratives to Hawaiian children. In C. B. Cazden, V. P. John, & D. Hymes (Eds.), *Functions of language in the classroom.* New York: Teachers College Press, 1972.

Boggs, S. T. Personal communication, 1977.

Brown, A. L. Knowing when, where, and how to remember: A problem of metacognition. In R. Glaser (Ed.), *Advances in instructional psychology.* Hillsdale, New Jersey: Laurence Erlbaum Associates, in press.

Cazden, C. B, Bond, J. T., Epstein, A. S., Matz, R.D., & Savignon, S.J. Language assessment: Where, what and how. *Anthropology and Education Quarterly,* 1977, *8*(2), 83–90.

Cazden, C. B., & John, V. P. Learning in American Indian children. In M.L. Wax, S. Diamond, & F. O. Gearing (Eds.), *Anthropological perspectives on education.* New York: Basic Books, 1971.

Ciborowski, T. The influence of formal education on rule learning and attribute identification in a West African society. *Journal of Cross-Cultural Psychology,* 1977, *1,* 17–32.

Cole, M., & Scribner, S. *Culture and thought: A psychological introduction.* New York: Wiley, 1974.

Cole, M., Sharp, D. W., & Lave, C. The cognitive consequences of education: Some empirical evidence and theoretical misgivings. *The Urban Review,* 1976, *9*(4), 218–233.

Crowell, D. *The use of minimum objectives in curriculum research and development, 1975–1976.* (Tech. Rep. No. 45). Honolulu, Hawaii: The Kamehameha Schools, The Kamehameha Early Education Program, 1976.

Crowell, D. *Description of the KEEP Reading Program for grades 1, 2, and 3: 1976–1977.* (Tech. Rep. No. 79). Honolulu, Hawaii: The Kamehameha Schools, The Kamehameha Early Education Program, 1977.

Day, R. *The acquisition of plurality and tense by pidgin-speaking children.* (Tech. Rep. No. 30). Honolulu, Hawaii: The Kamehameha Schools, The Kamehameha Early Education Program, 1975. (a)

Day, R. *The teaching of English to Hawaiian Creole-speaking children.* (Tech. Rep. No. 29.) Honolulu, Hawaii: The Kamehameha Schools, the Kamehameha Early Education Program, 1975. (b)

Erickson, F. Some approaches to inquiry in school-community ethnography. *Anthropology and Education Quarterly,* 1977, *8*(2), 58–69.

Gallimore, R. The role of dialect and general verbal/cognitive abilities in school performance of Hawaiian Creole speakers. In C. Jordan, R. G. Tharp, K. H. Au, T. S. Weisner, & R. Gallimore. *A multidisciplinary approach to research in education: The Kamehameha Early Education Program.* (Tech. Rep. No. 81.) Honolulu, Hawaii: The Kamehameha Schools. The Kamehameha Early Education Program, 1978.

Gallimore, R., Boggs, J. W., & Jordan, C. *Culture, behavior, and education: A study of Hawaiian-Americans.* Beverly Hills, California: Sage Publications, 1974.

Hostetler, J. A., & Huntington, G. E. *Children in Amish society: Socialization and community education.* New York: Holt, 1971.

Howard, A. Education in ʻAina Pumehana. In S. T. Kimball & J. H. Burnett (Eds.), *Learning and culture.* Seattle, Washington: American Ethnological Society, 1973.

Howard, A. *Ain't no big thing: Coping strategies in a Hawaiian-American community.* Honolulu, Hawaii: Univ. Press of Hawaii, 1974.

Jensen, A. R. How much can we boost I. Q. and scholastic achievement? *Harvard Educational Review,* 1969, *39,* 1–123.

Jordan, C. Teaching/learning interactions and school adaptation: The Hawaiian case. In C. Jordan, R. G. Tharp, K. H. Au, T. S. Weisner, & R. Gallimore. *A multidisciplinary approach to research in education: The Kamehameha Early Education Program.* (Tech. Rep. No. 81.) Honolulu, Hawaii: The Kamehameha Schools, The Kamehameha Early Education Program, 1978.

Keddie, N. (Ed.) *The myth of cultural deprivation.* Baltimore, Maryland: Penguin Books, 1973.

La Belle, T. J. Liberation, development, and rural nonformal education. *Council on Anthropology and Education Quarterly,* 1975, *6*(4), 20–27.

Lave, J. Cognitive consequences of traditional apprenticeship training in West Africa. *Anthropology and Education Quarterly,* 1977, *8*(3), 177–180. (a)

Lave, J. Tailor-made experiments and evaluating the intellectual consequences of apprenticeship training. *The Quarterly Newsletter of the Institute for Comparative Human Development,* 1977, *1*(2), 1–3. (b)

Leacock, E. B. Theoretical and methodological problems in the study of the schools. In M. L. Wax, S. Diamond, & F. O. Gearing (Eds.), *Anthropological Perspectives on Education.* New York: Basic Books, 1971.

Lein, L. You were talking through, oh yes, you was. *Council on Anthropology and Education Quarterly,* 1975, *6*(4), 1–11.

MacDonald, W. S. (with contributions by R. Gallimore) *Battle in the classroom: Innovations in classroom techniques.* Scranton, New York: Intext, 1971.

McDermott, R. P. Achieving school failure: An anthropological approach to illiteracy and social stratification. In G. D. Spindler (Ed.), *Education and cultural process: Toward an anthropology of education.* New York: Holt, 1974.

Olsen, D. R. The languages of instruction: The literate bias of schooling. In R. C. Anderson, R. J. Spiro, & W. E. Montague (Eds.), *Schooling and the acquisition of knowledge.* New York: Wiley, 1977.

O'Neal, K., & Bogert, K. *Classroom organization for the language arts teacher: A system for meeting learner needs through the use of work areas and small group instruction.* (Tech. Rep. No. 78.) Honolulu, Hawaii: The Kamehameha Schools, The Kamehameha Early Education Program, 1977.

Rosen, D. Multi-cultural education: An anthropological perspective. *Anthropology and Education Quarterly,* 1977, *8*(4), 221–229.

Rosenfeld, G. *"Shut those thick lips!" A study of slum school failure.* New York: Holt, 1971.

Scribner, S. *Cognitive consequences of literacy.* Paper presented at the meeting of the American Anthropological Association, Houston, Texas, December, 1977.

Scribner, S., & Cole, M. Cognitive consequences of formal and informal education. *Science,* 1973, *182,* 553–559.

Sloat, K. C. M., Tharp, R. G., & Gallimore, R. The incremental effectiveness of classroom-based teacher training techniques. *Behavior Therapy,* 1977, *8,* 810–818.

Sloggett, B. B. Behavior modification of the underachieving rural Hawaiian: An experimental classroom. *Pacific Anthropological Records,* 1969, *5,* 1–14.

Speidel, G. E. *The effect of group versus individual instruction on the acquisition of consonant sounds.* (Tech. Rep. No. 47). Honolulu, Hawaii: The Kamehameha Schools, The Kamehameha Early Education Program, 1976.

Speidel, G. E., & Tharp, R. G. Teacher training workshop strategy: Instructions, discrimination training, modeling, guided practice, and video feedback. *Behavior Therapy,* 1978, *9,* 735–739.

Tanaka-Matsumi, J., & Tharp, R. G. Teaching the teachers of Hawaiian children: Training and consultation strategies. *Topics in Culture Learning,* 1977, Aug., 92–106.

Tharp, R. G., Au, K. H., & O'Neal, K. Manuscript in progress. (Files of author.) Honolulu, Hawaii: The Kamehameha Schools, The Kamehameha Early Education Program, n.d.

Tharp, R. G., & Gallimore, R. *The uses and limits of social reinforcement and industriousness for learning to read.* (Tech. Rep. No. 60.) Honolulu: The Kamehameha Schools, The Kamehameha Early Education Program, 1976.

Thomas, R. K., & Wahrhaftig, A. L. Indians, hillbillies and the "education problem." In M. L. Wax, S. Diamond, & F. O. Gearing (Eds.), *Anthropological perspectives on education.* New York: Basic Books, 1971.

Torres-Trueba, H. Chicano bilingual–bicultural education. In C. J. Calhoun, & F. A. J. Ianni (Eds.), *The anthropological study of education.* The Hague: Mouton Publishers, 1976.

Valentine, C. A. Deficit, difference, & bicultural modes of Afro-American behavior. *Harvard Educational Review,* 1971, *41,* 137–157.

Watson-Gegeo, K. A., & Boggs, S. T. From verbal play to talk-story: The role of routines in speech events among Hawaiian children. In S. Ervin-Tripp & C. Mitchell-Kernan (Eds.), *Child discourse.* New York: Academic Press, 1977.

Wax, M. L., & Wax, R. H. Cultural deprivation as an educational ideology. In E. Leacock (Ed.), *The culture of poverty: A critique.* New York: Simon & Schuster, 1971.

Weisner, T. S. The Hawaiian-American cultural and familial context: What can it tell us? In C. Jordan, R. G. Tharp, K. H. Au, T. S. Weisner, & R. Gallimore, *A multidisciplinary approach to research in education: The Kamehameha Early Education Program.* (Tech. Rep. No. 81.) Honolulu, Hawaii: The Kamehameha Schools, The Kamehameha Early Education Program, 1978.

13

Orientation Programs for Cross-Cultural Preparation

RICHARD W. BRISLIN

Introduction

DESCRIPTION OF PROGRAMS

Cross-cultural orientation refers to short term programs designed to pre-pare people to live and work in a culture other than their own. Such programs usually have the goal of encouraging participants to learn about (and sometimes experience) another culture so that they will be able to live and work effectively, with a minimum of stress, when they actually en-counter the culture (Brislin & Pedersen, 1976). Usually offered before people are about to relocate themselves in a place foreign to their previous experiences, these programs have attracted the attention of administrators who deal with various types of cross-cultural encounters. These encounters include the problems and adjustments faced by such "audiences" as foreign students, overseas businessmen, technical assistance advisers, missionaries, tourists, diplomats, military in foreign posts, members of the Peace Corps, teachers in schools about to be desegregated, and so forth.

Three of the major assumptions in the design and execution of orientation programs are:

1. There are enough commonalities in cross-cultural encounters (e.g., culture shock, need to interpret unfamiliar interpersonal cues) that

287

lessons learned from one type of audience can be used in planning for another type.
2. Information and experiences can be conveyed in training that will make adjustment to another culture easier since trainees can use the relevant information when faced with an actual problematic situation.
3. The programs are more efficient substitutes for other means of learning about international contact.

For example, extensive travel and residence abroad are often cited as the best preparation for effective cross-cultural interaction. Yet these methods are too time consuming, too inefficient, and too expensive for widespread use.

Cross-cultural orientation programs can also be depicted through a series of descriptive phrases that summarize certain commonalities. Orientation programs are short term, rarely lasting more than two weeks, but often encompassing only a few hours. Training for Peace Corps volunteers was an exception, with programs lasting as long as 4 months. The programs center largely on the transmission of information, but sometimes include attempts to change attitudes and behavior. In cases where change per se is not a goal, there is often attention given to *expanding* attitudes and behavior. "Change" would be an inappropriate word as there is often no base point which can be modified, given that many people do not have any background with cultures other than their own. Programs are not handsomely budgeted and are often staffed by people for whom cross-cultural orientation is not a full time job. The programs are not always part of a widely accepted organizational structure. Rather, they are often dependent upon personnel who voluntarily add cross-cultural orientation to their jobs. The programs are not warmly greeted by potential users, partly because the need for cross-cultural preparation is not universally accepted by people who might benefit from it. This phenomenon may be related to people's lack of experience with cross-cultural matters previously mentioned.

Some Historical Trends

Some sort of orientation for overseas experience has undoubtedly taken place ever since people first started traveling outside their own country. "Old hands" might give a few hints to "first-timers," and some newcomers would undoubtedly seek out knowledgeable people who have had experience, sympathetic experts within the host culture, and so forth. For instance, Benjamin Franklin (1744) wrote about the movement of people between the English colonies and the American Indian cultures, and he detailed what changes can be expected of people from one culture who live for long

periods of time in the other. Systematic attempts at cross-cultural preparation, however, are much more recent. These attempts undoubtedly stem
from a growing awareness of international interdependence, the dangers of
isolationism, the demands for human rights expressed by minorities within
countries, and greater absolute amounts of international travel and residence. In addition, systematic attempts at cross-cultural training have
been dependent upon advances within the behavioral and social sciences.
Such central topics as (*a*) attitude change, (*b*) pedagogy, (*c*) value conflict,
(*d*) stress, and (*e*) the simple realization that people *can* be efficiently trained
in certain skills, have formed a literature from which cross-cultural administrators can borrow. Isolated empirical studies began to form a body of
literature in the 1950s. Unfortunately, the published literature emanates
almost entirely from the United States, and so there is an inevitable
ethnocentrism in any treatment of cross-cultural preparation. There is a real
need for non-American viewpoints and research.

Certain types of cross-cultural encounters have received more attention
than others, partially because of the sheer numbers that demanded attention
(foreign students), possibilities for funding of research (military, Peace
Corps), and less frequently, the realization that inattention to cross-cultural
contact can interfere with overseas business and development projects
(technical assistance advisers). Not all the work has dealt with orientation
itself, but it has dealt with the sorts of cross-cultural encounters that could
easily become part of a training program if someone was interested in
making the jump from *experience* to *preparation for experience*. Overseas
students (Scott, 1956; Spaulding & Flack, 1976), overseas businessmen
(Cleveland, Mangone, & Adams, 1960), technical assistance experts
(Goodenough, 1963; Arensberg & Niehoff, 1971), diplomats (Harmon, 1971),
Peace Corps volunteers (Textor, 1966), and military personnel (Humphrey,
1964) were the six audiences that received the most attention in the published literature.

The nature of the published literature is central to another important
historical point. Researchers and administrators, especially in government,
may have thought and written about cross-cultural preparation, but they did
not communicate widely since they did not publish in commonly available
journals. The field of cross-cultural training has always been plagued by the
''100-copy underground mimeographed press'' approach to dissemination,
which means no real dissemination at all. Some of the almost-published
literature has been reviewed (Brislin & Pedersen, 1976), but there is no way
to estimate what proportion of the literature was covered as there is no way
to delineate the total population of sources. A major breakthrough in cross-
cultural orientation came in the early 1960s when a large number of very
competent behavioral–social scientists became involved, especially in the
development of the Peace Corps. They did good research and published their

results (e.g., Guthrie & Zektick, 1967; Smith, Fawcett, Ezekiel, & Roth, 1963; Textor, 1966). Their efforts allowed others to examine the work, build upon it, and to advance the field in a normal way.

Types of Cross-Cultural Orientation Programs

Techniques used in orientation programs seem to be of five types, and these types are based on various select combinations of teacher roles, trainee roles, and materials. In most actual programs, more than one of these techniques would be used by the administrator or designer.

SELF-AWARENESS

In this method, people learn about the cultural bases of their own behavior. For example, in programs involving citizens of the United States and Japan, the Americans might discuss their own concern with individuality whereas the Japanese might discuss their concern with the individual as an integral part of a group. This approach would seem efficient as people in an orientation program could pursue self-awareness no matter what other country is to be the focus of their interaction in the future. Expenses might be greater if people are grouped according to country-of-assignment rather than country-of-background. A shortcoming of the approach is that there has been no clear demonstration that self-awareness leads to effective intercultural interaction.

One of the well developed self-awareness approaches is the "Contrast-American" technique (Stewart, 1966; Kraemer, 1969). The technique was designed for Americans about to live in another culture, but it is generalizable to trainees from any country. Americans interact with a person who has been carefully trained by the program administrator. This assistant acts in a manner that contrasts sharply with typical American behavior. Where the American stresses material goals, the "Contrast-American" stresses spiritual goals. Other contrasts are achieved versus ascribed status, and self-reliance versus reliance on superiors and patrons. The American has to interact with the assistant to solve a problem, and again the contrast becomes clear. Where the American brings a "let's all pitch in" attitude and a "let's do it now" orientation, the assistant prefers to wait for subordinates. Anecdotal reports indicate that Americans become quite frustated, but of course a moderate amount of frustration leads to learning. One of the researchers involved in the work (Stewart, 1978, personal communication) reports that trainees remember the experience 10 years after it happened.

"Self-awareness" is used here in the sense of learning about typical traits held by members of one's culture, whereas individual self-awareness refers to learning about one's own traits. Cross-cultural orientation deals with the former. The position of Brislin and Pedersen (1976) is that the development of individual self-awareness belongs in a clinical setting with well-trained therapists and counsellors as staff. Insufficient time and resources exist for developing individual self-awareness in orientation programs, and so touching upon the subject may be uncomfortable, and sometimes damaging, for participants. This view is not universally shared. In a well done analysis, Gudykunst, Hammer, and Wiseman (1977) included an individual self-awareness component in their typology of programs.

COGNITIVE TRAINING

In this approach, people are presented with various facts about other cultures. Program content may include information on topics as diverse as food, climate, male–female relations, economy, and decision-making styles. Programs of this type are currently the most common, and they are the easiest to prepare since information about various cultures is efficiently catalogued in libraries (e.g., through the Human Relations Area Files system). The disadvantage often reported by people who participate in the program is that the facts presented do not add up to a meaningful whole, and that nothing is said about what to *do* with the facts. If the cognitive approach is chosen, this is an inherent danger, and one of the administrator's responsibilities is to plan the whole program so that the danger is minimized.

My description of cognitive training, however, is not meant to be demeaning. There should be an important place in any program for a well-prepared presentation centering on key problems and issues that people are likely to encounter in a specific culture. Such a presentation in a cognitive training program can be in the form of guided reading, guided group discussion, a lecture, films, audio–video tapes, and so forth. If the lecture method is chosen, good resource people for such a component should have some of the following characteristics.

1. They should be knowledgeable people who have lived in the other culture, *and* who possess some flair or skill in public speaking.
2. They should be recently returned sojourners who may not have high-status credentials or even training in public speaking. However, the freshness of their experience will undoubtedly be exciting to them, and they will subsequently generate enthusiasm among the trainees.
3. They should be people who have faced and coped with problems similar to those the trainees will encounter.

One advantage of long-term organizational support for cross-cultural programs is that administrators can keep in contact with trainees. Some of these trainees can then be employed as resource people in future programs. Returned trainees can both explain about coping with problems, and they can constructively criticize the entire program from the point of view of "someone who has been there."

ATTRIBUTION TRAINING

Using this method, people learn the explanation of behavior from the point of view of people in other cultures. "Attribution" is a theoretical approach in social psychology (Jones, Kanhouse, Kelley, Nisbett, Valins, & Weiner, 1972; Harvey, Ickes, & Kidd, 1976), and it is concerned with how and why people make judgments about themselves and others. In cross-cultural encounters, of course, there may be many mistakes in attribution as people bring very different experiences to the encounters. The attribution approach eschews imposed explanations of behavior from people outside a given culture. For example, a student at the East-West Center from Laos once verbalized an imposed explanation, and his own explanation, for a certain behavior.

> I agree that Western observers complain about our indirect response to things. We consider it polite, Westerners consider it not frank but you have to bear in mind that among Laotians these are not problems. Being in that kind of society with these values, we have learned to understand the message that other people are sending without it being stated in words. It is not so much what you say but the way you say it that counts [Brislin & Holwill, 1977, p. 21].

The attribution method demands the preparation of materials for each culture in which people in a program are to interact. People from the other cultures must participate in the development of the materials. Such preparation is expensive and time-consuming but ideally the products will be first-rate materials that can be circulated and used in many different programs.

The best developed technique that has used attribution as a starting point is the "Culture Assimilator" (Fiedler, Mitchell, & Triandis, 1971). Materials are prepared by soliciting critical incidents involving people from two specific cultures, such as members of the white, middle-class, urban United States and people from rural Thailand. Different materials would have to be prepared for Americans interacting with members of another culture, or for members of other cultures interacting with rural Thais. In addition to the incidents, explanations of the incidents are gathered, and these explanations often take the form of attributions. That is, people from Culture A make attributions about members of Culture B, and these attributions may be correct or incorrect as seen by the B's. Various attributions that might seemingly explain the incident are listed, one of which is correct as judged by at least 80% of the people from Culture B. The goal of the culture assimilator approach is "isomorphic attribution," or agreement regarding judgments about behavior as seen by all parties involved.

One incident from the Thai assimilator (Foa, Mitchell, Santhai, Wichiarajote, & Wichiarajote, 1967: designed for Americans about to live and work in Thailand) is presented below to show the nature of the incidents, the alternatives, feedback about the alternatives, and methods of presenting information about Thailand. The danger of presenting just one incident is that readers may make generalizations about the whole approach based on idiosyncratic reactions to this one example. Readers are asked to keep in mind that a complete assimilator has over 100 incidents, and that any one major theme (e.g., family, interpersonal relations, superior–subordinate relations on the job) may be developed in 10 or more incidents.

To save space, alternatives are combined on a few pages here, whereas they are on separate pages in an actual culture assimilator.

(i)

Four American economic researchers went to two villages in the northern part of Thailand. The two Americans in one village participated in a welcoming ceremony which signified the strangers' respect for the spirits in which the villagers believed. On this occasion, the Americans' wrists and his Thai co-workers' wrists were wound with an unspun thread which was blessed by the Buddhist monks during the ceremony.

In the neighboring village, the other two Americans thanked the village headman but declined participation in this ceremony, saying that it was contrary to their beliefs. Later, when the two groups of Americans compared their information received from village informants, they found that the two Americans who participated in the ceremony had more specific and significant details and had had more important informants introduced to them by the friendly headman of the village. The other two Americans said that they did not have a very friendly village headman at all, and he was rather uncooperative.

What was the cause of these differences?

1. The villagers felt that one group of Americans had the spirits on their side and therefore felt more at ease with them. (Go to page ii)

2. The villagers who did not give much information were holding back due to orders from the headman who was insulted when the Americans refused to participate in the ceremony. (Go to page iii)

3. The Thai people are very hostile to Christianity and since one group refused to participate in their ceremony, they refused to cooperate. (Go to page iv)

4. The group that received the factual information had shown respect for the Thai customs. The villagers were pleased and relaxed by this gesture and gave the information freely because they considered the Americans to be close to them spiritually. (Go to page v)

(ii)

You selected 1:   The villagers felt that one group of Americans had the spirits on their side and therefore felt more at ease with them.

This is somewhat correct.

The Thais would have felt that the spirits had been respected, but this would not mean they were "on their side." There are more important things here than just being accepted by the spirits. Try again. (Go to page i)

(iii)

You selected 2:   The villagers who did not give much information were holding back due to orders from the headman who was insulted when the Americans refused to participate in the ceremony.

Incorrect.

The headman was probably displeased at the Americans' action, but it is doubtful that he would have told his villagers not to cooperate. The problem here concerns feeling held by all the villagers, not just the headman. Make another choice. (Go to page i)

(iv)

You selected 3:   The Thai people are very hostile to Christianity and since one group refused to participate in their ceremony, they refused to cooperate.

A better choice is available.

The Thais are very open-minded about their religious beliefs. Through the years, they have incorporated into their Buddhism beliefs of other religions and faiths that seemed to fit in, or those brought into the country by other peoples. Religious tolerance is therefore wide-spread. In this situation it is doubtful that the Thais would have been hostile to the Americans because they were Christians. Choose again. (Go to page i)

(v)

You selected 4:   The group that received the factual information had shown respect for the Thai customs. The villagers were pleased and relaxed by this gesture, and gave the information freely because they considered the Americans to be close to them spiritually.

An excellent choice.

The villagers, seeing that the Americans were showing respect for their beliefs, would feel that the Americans wanted to be informal and intimate with them, and would show their appreciation and friendliness toward the newcomers. This opportunity would give the Americans access to the people, particularly the influential village leaders who could facilitate the business by using their power and influences once the Americans had made themselves one of the clan.

Moreover, by going through such a ceremony, and from the villagers' point of view, the Americans have started out to undertake an important business after being blessed with a good omen. The ceremony of the *"Tham Kwan"* or the making of *kwan,* meaning soul or spirits, is performed for the welfare of the owner of the *kwan* which is believed to reside in a person. These northern Thai people believe that the *kwan* gives him or her health, success, and wealth, if it stays with the owner. Thus, when a distinguished guest arrives in the community, the *Tham Kwan* ceremony is performed in order to invite the guest's kwan to come and stay with him. (Go to the next incident.)

The culture assimilator is the best researched technique in the orientation programs literature (Fiedler, Mitchell, & Triandis, 1971; Albert & Adamapoulous, 1976; Triandis, 1977). Researchers have discovered, for instance, that trainees may "freeze up" after a program and may be somewhat fearful of interacting in another culture (O'Brien & Plooij, 1976). Whereas on the surface this may seem to be a disapointing result, in actuality such a response may reflect a healthy awareness of the difficulties of intercultural communication. Training also seems to be more effective for people who have already had an intercultural experience (O'Brien, Fiedler, & Hewett, 1971). Perhaps the structured materials provided by the culture assimilator help trainees to integrate their previous haphazard thoughts and feelings about their cross-cultural experience.

BEHAVIOR MODIFICATION

In this method, well-documented principles of learning are applied. David (1972) has used this approach by asking people to analyze the aspects of their own culture that they find rewarding and punishing. The people then study other cultures to determine which of these rewards and punishers are present, and how they can be obtained or avoided. For instance, people who enjoy long periods of privacy would analyze how to obtain this reward in cultures were norms of interpersonal interaction make deviates of people who isolate themselves for even short periods of time. The advantage of the approach is that a person's probable reaction to life in another culture is explicitly analyzed. The disadvantage is that the concepts of learning theory (many of the terms are those of Skinner) connote "control" and "loss of freedom" to many people, and so the entire approach is distasteful to them.

Application of behavior modification to cross-cultural training has not advanced since David's (1972) research. Howard Higginbotham (1978, personal communication) is familiar with recent developments in cognitive behavior modification and he has speculated on possible applications. The remaining material in this section closely follows a set of ideas that was contributed by him.

Behavior therapy procedures follow from an analysis of conditions, environmental and intraindividual, which gives rise to changeworthy (problem) behavior. It is meaningless to list an array of behavior change techniques (e.g., systematic desensitization, modeling, or assertion training) as being useful to cross-cultural orientation training without first establishing two conditions: (*a*) situational demands of cross-cultural traveling and living which evoke perceptions of discomfort, disorientation, and stress; and, (*b*) problem-solving behaviors and coping skills potentially available to sojourners that they might use to successfully meet problematic situations. The data base for designing orientation programs, thus, comes from understanding who failed in what situations. A microanalysis of the performance requirements for mastering a novel, foreign environment leads to hypotheses about the "nature of the deficit" in those individuals who somehow fail to "survive." An analysis of the deficit, pinpointing cognitive strategies and behavioral skills that the individual failed to produce in response to environmental demands, thus permits the trainer to select or create a treatment–training procedure dealing with those specific deficits.

The fruitfulness of employing this approach is borne out by Meichenbaum's research laying the foundation for a new thrust in behavior therapy—cognitive behavior modification (Meichenbaum, 1977). Meichenbaum's work is clearly relevant to assessing and treating problems of cross-cultural living. Viewing change processes as occuring in three stages (i.e., self-observation, production of incompatable thoughts and behaviors, generating appropriate cognitions concerning change), he has designed intervention programs to teach creative problem-solving, "inoculate" individuals against anxiety provoking, high stress situations, and to give individuals with chronic anger problems competency in anger control during provocation. Anger control, creative problem-solving, and stress inoculation procedures all deserve exploration as useful components for orientation programs. However, stress inoculation has potentially the widest application and is selected here for consideration.

The stress inoculation procedure exemplifies the current shift within behavior therapy from problem-specific interventions focused on discrete responses, to a concern with general coping skills applicable across settings, problems, and behaviors (e.g., Goldfried & Davidson, 1976). Meichenbaum (1977) proposes a three-phase program to increase tolerance for an impending stressful encounter. Phase 1 is education. The clients (trainees) are provided with a conceptual framework for understanding the nature of their stressful reactions. This initial conceptualization is of singular importance. It must provide a rationale, plausible to the clients, that, when accepted, leads to the development of specific exercises and the acquisition of coping techniques.

For example, the sojourner may report (or, be warned about) feeling extremely anxious and fearful while using public transport in many "developing" countries. Western travelers (including Higginbotham and Brislin) summarize their encounters with the bus system in certain Southeast Asian capital cities as follows: confusion about which bus to take; how to get on and off safely; how much to pay; disgust about being pressed against other people in crowded, unventilated, and scorching hot conditions; fear of pickpockets; the driver's seemingly suicidal handling of the bus; plus the constant stares directed at the individual by the other passengers.

Conceptualizing the "culture shock" reaction of using public transport, it is possible to point out two major elements, (a) heightened physiological arousal (heartbeat, body tension, sweating, acidic stomach); and (b) a set of self-statements sensitizing the traveler to the situation and heightening the dread (disgust at being touched; stared at; panic thoughts; desire to flee; images of being harmed from numerous sources). In the education phase, the trainer could then indicate that the program would be aimed at: (a) helping the traveler to control physiological arousal; and (b) changing the "dread" thoughts and images occupying his/her mind during the stressful situation.

Phase 2 provides the client with coping techniques to employ while preparing for a stressor, confronting it, possibly being overwhelmed, and reinforcing oneself for handling the stressor. Viable techniques might include self-guided relaxation exercises (deep muscle relaxation, deep breathing) to reduce physical arousal, and the creation of a series of coping self-statements that could be introduced to replace "dread" thoughts during the stress encounter. During the bus ride, the client's disturbing feelings become signals to "let go" physically; relax; take a deep, slow breath; and begin a coping internal dialogue (e.g., "I can manage this; watch what the others do, I can learn much about the people this way; at least it's cheap and makes a good story when I go home").

Application training, Phase 3, involves the testing of clients' coping skills by using them under stressful conditions approximating the phobic encounter. During the orientation program, the cross-cultural traveler could be given graded exposure to the trauma of public transport use through various experiences. With "imagery stress," vivid accounts of being in the situation could be visualized; or, stress inducing films might be used. Moreover, trainees, who may be accustomed to driving their own cars, could be asked to rely on public transport in their home city and imagine all the problems arising if they could not speak the language, read street signs, know the routes, and fear the other riders, etc.

The stress inoculation training, in summary, provides the orientation trainer with a conceptual framework for addressing negative emotional reactions predicted from encounters with various "culture shock" situations in cross-cultural living. Succinctly stated, "the training involves discussing the nature of emotional and stress reactions, rehearsing coping skills, and testing these skills under actual stressful conditions [Meichenbaum, 1977, p. 157]." The trainer can call upon a variety of behavior therapy techniques and weave them into a program dealing with specific incidents frequently reported as stressful, or focus on generating a basic coping repertoire that will hopefully serve sojourners well in most imagined or unimagined anxiety engendering spots they may encounter while abroad.

EXPERIENTIAL LEARNING

People actively participate in realistic simulations of other cultures with this approach. Sometimes called "total immersion," this approach involves all the senses of the participants, their cognitions *and* emotions, and their total cooperation in satisfying their everyday needs. For instance, contract teachers about to work in Micronesia have been trained in rural parts of Hawaii (Trifonovitch, 1973). There, they (*a*) provided their own food, (*b*) planned daily activities based on the tides and the sun rather than clocks, (*c*) rationed the available water, (*d*) made their own entertainment, and so forth. The point, of course, is that such activities are performed on a day-to-day basis by Micronesians and that outsiders must understand the behaviors to interact effectively in Micronesia. The advantage of this technique is that the relationship to reality is greater than any of the other approaches. The disadvantages are the expense of the preparations and the danger that some people will not be able to cope with such an intense experience.

Recently, an attempt was made to document people's reactions to a cross-cultural simulation of this type (Trifonovitch, Hamnett, Geschwind, & Brislin, 1978). The trainees were themselves program administrators who might incorporate such an approach into their own work. The major finding was that the same situation involving the activities listed as *a-d* in the previous paragraph led to quite different reactions. These reactions were seemingly based on individual differences in the perception of the similarity between their own culture and the simulated culture. For people seeing high similarity, the venture was a "boy-scout outing" and not an opportunity for cross-cultural learning. For people seeing medium-similarity, reactions were favorable. For people seeing little similarity, the situation was so unstructured (and perhaps so uncomfortable) that no learning took place. A certain number of people reported positive experiences such as the following:

> Learning about the amount of time necessary for food preparation early in day. Children have to participate, thus might be tired by time they get to American patterned schools.

> Different people in group took a leadership role, based on skills in this situation, in contrast to passive role in other types of cross-cultural orientation approaches.

> In societies this experience simulates, not much time for development of complex written records, or philosophical analyses, when so much time must be spent on subsistence activities.

> Experience gives some affective base for interpreting factually oriented material about subsistence societies.

There are other, less complex, experiential techniques that can be incorporated into orientation programs. Role playing is the most common approach. Trainees take the part of various individuals involved in a cross-cultural encounter and they develop a short scene that incorporates a problematic issue. Scenes can often be categorized as "experiential training" as participants determine what is done in the role plays and as the scenes can be emotional if sensitive topics are dealt with. For instance, the interaction between the American and contrast-American described previously under "self-awareness" incorporates role playing. In general, experiential techniques are more trainee centered than staff centered, and they incorporate the feelings and emotions of participants in addition to their cognitions.

The Timing of Orientation Programs

Although most of the examples in previous descriptions of orientation programs have dealt with preparations for a cross-cultural experience (such training is presently the most common type), orientation is useful at two other times. One is mid-way into a cross-cultural sojourn, and the second is prior to people's return to their host culture.

MID-TERM ORIENTATION

Perhaps the most well-established finding about the nature of overseas assignments is that people very often encounter a period of low morale and motivation, frustration, and a desire to go home. This is due to a combination of events. The honeymoon phase of excitement about living in another culture wears off. Minor frustrations due to a lack of familiarity with cultural patterns build up, and the individual feels that nothing is getting accomplished since (s)he has to fight so much tradition (Gullahorn & Gullahorn, 1963).

Social scientists have learned much about cross-cultural training from the experience of the Peace Corps, and mid-term training is a good example. Noting that American volunteers in a certain area of South America had adjustment problems, one of the directors started additional training based on the group discussion method. All Peace Corps members in the area were brought together frequently to discuss any issues that they desired. The fact that change comes so slow, and the feelings emanating from culture shock, were often voiced at the meetings. The groups also allowed the members to provide social support for each other. They could praise one member's project, try to lift another's spirits if (s)he was especially "down," or suggest means of implementing the goals of still another member. This additional training was apparently quite effective since the number of premature returns (volunteers who go back to the United States before their two-year assignment is completed) for the discussion group members was only 25% of the figure for nonparticipating volunteers in similar cultures (Arnold, 1967).

REORIENTATION TO HOME CULTURE

When people live in another culture for a significant length of time, their attitudes and outlook change. Many aspects of their home countries will also have changed, for instance, the attitudes of friends and family members and physical aspects of the environment that they remember. People also incorporate new ideas into their thinking, but these new ideas may conflict with tradition in the home culture. Returnees might not be able to find internationally-minded people with whom experiences can be shared, and job relations can be tense if people who were previously subordinates have moved into a supervisory position. Reverse culture shock has not been a common focus of training, but there have been some efforts in the 1970s (Brislin & Van Buren, 1974). In work with which I have been involved, training centers on critical incidents which are the product of interviews with returnees who have faced and coped with difficulties. Sessions within the program center on reactions of family and friends, professional relations, the difference between short and long term adjustment, nonverbal behavior and the nature of attribution, and the maintenance of international relations. Participants also role-play experiences they might face upon returning home. The assumption is that if trainees work through these issues and if they prepare for potential conflicts, they will have fewer problems after actually returning home. Re-entry problems are becoming increasingly recognized and the seminar approach has been recently adopted by a number of organizations as a partial solution (Marsh, 1975; National Association for Foreign Student Affairs, 1977).

Conclusions: Some Needed Research Emphases

While discussing the history, types, and timing of cross-cultural orientation programs, certain points were raised that seemed of critical importance. These points will be developed in more detail here, with special attention given to identifying gaps in our knowledge. Research that may possibly fill the gaps will also be suggested.

1. Cross-cultural training is not widely accepted (p. 288). One reason is that the people who might undergo such training are well-educated, self-confident people who do not always feel the need for additional expertise in human relations, cross-cultural or otherwise. Schnapper (1973) analyzed resistance to cross-cultural training, and found such factors as these:

(*a*) Host–national politeness to high status visitors interferes with honest communication about cross-national differences. The visitors never learn that their behavior may have caused problems, and so are unlikely to recommend training upon arrival back in their home country.

(*b*) Training is not a respected speciality within organizations, but rather is a "dead-end." This low status is easily communicated to potential trainees, making any training effort cumbersome from the start.

(*c*) Different cross-cultural trainers do not agree on what orientation is best and they bicker among themselves in a dogmatic manner. A potential user might overhear such bickering and consequently wonder what the trainers can offer if they are so feisty and intolerant. In addition, trainers sometimes communicate a "more holy (interculturally sensitive) than thou" attitude.

One possible research study would be to identify organizations in which cross-cultural training is, and is not accepted. Reasons for the difference would then be sought, perhaps in a similar way to the work by Caplan and Nelson (1973) on acceptance and rejection of findings from applied research projects.

2. There is a tendency for trainers to deal only with those aspects of other cultures that are clear and unambiguous. In reality, the unclear and the ambiguous will probably cause the most problems. For instance, the culture assimilator is based on incidents that yield 80% agreement as to correct explanation (p. 292). Such a procedure might eliminate crucial incidents about which there is disagreement *within* a culture, but which should be understood by trainees. The research suggestion is to incorporate such ambiguity into the development of cross-cultural training materials. Possibly, recent developments in applied multivariate statistics will help since these techniques reduce complex data to manageable proportions while retaining multidimensionality (e.g., multiple factors, multiple independent and dependent variables, multiple causation, and so forth).

3. Because trainees have very different reactions to cross-cultural orientation (p. 298), the training staff is always on the "firing line." The staff will constantly receive complaints, suggestions for improvement, proposals for a complete revision of a given session, and so forth. People selected to go overseas are bright, verbal, and questioning. Together with these basic qualities, they may displace some of their frustrations due to uncertainty about their future experience, and the training program is an easy target. Younger trainees, just out of college, may enjoy the role of vocal critic as they previously had to keep wraps on this potential so as not to irritate their professors. For whatever reason, the training staff constantly receives feedback, and this can be very frustrating when the staff is doing the best it can. Recently, Adler (1978) published feedback on an orientation program, much of it contradictory. One person said "too much detail"; another, "not enough." A third person said, "I liked the lectures," and a fourth complained "too many." Other complaints centered on the sex and ethnic balance of resource people, the weather, and on the ecological considerations of using paper plates at meals.

The point is that cross-cultural trainers are subject to such criticism by the very nature of their work. Research efforts can center on either (*a*) selecting people who enjoy the give-and-take of such criticism, and/or (*b*) training people to cope with it. One research approach would be to interview current trainers and to document how they deal with the constant barrage of criticisms and complaints.

4. The content of cross-cultural orientation is not always sophisticated and well-prepared. Too often, content centers on the superfluous, trivial, or obvious. For instance, the same gesture that means "hello" in one culture

and "good-bye" in another culture seems to pop up in many programs. The problem is due to the inherent difficulties in trainers' selection of program content. On the one hand they have only a short period of time in which to communicate content. This tempts trainers into presenting material that can be easily understood as too much content would cause a criticism of "over-load." On the other hand, training should have an impact on participants, and this suggests more complex material.

Research might center on the types of materials that can be incorporated by participants in programs of various lengths, and the methods for develop-ing various types of training materials. For the latter, trainers need guidelines for developing materials and various sources on which to draw, such as anthropological ethnographies (some of which are organized in the Human Relations Area Files), in-house reports on people's overseas experi-ence, and so forth.

5. There is a need to communicate to trainees the nature of stereotypes, *and* to prevent orientation programs from becoming lists of stereotypes (e.g., Americans are . . . ; Greeks do . . .). To further complicate the matter, trainers have to point out that people constantly engage in stereotyp-ical thinking. Stereotypes refer to any categorization of individual elements that masks the differences among those elements. Stereotypes are absolutely necessary for thinking and communicating since people cannot respond individually to the millions of isolated elements they perceive every day. They must group elements together into categories, and then respond to those categories. Stereotypes are a form of generalization that involve names of some group of people and statements about that group. Thus when people speak of "conservatives," or "academics," or "educators," they are using stereotypical categories that mask individual differences within those categories. Stereotypes will always be a factor in any sort of com-munication, a fact that must be realized in any analysis of communication between individuals from different backgrounds. Educators who would like to deal with this topic find difficulty in encouraging multicultural groups to discuss stereotypes because the link between prejudice and stereotypes has become so strong. Stereotypes have acquired a distasteful status (e.g., Bosmiajian, 1974) Refusal to deal with them, however, means a refusal to deal with one of the most basic aspects of thinking and communication.

Guidelines do not exist concerning how to deal with this problem except for the general suggestion that trainers emphasize the form, function, and pervasiveness of stereotypes, as indicated above. In addition, when trainers present a statement about members of a certain culture, they must have good evidence for their assertion. Oftentimes, the statements will be more com-plex than "Americans are . . . ." Rather, there will be more detailed arguments with limitations on generality according to sub-culture, age, sex, education, religion, and so forth. Such statements are more complex (and thus harder to communicate, see Point 4) but they are probably a more accurate reflection of reality. Since one goal of cross-cultural orientation is to encourage trainees to be more complex in their thinking, a presentation of this sort on stereotypes should be useful.

Summary

Cross-cultural orientation programs are meant to prepare people to live and work effectively in a culture other than their own. Because potential users are not familiar with the benefits of such training, orientation programs are not an established entity in all organizations that have dealings with numerous countries. Most developments in the field have occurred since World War II, due to increased recognition of international interdependence and developments in the *general* area of training people in various skills. Progress in the field has been plagued by a lack of openly published research. This problem has diminished since about 1965, and recent developments include the publication of books (e.g., Brislin & Pedersen, 1976), and the inauguration of a journal (*International Journal of Intercultural Relations*). There are five types of programs:

1. Self-awareness, in which people learn about the cultural bases of their own behavior. Such training is not concerned with individual self-awareness, but rather with typical traits held by members of one's own society. Keeping such analysis of traits from becoming a list of stereotypes is a difficult problem.
2. Cognitive training, in which people are presented various facts about another culture. Such programs are currently the most common, and the focus of training is on the trainer's presentation of information to trainees.
3. Attribution training, in which people learn the explanation of behavior from the point of view of people in other cultures. The attribution demands the preparation of materials for each culture in which people in a program are to interact, and for each culture from which trainees come.
4. Behavior modification, in which well-documented principles of learning are applied. For instance, trainees might be asked to analyze the rewards they enjoy and the punishments they avoid, and then to speculate how they might find and avoid these in another culture. Recent developments in cognitive behavior modification that center on analysis of stress in terms of education, coping, and testing may prove useful.
5. Experiential learning, in which people actively participate in realistic simulations of other cultures. "Intense" versions of such training include simulations in which participants have to behave like members of a certain culture to obtain their everyday needs. Less complex tech-

niques include role playing, in which people develop a short scenario involving a cross-cultural encounter that centers on a problematic issue.

Programs are most frequently held just before people leave their own country, or shortly after arrival in another culture. However, there are also advantages to mid-term orientation and to re-orientation seminars. The latter can prepare people for the reverse culture shock they may encounter upon their return home.

Some needed research emphases include (*a*) the analysis of the acceptance and rejection of training in various organizations; (*b*) the incorporation of the unclear and the ambiguous in training, since such issues are common and may cause the most difficulty; (*c*) investigations of how trainers deal with the constant barrage of criticism they receive as an inevitable part of their job; (*d*) development of methods to "translate" knowledge of other cultures from one form (e.g., anthropological ethnographies) to another (cross-cultural training materials); and (*e*) to incorporate analyses of stereotypes into training, but at the same time to prevent training itself from transmitting stereotypes.

REFERENCES

Adler, P. Orientation '77, *Impulse,* 1978, Winter Issue.
Albert, R., & Adamapoulous, J. An attributional approach to culture learning: the Culture Assimilator. *Topics in Culture Learning,* 1976, *4,* 53–60.
Arensberg, C., & Niehoff, A. *Introducing social change: A manual for community development* (2nd ed.). Chicago: Aldine-Atherton, 1971.
Arnold, D. Culture shock and a Peace Corps field mental health program. *Community Mental Health Journal,* 1967, *3,* 53–60.
Bosmajian, H. *The language of oppression.* Washington, D.C.: Public Affairs Press, 1974.
Brislin, R., and Holwill, F. Reactions of indigenous people to the writings of behavioral and social scientists. *International Journal of Intercultural Relations,* 1977, *1,* 15–34.
Brislin, R., & Pedersen, P. *Cross-cultural orientation programs.* New York: Wiley–Halsted, 1976.
Brislin, R., & Van Buren, H. Can they go home again? *International Educational and Cultural Exchange,* 1974, *9,* 19–24.
Caplan, N., & Nelson, S. On being useful: The nature and consequences of psychological research on social problems. *American Psychologist,* 1973, *28,* 199–211.
Cleveland, H., Mangone, G., & Adams, J. *The overseas Americans.* New York: McGraw-Hill, 1960.
David, K. Intercultural adjustment and applications of reinforcement theory to problems of "culture." *Trends,* 1972, *4,* 1–64.
Fiedler, F., Mitchell, T., & Triandis, H. The culture assimilator: An approach to cross-cultural training. *Journal of Applied Psychology,* 1971, *55,* 95–102.
Foa, U., Mitchell, T., Santhai, S., Wichiarajote, N., & Wichiarajote, W. *Thai Culture Assimilator.* Urbana, Illinois: Group Effectiveness Research Laboratory, 1967.
Franklin, B. Remarks concerning the savages of North America (pamphlet written concerning an event in 1744). In *The Works of Benjamin Franklin* (Vol. 2). Boston: Tappan & Dennet, 1844.

Goldfried, M., & Davison, G. *Clinical behavior therapy*. New York: Holt, 1976.

Goodenough, W. *Cooperation in change*. New York: Russell Sage, 1963.

Gudykunst, W., Hammer, M., & Wiseman, R. An analysis of an integrated approach to cross-cultural training. *International Journal of Intercultural Relations*, 1977, *1*, 99–110.

Gullahorn, J., & Gullahorn, J. An extension of the U-curve hypothesis. *Journal of Social Issues*, 1963, *19*, 33–47.

Guthrie, G., & Zektick, I. Predicting performance in the Peace Corps. *Journal of Social Psychology*, 1967, *71*, 11–21.

Harmon, R. *The art and practice of diplomacy: A selected and annotated guide*. Metuchen, New Jersey: The Scarecrow Press, 1971.

Harvey, J., Ickes, W., & Kidd, R. (Eds.). *New directions in attribution research*. New York: Wiley–Halsted, 1976.

Humphrey, R. *Fight the cold war: A handbook for overseas orientation officers*. Washington, D.C.: American Institutes for Research, August, 1964.

Jones, E., Kanhouse, D., Kelley, H., Nisbett, R., Valins, S., & Weiner, B. (Eds.). *Attribution: perceiving the causes of behavior*. Morristown, New Jersey: General Learning Press, 1972.

Kraemer, A. *The development of cultural self-awareness: Design of a program of instruction*. Human Resources Research Organization, Professional Paper, August, 1969, 27–29.

Marsh, H. Re-entry–transition seminars for overseas sojourners: Report on the Wingspread colloquium. *Topics in Culture Learning*, 1975, *3*, 39–51.

Meichenbaum, D. *Cognitive-behavior modification: An integrative approach*. New York: Plenum, 1977.

National Association for Foreign Student Affairs. Re-entry–transition workshops and materials. Washington, D.C. (1860 19th St., NW): National Association of Foreign Student Affairs, 1977.

O'Brien, G., & Plooij, D. Development of culture training manuals for medical workers with Pitjantjatjara Aboriginals: The relative effect of critical incident and prose training upon knowledge, attitudes, and motivation. In G. Kearney & D. McElwain (Eds.), *Aboriginal Cognition: Retrospect and prospect*. Canberra, Australia: Australian Institute for Aboriginal Studies, 1976.

O'Brien, G., Fiedler, F., & Hewett, T. The effects of programmed culture training upon the performance of volunteer medical teams in Central America. *Human Relations*, 1971, *24*, 209–231.

Schnapper, M. *Resistances to intercultural training*. Paper presented at the Thirteenth Annual Conference of the Society for International Development, San Jose, Costa Rica, February, 1973.

Scott, F. *The American experience of Swedish students*. Minneapolis: Univ. of Minnesota Press, 1956.

Smith, M., Fawcett, J., Ezekial, R., & Roth, S. A factorial study of morale among Peace Corps teachers in Ghana. *The Journal of Social Issues*, 1963, *14*, 10–32.

Spaulding, S., & Flack, M. *The world's students in the United States: A review and evaluation of research on foreign students*. New York: Praeger, 1976.

Stewart, E. The simulation of cultural differences. *Journal of Communication*, 1966, *16*, 291–304.

Textor, R. (Ed.). *Cultural frontiers of the Peace Corps*. Cambridge, Massachusetts: MIT Press, 1966.

Triandis, H. *Interpersonal behavior*. Belmont, California: Wadsworth, 1977.

Trifonovitch, G. On cross-cultural orientation techniques. *Topics in Culture Learning*, 1973, *1*, 38–47.

Trifonovitch, G., Hamnett, M., Geschwind, N., & Brislin, R. *Experiential cross-cultural training*. Paper delivered at the combined meetings of the Nineteenth International Congress of Applied Psychology and the International Association for Cross-Cultural Psychology, Munich, Germany, August, 1978.

14

Culture and Mental Health Services

HOWARD N. HIGGINBOTHAM

Introduction

This chapter is concerned with culture and mental health services. Culture affects the design and delivery of mental health services in several important ways. First, culture causes stress in the individual, as when a society undergoes change, modernization, or disintegration. Cultural stress relates to the rate and pattern of psychological problems, and hence to the need for therapeutic resources. Second, community definitions of problem behavior and adjustment are culturally determined. These definitions form the framework for judging whether or not to seek treatment, and from what type of healer. Culture gives rise to certain attitudes toward deviancy. The reaction may be one of tolerance or abandonment and the sick role may be viewed as transient or permanent. Third, expectations that people maintain about effective therapy and psychiatric agencies are influenced by culture. Patient and family may hold well-defined beliefs about the appropriate setting, techniques, therapeutic manner, and patient role required to foster healing. Fourth, the organizational structure of a mental health facility also reflects cultural forces. Finally, the cultural context influences the relationship of psychiatric programs to other health professionals, government departments, national priorities and policies.

Mental health planners in developing nations confront these relationships

PERSPECTIVES ON CROSS-CULTURAL PSYCHOLOGY

when they introduce new programs. Implantation of Western care in non-Western settings highlights the dynamic relationship between culture and therapeutic systems. Unfortunately, many cultural factors are ignored or overlooked by planners. Training in "modern" psychiatry fosters insensitivity to indigenous life styles when it provides planners with preconceived notions of appropriate service delivery. Implementing Western treatment diverts professional attention to the pressing problems of manpower shortages, drug availability, funding for residential care, comprehensive services, and so forth.

This chapter provides an interdisciplinary view of the relationship between culture and psychiatry. The second part accounts for the presence of Western therapeutics in developing regions by looking at national conditions during colonial times and at present. The third part appraises the present status of psychiatry in emerging nations and focuses on planning procedures, program implementation, and intervention problems. This is the longest part because intervention problems are innumerable, and the process of introducing psychiatry is sharply questioned. After a summary of the requirements for a new approach, the fourth part introduces a culture assessment and accommmodation framework for studying communities and planning helping services. A survey instrument, *The Ethno-Therapy and Culture Accommodation Scale,* is offered for designing and evaluating treatment programs. It also serves to identify community values and resources that should be strengthened to promote community competency.

Origins of Western Derived Treatment Systems in Developing Countries

The Western visitor to developing nations of Asia, Africa, and South America is often surprised to find that "modern" psychiatry has a firm foothold there. The surprise comes from two sources. First, an assumption that traditional societies have less stress, and hence fewer psychiatric problems. Secondly, from the discovery that psychiatry is readily exported to the non-industrialized world. What accounts for the presence of Western services in these regions, and the continuing efforts to plan and expand them? This section answers this question by examining historical and present conditions.

HISTORICAL

Colonial rulers left their stamp on all phases of human activity. Not only were systems of religion, economics, and education forcefully transplanted, but European concepts of mental illness and its treatment were brought to the colonies as well (Lambo, 1978). Quite likely, the empire builders who incarcerated disturbed individuals along with common criminals, had far less sophisticated therapeutics than native healers. Indigenous therapists usually treated the chronically ill among their familiar surroundings, avoiding stigmatization (Lambo, 1978).

Custodial care began in Southeast Asia at the same time it got underway in the United States. H. B. Murphy's (1971) search of records in Singapore yielded an 1841 decree to "lose no time in commencing the erection of an Insane Hospital [p. 14]." Twenty years after it opened, this hospital, accommodating 100 inpatients for a Colony of 82,000, was providing Singapore with a higher psychiatric bed ratio than that of the United States. By 1829, nearby Penang had its "lunatic asylum," populated by Chinese, Portugese, and Indians (Tan & Wagner, 1971). This preceded by a decade the opening of city mental hospitals in New York and Boston. It paralleled Dorothea Dix's quest to hospitalize every "insane" individual, ending the era of moral treatment.

By the close of the nineteenth century, colonial architects had created rambling, custodial enclaves stretching from India, through Thailand, down the Malay Penninsula to the Dutch controlled archipelago of Indonesia (Haq, 1975; Tan & Wagner, 1971). These facilities, isolated and alien, represented the end of the road for most referrals (Harding, 1975). This "last resort" image is a historical residue that even today shapes the perceptions of people in this region.

Present Conditions

Given the colonial roots of psychiatry, what contemporary forces perpetuate and expand its availability? Four factors insure its continued importation and expansion: (*a*) governmental request based on national development needs; (*b*) the unsettling impact on mental health of modernization; (*c*) the rationale that psychiatric medicine is transcultural; and, (*d*) international consultation and training of indigenous personnel. The following section examines these four factors.

GOVERNMENTAL REQUEST BASED ON NATIONAL DEVELOPMENT NEEDS

The quest for economic development organizes national priorities in most "underdeveloped" countries. To the extent that social welfare services can contribute to national development goals, such services will receive government attention. Kiev (1972, 1976) and Benyoussef, Collomb, Diop, and Zollner (1975) have made a strong case for including mental health as a national priority. They use a cost–benefit logic to argue that mental *ill* health is detrimental to socioeconomic development. Disordered people have a smaller chance to participate in the full range of productive economic roles. The most unaffordable loss arises from mental problems among college students, technical specialists, and government leaders. A recent report estimates 40 million untreated cases of mental illness in the world's developing regions, and trends show increasing survival rates for brain damaged children and disorders of the aged (WHO, 1975). These governments may soon weigh more carefully the contention that mental health be afforded higher priority.

STRESS FROM SOCIOCULTURAL CHANGE

Despite present priorities, indigenous professionals, international consultants and researchers all agree that psychological problems are on the upswing as a consequence of modernization (Burton-Bradley, 1973; Kiernan, 1976; Marsella, 1978; Sangsingkeo, 1966). This belief is the second stimulus for health leaders to request and plan for Western systems of care.

Concern for the mental health effects of industrialization and rapid social change has been stimulated by an extensive literature on this topic by Western writers. Frequently singled out for study are instances where the fabric of a society cannot endure the pace of change, and increased social pathology follows (see Marsella's 1978 review). Leighton and his colleagues began, in the early 1950s, to lay a theoretical foundation linking community disorganization with individual impairment (Leighton, 1959). Echoing this theme, social observers in developing countries lament and fear the passing of traditional cultural forms and institutions (Kiev, 1976; Sangsingkeo, 1966). Kamal (1975) notes the widespread abandonment of the stable, traditional ways of life that gave people security, identity, and perhaps immunity from mental breakdown. He asks if it is possible to preserve spiritual elements of traditional life without affecting the desired national progress.

Urbanization has other consequences. Recent migrants are at "high risk" of disorder as they seek to adjust, usually without a firm economic base, to conditions of overcrowding, poor housing, status loss, sex role changes, depersonalization, and crime (Ignacio, 1976; Kiev, 1972, 1976; Marsella, Escudero, & Gordon, 1972). The break in cultural continuity, from rural to urban, traditional to modern, especially effects child-rearing patterns (Prasetyo, 1977), and the family's capacity to care for its ill (Kiernan, 1976). Moreover, with urbanization, symptom patterns seem to "modernize." Several psychiatrists have noticed a shift in symptoms among local inhabitants toward those found in technologically more developed societies (Burton-Bradley, 1973; Lambo, 1978; Ko, 1975).

The revolution of rising expectations has also been identified as a determinant of disorder rates. Parker and Kleiner (1966) and Marsella, et al. (1972) theorize how the gap between an individual's aspirations in life and what is actually achieved leads to stress and psychiatric symptoms. Widespread frustration accrues when people view the goods, services, and life styles of developed countries, yet lack the economic means for securing them (Sangsingkeo, 1966; Sanvictores, 1976). As the gap remains unbridged, the incidence of disorder increases, along with pressure to provide psychiatric assistance.

Some authors dispute the scenario just depicted. Murphy (1961) points out that mental health can be either worsened or bettered in situations of change. Inkeles and Smith (1970) found that individual stress is not an inherent accompaniment of industrialization and urbanization. These authors agree with Lambo (1978) that village life can be just as stressful as the urban center. Irrespective of whether or not modernization per se is related to increases in adjustment problems, mental health workers believe it to be the case. They ask assistance from international agencies for manpower training and expanded services.

PSYCHIATRIC MEDICINE AS TRANSCULTURAL

A third reason for exporting psychiatry is the strong confidence that physicians have in the cross-cultural suitability of their methods (Draguns & Phillips, 1972). Physician–investigators assume that the basic disease process is not culturally determined and that treatment successful in one culture, should be successful in another (e.g., German, 1972). Psychiatrists around the world feel that an expansion of mental health services is overdue, and when available, will be viable and accepted (e.g., Giel & Harding, 1976).

CONSULTATION AND TRAINING FROM ABROAD

Lastly, psychiatry's involvement in these regions is traced to ongoing consultation by international agencies such as the World Health Organization (WHO), and the fact that influential health leaders received most or all of their professional training in Europe or the United States. Supporting this second point, Tan (1971) revealed that psychiatry started in Malaysia when the first psychiatrist returned from training in England. I found that among the 80 psychiatric professionals I interviewed in 34 Southeast Asian agencies, 50% received graduate diplomas abroad. Sethi, Thacore, and Gupta (1968) state that most qualified psychiatrists in India are Western trained, and have tried unsuccessfully to introduce Western models of teaching and practice. The trend of sending trainees abroad, supported by fellowships from WHO, USAID, and others, has not abated, although early returnees have built specialized courses within home universities and hospitals. Without resources for ongoing research, knowledge and practice brought back quickly grows stale, necessitating further trips abroad for updating and adding to the "brain drain" problem.

Regional consultants for WHO Mental Health Division have made a lasting impression with their advise and evaluations (e.g., Kiernan, 1976; Stoller, 1959). These experts draw upon current thinking in their own countries to recommend models of service delivery. An excellent example is E. C. Dax, who in 1962 and 1969 filed assignment reports for expanding psychiatric programs in Malaysia. His recommendations were modeled after the service that he had established for the State of Victoria in Australia (Tan, 1971). WHO influences the shape of national programs through site visits, evaluation of existing facilities, Expert Committee reports, and experimental projects. Recently, a new administrative body was introduced for coordinating mental health programs at local, regional, and global levels (WHO, 1976).

Current advice and guidance from WHO is summarized in *Organization of Mental Health Services in Developing Countries* (WHO, 1975). This report draws upon principles of social psychiatry to guide future planning of member states. Personnel at WHO believe there are successful solutions to bringing effective care to the 90% who are without it, but only if the structure of mental health services becomes clearly specified and their national priority reversed (Harding, 1975). Regarding structure, four components are thought essential. The service should be *comprehensive,* with a diversity of treatments and units. It must provide for *continuity* of care, with patients handled by a team of multidisciplinary staff, and operate with a *preventive* focus while being *accessible* to potential users. From this introduction of the origins of Western treatment in the Third World, we turn attention toward the services themselves, and the methods by which they are planned and implemented.

Status of Mental Health Services in Developing Countries: Planning, Implementation, and Problems

To appraise the status of mental health delivery in the nonindustrialized world, three topics are considered: (*a*) methods of planning; (*b*) existing programs; and, (*c*) problems of practitioners. This section draws upon writings from the culture and mental health literature. Data from a recent field survey to Southeast Asia are presented to illuminate the special problems of agencies in developing settings.

PLANNING

Consideration should be given first to the basis upon which treatment services are founded. Who decides the target problems, the kinds of intervention, and the type of information necessary to make these decisions? The potential participants in mental health planning include patients, their families, community leaders, professionals, outside consultants, and administrators. The trend in the United States is towards an increasing degree of citizen involvement through surveys or citizen advisory groups (Milford, 1976). The World Health Organization (1975) follows this trend in an effort to increase the acceptability of new services. The services now available did not originate through rational planning or surveys of user needs. Rather, they derived from historical accidents of the colonial era, the orientation of visiting advisors, and the type of foreign education received by local professionals. These factors, in combination with economic and political realities, are the actual determinants of the scope and role of clinical psychiatry.

Despite these constraints, there have been needs assessments undertaken to guide some phase of planning and document existing problems. The most frequently used methods of case finding have been epidemiological surveys and descriptions of patients in contact with agencies (e.g., Jayasundera, 1969). The epidemiological approach was used successfully by Lin in the late 1940s to argue for the creation of psychiatric care and training in Taiwan (Lin, 1961). This method can be used to document the extent of untreated disorder, "residual deviance," and provides ammunition for lobbying to secure more funds, manpower and facilities. It may also give impetus to a "seeking mode" of therapy (i.e., going out to find clients where they live and work).

The second method of uncovering mental health needs is to tabulate detailed information on those who find their way into the treatment system. Demographic data are useful for learning which sex, age, income, and ethnic groups use facilities, and from what areas they are drawn. Diagnostic data are instructive to the extent that they reflect the need for different types of staff, specialized units, and programs. A variation of this method is the case register which is: a standard, precoded questionnaire that is administered to all new admissions or outpatients.

Although the epidemiological and hospital register approaches appear useful to planners, they are strongly criticized on methodological and conceptual grounds (Draguns, 1973, 1977). Problems using epidemiological surveys center on three questions: How to identify cases in non-referred populations? What constitutes disorder for a group? And, what symptoms are required to surpass the threshold for labeling an individual impaired?

Inpatient and outpatient surveys are burdened with even more limitations. Data are biased by availability of facilities, community knowledge, and acceptance. The chronically ill do not regularly visit outpatient departments, but become wandering vagrants and beggers (Giel, 1975). Those seeking treatment with psychological problems may go unrecorded when handled by general practitioners and native healers. Giel (1975) also suggests that impoverished people are less willing to invoke the "sick role" and seek treatment for suffering. The poor cannot afford the time it takes to be ill, nor the expense of traveling even to "free" health clinics.

Beyond the methodological shortcomings of needs assessment, is the fundamental issue of how to conceptualize psychological problems. The medical view assumes that behavior or symptoms themselves have a specific meaning, and can be interpreted and diagnosed as pathological in any context. However, is it possible to extract behaviors from a sociocultural context, and identify them as dysfunctional, without examining their meaning from within the culture itself? One way to approach this question is to compare an indigenous taxonomy with the Western nosology, a step taken by Leighton's team in Nigeria (Leighton, Lambo, Hughes, Leighton, Murphy, & Macklin, 1963). Although these investigators report finding some convergence among natives and psychiatrists in recognizing major disorders, some Western-identified syndromes were not labeled as illness, nor was there overlap in theories of etiology.

These studies are preliminary. The labeling process is interactive, requiring longitudinal investigations of how it arises, its impact on the individual and his group relations, perceptions of changeworthiness, and so forth. In order to truly compare Western conceptions of psychopathology with that of another culture, it is necessary to determine the functional significance of "disturbing" behavior in the two settings. First, identify the conditions under which an action leads to the evaluation of "deviance" (Ullmann & Krasner, 1975). In order to accomplish this, four factors should be considered simultaneously: (*a*) the behavior itself; (*b*) the person's status and role expectations; (*c*) the setting, time, and circumstances; and, (*d*) the attributions made by observers as to why the person behaved in that manner. Second, the consequences of the action are taken into account. What meaning did it have for the individual and those around him? Did it lead to social sanctions—a label, stigmatization, outcaste status? Was there no response or was there acceptance, or praise? It is no longer legitimate to do epidemiological studies cross-culturally by focusing on extracted "symptoms." Needs assessment must take into account the cultural context before proceeding with statements about the incidence of problems in a community.

This topic will be considered again on page 325. Next, attention is focused on the intended product of needs assessment—the programs to handle psychiatric needs.

PROGRAM IMPLEMENTATION

The reports of consultants and indigenous professionals reveal an overall lack of clarity in program objectives and implementation plans. These reports fail to conceptualize how systematic criteria can be used to structure services and evaluate outcome (Higginbotham, 1976). The World Health Organization sought to handle this confusion through the publication of guidelines taken from social psychiatry (WHO, 1975). Nevertheless, there remains an absence of systematic procedures for designing appropriate therapeutic programs. Reviewing the existing programs, three basic models for service design emerge. These are "traditional" psychiatry, the public health approach, and programs sensitive to local conditions.

The first model represents the direct extension of traditional North American or European psychiatry, unmodified, to non-Western settings. Typically, inpatient or outpatient facilities are added to existing hospitals, or clinics are given consultation on "modern methods" (Lin, 1961; Thebaud, 1971). Residential facilities are emphasized—although, these remove people from the general population, tie up personnel and resources, and perpetuate chronicity through long-term confinement (Baasher, 1975; Collomb, 1975; Thong, 1976).

Treatment within these settings ranges from custodial management to active programs of work "therapy" (e.g., farming, woodshop, sewing, and daily chores around the hospital). For those newly admitted, or "acute" ward residents, therapy follows classic psychiatric formulae of psychotropic drugs and electroconvulsive shock (ECT). One-to-one psychotherapy is less common. It is absent from the training of practitioners, a luxury in terms of time and resources, and generally ineffective in producing changes (Bolman, 1968; Koptagel, 1971; Mehryar & Khajavi, 1974).

A second approach to the design of therapeutic systems, the public health approach, is presently receiving the most attention among writers (Argandoña & Kiev, 1972; Kiev, 1972). Community mental health programs in the United States are fundamentally derived from the public health model (Rappaport, 1977). A key article by Mehryar and Khajavi (1974) delineates the features of this approach which are common to the majority of programs recently established in developing countries (Jayasundera, 1969; Osborne, 1969; Thebaud, 1971): (*a*) emphasis on primary prevention; (*b*) training of paraprofessionals; (*c*) extension of professional resources through consultation and education activities; and (*d*) mobilization of community resources to maintain the patient outside the hospital. To this list can be added the current thrust among WHO planners to encourage integration of psychiatric with general health delivery (e.g., Aragon, 1977).

A third approach, the "village system," is attaining increased popularity in Africa through the work of Lambo (1966, 1978) and others (Collomb, 1972; Osborne, 1969). Lambo's original idea for village treatment developed independently, in response to his problems in establishing a Western-type center in Nigeria. In the village system, psychiatric patients live with a relative in a traditional community especially provided to handle such patients close to the mental clinic. Treatment progress is a function of the natural therapeutic elements of the village (confession, dancing, rituals, tolerance), use of native healers in case management, permissive therapeutic relationships, Western drugs, and group psychotherapy.

The village system concept was a direct outgrowth of practitioners facing monumental barriers to the implementation of European-type programs. As a final means of describing the current status of psychiatry in traditional settings, the barriers and problems confronting it follow.

PROBLEMS

In contrast with the diversity of opinion regarding treatment designs, a consensus emerges in recognizing the practical problems in implementing any service system. Paralleling the problematic aspects of treatment delivery are two important issues. First, the appropriateness of using a Western standard of comparison. Second, the ethics of using psychiatry as a tool for culture change; especially when it leads to a discontinuity between the cultural context and proposed service.

Socioeconomic Barriers

The socioeconomic exigencies of today's developing nations preclude the attainment of psychiatry's four standards: comprehensive, preventive, accessible, and continuous services. The feasibility of meeting these standards are mitigated by forces operating at the national level. The most critical of these is the low priority assigned social welfare services in general, and psychiatric services in particular (Davis, 1975). Only programs for dental care receive less attention during national budgeting for health service items. Projects for industrialization, rural development, food production, and defense have top priority in settings where at present 70–80% of the citizens reside in rural areas (Kiev, 1972; Neki, 1973). Neki found in 1973 that, for the Southeast Asia Region, public health funding was .6% of the national expenditure for Indonesia, 2.7% for Thailand, and 7% for India. Mental health was the lowest allocation within these budgets, with the money used to maintain large, custodial hospitals.

The political aspect of establishing mental health care is a study in and of itself. With scarce resources, general health providers lobby against psychiatry as premature in places where infectious disease remains unchecked (Harding, 1975). Competition fosters unwillingness to coordinate with other agencies, leading to interdepartmental conflict and turmoil that stalls mental health legislation (Dasnanjali, 1971; Kiev, 1972). National legislation outlining mental health goals and guidelines is clearly needed (Burton-Bradley, 1971; Harding, 1975). A permanent, directorate-level body is recommended for giving mental health political clout within the government machinery (Kiernan, 1976).

Insufficient infrastructure within emerging nations also affects the health arena. The structure for making decisions and supervising their execution within institutions, simply does not exist. Butwell (1975), a political scientist, bolsters this point by revealing that governments in Southeast Asia have generally been ones of men, not of institutions. Political, economic, or health programs fall with the figures who proposed them when viable governing structures fail to develop. Mismanagement of resources by incompetent administrators is a related problem (Benyoussef, *et al.*, 1975).

Adding anthropological insight into the functioning of these institutions, Foster (1977) observes that the culture of bureaucracies shapes medical service delivery. No one wants to work in the village, therefore, 75–90% of the mental health resources serve 10–20% of the population (Kiernan, 1976; Krapf & Moser, 1966). On these occasions, professional and client culture fail to overlap (Foster, 1977).

Mental Health Resources

The second problem domain arises from the acutely felt lack of mental health resources (Krapf & Moser, 1966; Neki, 1973; WHO, 1975). The shortage of manpower across all helping professions, especially supervisors, is the most lamented scarcity (Chaudhry, 1975). This condition, more than the medical model itself, imposes a rigid stamp upon the nature of client care. Psychiatrists feel their treatment options constricted when they face a ratio of .01 specialist per 100,000 (Neki, 1973). The *First Report* of the WHO Expert Committee on Mental Health (1950) called for one psychiatrist per 20,000 to provide satisfactory treatment. It is not surprising that patient management consists chiefly of drug therapy and brief somatotherapeutics applied to acute cases.

The source of manpower shortages lie in the absence of training facilities and university departments to prepare professional careers (Kiernan, 1976; Wig, 1975). Prejudice within academic medicine and traditions of non-specialization are also curtailing influences (Carstairs, 1975; Maguidad, 1964). Training programs fail to evolve through lack of interest within general medicine. Krapf and Moser (1966), in a survey of 33 countries, found psychiatric specialization unattractive to medical students because of poor quality courses, unattractive working conditions, and low status and salary.

The consequence of having few training opportunities at home is that advanced degrees must be sought abroad. This frequently leads to a loss of manpower when trainees remain overseas, attracted by higher paying positions (Quah, 1977). Elite applicants, receiving training at home, often graduate only to slip away to jobs in industrialized countries.

Shortages of facilities and inpatient beds are also important deficits (Benyoussef, *et al.*, 1975). Industrialized societies make available anywhere from one to six beds per 1000 population (Kiernan, 1976). In 1959, the WHO consultant Stroller estimated that Thailand needed an additional 70,000 beds. Twenty years later, the follow-up consultant, Kiernan (1976), estimated that a fourfold increase was needed. With referrals feeding into these limited residential facilities, overcrowding reaches 50–250% (Neki, 1973). Most specialty care (e.g., forensic, retardation, child) is extremely rare, and unobtainable in rural zones (WHO, 1975; Krapf & Moser, 1966). In addition,

WHO (1975) foresees no prospect in the next 10–20 years of providing enough specialized workers to meet even the basic needs.

Community Acceptance of Services

The third problem domain, acceptability of services by the community, is undoubtably linked to the problem of scarce resources. The negative evaluation of psychiatric care is provoked by several factors. First, the mental hospital organization remains a closed system to the larger community. Alien and isolated, its inhabitants are cut off from the surrounding pattern of social life (Baasher, 1975; Draguns, 1973, Thebaud, 1971). A vicious circle perpetuates the isolation. Existing prejudices force families to wait a long time before admitting the patient, who by then may have firmly established maladaptive behaviors. The overburdened staff make little headway with these established patterns, so chronicity and institutionalization evolve. When it becomes apparent that there is little hope of recovery, the family loses contact and abandons the patient. This is especially true if the person was violent, or severely upset his family and community. Thus, the prophesy is fulfilled: The hospital becomes the institution of last resort, reserved for conditions of extreme disturbance.

Another factor influencing psychiatry's acceptance is the community's perception of deviance. Centuries-old beliefs about the causes of disorder attribute them to punishment for sin, violation of taboo, and witchcraft (Asuni, 1975). The traditional family's reaction is panic (Koptagel, 1971). They fear that the person has sinned, or that someone in the village is using sorcery to bring illness to their kinsmen (Lieban, 1973). From this world view, psychiatry has little to offer. Indigenous healers are called to propitiate the malevolent spirit, or cast off the malicious spell and return the patient to his normal self without stigma (Kiev, 1976; Torrey, 1972).

The attitudes of other health workers towards psychiatry also determines its acceptance in developing countries (Baasher, 1975). Carstairs (1975) found a high degree of prejudice and ignorance among the professors of medicine he visited in eight Southeast Asian countries. These medical leaders maintained "outdated ideas about psychiatry, regarding it as exclusively concerned with the treatment of the insane in mad houses [Carstairs, 1975, p. 109]." The World Health Organization (1975) regards negative attitudes held by health personnel, planners, and politicians as a major obstacle to the development of rational mental health services.

Mental Health Workers Perceptions of Problems

The array of problems just reviewed was derived from the reports of hospital administrators and visiting consultants. However, to date, no attempt has been made to survey the full range of hospital staff to determine their perceptions of the seriousness of these problems. To gain this perspective, interviews were undertaken in Taiwan and the five emerging countries of the Association of Southeast Asian Nations (ASEAN) group. Questions were posed regarding socioeconomic, resource, and acceptability barriers to 83 professionals working in 34 psychiatric facilities. Table 14.1 summarizes the distribution of staff respondents across countries, facilities, and professions. The sampling was not random, but representatives of the different disciplines were sought within the agencies visited.

Table 14.2 presents results of this survey. The opinions of psychiatrists are displayed along with those of the other professionals. Hospital directors ($N = 24$), psychiatrist supervisors ($N = 18$), and medical line staff ($N = 9$), make up the first group. Psychologists ($N = 17$), supervisory nurses ($N = 5$), and occupational therapists–social workers ($N = 10$) comprise the second. Each respondent was asked to evaluate 31 potential problems in terms of their seriousness. Twelve items from this questionnaire were selected for Table 14.2, and the percentages of respondents endorsing the item as moderately or very serious are given.

Table 14.2 reveals that the professionals interviewed substantially agree that the problems raised in the literature are applicable to their own work site. Moreover, except for four items, both sets of staff responded in an almost identical pattern. Specifically, 50% of the total staff felt that socioeconomic barriers (low national priority) were significant. The staff furthest from the administrative level viewed money for present treatment as less of a problem, but concurred with the others that it was a problem for the future. The lack of resources was strongly endorsed by all, with lack of trained administrators being the highest endorsed item. Professional role made a difference regarding perceptions of treatment supplies. The nonmedical respondents apparently lack the tools of their trade—psychological tests, rehabilitation items—whereas drug supplies, the staple for psychiatrists, appear more available. The lack of a positive working relationship with other agencies and health professionals seems to be the least acutely felt problem. Those interviewed did not uniformly feel the intense prejudice from the leaders of medicine that Carstairs (1975) found in his earlier visit to

TABLE 14.1

Occupation of Respondents for Questionnaire Number 2: Staff Perceptions of Agency

Country	Psychiatrist	Psychologist	Social worker–occupational therapist	Nurse	Total
Taiwan	6(4)[a]	1(1)	1(2)	2(2)	10
Philippines	12(8)	5(4)	2(2)	3(3)	22
Thailand	10(6)	5(4)	1(1)	0	16
Malaysia	6(4)	2(2)	5(3)	0	13
Singapore	2(1)	1(1)	1(1)	0	4
Indonesia	15(6)	3(3)	0	0	18
Total	51(29)	17(15)	10(9)	5(5)	83(34)

[a] The number in parenthesis is the number of facilities from which responses were obtained.

TABLE 14.2
Percentage of Staff Endorsing the Stated Problem as Moderately Serious or Very Serious at Their Facility.

Problems	Psychiatrists	Other professionals
Socioeconomic		
1. Low priority; lack of help from government	52%	50%
2. Not enough money for present treatment	51%	38%
3. Not enough money for future treatment	57%	53%
Resources		
4. Lack of staff	63%	60%
5. Lack of administrators	70%	68%
6. Too many patients	57%	66%
7. Treatment supplies not enough	39%	60%
Professional isolation		
8. Lack of relationship with other agencies	41%	34%
9. Other professionals do not support	37%	22%
Acceptibility		
10. People do not know about or understand the program	63%	69%
11. Used as a last chance	51%	47%
12. People returning home are stigmatized	75%	78%
13. Folk healers are preferred	54%	41%

this area. What was confirmed is the perceived alienation and stigmatization of psychiatric care. Endorsement was 75 and 78% for the questionnaire item 12 in Table 14.2: "Patients returning home have problems because people know they were in a mental hospital." This is coupled with staff agreement that people do not know about the treatment program, and usually seek out folk doctors instead of visiting their agencies. In summary, these staff perceptions add credence to those concerns highlighted in the literature.

ISSUES IN DESIGNING WESTERN-ORIENTED MENTAL HEALTH SYSTEMS

A second set of concerns spring from an awareness that modern psychiatry may be unacceptable because its underlying assumptions are incongruent with cultural beliefs. The use of psychiatry as a force of innovation and culture change raises serious ethical questions when community members have no influence in the direction of that change. The impact of innovation is also questioned when it poses a threat to existing social relationships, and disrupts the integrated continuity of values and institutions. This section will explore these issues as a prelude to offering a potential solution to the dilemmas outlined.

Modern Psychiatry and Western Values

Visiting consultants and their native counterparts share a common education. Undergirding it are philosophical assumptions about the nature of man specific to the cultures of Europe and America. These assumptions have given shape to the course of psychiatric thought and practice. Definitions of disorder, intervention, and therapy goals, are all determined by culture-specific values, just as they are in traditional societies of Africa and Asia (Collomb, 1975; Neki, 1973). Many writers have commented on the cultural bias of modern psychiatry (e.g., Pande, 1968). For example, the emphasis in psychoanalysis on the growth of the individual at the expense of the larger social group, might be viewed as somewhat odd by members of kinship and group-centered cultures.

Draguns (1973) maintains that psychotherapy serves culture as a process of resocializing the person back to expected norms. To the extent that cultures differ, the goal and modality of resocialization differ as well. Indigenous professionals, trained abroad in psychotherapy, return home with interventions appropriate only to a sliver of the population whose educational backgrounds overlap their own. Overtrained returnees may have to unlearn newly acquired methods, and seek out approaches more congruent with the needs encountered (Kiev, 1972).

Modern Psychiatry and Culture Change

The preceding paragraphs noted that each system of curing is geared to fulfilling the sociocultural needs of its society. It cannot be transferred intact to another society (Asuni, 1975). With the transference well under way, something must be happening. Is the curing system being modified? Are elements in the host society changing to accept a better fit? Suggestions on how to modify psychiatry to make it acceptable have been offered recently (e.g., Asuni, 1975; Benyoussef, *et al.*, 1975). The cultural change potential of psychiatric interventions is considered first.

What elements in the host culture might suffer alteration with the introduction of Western care? A review of ethnographic and transcultural writings suggests several possibilities. First, prevailing notions about disease may be replaced (Kiev, 1972; Neki, 1973; Wolff, 1965). Second, cultural values and attitudes may come under attack. Ari Kiev (1976) warns against "psychiatric imperialism." Yet, at the same time, he advocates psychiatrists' involvement in leadership selection, educational planning, and suppression of tribal customs that impede the development of psychological autonomy among the young. Such customs, Kiev reasons, hinder modernization.

Social relationships are a third cultural element at risk of being altered. An established psychiatric service makes explicit role demands and the medical system is hierarchical. It prescribes role relationships among levels of staff, as well as between staff and patients, their families, and involved community agents. In taking the responsibility of caring for patients, the medical system competes with, and undermines, an intricate pattern of interpersonal relationships (Lewis, 1955). Most often, the family's authority for making decisions and overseeing patient recovery is sacrificed for the sake of medical expediency (Clark, 1959; Prasetyo, 1977).

Fourth, introducing services has implications for strengthening or weakening prevailing patterns of power within a society (Lewis, 1955; Lieban, 1973). In the West, some writers characterize psychiatry as a device for political and social control. They argue that its goals are to maintain the status quo, or to discredit and silence opponents of those in power (Laing, 1967). At present, the impact of modernization has been to stratify communities into a small Westernized elite, and a vast majority of traditional farmers and peasants (Neki, 1973). The authorities control how the treatment system will be introduced and used, ensuring that, at minimum, it will not disrupt the present status configuration.

The final element of a culture that may suffer alteration is the system of indigenous healing. The net result of importing a formal system of therapy may be less help for those in need. This arose in the United States when services to the poor were actually reduced as agencies stopped treating these clients and instead, referred them to the new community mental health centers which had little to offer as well (Rappaport, 1977). Creating an ineffective new institution results in less support for the community when legislation, official disapproval, and referral patterns combine to undermine the existing healing network. Native healing institutions are relied upon by all layers of society (Hartog, 1972; Jahoda, 1961). They are curative, serve important social functions, and assist in mediating the stress of rapid social change. Yet, practitioners of native medicine are dying out in many areas (Foster, 1977; Hartog, 1972). The formal programs intended to replace them are scarce, not well accepted, and suffer from other deficiencies enumerated earlier.

Cultural Continuity

The critical feature of folk healing that Western methods lack, is continuity with the values, beliefs, and customs of the local setting. This points to the major deficit of modern psychiatry, and indicates its most damaging repercusion—the disruptive effect on an integrated set of cultural elements governing perception and response to mental health problems. It still remains, however, to articulate the specific ways in which indigenous treatment provides cultural continuity and modern medicine does not.

The cultural continuity of traditional medicine begins with the folk healer. His personal manner, rituals, problems explanation, even style of dress and nonverbal messages, are all appropriate to the expectations of patient and audience (Clark, 1959; Frank, 1973; Kleinman, 1977). Meeting the patient's expectations of therapy, the healer ensures mobilization of hope, faith, and expectancy of success. He thus increases the chances of a positive outcome (Higginbotham, 1977). The folk healer is an observant member of his community. He knows how to inspire a group confidence in his cure and can mobilize family and friends as resources for the distressed person (Clark, 1959; Dean & Thong, 1972; Marriott, 1955). The traditional doctor provides what is desperately desired; whether it be firm assurance of cure, absolute faith in the medicine prescribed (Carstairs, 1955), or an extensive community ceremony to solve interpersonal disputes, cleanse, and reintegrate a person alienated from his kinsmen (Chen, 1975; Turner, 1964).

Traditional medicine maintains continuity with culture because the assumptions on which it operates are at the cultural core of society. Beliefs about mental illness are intimately linked with conceptions of religion, social values, norms, and ideals of human relationships (Lieban, 1973). These shared beliefs determine the nature of traditional medicine, and provide the medical framework for interpreting symptoms and guiding social action in response to them.

In summary, the issue of cultural continuity is critical for understanding the disruptive potential and failure of Western psychiatry. When modern medicine is imported to traditional societies, it fails to provide the ritual and philosophical basis considered necessary by members of such societies (Chen, 1975). Focusing exclusively on the disease process, rather than the total human, villagers view Western treatment as depersonalizing, mechanistic, and fragmented. Scientific doctors seem impersonal and uncaring of family and friends (Clark, 1959; Chen, 1975). Lambo (1978) advises that in Africa, Western medicine and modern science do not satisfy the basic metaphysical and social needs of many people, no matter how sophisticated they are. He concludes that "In Africa, healing is an integral part of society and religion, a matter in which the whole community is involved. To understand African psychotherapy one must understand African thought and its social roots [Lambo, 1978, p. 32]."

A Proposed Solution: The Culture Assessment and Culture Accommodation Approach to Planning Helping Services

ATTEMPTS TO COPE WITH AGENCY PROBLEMS

The current status of mental health delivery in developing countries is characterized by the limitations, problems, and sociocultural barriers effecting its introduction and acceptance. Low national priority, organizational deficits, shortages of training, manpower and treatment facilities, community ignorance and rejection of psychiatric care, all combine to severely restrict the availability and use of treatment centers. Recently, however, ethnopsychiatry has sought to come to terms with these problems (Draguns, 1975; Kiev, 1972, 1976; Lebra, 1976). The village system concept in Nigeria and Senegal is a clear example. In terms of training, Wig (1975) suggests that the best results arise when it is provided within the home country. If home training does not exist, then students should attend centers in neighboring countries where the culture and problems are relatively similar. Planning new services in strict collaboration with local leaders is an important recommendation (Bhaskaran, 1975). Making services accessible in terms of location, reduced waiting, and affordable fees, increases acceptability (Foster, 1977). Programs become more desirable when their personnel share a common background and language with the clients (Schmidt, 1965), or show the family dramatic results, quickly releasing the patient (Asuni, 1975). My (1976) survey of the literature found three strategies for dealing with problems of innovation:

1. The Western trained professional has most success as a consultant.
2. Integration of new services with well accepted helping systems appears advisable.
3. Model projects are useful for testing and demonstrating the efficacy of new programs.

THE REQUIREMENTS OF A NEW MODEL

Given the problematic status of mental health delivery, and the brave but fragmented attempts to adapt Western care, there remains a pressing need for a unified, culture-specific approach to guide the design of helping services. This new approach must be capable of resolving the critical dilemmas: resource availability, ethics, community acceptability, effectiveness, and continuity with culture. A proposal is now offered with solutions to these issues through a cultural assessment and accommodation framework. This framework emerged from an attempt to integrate concepts from the culture and psychopathology literature with the practices of professionals working in non-Western settings (Higginbotham, 1976). The purpose is to give practitioners explicit guidelines for planning and evaluating services from the perspective of the client's cultural context. To prepare guidelines, questions must first be directed toward the recipient community. A comprehensive set of questions was formulated based upon findings in the culture and mental health literature.

FOUNDATIONS OF THE CULTURE ASSESSMENT MODEL

The field of culture and psychopathology provides a point of departure for determining attributes of a cultural group prior to the design of a mental health system (Draguns, 1979). The literature offers three contributions: (*a*) culture-specific (emic) definitions of abnormality; (*b*) sociocultural causes of disorder; and (*c*) sociocultural responses to disorder, including healing and psychotherapy processes.

These three domains can be transformed into a set of assessment questions and administered through a survey of community recipients. Information from the survey serves as the foundation for determining the scope and operations of a mental health system. Briefly, the design of an emic program must follow an assessment of: cultural perceptions of problem behavior; norms of individual adjustment; the folk healing practices and network; and expected community relationship with the agency.

Analysis of Culturally Defined Problem

A typology of problem behavior is the first assessment component. One element in the typology is the classification scheme used by people to identify and label disturbing behaviors. An important consideration is the process of person–group interaction, and the covert rules governing the assignment of a label (Ullmann & Krasner, 1975). No behavior per se is deviant, but is evaluated as abnormal by an observer based on its violations of social expectations (Draguns, 1979).

Another element of the problem typology maps the perceived etiology of each disorder type. Some conditions are thought to be caused by a single agent, whereas others are attributed to multiple sources, such as sorcery, violation of tribal laws, family disharmony, ancestral ghosts, etc. (Cawte, 1974; Chen, 1975; Lebra, 1976). Intervention locations are determined by the problem's perceived origin. The therapist can either direct his ministrations toward the person, social group, supernatural world, or physical environment.

The last problematic typologic element is the social reaction or attitude toward each "type" of deviant. Social attitude may be the most crucial determinant of outcome (Lambo, 1978; Sangsingkeo, 1958; Waxler, 1974). In some cases, the individual is not held responsible, maintains family support, and quickly sheds the sick role (Dean & Thong, 1972; Waxler, 1974). In other cases, particularly when the patient has been violent or causes repeated suffering, this process is reversed. When the sick role stays with the person, along with an attitude of rejection, he is often banished from the village and institutionalized (Colson, 1971).

Norms of Personal Adjustment

The second component of culture assessment examines values and expectations of adjustment in the community. Treatment objectives are determined by knowledge of social roles and standards of interpersonal relations. This has been ignored in the past, with planners uncritically adopting therapeutic goals taken from medical criteria or personality theories. The behavioral qualities a person should ideally possess by community consensus are termed *areté* (Goldschmidt, 1971). It is towards the cultural *areté* that therapy attempts to resocialize the nonconformist. The *areté* is valuable as a general guideline. However, using it as the criterion of outcome should be balanced against ethical considerations of individual rights, client consent, and the long range benefits for the person in a changing society.

Expected Ways and Means of Curing

Analysis of the helping network is the third cultural assessment component. An attempt is made to understand how the *means* of social influence, employed by a therapist, brings about resocialization to community goals. Culture members have set expectations about the techniques of healing (Quah, 1977). These expectancies must be tapped and included in program operations to avoid the adverse effects of unmet expectations (Higginbotham, 1977).

Some writers postulate a universality in the behavior influence tactics used by therapists (Draguns, 1975; Frank, 1973; Torrey, 1972). The techniques are continuous with the style of social control relied upon in everyday life, whether authoritarian or self-generated (Draguns, 1975). A typology of tactics includes providing expert testimony, placebo manipulations, principles of reward and punishment, and could also involve physical exercise, or altered states of consciousness (Higginbotham, 1976).

The tactics of behavior change are put into operation formally through certain community sanctioned roles, including folk healer or shaman. However, other individuals in relationship with the identified patient may also apply social influence. These *sources of influence* are recognized as legitimate change agents due to their expertise, authority within the village, or kinship with the person (Tharp & Wetzel, 1969). Assessing the referral process is important for determining when the family will take the disturbed person to which source of influence.

Expected Community Relationship with Agency

Appraising the community's expected relationship with the agency is the final assessment component. Community members hold expectations about the preferred type of agency, and the nature of their interaction with it. Program acceptability is dependent upon the extent to which these are met. An example is the issue of community control. Have local leaders been called upon to sanction the service or review program objectives?

A second question concerns expectations of activities and organizational structures. Recipients have preferences regarding location, cost, treatment within the home, types of service units, and a facility's community-like atmosphere. The most important consideration is the family's expected involvement with the patient during agency contact. Families may insist on having a relative remain with the patient in the hospital and play an active role in rehabilitation (Kiev, 1972; Tung, 1972).

Community members have definite ideas about agency personnel. The question arises if indigenous healers should be allowed to care for certain patients or be employed as consultants (Wittkower & Warnes, 1974). Also, what knowledge are staff expected to have of folk disorders, their causes and cures? Finally, the importance of personnel characteristics like social distance, faith in therapy, and professional aloofness should be determined (Clark, 1959; Lieban, 1973; Marriott, 1955).

A Framework for Culture Assessment: The Ethnotherapy and Culture Accommodation Scale

PROCEDURES

The previous section laid the foundation for gathering culture-specific mental health data. A framework for organizing this information would be helpful to the planner. For this purpose, the author proposes the development of an Ethno-Therapy and Culture Accommodation Scale (ETCAS). Four phases of research are required to construct and validate the instrument. In Phase 1, "domain definition" or open-ended interviews of community leaders and knowledgeable sources are conducted to generate items for ETCAS. The topics addressed by the interviews include perceptions of problem behavior and causes, norms of adjustment, expected treatment techniques and healers, and expected relationship with agency. Phase 2 consists of an analysis of survey data to construct weighted items. The practices and expectations gathered from informants would be transformed into statement items. These items would then be compiled into a questionnaire and readministered to community informants. Weightings are assigned to each item by asking the respondents to endorse the statement in terms of their significance in providing appropriate care.

Phase 3 is the application phase. The weighted items are grouped according to priority, and summary statements are drafted indicating which mental health considerations are deemed most important. At this point, an existing program can be assessed in terms of its degree of congruity with ETCAS. Finally, Phase 4 appraises the criterion and predictive validity of the instrument. One way would be to correlate ETCAS scores obtained from evaluating a psychiatric facility with independent measures of accommodation and indices of community satisfaction.

APPLICATIONS

Potential uses of the ETCAS are threefold. First, it may be used in agency evaluation to determine the congruity between the community's expressed needs and the services actually provided. Existing programs may be modified to increase their attractiveness, use, and client satisfaction. Second, new programs can be designed based on community criteria. An accommodating treatment system would not usurp present indigenous care. Instead, it would fill the gaps where the community recognizes treatment is needed but is unavailable (Kiev, 1972).

Third, ETCAS may be used in identifying existing resources that need to be strengthened. This use closely follows the formulation for community psychology offered by Rappaport (1977). The aim of professional helpers is to aid in developing existing community values and strengths. This is done by making society's resources available to needy groups based on cultural relativity and diversity. In this manner, the ETCAS functions as an instrument for permitting a social group to enhance its inherent competency and retain its cultural continuity.

Conclusion

This chapter has given a broad overview of psychiatry and culture in developing regions of the world. The crux of the overview is that Western-style services are inappropriate, unaffordable, far beyond the horizon in terms of manpower, and potentially disruptive of integrated elements in the host culture. What *is* required is a treatment system continuous with cultural beliefs and existing patterns of helping. Through a cultural assessment, looking at community definitions of disorder and helping, a clear understanding of appropriate intervention can be established. The Ethno-Therapy and Culture Accommodation Scale is proposed for gathering and analyzing this information. As a device for judging program congruity with community preferences, ETCAS serves as a guideline for creating human services with a high level of cultural sensitivity. Secondly, ETCAS identifies healing networks that may be strengthened by the allocation of additional resources. The end product, in harmony with the aims of community psychology, is to create competent communities—communities capable of actualizing the values and goals they select for themselves.

References

Aragon, E. *Manual of operations on control of mental disorders.* Republic of the Philippines, Department of Health, Manila, 1977.
Argandoña, M., & Kiev, A. *Mental health in the developing world.* New York: The Free Press, 1972.
Asuni, T. Existing concepts of mental illness in different cultures and different forms of treatment. In T. A. Baasher, G. Carstairs, R. Giel & F. Hassler, (Eds.), *Mental health services in developing countries.* Geneva: WHO, 1975.

Baasher, T. A. Principles of psychiatric care. In T. A. Baasher, G. Carstairs, R. Giel & F. Hassler, (Eds.), *Mental health services in developing countries.* Geneva: WHO, 1975.

Benyoussef, A., Collomb, H., Diop, B., & Zollner, H. Demographic and economic aspects of mental health care in developing countries. In T. A. Baasher, G. Carstairs, R. Giel & F. Hassler, (Eds.), *Mental health services in developing countries.* Geneva: WHO, 1975.

Bhaskaran, K. Administration and organization. In T. A. Baasher, G. Carstairs, R. Giel & F. Hassler, (Eds.), *Mental health services in developing countries.* Geneva: WHO, 1975.

Bolman, W. Cross-cultural psychotherapy. *American Journal of Psychiatry,* 1968, *124,* 1237–1244.

Burton-Bradley, B. G. Psychiatry and the law in the developing country with special reference to the Territory of Papua and New Guinea. *Transcultural Psychiatric Research Review,* 1971, *18,* 140–144.

Burton-Bradley, B. G. Kava-Kava: Mental health in Papua, New Guinea. *World Medical Journal,* 1973, *20,* 110–112.

Butwell, R. *Southeast Asia: A political introduction.* New York: Praeger, 1975.

Carstairs, G. M. Medicine and faith in rural Rajasthan. In B. D. Paul (Ed.), *Health, culture and community.* New York: Russell Sage, 1955.

Carstairs, G. M. Psychiatric problems in developing countries. *British Journal of Psychiatry,* 1973, *123,* 271–277.

Carstairs, G. M. Psychiatry in basic medical education. In T. A. Baasher, G. Carstairs, R. Giel & F. Hassler, (Eds.), *Mental health in developing countries.* Geneva: WHO, 1975.

Cawte, J. *Medicine is law.* Honolulu, Hawaii: Univ. Press of Hawaii, 1974.

Chaudhry, M. R. Staffing requirements. In T. A. Baasher, G. Carstairs, R. Giel & F. Hassler, (Eds.), *Mental health in developing countries.* Geneva: WHO, 1975.

Chen, P. C. Y. Medical systems in Malaysia: Cultural bases and differential use. *Social Science and Medicine,* 1975, *9,* 171–180.

Clark, M. *Health in the Mexican-American culture.* Berkeley: Univ. of California Press, 1959.

Collomb, H. *Psychiatries sans psychiatres.* Cairo: Ed. Etudes Medicales, 1972.

Collomb, H. The future of psychiatry in Africa. *Transcultural Psychiatric Research Review,* 1975, *12,* 171–174.

Colson, A. C. The perception of abnormality in a Malay village. In N. N. Wagner & E. S. Tan (Eds.), *Psychological problems and treatment in Malaysia.* Kuala Lumpur: Univ. of Malaya Press, 1971.

Dasnanjali, R. Special problems in providing mental retardation services in a developing country. In R. De la Fuente & M. N. Weisman (Eds.), *5th World Congress of Psychiatry.* New York: American Elsevier, 1971.

Davis, A. J. Psychiatric problems and services in Kenya. *International Nursing Review,* 1975, *22,* 25–27.

Dax, E. *Assignment report for Malaya.* World Health Organization, Western Pacific Region, Report Number 303, Manila, Philippines, 1962.

Dax, E. *Assignment report for Malaysia.* World Health Organization, Western Pacific Region, Report Number 58, Manila, Philippines, 1969.

Dean, S. R., & Thong, D. Shamanism versus psychiatry in Bali, "Isle of the Gods,": Some modern implications. *American Journal of Psychiatry,* 1972, *129,* 91–94.

Draguns, J. G. Comparisons of psychopathology across cultures. *Journal of Cross-Cultural Psychology,* 1973, *4,* 9–47.

Draguns, J. G. Resocialization into culture: The complexities of taking a worldwide view of psychotherapy. In R. W. Brislin & W. J. Lonner (Eds.), *Cross-cultural perspectives on learning.* New York: Wiley, 1975.

Draguns, J. G. Advances in the methodology of cross-cultural psychiatric assessment. *Transcultural Psychiatric Research Review,* 1977, *14,* 125–143.

Draguns, J. G. Psychological disorders of clinical severity. In H. C. Triandis & J. G. Draguns

(Eds.), *Handbook of cross-cultural psychology* (Vol. 5). Rockleigh, New Jersey: Allyn & Bacon, 1979.

Draguns, J. G., & Phillips, L. *Culture and psychopathology: The quest for a relationship.* Morristown, New Jersey: General Learning Press, 1972.

Foster, G. M. Medical anthropology and international health planning. *Social Science and Medicine,* 1977, *11,* 527–534.

Frank, J. *Persuasion and healing.* New York: Schocken Books, 1973.

German, A. C. Aspects of clinical psychiatry in Sub-Saharan Africa. *British Journal of Psychiatry,* 1972, *212,* 461–479.

Giel, R. Problems of assessing the needs of the population. In T. A. Baasher, G. Carstairs, R. Giel & F. Hassler, (Eds.), *Mental health in developing countries.* Geneva: WHO, 1975.

Giel, R., & Harding, T. W. Psychiatric priorities in developing countries. *British Journal of Psychiatry,* 1976, *128,* 513–522.

Goldschmidt, W. *Areté*—motivation and models for behavior. In I. Galdston (Ed.), *The interface between psychiatry and anthropology.* New York: Brunner/Mazel, 1971.

Haq, S. M. Past and present trends in the development of psychiatric services in peninsular Malaysia. *The Family Practitioner,* 1975, *2*(1), 4–9.

Harding, T. W. Mental health services in the developing countries: Some issues involved. In T. A. Baasher, G. Carstairs, R. Giel & F. Hassler, (Eds.), *Mental health in developing countries.* Geneva: WHO, 1975.

Hartog, J. The intervention system for mental and social deviants in Malaysia. *Social Science and Medicine,* 1972, *6,* 211–220.

Higginbotham, H. A conceptual model for the delivery of psychological services in non-Western settings. In R. Brislin (Ed.), *Topics in culture learning* (Vol. 4). Hololulu, Hawaii: East–West Center, 1976.

Higginbotham, H. Culture and the role of client expectancy in psychotherapy. In R. Brislin & M. Hamnett (Eds.), *Topics in culture learning* (Vol. 5). Honolulu, Hawaii: East-West Center, 1977.

Ignacio, L. Effects of urbanization on mental health. *Philippine Journal of Mental Health,* 1976, *7,* 12–15.

Inkeles, A., & Smith, D. The fate of personal adjustment in the process of modernization. *International Journal of Comparative Sociology,* 1970, *11,* 81–114.

Jahoda, G. Traditional healers and other institutions concerned with mental illness in Ghana. *International Journal of Social Psychiatry,* 1961, *77,* 245–268.

Jayasundera, M. G. Mental health surveys in Ceylon. In W. Caudill & T. Y. Lin (Eds.), *Mental health research in Asia and the Pacific.* Honolulu, Hawaii: East–West Center, 1969.

Kamal, A. Principles of preventive action in mental health care. In T. A. Baasher, G. Carstairs, R. Giel & F. Hassler, (Eds.), *Mental health in developing countries.* Geneva: WHO, 1975.

Kiernan, W. E. S. Strengthening of mental health services in Thailand. Geneva: *WHO Field Visit Report,* South-East Asian Region, Mental Health Division, Report No. 34, August, 1976.

Kiev, A. *Transcultural psychiatry.* New York: Free Press, 1972.

Kiev, A. Psychiatry programs for the developing countries. In B. H. Kaplan & A. H. Leighton (Eds.), *Further explorations in social psychiatry.* New York: Basic Books, 1976.

Kleinman, A. M. Explaining the efficacy of indigenous therapies: The need for interdisciplinary research. *Culture, Medicine and Psychiatry,* 1977, *1,* 133–134.

Ko, Y.-H. Student mental health problems in two different industrialized cities. *Acta Psychologia Taiwanica,* 1975, *17,* 25–38.

Koptagel, G. Rehabilitation of the mentally handicapped in Turkey: Past and present. *Social Science and Medicine,* 1971, *5,* 603–606.

Krapf, E. E., & Moser, J. M. A survey of mental health resources. In H. P. David (Ed.), *International trends in mental health.* New York: McGraw-Hill, 1966.

Laing, R. D. *The politics of experience.* New York: Pantheon, 1967.

Lambo, T. A. Patterns of psychiatric care in developing African countries: The Nigerian program. In H. R. David (Ed.), *International trends in mental health.* New York: McGraw-Hill, 1966.

Lambo, T. A. Psychotherapy in Africa. *Human Nature,* 1928, *1,* 32–39.

Lebra, W. P. (Ed.). *Culture-bound syndromes, ethnopsychiatry, and alternate therapies.* Honolulu, Hawaii: Univ. Press of Hawaii, 1976.

Leighton, A. H. *My name is Legion.* New York: Basic Books, 1959.

Leighton, A. H., Lambo, T. A., Hughes, C. C., Leighton, D. C., Murphy, J. M., & Macklin, D. B. *Psychiatric disorder among the Yoruba.* Ithaca, New York: Cornell Univ. Press, 1963.

Lewis, O. Medicine and politics in a Mexican village. In B. D. Paul (Ed.), *Health, culture and community.* New York: Russell Sage, 1955.

Lieban, R. Medical anthropology. In J. Honigmann (Ed.), *Handbook of social and cultural anthropology.* Chicago: Rand McNally, 1973.

Lin, T.-Y. Evolution of a mental health programme in Taiwan. *American Journal of Psychiatry,* 1961, *117,* 961–971.

Maguidad, L. C. Psychiatry in the Philippines. *American Journal of Psychiatry,* 1964, *121,* 21–25.

Marriott, M. Western medicine in a village of Northern India. In B. D. Paul (Ed.), *Health, culture and community.* New York: Russell Sage, 1955.

Marsella, A. J. Modernization: Consequences for the individual. In D. Hoopes, P. Pedersen, & G. Renwick (Eds.), *Overview of intercultural education, training, and research: Special research areas* (Vol. 3). La Grange, Illinois: Intercultural Network, Inc., 1978.

Marsella, A. J., Escudero, M., & Gordon, P. Stresses, resources, and symptom patterns in urban Filipino men. In W. Lebra (Ed.), *Transcultural research in mental health.* Honolulu, Hawaii: East–West Center, 1972.

Mehryar, A., & Khajavi, F. Some implications of a community mental health model for developing countries. *International Journal of Social Psychiatry,* 1974, *21,* 45–52.

Milford, J. T. Human service needs assessment: Three non-epidemiological approaches. *Canadian Psychological Review,* 1976, *17,* 260–269.

Murphy, H. M. B. Social change and mental health. In *Causes of mental disorders: A review of the epidemiological knowledge.* New York: Milbank Memorial Fund, 1961.

Murphy, H. M. B. The beginnings of psychiatric treatment in the Peninsula. In N. N. Wagner & E. S. Tan (Eds.), *Psychological problems and treatment in Malaysia.* Kuala Lumpur: Univ. of Malaya, 1971.

Neki, J. S. Psychiatry in South-East Asia. *British Journal of Psychiatry,* 1973, *123,* 257–269.

Osborne, O. H. The Yoruba village as a therapeutic community. *Journal of Health and Social Behavior,* 1969, *10,* 187–200.

Pande, S. K. The mystique of Western psychotherapy: An Eastern interpretation. *Journal of Nervous and Mental Disease,* 1968, *146,* 425–432.

Parker, S., & Kleiner, R. J. *Mental illness in the urban Negro community.* New York: Free Press, 1966.

Prasetyo, J. *Child psychiatry in Indonesia.* Working paper, Subdivision of Child Psychiatry, Department of Psychiatry, School of Medicine, Univ. of Indonesia, Jakarta, 1977.

Quah, S. R. *The unplanned dimensions of health care in Singapore: Traditional healers and self-medication.* Sociology working paper No. 62. Department of Sociology, Univ. of Singapore, 1977.

Rappaport, J. *Community psychology: Values, research, action.* New York: Holt, 1977.

Sangsingkeo, P. Community attitudes in Thailand toward social treatment. *Journal of Social Therapy,* 1958, *4,* 197–200.

Sangsingkeo, P. Mental health in developing countries. In H. P. David (Ed.), *International trends in mental health.* New York: McGraw-Hill, 1966.

Sanvictores, L. L. Mental health and economic growth. *Philippine Journal of Mental Health,* 1976, *7,* 18–21.

Schmidt, K. E. Communication problems with psychiatric patients in the multilingual society of Sarawak. *Psychiatry,* 1965, *28,* 229–233.

Sethi; B. B., Thacore, V. R., & Gupta, V. R. Changing patterns of culture and psychiatry in India. *American Journal of Psychotherapy,* 1968, *22,* 46–54.

Stoller, A. Assignment report on mental health situation in Thailand. WHO project: Thailand 17, South-East Asia Region, Mental Health Division, Report No. 7, February, 1959.

Tan, E. S., & Wagner, N. N. Psychiatry in Malaysia. In N. N. Wagner & E. S. Tan (Eds.), *Psychological problems and treatment in Malaysia.* Kuala Lumpur: Univ. of Malaya Press, 1971.

Tharp, R., & Wetzel, R. *Behavior modification in the natural environment.* New York: Academic Press, 1969.

Thebaud, E. F. Some innovations in the establishment of psychiatric services in a developing country: The Liberian experiences. In R. De la Fuente & M. N. Weisman (Eds.), *5th World Congress of Psychiatry.* New York: American Elsevier, 1971.

Thong, D. Psychiatry in Bali. *Australian and New Zealand Journal of Psychiatry,* 1976, *10,* 95–97.

Torrey, E. F. *The mind game.* New York: Bantam Press, 1972.

Tung, T. M. The family and the management of mental health problems in Vietnam. In W. Lebra (Ed.), *Transcultural research in mental health.* Honolulu, Hawaii: Univ. Press of Hawaii, 1972.

Turner, V. W. A Ndembu doctor in practice. In A. Kiev (Ed.), *Magic, faith, and healing.* New York: Free Press, 1964.

Ullmann, L., & Krasner, L. *A psychological approach to abnormal behavior.* Englewood Cliffs, New Jersey: Prentice-Hall, 1975.

Waxler, N. E. Culture and mental illness: A social labeling perspective. *Journal of Nervous and Mental Disease,* 1974, *159,* 379–399.

WHO. Expert Committee on Mental Health, *First report.* Geneva: Technical Report Series, No. 9, 1950.

WHO. Organization of mental health services in developing countries. *Sixteenth Report of the Expert Committee on Mental Health,* 1975.

WHO. *Report of the first meeting of the coordinating group for the mental health programme.* World Health Organization, Geneva, Switzerland, Report No. 76.4, 1976.

Wig, N. N. Training of psychiatrists. In T. A. Baasher, G. Carstairs, R. Giel & F. Hassler, (Eds.), *Mental health services in developing countries.* Geneva: WHO, 1975.

Wittkower, E., & Warnes, H. Cultural aspects of psychotherapy. *American Journal of Psychotherapy,* 1974, *28,* 566–573.

Wolff, R. J. Modern medicine and traditional culture: Confrontation on the Malay Peninsula. *Human Organization,* 1965, *24,* 339–345.

15

Culture and Psychotherapy

WEN-SHING TSENG
JING HSU

Introduction

Based on several decades of knowledge and experience in modern psychology and psychiatry, various forms of counseling and psychotherapy have been developed to serve the mental health needs of contemporary society. However, if we define psychotherapy broadly as a special treatment in which psychological principles and means are utilized to solve a client's behavior or emotional problems, and if we extend our attention widely into every corner of the world, we will discover that numerous kinds of folk and/or modern psychotherapy are practiced in various cultural settings.

Modern psychology and psychiatry have reached a level of sophistication in which there is a concern for the cultural dimensions of human behavior and emotional problems, and an appreciation for the cultural aspects of psychotherapy (Tseng & McDermott, 1975). In our contemporary world, there is an increasing tendency for mental health workers to treat clients of different cultural backgrounds. There is both a theoretical and practical need for the study of various forms of psychotherapy existing in different cultures, cultural influences on the practice of psychotherapy, and cultural implications of psychotherapy, so that culturally relevant treatment can be carried out.

PERSPECTIVES ON CROSS-CULTURAL PSYCHOLOGY

Variations of Psychotherapy in Different Cultures

Modern psychotherapy can be categorized according to a theoretical framework (e.g., psychoanalytic psychotherapy, behavior therapy, existential therapy) or according to treatment goals (e.g., supportive therapy, re-education therapy, reconstructive therapy). In order to include various forms of both folk and modern psychotherapy from various cultures, a broader framework is necessary. Based on anthropological information and medical and psychiatric history, various forms of psychotherapy can be described according to their basic orientation.

SUPERNATURALLY ORIENTED HEALING SYSTEMS

This group of treatments is characterized by a belief in the existence of the supernatural. It is assumed that possession by an evil spirit, soul loss, a sorcerer's curse, or taboo violation are the causes of problems (Clements, 1932). Consequently, ritual performance, sacrifices, prayer, or exorcism are performed for the solution of the problems. At the psychological level, it is considered that relief of tension, group participation, induction of a hopeful attitude to problems, or other elements are working therapeutically for the clients (Murphy, 1964). Most of the healing ceremonies and types of faith healing belong to this category.

The trance-possession state for the healer, or the client, or both, may occur in the healing practice. In shamanism, the healer goes into a trance state in which he is "possessed" by a supernatural power. The client can then consult the supernatural through the spirit medium, the shaman, for instruction in dealing with problems. Sometimes it is the client who is induced into the possessed state. In this condition, the client reveals the cause of his problem and suggests the way to solve it (Lebra, 1976). Both the healer and the client may be possessed, as in the Zar cult (Prince, 1976), so that a dialogue between the healer and the client is carried out while both are in a dissociate state, and it is determined what the Zar, "the possessing spirit," wants in the way of gifts in order to alleviate the suffering of the client.

In addition to a dissociated state, other ways of searching for the cause of problems are utilized such as divination (Shelton, 1965; Dobkin, 1969; Beattie, 1967) or temple incubation as described in ancient Greece (Mora, 1967) in order to obtain supernatural illumination through divine instruction or dreams.

NATURALLY ORIENTED HEALING PRACTICES

In this group of practices, based on the concepts of microcosm and macrocosm, human life and behavior is considered as a part of the universe, and the nature of problems are explained in terms of imbalance or disharmony with the natural principles that rule the universe. Thus, the goal of treatment is to help the client find how to live compatibly and harmoniously with nature, and to adjust to the environment more appropriately according to natural principles.

Fortune-tellers, astrologists, and physiognomists are the healers in this group. These therapists are effective because the clients believe in them; they trust the "expert" in this field. The interpretation of the problem which is given is both an abstract concept and a reflection of the actual reality. Clients are relieved because they get reason for the cause of their trouble and obtain concrete instruction on how to cope with it (Tseng, 1976). The successful "therapists" in this group are not only skillful in providing answers for the clients, but through the process of interaction, their individualized interpretations with psychological insight achieve positive psychotherapeutic effects (Hsu, 1976).

MEDICAL-PHYSIOLOGICALLY ORIENTED TREATMENT PRACTICE

The treatment practice in this category is primarily based on the medical–physical concept that weakness, or exhaustion of the nervous system, or an imbalance of physiological conditions are the causes for mental disorders. Therefore, various remedies are given to strengthen or to balance the physiological system, even though many of those remedies also have psychological effects for the client.

This group of treatments can be illustrated by the practice of mesmerism, which hypothesized that a shortage of special magnetic fluid was the cause of mental illness. The treatment required the therapist to transmit and supplement the vital–magnetic power he possessed to his client by touching him. It has been speculated that suggestion is the psychological mechanism for the effectiveness of such treatment (Mora, 1967).

Another example is rest therapy as described in Morita Therapy. Based on the assumption that the client needs rest for his nervous exhaustion, a certain period of rest is prescribed for the client. A client usually experiences and perceives life and reality differently after going through the semi-sensory–social deprivation for two or three weeks. The permission for time out from the daily routine and/or the opportunity for self-examination through retreat may also be some of the factors involved in the improvement, in addition to the actual opportunity for rest (Kondo, 1953).

The practice of acupuncture for emotionally disturbed patients also belongs to this category. Although there is a folk anatomical interpretation and belief that there exist certain nerve–organ connections, and that needle stimulation of these locations will stimulate the function of certain organs, there is the effect of suggestion working for the clients.

SOCIOPSYCHOLOGICALLY ORIENTED
TREATMENT SYSTEMS

Most of the modern psychotherapeutic methods belong to this category. In this area, sociopsychological elements are considered as major etiological factors to emotional problems. Therefore, psychological processes, such as relearning and correcting errors in behavior therapy, or resolving conflicts in analytic therapy, are considered the essence of therapy. In meditation therapy, the aim is to obtain tranquility of the mind, whereas in Zen training, self-enlightenment and change of one's philosophical attitude are the ultimate goal of treatment.

In spite of the vast differences in the many types of folk and modern psychotherapies, scholars have pointed out the universal elements in all kinds of healing practices. The mobilization of hope (Frank, 1968), faith in the therapist (Opler, 1936), active participation of the client and his family (Carstairs, 1964), providing an authoritative figure (Lederer, 1959), and a warm personality quality of the therapist (Torrey, 1970), are some of the factors cited as necessary. From the operational point of view, the analysis and identification of the cause of the problem, no matter what the explanation, is always helpful to the client who is suffering from doubt and uncertainty about his problems. The prescription for change itself, again regardless of what is suggested, is always helpful to the client who needs guidance and support to cope with his problems. In spite of the common therapeutic elements, various forms of psychotherapy do differ in their referential systems, style of operation, and goals. Thus, there is the cultural divergence in practices.

Psychotherapy and Cultural Suitability

In view of the various forms of therapy present in different cultural settings, it is pertinent to ask whether there are any unique relationships between the particular form of therapy and the kind of cultural settings in which that form is practiced. From a sociological point of view, it has been pointed out that the nature of the sophistication of certain healing systems parallels the degree of the development of their social structure (Kiev, 1964). Namely, in simple food-gathering societies, the systematic organization of theories of healing systems is absent, and the healing practice is dominated only by simple magic methods; in more complex fishing–hunting societies, medical beliefs are more elaborated, and religious–medical therapy are available; in agricultural societies, illness is attributed more to sick individuals rather than to supernatural causes, and the healing system is more specialized.

Analysis of primitive societies has shown that the use of various therapies is often related to personality variables (Kiev, 1960). For example, "sacrifice" is most often used therapeutically in societies where aggressive behavior is severely prohibited for children. The same tendency is also found in regard to "bloodletting" treatment. In contrast to this, in a society where oral gratification is present, as manifested by over-indulgence of infants, delayed weaning, and nurture preoccupation, "tonic" supply and "recuperation" will be emphasized.

In a similar way it has been hypothesized (Wallace, 1959) that the need for a certain style of therapy is closely related to the sociocultural system. For example, in a highly organized sociocultural system in which regulation and control is overemphasized, institutionalized "catharsis" is needed; whereas in a poorly organized society, where lack of goal regulation and guidance is characteristic, "control" is the therapeutic approach used. It is therefore reasonable to consider that there is a certain kind of correlation or fitness between the form of therapy and the nature of the cultural system.

Client-centered therapy, with its relationship to American cultural norms, has been analyzed (Meadow, 1964) and is relevant to this subject. A study of this therapy pointed out that the fundamental assumptions that (*a*) the client has basic potentiality within him for growth and development; (*b*) the great emphasis of nondirective counseling approach is necessary in order to help the client to establish a feeling of equality with the therapist; and (*c*) particular attention must be paid to the client's need for autonomy and independence are reflections of an American ethos of democracy and independence. It was also pointed out (Harper, 1959) that the central philosophy of the person's potentiality for constructive change fits in well with the optimistic aspects of American culture and is one of the many reasons for the popularity of this type of therapy in the States.

Naikan Therapy, or introspection therapy (Murase, 1976), originated in Japan has been derived methodologically from a Buddhist philosophy. Technically, it is a process of continuous meditation and self-introspection. Under intense instruction, the client is requested to examine himself in relation to others, to recall the care and benevolence that he has received from his parents, siblings, teachers, or other important persons in his life, and then, to recall and examine his memories of what he has returned to that person.

As the treatment process goes on, the client becomes fully involved in such introspection and accepts the newly recognized guilt along with the feelings of self-criticism and repentance. These will bring an eventual improvement in the patient's interpersonal relationships. From a cultural point of view, it is necessary to note that for a Japanese to do harm to those close to him, such as his parents, is a severe violation of social morals. Thus, the acknowledgment of such misconduct produces especially strong guilt feelings in the Japanese. In other words, *Naikan* therapy seems to skillfully facilitate guilt-consciousness by reinforcing the sense of *On* obligation regarding one's mother, which may not be applicable to other cultural settings where obligation to parents is not emphasized. Because of variations in the referential system, techniques of treatment and, most importantly, the values emphasized in any particular healing system, point to a "cultural suitability" of therapy—that certain kinds of therapeutic practices are prevalent in certain cultural settings but not in other cultural settings.

Cultural Influence on Psychotherapy Practice

The influence of cultural factors on the practice of psychotherapy is enormous. Nevertheless, such impact is usually not explicit, nor is it observed unless the therapist is faced with the situation of treating a client of a different cultural background, or is practicing treatment in a very different cultural setting.

ORIENTATION TO THE TREATMENT SYSTEMS

The utilization of *healing systems* is very much determined by the client's socioeconomic background as well as his orientation to and expectations from the healing system. A client may visit a shaman if he believes his problem is a matter of evil possession which warrants a supernatural cure. However, he may consult a physiognomist if he perceives his difficulty as arising from a constitutional defect which can be corrected by some "naturalistic" alteration. If he understands his difficulty as a kind of nerve disorder, he then may call upon a "brain doctor" for medical treatment.

A client accustomed to visiting a fortune-teller would know *not* to reveal too much of his personal background except his birthdate and name so that accurate fortune-telling can be obtained. If such a client visited an analyst, he would surely find the therapy odd and disappointing, as he would have to tell the therapist a great deal about himself and, in return, be told nothing by the therapist.

Thus, it is obvious that the client's familiarity with, orientation to, and expectation from treatment will greatly determine the course of therapy and its effectiveness. Needless to say, cultural factors have a great impact on the orientation to the healing system, one of the core elements for the practice of psychotherapy.

EVALUATION OF PROBLEMS AND CULTURAL EMPATHY

One of the basic operations of treatment is the evaluation of the client's problems. The focus of evaluation may vary because of the referential system—a shaman may search for any evidence of spirit possession or violation of taboo; a fortune-teller, for accurate information of time and date of birth (which is considered an essential factor in determining a person's life and problems); and an analyst, unconscious material, such as dream content, or fantasy. Nevertheless, there is a common need to understand the client's background and source of problems so that effective treatment can be planned.

It has been pointed out that the process of empathy itself—understanding the client's situation, sharing the client's feelings, and showing genuine interest in him—has a therapeutic effect upon the client. However, in the process of empathy an issue emerges regarding the extent to which therapists can understand the client. Besides the therapist's professional sensitivity, there are always the factors of: actual life experience and knowledge, and familiarity of the setting ("cultural empathy") which greatly determines the genuineness of such understanding.

THERAPIST–CLIENT RELATIONSHIPS, CULTURAL TRANSFERENCE AND COUNTERTRANSFERENCE

The therapist–client relationship is of paramount importance to therapy, and although it usually varies for different modalities of treatment, there is always some reflection of authority–subordinate relationships as they exist in the particular cultural environment. That is, the client will expect to relate to the therapist in a manner mirrored by this culture. For example, a client who comes from a background where authority tends to be autocratic will expect the therapist to be active, instructive, assertive, and authoritative in the treatment session; whereas, another client, who is used to relating to authority in a democratic way, will prefer a more equal relationship and would not expect the therapist to command and manipulate him.

If we define analytic concepts of transference and countertransference in a broad sense, we could then perceive the complexities of the two phenomena as the client tends to project his own stereotypes regarding the ethnic–cultural background of the therapist, and relates to the therapist as such. In the same way, the therapist may react toward the client according to his culturally related stereotyped beliefs. Thus, this "cultural transference and countertransference" may further complicate the therapeutic process.

GOAL OF THERAPY AND CONCEPT OF HEALTH

The concepts of normality, health, and maturity are related to the final goal of treatment. How to help the client to become a healthy and mature person, and how to define this status, is certainly culturally related. Thus each term should be necessarily challenged from a cultural point of view. The process of psychotherapy can be viewed as a communication and exchange of values between two partners—the healer and the client. How a person should handle his aggression, manage his sexual life, or relate to his family or friends should all be discussed according to the cultural context within which the client is going to live and to adjust.

Cultural Implications of Psychotherapy

The nature of psychotherapy can be understood from various perspectives. From a psychological point of view it may be considered as a procedure of relearning (by behavior therapy), a way of working on resistance, or obtaining insight (by analysis). From a sociological point of view, it may be perceived as a process of resocialization, or the restoration of moralization. The nature of psychotherapy from a cultural point of view will be described in the following section.

DEFINITION OF NORMS, VALUES, AND GOALS FOR THE CLIENT

One of the frequently encountered anxieties among clients is the problem of uncertainty and unknowing. Although mental health implies a condition of maximum efficiency, happiness, and success in an individual's adjustment to his environment and the concepts of "normal," "healthy," and "success" are subject to value systems. In traditional healing practices or folk counseling, the therapist is usually considered the highest authority in the community and is respected for his wisdom and experience. As a healer, he is skillful in providing the answer, by defining the norms, values, and goals of the society for his client in order to help the client to eliminate his doubt and anxiety.

Influenced by the democratic ethos and the analytic nonimposing approach, modern therapists tend to minimize or deny the fact that they impose values on the client. However, no matter how neutral the therapist claims to be, his response is likewise based on some implicit, personal, value judgment. Thus one purpose of psychotherapeutic activity is for the therapist to function as a representative of the values of his society, as a priest or judge, to help the client find an appropriate value system for his behavior, decision, and adjustment. (Nelson, 1973).

REINFORCEMENT OF CULTURALLY SANCTIONED COPING MECHANISMS

Based on the personality style, the nature of the stress, and the environmental situation, there are divergent ways to cope with the stress, conflict, or maladjustment. In each society there is always a preferred, patterned, or sanctioned way of coping with problems. From a cultural point of view, one of the functions of psychotherapy can be understood as a process of reinforcing such culturally sanctioned coping patterns so that the client can be properly accepted and can be successfully adjusted to society.

Analysis of Chinese divination, a form of folk counseling, revealed that the majority of "divine" advice given to the clients, suggests that the client be satisfied with what he is and that he remain conservative. The client is usually warned not to be too ambitious or aggressive, or to do things that are inappropriate for his role and status. Thus, it reinforces the traditional Chinese way of remaining patient, unaggressive, and accepting of the situation, rather than rebelling against it (Hsu, 1976).

A basic principle of Western client-centered therapy emphasizes a nondirective counseling approach (i.e., minimizing the therapist's interpretation, suggestion, and advice). This approach helps the client to establish a sense of autonomy, independence, and a feeling of equality with the therapist. Thus, as a therapy, it reinforces a coping mechanism that is valued in American culture—learning to solve problems by oneself (Meadow, 1964).

PROVISION AND OPPORTUNITY FOR A CULTURAL "TIME OUT"

Another function of psychotherapy is to provide permission and opportunity for the client to have "time out" away from his cultural system. In each cultural system there are certain sets of regulations, restrictions, expectations, and limitations, and sometimes there is a great need for the client to have a temporal "vacation" or "freedom" from culturally expected behavior.

The cultural time out can take effect in various ways. The process of "therapeutic regression" provides the client an occasion to behave in a way which is normally not allowed in regular social life. The procedure of catharsis gives a client a chance to express socioculturally forbiden desires or feelings during the therapeutic session. By going into a possessed trance state, a client is given the opportunity to complain about, or to demand something which he is usually not allowed in ordinary life (Lebra, 1976). The kind of time out needed by the client may vary from society to society with the pattern of life. Regardless of the nature of the aberration, allowing clients this temporary vacation during the therapeutic situation, equips them to reenter ordinary cultural experience and to function better in it.

ALTERNATIVES TO CULTURE-DEFINED SOLUTIONS

Our methods of solving problems are strongly patterned by our customary thinking, social regulation, and cultural value systems; consequently, our solutions are culturally restricted or limited. Another purpose of psychotherapy is to help clients be more flexible and more aware of the possible alternatives beyond their present, culturally-limited coping spectrum so that they can have more choices regarding adjustment.

For example, a group of immigrated Hispanic American mothers, generally suffering from unsatisfactory marital relationships and a sense of emptiness in their lives, were overinvolved with their children. Because of their unhappy circumstances, the children seemed so important to them that some of the mothers had great difficulty setting standards of discipline. They often overextended themselves in making sacrifices for their children, and then felt hurt and rejected when the children did not reciprocate. Based on their traditional upbringing and the established importance of children in their culture, it seems that becoming such sacrificing mothers was the only fate destined to them. However, in such situations, the therapist may promote the idea that the "good" mother was one who could take time for herself to do activities that she enjoyed as an individual. Such a therapeutic suggestion may be culturally revolutionary from the client's point of view, but it may be extremely helpful. In this way therapists can reveal to clients the existence of many alternatives beyond the culturally accepted reaction-patterns experience and also give clients permission to use them.

PRESENTATION OF MISSING ELEMENTS IN THE EXISTING LIFE PATTERN

The cultural setting in which the client is living may be characterized in ways which emphasize certain cultural qualities and delete, or ignore other cultural elements. Thus the client may crave the "missing portions of the pie," and the nature of psychotherapy is to provide these missing elements.

For example, if a society overemphasizes the technical–material quality of life and tends to neglect the philosophical aspects of life, then psychotherapy focusing on existential problems may be needed. On the other hand, if a society is only interested in the search for the metaphysical meaning of life, and has very little concern with the practical aspects of living, treatment concentrated upon coping with more realistic needs may become essential. Within a society in which self-sufficiency and responsibility are highly idealized and autonomy and independence are greatly valued, it is often difficult to find or accept opportunities for the satisfaction of dependency needs except in a therapeutic setting. Thus, the purpose of psychotherapy is to provide any such missing element and to counteract, or buffer the already overemphasized elements.

EXPOSURE, EXCHANGE AND INCORPORATION OF CULTURAL SYSTEMS

Finally the process of psychotherapy could be perceived as the interaction of two value systems: the client's and the therapist's. The client's problems may be conceptualized as being rooted in the special "way of life" in which he was raised and by which he has patterned and coded all the responses and reactions in his experience. Such "ways of life," clinically referred to as "immature," "distorted," "neurotic," or "pathological" are ineffective guides for coping appropriately or adequately with a difficult situation or any other problems which occur. In contrast to this, the therapist is equipped with another "way of life," which usually leads a person to think, feel, and react in an appropriate and effective way. In the process of psychotherapy, the therapist exposes the client to the latter "way of life." Through the steps of exchange and incorporation, the client gradually absorbs the new "way of life" and the "healthier" value system and is able to react to situations in a more mature and successful way. Thus psychotherapy, here, is both the encounter and assimilation of a new cultural system.

Comments and Suggestions

There has been an increasing interest in the study of culture and psychotherapy in the last decade (Abel & Metraux, 1974). Numerous investigations have been carried out regarding indigenous, folk, or traditional psychotherapy in primitive, underdeveloped, or non-Western societies, with an attempt to learn the cultural aspects of psychotherapy through studies of the healing system in "other" cultures. Very little effort has been made to investigate how the modern psychotherapies in Western societies are related to cultural factors. We lack cultural insight about our own healing system, and more attention and investigation are needed regarding this matter.

Counseling across cultures has been concerned recently with the need for increased cultural sensitivity and modification of skills for helping clients of various cultural backgrounds (Pedersen, Lonner, & Draguns, 1976). There is a practical need to learn what kind of minimal cultural information and knowledge regarding the client is necessary, and how to obtain and utilize it in the process of treatment. Additionally, we need to know how the therapist can utilize his own cultural background to help the client. Again, from the experience of such intercultural psychotherapy, it is important for us to learn (a) how cultural factors influence the process of homocultural psychotherapy—psychotherapy with a client of the same cultural background; (b) what is the benefit and asset that can be utilized, and (c) what are the limitations and blind spots of which we should be aware? After all, one of the last things we discover is the invisible cultural dimensions surrounding ourselves.

References

Abel, T. M. & Metraux, R. *Culture and psychotherapy.* New Haven, Connecticut: College and University Press, 1974.

Beattie, J. H. Consulting a Nyoro diviner: The ethnologist as client. *Ethnology,* 1967, *6,* 57–65.

Carstairs, G. M. Healing ceremonies in primitive societies. *The Listener,* 1964, *72,* 195–197.

Clements, F. E. Primitive concepts of disease. *University of California Publications in American Archaeology and Ethnology,* 1932, *32,* 185–252.

Dobkin, M. Fortune's malice: Divination, psychotherapy, and folk medicine in Peru. *Journal of American Folklore,* 1969, *82,* 132–141.

Frank, J. D. The role of hope in psychotherapy. *International Journal of Psychiatry,* 1968, *5,* 383–412.

Harper, R. *Psychonanalysis and psychotherapy.* Englewood Cliffs, New Jersey: Prentice-Hall, 1959.

Hsu, J. Counseling in the Chinese temple: A psychological study of divination by *chien* drawing. In W. Lebra (Ed.), *Culture-bound syndromes, ethnopsychiatry, and alternate therapies.* Honolulu, Hawaii: Univ. Press of Hawaii, 1976.

Kiev, A. Primitive therapy: A cross-cultural study of the relationship between child training and therapeutic practices related to illness. In W. Muensterberg & W. Axebrad (Eds.), *The Psychoanalytic study of society.* New York: International Universities Press, 1960.

Kiev, A. The study of folk psychiatry. In A. Kiev (Ed.), *Magic, faith, and healing.* New York: Free Press, 1964.

Kondo, A. Morita therapy. *American Journal of Psychoanalysis,* 1953, *13,* 31–37.

Lebra, T. S. Taking the role of supernatural "other": Spirit possession in a Japanese healing cult. In W. Lebra (Ed.), *Culture-bound syndromes, ethnopsychiatry, and alternate therapies.* Honolulu, Hawaii: Univ. Press of Hawaii, 1976.

Lederer, W. Primitive psychotherapy. *Psychiatry,* 1959, *22,* 255–265.

Meadow, A. Client-centered therapy and the American ethos. *International Journal of Psychiatry,* 1964, *10,* 246–260.

Mora, G. History of psychiatry. In A. M. Freedman & H. I. Kaplan (Eds.), *Comprehensive textbook of psychiatry.* Baltimore, Maryland: Williams & Wilkins, 1967.

Murase, T. Naikan therapy. In W. Lebra (Ed.), *Culture-bound syndrome, ethnopsychiatry, and alternate therapies.* Honolulu Hawaii: Univ. Press of Hawaii, 1976.

Murphy, J. M. Psychotherapeutic aspects of shamanism on St. Lawrence Island, Alaska. In A. Kiev (Ed.), *Magic, faith and healing: Studies in primitive psychiatry today.* New York: Free Press, 1964.

Nelson, S. H. & Torrey, E. F. The religious function of psychiatry. *American Journal of Orthopsychiatry,* 1973, *43,* 362–367.

Opler, M. E. Some points of comparison and contrast between the treatment of functional disorders by Apache shamans and modern psychiatric practice. *American Journal of Psychiatry,* 1936, *92,* 1371–1387.

Pedersen, P., Lonner, W. J., & Draguns, J. G. (Eds.) *Counseling across cultures.* Honolulu Hawaii: Univ. Press of Hawaii, 1976.

Prince, R. *Variations in Psychotherapeutic Procedures.* Paper presented at the Conference of Cross-Cultural Research for Behavioral and Social Scientists, Culture Learning Institute, East–West Center, Honolulu, 1976.

Shelton, A. J. The meaning and method of Afa divination among the Northern Nsukka Ibo, *American Anthropologist,* 1965, *67,* 1441–1445.

Torrey, E. F. Indigenous psychotherapy: Theories and techniques. *Current Psychiatric Therapies.* 1970, *10,* 118–129.

Tseng, W. S. Folk Psychotherapy in Taiwan. In W. Lebra (Ed.), *Culture-bound syndromes, ethnopsychiatry, and alternate therapies*. Honolulu, Hawaii: Univ. Press of Hawaii, 1976.

Tseng, W. S., & McDermott, J. F., Jr. Psychotherapy: Historical roots, universal elements, and cultural variations. *American Journal of Psychiatry*, 1975, *132*, 378–384.

Wallace, A. F. C. The institutionalization of cathartic and control strategies in Iroquois religious psychotherapy. In M. D. Opler (Ed.), *Culture and mental health*. New York: Macmillan, 1959.

IV

FUTURE

16

A Cross-Cultural Odyssey:
Some Personal Reflections

GEORGE M. GUTHRIE

Introduction

In this chapter I am going to describe some of my experiences in 20 years of cross-cultural research (mostly in the Philippines) on child rearing and personality development, attitude change with modernization, and the adjustment of Americans who went to live in the Philippines as Peace Corps volunteers. The topics may not appear to follow one another logically, but the editors have asked me for a personal musing and a personal history of my cross-cultural research; apparently they believe something may be learned from it. Perhaps it may; I have certainly been influenced by my predecessors. In fact I will begin this chapter by thinking of some early workers in the field, and what their experiences have taught me. That will help to illustrate my notion of the nature of cross-cultural research. Then I can discuss the difficulties I have found, and end with a few suggestions.

Is Cross-Cultural Research Different?

Surely the methods of research one may use in cross-cultural studies are, at a very basic level, the same as those used in one's home setting. Taking those methods to an alien culture, however, is hazardous because the mate-

349

PERSPECTIVES ON CROSS-CULTURAL PSYCHOLOGY

rials, the tasks, and the relationship between subject and experimenter may be very different. Coping with those differences as well as extensive understanding or good advice about the new setting is the heart of the matter; that *is* the problem of cross-cultural research.

The specific methods one may choose depends on the problem one is studying, the characteristics of the subject population, the facilities available, and the skills of the researchers. Research methods in cross-cultural research are never satisfactory or poor by themselves; they are appropriate to the degree that they provide unambiguous answers to the questions the researcher has posed. The major problem that faces in cross-cultural research is that of determining whether differences found among samples from different societies are real or merely the artifacts of data-collection procedures that mean different things to people from different cultural backgrounds.

There is one important additional feature, however, which characterizes cross-cultural research: We seek to determine which cultural differences alter the *relationships* among the same variables in different societies. For instance, the life expectancy of women is several years more than that of men in the United States, but approximately the same as men in Russia. Or we might find that competition generates a greater improvement in performance over noncompetition for American subjects as compared to citizens of a second country. In the latter case the effect of cultural differences appears as the interaction term in a 2×2 design. In domestic research we are interested in cause–effect relationships among variables; in cross-cultural research we are asking whether those relationships are universal or are moderated by cultural features.

Methods have varied over time in a close relationship with the questions posed. In the late nineteenth century, psychologists were interested in sensory capacities. The Cambridge Expedition to the Torres Strait was staffed by people concerned with vision and hearing. Their accounts of their methods (Haddon, 1901) make fascinating reading because they attempted to make the tasks meaningful to subjects whose experiences were markedly different from subjects of Victoria's England. Shortly thereafter, others with different interests began to give intelligence tests. A teacher who later became an editor, A. V. H. Hartendorp, went from the United States to teach in the Philippines and carried group intelligence tests along to administer at teachers' conferences.

In the early stages of planning for her doctoral research on Samoa, Margaret Mead (1972) considered using galvanic-skin-response (GSR) apparatus which had recently been used in social science research. In the 1950s psychologists and psychologically oriented anthropologists used the Rorschach Test (Kaplan, 1961). In this case a procedure by which one could understand personality more fully led to much interest in the underlying personality structure of various groups. More recently the Semantic Differential, because it is available, has been employed many times; not so much because it provided an answer to a question, but because it was there.

One of the first tests in which theory was retained and test materials modified was the Thematic Aperception Test (TAT). Lagmay (1960), for instance, developed pictures with Filipino faces and scenes, replacing the European faces and settings of Murray's set of pictures. Decline in use of the TAT in cross-cultural research followed decline in use in the United States, and probably for similar reasons—researchers lost interest in the theory on which the TAT was based and were no longer interested in the responses which the pictures elicited.

The point of this brief venture into history is to suggest that cross-cultural research methods follow rather closely those of domestic research in North America and Europe. This is the case with respect to theory, designs, apparatus, and methods of analysis. But on closer examination much of the research done in alien cultural settings turns out to be not cross-cultural at all. Suppose that I am interested in neuroticism, memory span, or locus of control among Filipinos. Measuring these characteristics or skills and comparing them with data collected elsewhere is not significant cross-cultural research; it might be called *ethnometry* or the measurement of the characteristics of members of another cultural group. But few studies which merely report differences are published. Around the world with the Minnesota Multiphasic Personality Inventory may fool the Internal Revenue Service, but not anonymous reviewers.

What has been happening is that authors have been disguising their *ethnometry* by offering interpretations of the differences they have found. This can be detected by reading the last sentence of the abstract which may say "the differences were explained in terms of the different cultural backgrounds of members of the two societies." Unfortunately, cultural backgrounds, as complex as they are, can account for all sorts of differences or, with hypothesized compensatory processes, no differences.

The Question Is as Important as the Answer

We need to change the order of events in the research process. If we are interested in the instability of the nuclear family as it affects the development of self-control and favorable self-attitudes, we should look for a society in which nuclear families are very unstable and another where they are highly stable, hypothesize effects on children, and test those hypotheses. Our theories, for instance, are almost unanimous that stable, continuing relationships of parents with children promote stability in the child. Polynesia gives us an opportunity, with its child-rearing tradition of fosterage in which children move from one set of parents to another and to a third, to test our theory that discontinuity disposes to instability. My guess is that the apparent stability of Polynesian children would lead us to question or modify our theories of personality development in children, theories which stress the importance of stable relationships between parents and children.

Malinowski (1927) was one of the first to apply the idea that different cultures provided an opportunity to test theories about the importance of certain childhood events. He found a naturally occurring situation in which the male who fathered a child was not the same person as the male who was responsible for the child's discipline. This provided a test of Freud's theory of a universal oedipus complex, a test in which Freud's theory was not confirmed because Malinowski's Trobriand boys felt resentful toward their uncle–caretakers and not toward their mother's sexual partners.

In the ensuing debate in the journals (Jones, 1928), Malinowski's conclusions were questioned because he had not undergone psychoanalytic training and, without the support of other social scientists, Malinowski gave up his position. This was an unfortunate capitulation because it set a pattern that only the indoctrinated could comment on the validity of Freud's ideas from the perspective of data from other societies. It also established the doctrine that data from other societies did not bear on Freud's theories unless they were collected under conditions of psychoanalytic investigation or treatment.

Because psychoanalytic theory dominated theories about behavior for so long, data from other societies have had virtually no impact on theories of personality or of psychopathology. Pick up a dozen books on personality theory or textbooks of psychiatry and you will rarely find any indication of *cross-cultural* or its synonyms in the index.

Theory and Cross-Cultural Research

If the research of cross-cultural psychologists has had little impact on personality theory or other aspects of psychology, it is because research done in second cultures is not rooted in, and only slightly related to, current theories. Sechrest (1977a) has made a strong case for theoretical grounding of research, arguing that cross-cultural research is a method of studying phenomena and processes of interest to psychologists, and not an area of study in which one looks for or describes psychological differences between citizens of two societies. His differentiation between method of study and area of study parallels Cronbach's differentiation of experimental and descriptive psychology (1975).

One test of whether a given study is a test of theory or a description of behavior, is whether the experimenter explicitly sought a cultural group because they differed on a variable in which the experimenter was interested. Thus, if I choose to study stability in Polynesian children because Polynesians practice fosterage, I am following something approximating a cross-cultural method, but if I study child rearing in the Philippines merely because I happen to be there, I am engaged in largely atheoretical, descriptive research.

There are at least two problems one will encounter if one seeks to meet Sechrest's requirement: Establishing a relationship with and an understanding of an alien society requires a great deal of time, and, second, most psychological theories have no place for cultural factors to operate. In order to collect data in Polynesia on the effects of fosterage and the resultant instability of bonds between the child and parental figures, one would need to spend a year in Samoa or Tonga learning the language and otherwise laying the groundwork for collecting the data necessary to test the theory. A more desirable strategy would be to carry out each of the above steps and then to collaborate with a Polynesian social scientist who is native to the area. So far so good, but one study gives rise to another, and to study another aspect of the role of stability in parent–child bonds one might have to go to quite another site, an Israeli kibbutz for instance—and there goes another year or more of preparation. It is less efficient than Prince Charming searching for a maiden with the right-sized foot.

The second problem should also be borne in mind, even though it does not justify atheoretical studies of differences in child rearing or of modernity of attitudes. The major theories of personality and of disordered behavior—psychoanalytic, Rogerian, and behavioral—make no allowances for cultural differences. On the contrary, they emphasize the universality of the processes fundamental to their theories. Similarly, the "minitheories" with which social psychology abounds (e.g., cognitive dissonance, or attribution theory) make little if any provision for cultural factors; this in spite of the fact that cultural differences are fundamentally social differences. When authors of textbooks in social psychology cite cross-cultural data, they use descriptive material showing, for instance, that the members of one society are more aggressive than others. But, rarely do they cite data from experiments in alien societies because virtually no experiments have been replicated in non-Western settings.

One of the founders of social psychology, now largely forgotten, William McDougall, the author of an early textbook called *Social Psychology* (1908), was a participant in the Cambridge Expedition. But as he said in his autobiography, "So I passed on from the Torres Straits, after spending some five months in those remote islands, having greatly enjoyed the time, but having accomplished very little [McDougall, 1930, pp. 201–202]." He went on to Borneo where he spent some time with a district officer, Hose, and later helped him write the classic two-volume *Wild Tribes of Borneo* (Hose & McDougall, 1912). This was the same McDougall who later formulated lists of basic instincts, an enterprise which finally succumbed to contrary evidence from other cultures. The only reference to his extensive cross-cultural experience in his later writings that I could find was the terse statement that the upriver Dyaks have a stronger instinct of pugnacity than the downriver Dyaks. Unfortunately, social psychologists, in my opioion at least, have followed McDougall's example and have paid little attention to cross-cultural data. As a result, they have formulated theories that make no provision for the operation of cultural factors.

So I would offer a revision to Sechrest's hard line, without reducing the emphasis on the role of theory. It seems to me that one can only hope reasonably to work in one or two societies other than his own so that finding a society to test a theory will not often be a workable strategy. Once one has established contacts in and acquaintance with an alien society, one can use it to test some aspects of one's theories, but not all aspects because Society 2 may not differ from Society 1 in some of the characteristics in which one is interested. At the same time one can be making observations of processes in Society 2 of child rearing, socialization for sex roles, attitude formation and change, role acquisition of the aged, or whatever, and then evaluate the applicability of existent theories to these observations. In a sense it is a converse of Sechrest's seeking a society to fit the needs of testing a theory in that we would seek a theory which approximates or orders the observations—sometimes you check princesses and sometimes you check slippers.

Many of the problems I have discussed can be seen clearly if one examines the cross-cultural research on personality development. There are profound differences among societies in their child-rearing practices, and in their adult beliefs and behavior patterns. Furthermore, there are extensive theories about the relationship of childhood experiences to adult behavior. It should be a straightforward matter, therefore, to use data from other societies to replicate suspected relationships observed in our own, and to observe effects of childhood experiences that are higher or lower on some continuum that can be readily observed at home.

Some Examples from the Philippines

CHILD REARING AND PERSONALITY DEVELOPMENT

I would like to illustrate some of the problems one encounters in cross-cultural research on child rearing and personality development by reviewing my own early experience in the Philippines (Guthrie & Jacobs, 1966). It was my first cross-cultural research; with the support of the Fulbright program, I went to the Philippine Normal College in Manila in 1959 with a copy of Sears, Maccoby, and Levin (1957) in my luggage, and plans to do a comparative study of child-rearing practices. How lucky it was that I quickly met a Filipina, Pepita Jiménez Jacobs, who had just returned from a year of graduate study at Merill-Palmer. She understood her own country well, and she also understood and practiced careful research activities. Sears *et al.* had thoughtfully reproduced their interview in their appendix and we took the logical first step of using the interview with English-speaking mothers whose children were attending the Nursery School of the Philippine Normal College. My collaborator translated the interview into Tagalog, the Manila-area Philippine language.

And then the difficulties began. In preliminary work with the translated interview she discovered that many questions dealt with matters that were not in the experience of Philippine mothers, matters such as TV time, and pickiness about food. Even worse, the interview omitted elements important to Philippine mothers, such as the large nuclear family, the extended family, and the role of household helpers. Finally, two entire sections had to be added, one which dealt with the fears which children acquired of invisible creatures who populated various places at various times, and another on the behavior patterns of children that parents valued and for which they felt responsible.

Philippine mothers were so influenced by explicit standards of what a good child should be and felt so responsible for the child's development that parents' values became a very important determining factor in the behavior of Philippine mothers. American mothers, in contrast, regarded their role as the task of helping the child to develop his own potentialities. Philippine mothers were environmental determinists, whereas American mothers held implicitly that development was a matter of unfolding of the potentialities with which the child was born.

So we trained 30 college-senior education students to conduct the interview and they collected 10 interviews each, from mothers of first grade children in communities outside of Manila where the 30 students were on practice teaching assignments. They conducted the interview in Tagalog or English, recording the answers more or less verbatim. We developed an ad hoc coding system for the answers, developed the report from the tabulations, and illustrated our interpretations with direct quotations from mothers.

So far, so good; but when we tried to make comparisons we ran into another set of problems. We could make simple comparisons such as incidence and duration of breastfeeding, age of bowel-control training, the teaching of modesty, etc., but could not make any connections between these differences and differences in adulthood due to differences in the context within which differences in socialization appeared. Breastfeeding in one society is a choice and often a choice based on feelings of closeness to the baby, whereas, in the other, there is virtually no choice because it is the only feeding method a family can afford. Teaching a child to acquire control over bowel functions is one matter when the mother has daily diaper service from a laundry, and another where an older sibling has the responsibility to clean up the child who has not yet learned. A Vietnamese mother once told me that she had her children trained by three months of age. When I observed that this was remarkable by our standards she replied that our women would achieve similar results if they carried their babies on their backs, and it became a matter of getting wet if the mother and child had not learned.

MEASURING PARENTAL ATTITUDES

There are differences in socialization practices from one society to another, but the differences go on within a context of different environmental and social factors which is much broader than the socialization practices themselves. This would seem to imply that point-by-point comparisons are not interpretable, and that comparisons must be of configurations. An example of this is illustrated in our application of the Parental Attitude Research Inventory (PARI) (Guthrie, 1966) to samples of American and Philippine mothers. We found that scale-by-scale analyses of differences led to misinterpretations because the individual 5-item scales did not mean the same things in one country as in another. Factor analyses of the 23 PARI scales for American and Philippine mothers suggested that parental control was equated with stifling initiative for American mothers, while the same scale measured attitudes which involved acceptance of responsibility for the child's development among Filipino mothers. Acceptance of similar sentiments implied authoritarianism for one group, a loving concern for the child for the other.

The research on mothers' attitudes about child-rearing practices epitomizes a major problem in cross-cultural undertakings. Differences between societies are not just differences of degree, but are differences in configurations. We found this to be dramatically the case when Macalandong took the interview from our child-rearing book (Guthrie & Jacobs, 1966) and studied Maranao Muslim mothers in the southern Philippines. She found (Macalandong *et al.*, 1978) that from conception, Maranao mothers organized their attention around protecting the child from malevolent influences, and around helping the child develop a fierce sense of pride in his family. These central purposes pervade the Maranaos' practices to such an extent that intellectual development and emotional security are accorded minor status as goals. In the same way, rural Filipinos emphasize good interpersonal relations and a fine sense of knowing one's obligations to others, as goals in personality development and as signs of a good citizen. Individual achievement is not a central goal, as it is in middle class citizens of North America. Cross-cultural comparisons must, therefore, be of configurations and not of the strength of a single shared motive or goal. An approach by way of multivariate statistics suggests itself, but relatively little has been done of this sort.

Problems and Opportunities in
Cross-Cultural Research

As we have noted, one of the most obvious subjects of cross-cultural psychological research is that of child rearing and personality development. Many of our theories hold that the experiences of childhood have profound effects on both emotional and intellectual development. Such ideas are at the heart of psychoanalytic formulations but they are also key elements in other approaches to socialization and growth.

There is a lore but there are a few longitudinal data on the development of children in normal home settings, such as the children who were studied by Sears *et al.* (1957). McClelland, Constantian, Regalado, and Stone (1978) managed to locate 78 of the 379 children of the Sears *et al.* group 25 years after they had been seen and when they had reached an adult age of 31 years. McClelland's team was interested in "determining how the different ways they had been brought up had helped or hindered them in achieving social and moral maturity." Few of the expected correlations were better than chance and so they concluded that "most of what people do and think and believe as adults is not determined by specific techniques of child rearing in the first five years [p. 53]."

We infer that child-rearing practices may affect children's behavior, but so many new events intervene that they had no measurable effect on behavior two decades later. The McClelland study illustrates another problem of research in this domain: The antecedent and consequent behavior patterns are so vaguely defined that convincing demonstrations of causal relationships are impossible. If child-rearing practices and adult behavior patterns do not covary across one culture there is little reason to suppose that differences between societies in adult behavior patterns are due to child-rearing practices. Children who grow up in one society develop certain similarities as adults because they are exposed to common models, not because they experience similar training as infants. This becomes quite apparent if one follows children who are adopted into an alien society between 4- and 10-years-of-age and who quickly acquire the behavior patterns and personalities of the adopting society.

Early training and experiences with respect to sexual behavior are considered important by almost all who speculate in this area, Freudian or not in outlook. Because experimentation with children in any society, that is, the imposition of different childhood experiences is impossible, and with respect to sex training impossible and unacceptable, we must turn to other societies to find the variations we need in order to test our theories. Before we do, however, we should spell out from our theories the relationships we intend to check. What are the significant experiences which lead to definable patterns of adult behavior? When we begin to ask these questions we find that our theories equivocate.

Consider these matters, for instance—what childhood experiences, if any, led to homosexual behavior in adulthood? What patterns of treatment of male children predispose to male dominance in adult society? Are there patterns which predispose to a high incidence of sexual assault and rape? There is an extensive, poorly systematized lore which deals with these issues, but it rarely provides a basis for unambiguous assertions of cause-and-effect relationships that can be checked in other societies.

However, child-rearing practices may have more effect on fundamental aspects of personality and behavior. Consider homosexuality as a specific example. We have a number of theories about how homosexuality comes about, ranging from a failure to resolve oedipal conflicts, to faulty modeling of male roles. Homosexual behavior apparently takes place in most societies, but homosexuals experience markedly different reactions from others depending on the place and time in which they live. In some societies, homosexuality is treated very harshly, in others it is treated as a clinical problem which evokes shame in those near the sick one and sympathetic rejection by those further removed, and in still others it is looked upon as something that happens to some people, a something which they will likely grow out of. Our own society has been harsh and clinical by turns whereas the Filipinos, for instance, have been much more permissive (Hart, 1968; Fay, 1970).

These situations, provide an opportunity to study the impact of different shared definitions upon the reversibility of sexual orientation, and the degree to which self-referent ideas about homosexuality enter into symptoms of schizophrenia and depression and into causes of suicide. A cross-cultural analysis from this perspective has not been completed. Cross-cultural methods are especially appropriate because the already occuring differences in shared views about homosexual behavior cannot be achieved in the contrived circumstances of experiments. Cross-cultural data are most valuable when cultural factors are known or suspected to be of importance.

More Examples from The Philippines

ARE INTERVIEWS AND QUESTIONNAIRES USEFUL?

Response to interviews, standardized or open-ended, and to written schedules or scales are subject to as much distortion in foreign settings as they are in our own. Subjects may feel that their family or society is on trial, that their integrity or honor is threatened, or that they must please the person posing the questions.

Let me offer two illustrations: In one of the first pieces of research I did in the Philippines, I developed a self-report scale of teaching practices and teaching philosophy (Guthrie, 1961). Half of the items expressed ideas that might be found in a modern American textbook with a permissive, child-centered orientation, whereas the other half expressed more directive views, set in a context of traditional Filipino views. Our teacher-trainee respondents saw little contradiction, accepting both kinds of statements, even though they appeared to the investigator to be quite contradictory. As one respondent said, "I try all the new modern methods; and if they don't work, I pinch."

In the second example (Guthrie & Azores, 1968), we used a sentence completion test which had originally been used in Thailand by Phillips (1966). With some difficulty my collaborator translated the stems into Tagalog; The difficulty arose because the structure of Tagalog sentences is not the noun–verb–predicate of English, so that the stems would not ordinarily appear at the beginning of sentences in Tagalog. Having overcome this problem, we administered the test randomly in English or Tagalog to Filipinos who spoke both languages well. Using an ad hoc classification system, we found that people responded differently, invoking different values, depending on the language they were using. Parenthetically, the sentence completion method, as used by Phillips and later by us, is a very effective method if one is working with literate populations such as college students or those who have had at least eight years of education. With those whose literacy is lower, an interviewer can read the stems and record the answers.

The first of the foregoing examples entailed the construction of sets of items on the job, items with special reference to a specific problem in a specific society. For cross-cultural studies most investigators feel the need of standardized instruments; in actual operation this frequently turns out to be an instrument somebody else made up, as though the fact that an interview or attitude schedule attains some established proven status by having made it past a journal editor. The alienation scale by Srole (1956) and modernization scales by Inkeles (1974) are among the most common sources of such unsatisfactory measurement procedures. An aspiring investigator, without much thought about alienation or modernization among his target population, selects items from Srole's or Inkeles' research reports and with this "scale" proceeds to measure the characteristic in which he is interested.

Such a scale will have highly satisfactory reliability, guaranteed by response acquiescence. This internal consistency, plus face validity, are assumed to assure that the items measure the construct. But as Jackson (1971) and many others have demonstrated, using an internal consistency method maximizes responses biases. These problems are not overcome by applying Guttman's criteria of scalability. They can be recoginzed if one applies the rules of Campbell and Fiske (1959) that a scale not only correlate highly with some outside criterion other than self-reports, but that it not correlate highly with self-report scales which purport to measure other attitudes.

An example of a scale that must be distorted by acquiescence is Kahl's

Modernism II (1968) in which all eight items are stated so that agreement implies a traditional attitude. There is an extensive body of literature on scale construction and a significant amount on response bias that has been summarized by Berg (1967). There should be no reason to continue seeing reports published with poor measures. Researchers must learn measurement theory themselves; there is no justification for those planning research calling their social science colleagues with such a request as, "We are starting a study of economic development in Southeast Asia and we need scales which measures entrepreneurial outlook, need achievement, and modernity. Please send us short reliable measures of each, tomorrow."

WHAT WE SAY MAY NOT PREDICT WHAT WE DO

As if these problems were not enough, there is the more general problem that attitudes often bear little relation to behavior. This has been well described by Deutscher (1973). We found the paradoxical situation in the Philippines that tenant farmers expressed agreement with modern attitudes, but retained traditional patterns of living. Hundreds of KAP (knowledge, attitude, practices) surveys about family planning find that knowledge is extensive, attitudes are favorable but practice of family planning is very limited and frequently discontinued after it has been accepted.

Similar marked discrepancies appear in our own society in health-related behavior where we have positive attitudes toward good practices, and much information, but we smoke, use alcohol excessively, and fail to exercise. The discrepancies between attitudes and behavior haave proven to be so great that we should forget about attitudes and concentrate directly on behavior. This choice should be considered especially in social action programs.

There is another solution to the problem: One can use nonreactive or unobtrusive measures (Webb et al., 1966). Let me illustrate this by citing a study which a Filipino sociologist, Salvador Parco, and I planned. (It never happened; the funding agency had a more favorable attitude toward competing proposals.)

Our purpose was to study the effect of new high-yielding varieties of rice on the economic activities of Filipinos in a province on the rice plain north of Manila. Instead of asking farmers how they felt about the new rice, we planned to find out how it affected their behavior. We proposed to review such indices of economic activity as the volume of betting at the cock pit, sales of gasoline, payments to the church for special observations, volume of sales and number of vendors in the market, volume of passengers on the provincial buses, sales of fertilizer, sales of rice to the local government buyer, and improvement in the attendance rates of rural schoolchildren. All of this was based on the knowledge that any additional earnings of tenants would be spent quickly, and that the increases would reflect the present goals of the farmers. Such data would also provide indications of points in the rural economy where stimulation might be most effective. We proposed to follow this line of investigation because we were sure that asking the farmers themselves would yield the finding that they felt they had no more money to spend than previously. We were also of the opinion that they would not be able to give us a very accurate account of how their behavior was changing, if at all, as a result of increased rice yields.

In retrospect then, I have made a good deal of use of questionnaire and interview methods, which are also the methods used most commonly by others. Although these methods yield a good deal of information about the attitude and outlooks of the respondents, they are entirely descriptive and largely atheoretical. Additionally, though they may help us to understand better the members of the society of the respondents, they do not serve a cross-cultural purpose. They do not improve our understanding of the role of cultural factors in behavior because questionnaire data yield no understanding of the processes by which cultural differences alter the relationships between stimuli and responses. A better way must be found.

Theories and Experimental Analogs

WE HAVE TO IMPROVE OUR OBSERVATIONS

A great majority of cross-cultural research reports are essentially atheoretical, a matter that should not be surprising because descriptive research is light on theory. Sechrest (1977b), as was mentioned earlier, has emphasized the need for a theoretical problem as a reason for cross-cultural research. I would like to suggest that we make it a sort of process in which we begin with some observations, and then seek an experimentally based theory with which to organize the observations. The theory might suggest further observations and/or steps by which behavior might be modified in socially mandated ways. For instance, we observed (Guthrie, 1972) that rural Filipinos were resistant to change and reluctant to take steps which might reasonably improve their lot. These observations were fitted to Seligman's (1975) theory of learned helplessness. The theory in turn suggests that the condition can be reduced by improving the relationship between initiatives and outcomes. This theory is very similar to McClelland's (1978) emphasis on setting attainable goals. Such a fitting of theory based on laboratory research to field observation provides testable suggestions of ways to promote economic development.

Another example would be the poor civil discipline of peasant areas where hillsides are burned to feed a small group while great numbers suffer from the resultant flooding and erosion, or fish are taken by dynamite thereby increasing today's take but damaging the marine environment for years to come. This is the tragedy of the commons (Hardin, 1968). I have suggested that this resembles an N-person, zero-sum game (Guthrie, 1977) but we need more game theory and more observations of peasants to carry the matter further.

Another area of study that invites an integration of observational data and theory-based experiments is that of reciprocity. Peasant social organization features a great deal of reciprocity within extended families and in coalitions between families. The generality of laboratory findings would suggest new principles that could be tested, and implications for social programs that could be evaluated in the field. This last step is not just an idle hope. Many developing countries are willing to experiment in social action programs to achieve the goals they have selected. The opportunities are numerous for social scientists who want to participate in programs designed to improve the economic and physical welfare of their fellow citizens. It is not often that social scientists have an opportunity to put their ideas to work and to the test. In developing countries the citizens and their leaders do not feel that they can afford the luxury of social scientists who do research having no immediate utility, they expect social science research to yield steps by which the lot of citizens can be improved. Social scientists in developing countries reflect this orientation when they complain that they are exploited by visitors who do research which yields no demonstrable benefit to the host society.

Some Examples from the Peace Corps

STRANGERS IN A STRANGE LAND

There is another aspect of cross-cultural research often not included with descriptions of cross-cultural undertakings. This area is concerned with the impact upon an individual's behavior of living in an alien social setting. I have been a sojourner often, and would argue that this is a sort of natural experiment in which antecedent conditions are different to a greater extent and over a greater duration than can be achieved in laboratory experiments. At a simple level, we can ask what happens to an individual's behavior if we change greatly almost all aspects of his social environment. Again, we can ask more meaningful questions and gather more interpretable data if we operate within a theoretical system. I can illustrate this by summarizing our experience training and predicting the performance of Peace Corps volunteers who went to live for 2 years in the Philippines (Guthrie & Zektick, 1967).

The conceptual framework within which we are working in the early 1960s was essentially psychodynamic with its emphasis upon the inner determinants of behavior, and with the expectation that behavior could be predicted through careful assessment using tests, observations, and peer ratings. Stability in a psychiatric sense could be evaluated by trained psychiatrists so that, with careful selection, good performance could be assured. Two years later we were able to obtain independent evaluations of their performance from several Peace Corps staff members, and evaluations of a considerable number of our trainees from Filipinos under whose supervision they worked. Our pooled predictions correlated about .30 with the Americans' evaluation of the volunteer's performance and .004 with the evaluations obtained from Filipinos. Those volunteers whom the psychiatrists and we considered great psychiatric risks but who went anyway performed satisfactorily and completed their tours, whereas a small number without apparent psychiatric blemish in training experienced such difficulties that they returned home prematurely. Of equal importance, about 95% of those whom we selected completed their tour of duty and many extended for additional months or years.

Over the succeeding years, other psychologists assumed responsibility for selection and the percentage of those who were selected and who accomplished the objective of completing their tour of duty fell from year to year until about half of those who now go abroad complete the standard 2-year assignment. I would like to point with pride to our excellent performance in selection, but I cannot forget the coefficient of .004, even though it is positive. This experience persuaded me that situational determinants should be accorded much more importance and that inner determinants of behavior are less powerful than many of us had believed. I am also convinced that the fall in the effectiveness of selection was determined by a change in the social climate in our society: The idealism and optimism of the New Frontier was replaced by the realism and cynicism of the Vietnam era.

CULTURE SHOCK AND SHOCKING CULTURES

The social experiment of living and working in an alien society presents other opportunities to observe the effects of changes in antecedent conditions, changes which are much more extensive than can be achieved under laboratory conditions. The phenomenon of culture shock, or what I think might be better caled *culture fatigue* (Guthrie, 1967), is a superb experimental neurosis that has never been studied intensively. This is a situation in which persons with histories of stability and with emotional and intellectual resources adequate for the task develop a wide variety of symptoms including restlessness, depression, irritability, loss of initiative, loss of appetite, and inability to concentrate. No two sufferers are the same. The victim has little insight into the causes of his difficulties and has few ideas about how they can be alleviated. Fortunately, the symptoms subside almost immediately when he returns home. We could never achieve such an approximation of neurosis, even before the days of human-subjects review committees.

In the foregoing discussion it is apparent that placing an individual in another society for an extended period of time is an experiment in which cultural factors are modified, providing us with an opportunity to observe the effects of those modifications on behavior. When we study members of two or more societies in their various home environments, we are not altering social factors for any of the subjects beyond the acts of data collection. The former situation of placing people in new cultural settings approximates a true experiment in which independent variables are changed. The latter is descriptive research, in which we study causal or correlated factors as we find them. Studies of groups in their home environments is also the prototype of cross-cultural research. But moving people to another society is an imprecise experiment because a multitude of independent variables are altered simultaneously.

Making Use of What We Know in Psychology

There is an alternative approach to differences in behavior found in different societies, or induced when one moves from one society to another. This approach involves using laboratory research as a model to explain or order the observed different behavior, and then to deduce testable steps to change further the behavior of the members of the second society or the behavior of the sojourner. Let me illustrate: Those who live for periods of time in an alien society frequently experience intense negative emotional reactions, which can be called *culture fatigue,* after 6 months to a year in the new setting. Azrin, Hutchinson, and Hake (1966) have demonstrated that experimental animals manifest considerable aggressive behavior when they are placed on extinction schedules. The sojourner is on an extinction schedule, inasmuch as the new society does not reinforce many operants that have been reinforced at home. This analysis could be tested by restoring old reinforcement contingencies in the new setting.

Many members of peasant societies appear to be extremely passive and fatalistic, many sojourners develop intense feelings of futility in their new setting. These observations approximate those of Seligman (1975) of learned helplessness which comes about when reinforcements or benefits bear no apparent relationship to efforts. This analysis can be tested by making reinforcement more contingent on effort for either the peasant or the sojourner with the prediction that passivity will be reduced. The test should be controlled by the social scientist, if possible, but a less persuasive case can be made from observations of naturally occurring instances when rewards for effort are made more reliable and prompt.

Finally, sojourners who are experiencing culture fatigue frequently make markedly negative interpretations of the motives and character of the host nationals. This phenomenon is clarified by the research on attribution summarized by E. E. Jones (1976) in which a series of experiments demonstrated that a subject is convinced that his own behavior is a reaction to the demands of the situation, whereas another's behavior is primarily an expression of the other's inner character and dispositions. I have no experimental data to illustrate this process in the case of sojourners except the observation that those who are adjusting well in an alien society are able to see a wide range of individual differences in members of the host society and are able to describe, to some degree, the world as experienced by the host national.

What Have We Learned from These Experiences?

There is a good deal of ambiguity about what should be included in the field of cross-cultural psychology. It does not include simply descriptions or measurements of differences in traits, attitudes or other variables between samples of two societies. It is not the application, with or without modifications, of psychological techniques in an alien society. Cross-cultural psychology deals with the effects of cultural differences in a second society on relationships, causal or otherwise, demonstrated to exist in a first. Thus, cross-cultural research could be carried out in North America if one asked whether relationships found with white subjects also existed among blacks or Native Americans.

Culture is thus a moderator variable (Saunders, 1956), one which designates two or more groups where the predictors of performance are not equally weighted or equally effective. A moderator variable by itself is not a predictor, it separates a large sample into two or more groups where beta weights are different for the same variables predicting the same outcome. Sex is often a moderator variable when a given factor is a good predictor of coronary problems for members of one sex but not for the other. Age is a moderator variable if smoking is related to lung cancer in one age group but not in another. The treatment of sex-related differences in current research would be a good model for cross-cultural researchers, if the implications of sex-related differences were well worked out.

A frequent justification of cross-cultural research in the social sciences is that other societies provide natural experiments in which antecedent variables are found at intensities different than is the case in our own society. However, except for Malinowski (1927), to whom we have referred, there have been few reports of the results of these natural experiments. When such an approach is attempted it may involve backward reasoning such as why is there little stress among Samoan adolescents? There is one problem with the natural experiment approach, namely, many variables are different in addition to the one in which we may be especially interested and there is no logical or statistical way one can rule out alternative explanations of any differences that are found.

A more recent approach would be to ask whether or laboratory-based theories account for behavioral phenomena in other cultures. A body of research and theory, such as that of Seligman (1975), suggests new observations one might make where people are apparently apathetic and resistant to change and, even more importantly, suggests testable steps to reduce resistance to new activities. Research on reciprocity, zero-sum games, and conformity provide analytical frameworks for description and testable suggestions to change or strengthen certain activities. A great deterrent to this lend–lease arrangement between laboratory and second culture is the virtual absence of any provision for cultural factors in most of our social psychological theories.

Conclusions

My lack of satisfaction with the current status of cross-cultural research is apparent. I believe that the quality and significance of our research would be enhanced if we spent more time on the formulation of the questions we are asking, asked questions that have theoretical relevance, and treated culture as a moderator variable, instead of as a post hoc explanation of our results. These opinions may be the bruises left by hard knocks in my own research. Perhaps these reflections will save somebody from repeating some of the errors we have all made in the past. I certainly look forward to my next sojourn in the Philippines. For all its problems, I would not trade cross-cultural research for any other. I even look forward to the next decade's problems, whatever they turn out to be.

References

Azrin, N., Hutchinson, N., & Hake, D. Extinction-induced aggression. *Journal of the Experimental Analysis of Behavior,* 1966, *9,* 191–204.
Berg, I. A. (Ed.). *Response set in personality assessment.* Chicago: Aldine, 1967.
Brislin, R. W., Lonner, W. J., & Thorndike, R. W. *Cross-cultural research methods.* New York: Wiley, 1973.
Campbell, D. T., & Fiske, D. W. Convergent and discriminant validation in the multitrait–multimethod matrix. *Psychological Bulletin,* 1959, *56,* 81–105.
Cronbach, L. J. Beyond the two disciplines of scientific psychology. *American Psychologist,* 1975, *30,* 116–127.
Deutscher, I. *Why do they say one thing, do another?* Morristown, New Jersey: General Learning Press, 1973.
Fay, T. L. *Culture and differences in concepts of sex role and self.* Unpublished doctoral dissertation, Northwestern University, 1970.

Guthrie, G. M. *The Filipino child and Philippine society.* Manila: Philippine Normal College, 1961.

Guthrie, G. M. Structure of maternal attitudes in two cultures. *The Journal of Psychology,* 1966, *62,* 155–165.

Guthrie, G. M. Cultural preparation for the Philippines. In R. B. Textor (Ed.), *Cultural frontiers of the Peace Corps.* Cambridge, Massachusetts: MIT Press, 1967.

Guthrie, G. M. The shuttlebox of subsistence attitudes. In B. T. King, & E. McGinnies (Eds.), *Attitudes, conflict and social change.* New York: Academic Press, 1972.

Guthrie, G. M. A social-psychological analysis of modernization in the Philippines. *Journal of Cross-Cultural Psychology,* 1977, *8,* 177–205.

Guthrie, G., & Jacobs, P. *Child rearing and personality development in the Philippines.* University Park, Pennsylvania: Penn. State Univ. Press, 1966.

Guthrie, G. M., & Zektick, I. N. Predicting performance in the Peace Corps. *The Journal of Social Psychology,* 1967, *71,* 11–21.

Guthrie, G. M., & Azores, F. M. *Philippine interpersonal behavior patterns.* Manila: Ateneo de Manila University. Institute of Philippine Culture (IPC Papers No. 6), 1968.

Haddon, A. C. (Ed.) *Reports of the Cambridge anthropological expedition to the Torres straits* (6 vols.). Cambridge: Univ. Press, 1901–1935.

Hardin, G. The tragedy of the commons. *Science,* 1968, *162,* 1243–1248.

Hart, D. V. Homosexuality and transvestism in the Philippines. *Behavior Science Notes,* 1968, *3,* 211–248.

Hose, C., & McDougall, W. *The pagan tribes of Borneo.* New York: Barnes & Noble, 1966. (Originally published in 1912).

Inkeles, A., & Smith, D. H. *Becoming modern.* Cambridge, Massachusetts: Univ. Press, 1974.

Jackson, D. N. The dynamics of structured personality tests: 1971, *Psychological Review,* 1971, *78,* 229–248.

Jones, E. Book review of Malinowski's *Sex and repression in savage society. International Journal of Psycho-Analysis,* 1928, *4,* 364–374.

Jones, E. E. How do people perceive the causes of behavior? *American Scientist,* 1976, *64,* 300–305.

Kahl, J. A. *The measurement of modernism.* Austin, Texas: Univ. of Texas Press, 1968.

Kaplan, B. Cross-cultural use of projective techniques. In F. L. K. Hsu (Ed.), *Psychological Anthropology.* Homewood, Illinois: Dorsey, 1961.

Lagmay, A. *The Philippine Thematic Apperception Test.* Manila: Univ. of Philippines, 1960.

Macalandong, R. M., Masangkay, Z. S., Consolacion, M. I., & Guthrie, G. M. Protection and pride in Maranao childhood. *The Journal of Social Psychology,* 1978, *105,* 85–97.

Malinowski, B. *Sex and repression in savage society.* London: Kegan Paul, 1927.

McClelland, D. C. Managing motivation to expand human freedom. *American Psychologist,* 1978, *33,* 201–210.

McClelland, D. C., Constantian, C. A., Regalado, D., & Stone, C. Making it to maturity. *Psychology Today,* 1978, *12,*(July), 42–53.

McDougall, W. *An Introduction to Social Psychology.* London: Methuen, 1908.

McDougall, W. Autobiography. In C. Murchison (Ed.), *A history of psychology in autobiography* (Vol. 1). Worcester, Massachusetts: Clark Univ. Press, 1930.

Mead, M. *Blackberry winter.* New York: Morrow, 1972.

Phillips, H. P. *Thai peasant personality.* Berkeley, California: Univ. of California Press, 1966.

Saunders, D. R. Moderator variables in prediction. *Educational and Psychological Measurement,* 1956, *16,* 209–222.

Sears, R. R., Maccoby, E., & Levin, H. *Patterns of child rearing.* Evanston, Illinois: Harper, 1957.

Sechrest, L. On the dearth of theory in cross-cultural psychology: There is madness in our method. In Y. Poortinga (Ed.), *Basic problems in cross-cultural psychology.* Amsterdam: Swets and Zeitlinger, 1977. (a)

Sechrest, L. On the need for experimentation in cross-cultural research. *Annals of the New York Academy of Sciences,* 1977, *285,* 104–118. (b)

Seligman, M. *Helplessness.* San Francisco, California: Freeman, 1975.

Srole, L. Social integration and certain corollaries: An exploratory study. *American Sociological Review,* 1956, *30,* 709–716.

Webb, E. J., Campbell, D. T., Schwartz, R. D., & Sechrest, L. *Unobtrusive measures: Nonreactive research in the social sciences.* Chicago, Illinois: Rand McNally, 1966.

17

The Futures of Culture or Cultures of the Future

JAMES A. DATOR

Introduction

Interest in, and serious attempts to forecast, the future are by no means new. Nonetheless, what is now called "Futures Studies" (among other names) had its origin in a set of post-World War II forces set in motion simultaneously in most industrialized nations of the world:[1]

- A few military, corporate, and governmental decision-makers, recognizing that "the future isn't what it used to be," began to seek methods by which they could anticipate the presently unanticipated and plan for it more effectively.[2]

[1] There are two major organizations of future researchers. One is the World Future Society (4916 St. Elmo Avenue, Washington, D.C. 20014) which publishes *The Futurist* monthly as well as the World Future Society *Bulletin,* and special newsletters in the area of government, communications, education, business, and life styles. See also, Cornish (1977) and World Future Society (1977). The other is the World Future Studies Federation (Casella Postale 6203, Roma-Prati, Italy) which also publishes a Newsletter, and serves mainly as a clearinghouse for futures studies organizations around the world. In addition, the journal, *Futures* (IPC Science & Technology Press, 32 High Street, Guildford, Surrey, England) and *Technological Forecasting and Social Change* (52 Vanderbilt Avenue, New York 10017) are major publications in the area. See also McHale (1977) and Marien (1976).

[2] The largest number of members of the World Future Society would probably be in this area. They are "establishment futurists" concerned that the rapid rate of social change of industrial

369

- A variety of marginal groups in industrial societies began to envision—and attempt to create—a culture which was counter to the unsatisfactory dominant one they found around them.[3]
- Environmental and related groups came to believe that the limits to growth loomed in many socially-important sectors, and that alternative paths to the future had to be found.[4]
- Many professionals who interacted with people negatively affected by present, societal features—such professionals as social workers, public health workers, religious ministers, psychiatrists, psychologists, and the like—began to become unusually concerned with the future developments of society so that they might help prepare their charges to "cope" more adequately with things to come.[5]
- Science fiction began to be taken more seriously—not that it had ever waned significantly in popularity (Armytage, 1968; Ash, 1976; Clareson, 1977; Hollister, 1974; Ketterer, 1974; Phillips, 1972; Tompkins, 1977);
- Space buffs and space mystics began to look for the cosmic connection in the noosphere (Christian, 1976; Hubbard, E., 1976; Maruyama & Harkins, 1975; O'Neill, 1977; Stine, 1975).[6]
- Even some educators began to wonder just what sort of a world their students might actually have to live in—and whether or not present courses and curricula were more nearly past, rather than future oriented (Ciba Foundation, 1975; Henley & Yates, 1974; Kauffman, 1976a, 1976b; Marien & Ziegler, 1972).[7]

Thus, "Future Studies" is fed from many sources, none dominant, and is very far from being accepted as a legitimate, much less as an emerging, arena

---

societies makes it difficult for managers to predict the future only by reference to the past, following hunches, or muddling through. Most of these people are "conservative" in the sense that they live in, profit from, and seek to sustain "the system." They believe that futures research is necessary to keep the system moving in the right direction.

[3] Now relatively few, there was once hope (or fear?) that their way would increase in the late 1960s. They are not totally dead, however. *Coevolution Quarterly* (Box 428, Sausalito, California 94965) is an especially good place to look for examples of their ideas.

[4] Environmental concerns "suddenly" emerged in the early 1970s to replace "the counterculture" and to rival the establishment futurists. Although some of them are radical in their attack on continued economic growth, generally they are even more "conservative" than the establishment futurists in their reluctance to encourage more social or environmental change.

[5] The medical and paramedical practitioners who form the global membership of the Hawaii Health Net (1629 Wilder Avenue, Honolulu, Hawaii 96822) is one example, (see also Strode, 1977).

[6] The Committee for the Future (2325 Porter Street, NW, Washington, D.C. 20038) is especially interested in integrating spiritual and spatial dimensions.

[7] The World Future Society; the School of Education, University of Massachusetts, Amherst; and the University of Northern Iowa, Mason City, all have regular newsletters on the future of education and education for the future.

for serious scholarly discourse by many people. I would guess that the attitudes towards ''Futures Studies'' of most participants at a symposium range from amusement to disgust, with due allowance for the chance existence of a fellow-traveller or two—or perhaps even a practitioner of the ''Weird Arts.''

I, of course, am one of these practitioners myself, holding the semiofficial title, ''State Weird,'' being permanently perched in the Department of Political Science at the University of Hawaii. For the past 10 years, I have devoted most of my time to teaching and research in the area of Future Studies. What follows, then, is what seems to me to be ''the future of culture'' from my particular position of hindsight, oversight, and (although it is too much to expect) foresight.

I will *not* be predicting the future of cultures. I do not believe it is any longer possible (if it ever was) to predict the future of anything in any but the most trivial and most imminent circumstances. It is this belief that, among other things, separates ''futurists'' from astrologers (i.e., astrologers, who believe they *can* predict the future, consider ''futurists'' to be low-grade astrologers at best, and charlatans most likely. I do not say their belief is an error). What I will be doing in the pages that follow is first commenting on the notion of ''time'' in this and other cultures; outlining some of the more prominent of the varying images of the future that I believe exist at present, commenting on the assumptions about the future of culture that I find implied in these images, and then concluding with some observations about the future of culture from my own perspective. In doing this latter, I will first review a recent article, titled ''The Future of Culture,'' by no less a believable person than Sir Geoffrey Vickers (1977), because my conclusions differ from his significantly, though we seem to agree about many of the bases and causes of future culture change.

About Time

''It is by the meaning that it intuitively attaches to time that one culture is differentiated from another,'' said Spengler in *The Decline of the West,* and thus, Thomas Cottle and Stephen Klineberg ask, ''Do persons in [traditional] cultures . . . tend to experience the flow of time and to conceive of their personal futures in ways that contrast markedly with the perspectives held by members of complex, highly modernized societies? Ethnographic reports suggest that they do [Cottle & Klineberg, 1974, p. 160].''

Yet, Robert Maxwell warns that ''Anthropological theorizing about time perspectives and time-reckoning schemes is still in the formative stage. The cross-cultural study of time has not yet even been given a name, nor have 'schools' of thought about the subject emerged within the discipline [Maxwell, 1972, p. 47].'' Cottle and Klineberg (1974), moreover, comment that in the scant anthropological literatures

> The impression is often given of a frozen uniformity across the population and of cultural forms unchanged for decades and centuries. Rarely are efforts made to sample systematically the population in question, to explore the diversity of individual attri- butes, and to speak in terms of frequencies and percentages rather than absolutes. This material should therefore be approached with caution, especially by one who comes upon it from a different discipline and with different purposes in mind [Cottle & Klineberg, 1974, p. 16]

As I am coming "upon it from a different discipline and with different purposes in mind," I must be careful indeed!

In addition, the notion of "time" has been a central philosophical concept (Fraser, 1966) and is intimately linked with many aspects of psychology, sociology, political science, and of course the one wholly time-oriented discipline, history. Consider the relationship of concepts of time to causal- ity, to change, to thinking per se (e.g., memory, anticipation, foresight, language, human development, "abnormal" versus "normal" behavior, "split brain" theories, sex-related differences, etc.), to "biorhythms," to death, to religion (and the "after-life"), to anxiety, to fatalism, to the ability to delay gratification, to achievement orientation and the entire idea of "developed" versus "under-developed" nations, and to "the culture of poverty" and social class-related differences.

Although it is admittedly tricky business, it nevertheless seems most convenient to divide the various understandings of "time" into four arenas: biological time, psychological time, mechanical time, and memorialized time.[8]

BIOLOGICAL TIME

In the evolution of consciousness, one of the earliest notions that is likely to have occurred to humans was the awareness that two fundamental rhythms seemed to operate in nature. One was finite and lineal, represented by the birth, maturation, and death of apparently all living things, and the other was that of oscillation between heights and depths around some "golden mean," such as day and night, the lunar month, the seasons, or the continuity of species, though not of individuals, in the repeating cycle of birth, maturation, and death.

Thus, while most cultures seem to have been aware of the operation of both phenomena, some emphasized one more than the other.[9] Specifically,

---

[8] The BBC film, *Time Is,* is one of the best audio-visual treatments of the subject available.

[9] This is the contention of Bloch (1977, p. 278–292). He argues that many anthropologists (he uses Clifford Geertz's work in Bali as an example) overemphasize the "timeless" character of traditional societies. Bloch believes that a linear notion is extant also, though less dominant.

we seem to find a predominance of cultures that stressed the "timeless" or, at least, repetitive aspects of nature. Because they lived, or seemed to live, in environments marked by repeatability, and hence predictability, where events and sequences that had occurred before occurred over and over again, most traditional human groups structured their cultures around ideas of permanence, stability, predictability, and only cyclic conceptions of change.

For most such cultures, therefore, there was neither existential anxiety, nor future dread. An attitude of "que será, será," and "if winter comes, can spring be far behind?" seems typical. Probably only for those tribes that experienced traumatic discontinuities, which they memorialized in myths and rituals, was the future a place of anxious concern. Perhaps for this, or similar reasons, then, some few groups—most notably, but certainly not only, the Jews—developed a linear, historical, developmental, and future-uncertain sense of time and of their place in it.

PSYCHOLOGICAL TIME

Yet, individuals, at all places and times probably subjectively experience time differently. Time has a different "meaning" to a very young child, to a middle-aged adult, and to a very old person. Time "hangs heavy" on hot boring days; is lost and stops in profound concentration of thought and energy; speeds up "when you're having fun"; looses all "normal" sequencing in dreams and day dreams; is altered by drugs; and is different between "normal" and "abnormal" people (different senses of time—the inability to plan ahead, to defer gratification, to remember past events or persons,—are used to define certain "mental illnesses" or other "abnormalities").

MECHANICAL TIME

Time, for most modern people, however, is something that is measured, and hence is scarce. Time is money, and clocks and calendars are necessary to see that it is properly spent. Virtually all societies measure time in some way, but frequently biological or other natural events—rather than artificial contrivances—are used (e.g., the phases of the moon, the growth of trees, "when grandfather was a little boy, no taller than that bush over there," "after the great flood"). These biological or natural markers are the most typical units of measure, and they were entirely satisfactory for the needs of hunting and gathering, or early agricultural societies.

Clocks, calendars, and now even more precise measures seem equally

---

Hence, "primitive" and "modern" people do *not* have different senses of time in his opinion, other anthropologists to the contrary notwithstanding. Rather, different aspects of the same general sense are stressed or relaxed according to the needs of different cultures, he maintains.

necessary for the "split second" timing of industrial life and processes, and because time can in fact be "measured out in coffee spoons," so does it seem to have a different meaning in industrial societies when compared to preindustrial ones.

MEMORIALIZED TIME (Lynch, 1972)

It is memorialized time that is most likely to be overlooked in discussions of time, but that in many ways is the most important. There are, I believe, three major types of memorialized time: celebrated time, mediated time, and constructed time.

Celebrated time is found in birthdays, religious rites and holy days, national holidays, rites of passage, and the like. Generally, these are events that make the past present ("Do this in remembrance of me. On the night in which He was betrayed, He took bread. . . ."). Time is telescoped, or, perhaps more accurately, the present is expanded to bring in more of the "past." Some, such as the rites of passage, celebrate the future: the child admitted into adult company. The deceased is enfolded in the arms of God.

Mediated time is more hidden from us. It is the capturing of time that is the characteristic of all languages.[10] We cannot utter a thought—perhaps we cannot talk at all—without trying to express the present in the terms of the past. In those tribal areas where past, present, and future were essentially the same, this was satisfactory. Is it sufficient for the present and our future?

It was with the introduction of writing that mediated time took on even more significance, however. Civilization, and all its discontents, is extremely difficult to sustain without the colonization of time and space which written language makes possible. Whereas the reinterpretation of past events is relatively easy in oral cultures, it is very difficult in print-based cultures, especially when the ability to read and write is possessed by only a small number of persons, all of whom are supporting members of the elite structure.

Then, with the development of the printing press, the invention of dictionaries, the rise of the modern school system (based significantly upon "readin' and 'ritin' "), and state commissions on correct use of the national language, the domination of the past over the present seemed to be complete. But not quite. Next came "mass media" (originally meaning national newspapers and magazines, but now meaning primarily radio, television, and the cinema), wherein an even smaller number of ideas are shaped, packaged, and poured into the consciousnesses of "the mass" by a tiny minority who both possess the "means of (audio–visual) production," and is literate in its use.

[10] "[L]anguage is conservative. It seeks to assimilate everything that happens to that which has happened [Zinn, 1971, p. 31]."

The final form of memorialized time is constructed time—that which is around us in the form of buildings, monuments, viaducts, highways, and landscaping. Monuments are obviously conscious attempts to make the past present, but the effect of the coexistence of buildings erected at various times in the past in most of our great cities has a similar effect, an effect that is being enhanced by the rapid rise of many conservation and preservation groups in the United States and elsewhere.

Images of the Future

In my opinion, the most important thing necessary to understand in order to forecast the future is the idea of the future that exist in people's minds— their so-called "images of the future" (Bell & Mau, 1971; Polak, 1973.).[11] As the previous discussion of "time" indicates, humans evolved into cultures that predicted the future on the basis of their experiences in the past. This image of the future, which I call "traditional," still dominates in those parts of the world where traditional cultures themselves dominate. However, equally important, it resides at the base, as the tacit, unexamined, and residual image of the future, of all humans everywhere, because of their evolutionary heritance. It is thus the "natural" image of the future for all human beings. It is at least for this reason, then, that "steady state" futures are so appealing for many modern futurists: The present period of turmoil is seen as only a temporary stage, leading eventually to an "end of history" forever stable environment. This was the conception of St. Augustine, of several late Medieval thinkers, of Karl Marx, and now of many environmentalists, as we shall see.

The Traditional image has two main variants, similar to those that we saw described above in our discussion of time. One is a "flat" or timeless image. Time is not a relevant dimension in many traditional cultures. The future is known to be just like the present, because the present is known to be just like the past. Nothing of importance is likely to happen. Therefore, what was good enough for my father, and his father, and his father (as it was in the beginning is now, and ever more shall be, world without change, Ah Me!), is good enough for me, and my son, and his sons for all eternity.

Related to this, but perhaps stronger for agricultural societies than for hunting and gathering societies, is a cyclical image (i.e., 7 fat years followed by 7 lean years, followed by 7 fat years, and so on). Hence, the moral imperative of "The Golden Mean" and the idea that good things do not last forever, and that "haughty pride goeth before a fall" while, equally, that bad things do not last forever either, and that "behind the darkest cloud, the sun

---

[11] Other things are of course important as well—phenomena that exhibit measurable *trends*, and unanticipated *events* are the most obvious. But I believe images to be central.

doth shine." In general, the attitude is one of take no thought for the morrow because the morrow will take care of itself, sufficient to the day are the evils thereof, and just muddle through.

Although, as I say, these "flat" and "cyclical" images still persist very strongly (as the misquotations from religious sources indicate), they are not the "official" image of the future of our culture today.[12] We are a society based firmly on the notion of development—of progress, growth, going somewhere, building a stairway to paradise—of, in short, discontinuity with the past, and hence, uncertainty towards the future. That is what economic growth means: to sever the present from the past, and to make the future better than the present. This is the purpose of industrialization, whether it is achieved by a capitalist or a communist route (and whether one hops along on one leg, or strides forward on two).

Yet, although I consider this "Developmental" image to be orthodox, it is not beyond dispute, so in the pages that follow, I will present briefly three of the major alternative images of the future foreseen as the most likely future for industrial, and industrializing, societies, and then turn to what I personally see as the future of culture.

Alternative Futures

CONTINUED GROWTH

The most commonly-held view of the future—that which I would expect most participants in a symposium to exhibit if they were to undertake an essay on "the future of culture"—is that the future will be more or less a continuation of the trends of the past. What, then, are the important characteristics of the immediate past? For most people in the industrialized portions of the world, the past has been a period (real or imagined) of societal growth, progress, and development. Although individual or group fortunes may have differed from the social norm, even "culturally-deprived" and otherwise marginal members of most industrial societies seem to believe that the general movement of society over the last 200 years (or at least since the Second World War) has been "upward," and that, if they could only play their cards right, their own time of good fortune would also eventuate.

That is to say, "change" has characterized the past. Moreover, that "change" has been "good." Progress, development, and growth are viewed by most people as essentially good things which can and should be per-

---

[12] The modern analysis of cycles is becoming fashionable once again (is this a cyclic phenomena?). See especially Alcock (1978) and Dewey (1970) for further discussion. It could also be that recent studies in the variabilities of the "invariant sun" and the inconstant nature of the Meander Constant—which makes it possible to reevaluate several "crazy" sunspot theories—is responsible for this resurgence. Dewey, by the way, *does* blame it all on sunspots!

petuated. Thus the future will also be characterized by a continued growth of those things that have grown in the past, and a continued decline of those things that have been declining in the past.

It was from examining the future characteristics of these continuing growth curves, however, that one of the earliest manifestations of "Futures Studies" emerged. Solid members of the establishment—such as Daniel Bell of Columbia University, Herman Kahn of the Rand Corporation and later founder of the Hudson Institute, Theodore Gordon also of Rand and now of the Futures Group, and others—began to point out that a "surprise-free" continuation of the trends of the past or present would result in a very "surprising" future—not at all the flat, present-extended-to-a-later-time type of future that was in the minds of many ordinary citizens and decision-makers. Bell began popularizing the idea of a "postindustrial" society that, although different in important aspects from the present, nonetheless was clearly the product of, not revolution or willful change, but rather, the continuation of present normal activities of dominant institutions and social actors (Bell, 1973; Harrison & Gordon, 1972.).

Herman Kahn and Anthony Wiener's book, *The Year 2000* (1967) was one of the first and most influential of these projections, and Kahn, with other members of his Hudson Institute, have subsequently revised and refined that vision into many other books and reports that have influenced important political and economic decision-makers around the world.

Kahn is profoundly optimistic about the future. While admitting, of course, that many things could happen that would result in catastrophe, he believes the world is moving into a period of unprecedented economic prosperity, with the "gap" between East and West closing. He expects world population to level off by the end of the twenty-first century at between 10–28 billion, and average per capita income to be between $10,000 and $20,000 (Kahn & Brown, 1976).

Kahn thus sees the next 100–200 years as a continuation of the trends that have shaped the past 200 years. Just as world population has grown from one billion persons in 1850 to almost four billion today, so can we expect it to grow to almost thirty billion by 2100—and that will be all right!

Similarly, if per capita income was $300 in 1850 and $1,250 today, then we can expect it to be the equivalent of $20,000 by the end of the twenty-first century—and that will be great! And if scientific knowledge, bureaucratized organizations, friendly fascism, and institutionalized responses to social and personal problems have increased in the past 200 years, then we can expect them to increase even more dramatically for the future—and we want it that way!

Kahn (and others) believes that the period of the late 1960s was a temporary aberration in the overall swing of satisfaction with material and personal progress. He sees the discontent which arose in the 1960s, and still lingers on in a vocal minority of the population today, to be merely the manifestation of the personal and psychological inadequacies of a "New Class" of pseudointellectuals. So far from being a sign of things to come, this discontent and fear for the future will become decreasingly prevalent as economic prosperity continues and as traditional conservative values are restored.

From Kahn's point of view, then, the culture of the foreseeable future should also be a consequence of the continuation of the trends that have created the culture of the present. This was identified in *The Year 2000* (Kahn & Wiener, 1967) as deriving from the unfolding of the "long-range, multifold trend." His more recent book, *The Next 200 Years* (Kahn & Brown, 1976) also reiterates this faith.

The views of Herman Kahn and the Hudson Institute probably come closest to the hopes, if not always the stated expectations, of most citizens in most industrialized societies. Although Kahn's view are probably more optimistic and embody the expectation of substantially more social and personal change than would be true for most citizens and decision-makers, nonetheless, they are the sort of thing that we all want to hear: "Everything is basically OK. If you will just find a niche in the growing industrial state—if you will contribute to its growth by learning as much and working as hard as you can—then the future, although of course not perfect, will certainly be as good as anyone can possibly make it. Moreover, it will be much better than the present and (everything considered) vastly superior to what has ever existed before. As a culture, we are on the right track, headed for a glorious future. All of the rest of the world is eagerly going along with us. Our job is to do all that we can to see that we all get there, and to stop having so many second thoughts about it. We have nothing to fear but fear itself, and if we don't let the fears of the few spoil it for the rest of us, everything will be all right."

A NEW DARK AGES

Not everyone agrees, to say the least! One of the most eloquent statements of despair—a total refutation of Kahn's optimism and a good example of what Kahn considers to be the irresponsible wailings of the "New Class"—comes from the widely respected social economist, Robert Heilbroner:

> There is a question in the air, more sensed than seen, like the invisible approach of a distant storm, a question that I would hesitate to ask aloud did I not believe it existed unvoiced in the minds of many: "Is there hope for man?" [Heilbroner, 1974, p. 3].

Heilbroner insists that this is a real and urgent question—he is not setting up a strawman to knock down with Kahnian optimism. Rather, he examines all of the environmental, political, economic, resource, demographic, and psychological data available to him and concludes that the answer to his question must be, "no." There is no hope for mankind. And it does not matter whether one is living in a liberal democratic or a socialist country, or in a developed or an underdeveloped part of the world. The negative answer must apply to all people everywhere.

With the greatest reluctance, therefore, Heilbroner states that the only future he can imagine is one which sees a more or less rapid decline of the world into a condition of fiercely warring, local areas—armed camps that cannot even count on the loyalty and support of their own countryside, so severe will be the challenge and so drastic the need. Of course there is one possible way out, but Heilbroner does not expect it to come about: global dictatorship. Yet no government presently on earth—capitalist or socialist—is likely to be able to make the sacrifice necessary, Heilbroner concludes, and the struggle necessary to evoke such a global authoritarian government would itself be almost as catastrophic as the tragedy it would be asked to avoid.

The culture of the future from Heilbroner's perspective, then, is essentially a return to a dark ages—or worse. Because "science" and modern institutions based upon science will be understood to be responsible for getting us into this horrible predicament to begin with, science—and most of modern industrial culture—will be repudiated, and the practitioners and advocates of it perhaps liquidated as well. At best, we can expect the restoration (or rediscovery) of those values and folkways that characterized all successful cultures before the rise of industrialization (some would say, before the rise of agriculturally-based civilizations). Even worse—and more likely—we can expect to see the world plunged into a Hobbesian condition of the "war of all against all" until such time as regional strong men are able to emerge to exercise power and the peace of the sword in a profoundly depopulated, de-industrialized, fragmented and dispersed world (Taylor, 1975; Vacca, 1974).

THE CONSERVER SOCIETY

It is in response to the total variance between these two images of the future that a third alternative has recently emerged. Wishing to keep the world headed towards the bright future of Herman Kahn, yet fearful that our single-minded attempt to do so will only bring this fragile house of cards crashing down upon us, many serious captains of state are beginning to look for the creation of a "Conserver Society"—of a "Steady State"—in which the "Limits of Growth" are taken seriously and considered to be imminent, necessitating a rapid deceleration of growth—or rather the careful selection of what shall grow, and where; what shall stabilize, and how; and what shall be cut back and perhaps caused to die.

Much of the work sponsored by the Club of Rome is of this kind (Laszlo, 1977; Meadows, 1972; Mesarovic & Pestel, 1974; Peccei, 1977; Tingergen, 1976). Moreover, the Science Council of the government of Canada has recently completed a lengthy and extensive investigation into what might be the alternative ways in which a "Conserver Society" might be structured, and what the social consequences of those alternatives might be.

A "Conserver Society" is on principle against waste. Therefore, it is a society which:

- promotes economy of design of all systems (i.e., "doing more with less");
- favors reuse or recycling and wherever possible, reduction at the source;
- questions the ever-growing per capita demand for consumer goods, artificially encouraged by modern marketing techniques; and
- recognizes that a diversity of solutions in many systems, such as in energy and transportation might increase the overall economy, stability, and resiliency [Science Council of Canada, 1976, p. 1].

The Science Council commissioned a group of scholars from the Universities of Montreal and McGill to draw up a set of "Tentative Blueprints for a Conserver Society" (Valaskakis, 1975), and that group (called GAMMA) produced a mountain of provocative documents that indicate how a generalized Conserver Society might, in fact, take a variety of forms—similar to the way in which an automobile, with prespecified gas mileage, weight, and size limitations for example, might have a wide variety of specification-satisfying designs (Valaskakis, 1976).

Depending on how stringent the assumptions,[13] the implications for the future of culture of a Conserver Society are simply variations on the traditional themes of frugality, conservation, limited social and geographic mobility, decline of urbanization and the rise of rural communalism, decreased industrialization, marked decline in the necessity (or desirability) of what is now called "higher education," and the increased need for persons with manual, agricultural, craft, or repair skills and expectations. In short, a world more characteristic of the late preindustrial era than of the past 100 years in the West.

Let me say again that the three images I have put forward so far are by no means the only ones important for understanding the alternative futures of culture. Not only might I have chosen different people (or groups of people) to illustrate each of the three—and hence that given a somewhat different impression of each alternative—but there are many other alternatives which I simply am not mentioning at all. For example, there are various religious and spiritually-based images (Hubbard, 1976; Jantsch & Waddington, 1976;

---

[13] Not only might one strive to "do more with less," but one variant of the Conserver Society posits the advantage of "doing less with less"—what GAMMA calls the "Buddhist Variant" in deference to E. F. Schumacher's use of the term, "Buddhist Economics" in his popular book (1973).

Stulman & Laszlo, 1973), the more techno-optimistic utopian dreams (Beckerman, 1974; Berry, 1974; Esfandiary, 1973; Tuccille, 1975), Marxist or Third World alternatives (Kothari, 1975; Markovic, 1974; Mazrui, 1975), the common-sense practical view that all long-range imagining is ridiculous or dangerous and that the future can *only* be approached incrementally, by muddling through (Lindblom, 1977; Wildavsky, 1974), and many, many more, including the one you yourself hold dear. Nonetheless, I stand my ground by saying that of all the many images of the future that exist, and among that smaller set of images of persons who spend more time contemplating the future than do the rest of us, I consider the three described to be, in essence, the most important for understanding the alternative futures of culture from a Western or industrialized society's perspective.

Geoffrey Vickers and "The Future of Culture"

"By far the biggest question mark that hangs over the future is in my view the question of culture." This is the opening of Sir Geoffrey Vickers' essay on "The Future of Culture" (Linstone & Simmonds, 1977). The reason for Sir Geoffrey's concern is that he has profound doubts about the future of society, per se. He believes that certain characteristics in Western culture are bringing not only the West, but the entire world, to the brink of disaster.

Whereas until only very, very recently, most societies accepted the inevitability and human-unalterability of their cultural characteristics:

> all Western societies for the last two hundred years (an epoch which I regard as abruptly ending now) have exaggerated the scope for design open to their societies in the social no less than the technological field, and at the same time have fallen further short than they might have done of what might have been their more modest objectives. I have attributed this to their lack of understanding of systemic limitations. This understanding is now dawning austerely and rapidly in the technological field. It is far less in evidence and far more needed in the cultural field [Linstone & Simmonds, 1977, p. 39].

In other words, Vickers seems to be accepting a view finding more and more advocates in the modern world (Bateson, 1972; Thompson, 1974; von Weizsacker, 1975)—that, at least since the Industrial Revolution (but perhaps since Adam and Eve's tinkering with the environmental order of the Garden of Eden, and/or Prometheus' theft of fire), humans have sought to "improve" and "develop" the world in ways no other creatures on earth do. In the process, humans have overlooked the systemic–ecological principle that "everything is connected to everything else," and thus, seeking to do good in the here and now, have often (and unexpectedly) done ill in the there and then. Consequently, when they seek to remedy the imbalance that their own earlier action caused, they only precipitate yet another, more serious and unanticipated set of problems. This chain proceeds to the immediate future where we have so unravelled the single web of culture that we no longer have a culture, but only a set of rapidly-disintegrating threads.

Sir Geoffrey concludes that the future demands "a cultural revolution on a scale which has never yet been attempted or imagined, but which it is our duty to attempt even though we may be biologically unfit to achieve it sufficiently in the time available [1977]." His view, then, is similar to that of Heilbroner, but from a significantly different perspective. I share a portion of his view, but come to a very different prognosis.

A View of a Transformational Future

If I were asked to state which, of the billions of factors significantly shaping the future, I feel to be most important (Dator, 1978; Dator, 1974, 1975), I would say they lie in three areas.

The first area is the present and future continuance of efforts by both the protagonists of the "Continued Growth" and "Conserver Society" views of the future to determine policy along the lines they feel necessary and desirable. Neither side will "win," in my view (and neither side is "correct" in its view of what is wrong with the present and might be right for the future). Nonetheless, the future will, to an important extent, be shaped by the pincers effect of their opposing actions. It will emerge, from my viewpoint, as a synthesis of their thesis and antithesis.

The next factor is technology. I myself believe that the positive (rather than the negative) role of technology has been recently seriously downplayed. Early twentieth-century futurism was almost entirely technocentric, and was repudiated by many intellectuals for that reason. It is even less fashionable[14] to speak of technology as a positive social force today, but I find it impossible not to do so.

Let me clarify, if only briefly. First of all, by "technology," I mean not only "hard," "physical" tools (that I call physical technology), but also "biological technologies," (such as sexual intercourse as a method of human reproduction), and "social technologies" (such as modern educational systems). The frequently competing, and often replacing, nature of these three different types of technology needs much greater study than it has had so far, and my position is based upon only a partial, and perhaps erroneous, analysis of my own. Second, I believe it is necessary to make the distinction between "hardware" and "software"—between the tool itself and the rules

---

[14] In addition to the well-known complaints of Ellul, Mumford, and Roszak, Schumacher (1977) and the entire "Appropriate Technology" movement that he founded resonates throughout much of industrial society's "alienated humanity."

(often culture-specific) for its use. The software (instructions for use) is often what people object to about a tool, not the tool itself, though it is usually the hardware that is blamed.

Finally, whereas the common-sense view of technology is that it is "merely" a way to get something done and has no major cultural consequences (the view that leads Vickers to despair about the future of culture), and whereas the technophobic belief that we are systematically "dehumanized" by every increase in technological sophistication is presently dominant in many scholarly and fictional formulations,[15] I believe that the major way in which *humans* evolve (in contrast to the ways other creatures evolve) is by symbiotic interaction through their technologies with the environment around them. New technologies create new choices which make new actions, thoughts, and values possible. Exercising these new options frequently forecloses old ones, to be sure, but I would judge that more of us have more options before us now than, proportionately, was ever the case in the past. Furthermore, I believe that, generally, each new level of technology increases our overall options, and modifies our sense of what it means to be human.

I must admit (as Vickers implies) that this human characteristic might be an evolutionary pathology. Humans may be an evolutionary experiment of relatively short duration, and "nature" might very well be in the process of discarding us because of our systems-disturbing propensities. Or, at the very least, we may be "interacting with our environment through technology" at a rate too fast for us to cope. Far wiser heads than mine have come to that conclusion. But that is not my conclusion.

Rather, I believe that the systems-unsettling and new systems-creating ability of humans should be accepted, celebrated, and enhanced. I do not see any compelling argument that leads me to conclude that we are not able physiologically, psychologically, or culturally to withstand—indeed, thrive—in a period of rapid change. This does not mean that I advocate some blind form of "technological determinism": that "anything that is technologically possible should be realized." Such rhetoric to the contrary notwithstanding, that has *never* been the case, and it should not be.

Neither am I opposed to what is called "technology assessment." I applaud and participate in attempts to assess the probable multiple impacts from the diffusion of new technologies *before* they are diffused. This is a difficult, and some would say actually impossible, task. But whether it is done well or poorly, I am more likely to want to take the risks—personal as well as social—implied in new technologies, than to hold on to old ways and

---

[15] The "dehumanizing" theme seems to dominate novels and films—at least until very recently: *Star Wars* and especially *Close Encounters of the Third Kind* (which may be unique among films in having not an evil machine but rather the symbiosis of mystical and physical technology as its main theme) may be indicators of a significant departure.

values merely because we think we understand them better. Although there
certainly are some technologies for which that is not the case, I freely admit
to "aiglatson" as a general rule, rather than to "nostalgia."

If I am permitted to have this view of technology, then the second major
force I see shaping the future is in the emergence of four areas:

1. Electronic (and postelectronic) communications technologies—
   primarily their microminiaturization and eventual biological implantation, and in the eventual creation of what is now called "artificial
   intelligence."
2. Biological technologies—from recombinant DNA, through life-
   enhancement, to cloning, and "test-tube babies"—that is, the creation
   of a new category of human beings by new processes.
3. Space research, space colonization, and eventual contact (probably
   electronic, not direct) with extraterrestrial intelligence.
4. New social technologies, especially in the area of "government," that
   is, the social decision-making and conflict-resolution areas (the cultural
   area presently most profoundly backward and resistant to needed
   change—even more backward than "education," which should be
   sufficiently archaic and superfluous for anyone).

There no doubt will be new technologies that I have not identified here but
that will be even more future-potent. However, that technology is a force
crying out for analysis as dispassionate as humans should ever attempt to
undertake, I have no doubt.

Finally, the third major factor shaping our futures lies in the area of global,
political, and economic relations. I label this change, "The Decline of the
West, and the Rise of the Third World." It is a counterintuitive position,
strongly at odds with Herman Kahn (who sees all areas prospering, and the
"gap" between rich and poor narrowing because of continued industrial
growth everywhere) and that of Heilbroner (who sees the gap widening, and
the misery and despair of the poor being one of the factors leading to the
downfall of industrial society, and hence of the entire world). I will not seek
fully to defend my position here (any more than I have defended any other
aspects of my or other's positions). It is clear to me that both things might be
happening. That is to say, as Vickers exactly notes, Western culture seems
to be coming to an end. It is coming apart at the seams and nothing can repair
it—especially the futile attempts of heretofore dominant institutions (e.g.,
church, school, governmental bureaucracies) which are so much evident at
present, and which Kahn sees as going from glory to glory through the
twenty-first century.

I do not by any means take this probability of decline to signify the end of
the world, or the end of meaningful life on this planet or this hemisphere. It
could mean that, of course. Partly because of the growing wail of hysterical
voices, such as that of Sir Geoffrey and the entire mob of back-to-nature

advocates, it is certainly possible—and increasingly likely—that we will fail to understand what opportunities do in fact lie ahead for the creation of a new culture. This new culture (like a child from the womb of its mother) grows out of, but is distinctly different from, the present and the past. It is, in part, the product of the three forces I have mentioned to this point: the struggle between "growth" and "no-growth" advocates; new possibilities and problems brought by new technologies; and the vigorous reaffirmation of life springing from many parts of the world that have recently been living in the shadow—if not under the heel—of Western culture.

I view the "Rise of the Third World" with very mixed feelings, indeed. It is the most volatile, most possibly bloody of all the factors I find important. And yet, I hear a mighty sighing of relief all around the world as the monolith of Western values and institutions is lifted from the shoulders of humanity— in the West as well as in the non-West. Although many of us seem to think this relief is a horrible catastrophe that must be prevented, many others, at home as well as abroad, see this as a period of unusual opportunity for creativity and life-enhancing responses.[16] Such is my view.

So what do I see for the "future of culture"? Remember that (as do all "futurists") I am hedging my bets by saying, "if everything is equal . . ." or "barring unforeseen circumstances . . ." or "if everything works out for the best. . . ." I am not predicting. I am hoping. (Some of you will think I am merely "freaking out.")

What Sir Geoffrey (and others) sees as the disintegration of culture, I see as the transformation of culture to a new evolutionary stage. It is a stage as profoundly different from the culture of the past 200 (perhaps the past 10,000) years, as was the shift for paleolithic tribes to high civilization cities. It is the shift from community- and other-based cultural *dependence* to individual, experiential, transient, and personal culture-*creation*. The movement I see, and see as good, is *away* from the time and place when one's own culture (e.g., language, ideas, values, actions) derived necessarily

---

[16] This positive faith in the future (which finds its counterpart in responses to survey research questions in the Third World), is most eloquently expressed in a Discussion Paper of the Panel on Futurology of the Department of Science and Technology of the Government of India (1974):

> It may be interesting to note here that there is a lunatic fringe in our society which still believes that India will face many Malthusian catastrophes. It is said that there will be famines; there will be several other natural disasters, and our population will, there-fore, according to them not reach the projected figure of 960 million. We believe this is an unimaginative way to look at things. Different aspects of India's population can be seen if we classify them variously. The fact that should be taken note of is that presently 40% of our population is below the 15 age group. This is the population which is our biggest "resource" and, if like the Western countries, we can also train several millions of our young people, we give to ourselves enormous strength, for, with every mouth to feed, God sends a pair of hands which can work. More relevantly in the present conditions, He also sends a brain which can think [p. 6f].

and unconsciously from those people around one, and *towards* the situation where each person's culture will be increasingly distinct and private from those around them.

Less and less can any of us "be sure" of the language, values, and actions of those who happen to be our geographic neighbors. More and more frequently will we find ourselves in contact with people who differ significantly from ourselves—until that situation becomes itself a "new culture": the culture of self-actualizing, independent, but freely interrelating people.

In such a situation, misunderstandings will be frequent, conflicts will abound, and time will be scarce and frequently "wasted" on interpersonal probing and seeking to comprehend. It is not a world we have encountered before. Rather, it is not a world we have encountered for very long, as a permanent transforming feature, and it is not a world within which we have been able to retain our sanity if we have had to endure it for long. In fact, such a world seems to many of us to be a madhouse (as the present and past worlds seem to me). It may be a madhouse. It may be beyond our human ability to withstand—much less to thrive in. However, I am very optimistic about it. I believe it will be a "good" world for those who are able to live in it, though it may be that very few of us now are adaptable enough to be able to do so. But those who can, will; and they may look back upon us with the same patronizing amusement that we often lavish now of other "savages."

We are all aborigines in a new world, creating a new culture. Please do not misunderstand me. I did not say that I was responsible for causing this new world. I only say that this is the world I see. I see it as a liveable world; in fact, an exciting world. Not a trouble-free world of course (it is not a utopian dream), but not the sort of nightmare that is so fashionably portrayed now. Just different. Very different. And good.

One last point. Sir Geoffrey (and many, many others) believes that the world I see as good is actually unholy chaos, which must be prevented (though he doubts we have either the time or the will to do so—and thus despairs). I agree with him that it is highly unlikely that it will be prevented. I especially doubt that it is possible to create a new culture of the sort he prefers, which I take to be one where everything is tied together by commonly-understood threads: a new community. So many people are calling for the re-creation of community (yet I find it impossible to see how it can come about, and furthermore do not especially want it) that I can only conclude that I fail to see something vital that others see clearly.

Please enlighten me.

But if I should happen to see something that you do not see, what then?

References

Alcock, N. Cyclical analysis in global economic forecasting. *World Future Society Bulletin,* 1978, *12*, 7–13.

Armytage, W. *Yesterday's tomorrows: A historical survey of future societies.* Toronto: Univ. of Toronto Press, 1968.

Ash, B. *Who's who in science fiction.* New York: Taplinger, 1976.

Bateson, G. *Steps towards an ecology of mind.* San Francisco, California: Chandler, 1972.

Beckerman, W. *Two cheers for the affluent society.* London: St. Martin's Press, 1974.

Bell, D. *The coming of post-industrial society.* New York: Basic Books, 1973.

Bell, W. & Mau, J. (Eds.). *The sociology of the future.* New York: Russell Sage, 1971.

Berry, A. *The next ten thousand years.* New York: Dutton, 1974.

Bloch, M. The past and the present in the present. *Man,* 1977, *NS 12,* 278–292.

Christian, J. (Ed.). *Extra-terrestrial intelligence.* Buffalo, New York: Prometheus, 1976.

Ciba Foundation. *The future as an academic discipline.* New York: Elsevier, 1975.

Clareson, T. *Many futures, many worlds.* Kent, Ohio: Kent State Univ. Press, 1977.

Cornish, E. *The study of the future.* Washington, D.C.: World Future Society, 1977.

Cottle, T. & Klineberg, S. *The present of things future.* New York: Free Press, 1974.

Dator, J. Neither there nor then: A eutopian alternative to the "development" model of future society. In Rome World Special Conference on Futures Research (Ed.), *Human futures.* Guildford, England: IPC Science & Technology Press, 1974.

Dator, J. De-colonizing the future. In A. Spekke (Ed.), *The next 25 years.* Washington, D.C.: World Future Society, 1975.

Dator, J. The future of anticipatory democracy. In C. Bezold (Ed.), *Anticipatory democracy.* New York: Random House, 1978.

Dewey, E. *Cycles.* Pittsburgh: Pittsburgh Univ. Center for the Study of Cycles, 1970.

Esfandiary, F. *Up-wingers.* New York: John Day, 1973.

Fraser, J. (Ed.). *The voices of time.* New York: Braziller, 1966.

Government of India, Panel on Futurology of the Department of Science and Technology. *Discussion paper.* New Delhi: Author, 1974.

Harrison, H. & Gordon, T. (Eds.), *Ahead of time.* New York: Doubleday, 1972.

Heilbroner, R. *An inquiry into the human prospect.* New York: Norton, 1974.

Henley, S. & Yates, J. *Futurism in education: Methodologies.* New York: McCutchan, 1974.

Hollister, B. (Ed.). *Another tomorrow: A science fiction anthology.* New York: Pflaum, 1974.

Hubbard, B. *The hunger of Eve.* Harrisburg, Pennsylvania: Stackpole, 1976.

Hubbard, E. *Our need for new worlds.* New York: Transbooks, 1976.

Jantsch, E. & Waddington, C. (Eds.). *Evolution and consciousness.* Reading, Massachusetts: Addison-Wesley, 1976.

Kahn, H. & Brown, W. *The next 200 years.* New York: William Morrow, 1976.

Kahn, H. & Wiener, A. *The year 2000.* New York: Macmillan, 1967.

Kauffman, D., Jr. *Futurism and future studies: Developments in classroom instruction.* Washington, D.C.: National Education Association, 1976. (a)

Kauffman, D., Jr. *Teaching the future: A guide to future-oriented education.* New York: ETC Press, 1976. (b)

Ketterer, D. *New worlds for old: The apocalyptic imagination, science fiction, and American literature.* New York: Anchor, 1974.

Kothari, R. *Footsteps into the future.* New York: Free Press, 1975.

Laszlo, E. *Goals for mankind.* New York: Dutton, 1977.

Lindblom, C. *Politics and markets.* New York: Basic Books, 1977.

Linstone, H., & Simmonds, W. (Eds.). *Future research: New directions.* Reading, Massachusetts: Addison-Wesley, 1977.

Lynch, K. *What time is this place?* Cambridge, Massachusetts: MIT Press, 1972.

Marien, M. *Societal directions and alternatives: A critical guide to the literature.* Lafayette, New York: Information for Policy Design, 1976.

Marien, M. & Ziegler, W. (Eds.). *The potential of educational futures.* Worthington, Ohio: Charles A. Jones, 1972.

Markovic, M. *From affluence to praxis.* Ann Arbor: Univ. of Michigan Press, 1974.

Maruyama, M. & Harkins, A. (Eds.). *Cultures beyond the earth: The role of anthropology in outer space.* New York: Vintage, 1975.

Maxwell, R. Anthropological perspectives. In H. Yaker (Ed.), *The future of time.* New York: Anchor Books, 1972.

Mazrui, A. *A world federation of cultures.* New York: Free Press, 1975.

McHale, J. & McHale, M. *Futures directory.* New York: Westview Press, 1977.

Meadows, D., Meadows, D., Rander, J., & Behrens, W., III. *The limits to growth.* New York: New American Library, 1972.

Mesarovic, M. & Pestel, E. *Mankind at the turning point.* New York: Dutton, 1976.

O'Neill, G. *The high frontier: Human colonies in space.* New York: William Morrow, 1977.

Peccei, A. *Human quality.* New York: Pergamon Press, 1977.

Phillips, B. *Worlds of the future: Exercises in the sociological imagination.* Columbus, Ohio: Charles Merrill, 1972.

Polak, F. *The image of the future.* New York: Elsevier, 1973.

Schumacher, E. *Small is beautiful.* New York: Harper, 1973.

Schumacher, E. *A guide for the perplexed.* New York: Harper, 1977.

Science Council of Canada. *Toward a conserver society: A statement of concern.* Ottawa: Author, 1976.

Stine, G. *The third industrial revolution.* New York: Putnam, 1975.

Strode, W. An emerging medicine: Creating the new paradigm. *Earthrise Newsletter,* 1977, *f (6),* 299–303.

Stulman, J. & Laszlo, E. (Eds.). *Emergent man.* New York: Gordon & Breach, 1973.

Taylor, G. *How to avoid the future.* London: Secker & Warburg, 1975.

Thompkins, R. *Futurescapes: Explorations in fact and fiction.* London: Menthuen, 1977.

Thompson, W. *Passages about earth.* New York: Harper, 1974.

Thompson, W. *Evil and world order.* New York: Harper, 1976.

Tinbergen, J. *RIO, reshaping the international order.* New York: Dutton, 1976.

Tuccile, J. *Who's afraid of 1984?* London: St. Martin's Press, 1975.

Vacca, R. *The coming dark age.* New York: Doubleday, 1974.

Valaskakis, K. *Tentative blueprints for a conserver society in Canada.* Montreal, Canada: Univ. of Montreal, 1975.

Valaskakis, K. *The selective conserver society* (3 vols.). Montreal, Canada: Univ. of Montreal, 1976.

Vickers, G. The future of culture. In H. Linstone & W. Simmonds (Eds.), *Futures research: New directions.* Reading, Massachusetts: Addison-Wesley, 1977.

von Weizsacker, C. F. A sceptical contribution. In S. Mendlovitz (Ed.), *On the creation of a just world order.* New York: Free Press, 1975.

Wildavsky, A. *The politics of the budgetary process.* Boston: Little, Brown, 1974.

World Future Society. *Resources directory for America's third century.* Washington, D.C.: Author, 1977.

Zinn, H. The conspiracy of law. In P. Wolff (Ed.), *The rule of law.* New York: Simon & Schuster, 1971.

18

The Future of
Cross-Cultural Psychology[1]

HARRY C. TRIANDIS

Cross-cultural psychology has a future only if mankind has one. Osgood (1977), after attending a Pugwash conference, expressed serious doubts that mankind will reach the year 2000. These doubts are based on current trends, such as the continuing arms race, the proliferation of sophisticated weapons, the continuing environmental damages inflicted by modern technology, and the continuing competition for the world's resources.

Osgood's pessimism about mankind's future reflects in part, his analysis of psychological universals that emerge from cross-cultural research. Such an analysis suggests that while the technological changes of the last century have changed the physical environment more than humans changed it in the past two million years, the psychological changes are relatively small, and reflect basic processes established during the past million years of psychological evolution. Thus, man-made changes of the physical environment, including the capability to destroy large cities and entire regions of the world, have been phenomenal, whereas the psychological changes needed to survive on the physically changed planet are lagging sadly behind. Current attitudes were more appropriate for human survival in the prehistoric period than in modern times.

[1] John Adamopoulos, C. E. Osgood, and Pola Triandis made helpful suggestions concerning an earlier draft.

PERSPECTIVES ON CROSS-CULTURAL PSYCHOLOGY

Survival will require major changes in attitudes. For example, the crisis of limited resources requires that people in the overdeveloped world accept a lower standard of living; the crisis of interdependence and limited resources requires world government; the population explosion requires drastic reorganization of social structures in some countries. Yet, no signs can be seen that any of these changes are about to take place. In fact, present human attitudes about standards of living, world government, and social structure are very similar to the attitudes of Neanderthal Man. One basic psychological factor which apparently has not changed in the past 100,000 years of human development is what Osgood calls *Pollyannaism:* We find it easier to cognitively process affectively positive than affectively negative stimuli. Substantial cross-cultural evidence supports this conclusion. Furthermore, we have a tendency to process congruent information and to find incongruent information hard to deal with. This is the basis for many theoretical systems (e.g., Abelson, Aronson, McGuire, Newcomb, Rosenberg, & Tannenbaum, 1968) and what has been labeled a *psycho-logic*. Triandis (1968) found cognitive consistency operating not only in America, but also in Japanese and Indian responses, though the data were obtained from college students and consequently may not be widely representative. Yet in most cases, it is the college educated who will make the major decisions about war and peace, so the potential nonrepresentativeness of such data is not really relevant to the present argument. Furthermore, when humans live under great stress they tend to use old habits rather than invent new responses. As the various crises mentioned above become more salient, our creativity may be reduced.

Pessimism also is based on the realization that many important decisions are taken by committees which used "groupthink" (Janis, 1972) processes which lead to misperception and error. Additionally, as if this were not enough, humans are "wired" in such a way that immediate reinforcements influence behavior much more than reinforcements which are remote in time. Most of the required changes are symbolic in nature, cannot be reinforced by immediate events, and often must be reinforced by nonevents—such as *avoiding* a war. Humans are very poor at being reinforced by nonevents (such as avoiding a war), particularly nonevents that may take place many years after an action. So, the probability is very high that humans will not do those things that might save mankind from disaster.

Turning to our own particular situation in the United States, we must add other elements to this pessimistic analysis. Democracies are particularly vulnerable when the required action is unpopular. Cutting standards of living is not going to get votes for any politician. President Carter's difficulties with energy legislation are most instructive, and the fall of the dollar, in spite of clear signs of what actions are needed with respect to reductions of imports, heralds a list of future disasters.

Another source of pessimisms, as Osgood notes, is the way world leaders use language. For example, they argue that "mutual trust" between nations must be established before there is a reduction in international tensions, when in fact de-escalation in tensions would create mutual trust. They talk about "security" and "unlimited national sovereignty" at the same time, when the modern world requires interdependence, and security is likely only if there is limited sovereignty. Osgood gives many examples of how psychological dynamics of thinking and talking function as causes of inappropriate policy decisions on defence spending, energy, population policy, and so forth.

In summary, one strong possibility concerning the future of cross-cultural psychology is that there *is* no future. However, hopefully, Osgood's analysis has not considered all the factors that determine the future of mankind, so we might explore other futures. One assumption behind such an exploration must be that somehow, perhaps at the last minute before nuclear annihilation, mankind will change attitudes and move toward more interdependence, and a pluralistic, global society. Such a society would have both economic and political ties that would make war unthinkable. It will have to be a society in which remote symbolic goals are more powerful than immediate gratification. The interesting point, from our perspective, is that in such a society cross-cultural psychology will be one of the most important disciplines. How is the world to become interdependent, how is mankind to control the vast social processes that lead to technological suicide, unless humans learn a great deal about themselves, their relationships with one another, and their relationships with nature in the context of social systems? If humans are to learn those things, they will need to develop not only provincial psychology but global psychology, both the universals and the culture-specifics about psychological processes.

Consider the policy decisions that will have to be made. They will affect billions of people, and involve the full range of variation of cultural forms. Or, consider the interpersonal relationships that will be common. They will frequently involve persons of differing social and cultural backgrounds. Not only the political system may be global, but also the educational, economic, and communication systems. With educational satellites circling the globe, people all over the world will have common experiences. However, one cannot develop global programs without understanding cross-cultural psychological phenomena. Global communications will require understanding of what is comnon in human perception (Deregowski, 1979), thinking (Pick, 1979, learning and motivation (Kornadt, Eckensberger, & Emminghouse, 1979), the communication of emotion (Izard, 1979), social behavior (Gergen, Mores, & Gergen, 1979 and many other processes, well discussed by Lonner (1979). What culturally specific, cognitive processes (Price-Williams, 1979) are operating? Global entertainment will require a global perspective on aesthetics, which, fortunately, is beginning to emerge (Berlyne, 1979).

In short, the future of cross-cultural psychology is either nil or excellent.

If mankind survives, cross-cultural psychology will become a central activity for all psychology. Psychological theories will have to use universally valid propositions. However, such theories may well include parameters that reflect the major ecological, economic, and sociocultural variations.

As the world becomes more unified, with resource interdependence, some inequalities will be reduced—the rich will become poorer and the poor will become richer. As societies in the less developed world become modern, they will also develop greater capabilities in psychology. Psychology is now flourishing only in the developed part of the world; however, in the future, it is bound to become a universal enterprise. As psychology develops, it will guide human activities more and more. In the future people will be spending more time on psychological analyses and less time on economic or technological activities. They will also spend more time in self-examination than in economic and technological activities because the latter require energy, and this is bound to remain in short supply. Self-examination and many social activities do not require much energy. So, I expect that in the developed world, the twenty-first century will be characterized by much more activity in the domains of intra- and interpersonal processes, than in the domains of exploitation of the physical environment. As a result, cultures where self-examination is important now will become more important. Perhaps India or China will dominate the world, not in the sense of military domination, but in the way the United States is dominating the world in the twentieth century. We now find American products, including films, television programs, music, and science dominating activities in all but a few of the countries of the world. In the future other cultures may dominate.

For the first million years of human evolution, survival in the battle with nature was the central element. The man–nature relationship was thus central. With the development of social aggregates, man–man relationships became more important. With the industrial revolution, the last 200 years have focused on production. The next epoch will make problems of resource allocation of central concern. Such problems will require, for their solution, a much better understanding of the prerequisites for the development of social structures that lead to harmony, and feelings of satisfaction. This cannot be done without a deep understanding of social and psychological processes. Both cross-cultural universals and varieties of psychological laws that are the results of differing ecologies, subsistence patterns, social structures, and ideologies will have to be explored.

To summarize, then, two strong alternative possibilities seem to emerge: *Either mankind has no future, or cross-cultural psychology will become one of the most vital activities of mankind.* If we assume that mankind will survive, then we must explore the major areas of research that will be needed in the future. In the next section I will explore some areas of needed research, taking seriously the conditions of resource interdependence that must characterize a global society.

Some Areas of Needed Research in the Next Fifty Years

To start with basics, we need a much better understanding of the mechanisms of perception, cognition, learning, and motivation, as well as social behavior, from a cross-cultural perspective. Too much of what we know in these fields is based on data from American sophomores, and too little on data from illiterate, culturally diverse samples, living in very different ecologies.

Cross-cultural dimensions must become integrated in psychological laws, much as the laws of physics reflect parameters of the environment. An analogy might help. Consider the well-known relationship, Force equals Mass times Acceleration. For gravitational forces, acceleration is represented by g. Thus, gravitational forces are proportional to the mass of the object, and depend on g. But g is specific to the earth. If we are concerned with the gravitation of the moon, we must substitute another value for g. If we are concerned with gravitational forces near Jupiter, we need still another value. So, g is a parameter that takes into account where the object is located in the planetary system, and reflects the mass of the astronomical body near which the object that we are studying happens to be located. The point is that the parameter changes lawfully, and in fact, there are known relationships that can predict it anywhere in the universe. In the same way, psychological laws must incorporate parameters that can be predicted from other relationships. We must learn to analyze ecologies, subsistence patterns, social structures, etc., and to assign specific values to the variables that reflect variations in such entities.

Triandis (1978) outlined a framework of a future universal theory of social behavior and a methodology for the testing and development of this theory. Briefly, it is argued that the responses that humans make to social stimuli will be placed in computers. The computers will work on the data, to reflect the major psychological processes (e.g., selectivity in perception influenced by values, cognitive consistency, the avoidance of uncertainty). Using complex programs that will summarize these psychological processes, the computer will print predictions about the percentage of each sample of humans that is likely to engage in each type of action. Regional variations, reflecting cultural variables, will be entered in the computer both in the form of differences in the input data and parametric modifications of the equations that are used by the computer to elaborate the data. The methodology will consist of multimethod tests (e.g., Rohner, 1975) of the predictions of computers, with data from many cultures. The social utility of such a development will be enormous. It will allow social planners, for instance, to ask questions such as: "If we pass Law X, what will be the effects?" The computer will print out the structures of the probability distributions of different outcomes of this legal development, in different populations, and in different parts of the world. Thus, psychological laws will essentially be computer programs, with parameters reflecting cultural variations.

It is very likely that in the twenty-first century, a most important area of research will be concerned with the conditions that produce harmonious interpersonal and intergroup relationships. We will have to place those relationships within the context of developmental psychology, and learn how adjustment to different ecologies and different social structures is made easier or more difficult, depending on different kinds of socialization practices. Both cognitive and social adjustment will be investigated in the manner of experimental anthropology (e.g., Cole & Scribner, 1977) and with methodologies that reflect sensitivity to cultural variables (e.g., Ciborowski, 1979).

Problems of social organization (Tannenbaum, 1979) and group functioning (Mann, 1979) in situations where people differ in cultural backgrounds and points of view will be of even greater significance in the next century than in the present. The problem will be to investigate how people can negotiate, or reach decisions that are mutually satisfying. When war is no longer a viable option, other ways of resolving conflict will have to be invented.

Studies of global public opinion will become common. The first study of this kind is now in the planning stage, and the methodological, political and practical problems are formidable. However, I am confident that they will be resolved. Once the first study of this type is done, it is likely to have a great impact on the conceptions of political leaders. It will gradually become an accepted technique in the resolution of many issues, just as polling has become significant in Europe and North America. To study attitudes (Davidson & Thomson, 1979) and values (Zavalloni, 1979) cross-culturally, and relate the findings to social change (Berry, 1979) will be one of the major challenges of the next century.

A number of practical problems will also require input from cross-cultural psychology. For instance, how does one educate a global citizen? What is the linguistic policy that is most desirable? There is already much information about language learning (Bowerman, 1979) and also bilingual education and its effects on cognitive development. For example, there appears to exist some evidence that learning more than one language increases creativity (Segalowits, 1979). What does that imply about language policy? There is evidence that contact with Western educational systems increases certain kinds of cognitive skills (Heron & Dasen, 1979). What does this imply for a global educational policy? There is evidence that certain kinds of games reflect the structure of the culture in which they are played (Sutton-Smith & Roberts, 1979). What does this imply about the kinds of games that will have global significance in the twenty-first century? Certain kinds of physical environments are more conducive to satisfaction than other environments (Altman & Chemers, 1979). What does this imply about the architecture of the twenty-first century?

Whereas the overdeveloped countries may experience a drop in their standard of living, the underdeveloped will continue developing, and will emphasize applications. Important applied problems will be centered around agriculture, because larger crops will be essential to prevent famine. How will the farms of the less productive parts of the world be improved so they can produce at levels typical of the developed part of the world? To answer this question a much better understanding of attitudes and behavior in the area of methods of agricultural production will be required.

An important issue, in matters of development, is to understand what aspects of culture can be maintained, and what aspects must be changed in order to achieve modernization. The Japanese example suggests that it is possible to have a completely modern society, while maintaining many traditional cultural elements. But is that also true of other societies? Exactly what kinds of cultural elements can be meshed with modernity, and what elements are completely incompatible with it?

Economic development implies changes in culture. What are the effects of cultural change on human feelings of well being? We know that certain forms of rapid social change lead to anomie (Guthrie & Tanco, 1979). Cultures respond differentially to anxieties and tensions, and the symptoms of poor adjustment reflect, in part, cultural variables (Tseng & Hsu, 1979). When the individual has some predispositions and the environments is stressful, various behavioral disorders become manifest. What is the form of these disorders? Draguns (1979) explores whether these disorders are exaggerations of existing cultural patterns, contrast with existing cultural patterns, or have no relationships at all with such cultural patterns. More must be learned about such matters in order to assess the effects of cultural change. If cultural change means trading a better economic condition for a severe increase in behavioral disorders, it will be important to bring ethical, value and other elements into the discussion. Learning how to resolve value dilemmas is one of the highest priorities in the social sciences. When more severe disorders are under investigation, such as schizophrenia or depression (Marsella, 1979), again we need to know how various forms of cultural change may increase or decrease the probability of occurrence of the disorder. Also, once the disorders are present, how does one deal with them, providing a form of psychotherapy that is culturally appropriate (Prince, 1979). Much research is also needed in this direction.

But economic development may be prevented if population increases too fast. Thus, population psychology will become increasingly important. The relationship of population psychology to cross-cultural studies of attitudes and behavior is close (Davidson & Thomson, 1979), and in the future it is likely to become closer.

While the less developed countries will struggle to develop, the more developed will change mostly because of the electronics revolution which is bound to change the nature of transportation systems. In the future, many of us will probably not be going to work physically, but only electronically. We will give our lectures on closed-circuit TV from our homes, talk with students in the same network while sitting in the offices of our homes, and participate in committees, nationally and internationally, without moving physically. An important field of psychology will develop—communication psychology. It will deal with the special problems of interaction through the electronic media. These developments will solve, in part, the energy problem, as much of our present consumption is used for the physical movement of persons from point "a" to point "b." Electronic media use relatively trivial amounts of power, and are much more energy effective.

The computer revolution will also result in several new phenomena, including very high unemployment and too much free time. We will all have pocket computers, which will be plugged into the wiring systems of our homes and the electronic systems of international communication, to do many of the tasks that are done differently today. For example, mail will no longer be carried; it will be transmitted electronically. Routine actions will not require human concerns, and will be preprogrammed by the computer to take place at the proper time. The time is not far off when we might have "Personalized software" for our private computers, that will reflect our biases, prejudices, values, and personal idiosyncracies. Such computers will be able to reach decisions more effectively than we can by using ordinary "clinical judgments." The evidence of this is already overwhelming. More than 70 studies show the superiority of a computer program over clinical judgements. But once this technological development takes place, a major new activity will develop for psychologists. They will test people so that they can advise them about what software to buy for their personal computers, and how to write the programs for such computers. A major parameter of such programs will reflect culturally derived assumptions, values, and other aspects of subjective culture. To program a personal computer correctly, one will need to have an accurate understanding of the subjective culture of the group to which one belongs.

Automation, the electronics revolution, and overpopulation will create more severe problems characterized by anomie, unemployment, poor use of leisure time, and so on. Psychologists will be busy counseling people facing such problems. Part of the treatment may be to enrich one's client's perspective by developing a network of friendships in different parts of the world. People may have "electronic pals" all over the map, and communicate electronically, via satellites, with people from diverse cultures. Acquiring enough information about the other cultures to do this well may be both enjoyable and therapeutic.

The energy crisis, concern with pollution, and other technological developments are likely to change the nature of human habitation. We will probably move more and more in the direction already mapped by Paolo Solari, the visionary architect who is building a city in Arizona. The idea is that a single building will be a city, surrounded by gardens and farm areas.

Several thousand people will live in the building, where temperature, quality of air, and full climatic controls will be possible. The car will be eliminated, though people may rent cars for excursions away from the city. Such cities will be energy efficient (few losses into the air; no gas needed for transportation). They will include work, recreation, and living space in the same building, and all places will be easily accessible by elevator, moving sidewalk and by walking. However, they will produce new problems of crowding, sense of privacy, social relationships, and work–play organization. Psychologists will have a role in designing these new spaces. We already know something about these problems (Altman & Chemers, 1979) and need to learn a great deal more about them, in order to produce city designs that are likely to reduce anomie and increase the sense of well being.

As the world becomes more interdependent, a most important future activity will be the devising of new systems of law. If people arc going to live in harmony the discoveries of psychology must be reflected in these systems. The complexity of devising a legal system with international jurisdiction seems very high, yet for the control of global crime, global pollution, global epidemics, and so on, such a system is essential. National systems of law will of course continue, but they will deal with private and small group activities. As we move to global advertising, global corporations, global labor–management bargaining, global social mobility, and global political institutions we will need a well developed legal system with global jurisdiction.

Deciding that a new law is good may well become an empirical matter, using evaluation research. Uniform systems of data collection for divorce, suicide, delinquency, crime rates, and subjective culture measures (including ratings of life satisfaction) will be used as criteria in such evaluations. Cross-cultural psychologists will be central to such activities. How can one measure satisfaction on a global basis without consulting the methodologically most sophisticated profession on this point?

All of that, of course, is looking into a future of 50 or more years. I love to make such predictions because they cannot be verified and because I will not be around to be told that I was wrong! Much more difficult are predictions about the next 10 years. I will come to that point a little later in this chapter. But first, I want to examine what needs to be accomplished in the next 25 years.

Some Needed Developments for the Next Quarter Century

An essential aspect of any progress, in cross-cultural psychology, is to develop the competence of our colleagues in less developed countries to do creative work. At the present time the picture is gloomy. In most of the less developed countries the few psychologists graduating from local universities study textbooks that are sometimes 20 years old, have no opportunities to learn how to do independent research, and have no facilities for doing such research after they take a job.

Research requires many ingredients that are in short supply in the less developed world. First, it requires *time.* Yet, most of our colleagues are saddled with large teaching loads and many other responsibilities. In addition they must do other jobs, such as consulting, or teaching at more than one university in order to have a middle class income. Second, it requires *stimulation.* This can come from other psychologists, journals, or books. Yet, typically, many of our colleagues are alone and miss both books and journals. Third, it requires *social support* for the activity. This comes in the form of social approval, a higher salary, and other advantages connected with research activities. This too is missing in many less developed countries, where solving the practical problems of survival is more likely to be rewarded than knowledge for its own sake. Fourth, one needs *funds,* to pay for equipment, assistants, computers, and so on. These too are in short supply in the less developed part of the world. I truly do not see how we are going to develop a global psychology without solving some of the problems of our colleagues in the less prosperous half of the world.

A frequent strategy used by cross-cultural psychologists in the past was to ignore this problem and to collect data directly, without the help of local colleagues. This approach has important methodological (Triandis, 1972), ethical, and political (Warwick, 1979) limitations.

METHODOLOGICAL LIMITATIONS

No matter how well we study the language and culture of another society, we cannot know as much about it as a person who has spent many years living in that society. Although we may discover the obvious, we are likely to miss the subtle. Of course, an outsider does have some advantages. For example, an outsider can ask innocent questions, of the "What is Christmas?" variety, and get answers, whereas an insider often cannot ask such questions. An outsider can also see that the answer is completely obvious to an insider. But, an outsider is much more likely to misunderstand and misinterpret. In my own research, I have frequently analyzed data, written a discussion section, and then sent it to my colleagues in the other culture only to find that their interpretation was substantially different from my own. So, the same data, can mean different things to different people. Writing a discussion section for a paper, then, becomes a process of negotiation, or becomes the stimulus for a new study that will determine whose interpretation is correct. It is a most valuable experience. It is the kind of interplay between insider and outsider that is most likely to lead to new insights. It creates the conditions of what Kurt Lewin called "productive tension." It avoids important errors. In short, if one does not have insiders as collaborators, I, as a reader of a paper, do not completely trust the interpretation.

Another methodological problem is that many generalizations require data from many cultures. Even though there is some cross-cultural data available in existing ethnographic materials, such as the Human Relations Area Files (Barry, 1979), so that it is possible to do hologeistic studies (Naroll, Michick, & Naroll, 1979) in which the number of cultures are the number of data points, there are many situations in which fresh data must be collected. In such situations we want at least 6 (the major culture areas) and preferably 30 (for data stability) cultures, spread across the major cultural areas of the world. The arithmetic of learning that many languages and learning how to interpret data from that many cultures clearly limits the strategy of *the* investigator who works without insider collaborators.

ETHICAL LIMITATIONS

There is increasing acceptance of the principle that to take data from a culture involves an obligation to give something of value in return (Tapp, Kelman, Triandis, Wrightsman, & Coelho, 1974). The researcher has obligations toward the science, the people who give the information, and the people who help in the collection and interpretation of the data. Each of these obligations is multifaceted. Included in these obligations are (*a*) the duty to collect valid data that are free of artifacts; (*b*) to help those who give data by giving, in return, information, status, or money; and (*c*) to do at least as much for one's collaborators in the research enterprise. As a minimum, ethical conduct requires and demands that the subjects should not be hurt or exploited and the research site should remain "intact," so that future investigators will be able to return to it and be welcomed (Tapp *et al.*, 1974).

I still remember the emotions expressed by a Tunisian sociologist when he described how Western "colonialists" came to Tunisia, collected their data and disappeared, telling him nothing about what they had found. It was at a conference in Nigeria, and those present agreed that such behavior is not acceptable. Although having a collaborator in cultures where there are several ingroups of professionals fighting for limited resources, has many problems, at least it meets some of the objections expressed by this Tunisian. It does disseminate knowledge in the local culture about the findings and it does return something of value to the local culture.

POLITICAL LIMITATIONS

We are increasingly finding that information is a valuable commodity. Those who know more are able to take advantage of situations, not only in the stockmarket, but also when deciding how to run an election, when to present their demands, or when to settle and accept someone's offer in a dispute. In an increasingly interdependent world, with supernational policy making, mistakes will have colossal effects. Only accurate information will decrease the likelihood of such mistakes.

As governments come to recognize that information is a resource, it is natural for them to put restrictions on those who collect it. No matter how innocuous the information, local government officials will want to control some of it. Controlling the outsider is a lot more difficult than controlling the insider. So, as a minimum, such officials will want local people to collaborate with the outsider, after receiving local governmental permission.

CROSS-CULTURAL COLLABORATION

Several lines of argument mentioned earlier point to the need to develop collaborative relationships with colleagues who are inside the culture. One problem of such relationships is the inequality which often characterizes them. This can easily deteriorate into a neocolonial form of exploitation. It is desirable to plan such relationships so that when the outsider has some advantage, the insider has some other advantage. For example, if the outsider has prestige the insider should have money. It is up to foundations, and other funding agencies, to make sure that the funds are controlled in such a way as to create a more egalitarian relationship and to avoid colonial exploitation. Such funding agencies should identify one research center, with an energetic, competent leader, and fund it. There should be time, stimulation, rewards for creativity, and funds for equipment and research collaborators, *including outsiders,* attached to such research centers. Thus, the conditions of scientific activity will be adequate and we will be able to see some progress in the less developed part of the world. I have argued elsewhere (Triandis, 1977a) that we need to find ways to foster many such research centers. Unless we do so the future of cross cultural psychology will not be bright.

The Next Ten Years

BROAD METHODOLOGICAL PERSPECTIVES

We now come to the next immediate steps in the future of cross-cultural psychology. Here the predictions are going to be most difficult, and I may be around to hear that they were wrong! But I offer them, nevertheless.

A major trend should be the emphasis on multimethod, multiculture measurement of the same theoretical constructs. Relationships among such constructs should be established with a variety of methodologies. Ideally, convergence across methodologies will be observed and this will ensure that the relationship is not method bound. An example of such an approach is the work of Rohner (1975) who studies the relationship between parental acceptance–rejection at the individual level, in ethnographies, and in hologeistic studies, employing the Human Relations Area Files. Thus, future work might show convergence across observations (Longabaugh, 1979), survey data (Pareek & Rao, 1979), psychometric measures (Irvine & Carroll, 1979), projective measures (Holtzman, 1979), unobtrusive measures (Bochner, 1979) and content analyses of existing documents (Brislin, 1979). Both field and experimental tests of the central hypotheses will be needed to corroborate relationships, and to establish interactions between cultural and psychological variables (Goodenough, 1979; Ciborowski, 1979; Brown & Sechrest, 1979).

BROAD THEORETICAL PERSPECTIVES

In projecting the next 10 years, it is probably most useful to take a historical perspective (Klineberg, 1979) and extrapolate. There are a number of themes that historically were important and are likely to continue in significance, with certain modifications.

Basic Processes: Perception, Memory, Cognition, Motivation

Perception was one of the earliest foci of cross-cultural investigation (Klineberg, 1979) and is a rich and active area of current investigation (Deregowski, 1979). I doubt that any major shifts of emphasis will occur in this area. It is likely to remain a very active area, with continued refinement of hypotheses. The Segall, Campbell, and Herskovits (1966) study was a major contributor to the excitement in this area, and it is likely to continue to be the focus of controversy in the next few years.

Cognition is an area in which psychologists have made important contributions by emphasizing what is universal (see review by Pick, 1979), and anthropologists have contributed much concerning how specific cultures process different kinds of information (see Price-Williams, 1979). I am concerned, however, with the way psychologists have approached this area. It seems to me that they have *assumed* the psychic unity of mankind. While I am sympathetic to this assumption, I am concerned because an assumption cannot be "disproved." Thus, no data are being collected by Cole and other psychologists that can challenge this assumption. *If* culturally specific cognitive processes are operating (e.g., a view of time as circular versus linear, as some anthropologists strongly believe), psychologists, using their present procedures, will not discover them. The problem is to develop a methodology that can uncover culture-specific processes. The anthropologists who support the view that such processes exist employ highly emic (culture specific) methods of data collection. These methods are not comparative, and it is difficult for outsiders to check the statements made by the anthropologist. Also, there appears to be something of a gentlemen's agreement about not working in another anthropologist's territory, and that makes such checks more difficult. Yet, an essential aspect of science is independent verifiability. It is to be hoped that some methodological breakthroughs will occur in the near future that will allow us to check the assumption of psychic unity with etic procedures. It is hoped that advances in methodology will allow such etic procedures to reflect the kinds of phenomena that relativists believe suggest culture-specific ways of cognitive functioning. Although I see this as an item of high priority, I am not sure that there will be such a breakthrough in the next 10 years.

Another basic area in which there has been much interest is motivation, with need achievement, in particular, a most prominent focus of activity (Jahoda, 1979, Berry, 1979). An examination of this topic (Kornadt, Eckensberger, & Emminghouse, 1979) suggests that some of McClelland's well-known assumptions about the universality of achievement motivation are not adequate. Kornadt and his associates define a motive as a highly organized cognitive system of person–environment relationships. Furthermore, Kornadt and colleagues feel that people think the realization of such person–environment relationships can influence their actions. They point out that such cognitive systems tend to be culture specific and to reflect the subjective culture (Triandis, 1972) of those who hold them. People in different cultures do not necessarily organize their cognitions about person–environment events the same way.

What may be universal is the motive to resolve uncertainty. This motive may be the basis of other motives. Uncertainty may occur in different domains, and there is the possibility that cultures could have totally idiosyncratic motives (such as *philotimo* in Greece and *amae* in Japan). The way goals can be reached and what goals constitute achievement may also be culturally specific. So, while Kornadt and associates see a universality of motive structures at a high level of abstraction, they also see this universal structure as having different contents in different cultures. One of the probable focuses of research in motivation during the next 10 years will be testing these kinds of conceptions. Another will be an emphasis on differentiations among related motives (e.g., fear of failure–fear of success), and among different kinds of achievement.

Psychoanalysis

An early trend in cross-cultural psychology employed the framework supplied by psychoanalytic theory. This appears to be fading away, but there is evidence of an intermarriage with other systems, such as behaviorism (in the work of Whiting) and systems theory (in the work of Robert LeVine). My expectation is that the decline of psychoanalytic thinking will continue, but some of the specific theoretical concepts will be retained. For example, the idea of an "anal personality" as a coherent structure, with specific antecedents and consequences seems to be supported by data, and may survive, but the total Freudian system may not.

Related to these trends is the decline of projective tests. Their use reached a peak in the 1930s, and sharply declined after Lindzey's (1961) review. Other reviews, such as Kidder and Campbell's (1970), have certainly contributed to this decline, but some projectives, such as the Holtzman (1979) Inkblot Technique may continue to be used in the next several decades. It is probable, however, that when this methodology is used in the future, it will not be closely tied to psychoanalytic thinking, but will be used in conjunction with other measurement procedures, in carefully validated studies.

The Psychometric Framework

The psychometric approach is more of a methodology than a theoretical framework, though a number of theoretical perspectives, such as Cattell's, have emerged from this approach. Historically, the use of tests in other cultures started by simple translations of Western tests. Soon it was discovered that results from such efforts had low validity, and more rigorous approaches were advocated (Irvine & Carroll, 1979). The future of this activity will be the outgrowth of a marriage between psychometrics and cognitive psychology. In cognitive psychology specific abilities, such as the rotation of a 3-dimensional figure in space, and the correct identification of parts projected on a plane, are analyzed in terms of component cognitive processes. These component processes can be identified, and an assessment of the individual's skill and ability with respect to each component process can be obtained by means of psychometric procedures. In this way, the final test will reflect much more fundamental cognitive processes of universal significance. I see, in the future, a new generation of culture-appropriate tests measuring fundamental universal dimensions. Such tests will be subjected to rigorous construct validation, and will use culture-appropriate items for tapping the fundamental universal dimensions of cognitive ability.

National Character

Historically one of the important concerns of social scientists has been the study of national character. This concern was part of the great movement in the "culture and personality" area, and was also linked with interest in modal personality, national stereotypes, and the like. In my opinion, these studies will be replaced by studies of subjective culture (Triandis, 1972), in which specific populations, differing in age, sex, social class, and other demographics within each linguistically homogeneous community, will be representatively sampled. Such studies usually show that there is tremendous heterogeneity within any broad socially defined category. For example, although Americans consider race an important social category, my studies (Triandis, 1976) show that the variance in subjective culture within black society is much greater than the variance in subjective culture within the middle class, black or white. Thus, to talk about black subjective culture is a gross oversimplification, but to talk about the subjective culture of black, unemployed, young men is feasible. I suspect that in the future many more specific studies will be done, and many more demographic variables will be used, in conjunction with cultural variables, to define the subjective culture of segments of the population.

Subjective culture is related to behavior (Triandis, 1977b). However, behavior is also a function of situational variables. The usefullness of any data for the development of public policy is limited, unless the interactions of situation and person variables are taken seriously. The current disenchantment with personality research is, probably, mostly a reflection of the insufficient specification of the samples under study, in terms of demographic variables beyond culture, as well as the neglect of situational variables in making predictions.

An important event that should take place in the next 10 years is the publication by Osgood and his colleagues of chapters interpreting the *Atlas* data from his 20-year, 30-culture, 600-concepts project. This body of data should yield 10 volumes of interpretive analyses of various aspects of subjective culture, similar in character to the color chapter in the Osgood, May, and Miron (1975) volume.

The study of stereotypes will probably merge with attribution studies. After all, when we assign a particular attribute to a socially defined category we stereotype, and the basic processes of attribution should be rather similar to making other kinds of attributions. One major question will continue to be that of whether some stereotypes are valid.

Language and Thought

Historically (Klineberg, 1979) this was one of the important areas of interest in cross-cultural psychology. It remains an important area, but it is moving into more fundamental questions, such as "What is a category?" and "Are there natural and universal categories?" (Rosch, 1975). Osgood's work, leading to a universal structure of affective meaning (Osgood, May, & Miron, 1975) is strongly implying that, in some respects, thought is independent of language. Many human cognitive tendencies, such as (*a*) Pollyanaism, (*b*) semantic-feature opposition, (*c*) cognitive congruence, and (*d*) the tendency to pay more attention to negative than to positive stimuli in a stimulus array, are apparently independent of language.

Genetic Psychology

Piaget's theoretical framework is the focus of much study and will remain so. Certain aspects of the framework are apparently universal (Dasen, 1977) whereas other aspects require qualification, modification and/or are culture specific (Heron & Dasen, 1979). The universality of these stages of development appears well supported, but the exact sequence of these stages and the antecedents of each stage are still unclear. In the future, more complex designs (i.e., the use of multimethod measurement for the identification of the various stages, with materials that are culturally appropriate) will remove some of the method-boundedness of the findings and will permit a universal statement of the theory.

Psychological Differentiation

This has been an area of intensive interest (Witkin & Berry, 1975) and is particularly significant because it has developed within a broad ecological framework (Berry, 1976). It is likely to continue as an important area, but I hope it will become better articulated with studies of other cognitive abilities, and other measures of cognitive differentiation, such as those developed by Kelley (1975), Schroeder, Driver, and Streufert (1967), Foa and Foa (1974), and Scott (1969). Dawson's (1975) work is important here because it uses culture-appropriate methods of measurement that reflect culture-specific content. Dawson's work, therefore, supplements the content-free Witkin measures.

Biological Factors and Interaction with Culture

A selected set of phenomena, such as the study of intelligence, mental illness, color-blindness, physiologically based motives (e.g., hunger, thirst, elimination) have definite biological components (Thompson, 1979), although they are strongly influenced by cultural variables (Munroe & Munroe, 1979). Thompson examines evolution, diversity, adaptation, and how such processes are reflected in these phenomena. In my view this area is likely to become quite important in the next few years, as the methods of genetic counseling, genetic engineering, behavior genetics, and procedures for the determination of the sex of the fetus are more widely used in different cultures. Exciting interactions of genetics and environment are likely to improve our understanding of both kinds of influence. Intensive studies of nutrition and eating behavior are likely to become popular, as we discover that it is necessary to change the food habits of certain populations.

Another area of considerable importance will be the study of altered states of consciousness, not only hypnosis, but also many of the states popularized by Asian mystics. Drugs and their interactions with psychological processes will be major areas of research. In addition, as people become more and more concerned with their interpersonal relations, and want to understand more about who they are, such investigations will become more popular. Intensive investigations of religious systems, magic, and symbolic systems will also take place, while the altered states of consciousness are being investigated.

The Search for Universals

As mentioned earlier, a global society will require a much better understanding of psychological universals. Lonner (1979) has examined a number of such universals. Some others are very well established (e.g., affective processes, see Izard, 1979; or aesthetic judgments in Berlyne, 1979) while others are still tentative. I consider this one of the highest priority items for cross-cultural psychology. I devoted my presidential address to the Division of Personality and Social Psychology to this topic, attempting to discover the main strands of a universal theory of social behavior (Triandis, 1978). It is my hope that some aspects of this theory will be tested in the next 10 years and will be supported by evidence.

The Training of Cross-Cultural Psychologists

Much of what I have been discussing assumes that cross-cultural psychologists will be active in the next 10 years. If this is to take place they must prove themselves useful (Triandis, 1977a) and must be well trained. One concern is the increased specialization of both anthropologists and psychologists which has been taking place in the last half century. This trend must be reversed, otherwise we will soon reach the point where we will not be reading each other's work. I think we must seriously consider this particular problem soon, and develop interdisciplinary training for students. Eventually we will need to develop special departments in which both anthropologists and psychologists are members.

Summary

Cross-cultural psychology has a future only if mankind has one. Some of the psychological literature suggests that humans do not have a future, because they are still psychologically suited for the age when warfare had limited consequences. However, if humans *do* survive, cross-cultural psychology will become most important, because most of the institutions, and many human activities will be on a global scale. For example, there will be global communications, marketing, and government, but also there will be global pollution and crime. To deal with humans in such a culturally heterogeneous spaceship as earth, governments will require consultations from psychologists who have developed universally valid propositions.

This chapter discussed the future in both the short range (10 years) and the longer range. Methodological and theoretical changes in emphasis, and the training of psychologists, were discussed for the short range. Economic, population, habitat, and technological changes were discussed for the longer range. New activities by psychologists were seen as likely in the long run. For example, the development of electronic technologies will result in changes in life styles, and new jobs for psychologists who will counsel people who find culture change too swift, underemployment and too much leisure time burdensome, and their old friendship networks unworkable. Completely new roles for psychologists were described, which will use universally valid psychological theory modified by parameters that reflect the major economic, ecological, and sociocultural variations of mankind.

References

Abelson, R. R., Aronson, E., McGuire, W. J., Newcomb, T. M., Rosenberg, M. J., & Tannenbaum, P. H. *Theories of cognitive consistency. A sourcebook*. Chicago: Rand McNally, 1968.

Altman, I., & Chemers, M. M. Cultural aspects of environment–behavior relationships. In H. C. Triandis & R. Brislin (Eds.), *Handbook of Cross-Cultural Psychology* (Vol. 5). Rockleigh, New Jersey: Allyn & Bacon, 1979.

Barry, H. Description and uses of the Human Relations Area Files. In H. C. Triandis & J. Berry (Eds.), *Handbook of Cross-Cultural Psychology* (Vol. 2). Rockleigh, New Jersey: Allyn & Bacon, 1979.

Berlyne, D. Psychological aesthetics. In H. C. Triandis & W. Lonner (Eds.), *Handbook of Cross-Cultural Psychology* (Vol. 3). Rockleigh, New Jersey: Allyn & Bacon, 1979.

Berry, J. W. *Human ecology and cognitive style*. New York: Sage–Halsted, 1976.

Berry, J. W. Psychology and social change. In H. C. Triandis & R. Brislin (Eds.), *Handbook of Cross-Cultural Psychology* (Vol. 5). Rockleigh, New Jersey: Allyn & Bacon, 1979.

Bochner, S. Unobtrusive measures. In H. C. Triandis & J. W. Berry (Eds.), *Handbook of Cross-Cultural Psychology* (Vol. 2). Rockleigh, New Jersey: Allyn & Bacon, 1979.

Bowerman, M. Language development. In H. C. Triandis and A. Heron (Eds.), *Handbook of Cross-Cultural Psychology* (Vol. 4). Rockleigh, New Jersey: Allyn & Bacon, 1979.

Brislin, R. Oral and written materials: Content analysis and translation. In H. C. Triandis & J. W. Berry (Eds.), *Handbook of Cross-Cultural Psychology* (Vol. 2). Rockleigh, New Jersey: Allyn & Bacon, 1979.

Brown, E. D., & Sechrest, L. Experiments in cross-cultural research. In H. C. Triandis and J. W. Berry (Eds.), *Handbook of Cross-Cultural Psychology* (Vol. 2). Rockleigh, New Jersey: Allyn & Bacon, 1979.

Ciborowski, T. Cross-cultural experimentation. In H. C. Triandis & J. W. Berry (Eds.), *Handbook of Cross-Cultural Psychology* (Vol. 2). Rockleigh, New Jersey: Allyn & Bacon, 1979.

Cole, M., & Scribner, S. Developmental theories applied to cross-cultural cognitive research. In L. Adler (Ed.), *Issues in cross-cultural psychology*. New York Academy of Sciences, 1977.

Dasen, P. Cross-cultural cognitive development: The cultural aspects of Piaget's theory. In L. L. Adler (Eds.), *Issues in cross-cultural psychology*. New York Academy of Sciences, 1977.

Davidson, A. R., & Thomson, E. Cross-cultural studies of attitudes and beliefs. In H. C. Triandis and R. Brislin (Eds.), *Handbook of Cross-Cultural Psychology* (Vol. 5). Rockleigh, New Jersey: Allyn & Bacon, 1979.

Dawson, J. L. M. *Psychological effects of bio-social change in West Africa.* New Haven, Connecticut: HRAFlex Press, 1975.

Deregowski, J. Perception. In H. C. Triandis and W. Lonner (Eds.), *Handbook of Cross-Cultural Psychology* (Vol. 3). Rockleigh, New Jersey: Allyn & Bacon, 1979.

Draguns, J. Psychopathology. In H. C. Triandis & J. Draguns (Eds.), *Handbook of Cross-Cultural Psychology* (Vol. 6) Rockleigh, New Jersey: Allyn & Bacon, 1979.

Foa, U., & Foa, E. *Societal Structures of the Mind.* Springfield, Illinois: Thomas, 1974.

Gergen, K. J., Morse, S., & Gergen, M. Behavior exchange in cross-cultural perspective. In H. C. Triandis & R. Brislin (Eds.), *Handbook of Cross-Cultural Psychology* (Vol. 5). Rockleigh, New Jersey: Allyn & Bacon, 1979.

Goodenough, W. Field methods. In H. C. Triandis and J. W. Berry (Eds.), *Handbook of Cross-Cultural Psychology* (Vol. 2). Rockleigh, New Jersey: Allyn & Bacon, 1979.

Guthrie, G. & Tanco, P. P. Alienation and anomie. In H. C. Triandis & J. Draguns (Eds.), *Handbook of Cross-Cultural Psychology* (Vol. 6). Rockleigh, New Jersey: Allyn & Bacon, 1979.

Heron, A. & Dasen, P. Cross-cultural tests of Piaget's theory. In H. C. Triandis & A. Heron (Eds.), *Handbook of Cross-Cultural Psychology* (Vol. 4). Rockleigh, New Jersey: Allyn & Bacon, 1979.

Holtzman, W. H. Projective techniques. In H. C. Triandis & J. W. Berry (Eds.), *Handbook of Cross-Cultural Psychology* (Vol. 2). Rockleigh, New Jersey: Allyn & Bacon, 1979.

Irvine, S. H., & Carroll, W. K. Testing and assessment across cultures: Issues in methodology and theory. In H. C. Triandis & J. W. Berry (Eds.), *Handbook of Cross-Cultural Psychology* (Vol. 2). Rockleigh, New Jersey: Allyn & Bacon, 1979.

Izard, C. E. Cross-cultural perspectives on emotion and emotion communication. In H. C. Triandis & W. Lonner (Eds.), *Handbook of Cross-Cultural Psychology* (Vol. 3). Rockleigh, New Jersey: Allyn & Bacon, 1979.

Jahoda, G. Theoretical and systematic approaches in cross-cultural psychology. In H. C. Triandis and W. W. Lambert (Eds.), *Handbook of Cross-Cultural Psychology* (Vol. 1). Rockleigh, New Jersey: Allyn & Bacon, 1979.

Janis, I. L. *Victims of groupthink.* Boston: Houghton, 1972.

Kelly, G. A. *The psychology of personal constructs.* New York: W. W. Norton, 1955.

Kidder, L., & Campbell, D. T. The indirect testing of social attitudes. In G. F. Summers (Ed.), *Attitude measurement.* Chicago: Rand McNally, 1970.

Klineberg, O. Historical perspectives: Cross-cultural psychology before 1960. In H. C. Triandis & W. W. Lambert (Eds.), *Handbook of Cross-Cultural Psychology* (Vol. 1). Rockleigh, New Jersey: Allyn & Bacon, 1979.

Kornadt, H. J., Eckensberger, L. H. & Emminghause, W. B. Motivation. In H. C. Triandis & W. Lonner (Eds.), *Handbook of Cross-Cultural Psychology* (Vol. 3). Rockleigh, New Jersey: Allyn & Bacon, 1979.

Lindzey, G. *Projective techniques and cross-cultural research.* New York: Appleton, 1961.

Longabaugh, R. The systematic observation of behavior in naturalistic settings. In H. C. Triandis & J. W. Berry (Eds.), *Handbook of Cross-Cultural Psychology* (Vol. 2). Rockleigh, New Jersey: Allyn & Bacon, 1979.

Lonner, W. The search for psychological universals. In H. C. Triandis & W. W. Lambert (Eds.), *Handbook of Cross-Cultural Psychology* (Vol. 1). Rockleigh, New Jersey: Allyn & Bacon, 1979.

Mann, L. Cross-cultural studies of small groups. In H. C. Triandis & R. Brislin (Eds.), *Handbook of Cross-Cultural Psychology* (Vol. 5). Rockleigh, New Jersey: Allyn & Bacon, 1979.

Marsella, A. Depressive affect and disorder across cultures. In H. C. Triandis & J. Draguns (Eds.), *Handbook of Cross-Cultural Psychology* (Vol. 6). Rockleigh, New Jersey: Allyn & Bacon, 1979.

Munroe, R., & Munroe, R. Perspectives suggested by anthropological data. In H. C. Triandis & W. W. Lambert (Eds.), *Handbook of Cross-Cultural Psychology* (Vol. 1). Rockleigh, New Jersey: Allyn & Bacon, 1979.

Naroll, R., Michik, G. L., & Naroll, F. Hologeistic theory testing. In H. C. Triandis & J. W. Berry (Eds.), *Handbook of Cross-Cultural Psychology* (Vol. 2). Rockleigh, New Jersey: Allyn & Bacon, 1979.

Osgood, C. E. *Mankind 2000??* Presidential Address to International Peace Science Society, November, 1977.

Osgood, C. E., May, W., & Miron, M. *Cross-cultural universals of affective meaning.* Urbana, Illinois: Univ. of Illinois Press, 1975.

Pareek, U. & Rao, T. V. Cross-cultural surveys and interviewing. In H. C. Triandis & J. W. Berry (Eds.), *Handbook of Cross-Cultural Psychology* (Vol. 2). Rockleigh, New Jersey: Allyn & Bacon, 1979.

Pick, A. Cognition: Psychological perspectives. In H. C. Triandis & W. Lonner (Eds.), *Handbook of Cross-Cultural Psychology* (Vol. 3). Rockleigh, New Jersey: Allyn & Bacon, 1979.

Price-Williams, D. Cognition: Anthropological perspectives. In H. C. Triandis & W. Lonner (Eds.), *Handbook of Cross-Cultural Psychology* (Vol. 3). Rockleigh, New Jersey: Allyn & Bacon, 1979.

Prince, R. Variations in psychotherapeutic procedures. In H. C. Triandis & J. Draguns (Eds.), *Handbook of Cross-Cultural Psychology* (Vol. 6). Rockleigh, New Jersey: Allyn & Bacon, 1979.

Rohner, R. P. *They love me, they love me not: A world wide study of the effects of parental acceptance–rejection.* New Haven, Connecticut: Human Relations Area Files, 1975.

Rosch, E. Universals and cultural specifics in human categorization. In R. Brislin, S. Bochner, & W. Lonner (Eds.), *Cross-cultural perspectives on learning.* New York: Sage–Halsted, 1975.

Schroder, H. M., Driver, M. J., & Streufert, S. *Human information processing: Individual and group functioning in complex situations.* New York: Holt, 1967.

Scott, W. Structure of natural cognitions. *Journal of Personality and Social Psychology,* 1969, *12,* 261–278.

Segall, M., Campbell, D., & Herskovits, N. *The influence of culture on visual perception.* Indianapolis, Indiana: Bobbs-Merrill, 1966.

Segalowitz, N. S. Issues in the cross-cultural study of bilingual development. In H. C. Triandis & A. Heron (Eds.), *Handbook of Cross-Cultural Psychology* (Vol. 4). Rockleigh, New Jersey: Allyn & Bacon, 1979.

Sutton-Smith, B. & Roberts, J. M. Play, toys, games and sports. In H. C. Triandis & A. Heron (Eds.), *Handbook of Cross-Cultural Psychology* (Vol. 4). Rockleigh, New Jersey: Allyn & Bacon, 1979.

Tannenbaum, A. S. Organizational psychology. In H. C. Triandis and R. Brislin (Eds.), *Handbook of Cross-Cultural Psychology* (Vol. 5). Rockleigh, New Jersey: Allyn & Bacon, 1979.

Tapp, J. L., Kelman, H. C., Triandis, H. C., Wrightsman, L., & Coelho, G. Continuing concerns in cross-cultural ethics: A report. *International Journal of Psychology,* 1974, *9,* 231–249.

Thompson, W. R. Perspectives suggested by biological data. In H. C. Triandis and W. W. Lambert (Eds.), *Handbook of Cross-Cultural Psychology* (Vol. 1). Rockleigh, New Jersey: Allyn & Bacon, 1979.

Triandis, H. C. Some cross-cultural studies of cognitive consistency. In R. P. Abelson, E. Aronson, W. McGuire, T. Newcomb, M. Rosenberg, & P. Tannenbaum (Eds.), *Theories of cognitive consistence: A Sourcebook.* Chicago: Rand McNally, 1968.

Triandis, H. C. *The analysis of subjective culture.* New York: Wiley, 1972.

Triandis, H. C. (Ed.), *Variations in black and white perceptions of the social environment.* Urbana, Illinois: Univ. of Illinois Press, 1976.

Triandis, H. C. Impediments to the progress of cross-cultural psychology. Presidential address to the International Association of Cross Cultural Psychology, and in Y. H. Poortinga (Ed.), *Basic Problems in Cross-Cultural Psychology.* Amsterdam: Swets & Zeitlinger, 1977. (a)

Triandis, H. C. *Interpersonal behavior.* Monterey: Brooks–Cole, 1977. (b)

Triandis, H. C. Some universals of social behavior. *Personality and Social Psychology Bulletin,* 1978, *4,* 1–16.

Tseng, W. & Hsu, J. The cross-cultural study of subclinical variations. In H. C. Triandis & J. Draguns (Eds.), *Handbook of Cross-Cultural Psychology* (Vol. 6). Rockleigh, New Jersey: Allyn & Bacon, 1979.

Warwick, D. P. The politics and ethics of cross-cultural research. In H. C. Triandis & W. W. Lambert (Eds.), *Handbook of Cross-Cultural Psychology* (Vol. 1). Rockleigh, New Jersey: Allyn & Bacon, 1979.

Witkin, H. A., & Berry, J. W. Psychological differentiation in cross-cultural perspective. *Journal of Cross-Cultural Psychology,* 1975, *6,* 4–87.

Zavalloni, M. Values. In H. C. Triandis and R. Brislin (Eds.), *Handbook of Cross-Cultural Psychology* (Vol. 5). Rockleigh, New Jersey: Allyn & Bacon, 1979.

Index